VALUE AND OBLIGATION

VALUE AND OBLIGATION

Systematic Readings in Ethics

RICHARD B. BRANDT

Swarthmore College

© 1961 by Harcourt, Brace & World, Inc.

All rights reserved. No part of this book may be reproduced in any form or by any mechanical means, including mimeograph and typewriter, without permission in writing from the publisher.

Printed in the United States of America

Harcourt, Brace & World, Inc.

New York / Burlingame

PREFACE

Most people interested in the problems of ethics aspire to two kinds of knowledge, one systematic, the other historical. They wish a systematic understanding of the field: knowledge of what are the various problems and their interrelations and knowledge of what has been done toward the solution of these problems. They also wish to learn what the great historical philosophers—particularly those who have had the most important ideas about values and conduct—have said about the subject.

Value and Obligation is intended to enable the reader to approximate the achievement of these twin goals at once. It makes clear what the main issues are, and it distinguishes the important types of theory about the issues. At the same time, like the traditional anthologies of ethical literature, it permits various philosophers—especially the important classical figures—to put their own case for the answers they defend. The organization of the book is systematic, but the historically important essays are included. In recognition of the strides made by ethical theory in the present century, nearly half of the selections are taken from writings of the past fifty years.

The readings are divided into groups corresponding to seven major problems. Each group is prefaced by an introduction, written by the editor, which explains what the major problem is and provides an initial sketch of the types of theory to come. The various problems need not, however, be studied in exactly the order here presented. The last three chapters should not be read before the first two, but otherwise the order may be modified to taste, at the cost only of an occasional paragraph in the introductory pages being somewhat obscure. It is possible to omit the third and fourth chapters—on metaethics—altogether; or they may be postponed until the end. They may also be read at the very outset.

The editor's brief introduction to each reading aims to prepare for the following selection, more directly than does the general chapter introduction, by an indication of the kind of theory to be defended and its relation to what has gone before. The reader who wishes to make sure he has grasped the main points of the readings—and some of them are inevitably not easy—should pay careful attention to the questions at the end of each selection. These have been planned to touch on the main points of the author, and, where this is necessary, to hint at how he may sensibly be understood. The reader who is able to answer these questions need not worry about having overlooked important contributions of the selection. Each chapter is also equipped with a bibliography, for those who wish to pursue a given topic further.

The initial general introductory chapter explains the general character of ethical problems, the connections between "normative ethics" and "meta-ethics," and, in a rough way, the relations of the seven problems (and the corresponding groups of readings) to each other and to the main purposes of ethical theory.

Most of the readings are well within the comprehension of the beginning student. A few, however, are more difficult—readings from an important author who must be represented by a difficult selection or not at all, or discussions of a difficult problem that are preferable to easier material that evades the serious issues. If the reader finds a given selection difficult, he need not fear that he cannot proceed effectively to later selections before having mastered it; the later readings will be intelligible independently, and he can return to the difficult item later, when he will be in a better position to grasp it easily.

For their helpful advice, I am most grateful to Elizabeth Lane Beardsley, of Lincoln University; to William K. Frankena, of the University of Michigan; to John Hospers, of Brooklyn College; to Ernest Nagel, of Columbia University; and to J. Roland Pennock, of the Department of Political Science of Swarthmore College.

RICHARD B. BRANDT

March, 1961
Swarthmore, Pennsylvania

CONTENTS

VALUE AND OBLIGATION

INTRODUCTION:
THE SUBJECT MATTER
OF ETHICAL THEORY

1. *What questions are ethical questions?*

All of us frequently face problems it is natural to call "ethical." These problems are so multifarious, however, that it is by no means clear what they have in common that justifies calling them all "ethical." Much less is it clear that they can be neatly classified into a small number of types. If attention is paid, however, not to the *kind of situation* involved when an ethical problem is presented but to the *kind of question* for which an answer is sought, then we can see that the problems naturally called "ethical" do have something in common. What they have in common is the kind of question we are raising about the situations. Moreover, it is clear as well that ethical problems fall into a very few — in fact, three main — types, because there are just a very few types of questions raised when what we call "ethical problems" are faced.

In order to see what the distinctively ethical questions are, let us look at two typical ethical problem situations and the issues they raise.

The writer once knew a graduate student who was applying for an important fellowship which would enable him to complete his graduate work. Failure to receive the fellowship would mean that he must leave school and seek employment in industry, perhaps permanently. He knew that he and one other young man were, on account of their records, the chief contenders for the fellowship. The two of them, he believed, were accounted nearly equal by their teachers and decidedly superior to any others who might conceivably apply. It so happened that applications for this fellowship were due at twelve o'clock noon, every May 1. On the afternoon of April 30 the other contender, a liked acquaintance but not a close friend, came into my friend's room and asked if he were applying for the fellowship. On receiving an affirmative answer, he remarked that he too was making application and was planning to submit his application *sometime during the following week*. It at once occurred to my friend that, if the application were not in by the following noon, there would be only one contender for the fellowship.

Two questions arise about this situation, both of them "ethical." The first and most important — the one that was the serious issue for my friend — is: Would it be *wrong* for my friend to refrain from reminding the other student that applications were due the following day? Or, and it seems this is to ask the same thing in different words: Was my friend *morally obligated* to remind his fellow student of the date on which such applications must be on file? Questions like this we may call questions of *right* and *wrong*.

There is a second question we can raise about this same case. Let us suppose that in fact it was morally obligatory for my friend to remind the other of the terminal date for filing fellowship applications. And let us suppose that my friend did *not* do so; he kept silent. The second question is: Was this act *morally reprehensible*, or was he *morally to blame* (or *morally blameworthy*) for his omission? It might seem that the answer is obviously affirmative if we already agree he had a moral obligation to give the information. But matters turn out to be more complex when we examine them. For possibly there were circumstances which tended to excuse his action, partially or wholly. In the first place, he might, after sincere (but let us suppose, mistaken) reflection, have concluded it was *not* his obligation to give this aid. For instance, he might believe his competitor a wealthy person and argue that it would only be promoting injustice to do what might place a fellowship in the hands of a person who did not need it; or he might argue that in a competitive world it is everyone's duty to be on his toes looking out for his own interests and not the duty of other people to run one's affairs. If such was his sincere conclusion, reached without rationalization on account of his own preferences, is it proper for any one of us to condemn him for his action? It is not clear. Certainly we do not condemn a conscientious objector merely on the showing that he refuses to do something which we, as nonobjectors, consider to be our duty. In the second place, for instance, it may not be proper to condemn this individual if he was in a disorganized frame of mind on account of the death of his father the night before, or on account of a serious disappointment in love, or for other reasons ad infinitum. So it seems that we may not infer straightforwardly, from the premise that it was really someone's moral obligation to do something, that he was morally blameworthy — or that his act was morally reprehensible — if he failed to do this thing. The two questions are distinct. So there is a second set of ethical questions, which we may call questions of *blameworthiness* and *praiseworthiness*.

There is still a third type of question: the question, What things are *desirable* or *worthwhile*? To see what this question is, let us look at another case. Suppose, rather like one of the figures in *South Pacific*, you are a student who has been inducted into the marines. You find yourself at the end of the war on an island in the South Pacific, in love with a beautiful but simple native girl, who wants you to stay there and settle down as a trader or official in a concern which owns and runs plantations. Doing so will mean a kind of life very different from what you will experience if you go back to the girl in Philadelphia. Life in Philadelphia will be more strenuous and demanding; it may also be intellectually more enlarging. You will be apt to ask yourself: "Moral obligations aside, which life that I might live is the more desirable, the more worthwhile?" Reflection on this point will lead you to some more general questions: Is happiness — at least in the sense of enjoyments or contentment — the only thing worthwhile in life? Or are broad intellectual horizons worth something on their own account, over and above what they may add to the enjoyment of life? Is strenuous living, perhaps some important achievement, something a rational person will want? Should one wish to create things — perhaps in science or industry — assuming one's talents are such as to offer little chance of creation in the South Pacific?

This problem may sound unreal. But it is duplicated to some extent when we face a choice among various professions or when we must decide between pursuing the young lady who is primarily beautiful and pursuing the one who is primarily a brain. It is duplicated when we make our decision to apply at certain colleges, since we must choose, say, between a college with a liberal arts emphasis and an engineering school or a college with strong preprofessional training. Let us call this question the question What is *worthwhile* or *desirable*? Clearly it is different from the earlier questions.

You may feel less inclined to call the problem raised by this third question an "ethical" one at all. Whether or not it is so, it is convenient to call it so, since, as we shall see, these three types of question have a great deal in common and raise common problems. Philosophers who have written on one have usually written on all, and when a person writes on any one of them, he has traditionally been said to have written "on ethics." We shall follow the historical tradition on this point and call all of these questions "ethical," although of course they are different in important respects.

Are there any other types of question such that, when someone is raising one of them, we tend to say he has an "ethical problem"? Of course there are. Consider, for example: "Does everyone have a *moral right* to a college education if he can make good use of it?" "Are kleptomaniacs *morally responsible* for their actions?" "Is it *unfair* for people to get large incomes when they have done nothing to earn them?" In regard to these other questions, however, it can be argued with some force that they are just alternative ways of putting the three types of question we have already mentioned. For example, it may be argued that to ask whether one person has a moral right to something is really to ask whether some other persons (perhaps only one) have a moral obligation toward him, perhaps to provide conditions so that he can get the thing to which he is said to have a right, or at least not to stand in his way. Whether or not these and similar questions really are just alternative ways of putting the three types already mentioned is a matter worth discussion at a later point.

For the present, at least, it will be helpful to view our three questions as roughly defining the meaning of "ethical questions" or "ethical problem." That is, our proposal is that the occurrence of one of these questions is a mark of a problem being an "ethical" one or a mark of a problem being the kind which historically has been called "ethical." Not that one of these particular words — "right," "blameworthy," "worthwhile" and so on — needs be used. The question is an ethical one if in substance it raises a question of one of these sorts, if, in other words, it *could* be put in the words we have mentioned without losing its obvious point.

It is convenient to use this same criterion for the identification of an "ethical statement" or an "ethical assertion" — although these terms are rather technical and not much, if at all, in common currency. Any statement which implies a statement containing one of our mentioned words, or which could be contradicted by a statement containing one of them (of course, in an essential way), is usefully classified as an "ethical statement."

One might infer, from the examples we have offered, that ethical problems are always personal problems. Such an inference is incorrect. The largest issues of social policy are ethical issues. Often men in a position to decide such issues do not realize that they are ethical questions, but they are. Consider: "What are the obligations of the United States toward underdeveloped and underprivileged nations?" "Should corporate profits be exempt from tax and taxes be levied on individual income alone?" "To what level of welfare does an elderly person have a right?" "Should the racial stock be improved by sterilizing persons with an I.Q. below a certain level?" "Should medical services be provided for everyone without charge, through a system of 'socialized' medicine?" These are all ethical questions, either about whether a certain kind of system is a desirable system or about whether some individuals have an obligation to do or to work toward something. They are the most important ethical questions, although they are not questions of the kind most of us are frequently called upon to answer.

2. The philosophical theory of ethics

A. THE THEORY OF NORMATIVE ETHICS   But what has philosophy to do with such matters? Do philosophers espouse certain answers to ethical questions as part of their professional business? If so, do they claim to have quasi-mathematical demonstrations of their views?

There are some ethical questions which philosophers do not consider at all, at least as professional philosophers, although they must decide such questions all the time as persons, like everybody else. Such questions are *specific* questions about *specific* situations. Should my graduate student friend give the information to his fellow student? Should I stay in the South Pacific with my attractive young lady? Answering such questions is not the philosopher's business, as philosopher. What he is concerned with is only *general* issues, questions that are apt to come up repeatedly and that have answers which are clues to answering specific questions.

Evidently, however, general principles are highly relevant to the solution of specific problems. If I know that personal happiness is the only thing in life that is important, then I know something very important for telling whether, obligations aside, staying in the South Pacific is the desirable thing to do; the only further thing I need to know, in order to decide what is the more desirable of these alternatives, is whether I shall really be happier in one place than in the other. We do not, in practice, always answer specific ethical questions by reflecting on what is implied, for specific problems, by general principles we may happen to think correct; but we often do, and at any rate we usually appeal to such general principles if we try to meet some challenge to our conclusions.

Philosophers are concerned with which general ethical principles are true or valid or defensible. Of course, what general principles any philosopher happens to espouse is only a biographical fact about him, so far no more important than the ethical values of any other person. But philosophers also try, as part of their professional business, to give *reasons* for these principles. It is these reasons that make the philosophical enterprise important. The philosopher, moreover, is not aiming merely to give a few reasons that may convince you and me of this or that general principle; what he is aiming at is a *complete* set of general principles (or at least a general procedure for resolving such questions) and a *systematic* defense of these principles, which takes into account all the relevant evidence and pushes the offering of reasons — and the offering of reasons for the reasons — just as far as it can go, or as an intelligent person would expect it to go. In other words, while we need not interest ourselves in what general ethical principles any philosopher happens to believe, the philosopher does, or aims to, give a systematic defense of his principles. To his defense, if it be cogent, we must pay attention. For we wish to base our own ethical thinking on sound first principles or sound procedures; and if someone has shown that certain ethical principles are sound, we wish to know.

Philosophers have sometimes done, or tried to do, something more. They have produced arguments aimed to show why it is *reasonable* to take a right course of action rather than a wrong one or to live a better life rather than a worse one. Such reasoning is aimed at a problem which puzzles many people: Why we should fulfill our obligations if to do so is contrary to our personal interests, and why we should choose the theoretically "better" life if we don't happen to want it and prefer the theoretically "less worthwhile" life instead?

One may be puzzled about the kind of "defense" philosophers give for ethical principles. This is one thing the reader will shortly be finding out. But it may help to anticipate this much: Philosophers are doing essentially the same sort of thing all of us do to some extent. We all have views about the rightness of particular actions and about principles to which we may appeal in defense of the view that they are right, although we may not have formulated any explicit principles, much less have even tried to survey the total system of principles we think defensible. Moreover, most of us at some time have presumably attempted to offer some sort of defense for some general principle, for instance, "A person ought never to tell a lie" or "It is morally permissible to tell a lie when substantial injury will be done by speaking the truth." What *kind* of defenses do *we* normally offer for our conclusions about what ought to be done in a particular situation or for our acceptance of a certain principle? It is not easy to say. Sometimes we argue by citing some more general ethical principle which we think our critic will accept and claiming that the issue at hand can be viewed as a special case of this principle; sometimes we argue by showing that general acceptance of a certain principle would do a great deal of harm; probably sometimes we argue for a principle by saying that it is "human nature" to accept it or live by it or that it would not really be contested by thoughtful people who were not influenced by any special personal stake. Traditional philosophical defenses of moral judgments or principles have not been very different from such types of reasoning. The philosophers differ from nonphilosophers in large part simply in that they are systematic, comprehensive, thorough, and write in clear view of the historically important discussions of the subject. There is one possible exception to this statement. As we shall see, one part of the philosophic enterprise is to determine what ethical statements *mean* and what is their *function*. Philosophers' defenses of principle naturally take account of conclusions and controversies in this area, since evidently what a statement means may have extremely important implications for how it may intelligently be supported or criticized.

The ethical principles defended by the philosophers you will be reading are not mutually consistent, and therefore you cannot agree with all of them. Perhaps surprisingly, the disagreement is not limited to philosophers of earlier ages; there is controversy at the present moment. A great many controversies which agitated philosophers of earlier periods have now been settled; it has become clear that at least one party to the dispute — very often both — held a view that was hopelessly vague, or was based on mistaken assumptions about fact, or was involved in circular reasoning. (Some selections included in this book represent what are, in the writer's opinion, outmoded views, but ones which it is broadening to the mind to know about. For instance, it is at least enriching to one's view of human nature to know that it has seriously been contended that having power of some sort is the fundamental value in life.) But although many controversies have been settled, many have not been. About these the reader must make up his mind for himself which view is best supported and is the one best suited to guide his decisions. To make this statement, of course, is not to say that we are not now in a position to decide, with good reasons, which view is right. The reader, let us suppose, will — if he can — do just this!

B. CRITICAL ETHICS OR METAETHICS   The formulation and systematic defense of ethical principles is one job of philosophers, but it is by no means the only job. There is another one, and this second one has equal importance — indeed, in recent years more effort has been expended on it than on the first problem of ethics. What is this second problem?

This second problem, or at least part of it, is also one which nearly all of us have debated at some time or another; it is by no means a purely technical problem. All of us have heard it claimed that ethical beliefs are "only subjective opinions," that there are no solid reasons which can settle ethical controversies. This view, which we might call "ethical skepticism," is widespread today. Indeed, it is an incongruity of contemporary thought that, at the very time when people are debating — perhaps more seriously than ever before in history — such moral questions as racial segregation, warfare, and abnormal sexual behavior, ethical skepticism is more influential, probably, than it has ever been. Bertrand Russell is a perfect epitome of this incongruity in modern thought: theoretically a moral skeptic but also a vigorous debater on behalf of moral causes. Ethical skepticism, however, is by no means a purely twentieth century phenomenon; it was vigorously supported by thinkers among the Greeks.

The question of ethical skepticism, then, is not a technical philosopher's problem; it is one which most of us discuss even if we have never looked at a book on ethical theory. It is only a part of the second major problem of ethical theory. The whole second problem, the theory about which is often called "metaethics" or "critical ethics," can be divided — some secondary issues aside — into two main questions. The first is: What is the meaning, or main function or use, of ethical statements or questions? The second is: How and in what sense and to what extent may ethical statements be justified? Evidently ethical skepticism is one answer to the second question, an answer to the effect that ethical statements cannot be justified at all.

It is helpful to compare the relation between the first problem of ethics — the formulation of defensible ethical statements and the defense of them — and the problems of metaethics, with the relation between the job of the scientist and the job of the "philosopher of science." The scientist, of course, aims at formulating true statements about nature and at supporting them by a mass of evidence and reasoning, usually including experiment or observation of some sort. Obviously his job is like the one we are trying to perform when we are trying to resolve the first problem of ethics — what we may call "doing normative ethics." But then there are many questions about the work of the scientist. For instance, does his evidence ever really entail or imply the propositions about the world which he asserts? In other words, would it be logically consistent to admit his evidence and at the same time reject his conclusion? Exactly what is the logical relation between his evidence and his conclusion? Can the scientist's passage from evidence to conclusion be justified if the former does not actually entail the latter? What kind of justification might be given? These questions are closely parallel to the questions we raise about normative ethics when we are doing "metaethics." We are standing off and observing the arguments we tend to offer when we are doing normative ethics. We are asking whether, in view of the meaning of ethical statements, the evidence we offer for them actually entails the ethical statement. Or, we are asking what is the exact logical relation between the two, and whether the inference of one from the other is justified, and if so how. Metaethics raises much the same questions about the inferences or arguments of normative ethics that the philosophy of science raises about the inferences or arguments of the working scientist.

The two main questions of critical ethics are closely related, since information about the meaning or function of ethical statements will be highly relevant to how an ethical statement may intelligently be supported. This relation may not be obvious. But suppose you thought, as some do, that to say "Stealing is wrong" is really to issue a general command, "Don't steal — anybody, ever!" Then you would hardly expect to support such a statement by *evidence*. If someone says, "Please close the door" and we challenge his request, we do not ask, "What's your evidence?" Evidence is not relevant. Evidence is pertinent only if we are concerned with a statement the truth or falsity of which we wish to assess. Now it is absurd to say that "Please close the door" is true or false; and it would be equally absurd to say that "Stealing is wrong" is true or false if it means just the same as "Don't steal — anybody, ever!" Therefore, on this command theory of ethical statements, the "support" that we can sensibly give an ethical statement will not be the offering of evidence but something else. Just what else would be a question to be decided. Evidently, if we adopt a command theory of ethical statements, one kind of "support" will be sensible; whereas if we think that "Stealing is wrong" is like "Psychoses always are caused by chemical imbalance," then we shall offer a different kind of "support," the support of evidence, just as the scientist offers evidence for his assertions.

At first thought it may seem absurd to suppose that ethical statements are not true or false or that they are essentially unlike the statements of the empirical sciences. And it may seem absurd to take skepticism seriously. One may say that philosophers of science do not take skepticism seriously as a view about scientific theories. Why should we consider it any more seriously when we are reflecting on the inferences of normative ethics? It seems worthwhile, in order to be clear how very important critical ethics is, to have a brief look at one of the lines of reasoning which has led many into the camp of ethical skepticism. There are other such lines of reasoning, but we cannot include them here.

The skeptic, then, may argue that if any ethical belief is challenged, a thoughtful person will naturally defend it by appeal to accepted premises, much as a physicist backs his theory by pointing to experiments. But the skeptic will point out that some of these premises must themselves be ethical statements: for we can validly infer that something is right or wrong from given premises only if one of them states that something is right or wrong — just as Euclid's theorems about points and lines would not follow from his axioms unless the latter mentioned points and lines. At least there must be one such premise if our inference is to qualify as valid deductive or inductive reasoning, of the kind used in mathematics and the sciences. We are thus led to a disturbing conclusion: if valid reasoning in ethics is to be what it is in mathematics or science, there must be at least one ethical premise which is reasonably believed without backing by further reasoning from premises. Why is this conclusion "disturbing"? The reason is: What may be our reason for accepting such a basic premise? Not a reason such as we have for accepting premises in pure mathematics, that it is true by definition. Nor is it prima-facie plausible to say that a first ethical premise has grounds like those we have for the premises of natural science, that it simply describes a fact of experiment or observation. The alternative, the skeptic says, is thus inescapable: the ultimate premises which support our moral thinking themselves have *no* support, however committed to them we may be after years of training and habituation. Obviously the skeptic's argument is not merely foolish.

Whatever one's eventual assessment of the skeptic's reasoning may be, it is clear that the logical status of ethical principles, and the type of reasoning which may properly be offered in support of them, deserve careful attention. And not merely for the intrinsic interest of the puzzle, although it does have such interest. It is of interest because reflection on these issues may or will result in an ideal model for ethical reasoning, proper for us in thinking about normative ethics. Thus the conclusions of metaethics may show us what we sensibly can do and cannot do in the way of supporting our ethical judgments. Presumably we shall think more sensibly and clearly, in our ordinary reasoning about ethical judgments, because of familiarity with the theories of critical ethics.

Can we point to an agreed consensus among serious students of the problems of critical ethics more than we can among students of normative ethics? No, we cannot, although probably for a rather different reason: the issues are highly complex, and an accurate statement of the relevant facts is difficult to obtain. In any event, the fact is that there is lively controversy today, among philosophers, on the issues of critical ethics, and widely different views are held by otherwise sane and intelligent writers. The reader must, again, simply make his own assessment of the reasoning in support of the various views.

It might be inferred that, until the problems of critical ethics are settled, the discussion of normative ethics might as well be given up. For, it might be said, until we know the answers to the questions of critical ethics, we do not even have a clear idea what we are supposed to be proving or how we should go about it. Until we do, any complicated intellectual maneuvers made in formulation or support of ethical principles are bound to be merely confusing.

Such an inference would be unfortunate. It would be like saying we should suspend the activities of the scientist until we have solved all the problems of the philosopher of science. In the case of ethics, we admittedly do our normative thinking less effectively until we are straight in our taethical views. Nevertheless, we *must* do it as well as we can, for we have :isions to make, and we wish to make these decisions as intelligently as possible. We must not make the mistake of condemning better reasoning simply because it is not the best. There are two further important points which support the view that it is sensible to go ahead with our normative reflections even before we are convinced that the problems of metaethics are all solved. The first point I can only offer here as a suggestion, although I have argued it at length elsewhere.* It is that if there is some reasoning which, after most careful thought, we find ourselves willing to accept as weighty support for an ethical judgment, metaethical thinking will not be able to show, because of the very nature of its own necessary premises, that such reasoning is wrong or ought not to be accepted as weighty support. The second point is that in good part various metaethical theories do not differ about whether a form of reasoning, which we naturally feel is effective reasoning in support of an ethical principle, really is "good" or permissible reasoning; where they differ is in their theory about the kind of reason it is, whether it is a strict logical proof or rather like the kind of reason we offer in support of "Please close the door." In general, metaethical theories do not assert that reasoning about ethical judgments or principles is superfluous or irrelevant; what these theories do is make assertions about what is going on, or what may be going on, when we reason about ethics. A correct metaethical theory, then, is not a necessary precondition for effective ethical reasoning, although it is a means for doing it more self-consciously, more intelligently and successfully.

3. The plan of the present book

A study of the problems of ethical theory naturally must include the problems both of normative ethical theory and of metaethics.

What types of normative question should be considered? Since there are three main ethical concepts — the desirable or worthwhile, the right and wrong or obligatory, and the praiseworthy and blameworthy — a thorough study of normative theory will examine formulations of general principles corresponding to these three concepts, and of defenses or justifications which have been offered for these general principles. In the present book, general principles about the desirable are considered first, and then principles about right and wrong conduct. Principles about what is praiseworthy and blameworthy are examined in the final chapter, under the title of "Moral Responsibility," in connection with the problem of freedom and determinism, to which they are highly relevant.

Some philosophers, it should be noticed, would not agree to the third of these concepts being separable as a special topic. Some would say that the question when an action or an agent is praiseworthy or blameworthy is

* Richard Brandt, *Ethical Theory* (Englewood Cliffs, N. J.: Prentice-Hall, 1959), Ch. 10 and pp. 178-79.

simply the question when an action or an agent is *valuable or good* because of a certain quality or property; accordingly, this third issue is a special department of the first. Other philosophers would say that the question when an action or agent is praiseworthy or blameworthy is simply the question when it is *right* to praise or blame an agent for his conduct; in this case the third issue is a special department of the second. There are still other theories. In view of this disagreement, the reader should give special thought to the relations of these concepts.

There are two other major ethical concepts which, although I believe they are in some way reducible to those already mentioned and hence theoretically need not be discussed at length, are practically so important in the thinking of the contemporary world that they deserve separate discussion: human rights and justice.

At the present time many rights are often said to belong to every human being: the right to freedom of speech and to freedom of travel, the right to freedom of worship and to opportunity for employment commensurate with one's abilities. The student of ethical theory will want to be in a position to assess what can seriously be claimed to be a right of everyone and what cannot. Moreover, since there are institutions protecting rights — the law courts and the system of free public education, for instance — an examination of what are really rights is at the same time an examination of the ethical foundations of some institutions.

The concept of justice plays an equally important part in contemporary thought. Traditionally it has been felt that there are two distinct kinds, or at least problems, of justice: that concerning distribution of goods, especially economic goods ("distributive justice"), and that concerning the allocation of rewards and punishments, especially by the state, in view of past behavior ("retributive justice"). Certainly there are two exceedingly important and distinct practical questions here: How should economic goods, or any goods the distribution of which can be modified by human decision, be distributed? And, what is the proper treatment of individuals who have trampled on the rights of others? (Or, instead of this second question, we might ask, if we assume that the criminal law is primarily designed to prohibit infringing the rights of others, What principles should govern the framing of the criminal law, with its provisions for punishment of persons who behave in antisocial ways?) As with rights, an examination of the concept of justice and related principles is at once an examination of the ethical foundations of important institutions: the economic system (taken broadly to include the whole system of remuneration for services, ownership and production, and taxation) and criminal justice.

In the present book separate attention is given to both rights and justice, so that, in all, five kinds of normative concepts and principles are discussed: the desirable and undesirable, the right and wrong, the praiseworthy and blameworthy, human rights, and justice.

The problems of metaethics fall into two groups. First, there is the most

important question how, or to what extent, ethical statements can be justified or given rational support. Will a reasonable defense of them be like
the defense we might give for the principles of arithmetic, or those of
physics and psychology? Or are ethical statements corollaries of theology
or revelation? Or will rational support be of some entirely different kind?
Or perhaps can no such support at all be given? Theories supporting each of
these views must be considered. The examination of this issue will, of course,
include a discussion of what ethical statements mean or do. The second
question is quite different. Assuming some conclusion has been reached
on the first question, one must then ask: Are there really any ethical principles which can be regarded as universally valid? Many social scientists have
urged, on the basis of anthropological and psychological facts and theories,
that there are few, if any, universally valid ethical principles; they have suggested that very often an ethical principle is valid for some people or peoples
but that some quite different and conflicting principle is valid for some other
people or peoples.

Thus there are, in addition to the five normative topics we have
sketched, two metaethical subjects to be discussed. These seven themes
correspond, with one exception, to the divisions of the present book. The
exception is justice. In Chapter 6 the principles of justice, both distributive and retributive, are discussed. But they are discussed as examples of
a larger problem, that of the moral assessment of institutions generally. In
this same chapter three other issues, all rather closely related to justice, are
considered: the institution of the family, with its rights and duties; the
moral justification for private property; and the ethical basis for claims on
behalf of democratic government. Examination of these topics will give further insight into the way in which ethical theory may be applied to concrete problems.

Should we begin by reading normative ethics or critical ethics? Each
procedure has its advantages. If we begin with critical ethics, we shall be
more alive to what is going on when we turn to normative ethics; we shall
notice the confusions and assumptions of the various writers, and we shall
be able to classify the kinds of reasoning on which they rely. If we begin
with normative ethics, then we shall go to critical ethics with substantial
knowledge of how people have actually argued ethical questions, with concrete background which gives life to what otherwise might seem abstract
argument. In reading the selections in the present book, either method may
be adopted; the discussions and selections concerning both normative and
critical ethics have been prepared so as not to presuppose knowledge of the
other major topic. In the arrangement of the topics in the book, however,
a compromise has been adopted: the discussion of critical ethics is introduced after the readings on what is worthwhile and what is right and wrong,
but before the material on the three remaining normative problems.

Since a great many people, including most of the giants of intellectual
history, have concerned themselves seriously with the problems of ethics,

it has been difficult to decide which passages most merit assembly in the present volume, for the attention of the student. It is clear enough what general policy should guide the process of selection: those passages should appear which, in one way or another, contain the clearest statements and most cogently argued defenses of the several major, possible theories. (The editor has excluded his own writings on principle — and in particular his *Ethical Theory*,* in which his own conclusions and arguments are set forth.) The application of this policy, however, is not easy. The policy has led to the exclusion of sheer ethical teaching, even the teaching of the great religious figures. For the teachers of historically influential moral codes were not aiming at clear and precise formulations or concerned with giving rational support for their views; indeed, they seem to have had no meta-ethical theories at all. Nevertheless, the policy does not imply limiting ourselves to writings of the past few decades, excluding the large figures of the past. It would do so, presumably, if we were here studying some branch of the natural sciences. But philosophy does not require to be rewritten every time there is a new technical development. Thus, while contemporary writers naturally find it easier to be clear, assert what is defensible, and argue forcibly in favor of their views because they stand on the shoulders of earlier philosophers, it often happens that something said by Aristotle or Hume is as true and as forcibly defended as anything which has been said in recent years. Indeed, what is written by Aristotle or Hume often enjoys a distinct advantage over contemporary literature — that it is said more gracefully. There are no reasons why we need exclude all the literature of the past from our consideration, then; and there are sometimes aesthetic reasons for including it. In deference to the historical interests of the reader, in this book passages by important figures from the history of philosophy have been preferred to those by contemporary writers, when — but only when — the merits of the passages are roughly equal.

LITERATURE ON ETHICS

Textbooks

Out of the great number of books available, the following are mentioned as especially pertinent.

Baylis, Charles A. *Ethics: The Principles of Wise Choice.* New York: Holt, 1958. Lucid, reasonably comprehensive, of medium difficulty.

Brandt, Richard B. *Ethical Theory.* Englewood Cliffs, N. J.: Prentice-Hall, 1959. Clear and comprehensive.

Carritt, E. F. *Ethical and Political Thinking.* New York: Oxford Univ. Press, 1947. Brief, sharp, covers problems of special interest, too terse to be easy to read, from an intuitionist point of view.

Castell, Alburey. *An Elementary Ethics.* Englewood Cliffs, N. J.: Prentice-Hall, 1954. Not comprehensive, but clear and elementary.

* *Ibid.*

Dewey, John, and J. H. Tufts. *Ethics*. New York: Holt, 1938. Shows insight and is interesting because it is John Dewey.

Ewing, Alfred Cyril. *Ethics*. New York: Macmillan, 1953. Brief, clear, fairly elementary discussion of many problems.

Garnett, A. Campbell. *Ethics: A Critical Introduction*. New York: Ronald Press, 1960. Reasonably comprehensive.

Garvin, Lucius. *A Modern Introduction to Ethics*. Boston: Houghton Mifflin, 1953. Interesting material on student ideas.

Rashdall, Hastings. *Theory of Good and Evil*. New York: Oxford Univ. Press, 1924. 2 vols. An older book, but thorough and comprehensive; some chapters still worth looking at.

Sharp, F. C. *Ethics*. New York: Appleton-Century, 1928. Another older book; interesting partly because of rich illustrative material.

Titus, Harold H. *Ethics for Today*. New York: American Book, 1936. Practical emphasis.

Histories of ethical thought

Broad, C. D. *Five Types of Ethical Theory*. New York: Humanities Press, 1960. Critical analyses of five historical figures.

Copleston, F. *A History of Philosophy*. London: Burns, Oates & Washbourn Ltd., 1947. 7 vols. Excellent discussions of the ethical theories of the historic figures.

Rogers, A. K. *Morals in Review*. New York: Macmillan, 1927. A careful account of all the major figures.

Sidgwick, Henry. *Outlines of the History of Ethics*. 6th ed. London: Macmillan, 1931. Brief, sensible, quite complete coverage.

The reader will find it helpful to consult these histories on the historical figures whose work is cited below. The histories will not be mentioned in the lists of further readings provided in connection with the selections.

1

WHAT IS WORTHWHILE?

1. *The desirable, the desired, and the right*

It is a matter of universal agreement that there is sometimes a discrepancy between what people want and what is good for them to have or do. Every language, anthropologists tell us, contains words used to mark off what is considered really good or worthwhile from what people may like or want. Moreover, it is generally supposed that it is relatively easy for a person to know what he wants or would like to have but a much more difficult matter to learn what is worthwhile or what would be the objects of a reasonable desire.

This distinction between the desirable or worthwhile, and the desired or wanted, may seem obvious, but the two are often confused. It is especially easy to fall into the confusion if we talk of the subject in terms of "values." "What are the main values in life?" may mean "What are the things most worthwhile or desirable in life?" But the question "What are American values?" is apt to mean "What do Americans think are the most valuable or worthwhile things?" or perhaps something close to "What do Americans want?" or "What do Americans work for?" If we are careful, we shall see that the question "What are American values?" is one properly answered by the sociologist or anthropologist and by means of questionnaires or other means of ascertaining what people think or want. But answering this question does not tell us what Americans would want or think desirable if they were more rational or better informed. To think that the two questions are not distinct is like thinking that the question "Is there a God?" is the same question as "Do Americans think there is a God?"

There is also a more excusable reason for failing to distinguish the two questions: what people do in fact desire in some circumstances may be a clue to what is desirable. Probably most philosophers would agree that if nobody would desire a certain thing under any circumstances, then it is not desirable; and they would agree that if everybody would desire something under absolutely all circumstances, then it is desirable. But to say this, of course, is by no means to identify the desired with the desirable — although it does motivate us to think harder of what the relation between the two may properly be said to be. Just what this relation is, we shall leave for the chapter on critical ethics.

But if, when we ask if something is worthwhile, we are not just asking whether some or all people want or like it, then what are we asking? A correct answer is: to ask if something is worthwhile is to ask if it is a *good thing,* or a *desirable thing,* or a *valuable thing,* in at least one of the senses of each of these terms. Of course, to say this is not to say much; to say it is not to give any kind of analysis or definition of "worthwhile"; the statement does not explain or unravel the meaning of "worthwhile" in the way in which we explain the meaning of "square" by giving a definition in terms of lines or angles. At a later stage, in the chapter on meta-ethics, we shall include readings from philosophers who have tried to perform this further and harder feat; but what they have to say is controversial and somewhat technical, and we do well to postpone it. In any event, we should not forget that there is a sense in which we all already understand these words. We have been using them and hearing them used since we were small children. It is not as if these words were technical words which we need to learn to use or words in a language we do not understand; we can all be presumed to be familiar with their use.

Nevertheless, it may be helpful, despite our familiarity with these words, to contrast them with words of another group: "right," "wrong," and "obligation." The most important thing to notice about the difference is that it does not follow, from the fact that something is the *best thing* a person can do, that he is *obligated* to do it or that it is wrong for him to fail to do it. Some philosophers have thought that if something is worthwhile, a person is morally obligated to produce it if he can, provided doing so is not incompatible with his producing something better. Perhaps he is obligated; but it seems that to say that something is good or best is not yet to *say* that we are morally obligated to produce it, even if in fact we always are. Indeed, it seems that sometimes we are not so obligated: for instance, it may be that, everything considered, the most desirable thing for me to do this summer is to take a month off for vacation and drive to the West Coast; but surely, even if such a vacation is most desirable, I may well not be *obligated* to spend the summer in this way. The desirable or worthwhile, then, is a concept different from that of moral obligation; and the same can be said for its relation to the concepts of right and wrong. One fact that brings out this difference is that moral obligation involves possibility in a way in which desirability does not: we can say, for instance, that it is desirable for man to enjoy eternal youth, but we can hardly say there is a moral obligation for men to have it or for anyone to produce it — the most we could say is that a person would have a moral obligation to produce it *if* he could.

To say that the concept of the good or desirable is different from the concepts of the right and the obligatory, however, is by no means to deny that knowing what is good or desirable is of the greatest importance for deciding what is right or a matter of moral obligation. Many philosophers have thought that the *only* thing we have to know, in order to decide which act is right, is which act among all the acts we might perform would bring about the best total state of affairs. Such philosophers are often called *teleologists* (from the Greek *telos* meaning "end" or "purpose"), meaning that what is right is decided by the value or worth of the result achieved. Some philosophers (for instance, G. E. Moore in his *Principia Ethica*) have even said that what we *mean* when we say an act is right, is simply that it is the act which, among those we can perform, will produce the best results. This latter view, as we shall see later, is open to serious objections. But the main thesis of the teleologists must be taken very seriously — that the right act is in fact the one, of those an agent could perform, that will achieve the most valuable results. Moreover, practically all philosophers today would agree that even if the view of the teleologists is incorrect, whether an action will have good or bad results is at least very important for its being right or wrong; and presumably we should all agree that if an act would be very seriously harmful to other persons — for instance, might result even in their death — a strong presumption would have been raised that it was not right. To say that something is desirable or worthwhile, then, is not yet to say that it, or something else, is right or obligatory; but the question of what is right or obligatory is closely related to the question of what is worthwhile or good; and knowledge of what consequences, desirable or undesirable, an act will have is highly relevant for deciding whether it is right or wrong.

2. *The desirable and the intrinsically desirable*

So far we have not distinguished the concept of the *intrinsically* desirable. It is important to mark this concept, although it is not easy to state exactly what it is.

The concept is not just a philosopher's concept; we make use of it, at least vaguely, all the time. For instance, suppose a dentist is repairing a tooth which is decayed in a sensitive area. He and his patient may agree that a shot of novocaine would be a "good thing." Neither of them thinks, however, that a shot of novocaine is a good thing just for itself. It is good only for its effects: it is a good thing because it deadens pain. On the other hand, the dentist and his patient will agree that pain is an undesirable thing in itself. Unlike the novocaine shot, its badness is not a matter of its consequences. Perhaps pain *does* have bad consequences: perhaps a patient in severe pain will not sit still, and the dentist will do a bad job of repairing his tooth; or perhaps it will unnerve the patient and he will have to go home to bed. But we think that even if the pain did not have these consequences, it would still be bad. In much the same way, we think that attending a play we enjoy, or watching a sunset over a mountain lake, or spending Christmas day happily with our family or friends is something worthwhile, quite irrespective of consequences. Each of these things, or some part or aspect of them, we think desirable for itself.

To mark these distinctions, we shall say that pain is intrinsically undesirable and that watching a sunset or attending a play we enjoy is intrinsically desirable; whereas we shall say that having the novocaine (assuming the experience of having it is neither pleasant nor unpleasant) is neither the one nor the other — but, if we like, "instrumentally" desirable.*

A rough definition of "intrinsic value" might be phrased as follows. Something is intrinsically desirable if it would be properly valued or desired or chosen for its own sake, when considered independently of its consequences; and a thing is intrinsically undesirable if it would be properly avoided or disvalued for its own sake, in abstraction from its consequences.

It may not be clear why the distinction is of practical importance. Its importance lies in that it directs attention to something we tend to forget, that some things are *not* intrinsically valuable and that we are mistaken if we act as if they were. For instance, we might forget that money is not intrinsically worthwhile. Forgetting this fact, we might accept a new post because it paid us five thousand dollars more, even though in that post we should be doing what we do not wish to do, even though our present salary is quite adequate for all our wants, and even though what we could buy with the additional five thousand dollars is not anything greatly to be valued. (Everything would be changed, of course, if it could be shown that money is intrinsically worthwhile, at least in relation to persons of certain temperaments; I am assuming for the moment that this is not true.) Again, a student might set his heart on earning A's and spend so much time studying that he misses important parts of the education he might have had. But is getting an A an event of intrinsic value? One will hardly say so; and curiously, it is of relatively small instrumental value either, except for those who may need good records for purposes of acceptance and scholarship aid in a graduate school. Of course, one may well be pleased to receive an A: to receive it is assurance of merit of some kind. But it is hardly sensible to work for an A just for its own sake. People's lives generally would probably be much more effective, and their energies spent more efficiently, if there were periodic times of housecleaning — times for reassessment of plans and ambitions in view of their likelihood of achieving things of intrinsic value. Such a reassessment would probably show that many things we work for are neither intrinsic nor instrumental values. It is helpful to divide values into the intrinsic and the instrumental precisely because such a division may well show that some things we work for belong to neither class and are best forgotten!

Let us try to formulate our definition of "intrinsically desirable" a bit more precisely. First, it is clarifying to put our beliefs about things being desirable into a standard form, "It is desirable that . . ."; then we can say that what is desirable is the fact or event described in the that-clause. For

---

* There are complications. Pain is sometimes a necessary part of something that is good in view of its consequences, for instance, a life-saving operation in the days before anesthetics. And experience with pain may be necessary for ability to sympathize with others or for some kinds of aesthetic appreciation.

instance, suppose it is desirable that John be given a local anesthetic before his wound is sewn up; then, of course, we should say that what is desirable is that John be given a local anesthetic. Next, we can raise the question what it is that makes such things desirable, or more desirable, than they otherwise might have been. In the case of John's anesthetic, for example, evidently what makes this event desirable is such facts as that without an anesthetic, treatment of the wound will be painful and that without it the surgeon will be unable to do a job which will leave no scar. Now such facts that make an event desirable may or may not be different from the very fact or event originally said to be desirable and may be different from anything included in, or logically required or necessitated by, this fact or event. In our example both the reasons are different from that event which was said to be desirable — that John receive the anesthetic. If *all* the facts which make some event or fact desirable are different from it, we shall say that the thing which is desirable is not *intrinsically* desirable at all. However, in some cases one of the reasons something is desirable is just the kind of thing it is itself. For instance, suppose it is desirable for Lucy to know about Aquinas' theory of analogous predication. If you ask why, one reason properly given, perhaps, is that Lucy will be more sparkling at cocktail parties by reason of mastery of this branch of theological thought. But perhaps knowing about Aquinas' work is some reason in itself. At least, if it is a reason, then we shall say that her knowing this material is *to some extent intrinsically* desirable. In some cases, possibly the *only* reason for something being desirable is of this sort. For instance, suppose that enjoying a sunset over a mountain lake is desirable. Perhaps there is no reason why this enjoyment is desirable beyond itself. In this case, we shall say that this thing is *solely intrinsically* desirable.

Some facts or events, then, are desirable for no reason beyond their being what they are; they are solely intrinsically desirable. Other facts or events are desirable solely for reasons beyond themselves, usually their effects; they are not intrinsically desirable at all. Still other things are desirable partly just because of what they are but partly because of other things, pre-eminently their effects; they are in part intrinsically desirable but in part desirable for other reasons.

Our suggestion is that often it is clarifying and worthwhile to think through our values and try to decide which ones are intrinsic, wholly or partly, and which ones are not. Our suggestion is that sometimes such reflection will surprise us by disclosing that some things we had thought worthwhile are not worthwhile at all.

The facts that make something desirable need not themselves be intrinsically desirable. For instance, if we say that John's having an anesthetic is a good thing because otherwise the surgeon will not be able to do a job which will leave no scar, we can still ask, "Why is it desirable not to have a scar?" and more reasons will be forthcoming, perhaps aesthetic ones. It would seem, however, that if anything is desirable at all, it must be because some facts or events (perhaps the thing itself) are intrinsically desirable. But a person would not be contradicting himself if he denied this statement, and it is an interesting question for reflection what one should say to a person who did deny it. Of course, we need not say that any fact or event is *solely* intrinsically desirable; maybe the enjoyable contemplation of a sunset is a good thing partly because it changes our perspectives and makes us more relaxed.

3. *Proposals about what is desirable*

Almost any kind of fact or event can in some contexts be desirable. Therefore, if we are to set ourselves a task of manageable proportions, we had better confine ourselves to inquiring what kinds of thing are *intrinsically* desirable. Indeed, even more narrowly, we do well to confine ourselves to asking what are the *ultimate* intrinsic values, that is, things which are intrinsically valuable as wholes, not just because some part or aspect of them is so. (The enjoyable watching of a sunset might be intrinsically valuable only because it is enjoyable or because it is an enjoyable aesthetic experience — in which event we might do better to exclude things like watching sunsets from our list of intrinsic values.)

In the readings which follow, the important thing to consider is the proposals that are made about ultimate intrinsic values and what is offered in the way of argument to support such judgments. Not all the philosophers whose work is included made just the distinctions we have been making; in such cases we must be content with coming as close as possible to the material we want.

It is convenient to classify the things said to be intrinsically or ultimately desirable under the following heads: (1) states of consciousness; (2) states of individual living beings which are not states of consciousness; (3) states of individual nonliving beings; and (4) relational structures of which individual beings are components. An example of (1) might be pleasure or enjoyment; an example of (2) might be just life itself; an example of (3) might be the beauty of a landscape when seen by no one; and an example of (4) might be a distribution of happiness corresponding to merit or virtue. Some proposals about what is desirable are hard to locate in this scheme. For instance, suppose someone says that having knowledge (say, knowledge of mathematics) is intrinsically worthwhile. Is knowledge a state of consciousness? We may be inclined to say "Yes" when we reflect that we should not think a person knew something if he could never remember it and it never occurred to him in a relevant context; we are also inclined to say "No" when we reflect that it is at least odd to say that a person doesn't "know" something when he is asleep and thinking of nothing, provided he shows familiarity with the fact in question in relevant waking moments. The same thing is true of states of character, like generosity and conscientiousness. Perhaps we should introduce another category into the above scheme to accommodate such hybrids more naturally.

If a philosopher thinks that pleasure and *only pleasure* is intrinsically worthwhile, he is called a *hedonist* (after the Greek *hedone*, meaning "pleasure"). If he is not a hedonist, but thinks all the intrinsic values fall within classes (1) and (2), it is convenient to call him a *personal pluralist* about values. If he thinks that some intrinsic values fall within classes (3) and (4), it is convenient to call him an *impersonal pluralist*; but one should notice that an impersonal pluralist might also think there are intrinsic values under headings (1) and (2).

Epicurus (341-270 B.C.)

PLEASURE THE ONLY INTRINSIC VALUE

Epicurus was born in Samos, the son of an Athenian. He came to Athens in 306 B.C. and founded a school. Unlike Socrates, Plato, and Aristotle, he believed that pleasure is the only thing intrinsically desirable. He was not the first hedonist, however. Aristippus of Cyrene (*c.* 435-366 B.C.) had already started the Cyrenaic school, and Democritus (*c.* 460-370 B.C.) should probably also be counted as a hedonist. But Epicurus wrote widely and had much influence, notably on the Roman Lucretius, whose *De Rerum Natura* was an expression of Epicurus' ideas. Unlike many of the other hedonists of his day, Epicurus did not consider that a life of pleasure must be a life of indulgence; he believed that the pleasantest life is one of serenity (*ataraxia*).

Our chief source of information about his work is Diogenes Laertius' (*c.* A.D. 230) *Lives of Eminent Philosophers*, which has been translated into English by R. D. Hicks in the series of The Loeb Classical Library. The following selection is drawn from Book X, beginning with the very end of section 122. At this point Diogenes quotes a letter by Epicurus.

Reprinted by permission of the publishers and The Loeb Classical Library from Diogenes Laertius, *Lives of Eminent Philosophers*, translated by R. D. Hicks, Cambridge, Mass., Harvard University Press.

LIVES OF EMINENT PHILOSOPHERS

Epicurus to Menoeceus, greeting.

Let no one be slow to seek wisdom when he is young nor weary in the search thereof when he is grown old. For no age is too early or too late for the health of the soul. And to say that the season for studying philosophy has not yet come, or that it is past and gone, is like saying that the season for happiness is not yet or that it is now no more. Therefore, both old and young ought to seek wisdom, the former in order that, as age comes over him, he may be young in good things because of the grace of what has been, and the latter in order that, while he is young, he may at the same time be old, because he has no fear of the things which are to come. So we must exercise ourselves in the things which bring happiness, since, if that be present, we have everything, and, if that be absent, all our actions are directed toward attaining it. . . .

Accustom thyself to believe that death is nothing to us, for good and evil imply sentience, and death is the privation of all sentience; therefore a right understanding that death is nothing to us makes the mortality of life enjoyable, not by adding to life an illimitable time, but by taking away the yearning after immortality. For life has no terrors for him who has thoroughly apprehended that there are no terrors for him in ceasing to live. Foolish, therefore, is the man who says that he fears death, not because it will pain when it comes, but because it pains in the prospect. Whatsoever causes no annoyance when it is present, causes only a groundless pain in the expectation. . . .

We must also reflect that of desires some are natural, others are groundless; and that of the natural some are necessary as well as natural, and some natural only. And of the necessary desires some are necessary if we are to be happy, some if the body is to be rid of uneasiness, some if we are even to live. He who has a clear and certain understanding of these things will direct every preference and aversion toward securing health of body and tranquility of mind, seeing that this is the sum and end of a blessed life. For the end of all our actions is to be free from pain and fear, and, when once we have attained all this, the tempest of the soul is laid; seeing that the living creature has no need to go in search of something that is lacking, nor to look for anything else by which the good of the soul and of the body will be fulfilled. When we are pained because of the absence of pleasure, then, and then only, do we feel the need of pleasure. Wherefore we call pleasure the alpha and omega of a blessed life. Pleasure is our first and kindred good. It is the starting-point of every choice and of every aversion, and to it we come back, inasmuch as we make feeling the rule by which to judge of every good thing. And since pleasure is our first and native good, for that reason we do not choose every pleasure whatsoever, but ofttimes pass over many pleasures when a greater annoyance ensues from them. And ofttimes we consider pains superior to pleasures when submission to the pains for a long time brings us as a consequence a greater pleasure. While therefore all pleasure because it is naturally akin to us is good, not all pleasure is choiceworthy, just as all pain is an evil and yet not all pain is to be shunned. It is, however, by measuring one against another, and by looking at the conveniences and inconveniences, that all these matters must be judged. Sometimes we treat the good as an evil, and the evil, on the contrary, as a good. Again, we regard independence of outward things as a great good, not so as in all cases to use little, but so as to be contented with little if we have not much, being honestly persuaded that they have the sweetest enjoyment of luxury who stand least in need of it, and that whatever is natural is easily procured and only the vain and worthless hard to win. Plain fare gives as much pleasure as a costly diet, when once the pain of want has been removed, while bread and water confer the highest possible pleasure when they are brought to hungry lips. To habituate one's self, therefore, to simple and inexpensive diet supplies all that is needful for health, and enables a man to meet the necessary requirements of life without shrinking, and it places us in a better condition when we approach at intervals a costly fare and renders us fearless of fortune.

When we say, then, that pleasure is the end and aim, we do not mean the pleasures of the prodigal or the pleasures of sensuality, as we are understood to do by some through ignorance, prejudice, or wilful misrepresentation. By pleasure we mean the absence of pain in the body and of trouble in the soul. It is not an unbroken succession of drinking-bouts and of revelry, not sexual love, not the enjoyments of the fish and other delicacies of a luxurious table, which produce a pleasant life; it is sober reasoning, searching out the grounds of every choice and avoidance, and banishing those beliefs through which the greatest tumults take possession of the soul. Of all this the beginning and the greatest good is prudence. Wherefore prudence is a more precious thing even than philosophy; from it spring all the other virtues, for it teaches that we cannot lead a life of pleasure which is not also a life of prudence, honour, and justice; nor lead a life of prudence, honour, and justice, which is not also a life of pleasure. For the virtues have grown into one with a pleasant life, and a pleasant life is inseparable from them.

Who, then, is superior in thy judgment to such a man? He holds a holy belief concerning the gods, and is altogether free from the fear of death. He has diligently considered the end fixed by nature, and understands how easily the limit of good things can be reached and attained, and how either the duration or the intensity of evils is but slight. Destiny, which some introduce as sovereign over all things, he laughs to scorn, affirming rather that some things happen of necessity, others by chance, others through our own agency. For he sees that necessity destroys responsibility and that chance or fortune is inconstant; whereas our own actions are free, and it is to them that praise or blame naturally attach. . . .

Exercise thyself in these and kindred precepts day and night, both by thyself and with him who is like unto thee; then never, either in waking or in dream, wilt thou be disturbed, but wilt live as a god among men. For man loses all semblance of mortality by living in the midst of immortal blessings.

[After citing the above letter from Epicurus, Diogenes goes on to describe the ideas of Epicurus as follows:]

He differs from the Cyrenaics with regard to pleasure. They do not include under the term the pleasure which is a state of rest, but only that which consists in motion. Epicurus admits both; also pleasure of mind as well as of body. . . . The words of Epicurus in his work *On Choice* are: "Peace of mind and freedom from pain are pleasures which imply a state of rest; joy and delight are seen to consist in motion and activity."

He further disagrees with the Cyrenaics in that they hold that pains of body are worse than mental pains; at all events evil-doers are made to suffer bodily punishment; whereas Epicurus holds the pains of the mind to be the worse; at any rate the flesh endures the storms of the present alone, the mind those of the past and future as well as the present. In this way also he holds mental pleasures to be greater than those of the body. And as proof that pleasure is the end he adduces the fact that living things, so soon as they are born, are well content with pleasure and are at enmity with pain, by the prompting of nature and apart from any reason. . . .

And we choose the virtues too on account of pleasure and not for their own sake, as we take medicine for the sake of health. . . . Epicurus describes virtue as the *sine qua non* of pleasure, *i.e.* the one thing without which pleasure cannot be, everything else, food, for instance, being separable, *i.e.* not indispensable to pleasure.

Come, then, let me set the seal, so to say, on my entire work as well as on this philosopher's life by citing his Sovran Maxims, therewith bringing the whole work to a close and making the end of it to coincide with the beginning of happiness. . . . [Excerpts from the Maxims follow.]

3. The magnitude of pleasure reaches its limit in the removal of all pain. When pleasure is present, so long as it is uninterrupted, there is no pain either of body or of mind or of both together.

4. Continuous pain does not last long in the flesh; on the contrary, pain, if extreme, is present a very short time, and even that degree of pain which barely outweighs pleasure in the flesh does not last for many days together. Illnesses of long duration even permit of an excess of pleasure over pain in the flesh.

5. It is impossible to live a pleasant life without living wisely and well and justly, and it is impossible to live wisely and well and justly without living pleasantly. Whenever any one of these is lacking, when, for instance, the man is not able to live wisely, though he lives well and justly, it is impossible for him to live a pleasant life. . . .

7. Some men have sought to become famous and renowned, thinking that thus they would make themselves secure against their fellow-men. If, then, the life of such persons really was secure, they attained natural good; if, however, it was insecure, they have not attained the end which by nature's own prompting they originally sought.

8. No pleasure is in itself evil, but the things which produce certain pleasures entail annoyances many times greater than the pleasures themselves. . . .

10. If the objects which are productive of pleasures to profligate persons really freed them from fears of the mind, — the fears, I mean, inspired by celestial and atmospheric phenomena, the fear of death, the fear of pain; if, further, they taught them to limit their desires, we should never have any fault to find with such persons, for they would then be filled with pleas-

ures to overflowing on all sides and would be exempt from all pain, whether of body or mind, that is, from all evil. . . .

12. It would be impossible to banish fear on matters of the highest importance, if a man did not know the nature of the whole universe, but lived in dread of what the legends tell us. Hence without the study of nature there was no enjoyment of unmixed pleasures. . . .

14. When tolerable security against our fellow-men is attained, then on a basis of power sufficient to afford support and of material prosperity arises in most genuine form the security of a quiet private life withdrawn from the multitude. . . .

18. Pleasure in the flesh admits no increase when once the pain of want has been removed; after that it only admits of variation. The limit of pleasure in the mind, however, is reached when we reflect on the things themselves and their congeners which cause the mind the greatest alarms. . . .

21. He who understands the limits of life knows how easy it is to procure enough to remove the pain of want and make the whole of life complete and perfect. Hence he has no longer any need of things which are not to be won save by labour and conflict. . . .

26. All such desires as lead to no pain when they remain ungratified are unnecessary, and the longing is easily got rid of, when the thing desired is difficult to procure or when the desires seem likely to produce harm.

27. Of all the means which are procured by wisdom to ensure happiness throughout the whole of life, by far the most important is the acquisition of friends. . . .

29. Of our desires some are natural and necessary; others are natural, but not necessary; others, again, are neither natural nor necessary, but are due to illusory opinion.

[Epicurus regards as natural and necessary desires which bring relief from pain, as *e.g.* drink when we are thirsty; while by natural and not necessary he means those which merely diversify the pleasure without removing the pain, as *e.g.* costly viands; by the neither natural nor necessary he means desires for crowns and the erection of statues in one's honour. — SCHOLIUM.]

31. Natural justice is a symbol or expression of expediency, to prevent one man from harming or being harmed by another.

32. Those animals which are incapable of making covenants with one another, to the end that they may neither inflict nor suffer harm, are without either justice or injustice. And those tribes which either could not or would not form mutual covenants to the same end are in like case.

33. There never was an absolute justice, but only an agreement made in reciprocal intercourse in whatever localities now and again from time to time, providing against the infliction or suffering of harm. . . .

36. Taken generally, justice is the same for all, to wit, something found expedient in mutual intercourse; but in its application to particular cases

of locality or conditions of whatever kind, it varies under different circumstances.

37. Among the things accounted just by conventional law, whatever in the needs of mutual intercourse is attested to be expedient, is thereby stamped as just, whether or not it be the same for all; and in case any law is made and does not prove suitable to the expediencies of mutual intercourse, then this is no longer just. And should the expediency which is expressed by the law vary and only for a time correspond with the prior conception, nevertheless for the time being it was just, so long as we do not trouble ourselves about empty words, but look simply to the facts. . . .

QUESTIONS

1. Which of the following kinds of thing does Epicurus regard as intrinsically good? Pleasure, pain, banquets, fame, ignorance, death, life, friendships, scientific knowledge, honesty. Which ones does he regard as desirable because of their consequences?
2. Some philosophers have thought that enjoyment gained from reflection on the misfortune of others is a bad thing. Would Epicurus agree?
3. Does Epicurus think the best strategy for maximizing happiness is to satisfy all our desires, get rid of our desires, or do the former in some instances and the latter in others? Explain.
4. In what ways does he think scientific or philosophical knowledge can contribute to human happiness?
5. Does Epicurus offer any support for his view that pleasure is the one and only thing worthwhile in itself? If so, what is it? Is what he asserts about the direction of human desires correct? Whether or not it is, does it follow, logically, that pleasure is the good?
6. How much money does one need to be happy, in Epicurus' view?
7. What is the relation of justice, law, and compacts, according to him? Are just laws the same everywhere, or can a given law be just in one country and unjust in another, in his view?

SUGGESTIONS FOR FURTHER READING

Epicurus. *Epicurus, The Extant Remains*. Trans. by Cyril Bailey. New York: Oxford Univ. Press, 1926.

Oates, Whitney J., ed. *The Stoic and Epicurean Philosophers*. New York: Random House, 1940.

Bailey, Cyril. *The Greek Atomists and Epicurus*. New York: Oxford Univ. Press, 1928.

DeWitt, N. W. *Epicurus and His Philosophy*. Minneapolis: Univ. of Minnesota Press, 1954.

Hicks, R. D. *Stoic and Epicurean*. New York: Scribner, 1910.

Taylor, A. E. *Epicurus*. London: Constable, 1911.

Zeller, Eduard. *The Stoics, Epicureans, and Sceptics*. New York: Longmans, Green, 1892.

John Stuart Mill (1806-1873)

HAPPINESS THE BASIC STANDARD

John Stuart Mill was one of the outstanding figures in nine-teenth century thought. He was the son of James Mill, himself an important writer on philosophy, psychology, and economics. John Stuart Mill lived a highly active life, influential in politics as well as in intellectual circles — a life fascinatingly recorded in his *Autobiography*. His *System of Logic*, first published in 1843, was long the standard work in British and American institutions, and still receives a good deal of attention. His *An Examination of Sir William Hamilton's Philosophy* (1865) is a major work on epistemology and metaphysics. In moral and social philosophy he wrote *On Liberty* (1859), *Considerations on Representative Government* (1861), and *Utilitarianism* (1863), from which the following selections are drawn.

In Chapters 2 and 4 of this last book, most of which are reproduced here, Mill is dealing with two questions, only one of which was considered by Epicurus in a detailed way. Like Epicurus, Mill is trying to establish the view that pleasure is the only thing intrinsically worthwhile. But he is also trying to establish an entirely different point: an act is *right* if, and only if, it will, or probably will, or tends to, produce at least as much good as any other action the agent might have performed instead. In doing so, Mill is discussing an issue on which selections are presented in the following chapter; strictly, the question Which acts are right or wrong? is a quite different question from that of what is intrinsically worthwhile. Since his discussion of his views on what is intrinsically desirable can hardly be separated from the body of these chapters, we here present the whole. The reader should bear in mind, however, that a goodly part of the discussion is directed at a topic to be examined fully only later. Mill calls himself a "utilitarian," by which he means that he holds both that pleasure is the one and only intrinsic value and that the right act is the one which maximizes, or tends to maximize, intrinsic value. His use of the word "utilitarian," however, is inconvenient. In this book we shall mean by this word only the second of Mill's two theses, *viz.*, the view that an act is right if, and only if, it maximizes or tends to maximize intrinsic value. According to this usage, a utilitarian is not committed by his utilitarianism to any view about what is intrinsically desirable. The reader will find the word used in both ways in books on ethics, and he should be careful, when examining criticisms of utilitarianism, to note which doctrine is intended.

The reader should be particularly alert, in examining the following selection, to Mill's view on two issues. First, he should try to determine whether Mill thinks that an act is right if *it* will maximize intrinsic good or whether it is right if it is the kind of act the *general* performance of which in similar circumstances would maximize intrinsic good. Does Mill think, for instance, that we should lie whenever so doing promises to do most good? Second, the reader should pay attention to the *reasons* Mill gives for his ethical views, mostly in the last pages of the selection. Mill did not think he quite *demonstrated* his ethical views, but he did think he gave them support which should convince a reasonable man. It is well worth notice just exactly what he did.

From John Stuart Mill, *Utilitarianism,* first published 1863. Many editions, Chs. 2 and 4.

UTILITARIANISM

CHAPTER 2   WHAT UTILITARIANISM IS

A passing remark is all that needs be given to the ignorant blunder of supposing that those who stand up for utility as the test of right and wrong use the term in that restricted and merely colloquial sense in which utility is opposed to pleasure. An apology is due to the philosophical opponents of utilitarianism for even the momentary appearance of confounding them with anyone capable of so absurd a misconception; which is the more extraordinary, inasmuch as the contrary accusation, of referring everything to pleasure, and that, too, in its grossest form, is another of the common charges against utilitarianism: and, as has been pointedly remarked by an able writer, the same sort of persons, and often the very same persons, denounce the theory "as impracticably dry when the word 'utility' precedes the word 'pleasure,' and as too practicably voluptuous when the word 'pleasure' precedes the word 'utility.' " Those who know anything about the matter are aware that every writer, from Epicurus to Bentham, who maintained the theory of utility meant by it, not something to be contradistinguished from pleasure, but pleasure itself, together with exemption from pain; and instead of opposing the useful to the agreeable or the ornamental, have always declared that the useful means these, among other things. Yet the common herd, including the herd of writers, not only in newspapers and periodicals, but in books of weight and pretension, are perpetually falling into this shallow mistake. Having caught up the word "utilitarian," while knowing nothing whatever about it but its sound, they habitually express by it the rejection or the neglect of pleasure in some of its forms: of beauty, of ornament, or of amusement. Nor is the term thus ignorantly misapplied solely in disparagement, but occasionally in compliment, as though it implied superiority to frivolity and the mere pleasures of the moment. And this perverted use is the only one in which the word is popularly known, and the one from which the new generation are acquiring their sole notion of its meaning. Those who introduced the word, but who had for many years discontinued it as a distinctive appellation, may well feel themselves called upon to resume it if by doing so they can hope to contribute anything toward rescuing it from this utter degradation.

The creed which accepts as the foundation of morals "utility" or the "greatest happiness principle" holds that actions are right in proportion as they tend to promote happiness; wrong as they tend to produce the reverse of happiness. By happiness is intended pleasure and the absence of pain; by unhappiness, pain and the privation of pleasure. To give a clear view of the moral standard set up by the theory, much more requires to be said; in particular, what things it includes in the ideas of pain and pleasure, and to what extent this is left an open question. But these supplementary explanations do not affect the theory of life on which this theory of morality is grounded — namely, that pleasure and freedom from pain are the only things desirable as ends; and that all desirable things (which are as numerous in the utilitarian as in any other scheme) are desirable either for pleasure inherent in themselves or as means to the promotion of pleasure and the prevention of pain.

Now such a theory of life excites in many minds, and among them in some of the most estimable in feeling and purpose, inveterate dislike. To suppose that life has (as they express it) no higher end than pleasure — no better and nobler object of desire and pursuit — they designate as utterly mean and groveling, as a doctrine worthy only of swine, to whom the followers of Epicurus were, at a very early period, contemptuously likened; and modern holders of the doctrine are occasionally made the subject of equally polite comparisons by its German, French, and English assailants.

When thus attacked, the Epicureans have always answered that it is not they, but their accusers, who represent human nature in a degrading light, since the accusation supposes human beings to be capable of no pleasures except those of which swine are capable. If this supposition were true, the charge could not be gainsaid, but would then be no longer an imputation; for if the sources of pleasure were precisely the same to human beings and to swine, the rule of life which is good enough for the one would be good enough for the other. The comparison of the Epicurean life to that of beasts is felt as degrading, precisely because a beast's pleasures do not satisfy a human being's conceptions of happiness. Human beings have faculties more elevated than the animal appetites and, when once made conscious of them, do not regard anything as happiness which does not include their gratification. I do not, indeed, consider the Epicureans to have been by any means faultless in drawing out their scheme of consequences from the utilitarian principle. To do this in any sufficient manner, many Stoic, as well as Christian, elements require to be included. But there is no known Epicurean theory of life which does not assign to the pleasures of the intellect, of the feelings and imagination, and of the moral sentiments a much higher value as pleasures than to those of mere sensation. It must be admitted, however, that utilitarian writers in general have placed the superiority of mental over bodily pleasures chiefly in the greater permanency, safety, uncostliness, etc., of the former — that is, in their circumstantial advantages rather than in their intrinsic nature. And on all these points utilitarians have fully proved their case; but they might have taken the other and, as it may be called, higher ground with entire consistency. It is quite compatible with the principle of utility to recognize the fact that some kinds of pleasure are more desirable and more valuable than others. It would be absurd that, while in estimating all other things quality is considered as well as quantity, the estimation of pleasure should be supposed to depend on quantity alone.

If I am asked what I mean by difference of quality in pleasures, or what makes one pleasure more valuable than another, merely as a pleasure, except its being greater in amount, there is but one possible answer. Of two pleasures, if there be one to which all or almost all who have experience of both give a decided preference, irrespective of any feeling of moral obligation to prefer it, that is the more desirable pleasure. If one of the two is, by those who are competently acquainted with both, placed so far above the other that they prefer it, even though knowing it to be attended with a greater amount of discontent, and would not resign it for any quantity of the other pleasure which their nature is capable of, we are justified in ascribing to the preferred enjoyment a superiority in quality so far outweighing quantity as to render it, in comparison, of small account.

Now it is an unquestionable fact that those who are equally acquainted with and equally capable of appreciating and enjoying both do give a most marked preference to the manner of existence which employs their higher faculties. Few human creatures would consent to be changed into any of the lower animals for a promise of the fullest allowance of a beast's pleasures; no intelligent human being would consent to be a fool, no instructed person would be an ignoramus, no person of feeling and conscience would be selfish and base, even though they should be persuaded that the fool, the dunce, or the rascal is better satisfied with his lot than they are with theirs. They would not resign what they possess more than he for the most complete satisfaction of all the desires which they have in common with him. If they ever fancy they would, it is only in cases of unhappiness so extreme that to escape from it they would exchange their lot for almost

any other, however undesirable in their own eyes. A being of higher faculties requires more to make him happy, is capable probably of more acute
suffering, and certainly accessible to it at more points, than one of an inferior type; but in spite of these liabilities, he can never really wish to sink
into what he feels to be a lower grade of existence. We may give what
explanation we please of this unwillingness; we may attribute it to pride,
a name which is given indiscriminately to some of the most and to some
of the least estimable feelings of which mankind are capable; we may refer
it to the love of liberty and personal independence, an appeal to which
was with the Stoics one of the most effective means for the inculcation of
it; to the love of power or to the love of excitement, both of which do
really enter into and contribute to it; but its most appropriate appellation
is a sense of dignity, which all human beings possess in one form or other,
and in some, though by no means in exact, proportion to their higher faculties, and which is so essential a part of the happiness of those in whom
it is strong that nothing which conflicts with it could be otherwise than
momentarily an object of desire to them. Whoever supposes that this preference takes place at a sacrifice of happiness — that the superior being, in
anything like equal circumstances, is not happier than the inferior — confounds the two very different ideas of happiness and content. It is indisputable that the being whose capacities of enjoyment are low has the
greatest chance of having them fully satisfied; and a highly endowed being will always feel that any happiness which he can look for, as the world
is constituted, is imperfect. But he can learn to bear its imperfections, if
they are at all bearable; and they will not make him envy the being who
is indeed unconscious of the imperfections, but only because he feels not
at all the good which those imperfections qualify. It is better to be a human being dissatisfied than a pig satisfied; better to be Socrates dissatisfied
than a fool satisfied. And if the fool, or the pig, are of a different opinion,
it is because they only know their own side of the question. The other
party to the comparison knows both sides.

It may be objected that many who are capable of the higher pleasures occasionally, under the influence of temptation, postpone them to the
lower. But this is quite compatible with a full appreciation of the intrinsic
superiority of the higher. Men often, from infirmity of character, make their
election for the nearer good, though they know it to be the less valuable;
and this no less when the choice is between two bodily pleasures than when
it is between bodily and mental. They pursue sensual indulgences to the
injury of health, though perfectly aware that health is the greater good. It
may be further objected that many who begin with youthful enthusiasm
for everything noble, as they advance in years, sink into indolence and
selfishness. But I do not believe that those who undergo this very common
change voluntarily choose the lower description of pleasures in preference
to the higher. I believe that, before they devote themselves exclusively to
the one, they have already become incapable of the other. Capacity for the

nobler feelings is in most natures a very tender plant, easily killed, not only by hostile influences, but by mere want of sustenance; and in the majority of young persons it speedily dies away if the occupations to which their position in life has devoted them, and the society into which it has thrown them, are not favorable to keeping that higher capacity in exercise. Men lose their high aspirations as they lose their intellectual tastes, because they have not time or opportunity for indulging them; and they addict themselves to inferior pleasures, not because they deliberately prefer them, but because they are either the only ones to which they have access or the only ones which they are any longer capable of enjoying. It may be questioned whether anyone who has remained equally susceptible to both classes of pleasures ever knowingly and calmly preferred the lower, though many, in all ages, have broken down in an ineffectual attempt to combine both.

From this verdict of the only competent judges, I apprehend there can be no appeal. On a question which is the best worth having of two pleasures, or which of two modes of existence is the most grateful to the feelings, apart from its moral attributes and from its consequences, the judgment of those who are qualified by knowledge of both, or, if they differ, that of the majority among them, must be admitted as final. And there needs be the less hesitation to accept this judgment respecting the quality of pleasures, since there is no other tribunal to be referred to even on the question of quantity. What means are there of determining which is the acutest of two pains, or the intensest of two pleasurable sensations, except the general suffrage of those who are familiar with both? Neither pains nor pleasures are homogeneous, and pain is always heterogeneous with pleasure. What is there to decide whether a particular pleasure is worth purchasing at the cost of a particular pain, except the feelings and judgment of the experienced? When, therefore, those feelings and judgment declare the pleasures derived from the higher faculties to be preferable *in kind*, apart from the question of intensity, to those of which the animal nature, disjoined from the higher faculties, is susceptible, they are entitled on this subject to the same regard.

I have dwelt on this point as being a necessary part of a perfectly just conception of utility or happiness considered as the directive rule of human conduct. But it is by no means an indispensable condition to the acceptance of the utilitarian standard; for that standard is not the agent's own greatest happiness, but the greatest amount of happiness altogether; and if it may possibly be doubted whether a noble character is always the happier for its nobleness, there can be no doubt that it makes other people happier, and that the world in general is immensely a gainer by it. Utilitarianism, therefore, could only attain its end by the general cultivation of nobleness of character, even if each individual were only benefited by the nobleness of others, and his own, so far as happiness is concerned, were a sheer deduction from the benefit. But the bare enunciation of such an absurdity as this last renders refutation superfluous.

According to the greatest happiness principle, as above explained, the ultimate end, with reference to and for the sake of which all other things are desirable — whether we are considering our own good or that of other people — is an existence exempt as far as possible from pain, and as rich as possible in enjoyments, both in point of quantity and quality; the test of quality and the rule for measuring it against quantity being the preference felt by those who, in their opportunities of experience, to which must be added their habits of self-consciousness and self-observation, are best furnished with the means of comparison. This, being according to the utilitarian opinion the end of human action, is necessarily also the standard of morality, which may accordingly be defined "the rules and precepts for human conduct," by the observance of which an existence such as has been described might be, to the greatest extent possible, secured to all mankind; and not to them only, but, so far as the nature of things admits, to the whole sentient creation.

Against this doctrine, however, arises another class of objectors who say that happiness, in any form, cannot be the rational purpose of human life and action; because, in the first place, it is unattainable; and they contemptuously ask, What right hast thou to be happy? — a question which Mr. Carlyle clinches by the addition, What right, a short time ago, hadst thou even *to be?* Next they say that men can do *without* happiness; that all noble human beings have felt this, and could not have become noble but by learning the lesson of *Entsagen,* or renunciation; which lesson, thoroughly learned and submitted to, they affirm to be the beginning and necessary condition of all virtue.

The first of these objections would go to the root of the matter were it well founded; for if no happiness is to be had at all by human beings, the attainment of it cannot be the end of morality or of any rational conduct. Though, even in that case, something might still be said for the utilitarian theory, since utility includes not solely the pursuit of happiness, but the prevention or mitigation of unhappiness; and if the former aim be chimerical, there will be all the greater scope and more imperative need for the latter, so long at least as mankind think fit to live and do not take refuge in the simultaneous act of suicide recommended under certain conditions by Novalis. When, however, it is thus positively asserted to be impossible that human life should be happy, the assertion, if not something like a verbal quibble, is at least an exaggeration. If by happiness be meant a continuity of highly pleasurable excitement, it is evident enough that this is impossible. A state of exalted pleasure lasts only moments or in some cases, and with some intermissions, hours or days, and is the occasional brilliant flash of enjoyment, not its permanent and steady flame. Of this the philosophers who have taught that happiness is the end of life were as fully aware as those who taunt them. The happiness which they meant was not a life of rapture, but moments of such, in an existence made up of few and transitory pains, many and various pleasures, with a decided predominance of the active over the passive, and having as the foundation of the whole not to expect more from life than it is capable of bestowing. A life thus composed, to those who have been fortunate enough to obtain it, has always appeared worthy of the name of happiness. And such an existence is even now the lot of many during some considerable portion of their lives. The present wretched education and wretched social arrangements are the only real hindrance to its being attainable by almost all.

The objectors perhaps may doubt whether human beings, if taught to consider happiness as the end of life, would be satisfied with such a moderate share of it. But great numbers of mankind have been satisfied with much less. The main constituents of a satisfied life appear to be two, either of which by itself is often found sufficient for the purpose: tranquillity and excitement. With much tranquillity, many find that they can be content with very little pleasure; with much excitement, many can reconcile themselves to a considerable quantity of pain. There is assuredly no inherent impossibility of enabling even the mass of mankind to unite both, since the two are so far from being incompatible that they are in natural alliance, the prolongation of either being a preparation for, and exciting a wish for, the other. It is only those in whom indolence amounts to a vice that do not desire excitement after an interval of repose; it is only those in whom the need of excitement is a disease that feel the tranquillity which follows excitement dull and insipid, instead of pleasurable in direct proportion to the excitement which preceded it. When people who are tolerably fortunate in their outward lot do not find in life sufficient enjoyment to make it valuable to them, the cause generally is caring for nobody but themselves. To those who have neither public nor private affections, the excitements of life are much curtailed, and in any case dwindle in value as the time approaches when all selfish interests must be terminated by death; while those who leave after them objects of personal affection, and especially those who have also cultivated a fellow-feeling with the collective interests of mankind, retain as lively an interest in life on the eve of death as in the vigor of youth and health. Next to selfishness, the principal cause which makes life unsatisfactory is want of mental cultivation. A cultivated mind — I do not mean that of a philosopher, but any mind to which the fountains of knowledge have been opened, and which has been taught, in any tolerable degree, to exercise its faculties — finds sources of inexhaustible interest in all that surrounds it: in the objects of nature, the achievements of art, the imaginations of poetry, the incidents of history, the ways of mankind, past and present, and their prospects in the future. It is possible, indeed, to become indifferent to all this, and that too without having exhausted a thousandth part of it, but only when one has had from the beginning no moral or human interest in these things and has sought in them only the gratification of curiosity. . . .

And this leads to the true estimation of what is said by the objectors concerning the possibility and the obligation of learning to do without happiness. Unquestionably it is possible to do without happiness; it is done involuntarily by nineteen-twentieths of mankind, even in those parts of our present world which are least deep in barbarism; and it often has to be done voluntarily by the hero or the martyr, for the sake of something which he prizes more than his individual happiness. But this something, what is it, unless the happiness of others or some of the requisites of happiness? It is noble to be capable of resigning entirely one's own portion of happiness, or chances of it; but, after all, this self-sacrifice must be for some end; it is not its own end; and if we are told that its end is not happiness but virtue, which is better than happiness, I ask, would the sacrifice be made if the hero or martyr did not believe that it would earn for others immunity from similar sacrifices? Would it be made if he thought that his renunciation of happiness for himself would produce no fruit for any of his fellow creatures, but to make their lot like his and place them also in the condition of persons who have renounced happiness? All honor to those who can abnegate for themselves the personal enjoyment of life when by such renunciation they contribute worthily to increase the amount of happiness in the world; but he who does it or professes to do it for any other purpose is no more deserving of admiration than the ascetic mounted on his pillar. He may be an inspiriting proof of what men *can* do, but assuredly not an example of what they *should.*

Though it is only in a very imperfect state of the world's arrangements that anyone can best serve the happiness of others by the absolute sacrifice of his own, yet, so long as the world is in that imperfect state, I fully acknowledge that the readiness to make such a sacrifice is the highest virtue which can be found in man. I will add that in this condition of the world, paradoxical as the assertion may be, the conscious ability to do without happiness gives the best prospect of realizing such happiness as is attainable. For nothing except that consciousness can raise a person above the chances of life by making him feel that, let fate and fortune do their worst, they have not power to subdue him; which, once felt, frees him from excess of anxiety concerning the evils of life and enables him, like many a Stoic in the worst times of the Roman Empire, to cultivate in tranquillity the sources of satisfaction accessible to him, without concerning himself about the uncertainty of their duration any more than about their inevitable end.

Meanwhile, let utilitarians never cease to claim the morality of self-devotion as a possession which belongs by as good a right to them as either to the Stoic or to the Transcendentalist. The utilitarian morality does recognize in human beings the power of sacrificing their own greatest good for the good of others. It only refuses to admit that the sacrifice is itself a good. A sacrifice which does not increase or tend to increase the sum total of happiness, it considers as wasted. The only self-renunciation which it applauds is devotion to the happiness, or to some of the means of happiness, of others, either of mankind collectively or of individuals within the limits imposed by the collective interests of mankind.

I must again repeat what the assailants of utilitarianism seldom have the justice to acknowledge, that the happiness which forms the utilitarian standard of what is right in conduct is not the agent's own happiness but that of all concerned. As between his own happiness and that of others, utilitarianism requires him to be as strictly impartial as a disinterested and benevolent spectator. In the golden rule of Jesus of Nazareth, we read the complete spirit of the ethics of utility. "To do as you would be done by," and "to love your neighbor as yourself," constitute the ideal perfection of utilitarian morality. As the means of making the nearest approach to this ideal, utility would enjoin, first, that laws and social arrangements should place the happiness or (as, speaking practically, it may be called) the interest of every individual as nearly as possible in harmony with the interest of the whole; and, secondly, that education and opinion, which have so vast a power over human character, should so use that power as to establish in the mind of every individual an indissoluble association between his own happiness and the good of the whole, especially between his own happiness and the practice of such modes of conduct, negative and positive, as regard for the universal happiness prescribes; so that not only he may be unable to conceive the possibility of happiness to himself, consistently with conduct opposed to the general good, but also that a direct impulse to promote the general good may be in every individual one of the habitual motives of action, and the sentiments connected therewith may fill a large and prominent place in every human being's sentient existence. If the impugners of the utilitarian morality represented it to their own minds in this its true character, I know not what recommendation possessed by any other morality they could possibly affirm to be wanting to it; what more beautiful or more exalted developments of human nature any other ethical system can be supposed to foster, or what springs of action, not accessible to the utilitarian, such systems rely on for giving effect to their mandates.

The objectors to utilitarianism cannot always be charged with representing it in a discreditable light. On the contrary, those among them who entertain anything like a just idea of its disinterested character sometimes find fault with its standard as being too high for humanity. They say it is exacting too much to require that people shall always act from the inducement of promoting the general interests of society. But this is to mistake the very meaning of a standard of morals and confound the rule of action with the motive of it. It is the business of ethics to tell us what are our duties, or by what test we may know them; but no system of ethics requires that the sole motive of all we do shall be a feeling of duty; on the contrary, ninety-nine hundredths of all our actions are done from other motives, and rightly so done if the rule of duty does not condemn them. It is the more unjust to utilitarianism that this particular misapprehension should be made a ground of objection to it, inasmuch as utilitarian moralists have gone beyond almost all others in affirming that the motive has nothing to do with the morality of the action, though much with the worth of the agent. He who saves a fellow creature from drowning does what is morally right, whether his motive be duty or the hope of being paid for his trouble; he who betrays the friend that trusts him is guilty of a crime, even if his object be to serve another friend to whom he is under greater obligations. But to speak only of actions done from the motive of duty, and in direct obedience to principle: it is a misapprehension of the utilitarian mode of thought to conceive it as implying that people should fix their minds upon so wide a generality as the world, or society at large. The great majority of good actions are intended not for the benefit of the world, but for that of individuals, of which the good of the world is made up; and the thoughts of the most virtuous man need not on these occasions travel beyond the particular persons concerned, except so far as is necessary to assure himself that in benefiting them he is not violating the rights, that is, the legitimate and authorized expectations, of anyone else. The multiplication of happiness is, according to the utilitarian ethics, the object of virtue: the occasions on which any person (except one in a thousand) has it in his power to do this on an extended scale — in other words, to be a public benefactor — are but exceptional; and on these occasions alone is he called on to consider public utility; in every other case, private utility, the interest or happiness of some few persons, is all he has to attend to. Those alone the influence of whose actions extends to society in general need concern themselves habitually about so large an object. In the case of abstinences indeed — of things which people forbear to do from moral considerations, though the consequences in the particular case might be beneficial — it would be unworthy of an intelligent agent not to be consciously aware that the action is of a class which, if practiced generally, would be generally injurious, and that this is the ground of the obligation to abstain from it. The amount of regard for the public interest implied in this recognition is no greater than is demanded by every system of morals, for they all enjoin to abstain from whatever is manifestly pernicious to society.

The same considerations dispose of another reproach against the doctrine of utility, founded on a still grosser misconception of the purpose of a standard of morality and of the very meaning of the words "right" and "wrong." It is often affirmed that utilitarianism renders men cold and unsympathizing; that it chills their moral feelings toward individuals; that it makes them regard only the dry and hard consideration of the consequences of actions, not taking into their moral estimate the qualities from which those actions emanate. If the assertion means that they do not allow their judgment respecting the rightness or wrongness of an action to be influenced by their opinion of the qualities of the person who does it, this is a complaint not against utilitarianism, but against any standard of morality at all; for certainly no known ethical standard decides an action to be good or bad because it is done by a good or a bad man, still less because done by an amiable, a brave, or a benevolent man, or the contrary. These considerations are relevant, not to the estimation of actions, but of persons; and there is nothing in the utilitarian theory inconsistent with the fact that there are other things which interest us in persons besides the rightness and wrongness of their actions. The Stoics, indeed, with the paradoxical misuse of language which was part of their system, and by which they strove to raise themselves above all concern about anything but virtue, were fond of saying that he who has that has everything; that he, and only he, is rich, is beautiful, is a king. But no claim of this description is made for the virtuous man by the utilitarian doctrine. Utilitarians are quite aware that there are other desirable possessions and qualities besides virtue, and are perfectly willing to allow to all of them their full worth. They are also aware that a right action does not necessarily indicate a virtuous character, and that actions which are blamable often proceed from qualities entitled to praise. When this is apparent in any particular case, it modifies their estimation, not certainly of the act, but of the agent. I grant that they are, notwithstanding, of opinion that in the long run the best proof of a good character is good actions; and resolutely refuse to consider any mental disposition as good of which the predominant tendency is to produce bad conduct. This makes them unpopular with many people, but it is an unpopularity which they must share with everyone who regards the distinction between right and wrong in a serious light; and the reproach is not one which a conscientious utilitarian need be anxious to repel. . . .

It may not be superfluous to notice a few more of the common misapprehensions of utilitarian ethics, even those which are so obvious and gross that it might appear impossible for any person of candor and intelligence to fall into them; since persons, even of considerable mental endowment, often give themselves so little trouble to understand the bearings of any opinion against which they entertain a prejudice, and men are in general so little conscious of this voluntary ignorance as a defect that the vulgarest misunderstandings of ethical doctrines are continually met with in the deliberate writings of persons of the greatest pretensions both to high principle and to philosophy. We not uncommonly hear the doctrine of utility inveighed against as a *godless* doctrine. If it be necessary to say anything at all against so mere an assumption, we may say that the question depends upon what idea we have formed of the moral character of the Deity. If it be a true belief that God desires, above all things, the happiness of his creatures, and that this was his purpose in their creation, utility is not only not a godless doctrine, but more profoundly religious than any other. If it be meant that utilitarianism does not recognize the revealed will of God as the supreme law of morals, I answer that a utilitarian who believes in the perfect goodness and wisdom of God necessarily believes that whatever God has thought fit to reveal on the subject of morals must fulfill the requirements of utility in a supreme degree. But others besides utilitarians have been of opinion that the Christian revelation was intended, and is fitted, to inform the hearts and minds of mankind with a spirit which should enable them to find for themselves what is right, and incline them to do it when found, rather than to tell them, except in a very general way, what it is; and that we need a doctrine of ethics, carefully followed out, to *interpret* to us the will of God. Whether this opinion is correct or not, it is superfluous here to discuss; since whatever aid religion, either natural or revealed, can afford to ethical investigation is as open to the utilitarian moralist as to any other. He can use it as the testimony of God to the usefulness or hurtfulness of any given course of action by as good a right as others can use it for the indication of a transcendental law having no connection with usefulness or with happiness.

Again, utility is often summarily stigmatized as an immoral doctrine by giving it the name of "expediency," and taking advantage of the popular use of that term to contrast it with principle. But the expedient, in the sense in which it is opposed to the right, generally means that which is expedient for the particular interest of the agent himself; as when a minister sacrifices the interests of his country to keep himself in place. When it means anything better than this, it means that which is expedient for some immediate object, some temporary purpose, but which violates a rule whose observance is expedient in a much higher degree. The expedient, in this sense, instead of being the same thing with the useful, is a branch of the hurtful. Thus it would often be expedient, for the purpose of getting over some momentary embarrassment, or attaining some object immediately useful to ourselves or others, to tell a lie. But inasmuch as the cultivation in ourselves of a sensitive feeling on the subject of veracity is one of the most useful, and the enfeeblement of that feeling one of the most hurtful, things to which our conduct can be instrumental; and inasmuch as any, even unintentional, deviation from truth does that much toward weakening the trustworthiness of human assertion, which is not only the principal support of all present social well-being, but the insufficiency of which does more than any one thing that can be named to keep back civilization, virtue, everything on which human happiness on the largest scale depends — we feel that the violation, for a present advantage, of a rule of such transcendent expediency is not expedient, and that he who, for the sake of convenience to himself or to some other individual, does what depends on him to deprive mankind of the good, and inflict upon them the evil, involved in the greater or less reliance which they can place in each other's word, acts the part of one of their worst enemies. Yet that even this rule, sacred as it is, admits of possible exceptions is acknowledged by all moralists; the chief of which is when the withholding of some fact (as of information from a malefactor, or of bad news from a person dangerously ill) would save an individual (especially an individual other than oneself) from great and unmerited evil, and when the withholding can only be effected by denial. But in order that the exception may not extend itself beyond the need, and may have the least possible effect in weakening reliance on veracity, it ought to be recognized and, if possible, its limits defined; and, if the principle of utility is good for anything, it must be good for weighing these conflicting utilities against one another and marking out the region within which one or the other preponderates.

Again, defenders of utility often find themselves called upon to reply to such objections as this — that there is not time, previous to action, for calculating and weighing the effects of any line of conduct on the general happiness. This is exactly as if anyone were to say that it is impossible to guide our conduct by Christianity because there is not time, on every occasion on which anything has to be done, to read through the Old and New Testaments. The answer to the objection is that there has been ample time, namely, the whole past duration of the human species. During all that time mankind have been learning by experience the tendencies of actions; on which experience all the prudence as well as all the morality of life are dependent. People talk as if the commencement of this course of experience had hitherto been put off, and as if, at the moment when some man feels tempted to meddle with the property or life of another, he had to begin considering for the first time whether murder and theft are injurious to human happiness. Even then I do not think that he would find the question very puzzling; but, at all events, the matter is now done to his hand. It is truly a whimsical supposition that, if mankind were agreed in considering utility to be the test of morality, they would remain without any agreement as to what *is* useful, and would take no measures for having their notions on the subject taught to the young and enforced by law and opinion. There is no difficulty in proving any ethical standard whatever to work ill if we suppose universal idiocy to be conjoined with it; but on any hypothesis short of that, mankind must by this time have acquired positive beliefs as to the effects of some actions on their happiness; and the beliefs which have thus come down are the rules of morality for the multitude, and for the philosopher until he has succeeded in finding better. That philosophers might easily do this, even now, on many subjects; that the received code of ethics is by no means of divine right; and that mankind have still much to learn as to the effects of actions on the general happiness, I admit or rather earnestly maintain. The corollaries from the principle of utility, like the precepts of every practical art, admit of indefinite improvement, and, in a progressive state of the human mind, their improvement is perpetually going on. But to consider the rules of morality as improvable is one thing; to pass over the intermediate generalization entirely and endeavor to test each individual action directly by the first principle is another. It is a strange notion that the acknowledgment of a first principle is inconsistent with the admission of secondary ones. To inform a traveler respecting the place of his ultimate destination is not to forbid the use of landmarks and direction-posts on the way. The proposition that happiness is the end and aim of morality does not mean that no road ought to be laid down to that goal, or that persons going thither should not be advised to take one direction rather than another. Men really ought to leave off talking a kind of nonsense on this subject, which they would neither talk nor listen to on other matters of practical concernment. Nobody argues that the art of navigation is not founded on astronomy because sailors cannot wait to calculate the Nautical Almanac. Being rational creatures, they go to sea with it ready calculated; and all rational creatures go out upon the sea of life with their minds made up on the common questions of right and wrong, as well as on many of the far more difficult questions of wise and foolish. And this, as long as foresight is a human quality, it is to be presumed they will continue to do. Whatever we adopt as the fundamental principle of morality, we require subordinate principles to apply it by; the impossibility of doing without them, being common to all systems, can afford no argument against any one in particular; but gravely to argue as if no such secondary principles could be had, and as if mankind had remained till now, and always must remain, without drawing any general conclusions from the experience of human life is as high a pitch, I think, as absurdity has ever reached in philosophical controversy.

The remainder of the stock arguments against utilitarianism mostly consist in laying to its charge the common infirmities of human nature, and the general difficulties which embarrass conscientious persons in shaping their course through life. We are told that a utilitarian will be apt to make his own particular case an exception to moral rules, and, when under temptation, will see a utility in the breach of a rule, greater than he will see in its observance. But is utility the only creed which is able to furnish us with excuses for evil-doing and means of cheating our own conscience? They are afforded in abundance by all doctrines which recognize as a fact in morals the existence of conflicting considerations, which all doctrines do that have been believed by sane persons. It is not the fault of any creed, but of the complicated nature of human affairs, that rules of conduct cannot be so framed as to require no exceptions, and that hardly any kind of action can safely be laid down as either always obligatory or always condemnable. There is no ethical creed which does not temper the rigidity of its laws by giving a certain latitude, under the moral responsibility of the agent, for accommodation to peculiarities of circumstances; and under every creed, at the opening thus made, self-deception and dishonest casuistry get in. There exists no moral system under which there do not arise unequivocal cases of conflicting obligation. These are the real difficulties, the knotty points both in the theory of ethics and in the conscientious guidance of personal conduct. They are overcome practically, with greater or with less success, according to the intellect and virtue of the individual; but it can hardly be pretended that anyone will be the less qualified for dealing with them, from possessing an ultimate standard to which conflicting rights and duties can be referred. If utility is the ultimate source of moral obligations, utility may be invoked to decide between them when their demands are incompatible. Though the application of the standard may be difficult, it is better than none at all; while in other systems, the moral laws all claiming independent authority, there is no common umpire entitled to interfere between them; their claims to precedence one over another rest on little better than sophistry, and, unless determined, as they generally are, by the unacknowledged influence of consideration of utility, afford a free scope for the action of personal desires and partialities. We must remember that only in these cases of conflict between secondary principles is it requisite that first principles should be appealed to. There is no case of moral obligation in which some secondary principle is not involved; and if only one, there can seldom be any real doubt which one it is, in the mind of any person by whom the principle itself is recognized.

CHAPTER 4   OF WHAT SORT OF PROOF THE PRINCIPLE OF UTILITY IS SUSCEPTIBLE

. . . Questions of ultimate ends do not admit of proof, in the ordinary acceptation of the term. To be incapable of proof by reasoning is common to all first principles, to the first premises of our knowledge, as well as to those of our conduct. But the former, being matters of fact, may be the subject of a direct appeal to the faculties which judge of fact — namely, our senses and our internal consciousness. Can an appeal be made to the same faculties on questions of practical ends? Or by what other faculty is cognizance taken of them?

Questions about ends are, in other words, questions what things are desirable. The utilitarian doctrine is that happiness is desirable, and the only thing desirable, as an end; all other things being only desirable as means to that end. What ought to be required of this doctrine, what conditions is it requisite that the doctrine should fulfill — to make good its claim to be believed?

The only proof capable of being given that an object is visible is that people actually see it. The only proof that a sound is audible is that people hear it; and so of the other sources of our experience. In like manner, I apprehend, the sole evidence it is possible to produce that anything is desirable is that people do actually desire it. If the end which the utilitarian doctrine proposes to itself were not, in theory and in practice, acknowledged to be an end, nothing could ever convince any person that it was so. No reason can be given why the general happiness is desirable, except that each person, so far as he believes it to be attainable, desires his own happiness. This, however, being a fact, we have not only all the proof which the case admits of, but all which it is possible to require, that happiness is a good, that each person's happiness is a good to that person, and the general happiness, therefore, a good to the aggregate of all persons. Happiness has made out its title as *one* of the ends of conduct and, consequently, one of the criteria of morality.

But it has not, by this alone, proved itself to be the sole criterion. To do that, it would seem, by the same rule, necessary to show, not only that people desire happiness, but that they never desire anything else. Now it is palpable that they do desire things which, in common language, are decidedly distinguished from happiness. They desire, for example, virtue and the absence of vice no less really than pleasure and the absence of pain. The desire of virtue is not as universal, but it is as authentic a fact as the desire of happiness. And hence the opponents of the utilitarian standard deem that they have a right to infer that there are other ends of human action besides happiness, and that happiness is not the standard of approbation and disapprobation.

But does the utilitarian doctrine deny that people desire virtue, or maintain that virtue is not a thing to be desired? The very reverse. It maintains not only that virtue is to be desired, but that it is to be desired disinterestedly, for itself. Whatever may be the opinion of utilitarian moralists as to the original conditions by which virtue is made virtue, however they may believe (as they do) that actions and dispositions are only virtuous because they promote another end than virtue, yet this being granted, and it having been decided, from considerations of this description, what *is* virtuous, they not only place virtue at the very head of the things which are good as means to the ultimate end, but they also recognize as a psychological fact the possibility of its being, to the individual, a good in itself, without looking to any end beyond it; and hold that the mind is not in a right state, not in a state conformable to utility, not in the state most conducive to the general happiness, unless it does love virtue in this manner — as a thing desirable in itself, even although, in the individual instance, it should not produce those other desirable consequences which it tends to produce, and on account of which it is held to be virtue. This opinion is not, in the smallest degree, a departure from the happiness principle. The ingredients of happiness are very various, and each of them is desirable in itself, and not merely when considered as swelling an aggregate. The principle of utility does not mean that any given pleasure, as music, for instance, or any given exemption from pain, as for example health, is to be looked upon as means to a collective something termed happiness, and to be desired on that account. They are desired and desirable in and for themselves; besides being means, they are a part of the end. Virtue, according to the utilitarian doctrine, is not naturally and originally part of the end, but it is capable of becoming so; and in those who live it disinterestedly it has become so, and is desired and cherished, not as a means to happiness, but as a part of their happiness.

To illustrate this further, we may remember that virtue is not the only thing originally a means, and which if it were not a means to anything else would be and remain indifferent, but which by association with what it is a means to comes to be desired for itself, and that too with the utmost intensity. What, for example, shall we say of the love of money? There is nothing originally more desirable about money than about any heap of glittering pebbles. Its worth is solely that of the things which it will buy; the desires for other things than itself, which it is a means of gratifying. Yet the love of money is not only one of the strongest moving forces of human life, but money is, in many cases, desired in and for itself; the desire to possess it is often stronger than the desire to use it, and goes on increasing when all the desires which point to ends beyond it, to be compassed by it, are falling off. It may, then, be said truly that money is desired not for the sake of an end, but as part of the end. From being a means to happiness, it has come to be itself a principal ingredient of the individual's conception of happiness. The same may be said of the majority of the great objects of human life: power, for example, or fame, except that to each of these there is a certain amount of immediate pleasure annexed, which has at least the semblance of being naturally inherent in them — a thing which cannot be said of money. Still, however, the strongest natural attraction, both of power and of fame, is the immense aid they give to the attainment of our other wishes; and it is the strong association thus generated between them and all our objects of desire which gives to the direct desire of them the intensity it often assumes, so as in some characters to surpass in strength all other desires. In these cases the means have become a part of the end, and a more important part of it than any of the things which they are means to. What was once desired as an instrument for the attainment of happiness has come to be desired for its own sake. In being desired for its own sake it is, however, desired as *part* of happiness. The person is made, or thinks he would be made, happy by its mere possession; and is made unhappy by failure to obtain it. The desire of it is not a different thing from the desire of happiness any more than the love of music or the desire of health. They are included in happiness. They are some of the elements of which the desire of happiness is made up. Happiness is not an abstract idea but a concrete whole; and these are some of its parts. And the utilitarian standard sanctions and approves their being so. Life would be a poor thing, very ill provided with sources of happiness, if there were not this provision of nature by which things originally indifferent, but conducive to, or otherwise associated with, the satisfaction of our primitive desires, become in themselves sources of pleasure more valuable than the primitive pleasures, both in permanency, in the space of human existence that they are capable of covering, and even in intensity.

Virtue, according to the utilitarian conception, is a good of this description. There was no original desire of it, or motive to it, save its conduciveness to pleasure, and especially to protection from pain. But through the association thus formed it may be felt a good in itself, and desired as such with as great intensity as any other good; and with this difference between it and the love of money, of power, or of fame — that all of these may, and often do, render the individual noxious to the other members of the society to which he belongs, whereas there is nothing which makes him so much a blessing to them as the cultivation of the disinterested love of virtue. And consequently, the utilitarian standard, while it tolerates and approves those other acquired desires, up to the point beyond which they would be more injurious to the general happiness than promotive of it, enjoins and requires the cultivation of the love of virtue up to the greatest strength possible, as being above all things important to the general happiness.

It results from the preceding considerations that there is in reality nothing desired except happiness. Whatever is desired otherwise than as a means to some end beyond itself, and ultimately to happiness, is desired as itself a part of happiness, and is not desired for itself until it has become so. Those who desire virtue for its own sake desire it either because the consciousness of it is a pleasure, or because the consciousness of being without it is a pain, or for both reasons united; as in truth the pleasure and pain seldom exist separately, but almost always together — the same person feeling pleasure in the degree of virtue attained, and pain in not having attained more. If one of these gave him no pleasure, and the other no pain, he would not love or desire virtue, or would desire it only for the other benefits which it might produce to himself or to persons whom he cared for.

We have now, then, an answer to the question, of what sort of proof the principle of utility is susceptible. If the opinion which I have now stated is psychologically true — if human nature is so constituted as to desire nothing which is not either a part of happiness or a means of happiness — we can have no other proof, and we require no other, that these are the only things desirable. If so, happiness is the sole end of human action, and the promotion of it the test by which to judge of all human conduct; from whence it necessarily follows that it must be the criterion of morality, since a part is included in the whole.

And now to decide whether this is really so, whether mankind do desire nothing for itself but that which is a pleasure to them, or of which the absence is a pain, we have evidently arrived at a question of fact and experience, dependent, like all similar questions, upon evidence. It can only be determined by practiced self-consciousness and self-observation, assisted by observation of others. I believe that these sources of evidence, impartially consulted, will declare that desiring a thing and finding it pleasant, aversion to it and thinking of it as painful, are phenomena entirely inseparable or, rather, two parts of the same phenomenon — in strictness of language, two different modes of naming the same psychological fact; that to think of an object as desirable (unless for the sake of its consequences) and to think of it as pleasant are one and the same thing; and that to desire anything except in proportion as the idea of it is pleasant is a physical and metaphysical impossibility.

So obvious does this appear to me that I expect it will hardly be disputed; and the objection made will be, not that desire can possibly be directed to anything ultimately except pleasure and exemption from pain, but that the will is a different thing from desire; that a person of confirmed virtue or any other person whose purposes are fixed carries out his purposes without any thought of the pleasure he has in contemplating them or expects to derive from their fulfillment, and persists in acting on them, even though these pleasures are much diminished by changes in his character or decay of his passive sensibilities, or are outweighed by the pains which the pursuit of the purposes may bring upon him. All this I fully admit and have stated it elsewhere as positively and emphatically as anyone. Will, the active phenomenon, is a different thing from desire, the state of passive sensibility, and, though originally an offshoot from it, may in time take root and detach itself from the parent stock, so much so that in the case of a habitual purpose, instead of willing the thing because we desire it, we often desire it only because we will it. This, however, is but an instance of that familiar fact, the power of habit, and is nowise confined to the case of virtuous actions. Many indifferent things which men originally did from a motive of some sort they continue to do from habit. Sometimes this is done unconsciously, the consciousness coming only after the action; at other times with conscious volition, but volition which has become habitual and is put in operation by the force of habit, in opposition perhaps to the deliberate preference, as often happens with those who have contracted habits of vicious or hurtful indulgence. Third and last comes the case in which the habitual act of will in the individual instance is not in contradiction to the general intention prevailing at other times, but in fulfillment of it, as in the case of the person of confirmed virtue and of all who pursue deliberately and consistently any determinate end. The distinction between will and desire thus understood is an authentic and highly important psychological fact; but the fact consists solely in this — that will, like all other parts of our constitution, is amenable to habit, and that we may will from habit what we no longer desire for itself, or desire only because we will it. It is not the less true that will, in the beginning, is entirely produced by desire, including in that term the repelling influence of pain as well as the attractive one of pleasure. Let us take into consideration no longer the person who has a confirmed will to do right, but him in whom that virtuous will is still feeble, conquerable by temptation, and not to be fully relied on; by what means can it be strengthened? How can the will to be virtuous, where it does not exist in sufficient force, be implanted or awakened? Only by making the person *desire* virtue — by making him think of it in a pleasurable light, or of its absence in a painful one. It is by associating the doing right with pleasure, or the wrong with pain, or by eliciting and impressing and bringing home to the person's experience the pleasure naturally involved in the one or the pain in the other, that it is possible to call forth that will to be virtuous which, when confirmed, acts without any thought of either pleasure or pain. Will is the child of desire, and passes out of the dominion of its parent only to come under that of habit. That which is the result of habit affords no presumption of being intrinsically good; and there would be no reason for wishing that the purpose of virtue should become independent of pleasure and pain were it not that the influence of the pleasurable and painful associations which prompt to virtue is not sufficiently to be depended on for unerring constancy of action until it has acquired the support of habit. Both in feeling and in conduct, habit is the only thing which imparts certainty; and it is because of the importance to others of being able to rely absolutely on one's feelings and conduct, and to oneself of being able to rely on one's own, that the will to do right ought to be cultivated into this habitual independence. In other words, this state of the will is a means to good, not intrinsically a good; and does not contradict the doctrine that nothing is a good to human beings but in so far as it is either itself pleasurable or a means of attaining pleasure or averting pain.

But if this doctrine be true, the principle of utility is proved. Whether it is so or not must now be left to the consideration of the thoughtful reader.

QUESTIONS

1. Mill urges (p. 30) "that actions are right in proportion as they tend to promote happiness, wrong as they tend to produce the reverse of happiness." Later, however, he writes (p. 38): "In case of abstinences indeed — of things which people forbear to do from moral considerations, though the consequences in the particular case might be beneficial — it would be unworthy of an intelligent agent not to be consciously aware that the action is of a class which, if practised generally, would be generally injurious, and that this is the ground of the obligation to abstain from it." Are these passages consistent? State, as clearly as you can, when an act is right or wrong, according to Mill.

2. Mill says that one pleasure that is smaller in quantity than another may be preferable on account of its quality, and that we know that it is if people who have experienced both actually prefer it. It might be argued, however, that if people actually prefer the one pleasure to another, the preferred one *is* greater in quantity — that all it means, to say that one pleasure is greater than another, is that it is preferred. What do you think it means to say that one pleasure is "greater in quantity" than another?

3. Mill would probably say that the pleasure of an evening spent reading a good book is better than the pleasure of an evening's bowling. Critics have sometimes replied to this that what is preferable is reading the book as compared with bowling for an evening and that it is absurd to say that anything so elusive as the "pleasure" of the one is better than the "pleasure" of the other. Furthermore, it is argued that Mill is not really a hedonist because he allows in effect that the *source* of pleasure, whether reading or bowling, makes a difference to the total intrinsic value of the two experiences; so he is not saying that the *only* thing that is relevant to intrinsic worth is a thing's pleasantness. Are these criticisms just?

4. It is often said that people who have not been pigs ought not to venture judgments on whether someone who had been both human and porcine

would prefer to be a human being dissatisfied than a pig satisfied. Could Mill give a reasonable answer to this objection?

5. Does Mill's conception of a "happy life" differ in any important respects from Epicurus'?

6. What would Mill say should be the goal of moral education?

7. Mill asserts that "motive has nothing to do with the morality of the action, though much with the worth of the agent. He who saves a fellow creature from drowning does what is morally right, whether his motive be duty, or the hope of being paid for his trouble." If one employs the distinction, made in our introductory remarks (p. 2) between rightness and blameworthiness (or praiseworthiness), how might we state Mill's view about when an act is (a) right and (b) blameworthy? Or does he have a view on the latter issue? You might take into account this further remark (p. 39): "A right action does not necessarily indicate a virtuous character, and . . . actions which are blamable often proceed from qualities entitled to praise."

8. Can a utilitarian believe that God's will is the supreme law of morals?

9. Mill says (p. 43) that "questions of ultimate ends do not admit of proof, in the ordinary acceptation of the term." Critics have often found that Mill offers a proof, but a logically objectionable one, in the following lines: "The only proof capable of being given that an object is visible is that people actually see it. The only proof that a sound is audible, is that people hear it: and so of the other sources of our experience. In like manner, I apprehend, the sole evidence it is possible to produce that anything is desirable, is that people do actually desire it." Is there a logical error here? If so, where?

10. Critics have thought there is another and different logical error, in the same paragraph, in the reasoning which leads to "the general happiness, therefore, a good to the aggregate of all persons." Is there? If so, what is it?

11. Although Mill holds that pleasure alone is intrinsically desirable, he also admits that people do "desire things which, in common language, are decidedly distinguished from happiness," for instance, virtue, money, and fame. Mill reconciled the apparently contradictory statements by saying that the latter are in some sense "parts of happiness." He says that "The ingredients of happiness are very various, and each of them is desirable in itself . . ." But does it make sense to say that virtue is a "part of happiness"? If it doesn't, then is Mill logically committed to a nonhedonist conclusion?

12. Psychologists have sometimes held that we do, or decide to do, only what we most *want* to do. Would Mill agree with this? Who is right, in your opinion?

13. Mill, attempting to prove that virtue is desired *as a part of happiness*, says that those "who desire virtue for its own sake, desire it either because the consciousness of it is a pleasure, or because the consciousness of being without it is a pain, or for both reasons united." It might be replied that the consciousness of virtue being a pleasure (and so on) just *is* the fact that virtue is desired for itself, and is not an explanation *why* it is desired — much less a showing that what is really desired is pleasure. Is this criticism just? One might note what Mill says on the next page: "Desiring a thing and finding it pleasant, aversion to it and thinking of it as painful, are phenomena entirely inseparable, or rather two parts of the same phenomenon; in strictness of language, two different modes of naming the same psychological fact. . . ."

SUGGESTIONS FOR FURTHER READING

Mill, John Stuart. *Autobiography*. New York: Columbia Univ. Press, 1924.
————. *The Subjection of Women*. New York: Longmans, Green, 1924.

Anschutz, R. P. *The Philosophy of J. S. Mill*. New York: Oxford Univ. Press, 1953.
Cranston, Maurice. *John Stuart Mill* (Writers and Their Work Series No. 99). New York: British Book Centre, 1960. Valuable for bibliography.
MacCunn, John. *Six Radical Thinkers*. London: Arnold, 1910.
Plamenatz, John. *Mill's Utilitarianism*; reprinted with a study of the English Utilitarians. New York: Macmillan, 1949.
Russell, Bertrand. "John Stuart Mill." *Proceedings of the British Academy*, Vol. 41 (1955), pp. 43-59.
Stephen, James Fitzjames. *Liberty, Equality, Fraternity*. London: Smith, Elder, 1873.
Stephen, Sir Leslie. *The English Utilitarians*. Gloucester, Mass.: Peter Smith, 1950.

Charlie Dunbar Broad (1887-   )

A CRITIQUE OF HEDONISM

C. D. Broad, who recently retired from the Knightbridge Chair of Moral Philosophy at Cambridge University, has been, next to Bertrand Russell, the most prolific writer among contemporary British philosophers. In addition to *Physics, Perception, and Reality* (1914), *Scientific Thought* (1923), *The Mind and its Place in Nature* (1925), *Five Types of Ethical Theory* (1930), and *Examination of McTaggart's Philosophy* (1933-38), 3 vols., he has written a large number of shorter pieces. His work is throughout marked by unusual clarity of exposition and patient analysis.

The present selection is drawn from a chapter in which Broad formulates and criticizes the main views of the ablest of all hedonists (if not of all moral philosophers), Henry Sidgwick (1838-1900). In the fashion typical of his philosophical writings, Broad pursues the question of exactly what hedonists might mean by "pleasure" and uses the distinctions arrived at as weapons against the hedonist.

From Charlie Dunbar Broad, *Five Types of Ethical Theory*, published by Humanities Press Inc., New York, 1956, and reprinted with their permission.

FIVE TYPES OF ETHICAL THEORY

Is it the case that nothing is intrinsically good or bad except experiences, that no characteristic of an experience has any bearing on its intrinsic value except its pleasantness or painfulness, and that the measure of its intrinsic value is the nett balance of pleasantness over painfulness which characterises it? Sidgwick discusses this question in Book 3, Chapter 14.

It seems to me important to begin by trying to get a clear idea of what we mean by "a pleasure" and "a pain"; for, on this point psychologists, to my mind, are very confused. The old tripartite division subdivides all mental events into Cognitions, Conations, and Feelings. And it seems to identify "Feelings" with pleasures and pains. Now this seems to me to be a radically unsatisfactory and unscientific division. I would first divide mental events into those which are and those which are not directed to objects. If there be any members of the second class, and I think it is plausible to maintain that there are, I confine the name "Feelings" to them. In the first class would certainly come Cognitions, Conations, and Emotions. You cannot cognise without cognising something, or will without willing something, or have an emotion without having it towards something. As regards those mental events which are called "Sensations," it seems to me that some, *e.g.*, visual and auditory sensations, are plainly Cognitions, and therefore fall into the first class. With regard to others it is difficult in practice to decide whether they ought to go into the first or the second class, though it is certain that any one of them must in fact go into one class or the other. There are some "Sensations," *e.g.*, those which we get from processes in our bodies, which are often called "Feelings," and which it seems highly plausible, though not absolutely necessary, to put in the second class. . . .

We are now in a position to deal with pleasures and pains. It seems to me that there is a quality, which we cannot define but are perfectly well acquainted with, which may be called "Hedonic Tone." It has the two determinate forms of Pleasantness and Unpleasantness. And, so far as I can see, it can belong *both* to Feelings and to those Cognitions which are also Emotions or Conations. Whether it can belong to Cognitions which have neither an emotional nor a conative quality, if such there be, is more doubtful. "A pleasure" then is simply any mental event which has the pleasant form of hedonic tone, and "a pain" is simply any kind of mental event which has the unpleasant form of hedonic tone. There is not a special *kind* of mental events, called "pleasures and pains"; and to think that there is is as if one should solemnly divide human beings into men, women, and blondes. It is of course true that the commonest, and some of the most intense, pleasures and pains are feelings, in my sense of the word. But remorse, which is memory of certain events, having a certain emotional tone, is plainly a pain as much as toothache. And hope, which is expectation of certain events, having a certain emotional tone, is plainly as much a pleasure as the sensation of smell which we get from a rose or a violet.

Now any mental event which has hedonic quality will always have other qualities as well, and its specific hedonic quality will often be causally determined by its specific non-hedonic qualities. Thus the painfulness of remorse and the pleasantness of hope are determined respectively by the specific kinds of emotional quality which these two cognitions have. And this is even more obvious in the case of bodily feelings. Headaches and toothaches are both pains, for they both have unpleasant hedonic tone. But each has its own specific sensible quality of "headachiness" and "toothachiness," beside further modifications, such as "stabbingness," "throbbingness," etc., which may be common to both. And the painfulness of these feelings seems to be causally determined by their non-hedonic sensible qualities. At this point I cannot refrain from throwing out an interesting question which I must not pursue further. Is the connexion between such and such non-hedonic qualities and such and such a form of hedonic quality *merely* causal and logically *contingent,* or is it intrinsically necessary? Is it, *e.g.,* logically possible that there should have been minds which had experiences exactly like our experiences of acute toothache in all their *sensible* qualities, but in whom these sensations were *pleasantly* toned? The reader may find it amusing to speculate on this question for himself.

We can now deal with the question of pleasures and pains of different quality, which Mill raised, but which he and his critics have so lamentably failed to state clearly. We must first divide the characteristics of any experience into Pure Qualities and Relational Properties. We must then further subdivide the Pure Qualities into Hedonic and Non-hedonic, and the Relational Properties into Causal and Non-causal. Take, *e.g.,* remorse. Its hedonic quality is unpleasantness. It has, beside, that characteristic emotional quality in virtue of which we call it "remorse." It has the non-causal relational property of being a cognition of one's own past misdeeds. And it may have the causal property of tending to make us avoid in future such actions as we are now regretting. Now it is perfectly plain that there are "differences of quality" among pleasures and pains in the sense that two experiences which were exactly alike in hedonic quality might differ in non-hedonic quality (as a headache and a toothache do), or in non-causal relational property, or in causal property. The pure Hedonist holds that differences of non-hedonic quality and non-causal relational property make no difference to the intrinsic value of an experience. Nothing is relevant to the value of the experience except its hedonic quality and a certain one of its causal properties, viz., what Bentham called its "fecundity." Fecundity is the causal property of tending to produce other experiences which are pleasant or painful. Mill presumably held that, although no experience would have any intrinsic value, positive or negative, unless it were pleasant or painful, yet of two experiences which had precisely the same hedonic quality and precisely the same fecundity one might be better than the other in virtue of some difference in non-hedonic quality, or in non-causal relational property, or in some causal property other than fecundity. This view appears to be perfectly consistent logically, whether it be in fact true or not.

There is, however, another and more subtle sense in which it is conceivable that pleasures or pains might "differ in quality." It is commonly assumed that hedonic tone is a determinable quality having two and only two determinate forms under it, viz., pleasantness and unpleasantness, though of course each can be present in various degrees of intensity. This may very well be true; but there is another possibility which is at least worth mentioning. Is it not possible that there may be several different determinate forms of pleasantness and unpleasantness, just as there are several different shades of redness and several different shades of blueness? If this were admitted, it might be held that nothing is relevant to the goodness or badness of an experience except its hedonic quality and its fecundity, and yet that two experiences which had exactly the same degree of pleasantness and the same fecundity might differ in value because they had this pleasantness in different determinate forms. It is just conceivable that Mill may have meant this. He was so confused that he probably did not himself know precisely what he meant; very likely he was thinking in a vague way of both these entirely different senses of "qualities of pleasure," without ever clearly distinguishing them. A person who took the present view might be called a "pure hedonist" but not a "purely quantitative hedonist."

As regards the characteristics which make an experience intrinsically good or bad, Sidgwick is definitely a pure quantitative hedonist. . . . I do not propose to go into the details of Sidgwick's argument. In the end, as he is well aware, each man must decide such questions for himself by direct inspection. All that the philosopher can do is to make sure that no relevant facts have been ignored, that no logical fallacies are committed, and that the issue is not confused by verbal ambiguities. I will therefore put the matter as briefly and clearly as I can in my own way. The contention which we have to examine is that no relational property of an experience, and no quality of it except its hedonic quality, has any bearing on its intrinsic goodness or badness. If this were so, it would follow that no causal characteristic of it can have any bearing on its goodness or badness as a means except its fecundity, *i.e.*, its tendency to produce pleasant or painful experiences. I shall first try to convince the reader that this is not in fact true. And I shall then try to point out the kind of fallacy which is, I think, committed by those persons who profess to show that it is true.

(i) Since this is a general proposition, it can be refuted if we can produce a single convincing contrary instance. Now consider the state of mind which is called "malice." Suppose that I perceive or think of the undeserved misfortunes of another man with pleasure. Is it not perfectly plain that this is an intrinsically bad state of mind, not merely *in spite of*, but *because of*, its pleasantness? Is it not plain that any cognition which has the relational property of being a cognition of another's undeserved misfortunes and the hedonic quality of pleasantness will be *worse* in proportion as the pleasantness is more intense? No doubt malice is a state of mind which on the whole tends to increase human misery. But surely it is clear that we do not regard it as evil, simply as a means. Even if we were quite sure that all malice would be impotent, it seems clear to me that we should condemn it as intrinsically bad.

This example, if it be accepted, not only refutes the general contention of the pure hedonist, but also brings out an important positive fact. Malice is not intrinsically bad simply because it is pleasant; many pleasant states are intrinsically good. And it is not intrinsically bad simply because it has the relational property of being a cognition of another's undeserved happiness; the sorrowful cognition of such an object would not be intrinsically bad. The intrinsic badness of malice depends on the *combination* of being pleasant with having this particular kind of object. We must therefore be prepared for the possibility that there is no single simple characteristic which is necessary and sufficient to make an experience intrinsically good or bad. It may be that intrinsic goodness or badness always depends on the combination of certain characteristics in the same experience. Any experience which combined the characteristics c_1 and c_2 might be intrinsically good; any that combined c_2 and c_3 might be intrinsically bad; whilst experiences which combined c_3 and c_1 might be neutral.

(ii) Let us now consider what seems to me to be the fallacy in the arguments of pure hedonists. We must begin by remarking that it is logically impossible that an experience should have no characteristic except hedonic quality. It is as clear that no experience could be *merely* pleasant or painful as that nothing could be black or white without also having some shape and some size. Consequently the hedonist can neither produce nor conceive an instance of an experience which was just pleasant or painful and nothing more; and so he cannot judge by direct inspection that hedonic quality is necessary and sufficient to determine intrinsic value. He is therefore reduced to reflecting on instances in which hedonic quality is combined with non-hedonic characteristics. Now the utmost that he can do is this. He can take in turn each of the non-hedonic characteristics of experiences which could with any plausibility be thought to affect their intrinsic value. These can occur, or be conceived to occur, without hedonic quality, or with various degrees of pleasantness and various degrees of painfulness. He will claim to establish by inspection propositions of the following kind with regard to each of these non-hedonic characteristics. (*a*) When this characteristic is present and hedonic quality is absent the experience has no intrinsic value. (*b*) When this characteristic is present and hedonic quality is also present the experience has intrinsic value. (*c*) The determinate kind of value (goodness or badness) varies with the determinate kind of hedonic quality (pleasantness or unpleasantness), and its degree varies with the degree of the hedonic quality. Variations in the determinate form or in the degree of this non-hedonic characteristic make no difference to the determinate form or the degree of value of the experience.

I do not think that any hedonist could possibly claim more than to establish these propositions in turn about each non-hedonic characteristic of an experience which seemed worth considering. I have tried to show by a contrary instance that the third of them, at any rate, is not true. But suppose, for the sake of argument, that they were all true, what could legitimately be inferred? You could legitimately infer that hedonic quality is *necessary* to give intrinsic value to an experience. You could legitimately infer that none of these other characteristics is necessary to give intrinsic value to an experience; *i.e.*, that, if you take *any one* of them, an experience could be intrinsically good or bad without possessing *that one*. But it would not be legitimate to infer that any experience could have intrinsic value if it had *none* of these characteristics. For it might be that, although an experience which had hedonic quality could have intrinsic value without c_1 being present, and could have it without c_2 being present, . . . and could have it without c_n being present, yet it could not have intrinsic value unless *one or other* of the non-hedonic characteristics c_1, c_2, . . . c_n were present in addition to the hedonic quality. To take a parallel case; there is no area which a thing must have in order to be round, but it cannot be round without having some area or other. Thus, even if all the premises which the most optimistic hedonist could demand were granted to him, he would have no right to conclude that the hedonic quality of an experience is *sufficient* as well as *necessary* to give it intrinsic value. Even if the *variations* in intrinsic value were dependent on variations in hedonic quality and totally independent of variations in any non-hedonic characteristic, it might still be the case that intrinsic value would not be *present at all* unless there were some non-hedonic characteristic in addition to the hedonic quality. To take a parallel case; the variations in the time of swing of a pendulum are independent of variations in the mass of the pendulum-bob. But it would not swing at all if the bob had no mass.

All arguments for pure quantitative hedonism, including Sidgwick's, with which I am acquainted overlook these elementary logical points. I conclude then that the arguments for this doctrine are certainly fallacious, and that the doctrine itself is almost certainly false.

Here, if I were wise, I should leave the matter. But I cannot resist the temptation of starting one more hare before I turn to another topic. We have so far talked of pleasantness and painfulness as two determinate forms of a certain determinable *quality* (hedonic tone) which may belong to any kind of experience. We have noted that it is *a priori* impossible that any experience should have *only* hedonic quality; it must always have some non-hedonic quality (such as toothachiness, throbbingness, etc.), and this will determine its hedonic quality. Now this suggests the following possibility. Is it not possible that what we have called "hedonic *quality*" is really a *relational property* and not a quality at all? Is it not possible that the statement: "This experience of mine is pleasant" just means: "I like this experience for its non-hedonic qualities"? I may dislike the experience as a whole, because it will have causal and non-causal relational properties in addition to its non-hedonic qualities. I like the experience of malice for its emotional quality; but I cannot confine my attention to this. I have to consider also its relational property of having for its object the undeserved misfortunes of another; and my dislike for the combination of this emotional quality with this relational property overbalances my liking for the experience regarded simply as having the emotional quality. On this view we should no longer divide the qualities of an experience into hedonic and non-hedonic. All its qualities would be non-hedonic. But, if its qualities were such that I liked it *for them* it would be pleasant, and if its qualities were such that I disliked it *for them* it would be painful. And it would remain pleasant in the first case even though I disliked it *on the whole*, and painful in the second case even though I liked it *on the whole*. I think it is worth while to throw out this suggestion; but I do not wish to attach much weight to it. My argument against pure quantitative hedonism is independent of its truth or falsity.

QUESTIONS

1. Psychologists would prefer to speak of pleasantness as the opposite of unpleasantness, reserving the word "painful" for a special kind of sensation (which may be pleasant, in mild forms). They are also agreed that pleasure is not a special kind of element in experience, but attaches in some sense to different experiences such as joy, scratching a mosquito bite, eating ice cream, and so on. Taking for granted these assumptions, do you find Broad's account of pleasantness as hedonic *quality*, at the beginning of the selection, or the identification of it with the relational property *being liked* for its (non-hedonic) qualities, the more plausible?
2. In view of these distinctions, is Mill's view that pleasures differ both in quantity and quality still tenable? Or what might his view be explained to mean?
3. Would it be convincing to say, despite Broad's argument, that malice is not *intrinsically* bad, although we object to it because it is a quality of mind which in most cases produces bad consequences?
4. Assuming that Broad's other criticism of hedonism is correct, can you state a form of hedonist view, which seems to you important if true, which is not inconsistent with the point he makes?

Aristotle (384-322 B.C.)

RATIONAL ACTIVITY AS THE GOOD

Aristotle must count as one of the dozen greatest minds in history. His *Nicomachean Ethics,* from which the following selection is drawn, is probably the one, of the great classics on ethics, which one should read if one could read only one. Many of his other works are equally significant in their fields. His historical influence has been enormous. Among the topics on which he wrote extensively are logic, metaphysics, physics, psychology, biology, and political theory, in addition to ethics.

Aristotle was born in Stagira, the son of a physician. He studied at Plato's Academy from 366-347 B.C. and was taught by Plato. After Plato's death he removed from Athens for some years, during three of which he was tutor of Alexander of Macedon. He returned to Athens and founded a school of his own, the Lyceum, sometimes called the Peripatetic school.

He agreed with the hedonists that the good must be that which we desire for itself, and he affirmed that "happiness" (*eudaimonia*) is the good, but not happiness in the sense of enjoyments. We shall find what the good or happiness is, he thought, only through an examination of human nature, through a consideration of the "proper function" of man in the sense in which the bodily organs have functions. His conclusion is that rational activity is the good: primarily scientific reflection but also practical action in conformity with rational principles, or virtuous action. This is not to exclude enjoyment from the good, for Aristotle concluded that rational activity is necessarily pleasant, indeed is the finest kind of pleasure. Much of Aristotle's book is concerned with elaborating exactly what "virtuous action" is. (In Chapter 7 there appears an additional brief selection, on the subject of voluntary action.)

From Aristotle, *Ethics for English Readers,* trans. by H. Rackham, published by Basil Blackwell, Publisher, Oxford, 1952, and reprinted with their permission.

NICOMACHEAN ETHICS

BOOK I

The good is what is desired for itself and is that for the sake of attaining which everything else is chosen *

Every science and every investigation, and likewise every practical pursuit and undertaking, appears to aim at some good; and consequently the good has been well defined as the object at which all things aim. It is true that a certain variety can be observed among the ends aimed at; sometimes the mere activity of practising the pursuit is the object of pursuing it, whereas in other cases the end aimed at is some product over and above the pursuit itself; and in the pursuits that aim at certain objects besides their mere practice, those products are essentially superior in value to the activities that produce them. But as there are numerous pursuits and sciences and branches of knowledge, it follows that the ends at which they aim are correspondingly numerous. Medicine aims at producing health, naval architecture at building ships, strategic science at winning victories, economics at acquiring wealth. And many pursuits of this sort are subordinate to some single faculty — for instance bit-making and the other departments of the harness trade are subordinate to the art of horsemanship, and the latter together with every other military activity to the science of strategics, and similarly other arts to different arts again. Now in all these cases the ends of the master sciences are of higher value than the objects of the subordinate ones, the latter being only pursued for the sake of the former. Nor does it make any difference whether the end aimed at by the pursuit is the mere activity of pursuing it or something else besides this, as in the case of the sciences mentioned.

If, therefore, among the ends at which our conduct aims there is one which we will for its own sake, whereas we will the other ends only for the sake of this one, and if we do not choose everything for the sake of some other thing — that would clearly be an endless process, making all desire futile and idle —, it is clear that this one ultimate end will be the good, and the greatest good. Then will not a knowledge of this ultimate end be of more than theoretic interest? Will it not also have great practical importance for the conduct of life? Shall we not be more likely to attain our needs if like archers we have a target before us to aim at? If this be so, an attempt must be made to ascertain at all events in outline what precisely this supreme good is, and under which of the theoretical or practical sciences it falls.

* The italicized headings are interpolations by the present editor. The footnotes are by the translator.

*This subject should be of central concern for statesmen; so we
can say it is really a branch of political science*

Now it would be agreed that it must be the subject of the most
authoritative of the sciences — the one that is in the fullest sense of the
term a master-craft. This term clearly describes the science of politics, since
it is that which ordains which of the sciences ought to exist in states and
what branches of knowledge the various classes of citizens must study and
up to what point; we observe that even the most highly esteemed faculties, such as strategics and domestic economy and oratory, are subordinate
to political science. As then this science employs the rest of the sciences,
and as it moreover lays down laws prescribing what people are to do and
what things they are to abstain from, the end of political science must
comprise the ends of the other sciences. Consequently the good of man
must be the subject pursued by the science of politics. No doubt it is true
that the good is the same for the individual and for the state; but still
the good of the state is manifestly a greater and more perfect object both
to ascertain and to secure. To procure the good of only a single individual
is better than nothing; but to effect the good of a nation or a state is a
nobler and more divine achievement.

This then being the object of our present investigation, it is in a sense
the science of politics.

The present investigation therefore, as directed to these objects, may
be termed Political Science.

*Our subject is complex, and we cannot expect to come out with
generalizations as simple and accurate as we obtain in some other
branches of inquiry*

Our treatment of this science will be adequate if it achieves the
degree of accuracy that is appropriate to the subject. The same amount of
precision is not requisite in every department of philosophy, any more than
in every product of the arts and crafts. Questions of right and of justice,
which are the matters investigated by Political Science, involve much difference of opinion and much uncertainty; indeed this has given rise to the
view that such things are mere conventions, and not realities in the order
of nature. There is a similar uncertainty as to the meaning of the term
'good,' owing to the fact that good things may often lead to harmful consequences; before now people have been ruined by wealth, and courage has
been the undoing of others. Therefore in dealing with subjects and starting from conceptions so indefinite we must be content to obtain not more
than a rough outline of the truth, and to reach conclusions which, like the
matters dealt with and the principles postulated, have merely a general
validity. And accordingly the reader likewise must accept the various views
propounded in the same spirit. It is the mark of an educated mind to ex-

pect that degree of precision in each department which the nature of the subject allows: to demand rigorous demonstration from a political orator is on a par with accepting plausible probabilities from a mathematician. . . .

It is generally agreed that the good is happiness in a broad sense — in the sense of "well-being" or "satisfaction"; but people differ in their more specific conceptions of happiness

To resume: inasmuch as all study and all deliberate action is aimed at some good object, let us state what is the good which is in our view the aim of political science, and what is the highest of the goods obtainable by action.

Now as far as the name goes there is virtual agreement about this among the vast majority of mankind. Both ordinary people and persons of trained mind define the good as happiness. But as to what constitutes happiness opinions differ; the answer given by ordinary people is not the same as the verdict of the philosopher. Ordinary men identify happiness with something obvious and visible, such as pleasure or wealth or honour — everybody gives a different definition, and sometimes the same person's own definition alters: when a man has fallen ill he thinks that happiness is health, if he is poor he thinks it is wealth. And when people realise their own ignorance they regard with admiration those who propound some grand theory that is above their heads. The view has been held by some thinkers [1] that besides the many good things alluded to above there also exists something that is good in itself, which is the fundamental cause of the goodness of all the others.

Now to review the whole of these opinions would perhaps be a rather thankless task. It may be enough to examine those that are most widely held, or that appear to have some considerable argument in their favour. . . .

Reasons for doubting whether enjoyment, fame, virtue, or wealth is the whole good

To judge by men's mode of living, the mass of mankind think that good and happiness consist in pleasure, and consequently are content with a life of mere enjoyment. There are in fact three principal modes of life — the one just mentioned, the life of active citizenship and the life of contemplation. The masses, being utterly servile, obviously prefer the life of mere cattle; and indeed they have some reason for this, inasmuch as many men of high station share the tastes of Sardanapalus.[2] The better

[1] Plato and the Academy.

[2] A mythical Assyrian king; two versions of his epitaph are recorded, one containing the words 'Eat, drink, play, since all else is not worth that snap of the fingers,' the other ending 'I have what I ate, and the delightful deeds of wantonness and love in which I shared; but all my wealth is vanished.'

people, on the other hand, and men of action, give the highest value to honour, since honour may be said to be the object aimed at in a public career. Nevertheless, it would seem that honour is a more superficial thing than the good which we are in search of, because honour seems to depend more on the people who render it than on the person who receives it, whereas we dimly feel that good must be something inherent in oneself and inalienable. Moreover men's object in pursuing honour appears to be to convince themselves of their own worth; at all events they seek to be honoured by persons of insight and by people who are well acquainted with them, and to be honoured for their merit. It therefore seems that at all events in the opinions of these men goodness is more valuable than honour, and probably one may suppose that it has a better claim than honour to be deemed the end at which the life of politics aims. But even virtue appears to lack completeness as an end, inasmuch as it seems to be possible to possess it while one is asleep or living a life of perpetual inactivity, and moreover one can be virtuous and yet suffer extreme sorrow and misfortune; but nobody except for the sake of maintaining a paradox would call a man happy in those circumstances.

However, enough has been said on this topic, which has indeed been sufficiently discussed in popular treatises.

The third life is the life of contemplation, which we shall consider later.

The life of money-making is a cramped way of living, and clearly wealth is not the good we are in search of, as it is only valuable as a means to something else. Consequently a stronger case might be made for the objects previously specified, because they are valued for their own sake; but even they appear to be inadequate, although a great deal of discussion has been devoted to them. . . .

> *Reaffirmation that the good is the ultimate and self-sufficient object of desire and that "happiness" is the good*

What then is the precise nature of the practicable good which we are investigating? It appears to be one thing in one occupation or profession and another in another: the object pursued in medicine is different from that of military science, and similarly in regard to the other activities. What definition of the term 'good' then is applicable to all of them? Perhaps 'the object for the sake of attaining which all the subsidiary activities are undertaken.' The object pursued in the practice of medicine is health, in a military career victory, in architecture a building — one thing in one pursuit and another in another, but in every occupation and every pursuit it is the end aimed at, since it is for the sake of this that the subsidiary activities in all these pursuits are undertaken. Consequently if there is some one thing which is the end and aim of all practical activities whatsoever, that thing, or if there are several, those things, will constitute the practicable good.

Our argument has therefore come round again by a different route to the point reached before. We must endeavour to render it yet clearer.

Now the objects at which our actions aim are manifestly several, and some of these objects, for instance money, and instruments in general, we adopt as means to the attainment of something else. This shows that not all the objects we pursue are final ends. But the greatest good manifestly is a final end. Consequently if there is only one thing which is final, that will be the object for which we are now seeking, or if there are several, it will be that one among them which possesses the most complete finality.

Now a thing that is pursued for its own sake we pronounce to be more final than one pursued as a means to some other thing, and a thing that is never desired for the sake of something else we call more final than those which are desired for the sake of something else as well as for their own sake. In fact the absolutely final is something that is always desired on its own account and never as a means for obtaining something else. Now this description appears to apply in the highest degree to happiness, since we always desire happiness for its own sake and never on account of something else; whereas honour and pleasure and intelligence and each of the virtues, though we do indeed desire them on their own account as well, for we should desire each of them even if it produced no external result, we also desire for the sake of happiness, because we believe that they will bring it to us, whereas nobody desires happiness for the sake of those things, nor for anything else but itself.

The same result seems to follow from a consideration of the subject of self-sufficiency, which is felt to be a necessary attribute of the final good. The term self-sufficient denotes not merely being sufficient for oneself alone, as if one lived the life of a hermit, but also being sufficient for the needs of one's parents and children and wife, and one's friends and fellow-countrymen in general, inasmuch as man is by nature a social being.

Yet we are bound to assume some limit in these relationships, since if one extends the connexion to include one's children's children and friends' friends, it will go on *ad infinitum*. But that is a matter which must be deferred for later consideration. Let us define self-sufficiency as the quality which makes life to be desirable and lacking in nothing even when considered by itself; and this quality we assume to belong to happiness. Moreover when we pronounce happiness to be the most desirable of all things, we do not mean that it stands as one in a list of good things — were it so, it would obviously be more desirable in combination with even the smallest of the other goods, inasmuch as that addition would increase the total of good, and of two good things the larger must always be the more desirable.

Thus it appears that happiness is something final and complete in itself, as being the aim and end of all practical activities whatever.

For a more specific conception of the kind of "happiness" which is the good, we do well to examine whether nature intended man for anything, as it intended the eye for sight. What is distinctive of man is reason, so the happiness which is the good must be the exercise of reason in living.

Possibly, however, the student may feel that the statement that happiness is the greatest good is a mere truism, and he may want a clearer explanation of what the precise nature of happiness is. This may perhaps be achieved by ascertaining what is the proper function of man. In the case of flute-players or sculptors or other artists, and generally of all persons who have a particular work to perform, it is felt that their good and their well-being are found in that work. It may be supposed that this similarly holds good in the case of a human being, if we may assume that there is some work which constitutes the proper function of a human being as such. Can it then be the case that whereas a carpenter and a shoemaker have definite functions or businesses to perform, a man as such has none, and is not designed by nature to perform any function? Should we not rather assume that, just as the eye and hand and foot and every part of the body manifestly have functions assigned to them, so also there is a function that belongs to a man, over and above all the special functions that belong to his members? If so, what precisely will that function be? It is clear that the mere activity of living is shared by man even with the vegetable kingdom, whereas we are looking for some function that belongs specially to man. We must therefore set aside the vital activity of nutrition and growth. Next perhaps comes the life of the senses; but this also is manifestly shared by the horse and the ox and all the animals. There remains therefore what may be designated the practical life of the rational faculty.

But the term 'rational' life has two meanings: it denotes both the mere possession of reason, and its active exercise. Let us take it that we here mean the latter, as that appears to be the more proper signification of the term. Granted then that the special function of man is the active exercise of the mind's faculties in accordance with rational principle, or at all events not in detachment from rational principle, and that the function of anything, for example, a harper, is generally the same as the function of a good specimen of that thing, for example a good harper (the specification of the function merely being augmented in the latter case with the statement of excellence — a harper is a man who plays the harp, a good harper one who plays the harp well) — granted, I say, the truth of these assumptions, it follows that the good of man consists in the active exercise of the faculties in conformity with excellence or virtue, or if there are several virtues, in conformity with the best and most perfect among them.

Moreover, happiness requires an entire life-time. One swallow does not make a summer, nor does a single fine day; and similarly one day or a brief period of prosperity does not make a man supremely fortunate and happy.

Let this then stand as a first sketch of the good, since perhaps our right procedure is to begin by drawing a preliminary outline, and then to fill in the details later on. Given a good outline to start with, it would seem to be within anybody's capacity to carry on, and to put in all the details. In discovering these time is a good collaborator; and that is in fact the way in which advances in the arts and crafts have actually been achieved, as anybody is capable of filling in the gaps. . . .

Such a life will necessarily be pleasant

In consequence of this their life has no need of pleasure as an external appendage; it contains pleasures within itself. For in addition to what has been said, if a man does not enjoy performing noble actions he is not a good man at all. Nobody would call a man just who did not enjoy acting justly, nor liberal if he did not enjoy acting liberally, and similarly with the other virtues. But if this is so, actions in conformity with virtue will be intrinsically pleasant. Moreover, they are also good and noble; and good and noble in the highest degree, inasmuch as the virtuous man must be a good judge of these matters, and his judgement is as we have said.

Consequently happiness is at once the best and the noblest and the pleasantest thing there is, and these qualities do not exist in separate compartments, as is implied by the inscription at Delos:

> The noblest thing is justice, health the best,
> But getting your desire the pleasantest.

For all these qualities are combined in the highest activities, and it is these activities or the best one among them which according to our definition constitutes happiness. All the same it is manifest that happiness requires external goods in addition, since it is impossible, or at all events difficult, to perform noble actions without resources. Many of them require the aid of friends and of wealth and power in the state. Also a lack of such advantages as good birth or a fine family of children or good looks is a blot on a man's supreme felicity. A very ugly man or one of low birth or without children cannot be classed as completely happy; and still less perhaps can a man whose children or friends are utterly base, or though worthy have died. . . .

> *For a clearer concept of the excellence or "virtue" of mind, the exercise of which is true happiness and which we have characterized as "rational," we must classify the various aspects or activities of the mind. We are thus led to distinguish intellectual from moral "virtues."*

Happiness then we define as the active exercise of the mind in conformity with perfect goodness or virtue. It will therefore be necessary to investigate the nature of virtue, as to do so will contribute to our understanding the nature of happiness. Moreover it appears that the true statesman must have made a special study of virtue, because it is his aim to make the citizens good and law-abiding men. As an example of this we have the lawgivers of Crete and of Sparta, and the other founders of constitutions recorded in history. But if the investigation of the nature of virtue is a duty of statesmanship, that investigation will clearly fit in with the original plan of this treatise.

Now obviously the virtue which we have to investigate is human virtue, inasmuch as the good and the happiness which we set out to discover were human good and human happiness. And by human virtue we mean not bodily excellence but goodness of the mind; and happiness also we define as an activity of the mind. This being so, it is clearly necessary for the statesman to have some acquaintance with psychology — just as the doctor in order to cure an affection of the eye or any other part of the body must know their anatomical structure. This background of science is even more essential for the statesman, inasmuch as statesmanship is a higher and more honourable profession than medicine; and even physicians of a high standard give a great deal of time to studying anatomy and physiology. Consequently the student of politics must study psychology, though he must study it for its bearing on politics, and only so far as is sufficient to throw light on the matters which fall to him to consider. To pursue it to a greater degree of precision would be a more laborious task than his purpose requires.

Some topics of psychology are adequately dealt with in extraneous discourses,[3] and we may adopt a view that is put forward in them, that the mind has an irrational side and a rational — though whether these are actually separate parts, in the same way as the members of the body are separate and the parts of any other divisible structure, or whether although capable of being thought of separately, they are actually inseparable, like the convex and concave sides of the circumference of a circle, is a question of no importance for the matter in hand.

Of the irrational side again one part appears to be present in all living things, and to be of a vegetative nature — I mean the part which is the cause of nutrition and growth; a vital faculty of this nature must be assumed to exist in all creatures capable of receiving nourishment, even embryos, and must also be present in them when fully developed. This is a more reasonable view than to suppose that the nutritive principle in the adult is different from that in the embryo.

Now the virtue of this irrational mind is manifestly a virtue that belongs to all living creatures, and is not peculiar to man; for this part and this faculty appear to be most active during sleep, but while people are

[3] This phrase, which recurs elsewhere in Aristotle, may perhaps denote doctrines not peculiar to him, but also taught in some other school, possibly in the Academy of Plato.

asleep the good are indistinguishable from the bad, which is the reason for the saying that for half of his life a pauper is as good as a gentleman. This is a natural result of the fact that sleep is a cessation of that activity of the mind which characterizes it as good or bad, though with this reservation, that in a small degree some sense-impressions may penetrate to the mind during sleep; that is why men of high character have better dreams than the vulgar have.

This is enough on this subject; and we may omit the faculty of nutrition, as its nature does not participate in distinctively human virtue. But there is another factor in the mind which although irrational nevertheless appears in a manner to have an element of rationality in it.

In a self-restrained man and in one who lacks self-restraint there is a rational faculty, a rational part of their mind, which we praise for giving them right advice and exhorting them to pursue the best course of action. But on the other hand their nature appears also to contain an irrational element which combats and opposes their reason. We may compare the symptoms of paralysis; when a man suffering from this infirmity intends to move the limbs affected to the right, the opposite takes place and they swerve to the left. Similarly in the case of the mind, with persons who lack self-restraint the impulses run counter to the reason. But whereas in men's bodies we can see the erratic movement, in the case of the mind this is invisible. Nevertheless we must probably hold the view that the mind contains an irrational factor as well, which opposes and runs counter to the reason. But this factor also appears to have a share in reason, as we said; at all events in the self-restrained man it obeys the orders of reason; and doubtless in the self-controlled and courageous it is still more amenable, as these persons are completely rational.

It appears therefore that the irrational part of the mind also is twofold. Its vegetative factor has no share of reason at all, but the factor of appetite, the organ of desire in general, does in a way participate in reason, as being obedient to it and under its control. And the fact that the irrational part in some measure obeys reason is shown by our employment of moral admonition, and of reprimand and exhortation in general. If on the other hand it is correct to say that this factor also possesses reason, then the rational part will be twofold, one part of it possessing reason in the proper sense and inherently, the other part listening to reason as a child obeys its father.

And virtue also is divided into two corresponding groups, one group called the intellectual virtues and the other the moral virtues. Wisdom or intelligence and prudence belong to the former group, but liberality and self-control to the latter, inasmuch as in describing a person's moral nature we do not speak of him as wise or intelligent but as gentle or self-controlled. Still, we do also praise a man as wise in character; and praiseworthy qualities of character are what we designate virtues.

BOOK II

Intellectual excellence is acquired by education and experience, but moral excellence is a result of practice in acting rightly

Virtue, then, falls into two divisions, intellectual excellence and goodness of character. A good intellect is chiefly produced and fostered by education, and consequently requires experience and time, but moral goodness is formed mainly by training in habit. This shows that none of the moral virtues are implanted in us by nature, because natural characteristics can never be altered by training: for instance, a stone, which naturally moves downward, could not be trained to move upward even if one tried to accustom it to do so by throwing it up into the air ten thousand times; nor can a flame be trained to move downward, nor anything else that naturally acts in one way be educated to act in another way. Consequently the virtues are not formed in us by nature, but they result from our natural capacity to acquire them when that capacity has been developed by training.

Moreover in the case of the endowments given us by nature, we first receive the power of using them and exercise these powers in action subsequently. This is clear in the case of the sense-faculties: we did not acquire our sight and hearing by repeatedly seeing and hearing things, but the other way round: we started in possession of those senses and then began to use them, we did not acquire them by using them. But we acquire the virtues by first acting virtuously, just as in the case of the arts and crafts: we learn these by actually doing the things that we shall have to do when we have learnt them — for instance men become builders by building houses and harpers by playing the harp. Similarly by acting justly we become just, by acting temperately we become self-controlled, and by acting bravely we become courageous.

This is confirmed by what occurs in the state. Lawgivers make the citizens good by training them in good habits — at least that is every legislator's intention; and those who fail as legislators are those who do not establish a good system of education. In this lies the difference between a good constitution and a bad one.

Moreover all excellence is both produced and destroyed by the same means. This is the case with the arts and crafts; both good harpers and bad harpers are made by playing on the harp, and the same with building and all the other trades — a man will become a good builder by building well and a bad one by building badly. Were this not so, there would be no need of a period of apprenticeship, but people would all be born either good tradesmen or else bad ones.

Similarly with the virtues: it is by actually transacting business with our fellow-citizens that some of us become honest and others dishonest; it is by encountering danger and forming a habit of being frightened or else of keeping up our courage that some of us become brave men and others cowards; and the same is the case in regard to indulging the appetites and giving way to anger — people become self-controlled and gentle, or self-indulgent and passionate, from behaving in the one way or in the other in the fields of conduct concerned. To sum up, habits of character are formed as the result of conduct of the same kind. Consequently it is essential for us to give a certain quality to our actions, since differences of conduct produce differences of character. Hence the formation of habits, good or bad, from early childhood up is not a matter of small moment; on the contrary it is something of very great or more truly speaking of the supremest importance.

> *Moral excellence is in part a disposition to perform right actions; hence to acquire it we must know the principles of right action. The essential property of right action is avoidance of both excess and deficiency.*

The present investigation then, unlike our other studies, is not undertaken for the purpose of attaining knowledge in the abstract — we are not pursuing it in order to learn what virtue is but in order to become virtuous; otherwise it would be of no value. We are therefore bound to carry the enquiry further, and to ascertain the rules that govern right conduct, since, as we have said, our conduct determines our characters.

The rule of acting in conformity with right principle is generally accepted, and may be taken for granted. Let us also take it as agreed that ethics is not an exact science, any more than are medicine and the art of navigation; and consequently the rules of conduct that it lays down are only of general validity, and their application must vary with the circumstances of the particular occasion, and be modified by the discretion of the agent.

The first point to have in view then is that in matters of conduct both excess and deficiency are essentially detrimental. It is the same here as in the case of bodily health and strength. Our strength is impaired by taking too much exercise, and also by taking too little; and similarly too much and too little food and drink injure our health, while the right amount produces health and increases it and preserves it. This also applies to self-control and courage and the other virtues. The man who runs away from every danger and never stands his ground becomes a coward, and the man who is afraid of nothing whatever and walks into everything becomes foolhardy; and similarly one who partakes of every pleasure and refrains from no gratification becomes self-indulgent, while one who shuns all pleasures becomes a boor and a dullard. It follows that self-control and courage are unimpaired by excess and by deficiency and are preserved by moderation.

But not only are our states of character engendered and promoted by the same causes and from the same acts as those which tend to corrupt them, but they will also be actively exercised in the same circumstances as those in which they were originally formed. This is the case with other more visible qualities, for example muscular strength, which is produced by eating a great deal of food and taking a great deal of exercise, while at the same time it is the man that possesses muscular strength who is most capable of large meals and muscular exertion. The same holds good in the case of the virtues: it is by abstaining from pleasures that we acquire self-control, and when we have acquired self-control we are most capable of abstaining from pleasures; and so with courage — we become brave by training ourselves to despise and to endure things that are alarming, and we shall be best able to endure alarm when we have become brave. . . .

An act does not exhibit moral excellence merely by being right; its motivation must be moral

But someone may ask what we mean by saying that men have to become just by acting justly and self-controlled by acting with self-control; if they act justly and with self-control, they are just and self-controlled already, in the same way as those who write or sing correctly are scholars or musicians.

Perhaps however this is not really the case even in the arts and sciences. A boy may do an exercise correctly by luck, or by getting help from another boy. He will only be a scholar if he does scholarly work in a scholarly way, that is by means of his own scholarship. Also in this respect the virtues are not the same as the arts. The merit of a work of art is intrinsic, so that it is enough for it to possess a certain quality of its own. But actions outwardly virtuous are not just or controlled merely because of their own quality, but only if certain conditions are satisfied by the doer while performing them: first, he must be acting with knowledge; [4] secondly, he must be acting from deliberate choice, and the act must be chosen for its own sake; and thirdly, the act must be based on a fixed and permanent quality in his character. In judging competence in the arts in general these conditions (except the proviso that the action must be done knowingly) are not taken into consideration; but in regard to the virtues, whereas knowledge is of little or no importance, the other considerations so far from being unimportant are of the first moment, inasmuch as a just and controlled character is formed by repeated actions involving justice and self-control.

Thus although actions are pronounced to show justice and self-control when they are the sort of actions that a just or self-controlled man would perform, a person is not just or self-controlled because he performs them but because he performs them in the spirit in which just and self-controlled men perform them. It is therefore correct to say that a man becomes just by acting justly and self-controlled by acting with self-control; nor is it re-

---

[4] See p. 652 ff. where this phrase is explained as meaning that (1) the doer must know what he is doing — the act must not be accidental, and (2) he must know that the act is morally right.

motely possible for a man to become virtuous by means of anything but
virtuous conduct. . . .

> *Moral excellence or virtue is not any emotion or the capacity
> to feel emotions; it is a quality of character, the one which en-
> ables a man to perform his function well*

We must next consider the formal definition of virtue. The contents of our minds fall into three groups — emotions, capacities and dispositions of character; and virtue must be one of these. By the emotions
I mean appetite, anger, fear, boldness, envy, joy, friendship, hatred, desire,
jealousy, pity, and in general the feelings that are accompanied by pleasure
and pain. The capacities are the qualities in virtue of which we are described as liable to feel those emotions, for example given to feeling anger
or fear or pity. The dispositions are the characteristics in virtue of which
we stand well or badly in respect of the emotions — for example, we are
badly constituted in respect of anger if we get angry too violently or not
violently enough, and we are well constituted if we get angry in moderation; and similarly in regard to the other emotions.

Now the virtues and vices are not emotions, because we are not described as good men or bad men on account of our emotions as we are on
account of our virtues and vices, and because we are not praised or blamed
for our emotions — a man is not praised for feeling fear or for showing
anger, nor is he blamed merely for showing anger, but for showing it in
a certain way; but we are praised and blamed for virtues and vices. Again,
we do not deliberately choose to be angry or afraid; but the virtues are matters of will, or not without an element of will. Moreover we speak of ourselves as being 'moved' by emotions, but in regard to virtues and vices we
are not said to be 'moved' in a certain manner but to have a certain disposition. The same considerations also show that the virtues are not capacities, for we are not classed as good or bad merely on the ground of our
capacities for certain experiences. Moreover capacities are bestowed on us
by nature, but we are not born good or bad. If then the virtues are neither
emotions nor capacities, it remains that they are qualities of character.

We have therefore now stated to what class of things virtue belongs.

But it is not enough to merely define virtue as a quality of character.
We must also say what species of quality it is. Now it may be asserted that
the effect of all virtue or excellence is not only to render the object to
which it belongs perfect in itself but also to cause it to function perfectly:
for example excellence in the eye renders perfect both the structure of the
eye and its function — having good eyes causes us to see well; and similarly
excellence in a horse produces not merely a fine animal but a good racer
or hack or charger. If then this holds good in all cases, human virtue will
mean the quality that produces a good man and that will cause him to
perform his function well. The reason for this we have explained already;

but it may be further elucidated by considering what is the specific quality of virtue.

> *Moral excellence, or virtue, is a disposition to choose the middle course between deficiency and excess, as determined by a man with practical wisdom. But some actions and attitudes are essentially evil and are not simply cases of excess or deficiency; the moral man will avoid them.*

In the case of every whole that is divisible into parts, it is possible to take a larger or a smaller share of it, or an equal share; and those amounts may be measured either in relation to the thing itself or in relation to us. I mean that whereas the middle of an object is the point equally distant from each of its extremities, which is one and the same for everybody, the medium quantity in its relation to us is the amount that is not excessive and not deficient, and this is not the same for everybody. For instance, if ten is many and two is few, to take the actual middle amount between them gives six (because 6 is the arithmetical mean between 2 and 10: $6 - 2 = 10 - 6$); but a medium quantity relative to us cannot be arrived at in this way. For instance, supposing that for an athlete in training ten pounds of food is too large a ration and two pounds too small, the trainer will not necessarily advise six pounds, as possibly that will be too large or too small an allowance for the particular person — a small ration for a Milo [5] but a large one for a novice in athletics; and the same applies to the amount of running or wrestling prescribed in training. This is how every expert avoids excess and deficiency and adopts the middle amount — not the exact half of the object he is dealing with, but a medium quantity in relation to the person concerned.

Such then is the manner in which every kind of skill operates successfully, by looking to the middle point and making its products conform with it. This accounts for the remark commonly made about successful productions, that you cannot take anything away from them or add anything to them. The implication is that excess and deficiency impair excellence, and a middle quantity secures it. If then we are right in saying that good craftsmen when at work keep their eyes fixed on a middle point, and if virtue, no less than nature herself, surpasses all the arts and crafts in accuracy and excellence, it follows that excellence will be the faculty of hitting a middle point. I refer to moral excellence or virtue; and this is concerned with emotions and actions, in which it is possible to have excess, or deficiency, or a medium amount. For instance you can feel either more or less than a moderate amount of fear and boldness, and of desire and anger and pity, and of pleasant or painful emotions generally; and in both cases the feelings will be wrong. But to feel these emotions at the right time and on the right occasion and towards the right people and for the

[5] A famous wrestler.

right motives and in the right manner is a middle course, and the best course; and this is the mark of goodness. And similarly there is excess and deficiency or a middle amount in the case of actions. Now it is with emotions and actions that virtue is concerned; excess and deficiency in them are wrong, and a middle amount receives praise and achieves success, both of which are marks of virtue. It follows that virtue is a sort of middle state, in the sense that it aims at the middle.

Moreover, though it is possible to go wrong in many ways (according to the conjecture of the Pythagorean school evil is a property of the infinite and good of the finite), it is only possible to go right in one way:

> Goodness is one, but badness manifold.[6]

This is why to go wrong is easy but to go right difficult; it is easy to miss the target but difficult to hit it. Here then is another reason why vice is a matter of excess and deficiency and virtue a middle state.

It follows that virtue is a fixed quality of the will, consisting essentially in a middle state — middle in relation to ourselves, and as determined by principle, by the standard that a man of practical wisdom would apply. And it is a middle state between two vices, one of excess and one of deficiency: and this in view of the fact that vices either exceed or fall short of the right amount in emotions or actions, whereas virtue ascertains the mean and chooses that. Consequently while in its essence and by the principle defining its fundamental nature virtue is a middle state, in point of excellence and rightness it is an extreme.

But not every action or every emotion admits of a middle state: the very names of some of them suggest wickedness — for instance spite,[7] shamelessness, envy, and among actions, adultery, theft, murder; all of these and similar emotions and actions are blamed as being wicked intrinsically and not merely when practised to excess or insufficiently. Consequently it is not possible ever to feel or commit them rightly: they are always wrong, nor are the qualifications 'well' or 'ill' applicable to them — for instance, you cannot commit adultery with the right woman and at the right time and in the right place: the mere commission of adultery with any woman anywhere at any time is an offence. Similarly it is equally erroneous to think that there can be a middle amount and an excess and a deficiency of injustice or cowardice or self-indulgence, as that would mean that you can have a medium quantity of excess and deficiency or too much excess or too little deficiency. So just as there is no such thing as an excess or a deficiency of self-control and courage, because in these the middle is in a sense the top point, so there can be no middle amount or excess or deficiency of self-indulgence or cowardice, but actions of that sort however committed are an offence. There is no such thing as a medium amount of

[6] A quotation from an unknown poem.
[7] *Schadenfreude*, delight in the misfortunes of other people.

excess or deficiency, nor an excessive or insufficient amount of observance of a mean.

Some examples of virtues which are midway between undesirable extremes are the following

It is not enough, however, merely to give a general definition of moral goodness; it is necessary to show how our definition applies to particular virtues. In theories of conduct although general principles have a wider application, particular rules are more accurate, inasmuch as actual conduct deals with particular cases, and theory must be in agreement with these. Let us then take the particular virtues and vices from the diagram.[8]

The middle state as regards fear and boldness is courage. Excessive fearlessness has no name (as is the case with many types of character); excessive boldness is called rashness, and excessive fear and insufficient boldness cowardice.

In regard to pleasure, and in a less degree to pain, the middle state is self-control,[9] and the excess self-indulgence.[10] Persons deficient in sensibility to pleasure are scarcely to be found, so that this class has no recognized name; they may however be called insensitive.

The middle disposition in respect of giving and getting money is liberality; the excess and the deficiency are extravagance and meanness, both of these vices in opposite ways displaying both excess and deficiency — the extravagant man exceeds in spending money and is deficient in acquiring it, and the mean man exceeds in acquiring money but is deficient in spending it.

We are for the present giving a description of these characters in outline only, as that is sufficient for our present purpose. A more detailed account of them will be given later.

There are also other dispositions in regard to money — the middle state called munificence (which is not the same as liberality, as munificence is concerned with large sums of money whereas liberality is displayed in dealing with minor amounts), the excess which is tasteless vulgarity and the deficiency shabbiness in the use of money; the differences between the two latter will be stated later, and also two extremes corresponding with liberality.

The middle state in regard to honour and dishonour is pride;[11] the

---

[8] It appears that the lecturer here exhibited a table in which the virtues in the various fields of emotion and action were displayed as lying halfway between the two extremes of excess and deficiency in each.

[9] The Greek term, literally 'soundmindedness,' was represented in Latin by *temperantia,* and is commonly rendered 'temperance.'

[10] The usual translation 'profligacy' is too strong. The adjective means literally 'unchastized,' and it was applied to naughty children.

[11] The Greek term means literally 'greatness of soul,' but that expression bears a different shade of meaning in English from what it suggests in Greek. It was rendered in Latin by *magnanimitas,* but our 'magnanimity' again is different. As will be seen from what

excess is called conceit and the deficiency lack of spirit. There is another middle state which stands in the same relation to pride as that which was described as existing between generosity and munificence: pride being concerned with high honours, the state indicated is similarly concerned with minor honours. These also may be desired in a proper manner, or more than is proper, or less. The man who covets them to excess is called ambitious and the man who is too little desirous of them unambitious; but there is no name for the person in between, who has a proper desire for such honours. Consequently the two extremes both lay claim to the middle place; and in fact in our ordinary use of the words we sometimes call a man of middle character in this respect sometimes ambitious and sometimes unambitious: both words are occasionally employed as terms of approval.

The reason for this ambiguity will be stated later. For the present let me speak about the remaining characters, in pursuance of our plan.

There are also excess and deficiency and a middle disposition in regard to anger, but there are virtually no accepted names to denote them. However, we speak of the person of intermediate character in regard to anger as good-tempered, so let us call the middle state good temper; while of the two extremes the man who exceeds may be called irascible and his vice irascibility, and for the man who is deficient perhaps we may use the term spiritless, and call his deficiency lack of spirit.

There are also three other middle dispositions which somewhat resemble one another and yet are really distinct, as although they all are concerned with our daily intercourse with our fellows in conversation and in conduct, they differ in that one is a matter of sincerity in social intercourse and the others denote agreeableness, displayed either in hours of relaxation or in the business of life. These dispositions must also be dealt with, to bring it home to us that in all affairs the middle course is to be commended and the extremes are neither commendable nor right, but reprehensible.

These dispositions also for the most part have no names attached to them, but for the sake of clearness and to enable the reader to follow us more easily we must attempt to invent terms of our own to denote them, as we have done for the other dispositions.

In regard to sincerity, the middle person may be called frank and the middle disposition frankness. To exaggerate one's own merits is boastfulness and the person possessing that quality a boaster; to depreciate oneself is mock-modesty and the man who does so is mock-modest. In respect of being pleasant in giving amusement the middle person is witty and his characteristic wit; the excess is buffoonery and its possessor a buffoon, and the deficiency may be called boorishness and its possessor a boor. In regard to pleasantness in the affairs of life in general, one who is agreeable in the proper way is kindly and the middle state of character kindliness; one who

follows, the Greek word means lofty and dignified pride, justified by real distinction of character and position.

is agreeable to excess is obsequious if it is for no interested motive and a toady if he hopes to get something out of it; one who is deficient in kindliness and always disagreeable in intercourse may be called churlish or surly.

There are also middle dispositions in respect of the emotions. In these also one man is said to be of a middle character, another excessive. There is the bashful man who is ashamed of everything, whereas another is deficient or entirely devoid of the emotion in question, who is impudent; while the middle character is called modest; though modesty is not a virtue, 'modest' is a term of commendation.

Righteous indignation is the middle state between envy and malice in regard to pain or pleasure at what happens to one's neighbours. The righteously indignant man is distressed when they prosper undeservedly; the jealous man goes further, and feels aggrieved at any prosperity of others; the malicious man is so far from feeling distress at other people's misfortunes that they give him actual pleasure.

BOOK X

Aristotle then criticizes the arguments of both hedonists and their critics; in his view both parties go too far

Let us now review the theories on the subject of pleasure that have been put forward.

It was the opinion of Eudoxus,[12] that pleasure is the good. His reason was as follows. Observation showed him that all creatures, rational and irrational alike, desire to obtain pleasure, and he held the view that in every department of life what is desired is good, and what is most desired is the greatest good. Consequently, he argued, the fact that all things 'gravitate in the direction of' the same object proves that object to be the greatest good for all, inasmuch as everything finds out its own particular good, just as every creature discovers what food is nourishing for it; but that which is good for all things and which all things try to obtain must be *the* good. This argument won acceptance more because of its author's excellence of character than from its own merits. Eudoxus had the reputation of being an exceptionally temperate man, and so his theory was not supposed to be suggested by love of pleasure but to be a correct statement of the facts.

Eudoxus also held that the truth of this estimate of pleasure is equally attested by considering its opposite. Pain, he argued, was an object of intrinsic aversion to all living things, so that the opposite of pain must be intrinsically desirable. Moreover those things are most desirable which we choose for their own sake and not for the sake of something else, and to this class, he said, pleasure admittedly belongs, because we never ask anybody *why* he wants pleasure: we assume that pleasure is desirable in itself. He also argued that the value of just or temperate conduct is enhanced if

12 Eudoxus, a pupil of Plato, was an astronomer, and applied the language of physical science to ethics.

we enjoy acting justly or temperately; but a good thing can only be augmented by something else that is good.

But this argument at all events only seems to show that pleasure is *a*
good, not that it is a greater good than any other; for every good thing is
better and more desirable if some other good thing is added to it than it
is by itself. This argument resembles the one used by Plato to prove that
the good is not pleasure, since a pleasant life is more desirable if combined
with wisdom than it is without it, but if pleasure is improved by combination with something else, pleasure is not the good.

Those [13] who maintain that something which all creatures try to obtain
is not necessarily good are surely talking nonsense. We say that what all
consider to be good really is good, and he who controverts this assertion
will hardly carry conviction. If it were only irrational creatures that desired
pleasant things, there would be something in what they say; but if they are
desired by rational creatures also, how can there be any sense in it? Perhaps even the inferior orders have in them an instinct that is on a higher
level than themselves, which aims at obtaining the good appropriate to
them.

Nor does the argument about the opposite of pleasure appear to be
sound. This maintains that the fact of pain being evil does not prove
pleasure to be good, as one evil thing may be opposed to another, and
both to something neutral. This is correct enough, only it does not really
hold good of the matters in question. If pleasure and pain both were to
be classed as evils both would necessarily be objects of aversion, and if both
were neutrals, neither would be an object of aversion or else both would
be so equally. But as it is, people manifestly avoid one of them as evil and
choose the other as good. Therefore it must be as good and evil that they
are opposed. . . .

They also say that pain is a deficiency of the natural state and pleasure
its replenishment. But these are bodily experiences. If therefore pleasure is
the replenishment of the natural state, the thing in which that replenishment occurs would be the thing that felt the pleasure. This would therefore be the body. But this does not seem to be the case. Therefore pleasure
is not a replenishment, though one may feel pleasure while replenishment
is taking place, just as one feels pain during a surgical operation. This view
of pleasure seems to come from the pains and pleasures connected with
nutrition; having been in need of food and having felt pain beforehand we
are pleased by the replenishment. But this does not occur in the case of
all pleasures. The pleasure of study involves no antecedent pain, nor yet
do some among the pleasures of the senses, namely the pleasure of smell
and that of many sounds and sights, and of memories and hopes. If these
are processes, processes towards what? There has been no previous deficiency
of something that can be replenished.

[13] These were the Platonic School in Aristotle's day.

In reply to those who bring forward the degrading pleasures one might say that these are not really pleasant; if they are pleasant to ill-conditioned persons, it must not be thought that they are really pleasant, except to those persons, any more than the things that are wholesome for invalids or that taste sweet or bitter to them, or that look white to people suffering from disease of the eye, are really so. Or one might express the point by saying that, though pleasures are desirable, yet they are not desirable when derived from those sources, just as wealth is desirable, but not if won by treachery, and health, but not at the cost of eating any diet the doctor may prescribe. Or one might say that pleasures differ in kind, those derived from honourable sources not being the same as those from base sources; and that one cannot experience the pleasure of justice without being a just man, nor enjoy music without being a musician, and similarly with the other pleasures.

Moreover the difference that exists between a friend and a flatterer seems to show clearly that pleasure is not a good, or else that there are different kinds of pleasure. A friend is thought to aim at doing good to his associates, but a flatterer at giving them pleasure; to be a flatterer is a reproach, but a friend is praised, because his motives for seeking society are different. Also nobody would like to pass the whole of his life with the intellect of a child, however much pleasure he might get from things that please children, nor to enjoy doing something very disgraceful even though it brought no painful consequences. And there are many things that we should be eager to possess even if they brought us no pleasure, for instance, sight, memory, knowledge, virtue. If these things do as a matter of fact necessarily bring pleasure, that makes no difference; we should prefer to possess them even if we got no pleasure from them.

It seems therefore that pleasure is not the good, and also that not all pleasure is desirable, but that some pleasures of various kinds and derived from various sources are desirable in themselves.

> *Pleasure occurs when some sense or faculty is functioning well in relation to its proper object; pleasure consummates the activity. A natural inference is that there are different kinds of pleasure.*

We may ascertain the essential nature or the qualities of pleasure more clearly if we start again from the beginning. . . .

Each of the senses acts in relation to its object, and acts perfectly when in good condition and when directed to the finest of the objects that come under it — this seems to be the best description of a perfect activity, it being assumed that it makes no difference whether we speak of the sense itself acting or the organ which contains it. Consequently each of the senses acts best when its sense-organ is in its best condition and is directed to the best of its objects. And this activity will be the most complete and the most pleasant. For every sensation is accompanied by pleasure, as also are thought and contemplation, and the pleasantest sensation is the most complete. The most complete sensation is that of the sense-organ when in good condition and directed to its worthiest object; and the activity of sensation is completed by the pleasure, though not in the same way as it is completed by the combination of object and sense, both being in good condition, any more than health is the cause of a man's being healthy in the same sense as the doctor is the cause of it.

(It is clear that each of the senses has a particular pleasure corresponding to it; we speak of pleasant sights and sounds as well as of sweet tastes and scents. And it is also clear that the pleasure is greatest when the sense faculty is in the best condition and is directed to the best object; there will always be pleasure when there is an object to cause it and a subject to feel it, if both the object perceived and the percipient organ are good.)

But the pleasure completes the activity not in the way in which it is completed by a fixed disposition of character already present in the agent, but as a supervening consummation, in the same way as a good complexion gives a finishing touch to the young and healthy. Consequently the activity will be attended by pleasure as long as both the object thought of or perceived and the subject discerning or judging are in a proper condition, inasmuch as in any relationship as long as both the passive and the active parties remain the same and stand in the same position as regards each other, the same result is naturally produced.

How is it then that nobody can go on feeling a pleasure continuously? Is it that we grow tired? No human activity can continue working without a break, and consequently pleasure also is not continuous, as it accompanies the exercise of a faculty. Also some things give pleasure when they are new but do not give similar pleasure later, for the same reason; at the outset the mind is stimulated and acts vigorously in regard to the object, just as in the case of sight when people fix their gaze on something very intently. Subsequently however the activity is not so vigorous, but relaxes; and this damps down the pleasure which the activity gives.

It might be thought that all people aim at getting pleasure, because all people desire life, and life is a form of activity, and everybody is active in regard to the objects and employs the faculties that give him most pleasure. For instance, a musician uses his faculties in hearing music, and a student employs his intellect in study, and so on; and the pleasure adds completion to their activities, and therefore to life, which is the object of their desire. Consequently it is reasonable for them to pursue pleasure, because pleasure gives completeness to their life, and this is a desirable thing.

The question whether we desire life for the sake of pleasure or pleasure for the sake of life may for the present be set aside. Pleasure and life appear to be inseparably connected together, since pleasure is not experienced apart from activity, and every activity acquires additional completion from pleasure.

This moreover is a ground for believing that pleasures vary in specific quality. We feel that different kinds of things must have a different sort of perfection; we see this both with natural objects like animals and trees and with the products of art such as a picture or a statue or a building or an implement. Similarly we feel that the thing which perfects one kind of activity must itself be of a different sort from that which perfects another kind. But the activities of the intellect are different in kind from those of the senses, and also differ among themselves. So also therefore do the pleasures that complete them. . . .

> *Good pleasures are those connected with worthy activities. Since the good man sets the standard, real pleasures are what seem to him to be pleasures.*

Activities differ in moral value. Some are to be adopted, others to be avoided, and others are neutral. And the same is the case with the sort of pleasure they afford, as every activity has a special kind of pleasure connected with it. The pleasure of doing a worthy action is morally good and that of doing a base action is morally evil: in fact even to desire what is honourable is praiseworthy and to desire what is disgraceful is reprehensible; but the pleasures contained in our activities are more intimately connected with them than are the desires which prompt them: these are both separate in time and distinct in nature from the activities themselves, whereas the pleasures are closely united with them, and indeed they are so closely linked together as to make it difficult to distinguish the pleasure of doing a thing from the action itself. Nevertheless we must not regard pleasure as actually identical with the sensation or the thought which it accompanies — that would be absurd; although as they occur simultaneously, some people suppose that they are the same thing.

Thus pleasures differ from one another as do the activities that give rise to them. Sight excels touch, and hearing and smell excel taste, in purity; there is consequently a corresponding difference between the pleasures attaching to them. The pleasures of thought are superior to those of the senses; and there are also degrees of value in both groups. . . . The same things delight some people and annoy others, or are painful and disgusting to some and pleasant and agreeable to others. This applies even to taste; the same thing does not taste sweet to an invalid and to a man with a strong constitution. Also the same thing does not feel hot to a fever patient and to a person in good health. The same occurs with the other senses as well.

But we hold that in all such matters the thing really is what it appears to be to the good man. And if this rule is sound, as it is generally taken to be, and if the standard of everything is goodness or the good man as such, then the things that appear to him to be pleasures will be real pleasures and the things that he enjoys will be really pleasant. Nor need it surprise us if things which the good man dislikes seem pleasant to some people. Human nature is liable to many corruptions and perversions, and the things referred to are not really pleasant but only pleasant to people who are in a condition to fancy them to be pleasant. It is clear therefore that pleasures which are admittedly disgraceful cannot properly be called pleasant at all, but only pleasant to a corrupt taste.

But among those deemed respectable, which class of pleasures or which particular pleasure is to be considered the distinctively human pleasure? Perhaps this will appear if we consider the nature of human activity, since pleasure accompanies activity. Whether then there is one activity belonging to the perfect and supremely happy man, or whether there are several, it is the pleasures that perfect these activities which must be pronounced to be the characteristically human pleasures. All the others will be human only in a secondary or even lower degree, as are the activities which they accompany.

Aristotle recapitulates earlier conclusions about happiness, and asserts that happiness cannot be identified with amusement

We have now spoken about the different virtues and the various kinds of friendship and of pleasure. It remains to give some account of happiness, which we pronounce to be the aim and end of human life. Our account of it may be shortened by recapitulating what has been said previously.

We have stated that happiness is not a particular disposition of character, because if it were it might be possessed by a person who passed the whole of his time asleep, living the life of a vegetable, or by someone afflicted with the greatest misfortunes. We have to reject these implications as unsatisfactory, and must rather class happiness as an activity, as we said above. But there are two kinds of activity, one merely adopted as the necessary means for securing some other object, the other desirable in itself. And it is clear that happiness must be classed as a thing desirable in itself and not for the sake of something else, inasmuch as it is self-sufficient and complete.

Happiness . . . does not consist in amusement. Indeed it would be curious if amusement were our chief object, and if we toiled and suffered all our life long for the sake of play. Happiness is the one object which is not pursued as a means for obtaining something else, but is an end in itself. To strive and labour for the sake of securing more amusement seems foolish and childish in the extreme. The northern prince's [14] dictum, 'Play in order to be able to work better,' seems the right rule. Amusement is a kind of relaxation, and people need relaxation because they cannot go on working continuously without a break. Recreation therefore is not an end in itself; it is pursued as a means to greater activity. The happy life is thought to be a life of virtue, and this involves serious effort, and does not consist in mere play.

[14] Anacharsis, Scythian prince, sometimes reckoned one of the Seven Sages, visited Solon at Athens.

In our view serious things are on a higher level than amusements and sports, and the nobler a faculty or a person is, the more serious are their activities. Therefore the activity of the nobler faculty or the nobler person is on a higher level, and therefore more productive of happiness.

The pleasures of the body can be enjoyed by anyone — by a slave as much as by the best of us. But no one supposes that a slave can participate in real happiness, any more than he can have a life of his own.

These considerations show that happiness does not consist in pastimes and amusements, but in activities in conformity with virtue, as has been said above.

Aristotle argues that the intellect is the highest part of our nature and hence that the activity of contemplation is the most perfect form of happiness

But if happiness is activity in conformity with virtue, it is reasonable to suppose that it is in conformity with the highest virtue, which must be the virtue belonging to the highest part of our nature. This is our intellect, or whatever part of us is held to be our natural ruler and guide, and to apprehend things noble and divine, as being itself divine, or nearest to the divine of all the parts of our nature. It will consequently be the activity of this part, in conformity with the virtue that belongs to it, which will constitute perfect happiness; and it has already been stated that this activity is the activity of contemplation.

This view may be accepted as in agreement both with the conclusions reached before and with the truth. Contemplation is the highest form of activity, because the intellect is the highest part of our nature, and the things apprehended by it are the highest objects of knowledge. Also it is the most continuous form of activity; we can go on reflecting more continuously than we can pursue any form of practical activity. Moreover we feel that happiness is bound to contain an element of pleasure; but the activity of philosophic contemplation is admittedly the most pleasurable of all the activities in conformity with virtue. Philosophy is thought to comprise pleasures of marvellous purity and permanence; and it is reasonable to hold that the enjoyment of knowledge already acquired is a more pleasant occupation than research directed to the acquirement of new knowledge. Also the activity of contemplation will be found to possess in the highest degree the quality designated self-sufficiency. It is of course true that the wise man as well as the just man and those possessing all the other virtues requires the necessities of life; but given a sufficient supply of these, whereas the just man needs people towards whom and in partnership with whom he may act justly, and similarly the self-controlled man and the brave man and the others, the wise man can practise contemplation by himself, and the wiser he is the better he can do this. No doubt he can do this better if he has fellow-workers, but nevertheless he is the most self-sufficient of all men.

It would appear that philosophic speculation is the only occupation that is pursued for its own sake. It produces no result beyond the act of contemplation itself, whereas from our practical pursuits we look to gain more or less advantage apart from the activities themselves.

Also happiness is thought to involve leisure. We practice business in order to gain leisure, and we go to war in order to secure peace. Thus the practical virtues are exhibited in the activities of politics or of warfare, and the actions connected with these seem to be essentially unleisurely. Military activities are entirely a business matter: nobody goes to war for choice, just in order to have a war, or takes deliberate steps to cause one. A man would be thought to be an absolutely bloodthirsty person if he made war on a friendly state in order to bring about battles and bloodshed. The life of active citizenship also is devoid of leisure; besides the actual business of politics it aims at winning posts of authority and honour, or at all events at securing happiness for oneself and one's friends — objects which are clearly not the same thing as mere political activity in itself. We see therefore that the occupations connected with politics and with war, although standing highest in nobility and importance among activities in conformity with the virtues, are devoid of leisure, and are not adopted for their own sakes but as means to attaining some object outside themselves. But the exercise of the intellect in contemplation seems to be pre-eminent in point of leisure and to aim at no result external to itself; the pleasure it contains is inherent, and augments its activity. Consequently self-sufficiency and leisure, as well as such freedom from fatigue as lies within the capacity of human nature, and all the other advantages that we think of as belonging to complete bliss, appear to be contained in this activity. Therefore the activity of contemplation will be the perfect happiness of man, — provided that it continues throughout a complete lifetime, since in happiness there must be nothing incomplete.

But the life described will be above the level of humanity; a man will pursue it not in virtue of his human nature but by the power of a divine element that is in him. Also the activity described will excel those in which the other virtues are manifested as widely as that divine element stands out as the highest part of man's composite nature. If then the intellect is something divine as compared with man as a whole, it follows that the life of the intellect is divine in comparison with human life as a whole. Therefore we must not listen to those who advise us, because we are men, to think human thoughts and, because we are mortal, to think the thoughts of mortality. So far as is in our power we must achieve immortality, and use every effort to guide our lives by the best element in our natures. This element may be small in size, but in potency and value it far surpasses all the other parts of a man's personality. In fact as being the ruling part and the best part, it may be thought actually to *be* the man himself. It would be strange then if he chose to live the life of someone else and not his own life. Moreover what was said above will apply here as well. That which is best and pleasantest for any being is that which by nature specially belongs to it; and consequently the best and pleasantest life for man is the life of the intellect, inasmuch as the intellect pre-eminently *is* the man. This life therefore will be the happiest.

> *Practical activity which exhibits moral excellence is also happy; but perfect happiness is nevertheless the purely cognitive activity of the mind*

On the other hand the life of moral virtue is happy in a secondary degree; for the moral activities are purely human. Justice and courage and the other virtues we exercise in our relations with our fellows, when we are careful to give every man his due in contracts and services, and in our own various actions and also in our emotions; and all these seem to be purely human affairs. Some moral actions appear to arise out of our bodily constitution, and virtue seems to have an affinity at many points with the emotions. Also prudence is closely connected with moral virtue, and moral virtue with prudence, inasmuch as the first principles of prudence conform with the moral virtues, and the right standard in morals is given by prudence. Moreover, as being connected with our emotions the moral virtues seem to belong to our composite nature; but the virtues of our composite nature are human; so therefore are the life and the happiness which conform with those virtues. The excellence of the intellect is entirely separate — so much may be said about it here, to give a full and precise account of it would be a bigger task than our present undertaking requires. And intellectual excellence would also appear to require little external equipment, or less than is needed by moral virtue. It may be granted that both require equally the necessaries of life (although the statesman's work is more concerned with bodily needs and the like); for there is little difference between them in this. But there will be a great deal of difference in what they require for their special activities. The liberal man will need wealth in order to practice liberality, and even the just man will require some wealth in order to return the services rendered to him, since mere intentions are not visible to others, and even unjust men pretend to wish to act justly. The brave man will need power if he is to accomplish any deeds in conformity with his virtue, and the self-controlled man opportunity to exhibit self-control, as without opportunity how is he or any other of the virtuous characters to display their virtue? Also it is debated whether purpose or performance is a more important factor in virtue, which is taken to involve both. In order to be perfect, virtue clearly requires both; but doing things needs much equipment, and the greater and more honourable the deeds done the more equipment they require. The student on the other hand for the purpose of his activity needs nothing of this kind. In fact such things are almost an impediment to contemplation, although as a man living in the company of other men the student will choose to do virtuous deeds, and therefore will require accessories of this sort for the sake of his life as a human being.

The following consideration will also show that perfect happiness is found in contemplation. The gods as we conceive them are supremely blessed and happy. But what kind of actions must we attribute to them? Just actions? or would it not be absurd to imagine them as making contracts and repaying deposits and so on? Then shall we say brave actions — enduring alarms and facing dangers in a noble cause? Or liberal actions? but who will receive their gifts? Moreover it is curious to think of the gods as having money or tokens of value. And what would be the meaning in their case of conduct exhibiting self-control? would it not be a poor compliment to the gods to say that they have no base appetites? If we went through the whole list, all the various forms of virtuous conduct would appear to be too trivial to be worthy of divine beings. Nevertheless everybody conceives of the gods as at all events alive, and therefore active, — they are certainly not imagined as always asleep, like Endymion. But take away action, and particularly productive action, and what remains for a living being except contemplation? It follows that the divine activity, since it is supremely blissful, will be the activity of contemplation. Therefore among human activities the one most nearly akin to divine contemplation is the activity that contains the largest amount of happiness.

And it appears that one who lives the life of the mind, and cultivates his intellect and keeps that in its best condition, is the man whom the gods love best. It is the common belief that the gods pay heed to the affairs of men. If this is true, it is reasonable to assume that the gods take pleasure in what is best and most akin to themselves, namely man's intellect, and that they requite with benefits those who pay the highest respect to the life of the mind, because these men care for the things that are dear to themselves and these men act rightly and nobly. But manifestly all these attributes belong in the highest degree to the wise man. He therefore is the man dearest to the gods, and consequently it is he who will presumably be supremely happy. This is another indication that the philosopher is the happiest of mankind.

This is also shown by the fact that the lower animals have no share in real happiness, because activity of the kind described is entirely denied to them. The whole life of the gods is blissful; and the life of mankind is blessed in so far as it bears a resemblance to the divine activity described above; but none of the other animals possesses happiness, because they have no faculty of contemplation. Thus happiness is co-extensive with the power of contemplation, and those beings who are more fully endowed with that power enjoy more happiness, not as an accidental concomitant of contemplation but as inherent in it, because contemplation has essential value. It follows that happiness must be some form of contemplation.

QUESTIONS

1. When Aristotle says that the good is what men want or aim at, is he talking about all men or only some, perhaps the good or intelligent ones? Can he be accused of not conducting an objective inquiry if he thinks that only the opinions of those he calls "good" are relevant? In any event, does it *follow* from the fact that people desire something, that it is good?

2. Aristotle seems to assume that anything that is intrinsically good, or the ultimate good, must not be a means to anything else, must be self-sufficient, and permanent. Are not these assumptions wholly arbitrary?

3. We say a knife "functions well" if it does the thing it was made to do, or fulfills the purpose for which we have it. We say the heart "functions well" if it does what is necessary to keep the organism in health. Is it reasonable to say that man has a "function" in these senses? in some other sense?

4. Is there any reason why the most desirable activity of man should be distinctively human, some activity man does not share with the animals? Are there distinctively human activities (blushing?) which Aristotle ignores?

5. What does Aristotle mean by "happiness"? How is it related to pleasure or enjoyments?

6. Assuming that Aristotle was defending the values of Greek intellectuals, are there disparities between Greek values and your own? Would you ordinarily think of the traits he praises as parts of a "good character"?

7. Is there any reason to think that a person who applied reason in living would have traits of character fitting Aristotle's description of the "mean"?

8. Could a person who did not know what it was right to do in a given situation find out by utilizing the description of the "mean"? Does Aristotle think he could?

9. Is Aristotle correct in thinking that a morally good act must be not merely right but have some other characteristics? Which other ones?

10. Was Aristotle analyzing rightly our concept of "virtue" when he said it is not an emotion, or a disposition to have emotions, but a "quality of the will"?

11. Would Aristotle say that the chief value of science is its production of technological advances which relieve human misery and raise the standard of living? Must one say that Aristotle advocates that the thinker retreat to his ivory tower, denying any responsibility to improve the lives of others?

12. How frequently does Aristotle's argument depend on appeal to the "distinctive functions" of man, or to human nature? Does he often rest his case on what "intelligent people would choose" or "think"? When he does, is his argument a cogent one?

13. One might go to the opposite extreme and say that knowledge of human nature is totally irrelevant to ethics — for instance, that what we know about the effects of prison terms on criminals is irrelevant to how society should handle problems of crime. If this position seems to go too far, can you state what you think is proved, that is relevant to what should be done or is good, by information about human nature?

14. Why does Aristotle think statesmen should study ethics?

SUGGESTIONS FOR FURTHER READING

Aristotle. *Works*. Vol. 9, *Magna Moralia; Ethica Eudemia; De Virtutibus et Vitiis*. Ed. by W. D. Ross. New York: Oxford Univ. Press, 1925.

Jaeger, W. W. *Aristotle*. New York: Oxford Univ. Press, 1934.

Joachim, H. H. *Aristotle: The Nicomachean Ethics*. New York: Oxford Univ. Press, 1951.

Randall, J. H. *Aristotle*. New York: Columbia Univ. Press, 1960.

Ross, Sir William David. *Aristotle*. New York: Barnes & Noble, 1955. (Meridian Books.)

Steward, J. A. *Notes on the Nicomachean Ethics*. London: Oxford Univ. Press, 1892.

Stocks, J. L. *Aristotle's Definition of the Human Good*. Oxford: Blackwell, 1919.

The Stoics, the First Being Zeno (c. 300 B.C.)

RATIONAL CONFORMITY TO NATURE IS THE GOOD

"Stoic philosophy" is the name of a tradition of ideas begun by Zeno of Citium (*c*. 340-265 B.C.), who was a student of the Cynic Crates and thus indirectly influenced by Socrates. The philosophy became very popular in both Greece and Rome, where it was introduced in 155 B.C. The Roman philosophers Seneca, Epictetus, and Marcus Aurelius (the emperor) were Stoics. Different members of the school held somewhat different views; the following selection, drawn from Book VII of Diogenes Laertius' (*c*. A.D. 230) *Lives of Eminent Philosophers*, is primarily a description of the opinions of the earlier figures.

The practical recommendations of the Stoics, such as those for self-sufficiency and simple living, are not very different from those of Epicurus. The Stoics reject the hedonist ideal, however; they deny that the good is pleasure. Indeed, they urge that pleasure is not even a primary object of human desire. Their theory of the good is much closer to Aristotle. Well-being or the good, they say, is life *in accordance with reason or nature*; it is the "natural perfection of a rational being *qua* rational." This is rather indefinite language; but what it seems to mean is that the good is satisfaction of desire in so far as satisfaction is permitted, and in the manner permitted, by reason. But what does reason require? Diogenes tells us they say it requires taking care of one's parents, paying attention to the interest of one's country; we may speculate that they meant it requires doing everything which it would be disastrous for people in general to fail to do. A life lived in accordance with reason will be a virtuous life: a life with wisdom, temperance, courage, and justice. These and other virtues they say (according to Diogenes) are intrinsically good — although perhaps it would be more plausible to say rather that the life which exercises them is so. Contrariwise, the Stoics say that vicious actions, and gloom, despair, and excess of grief (almost all, we may note, qualities of mind which would not occur in one who sees that the real good is primarily virtuous living), are intrinsically evil. Other things they concede are good in a secondary sense — only in a secondary sense, since they can be harmful if improperly used and since we can enjoy life without them — : life, health, strength, wealth, noble birth, and pleasure. Some other things they also concede to be evil in a similar secondary sense: lack of ability, death, disease, poverty, ignominy, low birth. The rational life, the life with virtue, then — the kind of life open to anyone with character or a good will — is the good life. External fortunes, things beyond the power of the human will, are of only secondary importance; the wise man will not set great store by them nor feel he has missed the good life if they are not available to him: one can have well-being without them.

Reprinted by permission of the publishers and The Loeb Classical Library from Diogenes Laertius, *Lives of Eminent Philosophers*, translated by R. D. Hicks, Cambridge, Mass., Harvard University Press.

LIVES OF EMINENT PHILOSOPHERS

An animal's first impulse, say the Stoics, is to self-preservation, because nature from the outset endears it to itself, as Chrysippus affirms in the first book of his work *On Ends*: his words are, "The dearest thing to every animal is its own constitution and its consciousness thereof"; for it was not likely that nature should estrange the living thing from itself or that she should leave the creature she has made without either estrangement from or affection for its own constitution. We are forced then to conclude that nature in constituting the animal made it near and dear to itself; for so it comes to repel all that is injurious and give free access to all that is serviceable or akin to it.

As for the assertion made by some people that pleasure is the object to which the first impulse of animals is directed, it is shown by the Stoics to be false. For pleasure, if it is really felt, they declare to be a by-product, which never comes until nature by itself has sought and found the means suitable to the animal's existence or constitution; it is an aftermath comparable to the condition of animals thriving and plants in full bloom. And nature, they say, made no difference originally between plants and animals, for she regulates the life of plants too, in their case without impulse and sensation, just as also certain processes go on of a vegetative kind in us. But when in the case of animals impulse has been superadded, whereby they are enabled to go in quest of their proper aliment, for them, say the Stoics, Nature's rule is to follow the direction of impulse. But when reason by way of a more perfect leadership has been bestowed on the beings we call rational, for them life according to reason rightly becomes the natural life. For reason supervenes to shape impulse scientifically.

This is why Zeno was the first (in his treatise *On the Nature of Man*) to designate as the end "life in agreement with nature" (or living agreeably to nature), which is the same as a virtuous life, virtue being the goal towards which nature guides us. So too Cleanthes in his treatise *On Pleasure*, as also Posidonius, and Hecato in his work *On Ends*. Again, living virtuously is equivalent to living in accordance with experience of the actual course of nature, as Chrysippus says in the first book of his *De finibus*; for our individual natures are parts of the nature of the whole universe. And this is why the end may be defined as life in accordance with nature, or, in other words, in accordance with our own human nature as well as that of the universe, a life in which we refrain from every action forbidden by the law common to all things, that is to say, the right reason which pervades all things, and is identical with this Zeus, lord and ruler of all that is. And this very thing constitutes the virtue of the happy man and the smooth current of life, when all actions promote the harmony of the spirit dwelling in the individual man with the will of him who orders the universe. Diogenes then expressly declares the end to be to act with good reason in the selection of what is natural. Archedemus says the end is to live in the performance of all befitting actions.

By the nature with which our life ought to be in accord, Chrysippus understands both universal nature and more particularly the nature of man, whereas Cleanthes takes the nature of the universe alone as that which should be followed, without adding the nature of the individual.

And virtue, he holds, is a harmonious disposition, choice-worthy for its own sake and not from hope or fear or any external motive. Moreover, it is in virtue that happiness consists; for virtue is the state of mind which tends to make the whole of life harmonious. When a rational being is perverted, this is due to the deceptiveness of external pursuits or sometimes to the influence of associates. For the starting-points of nature are never perverse.

Virtue, in the first place, is in one sense the perfection of anything in general, say of a statue; again, it may be non-intellectual, like health, or intellectual, like prudence. For Hecato says in his first book *On the Virtues* that some are scientific and based upon theory, namely, those which have a structure of theoretical principles, such as prudence and justice; others are non-intellectual, those that are regarded as co-extensive and parallel with the former, like health and strength. For health is found to attend upon and be co-extensive with the intellectual virtue of temperance, just as strength is a result of building of an arch. These are called non-intellectual, because they do not require the mind's assent; they supervene and they occur even in bad men: for instance, health, courage. . . .

Amongst the virtues some are primary, some are subordinate to these. The following are the primary: wisdom, courage, justice, temperance. Particular virtues are magnanimity, continence, endurance, presence of mind, good counsel. And wisdom they define as the knowledge of things good and evil and of what is neither good nor evil; courage as knowledge of what we ought to choose, what we ought to beware of, and what is indifferent; justice . . . ; magnanimity as the knowledge or habit of mind which makes one superior to anything which happens, whether good or evil equally; continence as a disposition never overcome in that which concerns right reason, or a habit which no pleasures can get the better of; endurance as a knowledge or habit which suggests what we are to hold fast to, what not, and what is indifferent; presence of mind as a habit prompt to find out what is meet to be done at any moment; good counsel as knowledge by which we see what to do and how to do it if we would consult our own interests.

Similarly, of vices some are primary, others subordinate: *e.g.*, folly, cowardice, injustice, profligacy are accounted primary; but incontinence, stupidity, ill-advisedness subordinate. Further, they hold that the vices are forms of ignorance of those things whereof the corresponding virtues are the knowledge.

Good in general is that from which some advantage comes, and more particularly what is either identical with or not distinct from benefit. Whence it follows that virtue itself and whatever partakes of virtue is called good in these three senses — viz., as being (1) the source from which benefit results; or (2) that in respect of which benefit results, *e.g.*, the virtuous act; or (3) that by the agency of which benefit results, *e.g.*, the good man who partakes in virtue.

Another particular definition of good which they give is "the natural perfection of a rational being *qua* rational." To this answers virtue and, as being partakers in virtue, virtuous acts and good men; as also its supervening accessories, joy and gladness and the like. So with evils: either they are vices, folly, cowardice, injustice, and the like; or things which partake of vice, including vicious acts and wicked persons as well as their accompaniments, despair, moroseness, and the like. . . .

Again, goods are either of the nature of ends or they are the means to these ends, or they are at the same time end and means. A friend and the advantages derived from him are means to good, whereas confidence, high-spirit, liberty, delight, gladness, freedom from pain, and every virtuous act are of the nature of ends.

The virtues (they say) are goods of the nature at once of ends and of means. On the one hand, in so far as they cause happiness they are means, and on the other hand, in so far as they make it complete, and so are themselves part of it, they are ends. Similarly of evils some are of the nature of ends and some of means, while others are at once both means and ends. Your enemy and the harm he does you are means; consternation, abasement, slavery, gloom, despair, excess of grief, and every vicious action are of the nature of ends. Vices are evils both as ends and as means, since in so far as they cause misery they are means, but in so far as they make it complete, so that they become part of it, they are ends. . . .

The reason why they characterize the perfect good as beautiful is that it has in full all the "factors" required by nature or has perfect proportion. Of the beautiful there are (say they) four species, namely, what is just, courageous, orderly and wise; for it is under these forms that fair deeds are accomplished. . . . By the beautiful is meant properly and in an unique sense that good which renders its possessors praiseworthy, or briefly, good which is worthy of praise; though in another sense it signifies a good aptitude for one's proper function; while in yet another sense the beautiful is that which lends new grace to anything, as when we say of the wise man that he alone is good and beautiful.

And they say that only the morally beautiful is good. . . . They hold, that is, that virtue and whatever partakes of virtue consists in this: which is equivalent to saying that all that is good is beautiful, or that the term "good" has equal force with the term "beautiful," which comes to the same thing. "Since a thing is good, it is beautiful; now it is beautiful, therefore it is good." They hold that all goods are equal and that all good is desirable in the highest degree and admits of no lowering or heightening of intensity. Of things that are, some, they say, are good, some are evil, and some neither good nor evil (that is, morally indifferent). . . . Neutral (neither good nor evil, that is) are all those things which neither benefit nor harm a man: such as life, health, pleasure, beauty, strength, wealth, fair fame and noble birth, and their opposites, death, disease, pain, ugliness, weakness, poverty, ignominy, low birth, and the like. . . . For as the property of hot is to warm, not to cool, so the property of good is to benefit, not to injure; but wealth and health do no more benefit than injury, therefore neither wealth nor health is good. Further, they say that that is not good of which both good and bad use can be made; but of wealth and health both good and bad use can be made; therefore wealth and health are not goods. On the other hand, Posidonius maintains that these things too are among goods. Hecato in the ninth book of his treatise *On Goods*, and Chrysippus in his work *On Pleasure*, deny that pleasure is a good thing either; for some pleasures are disgraceful, and nothing disgraceful is good.

To benefit is to set in motion or sustain in accordance with virtue; whereas to harm is to set in motion or sustain in accordance with vice.

The term "indifferent" has two meanings: in the first it denotes the things which do not contribute either to happiness or to misery, as wealth, fame, health, strength, and the like; for it is possible to be happy without having these, although, if they are used in a certain way, such use of them tends to happiness or misery. In quite another sense those things are said to be indifferent which are without the power of stirring inclination or aversion; *e.g.*, the fact that the number of hairs on one's head is odd or even or whether you hold out your finger straight or bent. But it was not in this sense that the things mentioned above were termed indifferent, they being quite capable of exciting inclination or aversion. Hence of these latter some are taken by preference, others are rejected, whereas indifference in the other sense affords no ground for either choosing or avoiding.

Of things indifferent, as they express it, some are "preferred," others "rejected." Such as have value, they say, are "preferred," while such as have negative, instead of positive, value are "rejected." Value they define as, first, any contribution to harmonious living, such as attaches to every good; secondly, some faculty or use which indirectly contributes to the life according to nature: which is as much as to say "any assistance brought by wealth or health towards living a natural life"; thirdly, value is the full equivalent of an appraiser, as fixed by an expert acquainted with the facts — as when it is said that wheat exchanges for so much barley with a mule thrown in.

Thus things of the preferred class are those which have positive value, *e.g.*, amongst mental qualities, natural ability, skill, moral improvement, and the like; among bodily qualities, life, health, strength, good condition, soundness of organs, beauty, and so forth; and in the sphere of external things, wealth, fame, noble birth, and the like. To the class of things "rejected" belong, of mental qualities, lack of ability, want of skill, and the like; among bodily qualities, death, disease, weakness, being out of condition, mutilation, ugliness, and the like; in the sphere of external things, poverty, ignominy, low birth, and so forth. But again there are things belonging to neither class; such are not preferred, neither are they rejected.

Again, of things preferred some are preferred for their own sake, some for the sake of something else, and others again both for their own sake and for the sake of something else. To the first of these classes belong natural ability, moral improvement, and the like; to the second wealth, noble birth, and the like; to the last strength, perfect faculties, soundness of bodily organs. Things are preferred for their own sake because they accord with nature; not for their own sake, but for the sake of something else, because they secure not a few utilities. And similarly with the class of things rejected under the contrary heads.

Furthermore, the term Duty is applied to that for which, when done, a reasonable defence can be adduced, *e.g.*, harmony in the tenor of life's process, which indeed pervades the growth of plants and animals. For even in plants and animals, they hold, you may discern fitness of behaviour.

Zeno was the first to use this term καθῆκον of conduct. Etymologically it is derived from κατά τινας ἥκειν, *i.e.*, reaching as far as, being up to, or incumbent on so and so. And it is an action in itself adapted to nature's arrangements. For of the acts done at the prompting of impulse some, they observe, are fit and meet, others the reverse, while there is a third class which is neither the one nor the other.

Befitting acts are all those which reason prevails with us to do; and this is the case with honouring one's parents, brothers and country, and intercourse with friends. Unbefitting, or contrary to duty, are all acts that reason deprecates, *e.g.*, to neglect one's parents, to be indifferent to one's brothers, not to agree with friends, to disregard the interests of one's country, and so forth. Acts which fall under neither of the foregoing classes are those which reason neither urges us to do nor forbids, such as picking up a twig, holding a style or a scraper, and the like.

Again, some duties are incumbent unconditionally, others in certain circumstances. Unconditional duties are the following: to take proper care of health and one's organs of sense, and things of that sort. Duties imposed by circumstances are such as maiming oneself and sacrifice of property. And so likewise with acts which are violations of duty. Another division is into duties which are always incumbent and those which are not. To live in accordance with virtue is always a duty, whereas dialectic by question and answer or walking-exercise and the like are not at all times incumbent. The same may be said of the violations of duty. And in things intermediate also there are duties; as that boys should obey the attendants who have charge of them.

QUESTIONS

1. What reasons do the Stoics give for doubting whether pleasure is intrinsically desirable? Is any of them cogent?
2. What do you think they meant by conduct "in accordance with nature" in accordance with "right reason"?
3. What are some of the things they think intrinsically worthwhile? intrinsically bad? Do they think that moral virtues are *means* to the worthwhile, or constituents of what is worthwhile in itself, or worthwhile in themselves? Do they offer any reason for their view?
4. Do they think that some virtues are more desirable than others?
5. If pain is not itself a bad thing, how can cruelty be a vice?
6. In what sense do they hold that things like wealth and health are not good or evil? Are these totally irrelevant to "happiness" or "well-being"? Is this consistent with thinking that only qualities of mind or character are worthwhile in themselves?
7. Do you think they believe that virtues are good in themselves, or rather that only a life lived with virtue is good in itself?

8. What is the connection between their conception of moral virtue and their conception of duty?
9. When they say that wisdom is "the knowledge of things good and evil," what kind of knowledge do you think they have in mind?
10. Is not everything that happens "natural"? If so, how can it be helpful to suggest that human conduct ought to "conform to nature"?

SUGGESTIONS FOR FURTHER READING

Oates, Whitney J., ed. *The Stoic and Epicurean Philosophers*. New York: Random House, 1940.

Arnold, E. V. *Roman Stoicism*. New York: Macmillan (n. d.).
Bevan, E. R. *Stoics and Sceptics*. New York: Oxford Univ. Press, 1913.
Hicks, R. D. *Stoic and Epicurean*. New York: Scribner, 1910.
Murray, Gilbert. *Stoic, Christian, and Humanist*. London: Allen & Unwin, 1940.
Reesor, M. E. *The Political Theory of the Old and Middle Stoa*. Locust Valley, N. Y.: J. J. Augustin, 1951.
Wenley, R. M. *Stoicism and its Influence*. Boston: Marshall Jones, 1924.
Zeller, Eduard. *The Stoics, Epicureans, and Sceptics*. New York: Longmans, Green and Co., 1892.

Saint Augustine   (354-430)

GOD IS MAN'S HIGHEST GOOD

St. Augustine, a theologian with prodigious energy, whose contributions to Christian theology are equalled by those of few if any other persons, was born in Carthage. His mother was a Christian, but as a young man he was attracted first to the Manichaean religion and later to Neoplatonic mysticism. He studied in Rome and then, after going to Milan as a teacher of rhetoric, was converted to Christianity by the Bishop of Milan and was baptized in 387. Thereupon he returned to Africa where he spent the rest of his life. He was made Bishop of Hippo in 395. Among his best known works are his *Confessions, The City of God, Concerning the Trinity*, and *On the Freedom of the Will*; but he wrote a number of other influential works.

St. Augustine touches on ethical problems at many points in his writings, although he never wrote a full-scale treatise on the subject. The following essay, *The Morals of the Christian Church*, written in 388 as a tract against the Manichaeans, is the most complete single statement of his view. *The City of*

God, at the end, contains a fuller description of the beatific vision of God attainable in the after life. It is worthwhile to compare Augustine's view with that of Aristotle: Augustine's is a God-centered, otherworldly ethical theory; Aristotle's is naturalistic and this-worldly.

Saint Augustine. "The Morals of the Catholic Church." Trans. by R. Stothert. In Schaff, Philip, ed. *A Select Library of the Nicene and Post-Nicene Fathers of the Christian Church*. Buffalo, N. Y.: Christian Literature, 1887. Vol. 4.

From *Basic Writings of Saint Augustine*, ed. by Whitney J. Oates. Copyright 1948 by Random House, Inc. Reprinted by permission.

THE MORALS OF THE CATHOLIC CHURCH

CHAPTER III   HAPPINESS IS IN THE ENJOYMENT OF MAN'S CHIEF GOOD. TWO CONDITIONS OF THE CHIEF GOOD: 1ST, NOTHING IS BETTER THAN IT; 2ND, IT CANNOT BE LOST AGAINST THE WILL

How then, according to reason, ought man to live? We all certainly desire to live happily; and there is no human being but assents to this statement almost before it is made. But the title happy cannot, in my opinion, belong either to him who has not what he loves, whatever it may be, or to him who has what he loves if it is hurtful, or to him who does not love what he has, although it is good in perfection. For one who seeks what he cannot obtain suffers torture, and one who has got what is not desirable is cheated, and one who does not seek for what is worth seeking for is diseased. Now in all these cases the mind cannot but be unhappy, and happiness and unhappiness cannot reside at the same time in one man; so in none of these cases can the man be happy. I find, then, a fourth case, where the happy life exists — when that which is man's chief good is both loved and possessed. For what do we call enjoyment but having at hand the object of love? And no one can be happy who does not enjoy what is man's chief good, nor is there any one who enjoys this who is not happy. We must then have at hand our chief good, if we think of living happily.

We must now inquire what is man's chief good, which of course cannot be anything inferior to man himself. For whoever follows after what is inferior to himself, becomes himself inferior. But every man is bound to follow what is best. Wherefore man's chief good is not inferior to man. Is it then something similar to man himself? It must be so, if there is nothing above man which he is capable of enjoying. But if we find something which is both superior to man, and can be possessed by the man who loves it, who can doubt that in seeking for happiness man should endeavor to reach that which is more excellent than the being who makes the endeavor.

For if happiness consists in the enjoyment of a good than which there is nothing better, which we call the chief good, how can a man be properly called happy who has not yet attained to his chief good? or how can that be the chief good beyond which something better remains for us to arrive at? Such, then, being the chief good, it must be something which cannot be lost against the will. For no one can feel confident regarding a good which he knows can be taken from him, although he wishes to keep and cherish it. But if a man feels no confidence regarding the good which he enjoys, how can he be happy while in such fear of losing it?

CHAPTER V   MAN'S CHIEF GOOD IS NOT THE
CHIEF GOOD OF THE BODY ONLY, BUT
THE CHIEF GOOD OF THE SOUL

Now if we ask what is the chief good of the body, reason obliges us to admit that it is that by means of which the body comes to be in its best state. But of all the things which invigorate the body, there is nothing better or greater than the soul. The chief good of the body, then, is not bodily pleasure, not absence of pain, not strength, not beauty, not swiftness, or whatever else is usually reckoned among the goods of the body, but simply the soul. For all the things mentioned the soul supplies to the body by its presence, and, what is above them all, life. Hence I conclude that the soul is not the chief good of man, whether we give the name of man to soul and body together, or to the soul alone. For as, according to reason, the chief good of the body is that which is better than the body, and from which the body receives vigor and life, so whether the soul itself is man, or soul and body both, we must discover whether there is anything which goes before the soul itself, in following which the soul comes to the perfection of good of which it is capable in its own kind. If such a thing can be found, all uncertainty must be at an end, and we must pronounce this to be really and truly the chief good of man.

If, again, the body is man, it must be admitted that the soul is the chief good of man. But clearly, when we treat of morals — when we inquire what manner of life must be held in order to obtain happiness — it is not the body to which the precepts are addressed, it is not bodily discipline which we discuss. In short, the observance of good *customs* belongs to that part of us which inquires and learns, which are the prerogatives of the soul; so, when we speak of attaining to virtue, the question does not regard the body. But if it follows, as it does, that the body which is ruled over by a soul possessed of virtue is ruled both better and more honorably, and is in its greatest perfection in consequence of the perfection of the soul which rightfully governs it, that which gives perfection to the soul will be man's chief good, though we call the body man. For if my coachman, in obedience to me, feeds and drives the horses he has charge of in the most satisfactory manner, himself enjoying the more of my bounty in proportion to his good conduct, can any one deny that the good condition of the horses, as well as that of the coachman, is due to me? So the question seems to me to be not, whether soul and body is man, or the soul only, or the body only, but what gives perfection to the soul; for when this is obtained, a man cannot but be either perfect, or at least much better than in the absence of this one thing.

CHAPTER VI   VIRTUE GIVES PERFECTION TO THE SOUL; THE SOUL OBTAINS VIRTUE BY FOLLOWING GOD; FOLLOWING GOD IS THE HAPPY LIFE

No one will question that virtue gives perfection to the soul. But it is a very proper subject of inquiry whether this virtue can exist by itself or only in the soul. Here again arises a profound discussion, needing lengthy treatment; but perhaps my summary will serve the purpose. God will, I trust, assist me, so that, notwithstanding our feebleness, we may give instruction on these great matters briefly as well as intelligibly. In either case, whether virtue can exist by itself without the soul, or can exist only in the soul, undoubtedly in the pursuit of virtue the soul follows after something, and this must be either the soul itself, or virtue, or something else. But if the soul follows after itself in the pursuit of virtue, it follows after a foolish thing; for before obtaining virtue it is foolish. Now the height of a follower's desire is to reach that which he follows after. So the soul must either not wish to reach what it follows after, which is utterly absurd and unreasonable, or, in following after itself while foolish, it reaches the folly which it flees from. But if it follows after virtue in the desire to reach it, how can it follow what does not exist? or how can it desire to reach what it already possesses? Either, therefore, virtue exists beyond the soul, or if we are not allowed to give the name of virtue except to the habit and disposition of the wise soul, which can exist only in the soul, we must allow that the soul follows after something else in order that virtue may be produced in itself; for neither by following after nothing, nor by following after folly, can the soul, according to my reasoning, attain to wisdom.

This something else then, by following after which the soul becomes possessed of virtue and wisdom, is either a wise man or God. But we have said already that it must be something that we cannot lose against our will. No one can think it necessary to ask whether a wise man, supposing we are content to follow after him, can be taken from us in spite of our unwillingness or our persistence. God then remains, in following after whom we live well, and in reaching whom we live both well and happily. If any deny God's existence, why should I consider the method of dealing with them, when it is doubtful whether they ought to be dealt with at all? At any rate, it would require a different starting-point, a different plan, a different investigation from what we are now engaged in. I am now addressing those who do not deny the existence of God, and who, moreover, allow that human affairs are not disregarded by Him. For there is no one, I suppose, who makes any profession of religion but will hold that divine Providence cares at least for our souls.

CHAPTER VII   THE KNOWLEDGE OF GOD TO BE OBTAINED
FROM THE SCRIPTURE. THE PLAN AND
PRINCIPAL MYSTERIES OF THE DIVINE SCHEME
OF REDEMPTION

But how can we follow after Him whom we do not see? or how can we see Him, we who are not only men, but also men of weak understanding? For though God is seen not with the eyes but with the mind, where can such a mind be found as shall, while obscured by foolishness, succeed or even attempt to drink in that light? We must therefore have recourse to the instructions of those whom we have reason to think wise. Thus far argument brings us. For in human things reasoning is employed, not as of greater certainty, but as easier from use. But when we come to divine things, this faculty turns away; it cannot behold; it pants, and gasps, and burns with desire; it falls back from the light of truth, and turns again to its wonted obscurity, not from choice, but from exhaustion. What a dreadful catastrophe is this, that the soul should be reduced to greater helplessness when it is seeking rest from its toil! So, when we are hasting to retire into darkness, it will be well that by the appointment of adorable Wisdom we should be met by the friendly shade of authority, and should be attracted by the wonderful character of its contents, and by the utterances of its pages, which, like shadows, typify and attemper the truth.

What more could have been done for our salvation? What can be more gracious and bountiful than divine providence, which, when man had fallen from its laws, and, in just retribution for his coveting mortal things, had brought forth a mortal offspring, still did not wholly abandon him? For in this most righteous government, whose ways are strange and inscrutable, there is, by means of unknown connections established in the creatures subject to it, both a severity of punishment and a mercifulness of salvation. How beautiful this is, how great, how worthy of God, in fine, how true, which is all we are seeking for, we shall never be able to perceive, unless, beginning with things human and at hand, and holding by the faith and the precepts of true religion, we continue without turning from it in the way which God has secured for us by the separation of the patriarchs, by the bond of the law, by the foresight of the prophets, by the witness of the apostles, by the blood of the martyrs, and by the subjugation of the Gentiles. From this point, then, let no one ask me for my opinion, but let us rather hear the oracles, and submit our weak inferences to the announcements of Heaven.

CHAPTER VIII   GOD IS THE CHIEF GOOD,
WHOM WE ARE TO SEEK AFTER
WITH SUPREME AFFECTION

Let us see how the Lord Himself in the gospel has taught us to live; how, too, Paul the apostle — for the Manichaeans dare not reject these Scriptures. Let us hear, O Christ, what chief end Thou dost prescribe to us; and that is evidently the chief end after which we are told to strive with supreme affection. "Thou shalt love," He says, "the Lord thy God." Tell me also, I pray Thee, what must be the measure of love; for I fear lest the desire enkindled in my heart should either exceed or come short in fervor. "With all thy heart," He says. Nor is that enough. "With all thy soul." Nor is it enough yet. "With all thy mind." [1] What do you wish more? I might, perhaps, wish more if I could see the possibility of more. What does Paul say on this? "We know," he says, "that all things issue in good to them that love God." Let him, too, say what is the measure of love. "Who then," he says, "shall separate us from the love of Christ? shall tribulation, or distress, or persecution, or famine, or nakedness, or peril, or the sword?" [2] We have heard, then, what and how much we must love; this we must strive after, and to this we must refer all our plans. The perfection of all our good things and our perfect good is God. We must neither come short of this nor go beyond it: the one is dangerous, the other impossible.

CHAPTER XI   GOD IS THE ONE OBJECT OF LOVE;
THEREFORE HE IS MAN'S CHIEF GOOD.
NOTHING IS BETTER THAN GOD.
GOD CANNOT BE LOST AGAINST OUR WILL

Following after God is the desire of happiness; to reach God is happiness itself. We follow after God by loving Him; we reach Him, not by becoming entirely what He is, but in nearness to Him, and in wonderful and immaterial contact with Him, and in being inwardly illuminated and occupied by His truth and holiness. He is light itself; we get enlightenment from Him. The greatest commandment, therefore, which leads to happy life, and the first, is this: "Thou shalt love the Lord thy God with all thy heart, and soul, and mind." For to those who love the Lord all things issue in good. Hence Paul adds shortly after, "I am persuaded that neither death, nor life, nor angels, nor virtue, nor things present, nor things future, nor height, nor depth, nor any other creature, shall be able to separate us from the love of God, which is in Christ Jesus our Lord." [3] If, then, to those who love God all things issue in good, and if, as no one doubts,

[1] Matt. 22:37.   [2] Rom. 8:28, 35.
[3] Rom. 8:38, 39.

the chief or perfect good is not only to be loved, but to be loved so that nothing shall be loved better, as is expressed in the words, "With all thy soul, with all thy heart, and with all thy mind," who, I ask, will not at once conclude, when these things are all settled and most surely believed, that our chief good which we must hasten to arrive at in preference to all other things is nothing else than God? And then, if nothing can separate us from His love, must not this be surer as well as better than any other good? . . .

CHAPTER XII   WE ARE UNITED TO GOD BY LOVE, IN SUBJECTION TO HIM

"No other creature," he says, separates us. O man of profound mysteries! He thought it not enough to say, no creature: but he says no other creature; teaching that that with which we love God and by which we cleave to God, our mind, namely, and understanding, is itself a creature. Thus the body is another creature; and if the mind is an object of intellectual perception, and is known only by this means, the other creature is all that is an object of sense, which as it were makes itself known through the eyes, or ears, or smell, or taste, or touch, and this must be inferior to what is perceived by the intellect alone. Now, as God also can be known by the worthy, only intellectually, exalted though He is above the intelligent mind as being its Creator and Author, there was danger lest the human mind, from being reckoned among invisible and immaterial things, should be thought to be of *the same* nature with Him who created it, and so should fall away by pride from Him to whom it should be united by love. For the mind becomes like God, to the extent vouchsafed by its subjection of itself to Him for information and enlightenment. And if it obtains the greatest nearness by that subjection which produces likeness, it must be far removed from Him by that presumption which would make the likeness greater. It is this presumption which leads the mind to refuse obedience to the laws of God, in the desire to be sovereign, as God is.

The farther, then, the mind departs from God, not in space, but in affection and lust after things below Him, the more it is filled with folly and wretchedness. So by love it returns to God — a love which places it not along with God, but under Him. And the more ardor and eagerness there is in this, the happier and more elevated will the mind be, and with God as sole governor it will be in perfect liberty. Hence it must know that it is a creature. It must believe what is the truth — that its Creator remains ever possessed of the inviolable and immutable nature of truth and wisdom, and must confess, even in view of the errors from which it desires deliverance, that it is liable to folly and falsehood. But then again, it must take care that it be not separated by the love of the other creature, that is, of this visible world, from the love of God Himself, which sanctifies it in order that it may abide most happy. No other creature, then — for we are ourselves a creature — separates us from the love of God which is in Christ Jesus our Lord.

CHAPTER XIII   WE ARE JOINED INSEPARATELY TO GOD BY CHRIST AND HIS SPIRIT

Let this same Paul tell us who is this Christ Jesus our Lord. "To them that are called," he says, "we preach Christ the virtue of God, and the wisdom of God." [4] And does not Christ Himself say, "I am the truth?" If, then, we ask what it is to live well — that is, to strive after happiness by living well — it must assuredly be to love virtue, to love wisdom, to love truth, and to love with all the heart, with all the soul, and with all the mind; virtue which is inviolable and immutable, wisdom which never gives place to folly, truth which knows no change or variation from its uniform character. Through this the Father Himself is seen; for it is said, "No man cometh unto the Father but by me." [5] To this we cleave by sanctification. For when sanctified we burn with full and perfect love, which is the only security for our not turning away from God, and for our being conformed to Him rather than to this world; for "He has predestinated us," says the same apostle, "that we should be conformed to the image of His Son." [6]

CHAPTER XV   THE CHRISTIAN DEFINITION OF THE FOUR VIRTUES

As to virtue leading us to a happy life, I hold virtue to be nothing else than perfect love of God. For the fourfold division of virtue I regard as taken from four forms of love. For these four virtues (would that all felt their influence in their minds as they have their names in their mouths!), I should have no hesitation in defining them: that temperance is love giving itself entirely to that which is loved; fortitude is love readily bearing all things for the sake of the loved object; justice is love serving only the loved object, and therefore ruling rightly; prudence is love distinguishing with sagacity between what hinders it and what helps it. The object of this love is not anything, but only God, the chief good, the highest wisdom, the perfect harmony. So we may express the definition thus: that temperance is love keeping itself entire and incorrupt for God; fortitude is love bearing everything readily for the sake of God; justice is love serving God only, and therefore ruling well all else, as subject to man; prudence is love making a right distinction between what helps it towards God and what might hinder it.

---

[4] 1 Cor. 1:23, 24.   [5] John 14:6.   [6] Rom. 8:29.

CHAPTER XIX   DESCRIPTION OF THE DUTIES OF
TEMPERANCE, ACCORDING TO THE SACRED SCRIPTURES

It is now time to return to the four virtues, and to draw out and prescribe a way of life in conformity with them, taking each separately. First, then, let us consider temperance, which promises us a kind of integrity and incorruption in the love by which we are united to God. The office of temperance is in restraining and quieting the passions which make us pant for those things which turn us away from the laws of God and from the enjoyment of His goodness, that is, in a word, from the happy life. For there is the abode of truth; and in enjoying its contemplation, and in cleaving closely to it, we are assuredly happy; but departing from this, men become entangled in great errors and sorrows. For, as the apostle says, "The root of all evils is covetousness; which some having followed, have made shipwreck of the faith, and have pierced themselves through with many sorrows. . . ." [7]

CHAPTER XX   WE ARE REQUIRED TO DESPISE
ALL SENSIBLE THINGS, AND TO LOVE GOD ALONE

Bodily delights have their source in all those things with which the bodily sense comes in contact, and which are by some called the objects of sense; and among these the noblest is light, in the common meaning of the word, because among our senses also, which the mind uses in acting through the body, there is nothing more valuable than the eyes, and so in the Holy Scriptures all the objects of sense are spoken of as visible things. Thus in the New Testament we are warned against the love of these things in the following words: "While we look not at the things which are seen, but at the things which are not seen; for the things which are seen are temporal, but the things which are not seen are eternal." [8] This shows how far from being Christians those are who hold that the sun and moon are to be not only loved but worshipped. For what is seen if the sun and moon are not? But we are forbidden to regard things which are seen. The man, therefore, who wishes to offer that incorrupt love to God must not love these things too. This subject I will inquire into more particularly elsewhere. Here my plan is to write not of faith, but of the life by which we become worthy of knowing what we believe. God then alone is to be loved; and all this world, that is, all sensible things, are to be despised — while, however, they are to be used as this life requires.

---

[7] 1 Tim. 6:10.   [8] 2 Cor. 4:18.

CHAPTER XXI   POPULAR RENOWN AND INQUISITIVENESS
ARE CONDEMNED IN THE SACRED SCRIPTURES

Popular renown is thus slighted and scorned in the New Testament: "If I wished," says Saint Paul, "to please men, I should not be the servant of Christ." [9] Again, there is another production of the soul formed by imaginations derived from material things, and called the knowledge of things. In reference to this we are fitly warned against inquisitiveness to correct which is the great function of temperance. Thus it is said, "Take heed lest any one seduce you by philosophy." And because the word philosophy originally means the love and pursuit of wisdom, a thing of great value and to be sought with the whole mind, the apostle, with great prudence, that he might not be thought to deter from the love of wisdom, has added the words, "And the elements of this world." [10] For some people, neglecting virtues, and ignorant of what God is, and of the majesty of the nature which remains always the same, think that they are engaged in an important business when searching with the greatest inquisitiveness and eagerness into this material mass which we call the world. This begets so much pride, that they look upon themselves as inhabitants of the heaven of which they often discourse. The soul, then, which purposes to keep itself chaste for God must refrain from the desire of vain knowledge like this. For this desire usually produces delusion, so that the soul thinks that nothing exists but what is material; or if, from regard to authority, it confesses that there is an immaterial existence, it can think of it only under material images, and has no belief regarding it but that imposed by the bodily sense. We may apply to this the precept about fleeing from idolatry. . . .

CHAPTER XXII   FORTITUDE COMES FROM
THE LOVE OF GOD

On fortitude we must be brief. The love, then, of which we speak, which ought with all sanctity to burn in desire for God, is called temperance, in not seeking for earthly things, and fortitude, in bearing the loss of them. But among all things which are possessed in this life, the body is, by God's most righteous laws, for the sin of old, man's heaviest bond, which is well known as a fact, but most incomprehensible in its mystery. Lest this bond should be shaken and disturbed, the soul is shaken with the fear of toil and pain; lest it should be lost and destroyed, the soul is shaken with the fear of death. For the soul loves it from the force of habit, not knowing that by using it well and wisely its resurrection and reformation will, by the divine help and decree, be without any trouble made subject to its authority. But when the soul turns to God wholly in this love, it

[9] Gal. 1:10.   [10] Coll. 2:8.

knows these things, and so will not only disregard death, but will even desire it.

Then there is the great struggle with pain. But there is nothing, though
of iron hardness, which the fire of love cannot subdue. And when the mind
is carried up to God in this love, it will soar above all torture free and
glorious, with wings beauteous and unhurt, on which chaste love rises to
the embrace of God. Otherwise God must allow the lovers of gold, the
lovers of praise, the lovers of women, to have more fortitude than the lovers
of Himself, though love in those cases is rather to be called passion or lust.
And yet even here we may see with what force the mind presses on with
unflagging energy, in spite of all alarms, towards that it loves; and we learn
that we should bear all things rather than forsake God, since those men
bear so much in order to forsake Him. . . .

CHAPTER XXV   FOUR MORAL DUTIES REGARDING
THE LOVE OF GOD, OF WHICH LOVE THE REWARD IS ETERNAL LIFE
AND THE KNOWLEDGE OF THE TRUTH

I need say no more about right conduct. For if God is man's
chief good, which you cannot deny, it clearly follows, since to seek the chief
good is to live well, that to live well is nothing else but to love God with
all the heart, with all the soul, with all the mind; and, as arising from this,
that this love must be preserved entire and incorrupt, which is the part of
temperance; that it give way before no troubles, which is the part of fortitude; that it serve no other, which is the part of justice; that it be watch-
ful in its inspection of things lest craft or fraud steal in, which is the part
of prudence. This is the one perfection of man, by which alone he can
succeed in attaining to the purity of truth. . . .

Let us then, as many as have in view to reach eternal life, love God
with all the heart, with all the soul, with all the mind. For eternal life
contains the whole reward in the promise of which we rejoice; nor can the
reward precede desert, nor be given to a man before he is worthy of it.
What can be more unjust than this, and what is more just than God? We
should not then demand the reward before we deserve to get it. Here, perhaps, it is not out of place to ask what is eternal life; or rather let us hear
the Bestower of it: "This," He says, "is life eternal, that they should know
Thee, the true God, and Jesus Christ whom Thou hast sent." [11] So eternal
life is the knowledge of the truth. See, then, how perverse and preposterous
is the character of those who think that their teaching of the knowledge
of God will make us perfect, when this is the reward of those already perfect! What else, then, have we to do but first to love with full affection
Him whom we desire to know? Hence arises that principle on which we

[11] John 17:3.

have all along insisted, that there is nothing more wholesome in the Catholic Church than using authority before argument.

CHAPTER XXVI   LOVE OF OURSELVES AND OF OUR NEIGHBOR

To proceed to what remains. It may be thought that there is nothing here about man himself, the lover. But to think this, shows a want of clear perception. For it is impossible for one who loves God not to love himself. For he alone has a proper love for himself who aims diligently at the attainment of the chief and true good; and if this is nothing else but God, as has been shown, what is to prevent one who loves God from loving himself? And then, among men should there be no bond of mutual love? Yea, verily; so that we can think of no surer step towards the love of God than the love of man to man. . . .

Let the Lord then supply us with the other precept in answer to the question about the precepts of life; for He was not satisfied with one as knowing that God is one thing and man another, and that the difference is nothing less than that between the Creator and the thing created in the likeness of its Creator. He says then that the second precept is, "Thou shalt love thy neighbor as thyself." [12] Now you love yourself suitably when you love God better than yourself. What, then, you aim at in yourself you must aim at in your neighbor, namely, that he may love God with a perfect affection. For you do not love him as yourself, unless you try to draw him to that good which you are yourself pursuing. For this is the one good which has room for all to pursue it along with thee. From this precept proceed the duties of human society, in which it is hard to keep from error. But the first thing to aim at is, that we should be benevolent, that is, that we cherish no malice and no evil design against another. For man is the nearest neighbor of man.

But there is a sense in which these either rise together to fullness and perfection, or, while the love of God is first in beginning, the love of our neighbor is first in coming to perfection. For perhaps divine love takes hold of us more rapidly at the outset, but we reach perfection more easily in lower things. However that may be, the main point is this, that no one should think that while he despises his neighbor he will come to happiness and to the God whom he loves. And would that it were as easy to seek the good of our neighbor, or to avoid hurting him, as it is for one well trained and kind-hearted to love his neighbor! These things require more than mere good-will, and can be done only by a high degree of thoughtfulness and prudence, which belongs only to those to whom it is given by God, the source of all good. On this topic — which is one, I think, of great difficulty — I will try to say a few words such as my plan admits of, resting all my hope in Him whose gifts these are.

[12] Matt. 22:39.

CHAPTER XXVII   ON DOING GOOD TO THE BODY
OF OUR NEIGHBOR

Man, then, as viewed by his fellowman, is a rational soul with a mortal and earthly body in its service. Therefore he who loves his neighbor does good partly to the man's body, and partly to his soul. What benefits the body is called medicine; what benefits the soul, discipline. Medicine here includes everything that either preserves or restores bodily health. It includes, therefore, not only what belongs to the art of medical men, properly so called, but also food and drink, clothing and shelter, and every means of covering and protection to guard our bodies against injuries and mishaps from without as well as from within. For hunger and thirst, and cold and heat, and all violence from without, produce loss of that health which is the point to be considered.

Hence those who seasonably and wisely supply all the things required for warding off these evils and distresses are called compassionate, although they may have been so wise that no painful feeling disturbed their minds in the exercise of compassion. No doubt the word compassionate implies suffering in the heart of the man who feels for the sorrow of another. And it is equally true that a wise man ought to be free from all painful emotion when he assists the needy, when he gives food to the hungry and water to the thirsty, when he clothes the naked, when he takes the stranger into his house, when he sets free the oppressed, when, lastly, he extends his charity to the dead in giving them burial. Still the epithet compassionate is a proper one, although he acts with tranquillity of mind, not from the stimulus of painful feeling, but from motives of benevolence. There is no harm in the word compassionate when there is no passion in the case.

Fools, again, who avoid the exercise of compassion as a vice, because they are not sufficiently moved by a sense of duty without feeling also distressful emotion, are frozen into hard insensibility, which is very different from the calm of a rational serenity. God, on the other hand, is properly called compassionate; and the sense in which He is so will be understood by those whom piety and diligence have made fit to understand. There is a danger lest, in using the words of the learned, we harden the souls of the unlearned by leading them away from compassion instead of softening them with the desire of a charitable disposition. As compassion, then, requires us to ward off these distresses from others, so harmlessness forbids the infliction of them.

CHAPTER XXVIII   ON DOING GOOD TO THE SOUL
OF OUR NEIGHBOR. TWO PARTS OF DISCIPLINE, RESTRAINT
AND INSTRUCTION. THROUGH GOOD CONDUCT
WE ARRIVE AT THE KNOWLEDGE OF THE TRUTH

As regards discipline, by which the health of the mind is restored, without which bodily health avails nothing for security against misery, the subject is one of great difficulty. And as in the body we said it is one thing to cure diseases and wounds, which few can do properly, and another thing to meet the cravings of hunger and thirst, and to give assistance in all the other ways in which any man may at any time help another; so in the mind there are some things in which the high and rare offices of the teacher are not much called for — as, for instance, in advice and exhortation to give to the needy the things already mentioned as required for the body. To give such advice is to aid the mind by discipline, as giving the things themselves is aiding the body by our resources. But there are other cases where diseases of the mind, many and various in kind, are healed in a way strange and indescribable. Unless His medicine were sent from heaven to men, so heedlessly do they go on in sin, there would be no hope of salvation; and, indeed, even bodily health, if you go to the root of the matter, can have come to men from none but God, who gives to all things their being and their well-being. . . .

He, then, who loves his neighbor endeavors all he can to procure his safety in body and in soul, making the health of the mind the standard in his treatment of the body. And as regards the mind, his endeavors are in this order, that he should first fear and then love God. This is true excellence of conduct, and thus the knowledge of the truth is acquired which we are ever in the pursuit of.

QUESTIONS

1. Does Augustine think that happiness is desirable? What does he think are the conditions of being "happy"? Does he understand this word in its ordinary contemporary sense?
2. Do you think he is right in thinking we should seek what is the best possible? right in thinking that whatever is the best possible thing is available to anyone who really wants it?
3. Is he right in arguing that something must be the highest good for man if in seeking it the mind achieves the highest perfection of which it is capable? and that possessing this thing will at the same time be of most benefit to the body?
4. How does Augustine "prove" that the highest good must be real? Why does he identify that perfect being with God?
5. How far must we rely on revelation for knowing how we may seek after God?
6. If we seek God or the highest good by loving Him, what is the culmination of this search — the possession which is the highest good of man?
7. What does Augustine think can separate man from God?
8. Does Augustine identify loving God with loving wisdom, truth, and virtue? As far as you can make out, is this kind of love a condition of achieving a perfect life, or identical with having a perfect life?
9. How does Augustine relate love of God to the traditional virtues of temperance, fortitude, justice, and prudence?
10. What does Augustine think of bodily enjoyments and desire to possess material things? of fame? of philosophical or scientific knowledge?

11. What is fortitude, according to him?
12. What is "eternal life"? Do you think Augustine believes that the perfect thing we should pursue can be possessed in the present, earthly existence?
13. Can we love God without loving our neighbor? What does Augustine mean by "love of your neighbor"?
14. Does Augustine hold that a benevolent person will be moved by feelings of sympathy for others? How far do you think Augustine's conception of the ideal man is similar to that of the Stoics?
15. Does love of neighbor involve concern for his mind as well as his body?
16. How far is there a parallel between the general outlines of Aristotle's conception of the good life and that of Augustine?
17. As far as you can make out, what does Augustine mean by his advice that we are to "love God"? What in particular should we think of, or do, in order to cultivate or attain a state of loving God?

   The interested reader should consult Book XXII of *The City of God* for Augustine's account of the "beatific vision" of God which will come to the saved in the after life.

SUGGESTIONS FOR FURTHER READING

Bourke, V. J. *Augustine's Quest of Wisdom*. Milwaukee: Bruce, 1945.
Clark, Mother Mary Twibill. *Augustine, Philosopher of Freedom*. New York: Desclee, 1959.
D'Arcy, M. C., *et al*. *A Monument to St. Augustine*. New York: Sheed & Ward, 1931.

Friedrich Wilhelm Nietzsche   (1844-1900)

POWER NOT PLEASURE

   Friedrich Nietzsche was born in Röcken, Germany, and was brought up a Protestant. During his university years, however, when he studied the Greek writers and became familiar with the evolutionary conceptions of Darwin, he rebelled against Christianity, as well as against other patterns of philosophical thinking popular in his day. He was plagued by ill-health for most of his life, and his thinking may have been influenced by this; he was made professor at the University of Basel, Switzerland, at the age of twenty-four but eleven years later resigned his post on grounds of health and never held any other academic position. In 1889 his internal turmoil culminated in insanity from which he did not recover.

   He wrote prolifically. Perhaps the best-known of his works

are *The Birth of Tragedy* (1872), *Thus Spoke Zarathustra* (1883-85), *Beyond Good and Evil* (1886), and *Toward a Genealogy of Morals* (1887). Nietzsche was anything but a lucid and careful writer; the student who wishes a scholarly formulation and assessment of his views should consult Walter Kaufmann's *Nietzsche* (New York: Meridian Books, 1956).

Nietzsche was a violent critic of the conventional morality of his day, of Christianity and its values, and of the philosophers who were his contemporaries. He had nothing but contempt for hedonism and utilitarianism; he thought it perverse to value sympathy, kindness, and all the qualities called for by Jesus in the Sermon on the Mount. Just what was he for? This is not easy to say. Power in some sense. But exactly in what sense and why he was for it and against other things the reader had best decide for himself.

BEYOND GOOD AND EVIL

Paragraph 260

In a tour through the many finer and coarser moralities which have hitherto prevailed or still prevail on the earth, I found certain traits recurring regularly together, and connected with one another, until finally two primary types revealed themselves to me, and a radical distinction was brought to light. There is *master-morality* and *slave-morality*; — I would at once add, however, that in all higher and mixed civilisations, there are also attempts at the reconciliation of the two moralities; but one finds still oftener the confusion and mutual misunderstanding of them, indeed, sometimes their close juxtaposition — even in the same man, within one soul. The distinctions of moral values have either originated in a ruling caste, pleasantly conscious of being different from the ruled — or among the ruled class, the slaves and dependents of all sorts. In the first case, when it is the rulers who determine the conception "good," it is the exalted, proud disposition which is regarded as the distinguishing feature, and that which determines the order of rank. The noble type of man separates from himself the beings in whom the opposite of this exalted, proud disposition displays itself: he despises them. Let it at once be noted that in this first kind of morality the antithesis "good" and "bad" means practically the same as "noble" and "despicable"; — the antithesis "good" and *"evil"* is of a different origin. The cowardly, the timid, the insignificant, and those thinking merely of narrow utility are despised; moreover, also, the distrustful, with their constrained glances, the self-abasing, the dog-like kind of men who let themselves be abused, the mendicant flatterers, and above all the liars: — it is a fundamental belief of all aristocrats that the common people are untruthful. "We truthful ones" — the nobility in ancient Greece called themselves. It is obvious that everywhere the designations of moral value were at first applied to *men,* and were only derivatively and at a later period applied to actions; it is a gross mistake, therefore, when historians of morals start questions like, "Why have sympathetic actions been praised?" The noble type of man regards *himself* as a determiner of values; he does not require to be approved of; he passes the judgment: "What is injurious to me is injurious in itself"; he knows that it is he himself only who confers honour on things; he is a *creator of values.* He honours whatever he recognises in himself: such morality is self-glorification. In the foreground there is the feeling of plenitude, of power, which seeks to overflow, the happiness of high tension, the consciousness of a wealth which would fain give and bestow: — the noble man also helps the unfortunate, but not — or scarcely — out of pity, but rather from an impulse generated by the superabundance of power. The noble man honours in himself the powerful one, him also who has power over himself, who knows how to speak and how to keep silence, who takes pleasure in subjecting himself to severity and hardness, and has reverence for all that is severe and hard. "Wotan placed a hard heart in my breast," says an old Scandinavian Saga: it is thus rightly expressed from the soul of a proud Viking. Such a type of man is even proud of *not* being made for sympathy; the hero of the Saga therefore adds warningly: "He who has not a hard heart when young, will never have one." The noble and brave who think thus are the furthest removed from the morality which sees precisely in sympathy, or in acting for the good of others, or in *désintéressement,* the characteristic of the moral; faith in oneself, pride in oneself, a radical enmity and irony towards "selflessness," belong as definitely to noble morality, as do a careless scorn and precaution in presence of sympathy and the "warm heart." — It is the powerful who *know* how to honour, it is their art, their domain for invention. The profound reverence for age and for tradition — all law rests on this double reverence, — the belief and prejudice in favour of ancestors and unfavourable to newcomers, is typical in the morality of the powerful; and if, reversely, men of "modern ideas" believe almost instinctively in "progress" and the "future," and are more and more lacking in respect for old age, the ignoble origin of these "ideas" has complacently betrayed itself thereby. A morality of the ruling class, however, is more especially foreign and irritating to present-day taste in the sternness of its principle that one has duties only to one's equals; that one may act towards beings of a lower rank, towards all that is foreign, just as seems good to one, or "as the heart desires," and in any case "beyond good and evil": it is here that sympathy and similar sentiments can have a place. The ability and obligation to exercise prolonged gratitude and prolonged revenge — both only within the circle of equals, — artfulness in retaliation, *raffinement* of the idea in friendship, a certain necessity to have enemies (as outlets for the emotions of envy, quarrelsomeness, arrogance — in fact, in order to be a good *friend*): all these are typical characteristics of the noble morality, which, as has been pointed out, is not the morality of "modern ideas," and is therefore at present difficult to realise, and also to unearth and disclose. — It is otherwise with the second type of morality, *slave-morality*. Supposing that the abused, the oppressed, the suffering, the unemancipated, the weary, and those uncertain of themselves, should moralise, what will be the common element of their moral estimates? Probably a pessimistic suspicion with regard to the entire situation of man will find expression, perhaps a condemnation of man, together with his situation. The slave has an unfavourable eye for the virtues of the powerful; he has a scepticism and distrust, a *refinement* of distrust of everything "good" that is there honoured — he would fain persuade himself that the very happiness there is not genuine. On the other hand, *those* qualities which serve to alleviate the existence of sufferers are brought into prominence and flooded with light; it is here that sympathy, the kind, helping hand, the warm heart, patience, diligence, humility, and friendliness attain to honour; for here these are the most useful qualities, and almost the only means of supporting the burden of existence. Slave-morality is essentially the morality of utility. Here is the seat of the origin of the famous antithesis "good" and "evil": — power and dangerousness are assumed to reside in the evil, a certain dreadfulness, subtlety, and strength, which do not admit of being despised. According to slave-morality, therefore, the "evil" man arouses fear; according to master-morality, it is precisely the "good" man who arouses fear and seeks to arouse it, while the bad man is regarded as the despicable being. The contrast attains its maximum when, in accordance with the logical consequences of slave-morality, a shade of depreciation — it may be slight and well-intentioned — at last attaches itself to the "good" man of this morality; because, according to the servile mode of thought, the good man must in any case be the *safe* man: he is good-natured, easily deceived, perhaps a little stupid, *un bonhomme*. Everywhere that slave-morality gains the ascendency, language shows a tendency to approximate the significations of the words "good" and "stupid." — A last fundamental difference: the desire for *freedom*, the instinct for happiness and the refinements of the feeling of liberty belong as necessarily to slave-morals and morality, as artifice and enthusiasm in reverence and devotion are the regular symptoms of an aristocratic mode of thinking and estimating. — Hence we can understand without further detail why love *as a passion* — it is our European specialty — must absolutely be of noble origin; as is well known, its invention is due to the

Provençal poet-cavaliers, those brilliant, ingenious men of the *"gai saber,"* to whom Europe owes so much, and almost owes itself.

THE GENEALOGY OF MORALS

First essay, paragraphs 14 and 16

Will any one look a little into — right into — the mystery of how *ideals* are *manufactured* in this world? Who has the courage to do it? Come!

Here we have a vista opened into these grimy workshops. Wait just a moment, dear Mr. Inquisitive and Foolhardy; your eye must first grow accustomed to this false changing light — Yes! Enough! Now speak! What is happening below down yonder? Speak out! Tell what you see, man of the most dangerous curiosity — for now *I* am the listener.

"I see nothing, I hear the more. It is a cautious, spiteful, gentle whispering and muttering together in all the corners and crannies. It seems to me that they are lying; a sugary softness adheres to every sound. Weakness is turned to *merit*, there is no doubt about it — it is just as you say."

Further!

"And the impotence which requites not, is turned to 'goodness,' craven baseness to meekness, submission to those whom one hates, to obedience (namely, obedience to one of whom they say that he ordered this submission — they call him God). The inoffensive character of the weak, the very cowardice in which he is rich, his standing at the door, his forced necessity of waiting, gain here fine names, such as 'patience,' which is also called 'virtue'; not being able to avenge one's self, is called not wishing to avenge one's self, perhaps even forgiveness (for *they* know not what they do — we alone know what they do). They also talk of the 'love of their enemies' and sweat thereby."

Further!

"They are miserable, there is no doubt about it, all these whisperers and counterfeiters in the corners, although they try to get warm by crouching close to each other, but they tell me that their misery is a favour and distinction given to them by God, just as one beats the dogs one likes best; that perhaps this misery is also a preparation, a probation, a training; that perhaps it is still more something which will one day be compensated and paid back with a tremendous interest in gold, nay in happiness. This they call 'Blessedness.'"

Further!

"They are now giving me to understand, that not only are they better men than the mighty, the lords of the earth, whose spittle they have got to lick (*not* out of fear, not at all out of fear! But because God ordains that one should honour all authority) — not only are they better men, but that they also have a 'better time,' at any rate, will one day have a 'better time.' But enough! Enough! I can endure it no longer. Bad air! Bad air!

These workshops *where ideals are manufactured* — verily they reek with the crassest lies."

Nay. Just one minute! You are saying nothing about the masterpieces of these virtuosos of black magic, who can produce whiteness, milk, and innocence out of any black you like: have you not noticed what a pitch of refinement is attained by their *chef d'oeuvre*, their most audacious, subtle, ingenious, and lying artist-trick? Take care! These cellar-beasts, full of revenge and hate — what do they make, forsooth, out of their revenge and hate? Do you hear these words? Would you suspect, if you trusted only their words, that you are among men of resentment and nothing else?

"I understand, I prick up my ears again. . . . Now do I hear for the first time that which they have said so often: 'We good, *we are the righteous*' — what they demand they call not revenge but 'the triumph of *righteousness*'; what they hate is not their enemy, no, they hate 'unrighteousness,' 'godlessness'; what they believe in and hope is not the hope of revenge, the intoxication of sweet revenge (— 'sweeter than honey,' did Homer call it?), but the victory of God, of the *righteous* God over the 'godless'; what is left for them to love in this world is not their brothers in hate, but their 'brothers in love,' as they say, all the good and righteous on the earth."

And how do they name that which serves them as a solace against all the troubles of life — their phantasmagoria of their anticipated future blessedness?

"How? Do I hear right? They call it 'the last judgment' the advent of *their* kingdom, 'the kingdom of God' — but *in the meanwhile* they live 'in faith,' 'in love,' 'in hope.' "

Enough! Enough!

Let us come to a conclusion. The two *opposing values*, "good and bad," "good and evil," have fought a dreadful, thousand-year fight in the world, and though indubitably the second value has been for a long time in the preponderance, there are not wanting places where the fortune of the fight is still indecisive. It can almost be said that in the meanwhile the fight reaches a higher and higher level, and that in the meanwhile it has become more and more intense, and always more and more psychological; so that nowadays there is perhaps no more decisive mark of the *higher nature*, of the more psychological nature, than to be in that sense self-contradictory, and to be actually still a battleground for those two opposites. The symbol of this fight, written in a writing which has remained worthy of perusal throughout the course of history up to the present time, is called "Rome against Judaea, Judaea against Rome." Hitherto there has been no greater event than *that* fight, the putting of *that* question, *that* deadly antagonism. Rome found in the Jew the incarnation of the unnatural, as though it were its diametrically opposed monstrosity, and in Rome the Jew was held to be *convicted of hatred* of the whole human race: and rightly so, in so far as it is right to link the well-being and the future of the human race to the unconditional mastery of the aristocratic values, of the Roman values. What, conversely, did the Jews feel against Rome? One can surmise it from a thousand symptoms, but it is sufficient to carry one's mind back to the Johannian Apocalypse, that most obscene of all the written outbursts, which has revenge on its conscience. . . . The Romans were the strong and aristocratic; a nation stronger and more aristocratic has never existed in the world, has never even been dreamed of; every relic of them, every inscription enraptures, granted that one can divine *what* it is that writes the inscription. The Jews, conversely, were that priestly nation of resentment *par excellence*, possessed by a unique genius for popular morals: just compare with the Jews the nations with analogous gifts, such as the Chinese or the Germans, so as to realise afterwards what is first rate, and what is fifth rate.

Which of them has been provisionally victorious, Rome or Judaea? but there is not a shadow of doubt; just consider to whom in Rome itself nowadays you bow down, as though before the quintessence of all the highest values — to *three Jews*, as we know, and *one Jewess* (to Jesus of Nazareth, to Peter the fisher, to Paul the tentmaker, and to the mother of the aforesaid Jesus, named Mary). This is very remarkable: Rome is undoubtedly defeated. At any rate there took place in the Renaissance a brilliantly sinister revival of the classical ideal, of the aristocratic valuation of all things: Rome herself, like a man waking up from a trance, stirred beneath the burden of the new Judaised Rome that had been built over her, which presented the appearance of an oecumenical synagogue and was called the "Church": but immediately Judaea triumphed again, thanks to that fundamentally popular (German and English) movement of revenge, which is called the Reformation, and taking also into account its inevitable corollary, the restoration of the Church — the restoration also of the ancient graveyard peace of classical Rome. Judaea proved yet once more victorious over the classical ideal in the French Revolution, and in a sense which was even more crucial and even more profound: the last political aristocracy that existed in Europe, that of the *French* seventeenth and eighteenth centuries, broke into pieces beneath the instincts of a resentful populace — never had the world heard a greater jubilation, a more uproarious enthusiasm: indeed, there took place in the midst of it the most monstrous and unexpected phenomenon; the ancient ideal *itself* swept before the eyes and conscience of humanity with all its life and with unheard of splendour, and in opposition to resentment's lying war-cry of *the prerogative of the most*, in opposition to the will to lowliness, abasement, and equalisation, the will to a retrogression and twilight of humanity, there rang out once again, stronger, simpler, more penetrating than ever, the terrible and enchanting counter-war-cry of *the prerogative of the few!* Like a final signpost to other ways, there appeared Napoleon, the most unique and violent anachronism that ever existed, and in him the incarnate problem *of the aristocratic ideal in itself* — consider well what a problem it is: — Napoleon, that synthesis of Monster and Superman.

BEYOND GOOD AND EVIL

Paragraphs 225 and 228

Whether it be hedonism, pessimism, utilitarianism, or eudae-monism, all those modes of thinking which measure the worth of things according to *pleasure* and *pain*, that is, according to accompanying circumstances and secondary considerations, are plausible modes of thought and naïvetés, which every one conscious of *creative* powers and an artist's conscience will look down upon with scorn, though not without sympathy. Sympathy for *you!* — to be sure, that is not sympathy as you understand it: it is not sympathy for social "distress," for "society" with its sick and misfortuned, for the hereditarily vicious and defective who lie on the ground around us; still less is it sympathy for the grumbling, vexed, revolutionary slave-classes who strive after power — they call it "freedom." *Our* sympathy is a loftier and further-sighted sympathy: — we see how *man* dwarfs himself, how *you* dwarf him! and there are moments when we view *your* sympathy with an indescribable anguish, when we resist it, — when we regard your seriousness as more dangerous than any kind of levity. You want, if possible — and there is not a more foolish "if possible" — *to do away with suffering*; and we? — it really seems that *we* would rather have it increased and made worse than it has ever been! Well-being, as you understand it — is certainly not a goal; it seems to us an *end*; a condition which at once renders man ludicrous and contemptible — and makes his destruction *desirable!* The discipline of suffering, of *great* suffering — know ye not that it is only *this* discipline that has produced all the elevations of humanity hitherto? The tension of soul in misfortune which communicates to it its energy, its shuddering in view of rack and ruin, its inventiveness and bravery in undergoing, enduring, interpreting, and exploiting misfortune, and whatever depth, mystery, disguise, spirit, artifice, or greatness has been bestowed upon the soul — has it not been bestowed through suffering, through the discipline of great suffering? In man *creature* and *creator* are united: in man there is not only matter, shred, excess, clay, mire, folly, chaos; but there is also the creator, the sculptor, the hardness of the hammer, the divinity of the spectator, and the seventh day — do ye understand this contrast? And that *your* sympathy for the "creature in man" applies to that which has to be fashioned, bruised, forged, stretched, roasted, annealed, refined — to that which.must necessarily *suffer*, and *is meant* to suffer? And *our* sympathy — do ye not understand what our *reverse* sympathy applies to, when it resists your sympathy as the worst of all pampering and enervation? — So it is sympathy *against* sympathy! — But to repeat it once more, there are higher problems than the problems of pleasure and pain and sympathy; and all systems of philosophy which deal only with these are naïvetés. . . .

I hope to be forgiven for discovering that all moral philosophy hitherto has been tedious and has belonged to the soporific appliances — and that "virtue," in my opinion, has been *more* injured by the *tediousness* of its advocates than by anything else; at the same time, however, I would not wish to overlook their general usefulness. It is desirable that as few people as possible should reflect upon morals, and consequently it is *very* desirable that morals should not some day become interesting! But let us not be afraid! Things still remain today as they have always been: I see no one in Europe who has (or *discloses*) an idea of the fact that philosophising concerning morals might be conducted in a dangerous, captious, and ensnarling manner — that *calamity* might be involved therein. Observe, for example, the indefatigable, inevitable English utilitarians: how ponderously and respectably they stalk on . . . in the footsteps of Bentham. . . . No new thought, nothing of the nature of a finer turning or better expression of an old thought, not even a proper history of what has been previously thought on the subject: an *impossible* literature, taking it all in all, unless one knows how to leaven it with some mischief. . . . In the end, they all want *English* morality to be recognised as authoritative, inasmuch as mankind, or the "general utility," or "the happiness of the greatest number," — no! the happiness of *England*, will be best served thereby. They would like, by all means, to convince themselves that the striving after *English* happiness, I mean after *comfort* and *fashion* (and in the highest instance, a seat in Parliament), is at the same time the true path of virtue; in fact, that in so far as there has been virtue in the world hitherto, it has just consisted in such striving. Not one of those ponderous, conscience-stricken herding-animals (who undertake to advocate the cause of egoism as conducive to the general welfare) wants to have any knowledge or inkling of the facts that the "general welfare" is no ideal, no goal, no notion that can be at all grasped, but is only a nostrum, — that what is fair to one *may not* be fair to another, that the requirement of one morality for all is really a detriment to higher men, in short, that there is a *distinction of rank* between man and man, and consequently between morality and morality. They are an unassuming and fundamentally mediocre species of men, these utilitarian Englishmen, and, as already remarked, in so far as they are tedious, one cannot think highly enough of their utility. . . .

THE GAY SCIENCE

Paragraphs 283, 285, 290

Preparatory men. I welcome all signs that a more manly, a warlike, age is about to begin, an age which, above all, will give honor to valor once again. For this age shall prepare the way for one yet higher, and it shall gather the strength which this higher age will need one day — this age which is to carry heroism into the pursuit of knowledge and *wage wars* for the sake of thoughts and their consequences. To this end we now need many preparatory valorous men who cannot leap into being out of nothing — any more than out of the sand and slime of our present civilization and metropolitanism: men who are bent on seeking for that aspect in all things which must be *overcome*; men characterized by cheerfulness, patience, unpretentiousness, and contempt for all great vanities, as well as by magnanimity in victory and forbearance regarding the small vanities of the vanquished; men possessed of keen and free judgment concerning all victors and the share of chance in every victory and every fame; men who have their own festivals, their own weekdays, their own periods of mourning, who are accustomed to command with assurance and are no less ready to obey when necessary, in both cases equally proud and serving their own cause; men who are in greater danger, more fruitful, and happier! For, believe me, the secret of the greatest fruitfulness and the greatest enjoyment of existence is: to *live dangerously*! Build your cities under Vesuvius! Send your ships into uncharted seas! Live at war with your peers and yourselves! Be robbers and conquerors, as long as you cannot be rulers and owners, you lovers of knowledge! Soon the age will be past when you could be satisfied to live like shy deer, hidden in the woods! At long last the pursuit of knowledge will reach out for its due: it will want to *rule* and *own*, and you with it! . . .

Excelsior! "You will never pray again, never adore again, never again rest in endless trust; you deny yourself any stopping before ultimate wisdom, ultimate goodness, ultimate power, while unharnessing your thoughts; you have no perpetual guardian and friend for your seven solitudes; you live without a view of mountains with snow on their peaks and fire in their hearts; there is no avenger for you, no eventual improver; there is no reason any more in what happens, no love in what will happen to you; no resting place is any longer open to your heart, where it has only to find and no longer to seek; you resist any ultimate peace, you want the eternal recurrence of war and peace. Man of renunciation, do you want to renounce all this? Who will give you the necessary strength? Nobody yet has had this strength." There is a lake which one day refused to flow off and erected a dam where it had hitherto flowed off: ever since, this lake has been rising higher and higher. Perhaps that very renunciation will also lend us the strength to bear the renunciation itself; perhaps man will rise ever higher when he once ceases to *flow out* into a god. . . .

One thing is needful. "Giving style" to one's character — a great and rare art! It is exercised by those who see all the strengths and weaknesses of their own natures and then comprehend them in an artistic plan until everything appears as art and reason and even weakness delights the eye. Here a large mass of second nature has been added; there a piece of original nature has been removed: both by long practice and daily labor. Here the ugly which could not be removed is hidden; there it has been reinterpreted and made sublime. . . . It will be the strong and domineering natures who enjoy their finest gaiety in such compulsion, in such constraint and perfection under a law of their own; the passion of their tremendous will relents when confronted with stylized, conquered, and serving nature; even when they have to build palaces and lay out gardens, they demur at giving nature a free hand. Conversely, it is the weak characters without power over themselves who *hate* the constraint of style. . . . They become slaves as soon as they serve; they hate to serve. Such spirits — and they may be of the first rank — are always out to interpret themselves and their environment as *free* nature — wild, arbitrary, fantastic, disorderly, astonishing; and they do well because only in this way do they please themselves. For one thing is needful: that a human being attain his satisfaction with himself — whether it be by this or by that poetry and art; only then is a human being at all tolerable to behold. Whoever is dissatisfied with himself is always ready to revenge himself therefor; we others will be his victims, if only by always having to stand his ugly sight. For the sight of the ugly makes men bad and gloomy.

BEYOND GOOD AND EVIL

Paragraph 29

It is the business of the very few to be independent; it is a privilege of the strong. And whoever attempts it, even with the best right, but without being *obliged* to do so, proves that he is probably not only strong, but also daring beyond measure. He enters into a labyrinth, he multiplies a thousandfold the dangers which life in itself already brings with it; not the least of which is that no one can see how and where he loses his way, becomes isolated, and is torn piecemeal by some minotaur of conscience. Supposing such a one comes to grief, it is so far from the comprehension of men that they neither feel it, nor sympathize with it. And he cannot any longer go back! He cannot even go back again to the sympathy of men!

Paragraph 51

The mightiest men have hitherto always bowed reverently before the saint, as the enigma of self-subjugation and utter voluntary privation — why did they thus bow? They divined in him — and as it were behind the questionableness of his frail and wretched appearance — the superior force which wished to test itself by such a subjugation; the strength of will, in which they recognised their own strength and love of power, and knew how to honour it: they honoured something in themselves when they honoured the saint. In addition to this, the contemplation of the saint suggested to them a suspicion: such an enormity of self-negation and anti-naturalness will not have been coveted for nothing — they have said, inquiringly. There is perhaps a reason for it, some very great danger, about which the ascetic might wish to be more accurately informed through his secret interlocutors and visitors? In a word, the mighty ones of the world learned to have a new fear before him, they divined a new power, a strange, still unconquered enemy: — it was the "Will to Power" which obliged them to halt before the saint. They had to question him.

QUESTIONS

1. In addition to "Tell the truth!" what would be some of the provisions of the "master-morality," according to Nietzsche? What would be some provisions of the code of the "slave-morality"?
2. Is it consistent for Nietzsche to say that the noble man is a "creator of values"?
3. Identify some traits of character and some values, which Nietzsche associates with the noble person.
4. Does he think that people of unusual ability should have any special privileges in society? What privileges?
5. What is Nietzsche's theory of the source of the ideals of "slave-morality"? Is Christianity the only slave-morality, according to him? Is there any historical truth in Nietzsche's view?
6. Would Nietzsche regard Napoleon as a perfect example of the noble man?
7. Why is he opposed to hedonism and utilitarianism?
8. Does Nietzsche have in mind, when he speaks of noble or superior persons, anybody who has political or social position? Or are personal qualities a sufficient condition of nobility?
9. Does the "power" which Nietzsche favors include self-control? Is it more than this? Why does he think people tend to respect the saints?
10. What aims does Nietzsche recommend to persons of superior talent? Personal enjoyments? A career in science, philosophy, business, or what?

SUGGESTIONS FOR FURTHER READING

Kaufmann, Walter. *Nietzsche: Philosopher, Psychologist, Antichrist.* New York: Meridian Books, 1956.

Mann, Thomas. "Nietzsche's Philosophy in the Light of Contemporary Events" in Mann, T. *Last Essays.* New York: Knopf, 1959.

Morgan, G. A. *What Nietzsche Means.* Cambridge: Harvard Univ. Press, 1941.

Reyburn, H. A. *Nietzsche, The Story of a Human Philosopher.* New York: Macmillan, 1948.

Salter, W. M. *Nietzsche, the Thinker.* London: Palmer & Hayward, 1917.

Sir William David Ross (1877-)

MANY THINGS INTRINSICALLY GOOD

W. D. Ross is a contemporary, who only recently retired from teaching at Oxford, where he was Provost of Oriel College. He is a distinguished classical scholar, a translator of many Greek philosophical texts, and the author of first-rate books on both Plato and Aristotle. He is also one of the outstanding figures among writers on ethics in the present century, primarily on account of novel theories about obligation and rightness, his criticisms of utilitarianism, and detailed discussion of exactly what it is people are obligated to do and of the relation between fulfillment of obligation and praiseworthiness of motivation. His two books on ethics, *The Right and the Good* and *Foundations of Ethics* are among the dozen most important pieces of ethical writing of the past fifty years.

Ross's views about what is good are similar to those of various outstanding philosophers of the present century: in particular, G. E. Moore, E. F. Carritt, and C. D. Broad. In essence, all these writers agree with hedonists to the extent of conceding that pleasure, at least in some contexts, is intrinsically good. But other things are also good: such things as knowledge, good deeds and qualities of character, perhaps aesthetic contemplation. Moreover they go on to assert that some other things are intrinsically worthwhile which are not states of persons at all, such as a just distribution of happiness or welfare. This view is by no means universal today, but it represents an important type of contemporary thought.

The following selection is Chapter 5 from *The Right and the Good*.

From W. D. Ross, *The Right and the Good*, published by The Clarendon Press, Oxford, 1930, and reprinted with their permission.

THE RIGHT AND THE GOOD

WHAT THINGS ARE GOOD?

Our next step is to inquire what kinds of thing are intrinsically good. (1) The first thing for which I would claim that it is intrinsically good is virtuous disposition and action, i.e. action, or disposition to act, from any one of certain motives of which at all events the most notable are the desire to do one's duty, the desire to bring into being something that is good, and the desire to give pleasure or save pain to others. It seems clear that we regard all such actions and dispositions as having value in themselves apart from any consequence. And if any one is inclined to doubt this and to think that, say, pleasure alone is intrinsically good, it seems to me enough to ask the question whether, of two states of the universe holding equal amounts of pleasure, we should really think no better of one in which the actions and dispositions of all the persons in it were thoroughly virtuous than of one in which they were highly vicious. To this there can be only one answer. Most hedonists would shrink from giving the plainly false answer which their theory requires, and would take refuge in saying that the question rests on a false abstraction. Since virtue, as they conceive it, is a disposition to do just the acts which will produce most pleasure, a universe full of virtuous persons would be bound, they might say, to contain more pleasure than a universe full of vicious persons. To this two answers may be made. (*a*) Much pleasure, and much pain, do not spring from virtuous or vicious actions at all but from the operation of natural laws. Thus even if a universe filled with virtuous persons were bound to contain more of the pleasure and less of the pain that springs from human action than a universe filled with vicious persons would, that inequality of pleasantness might easily be supposed to be precisely counteracted by, for instance, a much greater incidence of disease. The two states of affairs would then, on balance, be equally pleasant; would they be equally good? And (*b*) even if we could not imagine any circumstances in which two states of the universe equal in pleasantness but unequal in virtue could exist, the supposition is a legitimate one, since it is only intended to bring before us in a vivid way what is really self-evident, that virtue is good apart from its consequences.

(2) It seems at first sight equally clear that pleasure is good in itself. Some will perhaps be helped to realize this if they make the corresponding supposition to that we have just made; if they suppose two states of the universe including equal amounts of virtue but the one including also widespread and intense pleasure and the other widespread and intense pain. Here too it might be objected that the supposition is an impossible one, since virtue always tends to promote general pleasure, and vice to promote general misery. But this objection may be answered just as we have answered the corresponding objection above.

Apart from this, however, there are two ways in which even the most austere moralists and the most anti-hedonistic philosophers are apt to betray the conviction that pleasure is good in itself. (*a*) One is the attitude which they, like all other normal human beings, take towards kindness and towards cruelty. If the desire to give pleasure to others is approved, and the desire to inflict pain on others condemned, this seems to imply the conviction that pleasure is good and pain bad. Some may think, no doubt, that the mere thought that a certain state of affairs would be *painful* for another person is enough to account for our conviction that the desire to produce it is bad. But I am inclined to think that there is involved the further thought that a state of affairs in virtue of being painful is *prima facie* (i.e. where other considerations do not enter into the case) one that a rational spectator would not approve, i.e. is *bad*; and that similarly our attitude towards kindness involves the thought that pleasure is good. (*b*) The other is the insistence, which we find in the most austere moralists as in other people, on the conception of merit. If virtue deserves to be rewarded by happiness (whether or not vice also deserves to be rewarded by unhappiness), this seems at first sight to imply that happiness and unhappiness are not in themselves things indifferent, but are good and bad respectively.

Kant's view on this question is not as clear as might be wished. He points out that the Latin *bonum* covers two notions distinguished in German as *das Gute* (the good) and *das Wohl* (well-being, i.e. pleasure or happiness); and he speaks of 'good' as being properly applied only to actions,[1] i.e. he treats 'good' as equivalent to 'morally good,' and by implication denies that pleasure (even deserved pleasure) is good. It might seem then that when he speaks of the union of virtue with the happiness it deserves as the *bonum consummatum* he is not thinking of deserved happiness as good but only as *das Wohl*, a source of satisfaction to the person who has it. But if this exhausted his meaning, he would have no right to speak of virtue, as he repeatedly does, as *das oberste Gut*; he should call it simply *das Gute*, and happiness *das Wohl*. Further, he describes the union of virtue with happiness not merely as 'the object of the desires of rational finite beings,' but adds that it approves itself 'even in the judgement of an impartial reason' as 'the whole and perfect good,' rather than virtue alone. And he adds that 'happiness, while it is pleasant to the possessor of it, is not of itself absolutely and in all respects good, but always presupposes morally right behaviour as its condition'; which implies that *when* that condition is fulfilled, happiness *is* good.[2] All this seems to point to the conclusion that in the end he had to recognize that while virtue alone is morally good, deserved happiness also is not merely a source of satisfaction to its possessor, but objectively good.

But reflection on the conception of merit does not support the view that pleasure is always good in itself and pain always bad in itself. For

---

[1] *Kritik der pr. Vernunft*, 59-60 (Akad. Ausgabe, vol. v), 150-1 (Abbott's Trans. ed. 6).

[2] *Ib* 110-11 (Akad. Ausgabe), 206-7 (Abbott).

while this conception implies the conviction that pleasure when deserved is good, and pain when undeserved bad, it also suggests strongly that pleasure when undeserved is bad and pain when deserved good.

There is also another set of facts which casts doubt on the view that pleasure is always good and pain always bad. We have a decided conviction that there are bad pleasures and (though this is less obvious) that there are good pains. We think that the pleasure taken either by the agent or by a spectator in, for instance, a lustful or cruel action is bad; and we think it a good thing that people should be pained rather than pleased by contemplating vice or misery.

Thus the view that pleasure is always good and pain always bad, while it seems to be strongly supported by some of our convictions, seems to be equally strongly opposed by others. The difficulty can, I think, be removed by ceasing to speak simply of pleasure and pain as good or bad, and by asking more carefully what it is that we mean. Consideration of the question is aided if we adopt the view (tentatively adopted already) that what is good or bad is always something properly expressed by a that-clause, i.e. an objective, or as I should prefer to call it, a *fact*. If we look at the matter thus, I think we can agree that the fact that a sentient being is in a state of pleasure is always in itself good, and the fact that a sentient being is in a state of pain always in itself bad, when this fact is not an element in a more complex fact having some other characteristic relevant to goodness or badness. And where considerations of desert or of moral good or evil do not enter, i.e. in the case of animals, the fact that a sentient being is feeling pleasure or pain is the whole fact (or the fact sufficiently described to enable us to judge of its goodness or badness), and we need not hesitate to say that the pleasure of animals is always good, and the pain of animals always bad, in itself and apart from its consequences. But when a moral being is feeling a pleasure or pain that is deserved or undeserved, or a pleasure or pain that implies a good or a bad disposition, the total fact is quite inadequately described if we say 'a sentient being is feeling pleasure, or pain.' The total fact may be that 'a sentient and moral being is feeling a pleasure that is undeserved, or that is the realization of a vicious disposition,' and though the fact included in this, that 'a sentient being is feeling pleasure' would be good if it stood alone, that creates only a presumption that the total fact is good, and a presumption that is outweighed by the other element in the total fact.

Pleasure seems, indeed, to have a property analogous to that which we have previously recognized under the name of conditional or *prima facie* rightness. An act of promise-keeping has the property, not necessarily of being right but of being something that is right if the act has no other morally significant characteristic (such as that of causing much pain to another person). And similarly a state of pleasure has the property, not necessarily of being good, but of being something that is good if the state has no other characteristic that prevents it from being good. The two characteristics that may interfere with its being good are (*a*) that of being contrary to desert, and (*b*) that of being a state which is the realization of a bad disposition. Thus the pleasures of which we can say without doubt that they are good are (i) the pleasures of non-moral beings (animals), (ii) the pleasures of moral beings that are deserved and are either realizations of good moral dispositions or realizations of neutral capacities (such as the pleasures of the senses).

In so far as the goodness or badness of a particular pleasure depends on its being the realization of a virtuous or vicious disposition, this has been allowed for by our recognition of virtue as a thing good in itself. But the mere recognition of virtue as a thing good in itself, and of pleasure as a thing *prima facie* good in itself, does not do justice to the conception of merit. If we compare two imaginary states of the universe, alike in the total amounts of virtue and vice and of pleasure and pain present in the two, but in one of which the virtuous were all happy and the vicious miserable, while in the other the virtuous were miserable and the vicious happy, very few people would hesitate to say that the first was a much better state of the universe than the second. It would seem then that, besides virtue and pleasure, we must recognize (3), as a third independent good, the apportion-ment of pleasure and pain to the virtuous and the vicious respectively. And it is on the recognition of this as a separate good that the recognition of the duty of justice, in distinction from fidelity to promises on the one hand and from beneficence on the other, rests.

(4) It seems clear that knowledge, and in a less degree what we may for the present call 'right opinion,' are states of mind good in themselves. Here too we may, if we please, help ourselves to realize the fact by supposing two states of the universe equal in respect of virtue and of pleasure and of the allocation of pleasure to the virtuous, but such that the persons in the one had a far greater understanding of the nature and laws of the universe than those in the other. Can any one doubt that the first would be a better state of the universe?

From one point of view it seems doubtful whether knowledge and right opinion, no matter what it is of or about, should be considered good. Knowl-edge of mere matters of fact (say of the number of stories in a building), without knowledge of their relation to other facts, might seem to be worth-less; it certainly seems to be worth much less than the knowledge of general principles, or of facts as depending on general principles—what we might call insight or understanding as opposed to mere knowledge. But on reflec-tion it seems clear that even about matters of fact right opinion is in itself a better state of mind to be in than wrong, and knowledge than right opinion.

There is another objection which may naturally be made to the view that knowledge is as such good. There are many pieces of knowledge which we in fact think it well for people *not* to have; e.g. we may think it a bad thing for a sick man to know how ill he is, or for a vicious man to know how he may most conveniently indulge his vicious tendencies. But it seems that in such cases it is not the knowledge but the consequences in the way of pain or of vicious action that we think bad.

It might perhaps be objected that knowledge is not a better state than right opinion, but merely a source of greater satisfaction to its possessor. It no doubt is a source of greater satisfaction. Curiosity is the desire to *know*, and is never really satisfied by mere opinion. Yet there are two facts which seem to show that this is not the whole truth. (*a*) While opinion recognized to be such is never thoroughly satisfactory to its possessor, there is another state of mind which is not knowledge—which may even be mistaken—yet which through lack of reflection is not distinguished from knowledge by its possessor, the state of mind which Professor Cook Wilson has called 'that of being under the impression that so-and-so is the case.' [3] Such a state of mind may be as great a source of satisfaction to its possessor as knowledge, yet we should all think it to be an inferior state of mind to knowledge. This surely points to a recognition by us that knowledge has a worth other than that of being a source of satisfaction to its possessor. (*b*) Wrong opinion, so long as its wrongness is not discovered, may be as great a source of satisfaction as right. Yet we should agree that it is an inferior state of mind, because it is to a less extent founded on knowledge and is itself a less close approximation to knowledge; which again seems to point to our recognizing knowledge as something good in itself.

Four things, then, seem to be intrinsically good — virtue, pleasure, the allocation of pleasure to the virtuous, and knowledge (and in a less degree right opinion). And I am unable to discover anything that is intrinsically good, which is not either one of these or a combination of two or more of them. And while this list of goods has been arrived at on its own merits, by reflection on what we really think to be good, it perhaps derives some support from the fact that it harmonizes with a widely accepted classification of the elements in the life of the soul. It is usual to enumerate these as cognition, feeling, and conation. Now knowledge is the ideal state of the mind, and right opinion an approximation to the ideal, on the cognitive or intellectual side; pleasure is its ideal state on the side of feeling; and virtue is its ideal state on the side of conation; while the allocation of happiness to virtue is a good which we recognize when we reflect on the ideal relation between the conative side and the side of feeling. It might of course be objected that there are or may be intrinsic goods that are not states of mind or relations between states of mind at all, but in this suggestion I can find no plausibility. Contemplate any imaginary universe from which you suppose mind entirely absent, and you will fail to find anything in it that you can call good in itself. That is not to say, of course, that the existence of a material universe may not be a necessary condition for the existence of many things that are good in themselves. Our knowledge and our true opinions are to a large extent about the material world, and to that extent

<hr>

[3] *Statement and Inference*, i. 113.

could not exist unless it existed. Our pleasures are to a large extent derived from material objects. Virtue owes many of its opportunities to the existence of material conditions of good and material hindrances to good. But the value of material things appears to be purely instrumental, not intrinsic.

Of the three elements virtue, knowledge, and pleasure are compounded all the complex states of mind that we think good in themselves. Aesthetic enjoyment, for example, seems to be a blend of pleasure with insight into the nature of the object that inspires it. Mutual love seems to be a blend of virtuous disposition of two minds towards each other, with the knowledge which each has of the character and disposition of the other, and with the pleasure which arises from such disposition and knowledge. And a similar analysis may probably be applied to all other complex goods.

QUESTIONS

1. What question does Ross raise in order to settle the issue whether something is intrinsically desirable? Does an affirmative answer to his question really settle the matter?
2. Would Ross's reply to critics of the view that pleasure is good be effective against the Stoics? Did the Stoics fall into the confusions of which Ross accuses Kant?
3. In what way does Ross think the view that pleasure is intrinsically good should be qualified?
4. What is the difference between "knowledge" and "right opinion"? Is every instance of knowledge intrinsically valuable, according to Ross?
5. Can you make plausible additions to Ross's final list of things intrinsically good? How about achievement over obstacles? creativeness? life with mind and memory, just as such? Should we make some deletions from Ross's list?

CHAPTER 1   SUGGESTIONS FOR FURTHER READING

Baylis, Charles A. *Ethics: The Principles of Wise Choice.* New York: Holt, 1958.

Blake, Ralph. "Why Not Hedonism?" *Ethics,* Vol. 37 (1926), pp. 1-18. Hedonism.

Brandt, Richard B. *Ethical Theory.* Englewood Cliffs, N. J.: Prentice-Hall, 1959, Chs. 12 and 13. An analysis of what is involved in a choice between hedonist and nonhedonist theories.

Ewing, A. C. *Ethics.* New York: Macmillan, 1953, Ch. 3. Brief criticism of hedonism.

Moore, G. E. *Ethics.* New York: Oxford Univ. Press, 1947, Chs. 1 and 2.

———. *Principia Ethica.* New York: Cambridge Univ. Press, 1959 (also paper). Ch. 6. Various things argued to be intrinsically good.

Rashdall, Hastings. *Theory of Good and Evil.* New York: Oxford Univ. Press, 1924. 2 vols., Vol. 1, Ch. 7. Defense of traits of character as being good; and other things in addition to pleasure.

Sharp, F. C. *Ethics.* New York: Appleton-Century, 1928, Ch. 19.

2

WHICH ACTS
ARE RIGHT?

The conclusions you may have reached about what things are intrinsically desirable still leave open the question "What acts are *right?*" At least they do if we are correct in thinking that "is right" means something different from "is desirable," whether intrinsically or instrumentally or both—a point already made and for which we shall argue further shortly. We shall now discuss the answer to "What acts are right?" This question, however, will be a familiar one to the reader, since the preceding chapter contained selections stating or implying several authors' answers to it— for instance, Mill's, Aristotle's, and Nietzsche's.

What need we know in order to have an adequate answer to this question? We cannot, of course, discuss all possible particular moral problems. It will be enough if we get clearly *all the general* principles about right and wrong. Indeed, we need less than this. It is enough to know the *fundamental* principles of right and wrong—a set of premises from which, given suitable factual information, we could infer all true general principles about right and wrong. (Actually, most philosophers would be content with much less than this—with a few typical principles and with clues for deciding other cases when need to decide arises.) Something else is important: to see the *reasoning* by which it may be shown that a given principle is a defensible or tenable principle.

The philosophers whose work is presented below differ rather widely among themselves, both on what the basic principles are and on the reasoning which can properly be used in support of them.

1. The concept of moral rightness

What exactly are we asking when we ask whether it would be *right* to do a certain thing? In Chapter 3 we shall see that there is much disagreement about this when we come to rather sophisticated points. But there are some things we can say in answer to this query about which there is relatively little dispute. It will be helpful to summarize some of these things so as to be sure we all know roughly what question is being debated.

The first thing to notice is that we are all familiar with the use of "right" and "wrong" in typical situations. What we are asking, when we ask which acts are right or wrong, is which acts are right or wrong *in the sense* these words bear in these typical situations. For instance, on p. 1 we described the case of a graduate student who wondered whether it would be wrong not to give another student certain information. It is this sense of "wrong" that we have in mind throughout the present chapter. Presumably the reader will be able to think of many situations in which he has used, or might use, the word in this sense.

A second thing we can do to make clear the sense of "right" and "wrong" we have in mind is to point out the relations of these words to other words with which the reader will be familiar. Let us look at some of these connections.

(1) Obviously "is morally right" is the contradictory of "is morally wrong": for if an act is not wrong it is right, and if it is not right it is wrong.

(2) How are these words related to "is morally obligatory, everything considered"? Take first "right." If it is morally obligatory to do something, then it is right to do it; but it does not follow from the fact that something is morally right (e.g., eating dinner at home with my family tonight) that it is morally obligatory. Now consider "wrong." If it is morally obligatory to do something, it is wrong not to do it; and, it seems, if it is wrong to do something, it is morally obligatory not to do it. Some writers have questioned this last, saying that it does not follow from something's being wrong that there are moral obligations at all. And they are right that sometimes it is wrong to do something when no obligations to anyone are involved—at least, obligations of the kind we have to someone to whom we have made a promise or who has done us a favor. Thus it may be wrong for a man to commit suicide, even though it is by no means clear that he has a corresponding obligation to anyone. But what is proved is merely that an act can be morally obligatory when there is no moral obligation to anyone; hence it can still be true, as we initially asserted, that whenever it is wrong to do something it is morally obligatory not to do it, even if there are no moral obligations to anyone.

(3) What is true of the relations of "it is right [wrong] to" and "it is morally obligatory to" is also true of the relations of "it would be right [wrong] to" and "one ought to" in one of the senses of "ought." The word "ought," however, is used in several different but closely related senses, and we shall not attempt to discuss all these different uses.

(4) Reasons have already been stated (pp. 16-17) for thinking that for an action to be right or wrong is different from its being desirable, even from its being "the best thing to do." But what is the difference?

The question is not easy, but I think you will agree, after reflection, that when you say "you are morally obligated to" you are saying "you are morally bound to," whereas you are not saying or implying this when you say "the best thing for you to do is to." We can bring this difference out in an example. It may be that the best thing to do, if I am planning a solo trip to Europe, is to include at least two weeks of Paris in my stay;

in one way or another, we may suppose, staying there would increase my long-range enjoyments more than anything else I could do. But surely I am morally free to choose otherwise if I wish; there is not an obligation to go to Paris, as there would be if I were a professor and had promised to give lectures there.

But in what sense am I "morally bound" if I am obligated? It is tempting to say that the laws of God *require* me, in the sense that I shall be punished if I do not do the thing. But, as we shall see in Chapter 3, this sense seems not to be what we mean. Some writers have thought that to be morally bound is to be *obliged by somebody*, by some sort of threat. This view, again, is mistaken; we can think we are morally bound when we do not suppose that anyone is requiring us. A much more convincing proposal is that to say that we are morally bound to do something is to say that failure to do the thing will show a defect of character, or that if we fail we shall be morally culpable or reprehensible or justly open to criticism. This view is much closer. Even so, however, it is only approximately true. For we are *not* necessarily morally culpable, open to just criticism, or convicted of a defect of character, if we fail to do what we are morally bound to do. These things are true, if we do what is wrong, *only if we have no valid excuse*. This qualification is an extremely important one. The most we can assert is that "you are morally bound to" means "if you fail, you will be morally culpable unless you have a valid excuse." This very qualification, however, helps to shed light on the difference between "you are morally obligated to" and "the best thing for you to do is." For one *needs no excuse* in order to defend one's character or to show that one is not morally culpable if one merely chooses to do what is not best when there was no obligation. One is free to do less than the best without reflection on one's character. Whereas, if an act is morally wrong, if there is an obligation not to do it, then one *does* need an excuse if one hopes to show that one's action is not open to criticism.

(5) The qualification just mentioned serves to highlight another mistaken identification against which we issued warnings earlier (p. 2). It is crucially important to distinguish—however closely related they may be—the concept of the morally obligatory, and the corresponding concepts of right and wrong, from the concepts of the morally culpable, the morally blameworthy, and the reprehensible. These concepts are distinct, although they are the more likely to be confused because the word "wrong" *is* sometimes used synonymously with "culpable" or "morally blameworthy." In order to mark the difference, it will be helpful to label the sense of "wrong" with which we are here concerned as the *objective sense* of "wrong" and to contrast it with that sense of "wrong" which is synonymous with "reprehensible" (what has sometimes been called the "subjective" and at other times the "putative" sense of "wrong").

Failure to mark this distinction leads to fatal confusions in moral thinking. To see this confusion, let us look at a piece of faulty reasoning which occurs all too often. Suppose a person believes, rightly, that he will not be morally culpable for doing something if he sincerely believes it to be right, and suppose he has come to believe it right independently of any rationalizations favoring himself or his personal preferences. He may then go on to infer that it is not morally wrong, in *any* sense, for him to do this thing. This inference is erroneous. The reason, obviously, is that one cannot infer, from knowing something is not wrong in the sense of "culpable," that it is not wrong in the objective sense. What the person has overlooked is that believing sincerely that something is right (and so on) is a valid defense against imputations of bad character and just disapproval even if what has been done is, objectively, really wrong. The availability of this excuse breaks down any inference from objective wrongdoing to culpability. But, conversely, its availability also breaks down inference from lack of culpability to objective rightness of the act. Thus we may be morally blameless, guiltless, not open to criticism, but still have done something objectively wrong. It must be emphasized: Doing what is objectively wrong does not necessarily result in being morally blameworthy; and not being morally blameworthy—in view of some excuse—does not mean that one has not done what is objectively wrong.

When we ask questions like that asked by the graduate student mentioned earlier, or when we ask whether racial segregation is morally right or whether it is right to cheat in an examination or to break dormitory rules, we are asking about what is objectively right. What we are concerned with in the present chapter is what is morally right or wrong in this objective sense—although we concede that some philosophers do not keep the distinction as clearly in mind as they should. Moral theories like utilitarianism are best construed as assertions about which acts are right or wrong in this objective sense.

It is hoped that the foregoing remarks will at least have served to identify, if not fully to explain, the sense in which, in this chapter, we are inquiring which acts are *right*. Some of the reader's further puzzles will, we hope, come in for discussion in Chapter 3.

2. Is moral wrongness a reason for action?

Students often raise a question it may be helpful to examine at this point. It is: "Suppose it is shown that it would be morally wrong, in the objective sense, to do so-and-so. Has a *good reason* been given me for not doing so-and-so if it happens that I *want* to do it — or if it is really to my personal interest to do it? If you think a reason has been given, please explain how, or in what sense, it has been."

The following readings include one discussion proposing an answer to this question. But some brief remarks here may be helpful.

The person who is troubled by this question should begin by asking what he means by it, what in principle he would accept as an answer to it. Will showing that something would be wrong be a "good reason" only if this "reason" will in fact *make you prefer* not to do it? If so, then you do not give an alcoholic a good reason for refusing a further drink by showing him that another will cost him his life, unless the showing makes him stop. Or is it enough, for giving a "good reason," that something be brought forward in view of which you would act in a certain way *if* you were in a calm and dispassionate frame of mind, and saw clearly everything that was involved? If the person who is troubled about this issue will make up his mind just what his problem is, perhaps it will resolve itself.

There are some further points to be made. (1) Doing what is right and having a well-developed trait of conscientiousness in one's character are highly likely to pay off, in terms of personal gains, in the long run. The life of one who shortchanges others is not apt to be a happy one. Of course, we cannot say that it is always to one's long-range advantage to do what is right. (2) Many people are so built that they simply *want* to do what is right; and one of their cherished personal goals is to be a person of good character, or at least not a person with a defective character. If you are one of these people, then showing that a certain action would be wrong will be showing a consideration in view of which you will not want to do it. (3) Most, or perhaps even all, defensible moral rules or principles are rules, the general acceptance of and conformity with which is important for the welfare of everyone. Now, if you are the kind of person who wishes to do his share of those unpleasant things, the general doing of which is essential for the welfare of everybody, then again the showing that some action would be wrong, or at least an infringement of a moral rule important for the welfare of all, will be the showing of a consideration in view of which you will not want to do it.

How far these points are an answer to any puzzle the reader has at this point, he will have to decide, after examining what really it is he wants to know. We are *not* claiming, however, that the above points show that *always* and *for everybody* doing what is right promotes personal advantage, is in line with what one wishes, or is even in line with what one would wish if one were dispassionate and had a clear view of what is involved.

3. Types of proposal about which acts are right

The historically important theories about the fundamental principles of right and wrong conduct are conveniently classified under four major headings.

Some philosophers have argued that the rightness of an act depends entirely on the intrinsic value of its results or consequences. Such theories may be called "result" or "teleological" theories. In contrast, other philosophers have claimed that at least in some instances something besides consequences is important for rightness or wrongness; sometimes, they say, the fact that an act satisfies some formal condition, or has a certain property such as the property of being the fulfilment of a promise, determines that it is right or wrong. This view is conveniently called "formalism" or "deontology."

Result theories are of two major species. Some have said that whether an act is right depends only on its effects on the *agent*; thus an act is said to be right if and only if it produces states for the agent which are at least as good, intrinsically, as those that would have been produced by anything else the agent might have done instead. Such a view is called *egoism*. Most result theories, however, assert that an act is right if and only if its total results *for everybody affected* are as desirable intrinsically as would have been produced by anything else the agent might have done. This view is called *universalism* or *utilitarianism*, although the term "utilitarian" usually is employed to imply that the individual thinks that the only thing intrinsically desirable is pleasure, happiness, or some state of personal welfare.

There is still another type of theory which stands midway between formalism and the universalist type of result theory. It holds that the rightness of an act is fixed by results. But it is not the results of a *particular act* that fix whether it is right or wrong; it is the consequences, roughly, of that kind of act being permitted or prohibited, morally, *in general*, or of that kind of act being generally recognized as being wrong. The writers who support this kind of theory assert that it has moral implications different from those of the straight universalist or utilitarian theories. They think, for instance, that sometimes a straight universalist theory would permit or even prescribe the telling of a lie when this other type of theory would forbid it — since, while the consequences would be good in this case, the consequences of recognizing such an action as morally permissible would be bad. This type of theory is conveniently called "rule-utilitarianism"; and for the sake of contrast we can call the straight universalist theory "act-utilitarianism."

Our four major theories are, then: formalism (deontology), egoism, act-utilitarianism, and rule-utilitarianism. All of these theories can consistently be combined with any of the hedonist or nonhedonist views represented in the preceding chapter. Naturally, it is very important which view about what is intrinsically desirable is adopted by anyone who accepts one of the result theories, for the view on this point has a direct implication for conclusions about what is right or wrong.

All four major theories are represented by the following readings. Butler, Kant, and Ross are all formalists, of different sorts. Thomas Hobbes is an egoist; Medlin is a critic of this view. Jeremy Bentham and J. S. Mill are often classified as act-utilitarians, although there is probably more to be said for construing them as rule-utilitarians; Bentham is also a hedonist, and Mill is very nearly so. John Rawls advocates a rule-utilitarian type of theory, and the view of St. Thomas Aquinas, while unique in some ways, is close to this type of theory.

Kurt Baier (1917-)

A PARADOX ABOUT RIGHT ACTION,
AND REASONS FOR ACTING RIGHTLY

The readings which follow concern two puzzles which we have just been discussing. The first arises in the following situation: Suppose a man ought, objectively, to do A but *thinks* that he ought, objectively, to do B, which is incompatible with doing A. The question then arises: "Should he do A or B?" We hesitate, on the one hand, to say a person ought to do something which he thinks he ought not; and, on the other hand, it seems odd to say that he ought to do something incompatible with what he objectively ought to do. Baier considers what we should say, in the first of the following two selections. His answer, in effect, is that the puzzle dissolves if we distinguish the two questions just distinguished above: the question of what a person objectively ought to do and the question of whether a person is morally blameworthy for what he has done.

The second puzzle is this: Suppose a man rightly thinks his moral obligation is to do A; but he also rightly thinks that the course which will contribute most to his own personal welfare is to do B, which is incompatible with doing A. The question then is: "Is there good reason for preferring A to B?" Many philosophers have thought this question just confused, supposing that once something has been shown to be morally obligatory, no more need be said, and that to suppose more can be said is simply to show one's misunderstanding of what it is to be morally obligated. Many people remain puzzled, however, and in response to such puzzlement Baier does try to say more; he thinks the puzzlement is legitimate but that it can be resolved.

Baier was born in Austria and has a degree from the University of Vienna. He also holds degrees from Oxford University and the University of Melbourne. He is professor of philosophy at Canberra University in Australia.

From Kurt Baier, *The Moral Point of View: A Rational Basis of Ethics*. Copyright 1958 by Cornell University, published by Cornell University Press, Ithaca, N.Y., and reprinted with their permission.

THE MORAL POINT OF VIEW

THE PARADOX OF "SUBJECTIVITY"

"But," it might now be objected, "are you not slurring over a problem here? Should you not say 'in accordance with what *are* the best reasons' rather than 'in accordance with what we *take to be* the best reasons'? For surely we could make a mistake, and then, if we act in accordance with what we *take* to be the best reasons, we may well be acting contrary to what *are* the best reasons. And that would never do, for we want to do what we should do and not what we think we should do." This is a variant of what, in ethics, is known as "the paradox of subjective duty." The paradox arises when we consider a case in which the agent has made a mistake in deliberation and we ask ourselves what the agent ought to do, that which he *thinks* he ought to do or that which he *really* ought to do. Neither answer seems tenable. If we say he ought to do what he thinks he ought to do, it follows that sometimes he *really* ought to do what he thinks *wrongly* he ought to do, that is, what he ought not to do. If we say he ought to do what he *really* ought to do, then it follows that he sometimes ought to do what he thinks (wrongly) he ought *not* to do, but he surely cannot be expected to do that.

Consider an example. Count O. believes his wife to have been unfaithful to him with Casanova. He believes he ought to kill both Casanova and the Countess. In fact, however, she has not been unfaithful to him and, therefore, he really ought not to kill either Casanova or the Countess. What, then, ought he to do? What he *thinks* he ought, "his subjective duty"? Or what he *really* ought, "his objective duty"?

The paradox disappears as soon as we remember that, in deliberation, the agent has to accomplish a theoretical and a practical task and that, in evaluating the agent's performance, we can criticize him on two quite different grounds, the inadequate performance either of his theoretical task or of his practical task. When this distinction is drawn, the paradoxical question vanishes. For all that we can in reason demand of the *agent* is that he should first complete, to the best of his ability, his theoretical task *and then act in accordance with* whatever answer he has arrived at in completing that task. The agent, therefore, can never ask himself, "Should I do what I *think* best or what *is* best?" For his theoretical task is to find out, to the best of his ability, what *is* best. The completion of his theoretical task will be what he thinks best. He cannot therefore *at the same time think another course of action to be the best.* Count O. can think either that killing Casanova and his wife is the best *or* that something else is the best. He cannot think that killing Casanova and his wife is what he *thinks* best and at the same time that not killing anybody *really* is the best. In the course of deliberation, only the question What is the best action? can arise. Thus, for the agent the paradoxical question is impossible.

But can it not arise for a critic or judge? Surely, after he has acted, Count O. himself, or another critic or judge, can ask the paradoxical question: ought Count O. to have done what he thought he ought or what he really ought? But now the cramp is felt only because we do not take into account the many different grounds on which an agent can be criticized. The paradoxical question suggests that there are only two alternatives: either he must be criticized *whenever* he does not do what he ought, or he must be criticized *whenever* he does not do what he thinks he ought. But this is not so. He can be criticized for the inadequate performance of any part of his complex task.

Moreover, the criticism may have to be modified in the light of yet further facts. We must, for instance, criticize Count O. if he was negligent or careless in the performance of his theoretical task, if he has not taken sufficient care in finding out whether his wife really was unfaithful to him and with whom. In a matter as serious as the killing of two people, the utmost care about the facts is surely indicated. Count O. would have to be condemned for killing Casanova and his wife, not because he ought not to have killed them — that is, because he failed in his "objective duty" — but because he was careless in establishing what that "duty" was. He would have to be condemned for what he did because he culpably failed in his theoretical task.

The case would be different if, after careful investigations, Count O. had come to the conclusion that he had insufficient evidence and must wait for proof before killing either Casanova or his wife. But one day, on meeting Casanova and his wife in suspicious circumstances, he stabs Casanova in a fit of jealousy. In this case, we condemn Count O., not because he did not do what he really ought, but because he did not do what he thought he ought to do. We do not think him a whit more justified in killing Casanova and his wife even if it were true that they had committed adultery. Our condemnation of Count O. in this case is modified only by our knowledge that neither Casanova nor the lady had any right to complain or to feel aggrieved. They got their deserts, but Count O. is to be condemned for unjustifiably administering them.

The following is an even more complicated case. Suppose Count O., having concluded that both ought to die, relents after killing Casanova. He is then guilty of a double failure: he has culpably failed in his theoretical and in his practical task. Nevertheless, we do not condemn him for sparing his wife. A great variety of considerations enters into this verdict: the fact that great harm was avoided, that his motive was good (he may have loved or felt pity for her or thought she was seduced by a great master of the art), and so on.

To sum up, the paradox vanishes when we realize that the question cannot arise for the agent at all and that, though it can arise for a critic, it does not then force on him condemnation on only one of two grounds, failure either in his "objective" or in his "subjective" duty. The reason why only these two alternatives are thought to be available is, of course, that the question is always construed as arising for the agent, who is imagined as wavering between doing what he thinks he ought and doing what he really ought. For between what other alternatives could the agent be wavering? But, of course, the agent cannot waver between these two alternatives at all, and the critic has other alternatives to consider. Hence no paradox.

The whole problem could never have arisen if moral philosophers had not so blatantly misused the words "right," "duty," and "ought." For then they could never have telescoped so many different questions into one, namely, "Ought he to do the subjectively or the objectively right act?" This question can perplex us only because we have no more than a confused understanding of its sense. As soon as we make clear to ourselves the various different things it can mean, the problem vanishes. If we mean "Does thinking that something is one's duty make it so?" the answer is obviously "No." If we mean "Does the moral man do what after careful consideration he has worked out to be what he ought to do?" the answer is, of course, "Yes." If it means "Should a person who has worked out what he ought to do as carefully and conscientiously as can be expected be rebuked for acting on his results?" the answer is plainly "No." If it means "Is a man ever to be rebuked for doing what he thought he ought to do?" the answer is, of course, "Yes, sometimes, for he may culpably have failed in his theoretical task."

Having shown that the so-called paradox of subjective duty is merely a muddle, we can ignore the above objection. Admittedly, when we ask, "What shall I do?" we want to know what we really ought to do. Hence we should make as careful and determined an effort as we can to complete our theoretical task. For then the chances are that what, as a result, we shall *think* the best course of action *really* will be so. But whatever in the light of later critical examination our success may be pronounced to have been, at the time we can of course follow nothing but the outcome of our careful deliberations. We can never be condemned for doing that, except when we have been careless in our theoretical task, and then we are not really condemned for following the outcome of our theoretical endeavors, but for not being careful in them. . . .

THE SUPREMACY OF MORAL REASONS

Are moral reasons really superior to reasons of self-interest as we all believe? Do we really have reason on our side when we follow moral reasons against self-interest? What reasons could there be for being moral? Can we really give an answer to "Why should we be moral?" It is obvious that all these questions come to the same thing. When we ask, "Should we be moral?" or "Why should we be moral?" or "Are moral reasons superior to all others?" we ask to be shown the reason for being moral. What is this reason?

Let us begin with a state of affairs in which reasons of self-interest are supreme. In such a state everyone keeps his impulses and inclinations in check when and only when they would lead him into behavior detrimental to his own interest. Everyone who follows reason will discipline himself to rise early, to do his exercises, to refrain from excessive drinking and smoking, to keep good company, to marry the right sort of girl, to work and study hard in order to get on, and so on. However, it will often happen that people's interests conflict. In such a case, they will have to resort to ruses or force to get their own way. As this becomes known, men will become suspicious, for they will regard one another as scheming competitors for the good things in life. The universal supremacy of the rules of self-interest must lead to what Hobbes called the state of nature. At the same time, it will be clear to everyone that universal obedience to certain rules overriding self-interest would produce a state of affairs which serves everyone's interest much better than his unaided pursuit of it in a state where everyone does the same. Moral rules are universal rules designed to override those of self-interest when following the latter is harmful to others. "Thou shalt not kill," "Thou shalt not lie," "Thou shalt not steal" are rules which forbid the inflicting of harm on someone else even when this might be in one's interest.

The very *raison d'être* of a morality is to yield reasons which overrule the reasons of self-interest in those cases when everyone's following self-interest would be harmful to everyone. Hence moral reasons are superior to all others.

"But what does this mean?" it might be objected. "If it merely means that we do so regard them, then you are of course right, but your contention is useless, a mere point of usage. And how could it mean any more? If it means that we not only do so regard them, but *ought* so to regard them, then there must be *reasons* for saying this. But there could not be any reasons for it. If you offer reasons of self-interest, you are arguing in a circle. Moreover, it cannot be true that it is always in my interest to treat moral reasons as superior to reasons of self-interest. If it were, self-interest and morality could never conflict, but they notoriously do. It is equally circular to argue that there are moral reasons for saying that one ought to treat moral reasons as superior to reasons of self-interest. And what other reasons are there?"

The answer is that we are now looking at the world from the point of view of *anyone*. We are not examining particular alternative courses of action before this or that person; we are examining two alternative worlds, one in which moral reasons are always treated by everyone as superior to reasons of self-interest and one in which the reverse is the practice. And we can see that the first world is the better world, because we can see that the second world would be the sort which Hobbes describes as the state of nature.

This shows that I ought to be moral, for when I ask the question "What ought I to do?" I am asking, "Which is the course of action supported by the best reasons?" But since it has just been shown that moral reasons are superior to reasons of self-interest, I have been given a reason for being moral, for following moral reasons rather than any other, namely, they are better reasons than any other.

But is this always so? Do we have a reason for being moral whatever the conditions we find ourselves in? Could there not be situations in which it is not true that we have reasons for being moral, that, on the contrary, we have reasons for ignoring the demands of morality? Is not Hobbes right in saying that in a state of nature the laws of nature, that is, the rules of morality, bind only *in foro interno?*

Hobbes argues as follows.

(i) To live in a state of nature is to live outside society. It is to live in conditions in which there are no common ways of life and, therefore, no reliable expectations about other people's behavior other than that they will follow their inclination or their interest.

(ii) In such a state reason will be the enemy of co-operation and mutual trust. For it is too risky to hope that other people will refrain from protecting their own interests by the preventive elimination of probable or even possible dangers to them. Hence reason will counsel everyone to avoid these risks by preventive action. But this leads to war.

(iii) It is obvious that everyone's following self-interest leads to a state of affairs which is desirable from no one's point of view. It is, on the contrary, desirable that everybody should follow rules overriding self-interest whenever that is to the detriment of others. In other words, it is desirable to bring about a state of affairs in which all obey the rules of morality.

(iv) However, Hobbes claims that in the state of nature it helps nobody if a single person or a small group of persons begins to follow the rules of morality, for this could only lead to the extinction of such individuals or groups. In such a state, it is therefore contrary to reason to be moral.

(v) The situation can change, reason can support morality, only when the presumption about other people's behavior is reversed. Hobbes thought that this could be achieved only by the creation of an absolute ruler with absolute power to enforce his laws. We have already seen that this is not true and that it is quite different if people live in a society, that is, if they have common ways of life, which are taught to all members and somehow enforced by the group. Its members have reason to expect their fellows generally to obey its rules, that is, its religion, morality, customs, and law, even when doing so is not, on certain occasions, in their interest. Hence they too have reason to follow these rules.

Is this argument sound? One might, of course, object to step (i) on the grounds that this is an empirical proposition for which there is little or no evidence. For how can we know whether it is true that people in a state of nature would follow only their inclinations or, at best, reasons of self-interest, when nobody now lives in that state or has ever lived in it?

However, there is some empirical evidence to support this claim. For in the family of nations, individual states are placed very much like individual persons in a state of nature. The doctrine of the sovereignty of nations and the absence of an effective international law and police force are a guarantee that nations live in a state of nature, without commonly accepted rules that are somehow enforced. Hence it must be granted that living in a state of nature leads to living in a state in which individuals act either on impulse or as they think their interest dictates. For states pay only lip service to morality. They attack their hated neighbors when the opportunity arises. They start preventive wars in order to destroy the enemy before he can deliver his knockout blow. Where interests conflict, the stronger party usually has his way, whether his claims are justified or not. And where the relative strength of the parties is not obvious, they usually resort to arms in order to determine "whose side God is on." Treaties are frequently concluded but, morally speaking, they are not worth the paper they are written on. Nor do the partners regard them as contracts binding in the ordinary way, but rather as public expressions of the belief of the governments concerned that for the time being their alliance is in the interest of the allies. It is well understood that such treaties may be canceled before they reach their predetermined end or simply broken when it suits one partner. In international affairs, there are very few examples of *Nibelungentreue*, although statesmen whose countries have profited from keeping their treaties usually make such high moral claims.

It is, moreover, difficult to justify morality in international affairs. For suppose a highly moral statesman were to demand that his country adhere to a treaty obligation even though this meant its ruin or possibly its extinction. Suppose he were to say that treaty obligations are sacred and must be kept whatever the consequences. How could he defend such a policy? Perhaps one might argue that someone has to make a start in order to create mutual confidence in international affairs. Or one might say that setting a good example is the best way of inducing others to follow suit. But such a defense would hardly be sound. The less skeptical one is about the genuineness of the cases in which nations have adhered to their treaties from a sense of moral obligation, the more skeptical one must be about the effectiveness of such examples of virtue in effecting a change of international practice. Power politics still govern in international affairs.

We must, therefore, grant Hobbes the first step in his argument and admit that in a state of nature people, as a matter of psychological fact, would not follow the dictates of morality. But we might object to the next step that knowing this psychological fact about other people's behavior constitutes a reason for behaving in the same way. Would it not still be immoral for anyone to ignore the demands of morality even though he knows that others are likely or certain to do so, too? Can we offer as a justification for morality the fact that no one is entitled to do wrong just because someone else is doing wrong? This argument begs the question whether it *is* wrong for anyone in this state to disregard the demands of morality. It cannot be wrong to break a treaty or make preventive war if we have no reason to obey the moral rules. For to say that it is wrong to do so is to say that we ought not to do so. But if we have no reason for obeying the moral rule, then we have no reason overruling self-interest, hence no reason for keeping the treaty when keeping it is not in our interest, hence it is not true that we have a reason for keeping it, hence not true that we ought to keep it, hence not true that it is wrong not to keep it.

I conclude that Hobbes's argument is sound. Moralities are systems of principles whose acceptance by everyone as overruling the dictates of self-interest is in the interest of everyone alike, though following the rules of a morality is not of course identical with following self-interest. If it were, there could be no conflict between a morality and self-interest and no point in having moral rules overriding self-interest. Hobbes is also right in saying that the application of this system of rules is in accordance with reason only in social conditions, that is, when there are well-established ways of behavior.

The answer to our question "Why should we be moral?" is therefore as follows. We should be moral because being moral is following rules designed to overrule self-interest whenever it is in the interest of everyone alike that everyone should set aside his interest. It is not self-contradictory to say this, because it may be in one's interest *not* to follow one's interest at times. We have already seen that enlightened self-interest acknowledges this point. But while enlightened self-interest does not require any genuine sacrifice from anyone, morality does. In the interest of the possibility of the good life for everyone, voluntary sacrifices are sometimes required from everybody. Thus, a person might do better for himself by following enlightened self-interest rather than morality. It is not possible, however, that *everyone* should do better for himself by following enlightened self-interest rather than morality. The best possible life *for everyone* is possible only by everyone's following the rules of morality, that is, rules which quite frequently may require individuals to make genuine sacrifices.

It must be added to this, however, that such a system of rules has the support of reason only where people live in societies, that is, in conditions in which there are established common ways of behavior. Outside society, people have no reason for following such rules, that is, for being moral. In other words, outside society, the very distinction between right and wrong vanishes.

QUESTIONS

1. What is "the paradox of subjective duty"?
2. What does Baier mean by distinguishing the "theoretical" from the "practical" task of an agent?

3. Why is it that the paradox cannot arise for the agent himself?

4. Why does Baier think it arises for a critic only if he fails to distinguish a number of different grounds for condemnation?

5. Suppose Count O. kills his wife's lover, mistakenly thinking this is what he objectively ought to do. Then for which moral offense should he be condemned: unjustifiable homicide, holding a false moral opinion through carelessness, both, or what?

6. Baier says, "Moral rules are universal rules designed to override those of self-interest when following the latter is harmful to others." Do you think this is obviously true of *all* moral rules?

7. Does Baier attempt to show that there is never really conflict between self-interest and obligation?

8. Suppose Baier and Hobbes are right that a world in which everyone follows moral rules would be better than a world in which everyone followed self-interest. Does their rightness prove there is good reason for me to follow moral rules?

9. Baier says: "We should be moral because being moral is following rules designed to overrule self-interest whenever it is in the interest of everyone alike that everyone should set aside his interest. . . . A person might do better for himself by following enlightened self-interest rather than morality. It is not possible, however, that *everyone* should do better for himself by following enlightened self-interest rather than morality." Does this statement resolve your puzzle? Why?

10. Baier says: "Outside society, people have no reason for . . . being moral. In other words, outside society, the very distinction between right and wrong vanishes." Do you think this is true? How about cruelty to animals?

Thomas Hobbes (1588-1679)

EGOISM AS AN IMPLICATION OF PSYCHOLOGY

We occasionally meet people who say it is right and reasonable for everyone to look out exclusively for his own interests and to pay no attention to the interests of others: or at least they say no one can prove that such conduct isn't right and reasonable. It is less frequent that we find someone who actually says each has a *moral obligation* to look only to his own interests; but such a position is a logical possibility, and it is amusing to ask ourselves how we might dispute such a view if we met it. It is convenient to label either of these views, both the more and the less extreme, with the term "ethical egoism,"

Nobody knows what the common-sense egoist would say in defense of his views, if they were challenged; very possibly he would argue that everyone naturally looks out for himself first and that it can scarcely be wrong to do what is natural for man and what everyone else does too.

Such a position was seriously defended, with some qualifications, by Thomas Hobbes, as one of the premises or foundations to which appeal may be made in an explanation why citizens are obligated to obey laws or commands of the sovereign civil authority. Hobbes's view has been the object of vigorous discussion for the past three centuries.

Hobbes, the son of a vicar, was a graduate of Magdalen College, Oxford, in 1608, at which time he became tutor (later secretary) to the son of William Cavendish, the first Earl of Devonshire. Hobbes spent most of his life in the household of the Devonshire family, but, in the course of trips abroad with his charges, he had opportunity to meet the leading intellectual figures of the continent, and the position of the family gave him frequent contact with the major personalities of English life. Hobbes wrote numerous works on the nature of man and of man's relation to government, the best known of which is *Leviathan*, published in 1651.

From Thomas Hobbes, *Philosophical Rudiments Concerning Government and Society*. First published in English in 1651. Reprinted in Hobbes, Thomas. *The English Works of Thomas Hobbes.* Ed. by Sir William Molesworth. London: Bohn, 1841, Vol. 2.

PHILOSOPHICAL RUDIMENTS CONCERNING GOVERNMENT AND SOCIETY

CHAPTER 1   OF THE STATE OF MEN WITHOUT CIVIL SOCIETY

1. The faculties of human nature may be reduced unto four kinds; bodily strength, experience, reason, passion. Taking the beginning of this following doctrine from these, we will declare, in the first place, what manner of inclinations men who are endued with these faculties bear towards each other, and whether, and by what faculty they are born apt for society, and to preserve themselves against mutual violence; then proceeding, we will shew what advice was necessary to be taken for this business, and what are the conditions of society, or of human peace; that is to say, (changing the words only), what are the fundamental *laws of nature*.

2. The greatest part of those men who have written aught concerning commonwealths, either suppose, or require us or beg of us to believe,

that man is a creature born fit[1] for society. The Greeks call him ζῷον πολιτικον; and on this foundation they so build up the doctrine of civil society, as if for the preservation of peace, and the government of mankind, there were nothing else necessary than that men should agree to make certain covenants and conditions together, which themselves should then call laws. Which axiom, though received by most, is yet certainly false; and an error proceeding from our too slight contemplation of human nature. For they who shall more narrowly look into the causes for which men come together, and delight in each other's company, shall easily find that this happens not because naturally it could happen no otherwise, but by accident. For if by nature one man should love another, that is, as man, there could no reason be returned why every man should not equally love every man, as being equally man; or why he should rather frequent those, whose society affords him honour or profit. We do not therefore by nature seek society for its own sake, but that we may receive some honour or profit from it; these we desire primarily, that secondarily. How, by what advice, men do meet, will be best known by observing those things which they do when they are met. For if they meet for traffic, it is plain every man regards not his fellow, but his business; if to discharge some office, a certain market-friendship is begotten, which hath more of jealousy in it than true love, and whence factions sometimes may arise, but good will never; if for pleasure and recreation of mind, every man is wont to please himself most with those things which stir up laughter, whence he may, according to the nature of that which is ridiculous, by comparison of another man's defects and infirmities, pass the more current in his own opinion. And although this be sometimes innocent and without offence, yet it is manifest they are not so much delighted with the society, as their own vain glory. But for

---

[1] *Born fit.*] Since we now see actually a constituted society among men, and none living out of it, since we discern all desirous of congress and mutual correspondence, it may seem a wonderful kind of stupidity, to lay in the very threshold of this doctrine such a stumbling block before the reader, as to deny *man to be born fit for society.* Therefore I must more plainly say, that it is true indeed, that to man by nature, or as man, that is, as soon as he is born, solitude is an enemy; for infants have need of others to help them to live, and those of riper years to help them to live well. Wherefore I deny not that men (even nature compelling) desire to come together. But civil societies are not mere meetings, but bonds, to the making whereof faith and compacts are necessary; the virtue whereof to children and fools, and the profit whereof to those who have not yet tasted the miseries which accompany its defects, is altogether unknown; whence it happens, that those, because they know not what society is, cannot enter into it; these, because ignorant of the benefit it brings, care not for it. Manifest therefore it is, that all men, because they are born in infancy, are born unapt for society. Many also, perhaps most men, either through defect of mind or want of education, remain unfit during the whole course of their lives; yet have they, infants as well as those of riper years, a human nature. Wherefore man is made fit for society not by nature, but by education. Furthermore, although man were born in such a condition as to desire it, it follows not, that he therefore were born fit to enter into it. For it is one thing to desire, another to be in capacity fit for what we desire; for even they, who through their pride, will not stoop to equal conditions, without which there can be no society, do yet desire it.

the most part, in these kinds of meeting we wound the absent; their whole life, sayings, actions are examined, judged, condemned. Nay, it is very rare but some present receive a fling as soon as they part; so as his reason was not ill, who was wont always at parting to go out last. And these are indeed the true delights of society, unto which we are carried by nature, that is, by those passions which are incident to all creatures, until either by sad experience or good precepts it so fall out, which in many it never happens, that the appetite of present matters be dulled with the memory of things past: without which the discourse of most quick and nimble men on this subject, is but cold and hungry.

But if it so happen, that being met they pass their time in relating some stories, and one of them begins to tell one which concerns himself; instantly every one of the rest most greedily desires to speak of himself too; if one relate some wonder, the rest will tell you miracles, if they have them; if not, they will feign them. Lastly, that I may say somewhat of them who pretend to be wiser than others: if they meet to talk of philosophy, look, how many men, so many would be esteemed masters, or else they not only love not their fellows, but even persecute them with hatred. So clear is it by experience to all men who a little more narrowly consider human affairs, that all free congress ariseth either from mutual poverty, or from vain glory, whence the parties met endeavour to carry with them either some benefit, or to leave behind them that same ἐυδοϰιμεῖν, some esteem and honour with those, with whom they have been conversant. The same is also collected by reason out of the definitions themselves of *will, good, honour, profitable*. For when we voluntarily contract society, in all manner of society we look after the object of the will, that is, that which every one of those who gather together, propounds to himself for good. Now whatsoever seems good, is pleasant, and relates either to the senses, or the mind. But all the mind's pleasure is either glory, (or to have a good opinion of one's self), or refers to glory in the end; the rest are sensual, or conducing to sensuality, which may be all comprehended under the word *conveniences*. All society therefore is either for gain, or for glory; that is, not so much for love of our fellows, as for the love of ourselves. But no society can be great or lasting, which begins from vain glory. Because that glory is like honour; if all men have it no man hath it, for they consist in comparison and precellence. Neither doth the society of others advance any whit the cause of my glorying in myself; for every man must account himself, such as he can make himself without the help of others. But though the benefits of this life may be much furthered by mutual help; since yet those may be better attained to by dominion than by the society of others, I hope no body will doubt, but that men would much more greedily be carried by nature, if all fear were removed, to obtain dominion, than to gain society. We must therefore resolve, that the original of all great and lasting societies consisted not in the mutual good will men had towards each other, but in the mutual fear [2] they had of each other.

3. The cause of mutual fear consists partly in the natural equality of men, partly in their mutual will of hurting: whence it comes to pass, that we can neither expect from others, nor promise to ourselves the least security. For if we look on men full-grown, and consider how brittle the frame of our human body is, which perishing, all its strength, vigour, and wisdom itself perisheth with it; and how easy a matter it is, even for the weakest man to kill the strongest: there is no reason why any man, trusting to his own strength, should conceive himself made by nature above others. They are equals, who can do equal things one against the other; but they who can do the greatest things, namely, kill, can do equal things. All men therefore among themselves are by nature equal; the inequality we now discern, hath its spring from the civil law.

4. All men in the state of nature have a desire and will to hurt, but not proceeding from the same cause, neither equally to be condemned. For one man, according to that natural equality which is among us, permits as much to others as he assumes to himself; which is an argument of a temperate man, and one that rightly values his power. Another, supposing himself above others, will have a license to do what he lists, and challenges respect and honour, as due to him before others; which is an argument of a fiery spirit. This man's will to hurt ariseth from vain glory, and the false esteem he hath of his own strength; the other's from the necessity of defending himself, his liberty, and his goods, against this man's violence.

5. Furthermore, since the combat of wits is the fiercest, the greatest discords which are, must necessarily arise from this contention. For in this case it is not only odious to contend against, but also not to consent. For not to approve of what a man saith, is no less than tacitly to accuse him of an error in that thing which he speaketh: as in very many things to dissent, is as much as if you accounted him a fool whom you dissent from. Which may appear hence, that there are no wars so sharply waged as be-

2 *The mutual fear.*] It is objected: it is so improbable that men should grow into civil societies out of fear, that if they had been afraid, they would not have endured each other's looks. They presume, I believe, that to fear is nothing else than to be affrighted. I comprehend in this word *fear*, a certain foresight of future evil; neither do I conceive flight the sole property of fear, but to distrust, suspect, take heed, provide so that they may not fear, is also incident to the fearful. They who go to sleep, shut their doors; they who travel, carry their swords with them, because they fear thieves. Kingdoms guard their coasts and frontiers with forts and castles; cities are compact with walls; and all for fear of neighbouring kingdoms and towns. Even the strongest armies, and most accomplished for fight, yet sometimes parley for peace, as fearing each other's power, and lest they might be overcome. It is through fear that men secure themselves by flight indeed, and in corners, if they think they cannot escape otherwise; but for the most part, by arms and defensive weapons; whence it happens, that daring to come forth they know each other's spirits. But then if they fight, civil society ariseth from the victory; if they agree, from their agreement.

tween sects of the same religion, and factions of the same commonweal, where the contestation is either concerning doctrines or politic prudence. And since all the pleasure and jollity of the mind consists in this, even to get some, with whom comparing, it may find somewhat wherein to triumph and vaunt itself; it is impossible but men must declare sometimes some mutual scorn and contempt, either by laughter, or by words, or by gesture, or some sign or other; than which there is no greater vexation of mind, and than from which there cannot possibly arise a greater desire to do hurt.

6. But the most frequent reason why men desire to hurt each other, ariseth hence, that many men at the same time have an appetite to the same thing; which yet very often they can neither enjoy in common, nor yet divide it; whence it follows that the strongest must have it, and who is strongest must be decided by the sword.

7. Among so many dangers therefore, as the natural lusts of men do daily threaten each other withal, to have a care of one's self is so far from being a matter scornfully to be looked upon, that one has neither the power nor wish to have done otherwise. For every man is desirous of what is good for him, and shuns what is evil, but chiefly the chiefest of natural evils, which is death; and this he doth by a certain impulsion of nature, no less than that whereby a stone moves downward. It is therefore neither absurd nor reprehensible, neither against the dictates of true reason, for a man to use all his endeavours to preserve and defend his body and the members thereof from death and sorrows. But that which is not contrary to right reason, that all men account to be done justly, and with right. Neither by the word *right* is anything else signified, than that liberty which every man hath to make use of his natural faculties according to right reason. Therefore the first foundation of natural right is this, that *every man as much as in him lies endeavour to protect his life and members.*

8. But because it is in vain for a man to have a right to the end, if the right to the necessary means be denied him, it follows, that since every man hath a right to preserve himself, he must also be allowed a right *to use all the means, and do all the actions, without which he cannot preserve himself.*

9. Now whether the means which he is about to use, and the action he is performing, be necessary to the preservation of his life and members or not, he himself, by the right of nature, must be judge. For if it be contrary to right reason that I should judge of mine own peril, say, that another man is judge. Why now, because he judgeth of what concerns me, by the same reason, because we are equal by nature, will I judge also of things which do belong to him. Therefore it agrees with right reason, that is, it is the right of nature that I judge of his opinion, that is, whether it conduce to my preservation or not.

10. Nature hath given to *every one a right to all*; that is, it was law-

ful for every man, in the bare state of nature,[3] or before such time as men had engaged themselves by any covenants or bonds, to do what he would, and against whom he thought fit, and to possess, use, and enjoy all what he would, or could get. Now because whatsoever a man would, it therefore seems good to him because he wills it, and either it really doth, or at least seems to him to contribute towards his preservation, (but we have already allowed him to be judge, in the foregoing article, whether it doth or not, insomuch as we are to hold all for necessary whatsoever he shall esteem so), and by the 7th article it appears that by the right of nature those things may be done, and must be had, which necessarily conduce to the protection of life and members, it follows, that in the state of nature, to have all, and do all, is lawful for all. And this is that which is meant by that common saying, *nature hath given all to all*. From whence we understand likewise, that in the state of nature profit is the measure of right.

11. But it was the least benefit for men thus to have a common right to all things. For the effects of this right are the same, almost, as if there had been no right at all. For although any man might say of every thing, *this is mine*, yet could he not enjoy it, by reason of his neighbour, who having equal right and equal power, would pretend the same thing to be his.

12. If now to this natural proclivity of men, to hurt each other, which they derive from their passions, but chiefly from a vain esteem of themselves, you add, the right of all to all, wherewith one by right invades, the other by right resists, and whence arise perpetual jealousies and suspicions on all hands, and how hard a thing it is to provide against an enemy invading us with an intention to oppress and ruin, though he come with a small number, and no great provision; it cannot be denied but that the

---

[3] *In the bare state of nature*.] This is thus to be understood: what any man does in the bare state of nature, is injurious to no man; not that in such a state he cannot offend God, or break the laws of nature; for injustice against men presupposeth human laws, such as in the state of nature there are none. Now the truth of this proposition thus conceived, is sufficiently demonstrated to the mindful reader in the articles immediately foregoing; but because in certain cases the difficulty of the conclusion makes us forget the premises, I will contract this argument, and make it most evident to a single view. Every man hath right to protect himself, as appears by the seventh article. The same man therefore hath a right to use all the means which necessarily conduce to this end, by the eighth article. But those are the necessary means which he shall judge to be such, by the ninth article. He therefore hath a right to make use of, and to do all whatsoever he shall judge requisite for his preservation; wherefore by the judgment of him that doth it, the thing done is either right or wrong, and therefore right. True it is therefore in the bare state of nature, &c. But if any man pretend somewhat to tend necessarily to his preservation, which yet he himself doth not confidently believe so, he may offend against the laws of nature, as in the third chapter of this book is more at large declared. It hath been objected by some: if a son kill his father, doth he him no injury? I have answered, that a son cannot be understood to be at any time in the state of nature, as being under the power and command of them to whom he owes his protection as soon as ever he is born, namely, either his father's or his mother's, or him that nourished him; as is demonstrated in the ninth chapter.

natural state of men, before they entered into society, was a mere war, and that not simply, but a war of all men against all men. For what is WAR, but that same time in which the will of contesting by force is fully declared, either by words or deeds? The time remaining is termed PEACE.

13. But it is easily judged how disagreeable a thing to the preservation either of mankind, or of each single man, a perpetual war is. But it is perpetual in its own nature; because in regard of the equality of those that strive, it cannot be ended by victory. For in this state the conqueror is subject to so much danger, as it were to be accounted a miracle, if any, even the most strong, should close up his life with many years and old age. They of America are examples hereof, even in this present age: other nations have been in former ages; which now indeed are become civil and flourishing, but were then few, fierce, short-lived, poor, nasty, and deprived of all that pleasure and beauty of life, which peace and society are wont to bring with them. Whosoever therefore holds, that it had been best to have continued in that state in which all things were lawful for all men, he contradicts himself. For every man by natural necessity desires that which is good for him: nor is there any that esteems a war of all against all, which necessarily adheres to such a state, to be good for him. And so it happens, that through fear of each other we think it fit to rid ourselves of this condition, and to get some fellows; that if there needs must be war, it may not yet be against all men, nor without some helps.

14. Fellows are gotten either by constraint, or by consent; by constraint, when after fight the conqueror makes the conquered serve him, either through fear of death, or by laying fetters on him: by consent, when men enter into society to help each other, both parties consenting without any constraint. But the conqueror may by right compel the conquered, or the strongest the weaker, (as a man in health may one that is sick, or he that is of riper years a child), unless he will choose to die, to give caution of his future obedience. For since the right of protecting ourselves according to our own wills, proceeded from our danger, and our danger from our equality, it is more consonant to reason, and more certain for our conservation, using the present advantage to secure ourselves by taking caution, than when they shall be full grown and strong, and got out of our power, to endeavour to recover that power again by doubtful fight. And on the other side, nothing can be thought more absurd, than by discharging whom you already have weak in your power, to make him at once both an enemy and a strong one. From whence we may understand likewise as a corollary in the natural state of men, that *a sure and irresistible power confers the right of dominion and ruling over those who cannot resist*; insomuch, as the right of all things that can be done, adheres essentially and immediately unto this omnipotence hence arising.

15. Yet cannot men expect any lasting preservation, continuing thus in the state of nature, that is, of war, by reason of that equality of power, and other human faculties they are endued withal. Wherefore to seek peace,

where there is any hopes of obtaining it, and where there is none, to enquire out for auxiliaries of war, is the dictate of right reason, that is, the law of nature; as shall be showed in the next chapter.

QUESTIONS

1. Does Hobbes think human beings are naturally altruistic?
2. Why does he think men fear one another and are motivated to aim at one another's hurt?
3. What does he think people mean when they call things "good" or "bad"? If he is right in his view, could there be such a thing as good or evil, good or bad conduct, apart from relation to human desires?
4. What is it which man desires "by a certain impulsion of nature, no less than that whereby a stone moves downward"?
5. What is Hobbes's inference, from this psychological premise, about what conduct is right, reasonable, and not reprehensible? What is the meaning of saying, "Nature hath given all to all"?
6. Why does Hobbes make an exception, asserting that a son has no natural right to kill his father in order to gain personal ends?
7. In what sense is the natural state of mankind one of perpetual war?
8. Given his premises, how do you suppose Hobbes might go on to support the claim that men are obligated to obey the laws of their own civil society?

SUGGESTIONS FOR FURTHER READING

Hobbes, Thomas. *Leviathan*. Ed. by M. Oakeshott. Oxford: Blackwell (n.d.).
Hobbes, Thomas. *English Works*. Ed. by Sir William Molesworth. London: Bohn, 1839-45.

Bowle, John. *Hobbes and His Critics*. New York: Oxford Univ. Press, 1952.
Laird, John. *Hobbes*. London: Benn, 1934.
Peters, Richard. *Hobbes*. Baltimore: Penguin Books, 1956.
Stephen, Sir Leslie. *Hobbes*. New York: Macmillan, 1914.
Strauss, Leo. *The Political Philosophy of Hobbes*. New York: Oxford Univ. Press, 1936.
Taylor, A. E. *Thomas Hobbes*. New York: Dodge, 1908.
Warrender, Howard. *The Political Philosophy of Hobbes*. New York: Oxford Univ. Press, 1957.

Brian Medlin   (1927-   )

ETHICAL EGOISM IS INCONSISTENT

A good many philosophers have thought that whatever the difficulties of establishing moral principles, at least egoism can be definitively refuted. The following selection is a vigorous defense of this view, by a young Australian philosopher. This discussion is printed here instead of somewhat similar ones because it makes a minimum of assumptions, so that the reader will hardly object to it because it takes too much for granted. Indeed, perhaps the author makes too few assumptions! (The reader, incidentally, need not assume that the author's account of what is "generally accepted" is correct; a great many philosophers would not agree that ethical principles are "arbitrary.") Even so, probably most philosophers would think there is a fatal defect in the argument, and the reader should be on the lookout for it. If the following discussion fails to prove that egoism is inconsistent, it may nevertheless suggest good reasons for rejecting egoism as one's fundamental ethical principle.

Medlin received his undergraduate training in philosophy at the University of Adelaide. He is currently (1960-61) a student at Corpus Christi College, Oxford, having served during 1959-60 as assistant lecturer in philosophy at the University College of Ghana.

From Brian Medlin, "Ultimate Principles and Ethical Egoism," *Australasian Journal of Philosophy*, Vol. 35 (1957), pp. 111-18. Reprinted by permission of the author and of the editor of the *Australasian Journal of Philosophy*.

ULTIMATE PRINCIPLES AND ETHICAL EGOISM

I believe that it is now pretty generally accepted by professional philosophers that ultimate ethical principles must be arbitrary. One cannot derive conclusions about what should be merely from accounts of what is the case; one cannot decide how people ought to behave merely from one's knowledge of how they do behave. To arrive at a conclusion in ethics one must have at least one ethical premiss. This premiss, if it be in turn a conclusion, must be the conclusion of an argument containing at least one ethical premiss. And so we can go back, indefinitely but not for ever. Sooner or later, we must come to at least one ethical premiss which is not deduced but baldly asserted. Here we must be a-rational; neither rational nor irrational, for here there is no room for reason even to go wrong.

But the triumph of Hume in ethics has been a limited one. What appears quite natural to a handful of specialists appears quite monstrous to the majority of decent intelligent men. At any rate, it has been my experience that people who are normally rational resist the above account of the logic of moral language, not by argument — for that can't be done — but by tooth and nail. And they resist from the best motives. They see the philosopher wantonly unravelling the whole fabric of morality. If our ultimate principles are arbitrary, they say, if those principles came out of thin air, then anyone can hold any principle he pleases. Unless moral assertions are statements of fact about the world and either true or false, we can't claim that any man is wrong, whatever his principles may be, whatever his behaviour. We have to surrender the luxury of calling one another scoundrels. That this anxiety flourishes because its roots are in confusion is evident when we consider that we don't call people scoundrels, anyhow, for being mistaken about their facts. Fools, perhaps, but that's another matter. Nevertheless, it doesn't become us to be high-up. The layman's uneasiness, however irrational it may be, is very natural and he must be reassured.

People cling to objectivist theories of morality from moral motives. It's a very queer thing that by doing so they often thwart their own purposes. There are evil opinions abroad, as anyone who walks abroad knows. The one we meet with most often, whether in pub or parlour, is the doctrine that everyone should look after himself. However refreshing he may find it after the high-minded pomposities of this morning's editorial, the good fellow knows this doctrine is wrong and he wants to knock it down. But while he believes that moral language is used to make statements either true or false, the best he can do is to claim that what the egoist says is false. Unfortunately, the egoist can claim that it's true. And since the supposed fact in question between them is not a publicly ascertainable one, their disagreement can never be resolved. And it is here that even good fellows waver, when they find they have no refutation available. The egoist's word seems as reliable as their own. Some begin half to believe that perhaps it is possible to supply an egoistic basis for conventional morality, some that it may be impossible to supply any other basis. I'm not going to try to prop up our conventional morality, which I fear to be a task beyond my strength, but in what follows I do want to refute the doctrine of ethical egoism. I want to resolve this disagreement by showing that what the egoist says is inconsistent. It is true that there are moral disagreements which can never be resolved, but this isn't one of them. The proper objection to the man who says 'Everyone should look after his own interests regardless of the interests of others' is not that he isn't speaking the truth, but simply that he isn't speaking.

We should first make two distinctions. This done, ethical egoism will lose much of its plausibility.

1. UNIVERSAL AND INDIVIDUAL EGOISM

Universal egoism maintains that everyone (including the speaker) ought to look after his own interests and to disregard those of other people except in so far as their interests contribute towards his own.

Individual egoism is the attitude that the egoist is going to look after himself and no one else. The egoist cannot promulgate that he is going to look after himself. He can't even preach that he *should* look after himself and preach this alone. When he tries to convince me that he should look after himself, he is attempting so to dispose me that I shall approve when he drinks my beer and steals Tom's wife. I cannot approve of his looking after himself and himself alone without so far approving of his achieving his happiness, regardless of the happiness of myself and others. So that when he sets out to persuade me that he should look after himself regardless of others, he must also set out to persuade me that I should look after him regardless of myself and others. Very small chance he has! And if the individual egoist cannot promulgate his doctrine without enlarging it, what he has is no doctrine at all.

A person enjoying such an attitude may believe that other people are fools not to look after themselves. Yet he himself would be a fool to tell them so. If he did tell them, though, he wouldn't consider that he was giving them *moral* advice. Persuasion to the effect that one should ignore the claims of morality because morality doesn't pay, to the effect that one has insufficient selfish motive and, therefore, insufficient motive for moral behaviour is not moral persuasion. For this reason I doubt that we should call the individual egoist's attitude an ethical one. And I don't doubt this in the way someone may doubt whether to call the ethical standards of Satan "ethical" standards. A malign morality is none the less a morality for being malign. But the attitude we're considering is one of mere contempt for all moral considerations whatsoever. An indifference to morals may be wicked, but it is not a perverse morality. So far as I am aware, most egoists imagine that they are putting forward a doctrine in ethics, though there may be a few who are prepared to proclaim themselves individual egoists. If the good fellow wants to know how he should justify conventional morality to an individual egoist, the answer is that he shouldn't and can't. Buy your car elsewhere, blackguard him whenever you meet, and let it go at that.

2. CATEGORICAL AND HYPOTHETICAL EGOISM

Categorical egoism is the doctrine that we all ought to observe our own interests, *because that is what we ought to do*. For the categorical egoist the egoistic dogma is the ultimate principle in ethics.

The hypothetical egoist, on the other hand, maintains that we all ought to observe our own interests, because . . . . If we want such and such an end, we must do so and so (look after ourselves). The hypothetical egoist is not a real egoist at all. He is very likely an unwitting utilitarian who believes mistakenly that the general happiness will be increased if each man looks wisely to his own. Of course, a man may believe that egoism is enjoined on us by God and he may therefore promulgate the doctrine and observe it in his conduct, not in the hope of achieving thereby a remote end, but simply in order to obey God. But neither is *he* a real egoist. He believes, ultimately, that we should obey God, even should God command us to altruism.

An ethical egoist will have to maintain the doctrine in both its universal and categorical forms. Should he retreat to hypothetical egoism he is no longer an egoist. Should he retreat to individual egoism his doctrine, while logically impregnable, is no longer ethical, no longer even a doctrine. He may wish to quarrel with this and if so, I submit peacefully. Let him call himself what he will, it makes no difference. I'm a philosopher, not a rat-catcher, and I don't see it as my job to dig vermin out of such burrows as individual egoism.

Obviously something strange goes on as soon as the ethical egoist tries to promulgate his doctrine. What is he doing when he urges upon his audience that they should each observe his own interests and those interests alone? Is he not acting contrary to the egoistic principle? It cannot be to his advantage to convince them, for seizing always their own advantage they will impair his. Surely if he does believe what he says, he should try to persuade them otherwise. Not perhaps that they should devote themselves to his interests, for they'd hardly swallow that; but that everyone should devote himself to the service of others. But is not to believe that someone should act in a certain way to try to persuade him to do so? Of course, we don't always try to persuade people to act as we think they should act. We may be lazy, for instance. But in so far as we believe that Tom should do so and so, we have a tendency to induce him to do so and so. Does it make sense to say: "Of course you should do this, but for goodness' sake don't"? Only where we mean: "You should do this for certain reasons, but here are even more persuasive reasons for not doing it." If the egoist believes ultimately that others should mind themselves alone, then, he must persuade them accordingly. If he doesn't persuade them, he is no universal egoist. It certainly makes sense to say: "I know very well that Tom should act in such and such a way. But I know also that it's not to my advantage that he should so act. So I'd better dissuade him from it." And this is just what the egoist must say, if he is to consider his own advantage and disregard everyone else's. That is, he must behave as an individual egoist, if he is to be an egoist at all.

He may want to make two kinds of objection here:

1. That it will not be to his disadvantage to promulgate the doctrine, provided that his audience fully understand what is to their ultimate advantage. This objection can be developed in a number of ways, but I think that it will always be possible to push the egoist into either individual or hypothetical egoism.

2. That it is to the egoist's advantage to preach the doctrine if the pleasure he gets out of doing this more than pays for the injuries he must endure at the hands of his converts. It is hard to believe that many people would be satisfied with a doctrine which they could only consistently promulgate in very special circumstances. Besides, this looks suspiciously like individual egoism in disguise.

I shall say no more on these two points because I want to advance a further criticism which seems to me at once fatal and irrefutable.

Now it is time to show the anxious layman that we have means of dealing with ethical egoism which are denied him; and denied him by just that objectivism which he thinks essential to morality. For the very fact that our ultimate principles must be arbitrary means they can't be anything we please. Just because they come out of thin air they can't come out of hot air. Because these principles are not propositions about matters of fact and cannot be deduced from propositions about matters of fact, they must be the fruit of our own attitudes. We assert them largely to modify the attitudes of our fellows but by asserting them we express our own desires and purposes. This means that we cannot use moral language cavalierly. Evidently, we cannot say something like 'All human desires and purposes are bad.' This would be to express our own desires and purposes, thereby committing a kind of absurdity. Nor, I shall argue, can we say 'Everyone should observe his own interests regardless of the interests of others.'

Remembering that the principle is meant to be both universal and categorical, let us ask what kind of attitude the egoist is expressing. Wouldn't that attitude be equally well expressed by the conjunction of an infinite number of avowals thus? —

I want myself to come out on top	and	I don't care about Tom, Dick, Harry . . .
and		and
I want Tom to come out on top	and	I don't care about myself, Dick, Harry . . .
and		and
I want Dick to come out on top	and	I don't care about myself, Tom, Harry . . .
and		and
I want Harry to come out on top	and	I don't care about myself, Dick, Tom . . .
etc.		etc.

From this analysis it is obvious that the principle expressing such an attitude must be inconsistent.

But now the egoist may claim that he hasn't been properly understood. When he says 'Everyone should look after himself and himself alone,' he means 'Let each man do what he wants regardless of what anyone else wants.' The egoist may claim that what he values is merely that he and Tom and Dick and Harry should each do what he wants and not care about what anyone else may want and that this doesn't involve his principle in any inconsistency. Nor need it. But even if it doesn't, he's no better off. Just what does he value? Is it the well-being of himself, Tom, Dick and Harry or merely their going on in a certain way regardless of whether or not this is going to promote their well-being? When he urges Tom, say, to do what he wants, is he appealing to Tom's self-interest? If so, his attitude can be expressed thus:

> I want myself to be happy   I want myself not to care
> and   and   about Tom, Dick,
> I want Tom to be happy   Harry . . .

We need go no further to see that the principle expressing such an attitude must be inconsistent. I have made this kind of move already. What concerns me now is the alternative position the egoist must take up to be safe from it. If the egoist values merely that people should go on in a certain way, regardless of whether or not this is going to promote their well-being, then he is not appealing to the self-interest of his audience when he urges them to regard their own interests. If Tom has any regard for himself at all, the egoist's blandishments will leave him cold. Further, the egoist doesn't even have his own interest in mind when he says that, like everyone else, he should look after himself. A funny kind of egoism this turns out to be.

Perhaps now, claiming that he is indeed appealing to the self-interest of his audience, the egoist may attempt to counter the objection of the previous paragraph. He may move into 'Let each man do what he wants and let each man disregard what others want when their desires clash with his own.' Now his attitude may be expressed thus:

> I want everyone to be happy   I want everyone to dis-
> and   regard the happiness
> of others when their
> happiness   clashes
> with his own.

The egoist may claim justly that a man can have such an attitude and also that in a certain kind of world such a man could get what he wanted. Our objection to the egoist has been that his desires are incompatible. And this is still so. If he and Tom and Dick and Harry did go on as he recommends by saying 'Let each man disregard the happiness of others, when their happiness conflicts with his own,' then assuredly they'd all be completely miserable. Yet he wants them to be happy. He is attempting to counter this by saying that it is merely a fact about the world that they'd make one another miserable by going on as he recommends. The world could conceivably have been different. For this reason, he says, this principle is not inconsistent. This argument may not seem very compelling, but I advance it on the egoist's behalf because I'm interested in the reply to it. For now we don't even need to tell him that the world isn't in fact like that. (What it's like makes no difference.) Now we can point out to him that he is arguing not as an egoist but as a utilitarian. He has slipped into hypothetical egoism to save his principle from inconsistency. If the world were such that we always made ourselves and others happy by doing one another down, then we could find good utilitarian reasons for urging that we should do one another down.

If, then, he is to save his principle, the egoist must do one of two things. He must give up the claim that he is appealing to the self-interest of his audience, that he has even his own interest in mind. Or he must admit that, in the conjunction on page 155, although 'I want everyone to be happy' refers to ends, nevertheless 'I want everyone to disregard the happiness of others when their happiness conflicts with his own' can refer only to means. That is, his so-called ultimate principle is really compounded of a principle and a moral rule subordinate to that principle. That is, he is really a utilitarian who is urging everyone to go on in a certain way so that everyone may be happy. A utilitarian, what's more, who is ludicrously mistaken about the nature of the world. Things being as they are, his moral rule is a very bad one. Things being as they are, it can only be deduced from his principle by means of an empirical premiss which is manifestly false. Good fellows don't need to fear him. They may rest easy that the world is and must be on their side and the best thing they can do is be good.

It may be worth pointing out that objections similar to those I have brought against the egoist can be made to the altruist. The man who holds that the principle 'Let everyone observe the interests of others' is both universal and categorical can be compelled to choose between two alternatives, equally repugnant. He must give up the claim that he is concerned for the well-being of himself and others. Or he must admit that, though 'I want everyone to be happy' refers to ends, nevertheless 'I want everyone to disregard his own happiness when it conflicts with the happiness of others' can refer only to means.

I have said from time to time that the egoistic principle is inconsistent. I have not said it is contradictory. This for the reason that we can, without contradiction, express inconsistent desires and purposes. To do so is not to say anything like 'Goliath was ten feet tall and not ten feet tall.' Don't we all want to eat our cake and have it too? And when we say we do we aren't asserting a contradiction. We are not asserting a contradiction whether we be making an avowal of our attitudes or stating a fact about them. We all have conflicting motives. As a utilitarian exuding benevolence I want the man who mows my landlord's grass to be happy, but as a slug-a-bed I should like to see him scourged. None of this, however, can do the egoist any good. For we assert our ultimate principles not only to express our own attitudes but also to induce similar attitudes in others, to dispose them to conduct themselves as we wish. In so far as their desires conflict, people don't know what to do. And, therefore, no expression of incompatible desires can ever serve for an ultimate principle of human conduct.

QUESTIONS

1. What is the difference between "universal egoism" and "individual egoism," according to Medlin? Why does he think individual egoism may be ignored? Why does he think it isn't even an ethical theory?
2. What is the difference between "categorical egoism" and "hypothetical egoism," according to him?
3. Why does he think it inconsistent for the categorical universal egoist to avow his own doctrine? Would it be inconsistent for such an egoist to be convinced of his own doctrine but to refrain from public pronouncements?
4. Why does he think that the egoist principle — assuming that moral pronouncements express the speaker's attitudes — must express inconsistent attitudes? Can you think of any consistent attitude it might be expressing? Perhaps it urges sympathetic favoring of the welfare of anyone who happens to be an agent, at least while he is acting?
5. Is Medlin's argument seriously weakened if we do not require the egoist to make a successful appeal to the self-interest of other persons on behalf of his view?
6. Why does Medlin think his argument applies equally well as a criticism of pure altruism?
7. Does Medlin claim there is any formal logical contradiction in the egoist's principle? If so, what is it?

Bishop Joseph Butler (1692-1752)

A CRITIQUE OF EGOIST PSYCHOLOGY

The preceding selection from Medlin attacks Hobbes's ethical conclusion. The present selection criticizes its psychological base. It is aimed, however, at a broader target than just Hobbes's cynical views about human motivation. It is directed in part at the general thesis that human motives are purely selfish, that people are moved to act only by the prospect of enhancing their own welfare or pleasure — "psychological egoism." (We may recall that Mill and others employed a form of this doctrine in their proof that happiness is the sole good.) Butler's critique is also intended to expose the misconceptions behind the widespread assumption that a person who concerns himself with the welfare of other people is apt to get less happiness for himself than is one who keeps his mind solely on his own welfare.

Butler's attack consists in trying to show that human beings have many desires, interests, or "appetites" — for food, drink, fame, children, and sometimes for the welfare of other persons — and that happiness or enjoyment comes in the satisfaction of these desires. Thus, far from it being the case that the only motivating desire is for one's own enjoyment or welfare, enjoyment or happiness presupposes desires for other things. Moreover, satisfaction of a desire for the welfare of others, he argues, is as real a form of personal happiness as any other.

Butler was a clergyman. He held various posts in England, including those of preacher at the Rolls Chapel, London, dean of St. Paul's Cathedral, London, and bishop of Bristol and of Durham. His major work was *The Analogy of Religion, Natural and Revealed, to the Constitution and Course of Nature.*

From Joseph Butler, *Fifteen Sermons upon Human Nature.* First printed 1726. 2nd ed. London, 1729.

FIFTEEN SERMONS

SERMON XI   UPON THE LOVE OF OUR
NEIGHBOUR (PREACHED ON ADVENT SUNDAY)

And if there be any other commandment, it is briefly comprehended in this saying, namely, Thou shalt love thy neighbour as thyself. — Rom. 13:9

It is commonly observed that there is a disposition in men to complain of the viciousness and corruption of the age in which they live, as greater than that of former ones; which is usually followed with this further observation that mankind has been in that respect much the same in all times. Now, not to determine whether this last be not contradicted by the accounts of history, thus much can scarce be doubted — that vice and folly take different turns, and some particular kinds of it are more open and avowed in some ages than in others; and I suppose it may be spoken of as very much the distinction of the present to profess a contracted spirit and greater regards to self-interest than appears to have been done formerly. Upon this account it seems worth while to inquire whether private interest is likely to be promoted in proportion to the degree in which self-love engrosses us, and prevails over all other principles, or whether the contracted affection may not possibly be so prevalent as to disappoint itself, and even contradict its own end, private good.

And since, further, there is generally thought to be some peculiar kind of contrariety between self-love and the love of our neighbour, between the pursuit of public and of private good, insomuch that when you are recommending one of these, you are supposed to be speaking against the other; and from hence arises a secret prejudice against and frequently open scorn of all talk of public spirit and real goodwill to our fellow creatures; it will be necessary to inquire what respect benevolence hath to self-love, and the pursuit of private interest to the pursuit of public; or whether there be anything of that peculiar inconsistency and contrariety between them, over and above what there is between self-love and other passions and particular affections, and their respective pursuits.

These inquiries, it is hoped, may be favorably attended to; for there shall be all possible concessions made to the favorite passion, which hath so much allowed to it, and whose cause is so universally pleaded: it shall be treated with the utmost tenderness and concern for its interests.

In order to this, as well as to determine the forementioned questions, it will be necessary to consider the nature, the object, and end of that self-love, as distinguished from other principles or affections in the mind and their respective objects.

Every man hath a general desire of his own happiness; and likewise a variety of particular affections, passions, and appetites, to particular external objects. The former proceeds from, or is, self-love, and seems inseparable from all sensible creatures, who can reflect upon themselves and their own interest or happiness, so as to have that interest an object to their minds: what is to be said of the latter is, that they proceed from, or together make up, that particular nature, according to which man is made. The object the former pursues is somewhat internal, our own happiness, enjoyment, satisfaction; whether we have or have not a distinct particular perception what it is, or wherein it consists: the objects of the latter are this or that particular external thing, which the affections tend towards, and of which it hath always a particular idea or perception. The principle we call self-love never seeks anything external for the sake of the thing, but only as a means of happiness or good: particular affections rest in the external things themselves. One belongs to man as a reasonable creature reflecting upon his own interest or happiness: the other, though quite distinct from reason, are as much a part of human nature.

That all particular appetites and passions are towards *external things themselves*, distinct from the *pleasure arising from them*, is manifested from hence, that there could not be this pleasure, were it not for that prior suitableness between the object and the passion: there could be no enjoyment or delight for one thing more than another, from eating food more than from swallowing a stone, if there were not an affection or appetite to one thing more than another.

Every particular affection, even the love of our neighbour, is as really our own affection, as self-love; and the pleasure arising from its gratification is as much my own pleasure, as the pleasure self-love would have from knowing I myself should be happy some time hence, would be my own pleasure. And if, because every particular affection is a man's own, and the pleasure arising from its gratification his own pleasure, or pleasure to himself, such particular affection must be called self-love. According to this way of speaking, no creature whatever can possibly act but merely from self-love; and every action and every affection whatever is to be resolved up into this one principle. But then this is not the language of mankind: or, if it were, we should want words to express the difference between the principle of an action, proceeding from cool consideration that it will be to my own advantage; and an action, suppose of revenge, or of friendship by which a man runs upon certain ruin, to do evil or good to another. It is manifest the principles of these actions are totally different, and so want different words to be distinguished by: all that they agree in is, that they both proceed from, and are done to gratify an inclination in a man's self. But the principle or inclination in one case is self-love; in the other, hatred, or love of another. There is then a distinction between the cool principle of self-love, or general desire of our own happiness, as one part of our nature, and one principle of action; and the particular affections towards particular external objects, as another principle of action. How much soever, therefore, is to be allowed to self-love, yet it cannot be allowed to be the whole of our inward constitution; because, you see, there are other parts or principles which come into it.

Further, private happiness or good is all which self-love can make us desire or be concerned about. In having this consists its gratification; it is an affection to ourselves — a regard to our own interest, happiness, and private good: and in the proportion a man hath this, he is interested, or a lover of himself. Let this be kept in mind, because there is commonly, as I shall presently have occasion to observe, another sense put upon these words. On the other hand, particular affections tend towards particular external things; these are their objects; having these is their end; in this consists their gratification: no matter whether it be, or be not, upon the whole, our interest or happiness. An action, done from the former of these principles, is called an interested action. An action, proceeding from any of the latter, has its denomination of passionate, ambitious, friendly, revengeful, or any other, from the particular appetite or affection from which it proceeds. Thus self-love, as one part of human nature, and the several particular principles as the other part, are themselves, their objects, and ends, stated and shown.

From hence it will be easy to see how far, and in what ways, each of these can contribute and be subservient to the private good of the individual. Happiness does not consist in self-love. The desire of happiness is no more the thing itself, than the desire of riches is the possession or enjoyment of them. People may love themselves with the most entire and unbounded affection, and yet be extremely miserable. Neither can self-love any way help them out, but by setting them on work to get rid of the causes of their misery, to gain or make use of those objects which are by nature adapted to afford satisfaction. Happiness or satisfaction consists only in the enjoyment of those objects which are by nature suited to our several particular appetites, passions, and affections. So that if self-love wholly engrosses us and leaves no room for any other principle, there can be absolutely no such thing at all as happiness or enjoyment of any kind whatever; since happiness consists in the gratification of particular passions, which supposes the having of them. Self-love then does not constitute *this* or *that* to be our interest or good; but our interest or good being constituted by nature and supposed self-love, only puts us upon obtaining and securing it. Therefore, if it be possible that self-love may prevail and exert itself in a degree or manner which is not subservient to this end, then it will not follow that our interest will be promoted in proportion to the degree in which that principle engrosses us, and prevails over others. Nay, further, the private and contracted affection, when it is not subservient to this end, private good, may, for anything that appears, have a direct contrary tendency and effect. And if we will consider the matter, we shall see that it often really has. Disengagement is absolutely necessary to enjoyment; and a person may have so steady and fixed an eye upon his own interest, whatever he places it in, as may hinder him from attending to many gratifications within his reach, which others have their minds free and open to. Overfondness for a child is not generally thought to be for its advantage; and, if there be any guess to be from appearances, surely that character we call *selfish* is not the most promising for happiness. Such a temper may plainly be, and exert itself in a degree and manner which may give unnecessary and useless solicitude and anxiety, in a degree and manner which may prevent obtaining the means and materials of enjoyment, as well as the making use of them. Immoderate self-love does very ill consult its own interest; and how much soever a paradox it may appear, it is certainly true, that, even from self-love, we should endeavour to get over all inordinate regard to, and consideration of, ourselves. Every one of our passions and affections hath its natural stint and bound, which may easily be exceeded; whereas our enjoyments can possibly be but in a determinate measure and degree. Therefore such excess of the affection, since it cannot procure any enjoyment, must in all cases be useless, but is generally attended with inconveniences, and often is down-right pain and misery. This holds as much with regard to self-love as to all other affections. The natural degree of it, so far as it sets us on work to gain and make use of the materials of satisfaction, may be to our real advantage; but beyond or beside this, it is in several respects an inconvenience and disadvantage. Thus it appears that private interest is so far from being likely to be promoted in proportion to the degree in which self-love engrosses us, and prevails over all other principles, that *the contracted affection may be so prevalent as to disappoint itself and even contradict its own end, private good.*

"But who, except the most sordidly covetous, ever thought there was any rivalship between the love of greatness, honour, power, or between sensual appetites, and self-love? No; there is a perfect harmony between them. It is by means of these particular appetites and affections that self-love is gratified in enjoyment, happiness, and satisfaction. The competition and rivalship is between self-love and the love of our neighbour. That affection which leads us out of ourselves, makes us regardless of our own interest, and substitute that of another in its stead." Whether then there be any peculiar competition and contrariety in this case, shall now be considered.

Self-love and interestedness was stated to consist in or be an affection to ourselves, a regard to our own private good: it is, therefore, distinct from benevolence, which is an affection to the good of our fellow creatures. But that benevolence is distinct from, that is, not the same thing with self-love, is no reason for its being looked upon with any peculiar suspicion, because every principle whatever, by means of which self-love is gratified, is distinct from it. And all things, which are distinct from each other, are equally so. A man has an affection or aversion to another: that one of these tends to, and is gratified by doing good, that the other tends to, and is gratified by doing harm, does not in the least alter the respect which either one or the other of these inward feelings has to self-love. We use the word *property* so as to exclude any other persons having an interest in that, of which we say a particular man has the property: and we often use the word *selfish* so as to exclude in the same manner all regards to the good of others. But the cases are not parallel: for though that exclusion is really part of the idea of property, yet such positive exclusion, or bringing this peculiar disregard to the good of others into the idea of self-love, is in reality adding to the idea, or changing it from what it was before stated to consist in, namely, in an affection to ourselves. This being the whole idea of self-love, it can no otherwise exclude good-will or love of others, than merely by not including it, no otherwise than it excludes love of arts, or reputation, or of anything else. Neither, on the other hand, does benevolence, any more than love of art or of reputation, exclude self-love. Love of our neighbour, then has just the same respect to, is no more distant from self-love, than hatred of our neighbour, or than love and hatred of anything else. Thus the principles, from which men rush upon certain ruin for the destruction of an enemy, and for the preservation of a friend, have the same respect to the private affection, are equally interested, or equally disinterested: and it is of no avail, whether they are said to be one or the other. Therefore, to those who are shocked to hear virtue spoken of as disinterested, it may be allowed, that it is indeed absurd to speak thus of it; unless hatred, several particular instances of vice, and all the common affections and aversions in mankind are acknowledged to be disinterested too. Is there any less inconsistence between the love of inanimate things, or of creatures merely sensitive, and self-love, than between self-love, and the love of our neighbour? Is desire of, and delight in the happiness of another any more a diminution of self-love, than desire of and delight in the esteem of another? They are both equally desire of and delight in somewhat external to ourselves: either both or neither are so. The object of self-love is expressed in the term self: and every appetite of sense, and every particular affection of the heart, are equally interested or disinterested, because the objects of them all are equally self or somewhat else. Whatever ridicule, therefore, the mention of a disinterested principle or action may be supposed to lie open to, must, upon the matter being thus stated, relate to ambition, and every appetite and particular affection, as much as to benevolence. And indeed all the ridicule, and all the grave perplexity, of which this subject hath had its full share, is merely from words. The most intelligible way of speaking of it seems to be this: that self-love, and the actions done in consequence of it, (for these will presently appear to be the same as to this question) are interested; that particular affections towards external objects, and the actions done in consequence of those affections, are not so. But every one is at liberty to use words as he pleases. All that is here insisted upon is, that ambition, revenge, benevolence, all particular passions whatever, and the actions they produce, are equally interested or disinterested.

Thus it appears, that there is no peculiar contrariety between self-love and benevolence; no greater competition between these, than between any other particular affections and self-love. This relates to the affections themselves. Let us now see whether there be any peculiar contrariety between the respective courses of life which these affections lead to; whether there be any greater competition between the pursuit of private and of public good, than between any other particular pursuits and that of private good.

There seems no other reason to suspect that there is any such peculiar contrariety, but only that the course of action which benevolence leads to, has a more direct tendency to promote the good of others, than that course of action, which love of reputation, suppose, or any other particular affection, leads to. But that any affection tends to the happiness of another, does not hinder its tending to one's own happiness too. That others enjoy the benefit of the air and the light of the sun, does not hinder but that these are as much one's own private advantage now, as they would be if we had the property of them exclusive of all others. So a pursuit which tends to promote the good of another, yet may have as great tendency to promote private interest, as a pursuit which does not tend to the good of another at all, or which is mischievous to him. All particular affections whatever, resentment, benevolence, love of the arts, equally lead to a course of action for their own gratification, i. e., the gratification of ourselves: and the gratification of each gives delight: so far, then, it is manifest they have all the same respect to private interest. Now, take into consideration further, concerning these three pursuits, that the end of the first is the harm; of the second, the good of another; of the last, somewhat indifferent: and is there any necessity, that these additional considerations

should alter the respect which we before saw these three pursuits had to
private interest; or render any one of them less conducive to it than any
other? Thus, one man's affection is to honour, as his end; in order to obtain which, he thinks no pains too great. Suppose another, with such a
singularity of mind, as to have the same affection to public good, as his
end, which he endeavours with the same labour to obtain. In case of success, surely the man of benevolence hath as great enjoyment as the man
of ambition; they both equally having the end, their affections, in the same
degree, tended to; but in case of disappointment, the benevolent man has
clearly the advantage; since endeavouring to do good, considered as a virtuous pursuit, is gratified by its own consciousness, i. e., is in a degree its
own reward.

And as to these two, or benevolence and any other particular passions
whatever, considered in a further view, is forming a general temper, which
more or less disposes us for enjoyment of all the common blessings of life,
distinct from their own gratification: is benevolence less the temper of
tranquility and freedom, than ambition or covetousness? Does the benevolent man appear less easy with himself, from his love to his neighbour?
Does he less relish his being? Is there any peculiar gloom seated on his
face? Is his mind less open to entertainment, or to any particular gratification? Nothing is more manifest, than that being in good humour, which
is benevolence whilst it last, is itself the temper of satisfaction and enjoyment.

Suppose, then, a man sitting down to consider how he might become
most easy to himself, and attain the greatest pleasure he could; all that
which is his real natural happiness; this can only consist in the enjoyment
of those objects which are by nature adapted to our several faculties. These
particular enjoyments make up the sum total of our happiness; and they
are supposed to arise from riches, honours, and the gratification of sensual
appetites. Be it so: yet none profess themselves so completely happy in
these enjoyments, but that there is room left in the mind for others, if
they were presented to them. Nay, these, as much as they engage us, are
not thought so high, but that human nature is capable even of greater.
Now there have been persons in all ages, who have professed that they
found satisfaction in the exercise of charity, in the love of their neighbour,
in endeavouring to promote the happiness of all they had to do with, and
in the pursuit of what is just, and right, and good, as the general bent of
their mind and end of their life; and that doing an action of baseness or
cruelty, would be as great violence to *their* self, as much breaking in upon
their nature, as any external force. Persons of this character would add, if
they might be heard, that they consider themselves as acting in the view
of an infinite Being, who is in a much higher sense the object of reverence and of love, than all the world besides; and, therefore, they could
have no more enjoyment from a wicked action done under his eye, than
the persons to whom they are making their apology could, if all mankind

were the spectators of it; and that the satisfaction of approving themselves
to his unerring judgment, to whom they thus refer all their actions, is a
more continued settled satisfaction than any this world can afford; as also
that they have, no less than others, a mind free and open to all the common innocent gratifications of it such as they are. And, if we go no further, does there appear any absurdity in this? Will any one take upon him
to say, that a man cannot find his account in this general course of life,
as much as in the most unbounded ambition, or the excesses of pleasure?
Or that such a person has not consulted so well for himself, for the satisfaction and peace of his own mind, as the ambitious or dissolute man?
And though the consideration, that God himself will in the end justify
their taste, and support their cause, is not formally to be insisted upon
here; yet thus much comes in, that all enjoyments whatever are much more
clear and unmixed, from the assurance that they will end well. Is it certain, then, that there is nothing in these pretensions to happiness, especially when there are not wanting persons, who have supported themselves
with satisfactions of this kind in sickness, poverty, disgrace, and in the very
pangs of death? whereas, it is manifest all other enjoyments fail in these
circumstances. This surely looks suspicious of having somewhat in it. Self-
love, methinks, should be alarmed. May she not possibly pass over greater
pleasures, than those she is so wholly taken up with?

The short of the matter is no more than this. Happiness consists in
the gratification of certain affections, appetites, passions, with objects which
are by nature adapted to them. Self-love may indeed set us on work to
gratify these: but happiness or enjoyment has no immediate connexion
with self-love, but arises from such gratification alone. Love of our neighbour is one of those affections. This, considered as a virtuous principle, is
gratified by a consciousness of endeavouring to promote the good of others:
but considered as a natural affection, its gratification consists in the actual
accomplishment of this endeavour. Now, indulgence or gratification of this
affection, whether in that consciousness, or this accomplishment, has the
same respect to interest, as indulgence of any other affection; they equally
proceed from, or do not proceed from, self-love; they equally include or
equally exclude, this principle. Thus it appears, that "benevolence and the
pursuit of public good have at least as great respect to self-love and the
pursuit of private good, as any other particular passions, and their respective pursuits."

Neither is covetousness, whether as a temper or pursuit, any exception
to this. For if by covetousness is meant the desire and pursuit of riches
for their own sake, without any regard to or consideration of the uses of
them; this hath as little to do with self-love, as benevolence hath. But by
this word is usually meant, not such madness and total distraction of mind,
but immoderate affection to and pursuit of riches as possessions, in order
to some further end; namely, satisfaction, interest, or good. This, therefore,

is not a particular affection, or particular pursuit, but it is the general principle of self-love, and the general pursuit of our own interest; for which reason, the word *selfish* is by every one appropriated to this temper and pursuit. Now, as it is ridiculous to assert that self-love and the love of our neighbour are the same; so neither is it asserted that following these different affections hath the same tendency and respect to our own interest. The comparison is not between self-love and the love of our neighbour; between pursuit of our own interest, and the interest of others; but between the several particular affections in human nature towards external objects, as one part of the comparison; and the one particular affection to the good of our neighbour, as the one part of it: and it has been shown, that all these have the same respect to self-love and private interest.

There is indeed frequently an inconsistence, or interfering between self-love or private interest, and the several particular appetites, passions, affections, or the pursuits they lead to. But this competition or interfering is merely accidental, and happens much oftener between pride, revenge, sensual gratifications, and private interest, than between private interest and benevolence. For nothing is more common than to see men give themselves up to a passion or an affection to their known prejudice and ruin, and in direct contradiction to manifest and real interest, and the loudest calls of self-love: whereas the seeming competitions and interfering between benevolence and private interest, relate much more to the materials or means of enjoyment, than to enjoyment itself. There is often an interfering in the former, where there is none in the latter. Thus, as to riches: so much money as a man gives away, so much less will remain in his possession. Here is a real interfering. But though a man cannot possibly give without lessening his fortune, yet there are multitudes might give without lessening their own enjoyment; because they may have more than they can turn to any real use or advantage to themselves. Thus, the more thought and time any one employs about the interests and good of others, he must necessarily have less to attend his own; but he may have so ready and large a supply of his own wants, that such thought might be really useless to himself, though of great service and assistance to others.

The general mistake, that there is some greater inconsistence between endeavouring to promote the good of another and self-interest, than between self-interest and pursuing anything else, seems, as hath already been hinted to arise from our notions of property; and to be carried on by this property's being supposed to be itself our happiness or good. People are so very much taken up with this one subject, that they seem from it to have formed a general way of thinking, which they apply to other things that they have nothing to do with. Hence, in a confused and slight way, it might well be taken for granted, that another's having no interest in an affection (*i. e.*, his good not being the object of it,) renders, as one may speak, the proprietor's interest in it greater; and that if another had an interest in it, this would render his less, or occasion that such affection could not be so friendly to self-love, or conducive to private good, as an affection or pursuit which has not a regard to the good of another. This, I say, might be taken for granted, whilst it was not attended to, that the object of every particular affection is equally somewhat external to ourselves: and whether it be the good of another person, or whether it be any other external thing, makes no alteration with regard to its being one's own affection, and the gratification of it one's own private enjoyment. And so far as it is taken for granted, that barely having the means and materials of enjoyment is what constitutes interest and happiness; that our interest and good consists in possessions themselves, in having the property of riches, houses, lands, gardens, not in the enjoyment of them; so far it will even more strongly be taken for granted, in the way already explained, that an affection's conducing to the good of another, must even necessarily occasion it to conduce less to private good, if not to be positively detrimental to it. For, if property and happiness are one and the same thing, as by increasing the property of another, you lessen your own property, so by promoting the happiness of another, you must lessen your own happiness. But whatever occasioned the mistake, I hope it has been fully proved to be one; as it has been proved, that there is no peculiar rivalship or competition between self-love and benevolence; that as there may be a competition between these two, so there may also between any particular affection whatever and self-love; that every particular affection, benevolence among the rest, is subservient to self-love, by being the instrument of private enjoyment; and that in one respect benevolence contributes more to private interest, i. e., enjoyment or satisfaction, than any other of the particular common affections, as it is in a degree its own gratification.

And to all these things may be added, that religion, from whence arises our strongest obligation to benevolence, is so far from disowning the principle of self-love, that it often addresses itself to that very principle, and always to the mind in that state when reason presides; and there can no access be had to the understanding, but by convincing men, that the course of life we would persuade them to is not contrary to their interest. It may be allowed, without any prejudice to the cause of virtue and religion, that our ideas of happiness and misery are, of all our ideas, the nearest and most important to us; that they will, nay, if you please, that they ought to prevail over those of order, and beauty, and harmony, and proportion, if there should ever be, as it is impossible there ever should be, any inconsistency between them; though these last, too, as expressing the fitness of action, are real as truth itself. Let it be allowed, though virtue or moral rectitude does indeed consist in affection to and pursuit of what is right and good, as such; yet that, when we sit down in a cool hour, we can neither justify to ourselves this or any other pursuit, till we are convinced that it will be for our happiness, or at least not contrary to it.

QUESTIONS

1. Is Butler right in thinking that people generally do have an interest in, or desire for, their own happiness and also have interests in particular things, such as security, being warm, and being loved by others, and that the former is different from all of the latter?
2. How does he show that "particular appetites" (e.g., a desire to be loved) are for external things, and not for pleasure arising from these?
3. Does the fact that it is enjoyable to gratify particular appetites make it unreasonable to distinguish them from interest in happiness?
4. Is there any reason why among "particular appetites" there should not be a desire for the welfare of a child or parent or friend or pet, or even of some group of persons, large or small?
5. Does Butler go too far in saying that happiness consists of the satisfaction of our "particular appetites"? Can you name exceptions?
6. Why does he think selfishness may be an impediment to happiness?
7. Is he right in saying there is no more competition between self-love and benevolence than between self-love and any particular appetite or affection? Can we be made happy by promoting the happiness of others?
8. Assess this statement: "The object of every particular affection is equally somewhat external to ourselves."
9. Is Butler right in suggesting that the fact that charity reduces our property does not mean that it reduces our happiness? Why?
10. Do people commonly have a particular appetite or affection for doing what is right and for never doing what is wrong?
11. How completely does Butler succeed in refuting the theses of Psychological Egoism and Psychological Hedonism: people are motivated to do only what they believe will profit their welfare, or people are motivated to do only what they believe will enhance their pleasure, enjoyment, or happiness?

Bishop Joseph Butler (1692-1752)

ABSOLUTE MORAL PROHIBITIONS KNOWN INTUITIVELY

The author of the foregoing selection was not merely an acute observer of human nature. He had a moral theory of his own and was a penetrating critic of utilitarianism.

Butler's ethical views remind one of the Ten Commandments: there are some things that must be done or avoided without exception. Thus there are absolute obligations to act in certain ways — truthfully, justly, kindly, showing gratitude to our benefactors, and so on. But his views are sharply different from what one might call the "Ten Commandments view" in two ways. First, of course, the kinds of action he asserts to be right or wrong are very different from those mentioned in the Ten Commandments. Second, he does not view moral obligations simply as revealed commandments of the Deity; he thinks we know we have certain obligations because we have an approving or disapproving faculty in us — conscience — which informs us of them and which tells us that persons who culpably fail in their obligations merit punishment.

The following selection may be confusing at first because it seems to be about what is blameworthy, not about what is objectively wrong. In fact it is about both. Butler's initial concern is with blameworthiness, and his point is that a person's character and actions are morally bad if they do not show commitment to good principles of conduct. But what are good principles of conduct? In answering this question he exhibits his views about the identity of objectively right acts. Utilitarianism, he says, is far too simple; immoral adultery, he says, may do no harm but it is still wrong.

From Joseph Butler, *The Analogy of Religion*. First printed 1736.

Revised by L. A. Selby-Bigge, in Selby-Bigge, L. A., ed., *British Moralists*, Vol. I, published by The Clarendon Press, Oxford, 1897. Reprinted by permission.

THE ANALOGY OF RELIGION

DISSERTATION II   OF THE NATURE OF VIRTUE

That which renders beings capable of moral government, is their having a moral nature, and moral faculties of perception and of action. Brute creatures are impressed and actuated by various instincts and propensions: so also are we. But additional to this, we have a capacity of reflecting upon actions and characters, and making them an object to our thought; and on doing this, we naturally and unavoidably approve some actions, under the peculiar view of their being virtuous and of good desert; and disapprove others, as vicious and of ill desert. That we have this moral approving and disapproving [1] faculty, is certain from our experiencing it in

---

[1] This way of speaking is taken from Epictetus (Arr. Epict., lib. i. cap. I) and is made use of as seeming the most full, and least liable to cavil. And the moral faculty may be understood to have these two epithets, δοκιμαστικὴ and ἀποδοκιμαστικὴ, upon a double account; because, upon a survey of actions, whether before or after they are done, it determines them to be good or evil; and also because it determines itself to be the guide of action and of life, in contradistinction from all other faculties, or natural

ourselves, and recognising it in each other. It appears from our exercising it unavoidably, in the approbation and disapprobation even of feigned characters: from the words, right and wrong, odious and amiable, base and worthy, with many others of like signification in all languages, applied to actions and characters: from the many written systems of morals which suppose it; since it cannot be imagined, that all these authors, throughout all these treatises, had absolutely no meaning at all to their words, or a meaning merely chimerical: from our natural sense of gratitude, which implies a distinction between merely being the instrument of good, and intending it: from the like distinction, every one makes, between injury and mere harm, which Hobbes says, is peculiar to mankind; and between injury and just punishment, a distinction plainly natural, prior to the consideration of human laws. It is manifest great part of common language, and of common behaviour over the world, is formed upon supposition of such a moral faculty; whether called conscience, moral reason, moral sense, or divine reason; whether considered as a sentiment of the understanding, or as a perception of the heart; or, which seems the truth, as including both. Nor is it at all doubtful, in the general, what course of action this faculty, or practical discerning power within us, approves, and what it disapproves. For as much as it has been disputed wherein virtue consists, or whatever ground for doubt there may be about particulars; yet, in general, there is in reality an universally acknowledged standard of it. It is that which all ages and all countries have made profession of in public; it is that which every man you meet puts on the show of; it is that which the primary and fundamental laws of all civil constitutions over the face of the earth make it their business and endeavour to enforce the practice of upon mankind; namely, justice, veracity, and regard to common good. It being manifest then, in general, that we have such a faculty or discernment as this, it may be of use to remark some things more distinctly concerning it.

First, It ought to be observed, that the object of this faculty is actions,[2] comprehending under that name active or practical principles; those principles from which men would act, if occasions and circumstances gave them power; and which, when fixed and habitual in any person, we call his character. It does not appear that brutes have the least reflex sense of actions, as distinguished from events; or that will and design, which constitute the very nature of actions as such, are at all an object to their perception. But to ours they are; and they are the object, and the only one, of the approving and disapproving faculty. Acting, conduct, behaviour, abstracted from all regard to what is, in fact and event, the consequence of

principles of action; in the very same manner as speculative reason *directly* and naturally judges of speculative truth and falsehood; and at the same time is attended with a consciousness upon *reflection*, that the natural right to judge of them belongs to it.

[2] "Οὐδὲ ἡ ἀρετὴ καὶ κακία . . . ἐν πείσει, ἀλλὰ ἐνεργείᾳ," M. Aurelius Anton. lib. ix. 16. "Virtutis laus omnis in actione consistit," Cic. Off. lib. i. cap. 6.

it, is itself the natural object of the moral discernment, as speculative truth and falsehood is of speculative reason. Intention of such and such consequences, indeed, is always included; for it is part of the action itself: but though the intended good or bad consequences do not follow, we have exactly the same sense of the action as if they did. In like manner, we think well or ill of characters, abstracted from all consideration of the good or the evil, which persons of such characters have it actually in their power to do. We never, in the moral way, applaud or blame either ourselves or others, for what we enjoy or what we suffer, or for having impressions made upon us which we consider as altogether out of our power; but only for what we do, or would have done, had it been in our power; or for what we leave undone, which we might have done, or would have left undone, though we could have done it.

Secondly: Our sense or discernment of actions as morally good or evil, implies in it a sense or discernment of them as of good or ill desert. It may be difficult to explain this perception, so as to answer all the questions which may be asked concerning it; but every one speaks of such and such actions as deserving punishment; and it is not, I suppose, pretended, that they have absolutely no meaning at all to the expression. Now the meaning plainly is not, that we conceive it for the good of society, that the doer of such actions should be made to suffer. For if unhappily it were resolved, that a man who, by some innocent action, was infected with the plague, should be left to perish, lest, by other people's coming near him, the infection should spread; no one would say he deserved this treatment. Innocence and ill desert are inconsistent ideas. Ill desert always supposes guilt; and if one be no part of the other, yet they are evidently and naturally connected in our mind. The sight of a man in misery raises our compassion towards him; and, if this misery be inflicted on him by another, our indignation against the author of it. But when we are informed that the sufferer is a villain, and is punished only for his treachery or cruelty, our compassion exceedingly lessens, and in many instances our indignation wholly subsides. Now what produces this effect is the conception of that in the sufferer, which we call ill desert. Upon considering then, or viewing together, our notion of vice and that of misery, there results a third, that of ill desert. And thus there is in human creatures an association of the two ideas, natural and moral evil, wickedness and punishment. If this association were merely artificial or accidental, it were nothing; but being most unquestionably natural, it greatly concerns us to attend to it, instead of endeavouring to explain it away.

It may be observed further, concerning our perception of good and of ill desert, that the former is very weak with respect to common instances of virtue. One reason of which may be, that it does not appear to a spectator, how far such instances of virtue proceed from a virtuous principle, or in what degree this principle is prevalent: since a very weak regard to virtue may be sufficient to make men act well in many common instances.

And on the other hand, our perception of ill desert in vicious actions lessens in proportion to the temptations men are thought to have had to such vices. For vice in human creatures consisting chiefly in the absence or want of the virtuous principle; though a man be overcome, suppose, by tortures, it does not from thence appear to what degree the virtuous principle was wanting. All that appears is, that he had it not in such a degree as to prevail over the temptation; but possibly he had it in a degree which would have rendered him proof against common temptations.

Thirdly: Our perception of vice and ill desert arises from, and is the result of, a comparison of actions with the nature and capacities of the agent. For the mere neglect of doing what we ought to do would, in many cases, be determined by all men to be in the highest degree vicious. And this determination must arise from such comparison, and be the result of it; because such neglect would not be vicious in creatures of other natures and capacities, as brutes. And it is the same also with respect to positive vices, or such as consist in doing what we ought not. For every one has a different sense of harm done by an idiot, madman, or child, and by one of mature and common understanding; though the action of both, including the intention, which is part of the action, be the same; as it may be, since idiots and madmen, as well as children, are capable not only of doing mischief, but also of intending it. Now this difference must arise from somewhat discerned in the nature or capacities of one, which renders the action vicious; and the want of which, in the other, renders the same action innocent or less vicious: and this plainly supposes a comparison, whether reflected upon or not, between the action and capacities of the agent, previous to our determining an action to be vicious. And hence arises a proper application of the epithets, incongruous, unsuitable, disproportionate, unfit, to actions which our moral faculty determines to be vicious.

Fourthly: It deserves to be considered, whether men are more at liberty, in point of morals, to make themselves miserable without reason, than to make other people so; or dissolutely to neglect their own greater good, for the sake of a present lesser gratification, than they are to neglect the good of others, whom nature has committed to their care. It should seem, that a due concern about our own interest or happiness, and a reasonable endeavour to secure and promote it, which is, I think, very much the meaning of the word prudence in our language; it should seem that this is virtue, and the contrary behaviour faulty and blameable; since, in the calmest way of reflection, we approve of the first, and condemn the other conduct, both in ourselves and others. This approbation and disapprobation are altogether different from mere desire of our own, or of their happiness, and from sorrow upon missing it. For the object or occasion of this last kind of perception is satisfaction or uneasiness; whereas the object of the first is active behaviour. In one case, what our thoughts fix upon is our condition; in the other, our conduct. It is true, indeed, that nature has not given us so sensible a disapprobation of imprudence and folly, either in *ourselves* or *others,* as of falsehood, injustice, and cruelty; I suppose, because that constant habitual sense of private interest and good, which we always carry about with us, renders such sensible disapprobation less necessary, less wanting, to keep us from imprudently neglecting our own happiness, and foolishly injuring ourselves, than it is necessary and wanting to keep us from injuring others, to whose good we cannot have so strong and constant a regard; and also, because imprudence and folly, appearing to bring its own punishment more immediately and constantly than injurious behaviour, it less needs the additional punishment, which would be inflicted upon it by others, had they the same sensible indignation against it, as against injustice, and fraud, and cruelty. Besides, unhappiness being in itself the natural object of compassion, the unhappiness which people bring upon themselves, though it be wilfully, excites in us some pity for them; and this, of course, lessens our displeasure against them. But still it is matter of experience, that we are formed so as to reflect very severely upon the greater instances of imprudent neglects and foolish rashness, both in ourselves and others. In instances of this kind, men often say of themselves with remorse, and of others with some indignation, that they deserved to suffer such calamities, because they brought them upon themselves, and would not take warning. Particularly when persons come to poverty and distress by a long course of extravagance, and after frequent admonitions, though without falsehood or injustice; we plainly do not regard such people as alike objects of compassion with those who are brought into the same condition by unavoidable accidents. From these things it appears, that prudence is a species of virtue, and folly of vice: meaning by *folly,* somewhat quite different from mere incapacity; a thoughtless want of that regard and attention to our own happiness, which we had capacity for. And this the word properly includes; and, as it seems, in its usual acceptation; for we scarcely apply it to brute creatures.

However, if any person be disposed to dispute the matter, I shall very willingly give him up the words virtue and vice, as not applicable to prudence and folly; but must beg leave to insist, that the faculty within us, which is the judge of actions, approves of prudent actions, and disapproves imprudent ones; I say prudent and imprudent *actions* as such, and considered distinctly from the happiness or misery which they occasion. And by the way, this observation may help to determine what justness there is in that objection against religion, that it teaches us to be interested and selfish.

Fifthly: Without inquiring how far, and in what sense, virtue is resolvable into benevolence, and vice into the want of it; it may be proper to observe, that benevolence, and the want of it, singly considered, are in no sort the whole of virtue and vice. For if this were the case, in the review of one's own character, or that of others, our moral understanding and moral sense would be indifferent to every thing, but the degrees in which benevolence prevailed, and the degrees in which it was wanting.

That is, we should neither approve of benevolence to some persons rather than to others, nor disapprove injustice and falsehood upon any other account, than merely as an overbalance of happiness was foreseen likely to be produced by the first, and of misery by the second. But now, on the contrary, suppose two men competitors for any thing whatever, which would be of equal advantage to each of them; though nothing, indeed, would be more impertinent, than for a stranger to busy himself to get one of them preferred to the other; yet such endeavour would be virtue, in behalf of a friend or benefactor, abstracted from all consideration of distant consequences: as that examples of gratitude, and the cultivation of friendship, would be of general good to the world. Again, suppose one man should, by fraud or violence, take from another the fruit of his labour, with intent to give it to a third, who he thought would have as much pleasure from it as would balance the pleasure which the first possessor would have had in the enjoyment, and his vexation in the loss of it; suppose, also, that no bad consequences would follow; yet such an action would surely be vicious. Nay, further, were treachery, violence, and injustice, no otherwise vicious, than as foreseen likely to produce an overbalance of misery to society; then, if in any case a man could procure to himself as great advantage by an act of injustice, as the whole foreseen inconvenience, likely to be brought upon others by it, would amount to, such a piece of injustice would not be faulty or vicious at all; because it would be no more than, in any other case, for a man to prefer his own satisfaction to another's in equal degrees. The fact then appears to be, that we are constituted so as to condemn falsehood, unprovoked violence, injustice, and to approve of benevolence to some preferably to others, abstracted from all consideration, which conduct is likeliest to produce an overbalance of happiness or misery. And therefore, were the Author of nature to propose nothing to himself as an end but the production of happiness, were his moral character merely that of benevolence; yet ours is not so. Upon that supposition, indeed, the only reason of his giving us the above-mentioned approbation of benevolence to some persons rather than others, and disapprobation of falsehood, unprovoked violence, and injustice, must be, that he foresaw this constitution of our nature would produce more happiness, than forming us with a temper of mere general benevolence. But still, since this is our constitution, falsehood, violence, injustice, must be vice in us, and benevolence to some, preferably to others, virtue; abstracted from all consideration of the overbalance of evil or good, which they may appear likely to produce.

Now if human creatures are endued with such a moral nature as we have been explaining, or with a moral faculty, the natural object of which is actions; moral government must consist in rendering them happy and unhappy, in rewarding and punishing them, as they follow, neglect, or depart from, the moral rule of action interwoven in their nature, or suggested and enforced by this moral faculty; in rewarding and punishing them upon account of their so doing.

I am not sensible that I have, in this fifth observation, contradicted what any author designed to assert. But some of great and distinguished merit have, I think, expressed themselves in a manner, which may occasion some danger, to careless readers, of imagining the whole of virtue to consist in singly aiming, according to the best of their judgment, at promoting the happiness of mankind in the present state; and the whole of vice, in doing what they foresee, or might foresee, is likely to produce an overbalance of unhappiness in it; than which mistakes none can be conceived more terrible. For it is certain, that some of the most shocking instances of injustice, adultery, murder, perjury, and even of persecution, may, in many supposable cases, not have the appearance of being likely to produce an overbalance of misery in the present state; perhaps sometimes may have the contrary appearance. For this reflection might easily be carried on, but I forbear — The happiness of the world is the concern of him who is the lord and the proprietor of it; nor do we know what we are about, when we endeavour to promote the good of mankind in any ways but those which he has directed; that is, indeed, in all ways not contrary to veracity and justice. I speak thus upon supposition of persons really endeavouring, in some sort, to do good without regard to these. But the truth seems to be, that such supposed endeavours proceed, almost always, from ambition, the spirit of party, or some indirect principle, concealed perhaps in great measure from persons themselves. And though it is our business and our duty to endeavour, within the bounds of veracity and justice, to contribute to the ease, convenience, and even cheerfulness and diversion of our fellow creatures; yet from our short views, it is greatly uncertain, whether this endeavour will, in particular instances, produce an overbalance of happiness upon the whole; since so many and distant things must come into the account. And that which makes it our duty is, that there is some appearance that it will, and no positive appearance sufficient to balance this, on the contrary side; and also, that such benevolent endeavour is a cultivation of that most excellent of all virtuous principles, the active principle of benevolence.

However, though veracity, as well as justice, is to be our rule of life, it must be added, otherwise a snare will be laid in the way of some plain men, that the use of common forms of speech, generally understood, cannot be falsehood; and, in general, that there can be no designed falsehood without designing to deceive. It must likewise be observed, that in numberless cases, a man may be under the strictest obligations to what he foresees will deceive, without his intending it. For it is impossible not to foresee, that the words and actions of men, in different ranks and employments, and of different educations, will perpetually be mistaken by each other; and it cannot but be so, whilst they will judge with the utmost carelessness, as they daily do, of what they are not, perhaps, enough informed to be competent judges of, even though they considered it with great attention.

QUESTIONS

1. What is the "approving faculty," according to Butler — a feeling or a judgment? Does he have evidence for thinking we are equipped with such a "faculty"?
2. Butler says conscience approves or disapproves "actions," not in the sense of what is brought about by what a person does, but in the sense of principle or intent. Causing harm accidentally, then, is not to be blamed. State in your own words what you think he has in mind when he speaks of an "action."
3. Is Butler right in believing we think wrong-doers should be punished for other reason than the social benefits of doing so?
4. Does he think a person's conduct is immoral if he could not help doing what he did or if he was intellectually incapable of seeing that his action was wrong?
5. Does Butler think imprudence is wrong? Why?
6. Why does Butler think that we have obligations other than that to benevolence, viz., to doing good?
7. When Butler says, at the end, that "the use of common forms of speech cannot be falsehood," is he in effect introducing exceptions to the proposal that we should *always* tell the truth?
8. Suppose you cannot tell the truth without injuring someone. How should one then behave, according to Butler's theory?

SUGGESTIONS FOR FURTHER READING

Broad, C. D. *Five Types of Ethical Theory.* New York: Humanities Press, 1960.
Duncan-Jones, Austin. *Butler's Moral Philosophy.* Harmondsworth, Middlesex: Penguin Books, 1952.
Mossner, E. C. *Bishop Butler and the Age of Reason.* New York: Macmillan, 1936.
Norton, W. J. *Bishop Butler: Moralist and Divine.* New Brunswick, N. J.: Rutgers Univ. Press, 1940.

Jeremy Bentham (1748-1832)

UTILITARIANISM

Jeremy Bentham, like John Stuart Mill, the son of his close friend James Mill, was an influential figure in British political life. His most important book was *Principles of Morals and Legislation* (1789). Among other significant works should be mentioned *A Fragment on Government* (1776) and *A Defence of*

Usury (1787). His discussion of the ethical justification of the various aspects of criminal law and procedure is well worth reading quite apart from its historical interest.

Bentham's version of utilitarianism is simpler than Mill's. There is no attempt to distinguish qualities of pleasure: an act is said to be right if it produces the greatest net amount of pleasure possible. Bentham is a psychological hedonist; but, unlike Mill, he does not pretend to derive ethical principles from his psychology. Mill sometimes disavows proofs of his fundamental principles; Bentham does the same, and more consistently. Yet unquestionably Bentham is trying, very elaborately, to offer considerations which will convince a reasonable man of his theory.

The following selection contains Bentham's general statement of his theory and especially, in the last pages, his proposal for deciding the rightness of an act by totalling up the pleasure and pain to be expected from it; the selection also includes typical reasoning in favor of utilitarianism.

The reader should bear in mind that Bentham uses "utilitarianism" to mean what we have been calling "hedonistic utilitarianism."

From Jeremy Bentham, *An Introduction to the Principles of Morals and Legislation*. First printed 1789. Rev. ed. London, 1823.

AN INTRODUCTION TO THE PRINCIPLES OF MORALS AND LEGISLATION

CHAPTER 1   OF THE PRINCIPLE OF UTILITY

I. Nature has placed mankind under the governance of two sovereign masters, *pain* and *pleasure*. It is for them alone to point out what we ought to do, as well as to determine what we shall do. On the one hand the standard of right and wrong, on the other the chain of causes and effects, are fastened to their throne. They govern us in all we do, in all we say, in all we think; every effort we can make to throw off our subjection, will serve but to demonstrate and confirm it. In words a man may pretend to abjure their empire: but in reality he will remain subject to it all the while. The *principle of utility* recognizes the subjection, and assumes it for the foundation of that system, the object of which is to rear the fabric of felicity by the hands of reason and of law. Systems which attempt to question it, deal in sounds instead of sense, in caprice instead of reason, in darkness instead of light.

But enough of metaphor and declamation: it is not by such means that moral science is to be improved.

II. The principle of utility is the foundation of the present work; it will be proper therefore at the outset to give an explicit and determinate account of what is meant by it. By the principle of utility is meant that principle which approves or disapproves of every action whatsoever, according to the tendency which it appears to have to augment or diminish the happiness of the party whose interest is in question; or, what is the same thing in other words, to promote or to oppose that happiness. I say of every action whatsoever; and therefore not only of every action of a private individual, but of every measure of government.

III. By utility is meant that property in any object, whereby it tends to produce benefit, advantage, pleasure, good, or happiness, (all this in the present case comes to the same thing) or (what comes again to the same thing) to prevent the happening of mischief, pain, evil, or unhappiness to the party whose interest is considered: if that party be the community in general, then the happiness of the community: if a particular individual, then the happiness of that individual.

IV. The interest of the community is one of the most general expressions that can occur in the phraseology of morals: no wonder that the meaning of it is often lost. When it has a meaning, it is this. The community is a fictitious *body*, composed of the individual persons who are considered as constituting as it were its *members*. The interest of the community then is, what? — the sum of the interests of the several members who compose it.

V. It is in vain to talk of the interest of the community, without understanding what is the interest of the individual. A thing is said to promote the interest, or to be *for* the interest, of an individual, when it tends to add to the sum total of his pleasures: or, what comes to the same thing, to diminish the sum total of his pains.

VI. An action then may be said to be conformable to the principle of utility, or, for shortness' sake, to utility, (meaning with respect to the community at large) when the tendency it has to augment the happiness of the community is greater than any it has to diminish it.

VII. A measure of government (which is but a particular kind of action, performed by a particular person or persons) may be said to be conformable to or dictated by the principle of utility, when in like manner the tendency which it has to augment the happiness of the community is greater than any which it has to diminish it.

VIII. When an action, or in particular a measure of government, is supposed by a man to be conformable to the principle of utility, it may be convenient, for the purposes of discourse, to imagine a kind of law or dictate, called a law or dictate of utility: and to speak of the action in question, as being conformable to such law or dictate.

IX. A man may be said to be a partizan of the principle of utility, when the approbation or disapprobation he annexes to any action, or to any measure, is determined by and proportioned to the tendency which he conceives it to have to augment or to diminish the happiness of the community: or in other words, to its conformity or unconformity to the laws or dictates of utility.

X. Of an action that is conformable to the principle of utility, one may always say either that it is one that ought to be done, or at least that it is not one that ought not to be done. One may say also, that it is right it should be done; at least that it is not wrong it should be done: that it is a right action; at least that it is not a wrong action. When thus interpreted, the words *ought*, and *right* and *wrong*, and others of that stamp, have a meaning: when otherwise, they have none.

XI. Has the rectitude of this principle been ever formally contested? It should seem that it had, by those who have not known what they have been meaning. Is it susceptible of any direct proof? It should seem not, for that which is used to prove everything else, cannot itself be proved; a chain of proofs must have their commencement somewhere. To give such proof is as impossible as it is needless.

XII. Not that there is or ever has been that human creature breathing, however stupid or perverse, who has not on many, perhaps on most occasions of his life, deferred to it. By the natural constitution of the human frame, on most occasions of their lives men in general embrace this principle, without thinking of it; if not for the ordering of their own actions, yet for the trying of their own actions, as well as of those of other men. There have been, at the same time, not many, perhaps, even of the most intelligent, who have been disposed to embrace it purely and without reserve. There are even few who have not taken some occasion or other to quarrel with it, either on account of their not understanding always how to apply it, or on account of some prejudice or other which they were afraid to examine into, or could not bear to part with. For such is the stuff that man is made of: in principle and in practice, in a right track and in a wrong one, the rarest of all human qualities is consistency.

XIII. When a man attempts to combat the principle of utility, it is with reason drawn, without his being aware of it, from that very principle itself. His arguments, if they prove anything, prove not that the principle is *wrong*, but that, according to the applications he supposes to be made of it, it is *misapplied*. Is it possible for a man to move the earth? Yes; but he must first find out another earth to stand upon.

XIV. To disapprove the propriety of it by arguments is impossible; but, from the causes that have been mentioned, or from some confused or partial view of it, a man may happen to be disposed not to relish it. Where this is the case, if he thinks the settling of his opinions on such a subject worth the trouble, let him take the following steps, and at length, perhaps, he may come to reconcile himself to it.

1. Let him settle with himself, whether he would wish to discard this principle altogether; if so, let him consider what it is that all his reasonings (in matters of politics especially) can amount to?

2. If he would, let him settle with himself, whether he would judge and act without any principle, or whether there is any other he would judge and act by?

3. If there be, let him examine and satisfy himself whether the principle he thinks he has found is really any separate intelligible principle; or whether it be not a mere principle in words, a kind of phrase, which at bottom expresses neither more nor less than the mere averment of his own unfounded sentiments; that is, what in another person he might be apt to call caprice?

4. If he is inclined to think that his own approbation or disapprobation, annexed to the idea of an act, without any regard to its consequences, is a sufficient foundation for him to judge and act upon, let him ask himself whether his sentiment is to be a standard of right and wrong, with respect to every other man, or whether every man's sentiment has the same privilege of being a standard to itself?

5. In the first case, let him ask himself whether his principle is not despotical, and hostile to all the rest of the human race?

6. In the second case, whether it is not anarchical, and whether at this rate there are not as many different standards of right and wrong as there are men? and whether even to the same man, the same thing, which is right today, may not (without the least change in its nature) be wrong tomorrow? and whether the same thing is not right and wrong in the same place at the same time? and in either case, whether all argument is not at an end? and whether, when two men have said, "I like this," and "I don't like it," they can (upon such principle) have anything more to say?

7. If he should have said to himself, No: for that the sentiment which he proposes as a standard must be grounded on reflection, let him say on what particulars the reflection is to turn? if on particulars having relation to the utility of the act, then let him say whether this is not deserting his own principle, and borrowing assistance from that very one in opposition to which he sets it up: or if not on those particulars, on what other particulars?

8. If he should be for compounding the matter, and adopting his own principle in part, and the principle of utility in part, let him say how far he will adopt it?

9. When he has settled with himself where he will stop, then let him ask himself how he justifies to himself the adopting it so far? and why he will not adopt it any farther?

10. Admitting any other principle than the principle of utility to be a right principle, a principle that it is right for a man to pursue; admitting (what is not true) that the word *right* can have a meaning without reference to utility, let him say whether there is any such thing as a *motive* that a man can have to pursue the dictates of it: if there is, let him say what that motive is, and how it is to be distinguished from those which

enforce the dictates of utility: if not, then lastly let him say what it is this other principle can be good for?

CHAPTER 2   OF PRINCIPLES ADVERSE TO THAT OF UTILITY

I. If the principle of utility be a right principle to be governed by, and that in all cases, it follows from what has been just observed, that whatever principle differs from it in any case must necessarily be a wrong one. To prove any other principle, therefore, to be a wrong one, there needs no more than just to show it to be what it is, a principle of which the dictates are in some point or other different from those of the principle of utility: to state it is to confute it.

II. A principle may be different from that of utility in two ways: 1. By being constantly opposed to it: this is the case with a principle which may be termed the principle of *asceticism*. 2. By being sometimes opposed to it, and sometimes not, as it may happen: this is the case with another, which may be termed the principle of *sympathy* and *antipathy*.

III. By the principle of asceticism I mean that principle, which, like the principle of utility, approves or disapproves of any action, according to the tendency which it appears to have to augment or diminish the happiness of the party whose interest is in question; but in an inverse manner: approving of actions in as far as they tend to diminish his happiness; disapproving of them in as far as they tend to augment it.

IX. The principle of asceticism seems originally to have been the reverie of certain hasty speculators, who having perceived, or fancied, that certain pleasures, when reaped in certain circumstances, have, at the long run, been attended with pains more than equivalent to them, took occasion to quarrel with everything that offered itself under the name of pleasure. Having then got thus far, and having forgot the point which they set out from, they pushed on, and went so much further as to think it meritorious to fall in love with pain. Even this, we see, is at bottom but the principle of utility misapplied.

X. The principle of utility is capable of being consistently pursued; and it is but tautology to say, that the more consistently it is pursued, the better it must ever be for humankind. The principle of asceticism never was, or ever can be, consistently pursued by any living creature. Let but one tenth part of the inhabitants of this earth pursue it consistently, and in a day's time they will have turned it into a hell.

XI. Among principles adverse to that of utility, that which at this day seems to have most influence in matters of government, is what may be called the principle of sympathy and antipathy. By the principle of sympathy and antipathy, I mean that principle which approves or disapproves of certain actions, not on account of their tending to augment the happiness, nor yet on account of their tending to diminish the happiness of the party whose interest is in question, but merely because a man finds himself disposed to approve or disapprove of them: holding up that approbation or disapprobation as a sufficient reason for itself, and disclaiming the necessity of looking out for any extrinsic ground. Thus far in the general department of morals; and in the particular department of politics, measuring out the quantum (as well as determining the ground) of punishment, by the degree of the disapprobation.

XII. It is manifest, that this is rather a principle in name than in reality; it is not a positive principle of itself, so much as a term employed to signify the negation of all principle. What one expects to find in a principle is something that points out some external consideration, as a means of warranting and guiding the internal sentiments of approbation and disapprobation; this expectation is but ill fulfilled by a proposition, which does neither more nor less than hold up each of those sentiments as a ground and standard for itself.

XIII. In looking over the catalogue of human actions (says a partizan of this principle) in order to determine which of them are to be marked with the seal of disapprobation, you need but to take counsel of your own feelings: whatever you find in yourself a propensity to condemn, is wrong for that very reason. For the same reason it is also meet for punishment: what proportion it is adverse to utility, or whether it be adverse to utility at all, is a matter that makes no difference. In that same *proportion* also is it meet for punishment; if you hate much, punish much; if you hate little, punish little; punish as you hate. If you hate not at all, punish not at all; the fine feelings of the soul are not to be overborne and tyrannized by the harsh and rugged dictates of political utility.

XIV. The various systems that have been formed concerning the standard of right and wrong, may all be reduced to the principle of sympathy and antipathy. One account may serve for all of them. They consist all of them in so many contrivances for avoiding the obligation of appealing to any external standard, and for prevailing upon the reader to accept of the author's sentiment or opinion as a reason for itself. The phrases different, but the principle the same.[1]

---

[1] It is curious enough to observe the variety of inventions men have hit upon, and the variety of phrases they have brought forward, in order to conceal from the world, and, if possible, from themselves, this very general and therefore very pardonable self-sufficiency.

1. One man says, he has a thing made on purpose to tell him what is right and what is wrong; and that it is called a *moral sense*: and then he goes to work at his ease, and says, such a thing is right, and such a thing is wrong — why? "because my moral sense tells me it is."

2. Another man comes and alters the phrase: leaving out *moral*, and putting in *common*, in the room of it. He then tells you, that his common sense teaches him what is right and wrong, as surely as the other's moral sense did: meaning by common sense, a sense of some kind or other, which, he says, is possessed by all mankind: the sense of those, whose sense is not the same as the author's, being struck out of the account as

XV. It is manifest, that the dictates of this principle will frequently coincide with those of utility, though perhaps without intending any such thing. Probably more frequently than not: and hence it is that the business of penal justice is carried on upon that tolerable sort of footing upon which we see it carried on in common at this day. For what more natural or more general ground of hatred to a practice can there be, than the mis-

not worth taking. This contrivance does better than the other; for a moral sense, being a new thing, a man may feel about him a good while without being able to find it out: but common sense is as old as the creation; and there is no man but would be ashamed to be thought not to have as much of it as his neighbours. It has another great advantage: by appearing to share power, it lessens envy: for when a man gets up upon this ground, in order to anathematize those who differ from him, it is not by a *sic volo sic jubeo*, but by a *velitis jubeatis*.

3. Another man comes, and says, that as to a moral sense indeed, he cannot find that he has any such thing: that however he has an *understanding*, which will do quite as well. This understanding, he says, is the standard of right and wrong: it tells him so and so. All good and wise men understand as he does: if other men's understandings differ in any point from his, so much the worse for them: it is a sure sign they are either defective or corrupt.

4. Another man says, that there is an eternal and immutable Rule of Right: that that rule of right dictates so and so: and then he begins giving you his sentiments upon anything that comes uppermost: and these sentiments (you are to take for granted) are so many branches of the eternal rule of right.

5. Another man, or perhaps the same man (it's no matter) says, that there are certain practices conformable, and others repugnant to the Fitness of Things; and then he tells you, at his leisure, what practices are conformable and what repugnant: just as he happens to like a practice or dislike it.

6. A great multitude of people are continually talking of the Law of Nature; and then they go on giving you their sentiments about what is right and what is wrong: and these sentiments, you are to understand, are so many chapters and sections of the Law of Nature.

7. Instead of the phrase, Law of Nature, you have sometimes, Law of Reason, Right Reason, Natural Justice, Natural Equity, Good Order. Any of them will do equally well. This latter is most used in politics. The last three are much more tolerable than the others, because they do not very explicitly claim to be anything more than phrases; they insist but feebly upon the being looked upon as so many positive standards of themselves, and seem content to be taken, upon occasion, for phrases expressive of the conformity of the thing in question to the proper standard, whatever that may be. On most occasions, however, it will be better to say *utility*: *utility* is clearer, as referring more explicitly to pain and pleasure.

8. We have one philosopher, who says, there is no harm in anything in the world but in telling a lie: and that if, for example, you were to murder your own father, this would only be a particular way of saying, he was not your father. Of course, when this philosopher sees anything that he does not like, he says, it is a particular way of telling a lie. It is saying, that the act ought to be done, or may be done, when, *in truth*, it ought not to be done.

9. The fairest and openest of them all is that sort of man who speaks out, and says, I am of the number of the Elect: now God himself takes care to inform the Elect what is right: and that with so good effect, that let them strive ever so, they cannot help not only knowing it but practising it. If therefore a man wants to know what is right and what is wrong, he has nothing to do but to come to me.

It is upon the principle of antipathy that such and such acts are often reprobated chieviousness of such practice? What all men are exposed to suffer by, all men will be disposed to hate. It is far yet, however, from being a constant ground: for when a man suffers, it is not always that he knows what it is he suffers by. A man may suffer grievously, for instance, by a new tax, without being able to trace up the cause of his sufferings to the injustice of some neighbour, who has eluded the payment of an old one.

XVI. The principle of sympathy and antipathy is most apt to err on the side of severity. It is for applying punishment in many cases which deserve none: in many cases which deserve some, it is for applying more than they deserve. There is no incident imaginable, be it ever so trivial, and so remote from mischief, from which this principle may not extract a ground of punishment. Any difference in taste: any difference in opinion: upon one subject as well as upon another. No disagreement so trifling which perseverance and altercation will not render serious. Each becomes in the other's

on the score of their being *unnatural*: the practice of exposing children, established among the Greeks and Romans, was an unnatural practice. Unnatural, when it means anything, means unfrequent: and there it means something; although nothing to the present purpose. But here it means no such thing: for the frequency of such acts is perhaps the great complaint. It therefore means nothing; nothing, I mean, which there is in the act itself. All it can serve to express is, the disposition of the person who is talking of it: the disposition he is in to be angry at the thoughts of it. Does it merit his anger? Very likely it may: but whether it does or no is a question, which to be answered rightly, can only be answered upon the principle of utility.

Unnatural, is as good a word as moral sense, or common sense; and would be as good a foundation for a system. Such an act is unnatural; that is, repugnant to nature: for I do not like to practise it: and, consequently, do not practise it. It is therefore repugnant to what ought to be the nature of everybody else.

This mischief common to all these ways of thinking and arguing (which, in truth, as we have seen, are but one and the same method, couched in different forms of words) is their serving as a cloke, and pretence, and aliment, to despotism: if not a despotism in practice, a despotism however in disposition: which is but too apt, when pretence and power offer, to show itself in practice. The consequence is, that with intentions very commonly of the purest kind, a man becomes a torment either to himself or his fellow creatures. If he be of the melancholy cast, he sits in silent grief, bewailing their blindness and depravity: if of the irascible, he declaims with fury and virulence against all who differ from him; blowing up the coals of fanaticism, and branding with the charge of corruption and insincerity, every man who does not think, or profess to think, as he does.

If such a man happens to possess the advantages of style, his book may do a considerable deal of mischief before the nothingness of it is understood.

These principles, if such they can be called, it is more frequent to see applied to morals than to politics: but their influence extends itself to both. In politics, as well as morals, a man will be at least equally glad of a pretence for deciding any question in the manner that best pleases him, without the trouble of inquiry. If a man is an infallible judge of what is right and wrong in the actions of private individuals, why not in the measures to be observed by public men in the direction of those actions? accordingly (not to mention other chimeras) I have more than once known the pretended law of nature set up in legislative debates, in opposition to arguments derived from the principle of utility.

'But is it never, then, from any other considerations than those of utility, that we eyes an enemy, and, if laws permit, a criminal. This is one of the circumstances by which the human race is distinguished (not much indeed to its advantage) from the brute creation.

XVII.　It is not, however, by any means unexampled for this principle to err on the side of lenity. A near and perceptible mischief moves antipathy. A remote and imperceptible mischief, though not less real, has no effect. Instances in proof of this will occur in numbers in the course of the work. It would be breaking in upon the order of it to give them here.

XVIII.　It may be wondered, perhaps, that in all this while no mention has been made of the *theological* principle; meaning that principle which professes to recur for the standard of right and wrong to the will of God. But the case is, this is not in fact a distinct principle. It is never anything more or less than one or other of the three before-mentioned principles presenting itself under another shape. The *will* of God here meant cannot be his revealed will, as contained in the sacred writings: for that is a system which nobody ever thinks of recurring to at this time of day, for

derive our notions of right and wrong?' I do not know: I do not care. Whether a moral sentiment can be originally conceived from any other source than a view of utility, is one question: whether upon examination and reflection it can, in point of fact, be actually persisted in and justified on any other ground, by a person reflecting within himself, is another: whether in point of right it can properly be justified on any other ground, by a person addressing himself to the community, is a third. The two first are questions of speculation: it matters not, comparatively speaking, how they are decided. The last is a question of practice: the decision of it is of as much importance as that of any can be.

'I feel in myself,' (say you) 'a disposition to approve of such or such an action in a moral view: but this is not owing to any notions I have of its being a useful one to the community. I do not pretend to know whether it be an useful one or not: it may be, for aught I know, a mischievous one.' 'But is it then,' (say I) 'a mischievous one? examine; and if you can make yourself sensible that it is so, then, if duty means any thing, that is, moral duty, it is your *duty* at least to abstain from it: and more than that, if it is what lies in your power, and can be done without too great a sacrifice, to endeavour to prevent it. It is not your cherishing the notion of it in your bosom, and giving it the name of virtue, that will excuse you.'

'I feel in myself,' (say you again) 'a disposition to detest such or such an action in a moral view; but this is not owing to any notions I have of its being a mischievous one to the community. I do not pretend to know whether it be a mischievous one or not: it may be not a mischievous one: it may be, for aught I know, an useful one.' — 'May it indeed,' (say I) 'an useful one? but let me tell you then, that unless duty, and right and wrong, be just what you please to make them, if it really be not a mischievous one, and any body has a mind to do it, it is no duty of yours, but, on the contrary, it would be very wrong in you, to take upon you to prevent him: detest it within yourself as much as you please; that may be a very good reason (unless it be also a useful one) for your not doing it yourself: but if you go about, by word or deed, to do any thing to hinder him, or make him suffer for it, it is you, and not he, that have done wrong: it is not your setting yourself to blame his conduct, or branding it with the name of vice, that will make him culpable, or you blameless. Therefore, if you can make yourself content that he shall be of one mind, and you of another, about that matter, and so continue, it is well: but if nothing will serve you, but that you and he must needs be of the same mind, I'll tell you what you have to do: it is for you to get the better of your antipathy, not for him to truckle to it.'

the details of political administration: and even before it can be applied to the details of private conduct, it is universally allowed, by the most eminent divines of all persuasions, to stand in need of pretty ample interpretations; else to what use are the works of those divines? And for the guidance of these interpretations, it is also allowed, that some other standard must be assumed. The will then which is meant on this occasion, is that which may be called the *presumptive* will: that is to say, that which is presumed to be his will on account of the conformity of its dictates to those of some other principle. What then may be this other principle? it must be one or other of the three mentioned above; for there cannot, as we have seen, be any more. It is plain, therefore, that, setting revelation out of the question, no light can ever be thrown upon the standard of right and wrong, by anything that can be said upon the question, what is God's will. We may be perfectly sure, indeed, that whatever is right is comformable to the will of God; but so far is that from answering the purpose of showing us what is right, that it is necessary to know first whether a thing is right, in order to know from thence whether it be conformable to the will of God.

XIX. There are two things which are very apt to be confounded, but which it imports us carefully to distinguish: — the motive or cause, which, by operating on the mind of an individual, is productive of any act and the ground or reason which warrants a legislator, or other bystander in regarding that act with an eye of approbation. When the act happens, in the particular instance in question, to be productive of effects which we approve of, much more if we happen to observe that the same motive may frequently be productive, in other instances, of the like effects, we are apt to transfer our approbation to the motive itself, and to assume, as the just ground for the approbation we bestow on the act, the circumstance of its originating from that motive. It is in this way that the sentiment of antipathy has often been considered as a just ground of action. Antipathy, for instance, in such or such a case, is the cause of an action which is attended with good effects; but this does not make it a right ground of action in that case, any more than in any other. Still farther. Not only the effects are good, but the agent sees beforehand that they will be so. This may make the action indeed a perfectly right action: but it does not make antipathy a right ground for action. For the same sentiment of antipathy, if implicitly deferred to, may be, and very frequently is, productive of the very worst effects. Antipathy, therefore, can never be a right ground of action. No more, therefore, can resentment, which, as will be seen more particularly hereafter, is but a modification of antipathy. The only right ground of action, that can possibly subsist, is, after all, the consideration of utility, which, if it is a right principle of action and of approbation, in any one case, is so in every other. Other principles in abundance, that is, other motives, may be the reasons why such and such an act *has* been done, that is, the reasons or causes of its being done; but it is this alone that can be the reason why it might or ought to have been done. Antipathy or resentment requires always to be regulated, to prevent its doing mischief: to be regulated by what? always by the principle of utility. The principle of utility neither requires nor admits of any other regulator than itself.

CHAPTER 4   VALUE OF A LOT OF PLEASURE OR PAIN, HOW TO BE MEASURED

I. Pleasures then, and the avoidance of pains, are the *ends* which the legislator has in view: it behoves him therefore to understand their *value*. Pleasures and pains are the *instruments* he has to work with: it behoves him therefore to understand their force, which is again, in other words, their valuc.

II. To a person considered *by himself*, the value of a pleasure or pain considered *by itself*, will be greater or less, according to the four following circumstances.

1. Its *intensity*.	3. Its *certainty* or *uncertainty*.
2. Its *duration*.	4. Its *propinquity* or *remoteness*.

III. These are the circumstances which are to be considered in estimating a pleasure or a pain considered each of them by itself. But when the value of any pleasure or pain is considered for the purpose of estimating the tendency of any *act* by which it is produced, there are two other circumstances to be taken into the account; these are,

5. Its *fecundity*, or the chance it has of being followed by sensations of the *same* kind: that is, pleasures, if it be a pleasure: pains, if it be a pain.

6. Its *purity*, or the chance it has of *not* being followed by sensations of the *opposite* kind: that is, pains, if it be a pleasure: pleasures, if it be a pain.

These two last, however, are in strictness scarcely to be deemed properties of the pleasures or the pain itself; they are not, therefore, in strictness to be taken into the account of the value of that pleasure or that pain. They are in strictness to be deemed properties only of the act, or other event, by which such pleasure or pain has been produced; and accordingly are only to be taken into the account of the tendency of such act or such event.

IV. To a *number* of persons, with reference to each of whom the value of a pleasure or a pain is considered, it will be greater or less, according to seven circumstances: to wit, the six preceding ones; *viz.*

1. Its *intensity*.	4. Its *propinquity* or *remoteness*.
2. Its *duration*.	5. Its *fecundity*.
3. Its *certainty* or *uncertainty*.	6. Its *purity*.

And one other; to wit:

7. Its *extent*; that is, the number of persons to whom it *extends*; or (in other words) who are affected by it.

V. To take an exact account then of the general tendency of any act, by which the interests of a community are affected, proceed as follows. Begin with any one person of those whose interests seem most immediately to be affected by it: and take an account,

1. Of the value of each distinguishable *pleasure* which appears to be produced by it in the *first* instance.

2. Of the value of each *pain* which appears to be produced by it in the *first* instance.

3. Of the value of each pleasure which appears to be produced by it *after* the first. This constitutes the *fecundity* of the first *pleasure* and the *impurity* of the first *pain*.

4. Of the value of each *pain* which appears to be produced by it after the first. This constitutes the *fecundity* of the first *pain*, and the *impurity* of the first pleasure.

5. Sum up all the values of all the *pleasures* on the one side, and those of all the pains on the other. The balance, if it be on the side of pleasure, will give the *good* tendency of the act upon the whole, with respect to the interests of that *individual* person; if on the side of pain, the *bad* tendency of it upon the whole.

6. Take an account of the *number* of persons whose interests appear to be concerned; and repeat the above process with respect to each. *Sum up* the numbers expressive of the degrees of *good* tendency, which the act has, with respect to each individual, in regard to whom the tendency of it is *good* upon the whole: do this again with respect to each individual, in regard to whom the tendency of it is *bad* upon the whole. Take the *balance;* which. if on the side of *pleasure*, will give the general *good* tendency of the act, with respect to the total number of community of individuals concerned; if on the side of pain the general *evil tendency*, with respect to the same community.

VI. It is not to be expected that this process should be strictly pursued previously to every moral judgment, or to every legislative or judicial operation. It may, however, be always kept in view: and as near as the process actually pursued on these occasions approaches to it, so near will such process approach to the character of an exact one.

VII. The same process is alike applicable to pleasure and pain in whatever shape they appear: and by whatever denomination they are distinguished: to pleasure, whether it be called *good* (which is properly the cause or instrument of pleasure), or *profit* (which is distant pleasure, or the cause or instrument of distant pleasure), or *convenience*, or *advantage, benefit, emolument, happiness,* and so forth: to pain, whether it be called *evil* (which corresponds to *good*), or *mischief*, or *inconvenience*, or *disadvantage*, or *loss*, or *unhappiness*, and so forth.

VIII. Nor is this a novel and unwarranted, any more than it is a useless theory. In all this there is nothing but what the practice of mankind, wheresoever they have a clear view of their own interest, is perfectly conformable to. An article of property, an estate in land, for instance, is valuable, on what account? On account of the pleasures of all kinds which it enables a man to produce, and what comes to the same thing, the pains of all kinds which it enables him to avert. But the value of such an article of property is universally understood to rise or fall according to the length or shortness of the time which a man has in it: the certainty or uncertainty of its coming into possession: and the nearness or remoteness of the time at which, if at all, it is to come into possession. As to the *intensity* of the pleasures which a man may derive from it, this is never thought of, because it depends upon the use which each particular person may come to make of it; which cannot be estimated till the particular pleasures he may come to derive from it, or the particular pains he may come to exclude by means of it, are brought to view. For the same reason, neither does he think of the *fecundity* or *purity* of those pleasures.

QUESTIONS

1. What does Bentham mean by the "principle of utility"?
2. What is "the interest of the community"?
3. When will Bentham say a man is a "partizan" of the principle of utility?
4. What does Bentham suggest is the *meaning* of "ought" and "right" and "wrong" — that is, if they *have* a meaning?
5. Does Bentham think the principle of utility can be proved? Why? Does he think practically everyone in fact accepts it?
6. Does he think there is a serious alternative principle of conduct? What view does he seem to regard as the most likely rival of his view?
7. Is it a sound argument for utilitarianism, to say that it would have best consequences for mankind, if everyone followed its principle?
8. What are his principal objections to the principles of "sympathy and antipathy"?
9. Why does he think the "theological principle" is not a separate principle at all?
10. What various things does Bentham think we must take into account in deciding whether one action will produce more or less pleasure than some alternative action? Can you think of practical, or theoretical, difficulties in the way of deciding whether one course of action would produce "more" pleasure than another, if the reckoning is done along the lines of Bentham's discussion?

SUGGESTIONS FOR FURTHER READING

Baumgardt, David. *Bentham and the Ethics of Today.* Princeton: Princeton Univ. Press, 1952.

Halévy, E. *The Growth of Philosophical Radicalism.* New York: Macmillan, 1928.

Stephen, Sir Leslie. *The English Utilitarians.* Gloucester, Mass.: Peter Smith, 1950.

Immanuel Kant   (1724-1804)

CONDUCT YOU DON'T WANT
MADE UNIVERSAL IS IMMORAL

Immanuel Kant had perhaps the most powerful and original mind in modern philosophy. More books and articles have been written about him than about any other philosopher of the modern era. He was born in Königsberg, East Prussia, of a Pietist family. He attended the University of Königsberg, and after serving as tutor in several households, became first *privat-docent* and later professor at Königsberg. His most important work was *The Critique of Pure Reason* (1781), but *The Fundamental Principles of the Metaphysic of Morals* (1785), from which our selection is taken, has been one of the most influential books on this subject.

This essay is not concerned solely with the question of which acts are right. Indeed, it emphasizes a question with which it begins: Which men and actions are morally praiseworthy? Kant's answer to this question is that what makes a man praiseworthy is not what he achieves but whether he acts from regard for duty as he sees it. The central part of the essay, however, is the formulation and defense of a general principle about right actions, essentially the following: Suppose a man is considering whether it would be right for him to perform an action of the kind A in circumstances which, as he sees matters, are BCD. Then, Kant says, doing A is morally permissible (right) if the man is willing for *everyone* to make it a rule to do A in circumstances BCD. Otherwise it is wrong and the man's duty to avoid it. This is the principle of duty, "the categorical imperative." Kant conceived that it is part of rationality to refrain from conduct which one would not be willing to have made the universal rule. In a sense, then, Kant is able to say that the concept of duty, and moral laws, are purely rational and can be derived from the concept of a rational being. Moral conflict is the conflict between a person's rational ideal for conduct and his own personal impulses and preferences. Kant thinks that the more stringent moral duties, those which should be enforced by law, are those to avoid conduct which not only cannot be seriously wanted as universal by the agent but which could not *possibly* for one reason or another, be made a universal law. Kant himself considered that his view could be put in quite another way but one which comes to the same thing in the end: it is always one's duty to treat human beings with respect, to treat them always as having value and dignity in themselves and not merely as instruments for realizing one's own ends. In the last two pages of our selection it is evident that Kant, confusingly, supposed that ability to choose a rational or moral course of action as opposed to the course of personal preference or impulse is identical with freedom of choice.

There are various historical influences apparent in Kant's theory: the Golden Rule, Stoicism, eighteenth-century enthusiasm for being rational.

Kant's proposal is somewhat abstract, and we may wonder what specific conclusions about right and wrong conduct it commits us to. Kant himself offers some examples; but his argument is rather loose, and his theory may be better than his applications. Kant himself was very critical of utilitarianism; but one wonders whether one might not accept Kant's principle and still be a utilitarian — or even an egoist. This possibility raises the question whether Kant's theory should be considered as a substantive answer to the question "Which acts are right?" at all or whether it is rather something more abstract and basic, perhaps a theory of the justification of ethical statements. If one classifies his view as "formalist," it is on the ground that it asserts that an act is right, not if and only if doing it will have the best consequences, but because it has the property of being an act which the agent is willing to accept as a universal law.

From Immanuel Kant, *Grundlegung zur Metaphysik der Sitten*. First published 1785.

The Fundamental Principles of the Metaphysic of Morals, by I. Kant, translated by H. J. Paton, 1948, by permission of the Hutchinson Group.

THE FUNDAMENTAL PRINCIPLES OF THE METAPHYSIC OF MORALS

CHAPTER 1   PASSAGE FROM ORDINARY RATIONAL KNOWLEDGE OF MORALITY TO PHILOSOPHICAL

[The good will]

It is impossible to conceive anything at all in the world, or even out of it, which can be taken as good without qualification, except a *good will*. Intelligence, wit, judgement, and any other *talents* of the mind we may care to name, or courage, resolution, and constancy of purpose, as qualities of *temperament*, are without doubt good and desirable in many respects;

but they can also be extremely bad and hurtful when the will is not good which has to make use of these gifts of nature, and which for this reason has the term *'character'* applied to its peculiar quality. It is exactly the same with *gifts of fortune*. Power, wealth, honour, even health and that complete well-being and contentment with one's state which goes by the name of *'happiness,'* produce boldness, and as a consequence often over-boldness as well, unless a good will is present by which their influence on the mind — and so too the whole principle of action — may be corrected and adjusted to universal ends; not to mention that a rational and impartial spectator can never feel approval in contemplating the uninterrupted prosperity of a being graced by no touch of a pure and good will, and that consequently a good will seems to constitute the indispensable condition of our very worthiness to be happy.

Some qualities are even helpful to this good will itself and can make its task very much easier. They have none the less no inner unconditioned worth, but rather presuppose a good will which sets a limit to the esteem in which they are rightly held and does not permit us to regard them as absolutely good. Moderation in affections and passions, self-control, and sober reflexion are not only good in many respects: they may even seem to constitute part of the *inner* worth of a person. Yet they are far from being properly described as good without qualification (however unconditionally they have been commended by the ancients). For without the principles of a good will they may become exceedingly bad; and the very coolness of a scoundrel makes him, not merely more dangerous, but also immediately more abominable in our eyes than we should have taken him to be without it.

[*The good will and its results*]

A good will is not good because of what it effects or accomplishes — because of its fitness for attaining some proposed end: it is good through its willing alone — that is, good in itself. Considered in itself it is to be esteemed beyond comparison as far higher than anything it could ever bring about merely in order to favour some inclination or, if you like, the sum total of inclinations. Even if, by some special disfavour of destiny or by the niggardly endowment of step-motherly nature, this will is entirely lacking in power to carry out its intentions; if by its utmost effort it still accomplishes nothing, and only good will is left (not, admittedly, as a mere wish, but as the straining of every means so far as they are in our control); even then it would still shine like a jewel for its own sake as something which has its full value in itself. Its usefulness or fruitlessness can neither add to, nor subtract from, this value. Its usefulness would be merely, as it were, the setting which enables us to handle it better in our ordinary dealings or to attract the attention of those not yet sufficiently expert, but not to commend it to experts or to determine its value. . . .

[The good will and duty]

We have now to elucidate the concept of a will estimable in itself and good apart from any further end. This concept, which is already present in a sound natural understanding and requires not so much to be taught as merely to be clarified, always holds the highest place in estimating the total worth of our actions and constitutes the condition of all the rest. We will therefore take up the concept of *duty*, which includes that of a good will, exposed, however, to certain subjective limitations and obstacles. These, so far from hiding a good will or disguising it, rather bring it out by contrast and make it shine forth more brightly.

[The motive of duty]

I will here pass over all actions already recognized as contrary to duty, however useful they may be with a view to this or that end; for about these the question does not even arise whether they could have been done *for the sake of duty* inasmuch as they are directly opposed to it. I will also set aside actions which in fact accord with duty, yet for which men have *no immediate inclination,* but perform them because impelled to do so by some other inclination. For there it is easy to decide whether the action which accords with duty has been done *from duty* or from some purpose of self-interest. This distinction is far more difficult to perceive when the action accords with duty and the subject has in addition an *immediate* inclination to the action. For example, it certainly accords with duty that a grocer should not over-charge his inexperienced customer; and where there is much competition a sensible shopkeeper refrains from so doing and keeps to a fixed and general price for everybody so that a child can buy from him just as well as anyone else. Thus people are served *honestly*; but this is not nearly enough to justify us in believing that the shopkeeper has acted in this way from duty or from principles of fair dealing; his interests required him to do so. We cannot assume him to have in addition an immediate inclination towards his customers, leading him, as it were out of love, to give no man preference over another in the matter of price. Thus the action was done neither from duty nor from immediate inclination, but solely from purposes of self-interest.

On the other hand, to preserve one's life is a duty, and besides this every one has also an immediate inclination to do so. But on account of this the often anxious precautions taken by the greater part of mankind for this purpose have no inner worth, and the maxim of their action is without moral content. They do protect their lives *in conformity with duty*, but not *from the motive of duty*. When on the contrary, disappointments and hopeless misery have quite taken away the taste for life; when a wretched man, strong in soul and more angered at his fate than faint-hearted or cast down, longs for death and still preserves his life without loving it — not from inclination or fear but from duty; then indeed his maxim has a moral content.

To help others where one can is a duty, and besides this there are many spirits of so sympathetic a temper that, without any further motive of vanity or self-interest, they find an inner pleasure in spreading happiness around them and can take delight in the contentment of others as their own work. Yet I maintain that in such a case an action of this kind, however right and however amiable it may be, has still no genuinely moral worth. It stands on the same footing as other inclinations — for example, the inclination for honour, which if fortunate enough to hit on something beneficial and right and consequently honourable, deserves praise and encouragement, but not esteem; for its maxim lacks moral content, namely, the performance of such actions, not from inclination, but *from duty*. Suppose then that the mind of this friend of man were overclouded by sorrows of his own which extinguished all sympathy with the fate of others, but that he still had power to help those in distress, though no longer stirred by the need of others because sufficiently occupied with his own; and suppose that, when no longer moved by any inclination, he tears himself out of this deadly insensibility and does the action without any inclination, for the sake of duty alone; then for the first time his action has its genuine moral worth. Still further: if nature had implanted little sympathy in this or that man's heart; if (being in other respects an honest fellow) he were cold in temperament and indifferent to the sufferings of others — perhaps because, being endowed with the special gift of patience and robust endurance in his own sufferings, he assumed the like in others or even demanded it; if such a man (who would in truth not be the worst product of nature) were not exactly fashioned by her to be a philanthropist, would he not still find in himself a source from which he might draw a worth far higher than any that a good-natured temperament can have? Assuredly he would. It is precisely in this that the worth of character begins to show — a moral worth and beyond all comparison the highest — namely, that he does good, not from inclination, but from duty. . . .

It is doubtless in this sense that we should understand too the passages from Scripture in which we are commanded to love our neighbour and even our enemy. For love out of inclination cannot be commanded; but kindness done from duty — although no inclination impels us, and even although natural and unconquerable disinclination stands in our way — is *practical*, and not *pathological*, love, residing in the will and not in the propensions of feeling, in principles of action and not of melting compassion; and it is this practical love alone which can be an object of command.

[The formal principle of duty]

Our second proposition is this: An action done from duty has its moral worth, *not in the purpose* to be attained by it, but in the maxim in accordance with which it is decided upon; it depends therefore, not on the realization of the object of the action, but solely on the *principle* of *volition* in accordance with which, irrespective of all objects of the faculty of desire, the action has been performed. That the purposes we may have in our actions, and also their effects considered as ends and motives of the will, can give to actions no unconditioned and moral worth is clear from what has gone before. Where then can this worth be found if we are not to find it in the will's relation to the effect hoped for from the action? It can be found nowhere but *in the principle of the will,* irrespective of the ends which can be brought about by such an action; for between its *a priori* principle, which is formal, and its *a posteriori* motive, which is material, the will stands, so to speak, at a parting of the ways; and since it must be determined by some principle, it will have to be determined by the formal principle of volition when an action is done from duty, where, as we have seen, every material principle is taken away from it.

[*Reverence for the law*]

Our third proposition, as an inference from the two preceding, I would express thus: *Duty is the necessity to act out of reverence for the law.* For an object as the effect of my proposed action I can have an *inclination,* but *never reverence,* precisely because it is merely the effect, and not the activity, of a will. Similarly for inclination as such, whether my own or that of another, I cannot have reverence: I can at most in the first case approve, and in the second case sometimes even love — that is, regard it as favourable to my own advantage. Only something which is conjoined with my will solely as a ground and never as an effect — something which does not serve my inclination, but outweighs it or at least leaves it entirely out of account in my choice — and therefore only bare law for its own sake, can be an object of reverence and therewith a command. Now an action done from duty has to set aside altogether the influence of inclination, and along with inclination every object of the will; so there is nothing left able to determine the will except objectively the *law* and subjectively *pure reverence* for this practical law, and therefore the maxim [1] of obeying this law even to the detriment of all my inclinations.

Thus the moral worth of an action does not depend on the result expected from it, and so too does not depend on any principle of action that needs to borrow its motive from this expected result. For all these results (agreeable states and even the promotion of happiness in others) could have been brought about by other causes as well, and consequently their production did not require the will of a rational being, in which, however, the highest and unconditioned good can alone be found. Therefore nothing but the *idea of the law* in itself, *which admittedly is present only in a rational*

---

[1] A *maxim* is the subjective principle of a volition: an objective principle (that is, one which would also serve subjectively as a practical principle for all rational beings if reason had full control over the faculty of desire) is a practical *law.*

being — so far as it, and not an expected result, is the ground determining the will — can constitute that pre-eminent good which we call moral, a good which is already present in the person acting on this idea and has not to be awaited merely from the result.

[*The categorical imperative*]

But what kind of law can this be the thought of which, even without regard to the results expected from it, has to determine the will if this is to be called good absolutely and without qualification? Since I have robbed the will of every inducement that might arise for it as a consequence of obeying any particular law, nothing is left but the conformity of actions to universal law as such, and this alone must serve the will as its principle. That is to say, I ought never to act except in such a way *that I can also will that my maxim should become a universal law.* Here bare conformity to universal law as such (without having as its base any law prescribing particular actions) is what serves the will as its principle, and must so serve it if duty is not to be everywhere an empty delusion and a chimerical concept. The ordinary reason of mankind also agrees with this completely in its practical judgements and always has the aforesaid principle before its eyes.

Take this question, for example. May I not, when I am hard pressed, make a promise with the intention of not keeping it? Here I readily distinguish the two senses which the question can have — Is it prudent, or is it right, to make a false promise? The first no doubt can often be the case. I do indeed see that it is not enough for me to extricate myself from present embarrassment by this subterfuge: I have to consider whether from this lie there may not subsequently accrue to me much greater inconvenience than that from which I now escape, and also — since, with all my supposed *astuteness,* to foresee the consequences is not so easy that I can be sure there is no chance, once confidence in me is lost, of this proving far more disadvantageous than all the ills I now think to avoid — whether it may not be a *more prudent* action to proceed here on a general maxim and make it my habit not to give a promise except with the intention of keeping it. Yet it becomes clear to me at once that such a maxim is always founded solely on fear of consequences. To tell the truth for the sake of duty is something entirely different from doing so out of concern for inconvenient results; for in the first case the concept of the action already contains in itself a law for me, while in the second case I have first of all to look around elsewhere in order to see what effects may be bound up with it for me. When I deviate from the principle of duty, this is quite certainly bad; but if I desert my prudential maxim, this can often be greatly to my advantage, though it is admittedly safer to stick to it. Suppose I seek, however, to learn in the quickest way and yet unerringly how to solve the problem 'Does a lying promise accord with duty?' I have then to ask myself 'Should I really be content that my maxim (the maxim of getting out of a difficulty by a false promise) should hold as a universal law (one valid both for myself and others)? And could I really say to myself that every one may make a false promise if he finds himself in a difficulty from which he can extricate himself in no other way?' I then become aware at once that I can indeed will to lie, but I can by no means will a universal law of lying; for by such a law there could properly be no promises at all, since it would be futile to profess a will for future action to others who would not believe my profession or who, if they did so over-hastily, would pay me back in like coin; and consequently my maxim, as soon as it was made a universal law, would be bound to annul itself.

Thus I need no far-reaching ingenuity to find out what I have to do in order to possess a good will. Inexperienced in the course of world affairs and incapable of being prepared for all the chances that happen in it, I ask myself only 'Can you also will that your maxim should become a universal law?' Where you cannot, it is to be rejected, and that not because of a prospective loss to you or even to others, but because it cannot fit as a principle into a possible enactment of universal law. For such an enactment reason compels my immediate reverence, into whose grounds (which the philosopher may investigate) I have as yet no *insight*, although I do at least understand this much: reverence is the assessment of a worth which far outweighs all the worth of what is commended by inclination, and the necessity for me to act out of *pure* reverence for the practical law is what constitutes duty, to which every other motive must give way because it is the condition of a will good *in itself*, whose value is above all else.

[Ordinary practical reason]

In studying the moral knowledge of ordinary human reason we have now arrived at its first principle. This principle it admittedly does not conceive thus abstractly in its universal form; but it does always have it actually before its eyes and does use it as a norm of judgement. It would be easy to show here how human reason, with this compass in hand, is well able to distinguish, in all cases that present themselves, what is good or evil, right or wrong — provided that, without the least attempt to teach it anything new, we merely make reason attend, as Socrates did, to its own principle; and how in consequence there is no need of science or philosophy for knowing what man has to do in order to be honest and good, and indeed to be wise and virtuous.

CHAPTER 2   PASSAGE FROM POPULAR MORAL PHILOSOPHY TO A METAPHYSIC OF MORALS

[The use of examples]

If so far we have drawn our concept of duty from the ordinary use of our practical reason, it must by no means be inferred that we have treated it as a concept of experience. On the contrary, when we pay attention to our experience of human conduct, we meet frequent and — as we ourselves admit — justified complaints that we can adduce no certain examples of the spirit which acts out of pure duty, and that, although much may be done *in accordance with* the commands of *duty*, it remains doubtful whether it really is done *for the sake of duty* and so has a moral value. Hence at all times there have been philosophers who have absolutely denied the presence of this spirit in human actions and have ascribed everything to a more or less refined self-love. Yet they have not cast doubt on the rightness of the concept of morality. They have spoken rather with deep regret of the frailty and impurity of human nature, which is on their view noble enough to take as its rule an Idea so worthy of reverence, but at the same time too weak to follow it: the reason which should serve it for making laws it uses only to look after the interest of inclinations, whether singly or — at the best — in their greatest mutual compatibility.

In actual fact it is absolutely impossible for experience to establish with complete certainty a single case in which the maxim of an action in other respects right has rested solely on moral grounds and on the thought of one's duty. It is indeed at times the case that after the keenest self-examination we find nothing that without the moral motive of duty could have been strong enough to move us to this or that good action and to so great a sacrifice; but we cannot infer from this with certainty that it is not some secret impulse of self-love which has actually, under the mere show of the Idea of duty, been the cause genuinely determining our will. We are pleased to flatter ourselves with the false claim to a nobler motive, but in fact we can never, even by the most strenuous self-examination, get to the bottom of our secret impulses; for when moral value is in question, we are concerned, not with the actions which we see, but with their inner principles, which we cannot see.

Furthermore, to those who deride all morality as the mere phantom of a human imagination which gets above itself out of vanity we can do no service more pleasing than to admit that the concepts of duty must be drawn solely from experience (just as out of slackness we willingly persuade ourselves that this is so in the case of all other concepts); for by so doing we prepare for them an assured triumph. Out of love for humanity I am willing to allow that most of our actions may accord with duty; but if we look more closely at our scheming and striving, we everywhere come across the dear self, which is always turning up; and it is on this that the purpose of our actions is based — not on the strict command of duty, which would often require self-denial. One need not be exactly a foe to virtue, but merely a dispassionate observer declining to take the liveliest wish for goodness straight away as its realization, in order at certain moments (particularly with advancing years and with a power of judgement at once made shrewder by experience and also more keen in observation) to become doubtful whether any genuine virtue is actually to be encountered in the world. And then nothing can protect us against a complete falling away from our Ideas of duty, or can preserve in the soul a grounded reverence for its law, except the clear conviction that even if there never have been actions springing from such pure sources, the question at issue here is not whether this or that has happened; that, on the contrary, reason by itself and independently of all appearances commands what ought to happen; that consequently actions of which the world has perhaps hitherto given no example — actions whose practicability might well be doubted by those who rest everything on experience — are nevertheless commanded unrelentingly by reason; and that, for instance, although up to now there may have existed no loyal friend, pure loyalty in friendship can be no less required from every man, inasmuch as this duty, prior to all experience, is contained as duty in general in the Idea of a reason which determines the will by *a priori* grounds.

It may be added that unless we wish to deny to the concept of morality all truth and all relation to a possible object, we cannot dispute that its law is of such widespread significance as to hold, not merely for men, but for all *rational beings as such* — not merely subject to contingent conditions and exceptions, but *with absolute necessity*. It is therefore clear that no experience can give us occasion to infer even the possibility of such apodeictic laws. For by what right can we make what is perhaps valid only under the contingent conditions of humanity into an object of unlimited reverence as a universal precept for every rational nature? And how could laws for determining *our* will be taken as laws for determining the will of a rational being as such — and only because of this for determining ours — if these laws were merely empirical and did not have their source completely *a priori* in pure, but practical, reason?

What is more, we cannot do morality a worse service than by seeking to derive it from examples. Every example of it presented to me must first itself be judged by moral principles in order to decide if it is fit to serve as an original example — that is, as a model: it can in no way supply the prime source for the concept of morality. Even the Holy One of the gospel must first be compared with our ideal of moral perfection before we can recognize him to be such. He also says of himself: 'Why callest thou me (whom thou seest) good? There is none good (the archetype of the good) but one, that is, God (whom thou seest not).' But where do we get the concept of God as the highest good? Solely from the *Idea* of moral perfection, which reason traces *a priori* and conjoins inseparably with the concept of a free will. Imitation has no place in morality, and examples serve us only for encouragement. . . .

[*Review of conclusions*]

From these considerations the following conclusions emerge. All moral concepts have their seat and origin in reason completely *a priori*, and indeed in the most ordinary human reason just as much as in the most highly speculative: they cannot be abstracted from any empirical, and therefore merely contingent, knowledge. In this purity of their origin is to be found their very worthiness to serve as supreme practical principles, and everything empirical added to them is just so much taken away from their genuine influence and from the absolute value of the corresponding actions. It is not only a requirement of the utmost necessity in respect of theory, where our concern is solely with speculation, but is also of the utmost practical importance, to draw these concepts and laws from pure reason, to set them forth pure and unmixed, and indeed to determine the extent of this whole practical, but pure, rational knowledge — that is, to determine the whole power of pure practical reason. We ought never — as speculative philosophy does allow and even at times finds necessary — to make principles depend on the special nature of human reason. Since moral laws have to hold for every rational being as such, we ought rather to derive our principles from the general concept of a rational being as such, and on this basis to expound the whole of ethics — which requires anthropology for its *application* to man — at first independently as pure philosophy, that is, entirely as metaphysics (which we can very well do in this wholly abstract kind of knowledge). We know well that without possessing such a metaphysics it is a futile endeavour, I will not say to determine accurately for speculative judgement the moral element of duty in all that accords with duty — but that it is impossible, even in ordinary and practical usage, particularly in that of moral instruction, to base morals on their genuine principles and so to bring about pure moral dispositions and engraft them on men's minds for the highest good of the world.

In this task of ours we have to progress by natural stages, not merely from ordinary moral judgement (which is here worthy of great respect) to philosophical judgement, as we have already done, but from popular philosophy, which goes no further than it can get by fumbling about with the aid of examples, to metaphysics. (This no longer lets itself be held back by anything empirical, and indeed — since it must survey the complete totality of this kind of knowledge — goes right to Ideas, where examples themselves fail.) For this purpose we must follow — and must portray in detail — the power of practical reason from the general rules determining it right up to the point where there springs from it the concept of duty.

[Imperatives in general]

Everything in nature works in accordance with laws. Only a rational being has the power to act *in accordance with his idea* of laws — that is, in accordance with principles — and only so has he a *will*. Since *reason* is required in order to derive actions from laws, the will is nothing but practical reason. If reason infallibly determines the will, then in a being of this kind the actions which are recognized to be objectively necessary are also subjectively necessary — that is to say, the will is then a power to choose *only that* which reason independently of inclination recognizes to be practically necessary, that is, to be good. But if reason solely by itself is not sufficient to determine the will; if the will is exposed also to subjective conditions (certain impulsions) which do not always harmonize with the objective ones; if, in a word, the will is not *in itself* completely in accord with reason (as actually happens in the case of men); then actions which are recognized to be objectively necessary are subjectively contingent, and the determining of such a will in accordance with objective laws is *necessitation*. That is to say, the relation of objective laws to a will not good through and through is conceived as one in which the will of a rational being, although it is determined by principles of reason, does not necessarily follow these principles in virtue of its own nature.

The conception of an objective principle so far as this principle is necessitating for a will is called a command (of reason), and the formula of this command is called an *Imperative*.

All imperatives are expressed by an '*ought*' (*Sollen*). By this they mark the relation of an objective law of reason to a will which is not necessarily determined by this law in virtue of its subjective constitution (the relation of necessitation). They say that something would be good to do or to leave undone; only they say it to a will which does not always do a thing because it has been informed that this is a good thing to do. . . .

A perfectly good will would thus stand quite as much under objective laws (laws of the good), but it could not on this account be conceived as *necessitated* to act in conformity with law, since of itself, in accordance with its subjective constitution, it can be determined only by the concept of the good. Hence for the *divine* will, and in general for a *holy* will, there are no imperatives: 'I ought' is here out of place, because 'I *will*' is already of itself necessarily in harmony with the law. Imperatives are in consequence only formulae for expressing the relation of objective laws of willing to the subjective imperfection of the will of this or that rational being — for example, of the human will.

[Classification of imperatives]

All *imperatives* command either *hypothetically* or *categorically*. Hypothetical imperatives declare a possible action to be practically necessary as a means to the attainment of something else that one wills (or that one may will). A categorical imperative would be one which represented an action as objectively necessary in itself apart from its relation to a further end. . . . [Hence] if the action would be good solely as a means *to something else*, the imperative is *hypothetical*; if the action is represented as good *in itself* and therefore as necessary, in virtue of its principle, for a will which of itself accords with reason, then the imperative is *categorical*.

An imperative therefore tells me which of my possible actions would be good; and it formulates a practical rule for a will that does not perform an action straight away because the action is good — whether because the subject does not always know that it is good or because, even if he did know this, he might still act on maxims contrary to the objective principles of practical reason.

A hypothetical imperative thus says only that an action is good for some purpose or other, either *possible* or *actual*. In the first case it is a *problematic* practical principle; in the second case an *assertoric* practical principle. A categorical imperative, which declares an action to be objectively necessary in itself without reference to some purpose — that is, even without any further end — ranks as an *apodeictic* practical principle. . . .

All sciences have a practical part consisting of problems which suppose that some end is possible for us and of imperatives which tell us how it is to be attained. Hence the latter can in general be called imperatives of *skill*. Here there is absolutely no question about the rationality or goodness of the end, but only about what must be done to attain it. A prescription required by a doctor in order to cure his man completely and one required by a poisoner in order to make sure of killing him are of equal value so far as each serves to effect its purpose perfectly. Since in early youth we do not know what ends may present themselves to us in the course of life, parents seek above all to make their children learn things *of many kinds*; they provide carefully for *skill* in the use of means to all sorts of *arbitrary* ends, of none of which can they be certain that it could not in the future become an actual purpose of their ward, while it is always *possible* that he might adopt it. Their care in this matter is so great that they commonly neglect on this account to form and correct the judgement of their children about the worth of the things which they might possibly adopt as ends.

There is, however, *one* end that can be presupposed as actual in all rational beings (so far as they are dependent beings to whom imperatives apply); and thus there is one purpose which they not only *can* have, but which we can assume with certainty that they all *do* have by a natural necessity — the purpose, namely, of *happiness*. A hypothetical imperative which affirms the practical necessity of an action as a means to the furtherance of happiness is *assertoric*. We may represent it, not simply as necessary to an uncertain, merely possible purpose, but as necessary to a purpose which we can presuppose *a priori* and with certainty to be present in every man because it belongs to his very being. Now skill in the choice of means to one's own greatest well-being can be called *prudence* in the narrowest sense. Thus an imperative concerned with the choice of means to one's own happiness — that is, a precept of prudence — still remains *hypothetical*: an action is commanded, not absolutely, but only as a means to a further purpose.

Finally, there is an imperative which, without being based on, and conditioned by, any further purpose to be attained by a certain line of conduct, enjoins this conduct immediately. This imperative is *categorical*. It is concerned, not with the matter of the action and its presumed results, but with its form and with the principle from which it follows; and what is essentially good in the action consists in the mental disposition, let the consequences be what they may. This imperative may be called the imperative of *morality*. . . .

[*How are imperatives possible?*]

The question now arises 'How are all these imperatives possible?' This question does not ask how we can conceive the execution of an action commanded by the imperative, but merely how we can conceive the necessitation of the will expressed by the imperative in setting us a task. How an imperative of skill is possible requires no special discussion. Who wills the end, wills (so far as reason has decisive influence on his actions) also the means which are indispensably necessary and in his power. So far as willing is concerned, this proposition is analytic: for in my willing of an object as an effect there is already conceived the causality of myself as an acting cause — that is, the use of means; and from the concept of willing an end the imperative merely extracts the concept of actions necessary to this end. (Synthetic propositions are required in order to determine the means to a proposed end, but these are concerned, not with the reason for performing the act of will, but with the cause which produces the object.) That in order to divide a line into two equal parts on a sure principle I must from its ends describe two intersecting arcs — this is admittedly taught by mathematics only in synthetic propositions; but when I know that the aforesaid effect can be produced only by such an action, the proposition 'If I fully will the effect, I also will the action required for it' is analytic; for it is one and the same thing to conceive something as an effect possible in a certain way through me and to conceive myself as acting in the same way with respect to it. . . .

[With the] categorical imperative or law of morality the reason for our difficulty (in comprehending its possibility) is a very serious one. We have here a synthetic *a priori* practical proposition,[2] and since in theoretical knowledge there is so much difficulty in comprehending the possibility of propositions of this kind, it may readily be gathered that in practical knowledge the difficulty will be no less.

[*The Formula of Universal Law*]

In this task we wish first to enquire whether perhaps the mere concept of a categorical imperative may not also provide us with the formula containing the only proposition that can be a categorical imperative; for even when we know the purport of such an absolute command, the

---

2 Without presupposing a condition taken from some inclination I connect an action with the will *a priori* and therefore necessarily (although only objectively so — that is, only subject to the Idea of a reason having full power over all subjective impulses to action). Here we have a practical proposition in which the willing of an action is not derived analytically from some other willing already presupposed (for we do not possess any such perfect will), but is on the contrary connected immediately with the concept of the will of a rational being as something which is not contained in this concept.

question of its possibility will still require a special and troublesome effort, which we postpone to the final chapter.

When I conceive a *hypothetical* imperative in general, I do not know beforehand what it will contain — until its condition is given. But if I conceive a *categorical* imperative, I know at once what it contains. For since besides the law this imperative contains only the necessity that our maxim [3] should conform to this law, while the law, as we have seen, contains no condition to limit it, there remains nothing over to which the maxim has to conform except the universality of a law as such; and it is this conformity alone that the imperative properly asserts to be necessary.

There is therefore only a single categorical imperative and it is this: '*Act only on that maxim through which you can at the same time will that it should become a universal law.*'

Now if all imperatives of duty can be derived from this one imperative as their principle, then even although we leave it unsettled whether what we call duty may not be an empty concept, we shall still be able to show at least what we understand by it and what the concept means.

[The Formula of the Law of Nature]

Since the universality of the law governing the production of effects constitutes what is properly called *nature* in its most general sense (nature as regards its form) — that is, the existence of things so far as determined by universal laws — the universal imperative of duty may also run as follows: '*Act as if the maxim of your action were to become through your will a universal law of nature.*'

[Illustrations]

We will now enumerate a few duties, following their customary division into duties towards self and duties towards others and into perfect and imperfect duties.

1. A man feels sick of life as the result of a series of misfortunes that has mounted to the point of despair, but he is still so far in possession of his reason as to ask himself whether taking his own life may not be contrary to his duty to himself. He now applies the test 'Can the maxim of my action really become a universal law of nature?' His maxim is 'From self-love I make it my principle to shorten my life if its continuance threatens more evil than it promises pleasure.' The only further question to ask is whether this principle of self-love can become a universal law of nature. It is then seen at once that a system of nature by whose law the very same

---

[3] A *maxim* is a subjective principle of action and must be distinguished from an *objective principle* — namely, a practical law. The former contains a practical rule determined by reason in accordance with the conditions of the subject (often his ignorance or again his inclinations): it is thus a principle on which the subject *acts*. A law, on the other hand, is an objective principle valid for every rational being; and it is a principle on which he *ought to act* — that is, an imperative.

feeling whose function (*Bestimmung*) is to stimulate the furtherance of life should actually destroy life would contradict itself and consequently could not subsist as a system of nature. Hence this maxim cannot possibly hold as a universal law of nature and is therefore entirely opposed to the supreme principle of all duty.

2. Another finds himself driven to borrowing money because of need. He well knows that he will not be able to pay it back; but he sees too that he will get no loan unless he gives a firm promise to pay it back within a fixed time. He is inclined to make such a promise; but he has still enough conscience to ask 'Is it not unlawful and contrary to duty to get out of difficulties in this way?' Supposing, however, he did resolve to do so, the maxim of his action would run thus: 'Whenever I believe myself short of money, I will borrow money and promise to pay it back, though I know that this will never be done.' Now this principle of self-love or personal advantage is perhaps quite compatible with my own entire future welfare; only there remains the question 'Is it right?' I therefore transform the demand of self-love into a universal law and frame my question thus: 'How would things stand if my maxim became a universal law?' I then see straight away that this maxim can never rank as a universal law of nature and be self-consistent, but must necessarily contradict itself. For the universality of a law that every one believing himself to be in need can make any promise he pleases with the intention not to keep it would make promising, and the very purpose of promising, itself impossible, since no one would believe he was being promised anything, but would laugh at utterances of this kind as empty shams.

3. A third finds in himself a talent whose cultivation would make him a useful man for all sorts of purposes. But he sees himself in comfortable circumstances, and he prefers to give himself up to pleasure rather than to bother about increasing and improving his fortunate natural aptitudes. Yet he asks himself further 'Does my maxim of neglecting my natural gifts, besides agreeing in itself with my tendency to indulgence, agree also with what is called duty?' He then sees that a system of nature could indeed always subsist under such a universal law, although (like the South Sea Islanders) every man should let his talents rust and should be bent on devoting his life solely to idleness, indulgence, procreation, and, in a word, to enjoyment. Only he cannot possibly *will* that this should become a universal law of nature or should be implanted in us as such a law by a natural instinct. For as a rational being he necessarily wills that all his powers should be developed, since they serve him, and are given him, for all sorts of possible ends.

4. Yet a *fourth* is himself flourishing, but he sees others who have to struggle with great hardships (and whom he could easily help); and he thinks 'What does it matter to me? Let every one be as happy as Heaven wills or as he can make himself; I won't deprive him of anything; I won't even envy him; only I have no wish to contribute anything to his well-

being or to his support in distress!' Now admittedly if such an attitude were a universal law of nature, mankind could get on perfectly well — better no doubt than if everybody prates about sympathy and goodwill, and even takes pains, on occasion, to practise them, but on the other hand cheats where he can, traffics in human rights, or violates them in other ways. But although it is possible that a universal law of nature could subsist in harmony with this maxim, yet it is impossible to *will* that such a principle should hold everywhere as a law of nature. For a will which decided in this way would be in conflict with itself, since many a situation might arise in which the man needed love and sympathy from others, and in which, by such a law of nature sprung from his own will, he would rob himself of all hope of the help he wants for himself.

[*The canon of moral judgement*]

These are some of the many actual duties — or at least of what we take to be such — whose derivation from the single principle cited above leaps to the eye. We must *be able to will* that a maxim of our action should become a universal law — this is the general canon for all moral judgement of action. Some actions are so constituted that their maxim cannot even be *conceived* as a universal law of nature without contradiction, let alone be *willed* as what *ought* to become one. In the case of others we do not find this inner impossibility, but it is still impossible to *will* that their maxim should be raised to the universality of a law of nature, because such a will would contradict itself. It is easily seen that the first kind of action is opposed to strict or narrow (rigorous) duty, the second only to wider (meritorious) duty; and thus that by these examples all duties — so far as the type of obligation is concerned (not the object of dutiful action) — are fully set out in their dependence on our single principle.

If we now attend to ourselves whenever we transgress a duty, we find that we in fact do not will that our maxim should become a universal law — since this is impossible for us — but rather that its opposite should remain a law universally: we only take the liberty of making an *exception* to it for ourselves (or even just for this once) to the advantage of our inclination. . . .

We have thus at least shown this much — that if duty is a concept which is to have meaning and real legislative authority for our actions, this can be expressed only in categorical imperatives and by no means in hypothetical ones. At the same time — and this is already a great deal — we have set forth distinctly, and determinately for every type of application, the content of the categorical imperative, which must contain the principle of all duty (if there is to be such a thing at all). But we are still not so far advanced as to prove *a priori* that there actually is an imperative of this kind — that there is a practical law which by itself commands absolutely and without any further motives, and that the following of this law is duty. . . .

Our question therefore is this: 'Is it a necessary law *for all rational beings* always to judge their actions by reference to those maxims of which they can themselves will that they should serve as universal laws?' If there is such a law, it must already be connected (entirely *a priori*) with the concept of the will of a rational being as such. But in order to discover this connexion we must, however much we may bristle, take a step beyond it — that is, into metaphysics, although into a region of it different from that of speculative philosophy, namely, the metaphysic of morals. . . . Here . . . we are discussing objective practical laws, and consequently the relation of a will to itself as determined solely by reason. Everything related to the empirical then falls away of itself; for if *reason entirely by itself* determines conduct (and it is the possibility of this which we now wish to investigate), it must necessarily do so *a priori*.

[*The Formula of the End in Itself*]

The will is conceived as a power of determining oneself to action *in accordance with the idea of certain laws*. And such a power can be found only in rational beings. Now what serves the will as a subjective ground of its self-determination is an *end*; and this, if it is given by reason alone, must be equally valid for all rational beings. What, on the other hand, contains merely the ground of the possibility of an action whose effect is an end is called a *means*. The subjective ground of a desire is an *impulsion* (*Triebfeder*); the objective ground of a volition is a *motive* (*Bewegungsgrund*). Hence the difference between subjective ends, which are based on impulsions, and objective ends, which depend on motives valid for every rational being. Practical principles are *formal* if they abstract from all subjective ends; they are *material*, on the other hand, if they are based on such ends and consequently on certain impulsions. Ends that a rational being adopts arbitrarily as *effects* of his action (material ends) are in every case only relative; for it is solely their relation to special characteristics in the subject's power of appetition which gives them their value. Hence this value can provide no universal principles, no principles valid and necessary for all rational beings and also for every volition — that is, no practical laws. Consequently all these relative ends can be the ground only of hypothetical imperatives.

Suppose, however, there were something *whose existence* has *in itself* an absolute value, something which as *an end in itself* could be a ground of determinate laws; then in it, and in it alone, would there be the ground of a possible categorical imperative — that is, of a practical law.

Now I say that man, and in general every rational being, *exists* as an end in himself, *not merely as a means* for arbitrary use by this or that will: he must in all his actions, whether they are directed to himself or to other rational beings, always be viewed *at the same time as an end*. All the objects of inclination have only a conditioned value; for if there were not these inclinations and the needs grounded on them, their object would be valueless. Inclinations themselves, as sources of needs, are so far from having an absolute value to make them desirable for their own sake that it must rather be the universal wish of every rational being to be wholly free from them. Thus the value of all objects that can *be produced* by our action is always conditioned. Beings whose existence depends, not on our will, but on nature, have none the less, if they are non-rational beings, only a relative value as means and are consequently called *things*. Rational beings, on the other hand, are called *persons* because their nature already marks them out as ends in themselves — that is, as something which ought not to be used merely as a means — and consequently imposes to that extent a limit on all arbitrary treatment of them (and is an object of reverence). Persons therefore, are not merely subjective ends whose existence as an object of our actions has a value *for us*: they are *objective ends* — that is, things whose existence is in itself an end, and indeed an end such that in its place we can put no other end to which they should serve *simply* as means; for unless this is so, nothing at all of *absolute* value would be found anywhere. But if all value were conditioned — that is, contingent — then no supreme principle could be found for reason at all.

If then there is to be a supreme practical principle and — so far as the human will is concerned — a categorical imperative, it must be such that from the idea of something which is necessarily an end for every one because it is an *end in itself* it forms an *objective* principle of the will and consequently can serve as a practical law. The ground of this principle is: *Rational nature exists as an end in itself*. This is the way in which a man necessarily conceives his own existence: it is therefore so far a *subjective* principle of human actions. But it is also the way in which every other rational being conceives his existence on the same rational ground which is valid also for me; hence it is at the same time an *objective* principle, from which, as a supreme practical ground, it must be possible to derive all laws for the will. The practical imperative will therefore be as follows: *Act in such a way that you always treat humanity, whether in your own person or in the person of any other, never simply as a means, but always at the same time as an end*. We will now consider whether this can be carried out in practice.

[Illustrations]

Let us keep to our previous examples.

First, as regards the concept of necessary duty to oneself, the man who contemplates suicide will ask 'Can my action be compatible with the Idea of humanity *as an end in itself*?' If he does away with himself in order to escape from a painful situation, he is making use of a person merely as *a means* to maintain a tolerable state of affairs till the end of his life. But man is not a thing — not something to be used *merely* as a means: he must always in all his actions be regarded as an end in himself. Hence I cannot dispose of man in my person by maiming, spoiling, or killing. (A more precise determination of this principle in order to avoid all misunderstanding — for example, about having limbs amputated to save myself or about exposing my life to danger in order to preserve it, and so on — I must here forego: this question belongs to morals proper.)

Secondly, so far as necessary or strict duty to others is concerned, the man who has a mind to make a false promise to others will see at once that he is intending to make use of another man *merely as a means* to an end he does not share. For the man whom I seek to use for my own purposes by such a promise cannot possibly agree with my way of behaving to him, and so cannot himself share the end of the action. This incompatibility with the principle of duty to others leaps to the eye more obviously when we bring in examples of attempts on the freedom and property of others. For then it is manifest that a violator of the rights of man intends to use the person of others merely as a means without taking into consideration that, as rational beings, they ought always at the same time to be rated as ends — that is, only as beings who must themselves be able to share in the end of the very same action.

Thirdly, in regard to contingent (meritorious) duty to oneself, it is not enough that an action should refrain from conflicting with humanity in our own person as an end in itself: it must also *harmonize with this end.* Now there are in humanity capacities for greater perfection which form part of nature's purpose for humanity in our person. To neglect these can admittedly be compatible with the *maintenance* of humanity as an end in itself, but not with the *promotion* of this end.

Fourthly, as regards meritorious duties to others, the natural end which all men seek is their own happiness. Now humanity could no doubt subsist if everybody contributed nothing to the happiness of others but at the same time refrained from deliberately impairing their happiness. This is, however, merely to agree negatively and not positively with *humanity as an end in itself* unless every one endeavours also, so far as in him lies, to further the ends of others. For the ends of a subject who is an end in himself must, if this conception is to have its *full* effect in me, be also, as far as possible, *my* ends.

[The Formula of Autonomy]

This principle of humanity, and in general of every rational agent, *as an end in itself* (a principle which is the supreme limiting condition of every man's freedom of action) is not borrowed from experience; firstly, because it is universal, applying as it does to all rational beings as such, and no experience is adequate to determine universality; secondly, because in it humanity is conceived, not as an end of man (subjectively) — that is, as an object which, as a matter of fact, happens to be made an end — but as an objective end — one which, be our ends what they may, must, as a law, constitute the supreme limiting condition of all subjective ends and so must spring from pure reason. That is to say, the ground for every enactment of practical law lies *objectively in the rule* and in the form of universality which (according to our first principle) makes the rule capable of being a law (and indeed a law of nature); *subjectively*, however, it lies in the *end*; but (according to our second principle) the subject of all ends is to be found in every rational being as an end in himself. From this there now follows our third practical principle for the will — as the supreme condition of the will's conformity with universal practical reason — namely, the Idea *of the will of every rational being as a will which makes universal law.*

By this principle all maxims are repudiated which cannot accord with the will's own enactment of universal law. The will is therefore not merely subject to the law, but is so subject that it must be considered as also *making the law* for itself and precisely on this account as first of all subject to the law (of which it can regard itself as the author).

[The exclusion of interest]

Imperatives as formulated above — namely, the imperative enjoining conformity of actions to universal law on the analogy of a *natural order* and that enjoining the universal *supremacy* of rational beings in themselves *as ends* — did, by the mere fact that they were represented as categorical, exclude from their sovereign authority every admixture of interest as a motive. They were, however, merely *assumed* to be categorical because we were bound to make this assumption if we wished to explain the concept of duty. That there were practical propositions which commanded categorically could not itself be proved, any more than it can be proved in this chapter generally; but one thing could have been done — namely, to show that in willing for the sake of duty renunciation of all interest, as the specific mark distinguishing a categorical from a hypothetical imperative, was expressed in the very imperative itself by means of some determination inherent in it. This is what is done in the present third formulation of the principle — namely, in the Idea of the will of every rational being as *a will which makes universal law.*

Once we conceive a will of this kind, it becomes clear that while a will *which is subject to law* may be bound to this law by some interest, nevertheless a will which is itself a supreme lawgiver cannot possibly as such depend on any interest; for a will which is dependent in this way would itself require yet a further law in order to restrict the interest of self-love to the condition that this interest should itself be valid as a universal law.

Thus the *principle* that every human will is *a will which by all its maxims enacts universal law* — provided only that it were right in other ways

— would be *well suited* to be a categorical imperative in this respect: that precisely because of the Idea of making universal law it is *based on no interest* and consequently can alone among all possible imperatives be *unconditioned.* . . .

We need not now wonder, when we look back upon all the previous efforts that have been made to discover the principle of morality, why they have one and all been bound to fail. Their authors saw man as tied to laws by his duty, but it never occurred to them that he is subject only to *laws which are made by himself* and yet are *universal*, and that he is bound only to act in conformity with a will which is his own but has as nature's purpose for it the function of making universal law. For when they thought of man merely as subject to a law (whatever it might be), the law had to carry with it some interest in order to attract or compel, because it did not spring as a law from *his own* will: in order to conform with the law his will had to be necessitated by *something else* to act in a certain way. This absolutely inevitable conclusion meant that all the labour spent in trying to find a supreme principle of duty was lost beyond recall; for what they discovered was never duty, but only the necessity of acting from a certain interest. This interest might be one's own or another's; but on such a view the imperative was bound to be always a conditioned one and could not possibly serve as a moral law. I will therefore call my principle the principle of the *Autonomy* of the will in contrast with all others, which I consequently class under *Heteronomy*.

[The Formula of the Kingdom of Ends]

The concept of every rational being as one who must regard himself as making universal law by all the maxims of his will, and must seek to judge himself and his actions from this point of view, leads to a closely connected and very fruitful concept — namely, that of *a kingdom of ends*.

I understand by a *'kingdom'* a systematic union of different rational beings under common laws. Now since laws determine ends as regards their universal validity, we shall be able — if we abstract from the personal differences between rational beings, and also from all the content of their private ends — to conceive a whole of all ends in systematic conjunction (a whole both of rational beings as ends in themselves and also of the personal ends which each may set before himself); that is, we shall be able to conceive a kingdom of ends which is possible in accordance with the above principles.

For rational beings all stand under the *law* that each of them should treat himself and all others, *never merely as a means*, but always *at the same time as an end in himself*. But by so doing there arises a systematic union of rational beings under common objective laws — that is, a kingdom. Since these laws are directed precisely to the relation of such beings to one another as ends and means, this kingdom can be called a kingdom of ends (which is admittedly only an Ideal).

A rational being belongs to the kingdom of ends as a *member*, when, although he makes its universal laws, he is also himself subject to these laws. He belongs to it as its *head*, when as the maker of laws he is himself subject to the will of no other.

A rational being must always regard himself as making laws in a kingdom of ends which is possible through freedom of the will — whether it be as member or as head. The position of the latter he can maintain, not in virtue of the maxim of his will alone, but only if he is a completely independent being, without needs and with an unlimited power adequate to his will.

Thus morality consists in the relation of all action to the making of laws whereby alone a kingdom of ends is possible. This making of laws must be found in every rational being himself and must be able to spring from his will. The principle of his will is therefore never to perform an action except on a maxim such as can also be a universal law, and consequently such *that the will can regard itself as at the same time making universal law by means of its maxim.* Where maxims are not already by their very nature in harmony with this objective principle of rational beings as makers of universal law, the necessity of acting on this principle is practical necessitation — that is, *duty.* Duty does not apply to the head in a kingdom of ends, but it does apply to every member and to all members in equal measure. . . .

What is it then that entitles a morally good attitude of mind — or virtue — to make claims so high? It is nothing less than the *share* which it affords to a rational being *in the making of universal law*, and which therefore fits him to be a member in a possible kingdom of ends. For this he was already marked out in virtue of his own proper nature as an end in himself and consequently as a maker of laws in the kingdom of ends — as free in respect of all laws of nature, obeying only those laws which he makes himself and in virtue of which his maxims can have their part in the making of universal law (to which he at the same time subjects himself). For nothing can have a value other than that determined for it by the law. But the law-making which determines all value must for this reason have a dignity — that is, an unconditioned and incomparable worth — for the appreciation of which, as necessarily given by a rational being, the word *'reverence'* is the only becoming expression. *Autonomy* is therefore the ground of the dignity of human nature and of every rational nature.

The aforesaid three ways of representing the principle of morality are at bottom merely so many formulations of precisely the same law, one of them by itself containing a combination of the other two.

CHAPTER 3   PASSAGE FROM A METAPHYSIC
OF MORALS TO A CRITIQUE OF PURE
PRACTICAL REASON

The concept of freedom is the key to explain autonomy of the will

Will is a kind of causality belonging to living beings so far as they are rational. *Freedom* would then be the property this causality has of being able to work independently of *determination* by alien causes; just as *natural necessity* is a property characterizing the causality of all non-rational beings — the property of being determined to activity by the influence of alien causes.

The above definition of freedom is *negative* and consequently unfruitful as a way of grasping its essence; but there springs from it a *positive* concept, which, as positive, is richer and more fruitful. The concept of causality carries with it that of *laws* (*Gesetze*) in accordance with which, because of something we call a cause, something else — namely, its effect — must be posited (*gesetzt*). Hence freedom of will, although it is not the property of conforming to laws of nature, is not for this reason lawless: it must rather be a causality conforming to immutable laws, though of a special kind; for otherwise a free will would be self-contradictory. Natural necessity, as we have seen, is a heteronomy of efficient causes; for every effect is possible only in conformity with the law that something else determines the efficient cause to causal action. What else then can freedom of will be but autonomy — that is, the property which will has of being a law to itself? The proposition 'Will is in all its actions a law to itself' expresses, however, only the principle of acting on no maxim other than one which can have for its object itself as at the same time a universal law. This is precisely the formula of the categorical imperative and the principle of morality. Thus a free will and a will under moral laws are one and the same.

Consequently if freedom of the will is presupposed, morality, together with its principle, follows by mere analysis of the concept of freedom. . . .

How is a categorical imperative possible?

A rational being counts himself, *qua* intelligence, as belonging to the intelligible world, and solely *qua* efficient cause belonging to the intelligible world does he give to his causality the name of '*will.*' On the other side, however, he is conscious of himself as also a part of the sensible world, where his actions are encountered as mere appearances of this causality. Yet the possibility of these actions cannot be made intelligible by means of such causality, since with this we have no direct acquaintance; and instead these actions, as belonging to the sensible world, have to be understood as determined by other appearances — namely, by desires and inclinations. Hence, if I were solely a member of the intelligible world, all my actions would be in perfect conformity with the principle of the autonomy of a pure will; if I were solely a part of the sensible world, they would have to be taken as in complete conformity with the law of nature governing desires and inclinations — that is, with the heteronomy of nature. (In the first case they would be grounded on the supreme principle of morality; in the second case on that of happiness.) *But the intelligible world contains the ground of the sensible world and therefore also of its laws;* and so in respect of my will, for which (as belonging entirely to the intelligible world) it gives laws immediately, it must also be conceived as containing such a ground. Hence, in spite of regarding myself from one point of view as a being that belongs to the sensible world, I shall have to recognize that, *qua* intelligence, I am subject to the law of the intelligible world — that is, to the reason which contains this law in the Idea of freedom, and so to the autonomy of the will — and therefore I must look on the laws of the intelligible world as imperatives for me and on the actions which conform to this principle as duties.

And in this way categorical imperatives are possible because the Idea of freedom makes me a member of an intelligible world. This being so, if I were solely a member of the intelligible world, all my actions *would* invariably accord with the autonomy of the will; but because I intuit myself at the same time as a member of the sensible world, they *ought* so to accord. This *categorical* 'ought' presents us with a synthetic *a priori* proposition, since to my will as affected by sensuous desires there is added the Idea of the same will, viewed, however, as a pure will belonging to the intelligible world and active on its own account — a will which contains the supreme condition of the former will, so far as reason is concerned. This is roughly like the way in which concepts of the understanding, which by themselves signify nothing but the form of law in general, are added to intuitions of the sensible world and so make synthetic *a priori* propositions possible on which all our knowledge of nature is based.

The practical use of ordinary human reason confirms the rightness of this deduction. There is no one, not even the most hardened scoundrel — provided only he is accustomed to use reason in other ways — who, when presented with examples of honesty in purpose, of faithfulness to good maxims, of sympathy, and of kindness towards all (even when these are bound up with great sacrifices of advantage and comfort), does not wish that he too might be a man of like spirit. He is unable to realize such an aim in his own person — though only on account of his desires and impulses; but yet at the same time he wishes to be free from these inclinations, which are a burden to himself. By such a wish he shows that having a will free from sensuous impulses he transfers himself in thought into an order of things quite different from that of his desires in the field of sensibility; for from the fulfilment of this wish he can expect no gratification of his sensuous desires and consequently no state which would satisfy any of his actual or even conceivable inclinations (since by such an expectation the very Idea which elicited the wish would be deprived of its superiority); all he can expect is a greater inner worth of his own person. This better person he believes himself to be when he transfers himself to the standpoint of a member of the intelligible world. He is involuntarily constrained to do so by the Idea of freedom — that is, of not being dependent on *determination* by causes in the sensible world; and from this standpoint he is conscious of possessing a good will which, on his own admission, constitutes the law for the bad will belonging to him as a member of the sensible world — a law of whose authority he is aware even in transgressing it. The moral 'I ought' is thus an 'I will' for man as a member of the intelligible world; and it is conceived by him as an 'I ought' only in so far as he considers himself at the same time to be a member of the sensible world.

QUESTIONS

1. What does Kant mean when he says that only a good will is "good without qualification"? What reasons does he offer for this conclusion?
2. According to Kant, which ones of the following are praiseworthy: (a) actions inconsistent with duty; (b) actions consistent with duty but done because they are expected to serve personal ends; (c) kindly actions done from sympathy with other human beings; (d) actions consistent with duty done solely because the agent thinks them morally obligatory? Does Kant's view seem to you defensible?
3. What does he mean by saying that the moral value of an action is not a function of its aim or results but of "its maxim" or "the principle of the will"?
4. In the case of an action done on account of duty, is the maxim, "In circumstances *ABC*, do *D*" or is it rather like "Since in circumstances *ABC* it would be wrong to do non-*D*, therefore do *D*"? Or is the answer not clear?
5. Why does Kant say that it is possible to have *respect* for law but not for the objects of our preferences? Does this claim make any sense?
6. Explain the reasoning behind this conclusion: "Nothing remains to serve as a principle of the will except universal conformity of its action to law as such. That is, I should never act in such a way that I could not also will that my maxim should be universal law."
7. Is Kant right in thinking that intelligent people use this principle as the standard for moral assessments?
8. Why does Kant think it is important to show that moral laws can be derived from the concept of a rational being in general?
9. What is an "objective principle"? an "imperative"? a "hypothetical imperative"? a "categorical imperative"? How are imperatives related to the conception of a good action — good either as a means or in itself?
10. Show how the two kinds of hypothetical imperative are related to the imperatives of skill and prudence and to the categorical imperative of morality.

11. Kant, in answering the question how these imperatives are possible (*i.e.*, how the imperatives constrain choice) says that in a sense the effect of the hypothetical imperatives is analytic, whereas that of the categorical imperative is synthetic. Explain what he means. (Clue: There is a parallel with synthetic propositions, in which the concept of the subject of the judgment does not contain the concept of the predicate. In the present context, however, Kant is talking about *choices* and *principles*.)

12. Take the statement: "To perform one's duty is always to follow the categorical imperative." Does Kant regard this as an analytic or a synthetic statement?

13. Kant says some maxims can't even be *conceived*, without contradiction, as universal laws for conduct (or of nature), whereas others can't be *chosen* as such, without the person contradicting himself. Explain the distinction, and decide which of Kant's examples appears to fall into each category. Does he fail to show either kind of impossibility for some of his examples?

14. How does he relate the categorical imperative, as stated, by means of the view that rational beings have absolute worth, to the second form of the moral imperative: "Act so as to treat humanity . . . always as an end and never only as a means"? Does Kant offer any reasons for thinking rational beings have absolute worth? Does he think this conclusion can be proved by observation?

15. What is the "realm of ends"? How is it related to his concept of the moral law?

16. How does Kant define "freedom of the will"? Will a "free" will naturally be moral, according to him? Is morality what people ordinarily mean when they speak of "free choice"?

17. Why does Kant think that the idea of freedom leads to the view that we are members of an intelligible world, whose laws are imperatives of duty for us?

18. Might a choice be free in Kant's sense but at the same time be the necessary outcome, as a matter of causal laws, of a prior state of affairs?

19. What is the difference, if any, between Kant's categorical imperative and the Golden Rule?

20. Suppose someone argued that the categorical imperative is obviously no test for *objective* duty. For, according to Kant, the agent is to consider whether in the situation as he *thinks* it is, a possible action with the consequences he *thinks* it would have, can consistently be chosen by him as a universal rule for action. (Or is the question whether he *thinks* he can choose it as such a rule?) But objective duty clearly can't depend so heavily on what somebody *thinks*; according to Kant, the very same action in the same circumstances might be right for one person and wrong for another. What would you reply to this argument? Could Kant be defended successfully as giving an account of objective duty?

21. Suppose it is said that what one person can will as a universal rule for conduct may well differ from what another person can will. In particular, a person's choices about rules for charity will depend on his own situation, how likely he is to be in need of charity. Does this dependence mean that Kant's theory does not give any universally valid concrete moral principles?

SUGGESTIONS FOR FURTHER READING

Kant, Immanuel. *Critique of Practical Reason and Other Writings in Moral Philosophy.* Trans. and ed. by L. W. Beck. Chicago: Univ. of Chicago Press, 1949.
————. *Kant's Critique of Practical Reason and Other Works on the Theory of Ethics.* Trans. by T. K. Abbott. New York: Longmans, Green, 1909.
Brandt, Richard B. *Ethical Theory.* Englewood Cliffs, N. J.: Prentice-Hall, 1959, Ch. 2.
Broad, C. D. *Five Types of Ethical Theory.* New York: Humanities Press, 1960.
Harrison, J. "Kant's Examples of the First Formulation of the Categorical Imperative," *Philosophical Quarterly,* Vol. 7 (1957), pp. 50-62.
Körner, S. *Kant.* Baltimore: Penguin Books, 1955.
Paton, H. J. *The Categorical Imperative.* London: Hutchinson, 1953.
Ross, Sir William David. *Kant's Ethical Theory.* New York: Oxford Univ. Press, 1954.

Sir William David Ross (1877-   )

MANY DIFFERENT PRIMA FACIE OBLIGATIONS

We have already met with the work of W. D. Ross (*supra,* pp. 119-25). We now come to his most important contribution, the one on which his historical place as a moral philosopher primarily rests.

Ross is not convinced by contemporary utilitarianism, any more than Butler was convinced by the utilitarianism of his day. They agree that it is too simple to say that our only obligation is to do as much good as we can. On the one hand, Ross thinks this even when the utilitarian is not a hedonist but, like Ross himself, believes that various things, such as knowledge, have intrinsic worth. On the other hand, Ross believes that many formalists (like Butler and Kant) go too far in asserting that certain kinds of action are always wrong, or obligatory, without exception. Ross thinks that, *other things being equal,* we are obligated to keep a promise; but he agrees that sometimes other things aren't equal and then sometimes it is our duty to break a promise. It cannot be, he thinks, that we are *always* obligated to follow several different moral rules (like the Ten Commandments), for then we should be obligated to do impossible things when the rules conflict. Ross concludes by offering a kind of compromise between extreme formalism and utilitarianism. Certain kinds of situation (such as having made a promise) create *prima facie* obligations, which lay some claim on us. Among these kinds is the fact that we are sometimes in a position to do good — hence there is a prima facie obligation to do good (and so far Ross concedes truth in utilitarianism). Where there is a prima facie obligation, it ought to be fulfilled, except when there is a conflicting obligation. (This exception is his qualification of extreme formalism.) When obligations conflict, we must just use moral judgment to decide what we ought to do; there are no general rules which can give direction.

Ross has also been one of the foremost advocates of the view that some ethical principles are self-evident and hence do not require to be established or demonstrated. This view is one we shall be assessing in the following chapter, and the reader will wish to return to parts of the present selection, which set forth this theory, at a later point.

From W. D. Ross, *The Right and the Good*, published by The Clarendon Press, Oxford, 1930, and reprinted with their permission.

THE RIGHT AND THE GOOD

WHAT MAKES RIGHT ACTS RIGHT?

The real point at issue between hedonism and utilitarianism on the one hand and their opponents on the other is not whether 'right' means 'productive of so and so'; for it cannot with any plausibility be maintained that it does. The point at issue is that to which we now pass, viz. whether there is any general character which makes right acts right, and if so, what it is. Among the main historical attempts to state a single characteristic of all right actions which is the foundation of their rightness are those made by egoism and utilitarianism. But I do not propose to discuss these, not because the subject is unimportant, but because it has been dealt with so often and so well already, and because there has come to be so much agreement among moral philosophers that neither of these theories is satisfactory. A much more attractive theory has been put forward by Professor Moore: that what makes actions right is that they are productive of more *good* than could have been produced by any other action open to the agent.

This theory is in fact the culmination of all the attempts to base rightness on productivity of some sort of result. The first form this attempt takes is the attempt to base rightness on conduciveness to the advantage or pleasure of the agent. This theory comes to grief over the fact, which stares us in the face, that a great part of duty consists in an observance of the rights and a furtherance of the interests of others, whatever the cost to ourselves may be. Plato and others may be right in holding that a regard for the rights of others never in the long run involves a loss of happiness for the agent, that 'the just life profits a man.' But this, even if true, is irrelevant to the rightness of the act. As soon as a man does an action *because* he thinks he will promote his own interests thereby, he is acting not from a sense of its rightness but from self-interest.

To the egoistic theory hedonistic utilitarianism supplies a much-needed amendment. It points out correctly that the fact that a certain pleasure will be enjoyed by the agent is no reason why he *ought* to bring it into being rather than an equal or greater pleasure to be enjoyed by another, though, human nature being what it is, it makes it not unlikely that he *will* try to bring it into being. But hedonistic utilitarianism in its turn needs a correction. On reflection it seems clear that pleasure is not the only thing in life that we think good in itself, that for instance we think the possession of a good character, or an intelligent understanding of the world, as good or better. A great advance is made by the substitution of 'productive of the greatest good' for 'productive of the greatest pleasure.'

Not only is this theory more attractive than hedonistic utilitarianism, but its logical relation to that theory is such that the latter could not be true unless *it* were true, while it might be true though hedonistic utilitarianism were not. It is in fact one of the logical bases of hedonistic utilitarianism. For the view that what produces the maximum pleasure is right has for its bases the views (1) that what produces the maximum good is right, and (2) that pleasure is the only thing good in itself. . . . If, therefore, it can be shown that productivity of the maximum good is not what makes all right actions right, we shall *a fortiori* have refuted hedonistic utilitarianism.

When a plain man fulfils a promise because he thinks he ought to do so, it seems clear that he does so with no thought of its total consequences, still less with any opinion that these are likely to be the best possible. He thinks in fact much more of the past than of the future. What makes him think it right to act in a certain way is the fact that he has promised to do so — that and, usually, nothing more. That his act will produce the best possible consequences is not his reason for calling it right. What lends colour to the theory we are examining, then, is not the actions (which form probably a great majority of our actions) in which some such reflection as 'I have promised' is the only reason we give ourselves for thinking a certain action right, but the exceptional cases in which the consequences of fulfilling a promise (for instance) would be so disastrous to others that we judge it right not to do so. It must of course be admitted that such cases exist. If I have promised to meet a friend at a particular time for some trivial purpose, I should certainly think myself justified in breaking my engagement if by doing so I could prevent a serious accident or bring relief to the victims of one. And the supporters of the view we are examining hold that my thinking so is due to my thinking that I shall bring more good into existence by the one action than by the other. A different account may, however, be given of the matter, an account which will, I believe, show itself to be the true one. It may be said that besides the duty of fulfilling promises I have and recognize a duty of relieving distress, and that when I think it right to do the latter at the cost of not doing the former, it is not because I think I shall produce more good thereby but because I think it the duty which is in the circumstances more of a duty. This account surely corresponds much more closely with what we really think in such a situation. If, so far as I can see, I could bring equal amounts of good into being by fulfilling my promise and by helping some one to whom I had made no promise, I should not hesitate to regard the former as my duty. Yet on the view that what is right is right because it is productive of the most good I should not so regard it.

There are two theories, each in its way simple, that offer a solution of such cases of conscience. One is the view of Kant, that there are certain duties of perfect obligation, such as those of fulfilling promises, of paying debts, of telling the truth, which admit of no exception whatever in favour of duties of imperfect obligation, such as that of relieving distress. The other is the view of, for instance, Professor Moore and Dr. Rashdall, that there is only the duty of producing good, and that all 'conflicts of duties' should be resolved by asking 'by which action will most good be produced?' But it is more important that our theory fit the facts than that it be simple, and the account we have given above corresponds (it seems to me) better than either of the simpler theories with what we really think, viz. that normally promise-keeping, for example, should come before benevolence, but that when and only when the good to be produced by the benevolent act is very great and the promise comparatively trivial, the act of benevolence becomes our duty.

In fact the theory of 'ideal utilitarianism,' if I may for brevity refer so to the theory of Professor Moore, seems to simplify unduly our relations to our fellows. It says, in effect, that the only morally significant relation in which my neighbours stand to me is that of being possible beneficiaries by my action.[1] They do stand in this relation to me, and this relation is morally significant. But they may also stand to me in the relation of promisee to promiser, of creditor to debtor, of wife to husband, of child to parent, of friend to friend, of fellow countryman to fellow countryman, and the like; and each of these relations is the foundation of a *prima facie* duty, which is more or less incumbent on me according to the circumstances of the case. When I am in a situation, as perhaps I always am, in which more than one of these *prima facie* duties is incumbent on me, what I have to do is to study the situation as fully as I can until I form the considered opinon (it is never more) that in the circumstances one of them is more incumbent

---

[1] Some will think it, apart from other considerations, a sufficient refutation of this view to point out that I also stand in that relation to myself, so that for this view the distinction of oneself from others is morally insignificant.

than any other; then I am bound to think that to do this *prima facie* duty is my duty *sans phrase* in the situation.

I suggest '*prima facie* duty' or 'conditional duty' as a brief way of referring to the characteristic (quite distinct from that of being a duty proper) which an act has, in virtue of being of a certain kind (e.g. the keeping of a promise), of being an act which would be a duty proper if it were not at the same time of another kind which is morally significant. Whether an act is a duty proper or actual duty depends on *all* the morally significant kinds it is an instance of. . . .

There is nothing arbitrary about these *prima facie* duties. Each rests on a definite circumstance which cannot seriously be held to be without moral significance. Of *prima facie* duties I suggest, without claiming completeness or finality for it, the following division.[2]

(1) Some duties rest on previous acts of my own. These duties seem to include two kinds, (*a*) those resting on a promise or what may fairly be called an implicit promise, such as the implicit undertaking not to tell lies which seems to be implied in the act of entering into conversation (at any rate by civilized men), or of writing books that purport to be history and not fiction. These may be called the duties of fidelity. (*b*) Those resting on a previous wrongful act. These may be called the duties of reparation. (2) Some rest on previous acts of other men, i.e. services done by them to me. These may be loosely described as the duties of gratitude. (3) Some rest on the fact or possibility of a distribution of pleasure or happiness (or of the means thereto) which is not in accordance with the merit of the persons concerned; in such cases there arises a duty to upset or prevent such a distribution. These are the duties of justice. (4) Some rest on the mere fact that there are other beings in the world whose condition we can make better in respect of virtue, or of intelligence, or of pleasure. These are the duties of beneficence. (5) Some rest on the fact that we can improve our own condition in respect of virtue or of intelligence. These are the duties of self-improvement. (6) I think that we should distinguish from (4) the duties that may be summed up under the title of 'not injuring others.' No doubt to injure others is incidentally to fail to do them good; but it seems to me clear that non-maleficence is apprehended as a duty distinct from that of

[2] I should make it plain at this stage that I am *assuming* the correctness of some of our main convictions as to *prima facie* duties, or, more strictly, am claiming that we *know* them to be true. To me it seems as self-evident as anything could be, that to make a promise, for instance, is to create a moral claim on us in someone else. Many readers will perhaps say that they do *not* know this to be true. If so, I certainly cannot prove it to them; I can only ask them to reflect again, in the hope that they will ultimately agree that they also know it to be true. The main moral convictions of the plain man seem to me to be, not opinions which it is for philosophy to prove or disprove, but knowledge from the start; and in my own case I seem to find little difficulty in distinguishing these essential convictions from other moral convictions which I also have, which are merely fallible opinions based on an imperfect study of the working for good or evil of certain institutions or types of action.

beneficence, and as a duty of a more stringent character. It will be noticed that this alone among the types of duty has been stated in a negative way. An attempt might no doubt be made to state this duty, like the others, in a positive way. It might be said that it is really the duty to prevent ourselves from acting either from an inclination to harm others or from an inclination to seek our own pleasure, in doing which we should incidentally harm them. But on reflection it seems clear that the primary duty here is the duty not to harm others, this being a duty whether or not we have an inclination that if followed would lead to our harming them; and that when we have such an inclination the primary duty not to harm others gives rise to a consequential duty to resist the inclination. The recognition of this duty of non-maleficence is the first step on the way to the recognition of the duty of beneficence; and that accounts for the prominence of the commands 'thou shalt not kill,' 'thou shalt not commit adultery,' 'thou shalt not steal,' 'thou shalt not bear false witness,' in so early a code as the Decalogue. But even when we have come to recognize the duty of beneficence, it appears to me that the duty of non-maleficence is recognized as a distinct one, and as *prima facie* more binding. We should not in general consider it justifiable to kill one person in order to keep another alive, or to steal from one in order to give alms to another.

The essential defect of the 'ideal utilitarian' theory is that it ignores, or at least does not do full justice to, the highly personal character of duty. If the only duty is to produce the maximum of good, the question who is to have the good — whether it is myself, or my benefactor, or a person to whom I have made a promise to confer that good on him, or a mere fellow man to whom I stand in no such special relation — should make no difference to my having a duty to produce that good. But we are all in fact sure that it makes a vast difference. . . .

If the objection be made, that this catalogue of the main types of duty is an unsystematic one resting on no logical principle, it may be replied, first, that it makes no claim to being ultimate. It is a *prima facie* classification of the duties which reflection on our moral convictions seems actually to reveal. And if these convictions are, as I would claim that they are, of the nature of knowledge, and if I have not misstated them, the list will be a list of authentic conditional duties, correct as far as it goes though not necessarily complete. The list of *goods* put forward by the rival theory is reached by exactly the same method — the only sound one in the circumstances — viz. that of direct reflection on what we really think. Loyalty to the facts is worth more than a symmetrical architectonic or a hastily reached simplicity. If further reflection discovers a perfect logical basis for this or for a better classification, so much the better.

It may, again, be objected that our theory that there are these various and often conflicting types of *prima facie* duty leaves us with no principle upon which to discern what is our actual duty in particular circumstances. But this objection is not one which the rival theory is in a position to bring forward. For when we have to choose between the production of two hetero-geneous goods, say knowledge and pleasure, the 'ideal utilitarian' theory can only fall back on an opinion, for which no logical basis can be offered, that one of the goods is the greater; and this is no better than a similar opinion that one of two duties is the more urgent. And again, when we consider the infinite variety of the effects of our actions in the way of pleasure, it must surely be admitted that the claim which *hedonism* sometimes makes, that it offers a readily applicable criterion of right conduct, is quite illusory.

I am unwilling, however, to content myself with an *argumentum ad hominem*, and I would contend that in principle there is no reason to an-ticipate that every act that is our duty is so for one and the same reason. Why should two sets of circumstances, or one set of circumstances, *not* pos-sess different characteristics, any one of which makes a certain act our *prima facie* duty? When I ask what it is that makes me in certain cases sure that I have a *prima facie* duty to do so and so, I find that it lies in the fact that I have made a promise; when I ask the same question in another case, I find the answer lies in the fact that I have done a wrong. And if on reflection I find (as I think I do) that neither of these reasons is reducible to the other, I must not on any *a priori* ground assume that such a reduction is pos-sible. . . .

It is necessary to say something by way of clearing up the relation be-tween *prima facie* duties and the actual or absolute duty to do one particular act in particular circumstances. If, as almost all moralists except Kant are agreed, and as most plain men think, it is sometimes right to tell a lie or to break a promise, it must be maintained that there is a difference between *prima facie* duty and actual or absolute duty. When we think ourselves jus-tified in breaking, and indeed morally obliged to break, a promise in order to relieve some one's distress, we do not for a moment cease to recognize a *prima facie* duty to keep our promise, and this leads us to feel, not indeed shame or repentance, but certainly compunction, for behaving as we do; we recognize, further, that it is our duty to make up somehow to the prom-isee for the breaking of the promise. We have to distinguish from the char-acteristic of being our duty that of tending to be our duty. Any act that we do contains various elements in virtue of which it falls under various cate-gories. In virtue of being the breaking of a promise, for instance, it tends to be wrong; in virtue of being an instance of relieving distress it tends to be right. Tendency to be one's duty may be called a parti-resultant attribute, i.e. one which belongs to an act in virtue of some one component in its nature. *Being* one's duty is a toti-resultant attribute, one which belongs to an act in virtue of its whole nature and of nothing less than this. . . .

Another instance of the same distinction may be found in the operation of natural laws. *Qua* subject to the force of gravitation towards some other body, each body tends to move in a particular direction with a particular velocity; but its actual movement depends on *all* the forces to which it is subject. It is only by recognizing this distinction that we can preserve the absoluteness of laws of nature, and only by recognizing a corresponding dis-tinction that we can preserve the absoluteness of the general principles of morality. But an important difference between the two cases must be pointed out. When we say that in virtue of gravitation a body tends to move in a certain way, we are referring to a causal influence actually exercised on it by another body or other bodies. When we say that in virtue of being de-liberately untrue a certain remark tends to be wrong, we are referring to no causal relation, to no relation that involves succession in time, but to such a relation as connects the various attributes of a mathematical figure. And if the word 'tendency' is thought to suggest too much a causal relation, it is better to talk of certain types of act as being *prima facie* right or wrong (or of different persons as having different and possibly conflicting claims upon us), than of their tending to be right or wrong.

Something should be said of the relation between our apprehension of the *prima facie* rightness of certain types of act and our mental attitude to-wards particular acts. It is proper to use the word 'apprehension' in the former case and not in the latter. That an act, *qua* fulfilling a promise, or *qua* effecting a just distribution of good, or *qua* returning services rendered, or *qua* promoting the good of others, or *qua* promoting the virtue or insight of the agent, is *prima facie* right, is self-evident; not in the sense that it is evident from the beginning of our lives, or as soon as we attend to the proposition for the first time, but in the sense that when we have reached sufficient mental maturity and have given sufficient attention to the propo-sition it is evident without any need of proof, or of evidence beyond itself. It is self-evident just as a mathematical axiom, or the validity of a form of inference, is evident. The moral order expressed in these propositions is just as much part of the fundamental nature of the universe (and, we may add, of any possible universe in which there were moral agents at all) as is the spatial or numerical structure expressed in the axioms of geometry or arith-metic. In our confidence that these propositions are true there is involved the same trust in our reason that is involved in our confidence in mathe-matics; and we should have no justification for trusting it in the latter sphere and distrusting it in the former. In both cases we are dealing with proposi-tions that cannot be proved, but that just as certainly need no proof. . . .

Our judgements about our actual duty in concrete situations have none of the certainty that attaches to our recognition of the general principles of duty. A statement is certain, i.e. is an expression of knowledge, only in one or other of two cases: when it is either self-evident, or a valid conclusion from self-evident premises. And our judgements about our particular duties have neither of these characters. (1) They are not self-evident. Where a pos-sible act is seen to have two characteristics, in virtue of one of which it is *prima facie* right, and in virtue of the other *prima facie* wrong, we are (I think) well aware that we are not certain whether we ought or ought not to do it; that whether we do it or not, we are taking a moral risk. We come in the long run, after consideration, to think one duty more pressing than the other, but we do not feel certain that it is so. And though we do not always recognize that a possible act has two such characteristics, and though there *may* be cases in which it has not, we are never certain that any particular possible act has not, and therefore never certain that it is right, nor certain that it is wrong. For, to go no further in the analysis, it is enough to point out that any particular act will in all probability in the course of time contribute to the bringing about of good or of evil for many human beings, and thus have a *prima facie* rightness or wrongness of which we know nothing. (2) Again, our judgements about our particular duties are not logical conclusions from self-evident premisses. The only possible premisses would be the general principles stating their *prima facie* rightness or wrongness *qua* having the different characteristics they do have; and even if we could (as we cannot) apprehend the extent to which an act will tend on the one hand, for example, to bring about advantages for our benefactors, and on the other hand to bring about disadvantages for fellow men who are not our benefactors, there is no principle by which we can draw the conclusion that it is on the whole right or on the whole wrong. In this respect the judgement as to the rightness of a particular act is just like the judgement as to the beauty of a particular natural object or work of art. A poem is, for instance, in respect of certain qualities beautiful and in respect of certain others not beautiful; and our judgement as to the degree of beauty it possesses on the whole is never reached by logical reasoning from the apprehension of its particular beauties or particular defects. Both in this and in the moral case we have more or less probable opinions which are not logically justified conclusions from the general principles that are recognized as self-evident.

There is therefore much truth in the description of the right act as a fortunate act. If we cannot be certain that it is right, it is our good fortune if the act we do is the right act. This consideration does not, however, make the doing of our duty a mere matter of chance. There is a parallel here between the doing of duty and the doing of what will be to our personal advantage. We never *know* what act will in the long run be to our advantage. Yet it is certain that we are more likely in general to secure our advantage if we estimate to the best of our ability the probable tendencies of our actions in this respect, than if we act on caprice. And similarly we are more likely to do our duty if we reflect to the best of our ability on the *prima facie* rightness or wrongness of various possible acts in virtue of the characteristics we perceive them to have, than if we act without reflection. With this greater likelihood we must be content.

Many people would be inclined to say that the right act for me is not that whose general nature I have been describing, viz. that which if I were omniscient I should see to be my duty, but that which on all the evidence available to me I should think to be my duty. But suppose that from the state of partial knowledge in which I think act A to be my duty, I could pass to a state of perfect knowledge in which I saw act *B* to be my duty, should I not say 'act *B* was the right act for me to do'? I should no doubt add 'though I am not to be blamed for doing act *A*.' But in adding this, am I not passing from the question 'what is right' to the question 'what is morally good'? At the same time I am not making the *full* passage from the one notion to the other; for in order that the act should be morally good, or an act I am not to be blamed for doing, it must not merely be the act which it is reasonable for me to think my duty; it must also be done for that reason, or from some other morally good motive. Thus the conception of the right act as the act which it is reasonable for me to think my duty is an unsatisfactory compromise between the true notion of the right act and the notion of the morally good action.

The general principles of duty are obviously not self-evident from the beginning of our lives. How do they come to be so? The answer is, that they come to be self-evident to us just as mathematical axioms do. We find by experience that this couple of matches and that couple make four matches, that this couple of balls on a wire and that couple make four balls; and by reflection on these and similar discoveries we come to see that it is of the nature of two and two to make four. In a precisely similar way, we see the *prima facie* rightness of an act which would be the fulfilment of a particular promise, and of another which would be the fulfilment of another promise, and when we have reached sufficient maturity to think in general terms, we apprehend *prima facie* rightness to belong to the nature of any fulfilment of promise. What comes first in time is the apprehension of the self-evident *prima facie* rightness of an individual act of a particular type. From this we come by reflection to apprehend the self-evident general principle of *prima facie* duty. From this, too, perhaps along with the apprehension of the self-evident *prima facie* rightness of the same act in virtue of its having another characteristic as well, and perhaps in spite of the apprehension of its *prima facie* wrongness in virtue of its having some third characteristic, we come to believe something not self-evident at all, but an object of probable opinion, viz. that this particular act is (not *prima facie* but) actually right. . . .

Supposing it to be agreed, as I think on reflection it must, that no one *means* by 'right' just 'productive of the best possible consequences,' or 'optimific,' the attributes 'right' and 'optimific' might stand in either of two kinds of relation to each other. (1) They might be so related that we could apprehend *a priori*, either immediately or deductively, that any act that is optimific is right and any act that is right is optimific, as we can apprehend that any triangle that is equilateral is equiangular and *vice versa*. Professor Moore's view is, I think, that the coextensiveness of 'right' and 'optimific' is apprehended immediately. He rejects the possibility of any proof of it. Or (2) the two attributes might be such that the question whether they are invariably connected had to be answered by means of an inductive inquiry. Now at first sight it might seem as if the constant connexion of the two attributes could be immediately apprehended. It might seem absurd to suggest that it could be right for any one to do an act which would produce consequences less good than those which would be produced by some other act in his power. Yet a little thought will convince us that this is not absurd. The type of case in which it is easiest to see that this is so is, perhaps, that in which one has made a promise. In such a case we all think that *prima facie* it is our duty to fulfil the promise irrespective of the precise goodness of the total consequences. And though we do not think it is necessarily our actual or absolute duty to do so, we are far from thinking that any, even the slightest, gain in the value of the total consequences will necessarily justify us in doing something else instead. Suppose, to simplify the case by abstraction, that the fulfilment of a promise to A would produce 1,000 units of good [3] for him, but that by doing some other act I could produce 1,001 units of good for B, to whom I have made no promise, the other consequences of the two acts being of equal value; should we really think it self-evident that it was our duty to do the second act and not the first? I think not. We should, I fancy, hold that only a much greater disparity of value between the total consequences would justify us in failing to discharge our *prima facie* duty to A. After all, a promise is a promise, and is not to be treated so lightly as the theory we are examining would imply. What, exactly, a promise is, is not so easy to determine, but we are surely agreed that it constitutes a serious moral limitation to our freedom of action. To produce the 1,001 units of good for B rather than fulfil our promise to A would be to take, not perhaps our duty as philanthropists too seriously, but certainly our duty as makers of promises too lightly. . . .

Such instances — and they might easily be added to — make it clear that there is no self-evident connexion between the attributes 'right' and 'optimific.' The theory we are examining has a certain attractiveness when applied to our decision that a particular act is our duty (though I have tried to show that it does not agree with our actual moral judgements even here). But it is not even plausible when applied to our recognition of *prima facie* duty. For if it were self-evident that the right coincides with the optimific, it should be self-evident that what is *prima facie* right is *prima facie* optimific. But whereas we are certain that keeping a promise is *prima facie* right, we are not certain that it is *prima facie* optimific (though we are perhaps certain that it is *prima facie* bonific). Our certainty that it is *prima facie* right depends not on its consequences but on its being the fulfilment of a promise. The theory we are examining involves too much difference between the evident ground of our conviction about *prima facie* duty and the alleged ground of our conviction about actual duty. . . .

[3] I am assuming that good is objectively quantitative, but not that we can accurately assign an exact quantitative measure to it. Since it is of a definite amount, we can make the *supposition* that its amount is so-and-so, though we cannot with any confidence *assert* that it is.

I conclude that the attributes 'right' and 'optimific' are not identical, and that we do not know either by intuition, by deduction, or by induction that they coincide in their application, still less that the latter is the foundation of the former. It must be added, however, that if we are ever under no special obligation such as that of fidelity to a promisee or of gratitude to a benefactor, we ought to do what will produce most good; and that even when we are under a special obligation the tendency of acts to promote general good is one of the main factors in determining whether they are right.

In what has preceded, a good deal of use has been made of 'what we really think' about moral questions; a certain theory has been rejected because it does not agree with what we really think. It might be said that this is in principle wrong; that we should not be content to expound what our present moral consciousness tells us but should aim at a criticism of our existing moral consciousness in the light of theory. Now I do not doubt that the moral consciousness of men has in detail undergone a good deal of modification as regards the things we think right, at the hands of moral theory. But if we are told, for instance, that we should give up our view that there is a special obligatoriness attaching to the keeping of promises because it is self-evident that the only duty is to produce as much good as possible, we have to ask ourselves whether we really, when we reflect, *are* convinced that this is self-evident, and whether we really *can* get rid of our view that promise-keeping has a bindingness independent of productiveness of maximum good. In my own experience I find that I cannot, in spite of a very genuine attempt to do so; and I venture to think that most people will find the same, and that just because they cannot lose the sense of special obligation, they cannot accept as self-evident, or even as true, the theory which would require them to do so. In fact it seems, on reflection, self-evident that a promise, simply as such, is something that *prima facie* ought to be kept, and it does *not*, on reflection, seem self-evident that production of maximum good is the only thing that makes an act obligatory. And to ask us to give up at the bidding of a theory our actual apprehension of what is right and what is wrong seems like asking people to repudiate their actual experience of beauty, at the bidding of a theory which says 'only that which satisfies such and such conditions can be beautiful.' If what I have called our actual apprehension is (as I would maintain that it is) truly an apprehension, i.e. an instance of knowledge, the request is nothing less than absurd.

I would maintain, in fact, that what we are apt to describe as 'what we think' about moral questions contains a considerable amount that we do not think but know, and that this forms the standard by reference to which the truth of any moral theory has to be tested, instead of having itself to be tested by reference to any theory. I hope that I have in what precedes indicated what in my view these elements of knowledge are that are involved in our ordinary moral consciousness.

It would be a mistake to found a natural science on 'what we really think,' i.e. on what reasonably thoughtful and well-educated people think about the subjects of the science before they have studied them scientifically. For such opinions are interpretations, and often misinterpretations, of sense-experience; and the man of science must appeal from these to sense-experience itself, which furnishes his real data. In ethics no such appeal is possible. We have no more direct way of access to the facts about rightness and goodness and about what things are right or good, than by thinking about them; the moral convictions of thoughtful and well-educated people are the data of ethics just as sense-perceptions are the data of a natural science. Just as some of the latter have to be rejected as illusory, so have some of the former; but as the latter are rejected only when they are in conflict with other more accurate sense-perceptions, the former are rejected only when they are in conflict with other convictions which stand better the test of reflection. The existing body of moral convictions of the best people is the cumulative product of the moral reflection of many generations, which has developed an extremely delicate power of appreciation of moral distinctions; and this the theorist cannot afford to treat with anything other than the greatest respect. The verdicts of the moral consciousness of the best people are the foundation on which he must build; though he must first compare them with one another and eliminate any contradictions they may contain.

QUESTIONS

1. Which one of the result (teleological) theories does Ross think most plausible? Why?
2. Why does Ross say that utilitarianism can, with some plausibility, be asserted to be the principle we use in deciding which of *conflicting* obligations has the most claim on us, but can hardly be asserted to be the one we use in deciding whether we ought to keep a promise?
3. In what way does ideal utilitarianism "ignore the highly personal character of duty," according to Ross?
4. What is a "prima facie duty"? What types of prima facie duty does Ross list? Can you think of important omissions from Ross's list? For instance, do you think there is a prima facie duty not to commit incest?
5. Why does he not consider it an objection that his theory gives no rule about the right solution for conflicts of prima facie obligations?
6. In what respect does Ross think that the status of principles about prima facie obligation is similar to that of principles of mathematics? Is the same status enjoyed by beliefs about what is the right thing to do in a particular situation where there is a conflict of prima facie obligations?
7. By what argument does Ross attempt to undermine the utilitarian view that it is always right to do whatever will produce the most good? Can you propose a more realistic example than Ross's?

8. What difference does Ross find between the method proper for testing ethical principles and the method proper for testing scientific theories?

John Rawls (1921-)

RULE-UTILITARIANISM

Many contemporary philosophers with utilitarian leanings concede that there is much force in the arguments of such formalists as Ross. They are willing to concede, on the one hand, that an act is not right if, and only if, its performance maximizes intrinsic good. That view is too simple — and perhaps the great classic utilitarians never quite held such a theory. On the other hand, these philosophers find formalism repulsive: formalism, to their minds, makes moral right and wrong a matter of mysterious, arbitrary proscriptions; and if it recognizes general rules at all, it has no proposal to make about what is right or obligatory when the general rules give conflicting instructions.

Out of this impasse has arisen, in the past few years, a novel type of utilitarian theory — or else, perhaps, a great deal of interest in one aspect of classical utilitarian theory, depending on how one interprets the classical figures. This theory may be called "rule-utilitarianism." It has taken several different forms. Roughly what these forms have in common is the view that the rightness of an act is not fixed by *its* relative utility but by conformity with general rules or principles, and that the correctness of these rules or principles is fixed in some way by the utility of the general acceptance and recognition of them. Utility is relevant to the assessment of general moral rules, to deciding whether a given moral rule should command general assent, not to the assessment of particular actions except in special kinds of cases.

The rule-utilitarian view is defended, in part and with qualifications, in the following selection, taken from a recent paper by John Rawls. Rawls is a young American philosopher, who has written widely on ethical theory. After receiving his Ph.D. in philosophy from Princeton University, Rawls has taught at Cornell University and at Harvard University. He is now professor of philosophy at the Massachusetts Institute of Technology.

From John Rawls, "Two Concepts of Rules," *The Philosophical Review*, Vol. 64 (1955), pp. 3-32. Reprinted by permission of the author and of the editors of *The Philosophical Review*.

TWO CONCEPTS OF RULES

In this paper I want to show the importance of the distinction between justifying a practice and justifying a particular action falling under it, and I want to explain the logical basis of this distinction and how it is possible to miss its significance. While the distinction has frequently been made, and is now becoming commonplace, there remains the task of explaining the tendency either to overlook it altogether, or to fail to appreciate its importance.

To show the importance of the distinction I am going to defend utilitarianism against those objections which have traditionally been made against it in connection with punishment and the obligation to keep promises. I hope to show that if one uses the distinction in question then one can state utilitarianism in a way which makes it a much better explication of our considered moral judgments than these traditional objections would seem to admit. Thus the importance of the distinction is shown by the way it strengthens the utilitarian view regardless of whether that view is completely defensible or not.

To explain how the significance of the distinction may be overlooked, I am going to discuss two conceptions of rules. One of these conceptions conceals the importance of distinguishing between the justification of a rule or practice and the justification of a particular action falling under it. The other conception makes it clear why this distinction must be made and what is its logical basis. . . .

I I

I shall now consider the question of promises. The objection to utilitarianism in connection with promises seems to be this: it is believed that on the utilitarian view when a person makes a promise the only ground upon which he should keep it, if he should keep it, is that by keeping it he will realize the most good on the whole. So that if one asks the question "Why should I keep *my* promise?" the utilitarian answer is understood to be that doing so in *this* case will have the best consequences. And this answer is said, quite rightly, to conflict with the way in which the obligation to keep promises is regarded.

Now of course critics of utilitarianism are not unaware that one defense sometimes attributed to utilitarians is the consideration involving the practice of promise-keeping.[1] In this connection they are supposed to argue something like this: it must be admitted that we feel strictly about keeping

---

[1] Ross, *The Right and the Good*, pp. 37-39, and *Foundations of Ethics* (Oxford, 1939), pp. 92-94. I know of no utilitarian who has used this argument except W. A. Pickard-Cambridge in "Two Problems about Duty," *Mind*, n.s., XLI (April, 1932), 153-157, although the argument goes with G. E. Moore's version of utilitarianism in *Principia Ethica* (Cambridge, 1903). To my knowledge it does not appear in the classical utilitarians; and if one interprets their view correctly this is no accident.

promises, more strictly than it might seem our view can account for. But when we consider the matter carefully it is always necessary to take into account the effect which our action will have on the practice of making promises. The promisor must weigh, not only the effects of breaking his promise on the particular case, but also the effect which his breaking his promise will have on the practice itself. Since the practice is of great utilitarian value, and since breaking one's promise always seriously damages it, one will seldom be justified in breaking one's promise. If we view our individual promises in the wider context of the practice of promising itself we can account for the strictness of the obligation to keep promises. There is always one very strong utilitarian consideration in favor of keeping them, and this will insure that when the question arises as to whether or not to keep a promise it will usually turn out that one should, even where the facts of the particular case taken by itself would seem to justify one's breaking it. In this way the strictness with which we view the obligation to keep promises is accounted for.

Ross has criticized this defense as follows: however great the value of the practice of promising, on utilitarian grounds, there must be some value which is greater, and one can imagine it to be obtainable by breaking a promise. Therefore there might be a case where the promisor could argue that breaking his promise was justified as leading to a better state of affairs on the whole. And the promisor could argue in this way no matter how slight the advantage won by breaking the promise. If one were to challenge the promisor his defense would be that what he did was best on the whole in view of all the utilitarian considerations, which in this case *include* the importance of the practice. Ross feels that such a defense would be unacceptable. I think he is right insofar as he is protesting against the appeal to consequences in general and without further explanation. Yet it is extremely difficult to weigh the force of Ross's argument. The kind of case imagined seems unrealistic and one feels that it needs to be described. One is inclined to think that it would either turn out that such a case came under an exception defined by the practice itself, in which case there would not be an appeal to consequences in general on the particular case, or it would happen that the circumstances were so peculiar that the conditions which the practice presupposes no longer obtained. But certainly Ross is right in thinking that it strikes us as wrong for a person to defend breaking a promise by a general appeal to consequences. For a general utilitarian defense is not open to the promisor: it is not one of the defenses allowed by the practice of making promises.

Ross gives two further counterarguments: First, he holds that it overestimates the damage done to the practice of promising by a failure to keep a promise. One who breaks a promise harms his own name certainly, but it isn't clear that a broken promise always damages the practice itself sufficiently to account for the strictness of the obligation. Second, and more important, I think, he raises the question of what one is to say of a promise which isn't known to have been made except to the promisor and the promisee, as in the case of a promise a son makes to his dying father concerning the handling of the estate. In this sort of case the consideration relating to the practice doesn't weigh on the promisor at all, and yet one feels that this sort of promise is as binding as other promises. The question of the effect which breaking it has on the practice seems irrelevant. The only consequence seems to be that one can break the promise without running any risk of being censured; but the obligation itself seems not the least weakened. Hence it is doubtful whether the effect on the practice ever weighs in the particular case; certainly it cannot account for the strictness of the obligation where it fails to obtain. It seems to follow that a utilitarian account of the obligation to keep promises cannot be successfully carried out. . . .

These arguments and counterarguments . . . fail to make the distinction between the justification of a practice and the justification of a particular action falling under it, and therefore they fall into the mistake of taking it for granted that the promisor . . . is entitled without restriction to bring utilitarian considerations to bear in deciding whether to keep *his* promise. But if one considers what the practice of promising is one will see, I think, that it is such as not to allow this sort of general discretion to the promisor. Indeed, the point of the practice is to abdicate one's title to act in accordance with utilitarian and prudential considerations in order that the future may be tied down and plans coordinated in advance. There are obvious utilitarian advantages in having a practice which denies to the promisor, as a defense, any general appeal to the utilitarian principle in accordance with which the practice itself may be justified. There is nothing contradictory, or surprising, in this: utilitarian (or aesthetic) reasons might properly be given in arguing that the game of chess, or baseball, is satisfactory just as it is, or in arguing that it should be changed in various respects, but a player in a game cannot properly appeal to such considerations as reasons for his making one move rather than another. It is a mistake to think that if the practice is justified on utilitarian grounds then the promisor must have complete liberty to use utilitarian arguments to decide whether or not to keep his promise. The practice forbids this general defense; and it is a purpose of the practice to do this. Therefore what the above arguments presuppose — the idea that if the utilitarian view is accepted then the promisor is bound if, and only if, the application of the utilitarian principle to his own case shows that keeping it is best on the whole — is false. The promisor is bound because he promised: weighing the case on its merits is not open to him.

Is this to say that in particular cases one cannot deliberate whether or not to keep one's promise? Of course not. But to do so is to deliberate whether the various excuses, exceptions and defenses, which are understood by, and which constitute an important part of, the practice, apply to one's own case. Various defenses for not keeping one's promise are allowed, but among them there isn't the one that, on general utilitarian grounds, the promisor (truly) thought his action best on the whole, even though there may be the defense that the consequences of keeping one's promise would have been *extremely* severe. While there are too many complexities here to consider all the necessary details, one can see that the general defense isn't allowed if one asks the following question: what would one say of someone who, when asked why he broke his promise, replied simply that breaking it was best on the whole? Assuming that his reply is sincere, and that his belief was reasonable (i.e., one need not consider the possibility that he was mistaken), I think that one would question whether or not he knows what it means to say "I promise" (in the appropriate circumstances). It would be said of someone who used this excuse without further explanation that he didn't understand what defenses the practice, which defines a promise, allows to him. If a child were to use this excuse one would correct him; for it is part of the way one is taught the concept of a promise to be corrected if one uses this excuse. The point of having the practice would be lost if the practice did allow this excuse.

It is no doubt part of the utilitarian view that every practice should admit the defense that the consequences of abiding by it would have been extremely severe; and utilitarians would be inclined to hold that some reliance on people's good sense and some concession to hard cases is necessary. They would hold that a practice is justified by serving the interests of those who take part in it; and as with any set of rules there is understood a background of circumstances under which it is expected to be applied and which need not — indeed which cannot — be fully stated. Should these circumstances change, then even if there is no rule which provides for the case, it may still be in accordance with the practice that one be released from one's obligation. But this sort of defense allowed by a practice must not be confused with the general option to weigh each particular case on utilitarian grounds which critics of utilitarianism have thought it necessarily to involve. . . .

III

So far I have tried to show the importance of the distinction between the justification of a practice and the justification of a particular action falling under it by indicating how this distinction might be used to defend utilitarianism against two long-standing objections. One might be tempted to close the discussion at this point by saying that utilitarian considerations should be understood as applying to practices in the first instance and not to particular actions falling under them except insofar as the practices admit of it. One might say that in this modified form it is a better account of our considered moral opinions and let it go at that. But to stop here would be to neglect the interesting question as to how one can fail to appreciate the significance of this rather obvious distinction and can take it for granted that utilitarianism has the consequence that particular cases may always be decided on general utilitarian grounds. I want to argue that this mistake may be connected with misconceiving the logical status of the rules of practices; and to show this I am going to examine two conceptions of rules, two ways of placing them within the utilitarian theory.

The conception which conceals from us the significance of the distinction I am going to call the summary view. It regards rules in the following way: one supposes that each person decides what he shall do in particular cases by applying the utilitarian principle; one supposes further that different people will decide the same particular case in the same way and that there will be recurrences of cases similar to those previously decided. Thus it will happen that in cases of certain kinds the same decision will be made either by the same person at different times or by different persons at the same time. If a case occurs frequently enough one supposes that a rule is formulated to cover that sort of case. I have called this conception the summary view because rules are pictured as summaries of past decisions arrived at by the *direct* application of the utilitarian principle to particular cases. Rules are regarded as reports that cases of a certain sort have been found on *other* grounds to be properly decided in a certain way (although, of course, they do not *say* this).

There are several things to notice about this way of placing rules within the utilitarian theory.

1. The point of having rules derives from the fact that similar cases tend to recur and that one can decide cases more quickly if one records past decisions in the form of rules. If similar cases didn't recur, one would be required to apply the utilitarian principle directly, case by case, and rules reporting past decisions would be of no use. . . .

3. Each person is in principle always entitled to reconsider the correctness of a rule and to question whether or not it is proper to follow it in a particular case. As rules are guides and aids, one may ask whether in past decisions there might not have been a mistake in applying the utilitarian principle to get the rule in question, and wonder whether or not it is best in this case. The reason for rules is that people are not able to apply the utilitarian principle effortlessly and flawlessly; there is need to save time and to post a guide. On this view a society of rational utilitarians would be a society without rules in which each person applied the utilitarian principle directly and smoothly, and without error, case by case. On the other hand, ours is a society in which rules are formulated to serve as aids in reaching these ideally rational decisions on particular cases, guides which have been built up and tested by the experience of generations. If one applies this view to rules, one is interpreting them as maxims, as "rules of thumb"; and it is doubtful that anything to which the summary conception did apply would be called a *rule*. Arguing as if one regarded rules in this way is a mistake one makes while doing philosophy.

4. The concept of a *general* rule takes the following form. One is pictured as estimating on what percentage of the cases likely to arise a given rule may be relied upon to express the correct decision, that is, the decision that would be arrived at if one were to correctly apply the utilitarian principle case by case. If one estimates that by and large the rule will give the correct decision, or if one estimates that the likelihood of making a mistake by applying the utilitarian principle directly on one's own is greater than the likelihood of making a mistake by following the rule, and if these considerations held of persons generally, then one would be justified in urging its adoption as a general rule. In this way *general* rules might be accounted for on the summary view. It will still make sense, however, to speak of applying the utilitarian principle case by case, for it was by trying to foresee the results of doing this that one got the initial estimates upon which acceptance of the rule depends. That one is taking a rule in accordance with the summary conception will show itself in the naturalness with which one speaks of the rule as a guide, or as a maxim, or as a generalization from experience, and as something to be laid aside in extraordinary cases where there is no assurance that the generalization will hold and the case must therefore be treated on its merits. Thus there goes with this conception the notion of a particular exception which renders a rule suspect on a particular occasion.

The other conception of rules I will call the practice conception. On this view rules are pictured as defining a practice. Practices are set up for various reasons, but one of them is that in many areas of conduct each person's deciding what to do on utilitarian grounds case by case leads to confusion, and that the attempt to coordinate behavior by trying to foresee how others will act is bound to fail. As an alternative one realizes that what is required is the establishment of a practice, the specification of a new form of activity; and from this one sees that a practice necessarily involves the abdication of full liberty to act on utilitarian and prudential grounds. It is the mark of a practice that being taught how to engage in it involves being instructed in the rules which define it, and that appeal is made to those rules to correct the behavior of those engaged in it. Those engaged in a practice recognize the rules as defining it. The rules cannot be taken as simply describing how those engaged in the practice in fact behave: it is not simply that they act as if they were obeying the rules. Thus it is essential to the notion of a practice that the rules are publicly known and understood as definitive; and it is essential also that the rules of a practice can be taught and can be acted upon to yield a coherent practice. On this conception, then, rules are not generalizations from the decisions of individuals applying the utilitarian principle directly and independently to recurrent particular cases. On the contrary, rules define a practice and are themselves the subject of the utilitarian principle. . . .

If one compares the two conceptions of rules I have discussed, one can see how the summary conception misses the significance of the distinction between justifying a practice and justifying actions falling under it. On this view rules are regarded as guides whose purpose it is to indicate the ideally rational decision on the given particular case which the flawless application of the utilitarian principle would yield. One has, in principle, full option to use the guides or to discard them as the situation warrants without one's moral office being altered in any way: whether one discards the rules or not, one always holds the office of a rational person seeking case by case to realize the best on the whole. But on the practice conception, if one holds an office defined by a practice then questions regarding one's actions in this office are settled by reference to the rules which define the practice. If one seeks to question these rules, then one's office undergoes a fundamental change: one then assumes the office of one empowered to change and criticize the rules, or the office of a reformer, and so on. The summary conception does away with the distinction of offices and the various forms of argument appropriate to each. On that conception there is one office and so no offices at all. It therefore obscures the fact that the utilitarian principle must, in the case of actions and offices defined by a practice, apply to the practice, so that general utilitarian arguments are not available to those who act in offices so defined. . . .[2]

I have tried to show that when we fit the utilitarian view together with the practice conception of rules, where this conception is appropriate, we can formulate it in a way which saves it from several traditional objections. I have further tried to show how the logical force of the distinction between justifying a practice and justifying an action falling under it is connected with the practice conception of rules and cannot be understood as long as one regards the rules of practices in accordance with the summary view. . . .

QUESTIONS

1. What criticism against utilitarianism, when defined as the view that an action is right if, and only if, performing it will maximize welfare, does Rawls regard as just for the case of promise-keeping?
2. How well would this criticism be met if the utilitarian said that moral *rules*

---

[2] How do these remarks apply to the case of the promise known only to father and son? Well, at first sight the son certainly holds the office of promisor, and so he isn't allowed by the practice to weigh the particular case on general utilitarian grounds. Suppose instead that he wishes to consider himself in the office of one empowered to criticize and change the practice, leaving aside the question as to his right to move from his previously assumed office to another. Then he may consider utilitarian arguments as applied to the practice; but once he does this he will see that there are such arguments for not allowing a general utilitarian defense in the practice for this sort of case. For to do so would make it impossible to ask for and to give a kind of promise which one often wants to be able to ask for and to give. Therefore he will not want to change the practice, and so as a promisor he has no option but to keep his promise.

should be judged by their utility but that *particular actions* should be judged by conformity with moral rules?

3. In the rule-utilitarian view, should the agent take the effects of his decision on human welfare into account at all in deciding what he should do?

4. Are the implications of the rule-utilitarian theory more, or less, in conformity with what appear to be reasonable conclusions about moral issues and principles than are the implications of the more traditional type of utilitarianism?

5. Can you think of any situation in which some action would, to your mind, be clearly wrong but would be right according to the rule-utilitarian?

6. In what ways is the rule-utilitarian conception of "moral rules" different from the "summary" conception?

7. Might the rule-utilitarian believe that one "practice" is the rule that people should help others when they can do so without comparable inconvenience to themselves? Or would this rule not qualify at all as a "practice" in the sense in which there is a "practice" surrounding the making and keeping of promises and agreements?

Saint Thomas Aquinas (1225-74)

MORAL LAW IS NATURAL AND RATIONAL

St. Thomas was born near Naples, Italy, but went to Paris for study shortly after entering the Dominican order in 1244. Except for a ten-year stay in Italy as adviser to the papal court, he remained in Paris until nearly the end of his life.

St. Thomas is one of the great figures in intellectual history. He was perhaps not as original in the grand manner as were Plato and Aristotle, but he merits comparison with them on account of his scope, judgment, subtle insight on details, erudition, and power to think systematically. As a philosopher, he towers above all others closely identified with Christian theology. Even today, after centuries of discussion of his work, moral philosophers can still find helpful ideas in St. Thomas.

In its broad outlines the moral philosophy of St. Thomas was a synthesis of Christian and Aristotelian conceptions. God is the law-giver, as He is depicted in the Bible; God's laws and moral obligation coincide in extent and perhaps in conception. But these laws are rational; they are rules which all must follow if the best life for men in a community is to be realized. In a sense these laws are also natural: they are imprinted on man's instinctive inclinations and conceptions of what is obviously morally necessary. Like Aristotle, St. Thomas thinks that what is good is what will elicit desire or satisfaction in men; and what is good must thus be ascertained by study of man's natural wants, both animal and specifically human. Unlike Aristotle, however, St. Thomas sees man as having a supernatural, or heavenly, destiny; hence he infers, though not in the following selection, moral obligations which would have seemed strange to Aristotle. In the final paragraphs of our selection, St. Thomas is struggling with the difficulty, common to both formalist and rule-utilitarian theories, of finding a method by which a set of rules can be formulated which can seriously be said to give direction for all cases. It will be useful to compare his conclusions with those of John Rawls and W. D. Ross.

Saint Thomas Aquinas, *Summa Theologica*. First Part of the Second Part, Questions 90-94. Trans. by the Fathers of the English Dominican Province. First published London: Burns, Oates & Washbourne, 1915. Revised by Anton C. Pegis (see below).

From *Basic Writings of St. Thomas Aquinas*, ed. by Anton C. Pegis. Copyright 1945 by Random House, Inc. Reprinted by permission. Also reprinted by permission of Burns & Oates Ltd., London.

SUMMA THEOLOGICA

QUESTION 90

First Article: Whether law is something pertaining to reason?

. . . It belongs to the law to command and to forbid. But it belongs to reason to command, as was stated above. Therefore law is something pertaining to reason. . . . Law is a rule and measure of acts, whereby man is induced to act or is restrained from acting; for *lex* (*law*) is derived from *ligare* (*to bind*), because it binds one to act. Now the rule and measure of human acts is the reason, which is the first principle of human acts, as is evident from what has been stated above. For it belongs to the reason to direct to the end, which is the first principle in all matters of action. . . .

Second Article: Whether law is always directed to the common good?

. . . Isidore says that *laws are enacted for no private profit, but for the common benefit of the citizens.* . . . As we have stated above, law belongs to that which is a principle of human acts, because it is their rule and measure. Now as reason is a principle of human acts, so in reason itself there is something which is the principle in respect of all the rest. Hence to this principle chiefly and mainly law must needs be referred. Now the first principle in practical matters, which are the object of the practical reason, is the last end: and the last end of human life is happiness or beatitude, as we have stated above. Consequently, law must needs concern itself mainly with the order that is in beatitude. Moreover, since every part is ordained to the whole as the imperfect to the perfect, and since one man is a part of the perfect community, law must needs concern itself properly with the order directed to universal happiness. Therefore the Philosopher, in the above definition of legal matters, mentions both happiness and the body politic, since he says that we call those legal matters *just which are adapted to produce and preserve happiness and its parts for the body politic.* For the state is a perfect community, as he says in *Politics* i. . . . Since law is chiefly ordained to the common good, any other precept in regard to some individual work must needs be devoid of the nature of a law, save in so far as it regards the common good. Therefore every law is ordained to the common good. . . .

Third Article: Whether the reason of any man is competent to make laws?

. . . Isidore says, and the *Decretals* repeat: A *law is an ordinance of the people, whereby something is sanctioned by the Elders together with the Commonalty.* Therefore not everyone can make laws. . . . A law, properly speaking, regards first and foremost the order to the common good. Now to order anything to the common good belongs either to the whole people, or to someone who is the viceregent of the whole people. Hence the making of a law belongs either to the whole people or to a public personage who has care of the whole people; for in all other matters the directing of anything to the end concerns him to whom the end belongs. . . .

As was stated above, a law is in a person not only as in one that rules, but also, by participation, as in one that is ruled. In the latter way, each one is a law to himself, in so far as he shares the direction that he receives from one who rules him. Hence the same text goes on: *Who show the work of the law written in their hearts* (Rom. 2:15).

Fourth Article: Whether promulgation is essential to law?

. . . It is laid down in the *Decretals* that *laws are established when they are promulgated.* . . . As was stated above, a law is imposed on others as a rule and measure. Now a rule or measure is imposed by being applied to those who are to be ruled and measured by it. Therefore, in order that a law obtain the binding force which is proper to a law, it must needs be applied to the men who have to be ruled by it. But such application is made by its being made known to them by promulgation. Therefore promulgation is necessary for law to obtain its force. . . . Law is nothing else than an ordinance of reason for the common good, promulgated by him who has the care of the community. . . .

The natural law is promulgated by the very fact that God has instilled it into man's mind so as to be known by him naturally. . . .

QUESTION 91

First Article: Whether there is an eternal law?

. . . As we have stated above, law is nothing else but a dictate of practical reason emanating from the ruler who governs a perfect community. Now it is evident, granted that the world is ruled by divine providence, as was stated in the First Part, that the whole community of the universe is governed by the divine reason. Therefore the very notion of the government of things in God, the ruler of the universe, has the nature of a law. And since the divine reason's conception of things is not subject to time, but is eternal, according to *Prov.* 8:23, therefore it is that this kind of law must be called eternal. . . .

Promulgation is made by word of mouth or in writing, and in both ways the eternal law is promulgated, because both the divine Word and the writing of the Book of Life are eternal. . . .

Second Article: Whether there is in us a natural law?

. . . The *Gloss* on *Rom.* 2:14 (*When the Gentiles, who have not the law, do by nature those things that are of the law*) comments as follows: *Although they have no written law, yet they have the natural law, whereby each one knows, and is conscious of, what is good and what is evil.* . . . As we have stated above, law, being a rule and measure, can be in a person in two ways: in one way, as in him that rules and measures; in another way, as in that which is ruled and measured, since a thing is ruled and measured in so far as it partakes of the rule or measure. Therefore, since all things subject to divine providence are ruled and measured by the eternal law, as was stated above, it is evident that all things partake in some way in the eternal law, in so far as, namely, from its being imprinted on them, they derive their respective inclinations to their proper acts and ends. Now among all others, the rational creature is subject to divine providence in a more excellent way, in so far as it itself partakes of a share of providence, by being provident both for itself and for others. Therefore it has a share of the eternal reason, whereby it has a natural inclination to its proper act and end; and this participation of the eternal law in the rational creature is called the natural law. Hence the Psalmist, after saying (*Ps.* 4:6): *Offer up the sacrifice of justice,* as though someone asked what the works of justice are, adds: *Many say, Who showeth us good things?* in answer to which question he says: *The light of Thy countenance, O Lord, is signed upon us.* He thus implies that the light of natural reason, whereby we discern what is good and what is evil, which is the function of the natural law, is nothing else than an imprint on us of the divine light. It is therefore evident that the natural law is nothing else than the rational creature's participation of the eternal law.

Third Article: Whether there is a human law?

. . . Augustine distinguishes two kinds of law, the one eternal, the other temporal, which he calls human. . . . As we have stated above, a law is a dictate of the practical reason. . . . Accordingly, we conclude that, just as in the speculative reason, from naturally known indemonstrable principles we draw the conclusions of the various sciences, the knowledge of which is not imparted to us by nature, but acquired by the efforts of reason, so too it is that from the precepts of the natural law, as from common and indemonstrable principles, the human reason needs to proceed to the more particular determination of certain matters. These particular determinations, devised by human reason, are called human laws, provided that the other essential conditions of law be observed, as was stated above. Therefore Tully says in his *Rhetoric* that *justice has its source in nature; thence certain things came into custom by reason of their utility; afterwards these things which emanated from nature, and were approved by custom, were sanctioned by fear and reverence for the law.* . . . Just as on the part of the speculative reason, by a natural participation of divine wisdom, there is in us the knowledge of certain common principles, but not a proper knowledge of each single truth, such as that contained in the divine wisdom, so, too, on the part of the practical reason, man has a natural participation of the eternal law, according to certain common principles, but not as regards the particular determinations of individual cases, which are, however, contained in the eternal law. Hence the need for human reason to proceed further to sanction them by law.

Fourth Article: Whether there was any need for a divine law?

. . . Besides the natural and the human law it was necessary for the directing of human conduct to have a divine law. And this for four reasons. First, because it is by law that man is directed how to perform his proper acts in view of his last end. Now if man were ordained to no other end than that which is proportionate to his natural ability, there would be no need for man to have any further direction, on the part of his reason, in addition to the natural law and humanly devised law which is derived from it. But since man is ordained to an end of eternal happiness which exceeds man's natural ability, as we have stated above, therefore it was necessary that, in addition to the natural and the human law, man should be directed to his end by a law given by God.

Secondly, because, by reason of the uncertainty of human judgment, especially on contingent and particular matters, different people form different judgments on human acts; whence also different and contrary laws result. In order, therefore, that man may know without any doubt what he ought to do and what he ought to avoid, it was necessary for man to be directed in his proper acts by a law given by God, for it is certain that such a law cannot err.

Thirdly, because man can make laws in those matters of which he is competent to judge. But man is not competent to judge of interior movements, that are hidden, but only of exterior acts which are observable; and yet for the perfection of virtue it is necessary for man to conduct himself rightly in both kinds of acts. Consequently, human law could not sufficiently curb and direct interior acts, and it was necessary for this purpose that a divine law should supervene.

Fourthly, because, as Augustine says, human law cannot punish or forbid all evil deeds, since, while aiming at doing away with all evils, it would do away with many good things, and would hinder the advance of the common good, which is necessary for human living. In order, therefore, that no evil might remain unforbidden and unpunished, it was necessary for the divine law to supervene, whereby all sins are forbidden.

Fifth Article: Whether there is but one divine law?

. . . Things may be distinguished in two ways. First, as those things that are altogether specifically different, *e.g.*, a horse and an ox. Secondly, as perfect and imperfect in the same species, *e.g.*, a boy and a man; and in this way the divine law is distinguished into Old and New. Hence the Apostle (*Gal.* 3:24, 25) compares the state of man under the Old Law to that of a child *under a pedagogue*; but the state under the New Law, to that of a full grown man, who is *no longer under a pedagogue*.

Now the perfection and imperfection of these two laws is to be taken in connection with the three conditions pertaining to law, as was stated above. For, in the first place, it belongs to law to be directed to the common good as to its end, as was stated above. This good may be twofold. It may be a sensible and earthly good, and to this man was directly ordained by the Old Law. Hence it is that, at the very outset of the Law, the people were invited to the earthly kingdom of the Chananaeans (*Exod.* 3:8, 17). Again it may be an intelligible and heavenly good, and to this, man is ordained by the New Law. Therefore, at the very beginning of His preaching, Christ invited men to the kingdom of heaven, saying (*Matt.* 4:17): *Do penance, for the kingdom of heaven is at hand*. Hence Augustine says that *promises of temporal goods are contained in the Old Testament, for which reason it is called old; but the promise of eternal life belongs to the New Testament*.

Secondly, it belongs to law to direct human acts according to the order of justice; wherein also the New Law surpasses the Old Law, since it directs our internal acts, according to *Matt.* 5:20: *Unless your justice abound more than that of the Scribes and Pharisees, you shall not enter into the kingdom of heaven*. Hence the saying that *the Old Law restrains the hand, but the New Law controls the soul*.

Thirdly, it belongs to law to induce men to observe its commandments. This the Old Law did by the fear of punishment, but the New Law, by love, which is poured into our hearts by the grace of Christ, bestowed in the New Law, but foreshadowed in the Old. Hence Augustine says that *there is little difference between the Law and the Gospel — fear* [timor] *and love* [amor]. . . .

QUESTION 94

Second Article: Whether the natural law contains several precepts, or only one?

. . . The precepts of the natural law are to the practical reason what the first principles of demonstrations are to the speculative reason, because both are self-evident principles. Now a thing is said to be self-evident in two ways: first, in itself; secondly, in relation to us. Any proposition is said to be self-evident in itself, if its predicate is contained in the notion of the subject; even though it may happen that to one who does not know the definition of the subject, such a proposition is not self-evident. For instance, this proposition, *Man is a rational being*, is, in its very nature, self-evident, since he who says *man*, says *a rational being*; and yet to one who does not know what a man is, this proposition is not self-evident. Hence it is that, as Boethius says, certain axioms or propositions are universally self-evident to all; and such are the propositions whose terms are known to all, as, *Every whole is greater than its part*, and *Things equal to one and the same are equal to one another*. But some propositions are self-evident only to the wise, who understand the meaning of the terms of such propositions. Thus to one who understands that an angel is not a body, it is self-evident that an angel is not circumscriptively in a place. But this is not evident to the unlearned, for they cannot grasp it.

Now a certain order is to be found in those things that are apprehended by men. For that which first falls under apprehension is *being*, the understanding of which is included in all things whatsoever a man apprehends. Therefore the first indemonstrable principle is that *the same thing cannot be affirmed and denied at the same time*, which is based on the notion of *being and not-being*: and on this principle all others are based, as is stated in *Metaph*. iv. Now as *being* is the first thing that falls under the apprehension absolutely, so *good* is the first thing that falls under the apprehension of the practical reason, which is directed to action (since every agent acts for an end, which has the nature of good). Consequently, the first principle in the practical reason is one founded on the nature of good, viz., that *good is that which all things seek after*. Hence this is the first precept of law, that *good is to be done and promoted, and evil is to be avoided*. All other precepts of the natural law are based upon this; so that all the things which the practical reason naturally apprehends as man's good belong to the precepts of the natural law under the form of things to be done or avoided.

Since, however, good has the nature of an end, and evil, the nature of the contrary, hence it is that all those things to which man has a natural inclination are naturally apprehended by reason as being good, and consequently as objects of pursuit, and their contraries as evil, and objects of avoidance. Therefore, the order of the precepts of the natural law is according to the order of natural inclinations. For there is in man, first of all, an inclination to good in accordance with the nature which he has in common with all substances, inasmuch, namely, as every substance seeks the preservation of its own being, according to its nature; and by reason of this inclination, whatever is a means of preserving human life, and of warding off its obstacles, belongs to the natural law. Secondly, there is in man an inclination to things that pertain to him more specially, according to that nature which he has in common with other animals; and in virtue of this inclination, those things are said to belong to the natural law *which nature has taught to all animals*, such as sexual intercourse, the education of offspring and so forth. Thirdly, there is in man an inclination to good according to the nature of his reason, which nature is proper to him. Thus man has a natural inclination to know the truth about God, and to live in society; and in this respect, whatever pertains to this inclination belongs to the natural law: *e.g.*, to shun ignorance, to avoid offending those among whom one has to live, and other such things regarding the above inclination. . . .

All these precepts of the law of nature have the character of one natural law, inasmuch as they flow from one first precept. . . .

All the inclination of any parts whatsoever of human nature, *e.g.*, of the concupiscible and irascible parts, in so far as they are ruled by reason, belong to the natural law, and are reduced to one first precept, as was stated above. And thus the precepts of the natural law are many in themselves, but they are based on one common foundation. . . .

> *Third Article: Whether all the acts of the virtues are prescribed by the natural law?*

. . . We may speak of virtuous acts in two ways: first, in so far as they are virtuous; secondly, as such and such acts considered in their proper species. If, then, we are speaking of the acts of the virtues in so far as they are virtuous, thus all virtuous acts belong to the natural law. For it has been stated that to the natural law belongs everything to which a man is inclined according to his nature. Now each thing is inclined naturally to an operation that is suitable to it according to its form: *e.g.*, fire is inclined to give heat. Therefore, since the rational soul is the proper form of man, there is in every man a natural inclination to act according to reason; and this is to act according to virtue. Consequently, considered thus, all the acts of the virtues are prescribed by the natural law, since each one's reason naturally dictates to him to act virtuously. But if we speak of virtuous acts, considered in themselves, *i.e.*, in their proper species, thus not all virtuous acts are prescribed by the natural law. For many things are done virtuously, to which nature does not primarily incline, but which, through the inquiry of reason, have been found by men to be conducive to well-living. . . .

Temperance is about the natural concupiscences of food, drink and sexual matters, which are indeed ordained to the common good of nature, just as other matters of law are ordained to the moral common good. . . .

By human nature we may mean either that which is proper to man, and in this sense all sins, as being against reason, are also against nature, as Damascene states; or we may mean that nature which is common to man and other animals, and in this sense, certain special sins are said to be against nature: *e.g.* contrary to sexual intercourse, which is natural to all animals, is unisexual lust, which has received the special name of the unnatural crime. . . .

Fourth Article: Whether the natural law is the same in all men?

. . . As we have stated above, to the natural law belong those things to which a man is inclined naturally; and among these it is proper to man to be inclined to act according to reason. Now it belongs to the reason to proceed from what is common to what is proper, as is stated in *Physics* i. The speculative reason, however, is differently situated, in this matter, from the practical reason. For, since the speculative reason is concerned chiefly with necessary things, which cannot be otherwise than they are, its proper conclusions, like the universal principles, contain the truth without fail. The practical reason, on the other hand, is concerned with contingent matters, which is the domain of human actions; and, consequently, although there is necessity in the common principles, the more we descend towards the particular, the more frequently we encounter defects. Accordingly, then, in speculative matters truth is the same in all men, both as to principles and as to conclusions; although the truth is not known to all as regards the conclusions, but only as regards the principles which are called *common notions*. But in matters of action, truth or practical rectitude is not the same for all as to what is particular, but only as to the common principles; and where there is the same rectitude in relation to particulars, it is not equally known to all.

It is therefore evident that, as regards the common principles whether of speculative or of practical reason, truth or rectitude is the same for all, and is equally known by all. But as to the proper conclusions of the speculative reason, the truth is the same for all, but it is not equally known to all. Thus, it is true for all that the three angles of a triangle are together equal to two right angles, although it is not known to all. But as to the proper conclusions of the practical reason, neither is the truth or rectitude the same for all, nor, where it is the same, is it equally known by all. Thus, it is right and true for all to act according to reason, and from this principle it follows, as a proper conclusion, that goods entrusted to another should be restored to their owner. Now this is true for the majority of cases. But it may happen in a particular case that it would be injurious, and therefore unreasonable, to restore goods held in trust; for instance, if they are claimed for the purpose of fighting against one's country. And this principle will be found to fail the more, according as we descend further towards the particular, e.g., if one were to say that goods held in trust should be restored with such and such a guarantee, or in such and such a way; because the greater the number of conditions added, the greater the number of ways in which the principle may fail, so that it be not right to restore or not to restore.

Consequently, we must say that the natural law, as to the first common principles, is the same for all, both as to rectitude and as to knowledge. But as to certain more particular aspects, which are conclusions, as it were, of those common principles, it is the same for all in the majority of cases, both as to rectitude and as to knowledge; and yet in some few cases it may fail, both as to rectitude, by reason of certain obstacles (just as natures subject to generation and corruption fail in some few cases because of some obstacle), and as to knowledge, since in some the reason is perverted by passion, or evil habit, or an evil disposition of nature. Thus at one time theft, although it is expressly contrary to the natural law, was not considered wrong among the Germans, as Julius Caesar relates.

QUESTIONS

1. According to St. Thomas, is there any necessary connection between just law and the conditions of community welfare?
2. Is a law binding, according to St. Thomas, if it does not have the consent of the governed?
3. What is the relation of the moral law to enacted law, according to St. Thomas? Is enacted law binding if it is immoral? Is there any source of authority of the moral law?
4. Is it a part of "natural law" that man do those things which he is instinctively inclined to do? Since man is inherently rational, does St. Thomas infer that it is part of the "natural law" that man do whatever reflection indicates is necessary for the common good?
5. If the moral law is somehow naturally imprinted in man — either in the natural inclinations or in his reason — why is enacted law, or the law stated in the Old Testament and the New Testament, a necessity?
6. Does St. Thomas find any important difference between the moral teaching of the Old Testament and that of the New Testament?
7. What is the basic principle of the natural moral law, according to St. Thomas? State some examples of human values he recognizes and of moral laws based on them, according to him.
8. Does St. Thomas think man has a natural inclination to be temperate? If not, how does he justify belief that we should exercise temperance?
9. Does St. Thomas think that moral principles, precise enough to direct ac-

tion, can be formulated in such a way as to be universally valid? If not, by what principle are we to admit exceptions, or to decide which rules are valid for the most part as contrasted with ones not valid at all?

10. Was St. Thomas aware of the fact that different peoples recognize different and conflicting moral principles? Does he infer from this fact that different moral principles are true in different countries?

SUGGESTIONS FOR FURTHER READING

Thomas Aquinas, Saint. *Summa Theologica*. Literally trans. by Fathers of the English Dominican province. London: Burns, Oates, & Washbourne, 1916-37.

Copleston, F. C. *Aquinas*. Baltimore: Penguin Books, 1955.
D'Arcy, M. C. *Thomas Aquinas*. London: Benn, 1930.
Gilson, Etienne. *Moral Values and the Moral Life*. St. Louis: Herder, 1931.
———. *The Philosophy of St. Thomas Aquinas*. St. Louis: Herder, 1929.
Maritain, Jacques. *St. Thomas Aquinas, Angel of the Schools*. London: Sheed & Ward, 1933.

CHAPTER 2 SUGGESTIONS FOR FURTHER READING

Brandt, Richard B. *Ethical Theory*. Englewood Cliffs, N. J.: Prentice-Hall, 1959, Chs. 14 and 15. The meaning of "obligation" and its senses; egoism, utilitarianisms, formalism; whether it is prudent to act rightly.
Broad, C. D., in Schilpp, P., ed., *The Philosophy of G. E. Moore*. Evanston, Ill.: Northwestern Univ. Press, 1942, pp. 43-57. Discussion whether egoism is self-contradictory.
Ewing, A. C. *Ethics*. New York: Macmillan, 1953.
McCloskey, H. J. "An Examination of Restricted Utilitarianism." *Philosophical Review*, Vol. 66 (1957), pp. 466-85. Critique of both types of utilitarianism.
Moore, G. E. *Ethics*. New York: Oxford Univ. Press, 1947, Ch. 5. Discussion of the meaning and senses of right; brief but lucid.
Ross, Sir William David. *Foundations of Ethics* (Gifford lectures). New York: Oxford Univ. Press, 1939, Chs. 4-6, 7.
Sharp, F. C. *Ethics*. New York: Appleton-Century, 1928, Chs. 22 and 23. An attempt to show that it is not disadvantageous to be moral.
Sidgwick, Henry. *The Methods of Ethics*. 7th ed. New York: Macmillan, 1922, Bk. 1, Ch. 9; Bk. 2, Ch. 1; Bk. 3, Chs. 11, 13; Bk. 4, Chs. 2-5. The most serious defense of the classical utilitarian view.
Smart, J. J. C. "Extreme and Restricted Utilitarianism." *Philosophical Quarterly*, Vol. 6 (1956), pp. 344-54. Criticism of rule-utilitarianism from traditional utilitarian point of view.
Urmson, J. O. "The Interpretation of the Philosophy of J. S. Mill." *Philosophical Quarterly*, Vol. 3 (1953), pp. 33-40. Interpretation of Mill as a rule-utilitarian.
Williams, G. "Normative Naturalistic Ethics." *Journal of Philosophy*, Vol. 47 (1950), pp. 324-30. An egoist position.

3 THE JUSTIFICATION OF ETHICAL BELIEFS

All but one of the foregoing philosophical pieces fall, wholly or in large part, under the heading of "normative ethics." That is, they are statements of principles, some about what is intrinsically good and others about what is right and wrong, which the authors advocate as true ethical principles. And they are defenses of these principles; in most cases the authors marshalled reasons of some sort or other, intended to show the truth of the principles or to render them acceptable to a reasonable person.

The reasons offered by these writers for various ethical principles are of several different types. Without making any attempt to be complete, we may review some of these with profit.

(1) As you may have noticed, sometimes the author simply invites the reader to consider whether he does not agree that a certain principle is self-evident.

(2) Or, what is not much different, the author poses some rather concrete examples of ethical situations and takes for granted that it will be agreed that certain judgments about them are correct; he then condemns some principle being considered, because it is inconsistent with these judgments, or urges a principle, because it is compatible with them.

(3) Somewhat more complex types of reasoning begin with a proposal about the meaning of some ethical term like "good" or "right." (a) For instance, it may be said, with Hobbes, that we call a thing "good" if we want it or take an interest in it; and from this premise the writer goes on to show why certain things are then properly called "good." (b) Or it may be said that at least we *ought* to call a thing "good" or "right" only under certain conditions — perhaps, with Bentham, because otherwise "right" would have no clear meaning or, with Kant, because only when used in this sense would the right properly command universal respect — and then the argument may proceed as before.

(4) Quite a different line of reasoning is the condemnation of a principle on the showing that a person who accepted it could not consistently proclaim it.

(5) Then there is a more historical train of thinking: the author assembles the major types of competing principle and raises objections to all but one — perhaps on grounds of vagueness — with the result that his own

principle is left the only competitor in the field. Bentham, for instance, argued in this way.

(6) Sometimes, in quite different vein, a principle is supported simply by commending it to the benevolent instincts of the reader; it may be pointed out, for instance, how much human welfare would be enhanced if only everyone adopted some principle — say, the utilitarian one —; and such a commendation is felt to be considerable or even sufficient support in itself.

(7) Sometimes there is an appeal to human nature — although such an appeal is perhaps properly classified as simply the claim that a general principle relating the good or the right to human nature is self-evident. The appeal to human nature may take the form of asserting that some kind of action cannot be wrong if it is action of a kind human beings simply cannot avoid performing — such, for instance, as defending their own lives. Or it may take the form of arguing that some kind of activity, such as rational activity, is good because it is the exercise of a capacity that is uniquely human; it may be said that it is "the function" of a human being to act in this way.

(8) A closely related type of argument — one not exemplified in the foregoing selections but which is important enough to deserve mention — is the claim that some general, perhaps utilitarian, principle must be accepted because it is the only one that is compatible with the social function of moral principles and moral reasoning itself; and this social function is said to be the harmonizing of human conduct, to the end of greater welfare, by the promulgation of, promotion of, and obedience to, general rules.

Such are major types of reasoning which historically have been offered for ethical principles. They are not the only types. It would be useful to be able to provide an exhaustive survey of the fundamentally different types of support which historically have been used; but a satisfactory analysis of this sort is still a matter for the future.

1. The problem: The assessment of first principles

Most of the above lines of thinking will strike the reader as having some force. But they also leave us puzzled. We naturally ask: Which ones, if any, would a reasonable person, one infallible at spotting logical pitfalls and fully informed of scientific facts about man and nature, find persuasive or acceptable? The answer to this question is not obvious. One possible answer — that of the sceptic — is, "None at all."

The problem of assessing these types of reasoning to an ethical conclusion would be quite different if they *started with ethical premises,* as do many arguments which are aimed to establish an ethical conclusion. The latter are properly tested by the ordinary standards of inductive or deductive reasoning. For instance, suppose I am reflecting on the reasons for buying my son a second-hand car. I might set out my reasons as follows.

Premise 1: One *ought always to do* what will maximize the happiness of all concerned.
Premise 2: Purchase of a car for my son will increase happiness more than would any other use to which I could put my money.
Conclusion: I *ought to buy* my son a car.

No one questions the rigor of this argument; it is a correct piece of ordinary deductive reasoning. The conclusion is an ethical judgment; and the first premise is also an ethical judgment ("ought to" appearing in both). But the cases of reasoning to an ethical conclusion in which we are interested are different; they aim to justify acceptance of an ethical principle *without* use of a further ethical premise. This reasoning cannot be that of simple deduction (or induction).

Some philosophers have suggested that we need not concern ourselves with assessing *first* principles in ethics, that is, with justifying acceptance of ethical conclusions without use of some ethical premises. They say no one really, in any specific context, doubts *all* ethical principles; and there is no reason why one should. Hence there is a practical need only to support *some* ethical principles, the ones which are seriously in doubt in the context. For this purpose there is no objection to using as premises ethical principles not in doubt in the context. It just never happens, in practice, that we need to establish an ethical conclusion from premises none of which is an ethical judgment.

Most of us, however, will not be content to leave matters at this point. We want to answer the question: What is the basis or justification for the whole system of our ethical beliefs? The facts of experiment or observation are a justification for scientific beliefs, and anyone who rejects physics can be forced to capitulate by being faced with these facts. Is there a comparable basis for ethical beliefs? Can we compel a reasonable person to change his ethical views, at least sometimes, by confronting him with facts and reasoning?

Moral philosophy of the past thirty years has been almost exclusively preoccupied with this topic. As a result of the discussion, the conclusion has emerged that there are roughly four possible reasonable types of answer to the question. These four types of answer are briefly sketched below and are represented in the readings that follow. Philosophers have concluded that types of reasoning which do not fall into one of these four general patterns are mistaken and failures. Take, for instance, the attempt to justify the conclusion that rational activity is good simply by urging as a premise (and perhaps a true one) that rational activity is a uniquely human capacity. Such reasoning, if offered as an argument, it would now be agreed is a failure. The conclusion does not *follow* logically; you would not be contradicting yourself if you conceded the premise but denied the conclusion. Such an "argument," unless it is somehow supplemented, simply is not cogent.

2. The types of contemporary theory

The four possible types of reasonable answer to the above question are: naturalism, supernaturalism, nonnaturalism, and noncognitivism. Of these, the first and fourth enjoy by far the greatest amount of popularity among contemporary philosophers.

A. NATURALISM   Naturalists believe that there is, in a sense, no special problem about justifying belief in ethical principles. For they are confirmable *by observation*, by the methods of the empirical sciences, in a manner substantially like the principles of chemistry and psychology. This view may seem surprising; but its advocates say that it is surprising only because we have not examined sufficiently carefully what we *mean* by ethical statements. Consider an example. Some naturalists say that "is intrinsically desirable" just *means* "is a pleasant experience." Of course, if this is true, if what I have to know, in order to know whether something is intrinsically desirable, is just that it is a pleasant experience, then I can know whether something is intrinsically desirable by observation and scientific methods. Take another example. Some naturalists say that "is right" just means "will produce at least as much happiness as any other course of action open to the agent." Again, of course, if this claim about meanings is true, so that what I have to know, in order to know if some act is right, is simply whether it will maximize happiness, then I can know whether something is right by observation and the methods of the sciences. The essence of naturalism is the proposal that the meaning of every ethical statement is such that the truth of the statement can be determined in this general sort of way by observation and the methods of science.

We could put this view in another way. We could say that the contention of the naturalist is that the meaning of ethical words is such that some general principles, linking ethical properties with observable properties, are true *by definition*. Examples are: "Something is intrinsically desirable if, and only if, it is a pleasant experience" and "An act is right if, and only if, performing it will produce at least as much happiness as any other course of action open to the agent."

There is difference of opinion among naturalists as to what exactly ethical words like "desirable" and "right" and "reprehensible" do mean, and therefore disagreement as to exactly which principles, like the above, are true by definition. This disagreement points to a fact which may already have struck the reader: it is certainly not *obvious* that either of the naturalistic definitions just cited is correct, or even that any definition along these lines is correct. (It is not obvious in the way in which "Everyone ought to do his duty" may be true by definition.) Naturalists themselves are, of course, aware of the differences in their ranks and of the fact that it is not obvious that ethical terms mean what naturalist definitions say they do. Some naturalists, as in the following reading from F. C. Sharp, are inclined to retort, if one raises this point as a puzzle, that we need to reflect carefully on our actual linguistic usages; they say that when we do so we shall see that their proposals about the meanings of ethical statements are correct after all. Other naturalists take a slightly different line. They claim, at least sometimes, that some statements like the above *would be* true by definition *if* we used our ethical terms in a thoughtful way, if we had ethical concepts adapted to the job ethical reasoning should perform. So, they say, ethical principles like the above would be true by definition, or confirmable by observation, if they meant what a clear-headed person would mean by them. Part of the reading by R. B. Perry represents this view.

B. SUPERNATURALISM   The second view is very similar to naturalism. Only, in place of some definition of ethical terms like "is a pleasant experience" — a phrase referring to an observable property or occurrence — the supernaturalist proposes a definition like "is approved by God." In other words, ethical properties are equated with theological properties. As a result, instead of the naturalist view that ethical statements can be confirmed by observation and the methods of science, the supernaturalist says that we can decide the truth of ethical statements by determining the truth of theological statements about the will of God. He asserts that some statement like the following is true by definition: "An act is wrong if and only if it conflicts with the commands of God."

The reader may think that the supernaturalist view leaps from the frying pan into the fire. If there is a puzzle about the logical foundation of ethics, he may ask, is it a solution to turn to theology? Aren't theological propositions even more in need of a logical foundation than ethical ones? Don't we have to decide what is God's will, very often, by first making up our minds about what is right? The supernaturalist is well aware of the fact that his view is not a simple one. But he thinks his view is the right one, just the same.

C. NONNATURALISM   The nonnaturalist rejects the main points of both the naturalist and the supernaturalist. In his view, the claims of both these groups about the meaning of ethical words are just plain false. The nonnaturalist may admit that ethical words are so used that some ethical statements are true by definition, say, a statement like "Everyone ought to do his duty," but not the statements these other philosophers think are true by definition.

What is the nonnaturalist's answer to the question, How may ethical statements be supported? His answer is an old one, which harks back to views we have already noted — just as naturalism harks back to views like those held by Hobbes and perhaps by Bentham and Mill. In essence, the nonnaturalist view is that ethical first principles can't be given support by anything else. They are principles one can't prove by deduction from any other kind of principle. But, all the same, we can know them to be true — by reflecting on them. The nonnaturalist knows full well that many people today do not put any faith in reflection as a way of knowing principles (except for tautologies, or statements which are true by definition). But he regards this lack of faith as a mistake, a failure of understanding. There are many principles outside ethics which we cannot seriously question and which we know only through reflection. Among such propositions he counts the axioms of logic, perhaps principles of geometry such as "One and only one straight line connects any two points," and principles such as "If anything is red all over, then it is not at the same time green all over."

Sometimes nonnaturalists take a somewhat different line. They say that what is the basis of ethical knowledge is quasi-perceptual intuition, or feeling, of a particular action being right or called for in a particular case, or of particular things being good or bad. We don't know these things with our eyes or ears, but we know them all the same — sometimes, it is said, through our feelings.

D. NONCOGNITIVISM   The fourth view is essentially the child of the twentieth century; it has no tradition behind it. But it is a very popular view today. The essence of it is that ethical statements are misunderstood if they are construed as describing or asserting anything at all. Unlike the statements made by the scientist, ethical statements do not *fail* of truth, do not *fail* to correspond with the facts as they are, because they do not *purport* to state any facts. Hence, it is misleading to ask "how we know" them; and it is misguided to look for confirmation or logical support.

Writers of this persuasion do not speak with one voice when they come to their positive views. Ethical statements are said by some to be expressions of feelings, rather like "Alas!" or "Hurrah!" Then "Generosity is good" amounts to something like "Hurrah for generosity!" Or, ethical statements are said to be ways of expressing long-term attitudes. Not very different is a proposal that such statements are very like optative sentences: for instance, "Generosity is good" is construed as "Would that people were generous!" Another view is that they are essentially declarations of resolve, so that "Adultery is wrong" is rather like "Be it hereby known that I am resolved to abstain from adultery myself and to discourage and disapprove adultery on the part of others." Sometimes ethical statements are said to function as commands: then "Stealing is wrong" is taken as approximately identical with "Don't steal!" All these writers share the view that ethical statements are better understood as, in effect, optatives, imperatives, or exclamations, rather than as indicative descriptions or explanations like the statements of science.

Most noncognitivists today would wish to say that the simple translations suggested in the preceding paragraph are not quite accurate; there is something special about ethical language — if there weren't something special, language would never have developed specifically ethical terminology. What is this something special? Different writers have had various suggestions to make. One important proposal is that ethical statements all speak to some general issue or somehow are addressed to everybody. For instance, it may be said that "Stealing is wrong" is different from "Don't you steal!" but quite close to "Don't anyone, ever, anywhere steal — and this includes me!" Or again, "That's wrong" is said to mean less "Boo for that!" than "Boo for that and for anything pretty much like it!" Another important proposal is that the use of ethical words carries special implications: to the effect that the feelings or attitudes expressed are carefully considered, or that they are shared by most other people, or that they can be supported by appropriate considerations. Or, it is sometimes said that the use of moral language implies that the attitude expressed is an impartial one, uninfluenced by personal stakes in the issue being appraised. These various proposals (and others) may be combined in various ways.

Where does this radically novel view leave our questions whether and how ethical beliefs may be justified? Of course, one implication is that they are not supportable by *evidence* in the way in which scientific beliefs can be supported. Yet noncognitivism has room for two important different views about the possibility of justification of ethical beliefs.

Some writers are content with a skeptical answer: it cannot ever be shown that one of two conflicting views is better, more justified, than its contradictory. All we can say is that some people feel one way, others another. *De gustibus non est disputandum.* Of course, there are various things we can do to *convince* people (including ourselves), and these activities are effective in removing disagreements in ethics: we can show a person how his ethical views are inconsistent, show him how his interests will be promoted if he supports a certain principle or cause, or just use our prestige or play on his feelings. But it is said, the view to which one is converted by such methods is no more correct than was the initial view.

It is possible, however, to take a quite different line and to say that, while "true" and "verified" don't apply to ethical statements, nevertheless, in a sense, some statements are better justified than others. Some ethical statements are relatively thoughtless: the attitudes they express would not have been formed if the person had familiarized himself with the facts and reflected on them or if he had seen what it would really be like to have the kind of world he advocates. Again, some ethical statements just mislead one or misuse language: as employing moral words they purport to express an impartial attitude or one directed at a general issue, but in fact it may be no more than that their speaker has a personal wish or is advocating something for reasons of personal advantage. He says, "It is morally obligatory to . . . ," although the language properly used to express his state of mind would be simply, "I personally would like. . . ." In other words, some writers, while abstaining from claims that ethical statements are true or can be supported by evidence like science, are prepared to say that some ethical statements are objectionable in some way and that there is a sense in which some ethical statements, or beliefs, are better established or supported or justified than are others. Such writers are not skeptics.

Frank Chapman Sharp   (1866-1943)

THE IDEAL OBSERVER THEORY

What it means to say that an act is right, according to F. C. Sharp, is that the act is of a kind one would approve of anyone's performing in similar circumstances if one were fully acquainted with all the foreseeable consequences. Or, in other words, "x is right" means "If I were impartial and fully informed about relevant facts, I would approve of doing x in these circumstances." Sharp held a somewhat similar view about the meaning of "is desirable" or "is good." To say that an experience is intrinsically good, he thinks, is to say that it could become the object of "reflective desire" in the sense that one would want it in calm moments when one was clear about what the object is and was facing the fact that its attainment is incompatible with the attainment of other desires. Evidently Sharp was a naturalist: for he thought we can find out what is right or good by the methods of science — by seeing what a person would approve of if he were impartial and informed or by seeing what he would want in reflective moments. Sharp did not, of course, claim that it is a simple matter to find out these things.

This theory has attracted various philosophers in recent years. It has been advocated or suggested in much more sophisticated form by C. D. Broad and Roderick Firth. It was accepted by Adam Smith in the eighteenth century; it is possible to interpret David Hume (see below) as a defender of it; and the student of Kant will find that it has much in common with Kant's views.

F. C. Sharp graduated from Amherst College and received his Ph.D. degree from the University of Berlin in 1892. He taught at the University of Wisconsin from 1893 until his retirement in 1936. One of his strong philosophical ambitions was to support philosophical analyses of ordinary moral concepts by objective procedures — by questionnaires and interviews. He experimented widely with such procedures. Among his more important books are *The Influence of Custom on the Moral Judgment* (1908), *Ethics* (1928), *Business Ethics* (1937), and a posthumous volume, *Good Will and Ill Will* (1950).

The passage below, drawn from the last-named of these books, is concerned wholly with an analysis of the concepts of "right" and "wrong." His views about "good" are contained in his *Ethics*, Chapter 19.

Reprinted from *Good Will and Ill Will* by Frank Chapman Sharp by permission of The University of Chicago Press. Copyright, 1950 by The University of Chicago.

GOOD WILL AND ILL WILL

The moral judgment takes the form: Action *S* is right — or wrong. It thus consists in the application of the predicate "right" to conduct. We have now to inquire into the meaning of this predicate.

The subject matter of our studies is still the man on the street. It is what *he* means by "right" that interests us. And the difficulty we face is that he cannot tell us. Ask him to define the term, and he will not even understand what you are driving at. This difficulty, however, is not one peculiar to the vocabulary of ethics. John Smith cannot tell you what he means by "cause," "probable," or "now"; he cannot give a really satisfactory answer to so apparently simple a question as "What is 'money'?"

This difficulty we can meet today as we met it again and again when we were three years old. We heard the people about us using such terms as "very" or "if"; and we wanted to know what they meant. Undoubtedly we were very far from persistent or systematic in our search for enlightenment; indeed, perhaps we did not *search* at all. But, at any rate, when we had been told that this milk was very hot, this stool very heavy, this glass very easily broken, and that we had been very naughty, the meaning of "very" dawned upon our minds, not in the sense that we could define it but that we could use it intelligently. It is in precisely this same way that we can discover what the layman means by the fundamental terms in the moral vocabulary. We watch his use of them. Thereupon, proceeding one step farther than the child, we generalize our observations and in doing so form a definition.

It is indeed a curious fact that men can go through life using words with a fair degree of definiteness and consistency with no formulated definition before the mind. But it is fact, nonetheless. "I cannot define poetry," says A. E. Housman in effect, "but I know it when I see it. In the same way a terrier cannot define rat, but he knows one when he sees it."

If the analysis of this chapter is correct, "right" must be definable in terms of desire, or approbation, that is to say, in terms of "feeling." When John Smith calls an action "right" or "wrong," however, he means something other than that he happens to feel about it in a certain way at that particular moment. This was clearly pointed out by Hume two hundred years ago and should have become commonplace among moralists by this time. A successful swindle may arouse feelings of very different intensity according to who happens to be the victim — myself, my son, my intimate friend, an acquaintance, a stranger, a foreigner, a man who died a hundred years ago. Indeed, in some of the latter cases the feeling component may drop out entirely. Again, an incident I myself have witnessed, such as an act of malicious cruelty or the bullying of the weak by the strong, makes me feel very different from that about which I have only read or heard. And my feelings in the latter case are likely to depend on the vividness and complete- ness with which the narrator brings the situation home to my imagination. An incident which I can realize because I have been through just such an experience myself appeals to me far otherwise than one which I know only through having viewed it from the outside. The robbery or oppression of those whom I see from day to day or am personally acquainted with arouses in me far more indignation than if they are merely unknown people living for all practical purposes in a world other than my own. With all these variations in my feelings, I recognize upon reflection that what is really right or wrong in the premises remains unchanged. Wrong does not become innocent or right merely because the act took place a hundred years ago instead of this morning, because I did not happen to see it myself, because I myself have never happened to be in that position, or because one of the persons involved happens to be an acquaintance, a member of my family, or myself.

In view of these facts, we must define "right," if we are to use the term in the sense in which the ordinary man uses it, as *that which arouses appro- bation under certain conditions.* Accordingly the question arises: What are these conditions?

We shall not expect to discover them by asking John Smith to enu- merate and describe them. The man in the street does not carry about with him in his mental kit a set of formulas covering these conditions, any more than when he cuts a corner he says to himself, "A straight line is the shortest distance between two points." That the conditions in question represent real forces may be shown empirically by what John Smith does when in doubt or when he changes his mind or when the correctness of his predication is challenged by others.

In the first place, then, John Smith does not apply the predicates right and wrong to conduct unless he supposes himself to be viewing it from an impersonal standpoint. This means that he supposes, negatively, that his attitude is not determined by his egoistic interests or by any purely personal relations to the parties concerned; positively, that the act is one that he would approve of anyone's performing under the same conditions. This attitude is expressed in the familiar maxim: What is right for one is right for every- one else under the same conditions. This maxim is an analytic, not a syn- thetic, proposition. It is no discovery of moralists, least of all of Kant, to whom it is often attributed, for its governing role in the moral world was noted in effect by Cumberland and quite explicitly by Clarke before Kant was born. As a matter of fact, the "discovery" has been made countless mil- lions of times, for it is a dull-witted seven-year-old who does not remind his parents on occasions that what they require him to do they are bound to do themselves.

Here, again, enters the all-important distinction between correct and incorrect moral judgments, or, as I should prefer to say, between valid and invalid; for, as we have seen in this chapter, John Smith frequently regards an action as innocent or even obligatory when he profits by it and wrong when he happens to be the sufferer. In calling it "wrong" instead of "harmful," he implies that it is an act which, performed under the conditions, he would condemn in anyone, including himself. His supposition being false, his judgment expresses an opinion which can only be called "incorrect."

As soon as John Smith realizes this lack of impersonality, he recognizes at once the incorrectness of the judgment and therewith the necessity of modifying or abandoning it. In a certain city, the university YMCA, having included a barber shop among the attractions of its new building, engaged as its manager the popular head-barber of the city's leading "tonsorial parlor"; whereupon the proprietor complained loudly of the action of the association in attracting his most valuable employee away from him as being "unfair." When he was reminded that he himself had obtained this same employee in precisely the same way, by attracting him from another shop by a better financial offer, nothing more was heard from him on this subject.

Common sense thus recognizes the existence of such a thing as a mistaken moral judgment. Those moralists who ignore this fact thereby show that their picture of the workings of the moral consciousness is an arbitrary construction, out of touch with the realities of life.

Impersonality, however, is not the only condition which John Smith recognizes the moral judgment must meet if it is to conform to the implications involved in this conception of right. The second condition is a consequence of the essential character of the evaluating judgment as such. When we pass judgment upon anything whatever, whether it be a candidate for public office or Titian's "Assumption of the Virgin," we suppose that we know what it is. Really to know what anything is, is to have an apprehension of its nature, which is at once accurate and complete. In practice, of course, this ideal is ordinarily incapable of attainment. But, in proportion as we approach certainty of conviction, our confidence increases that our view possesses an amount of accuracy and completeness such that any correction of or addition to the data in our possession would make no difference in the conclusion reached. And our task is lightened by growing insight into what kinds of data are relevant and what are not. A datum is relevant when its introduction would tend to make any difference in the resulting judgment.

The application of these observations to the moral judgment is obvious. The subject of the moral judgment is voluntary action. A voluntary act is an attempt to produce certain effects. The moral judgment, accordingly, is supposed, with varying degrees of confidence, by the judger to be based upon an accurate and complete knowledge of these effects or upon as much knowledge as would involve no change of opinion if the rest of the effects were displayed accurately and in order before the mind's eye. If this supposition is true, the judgment is in so far forth correct or valid. On the other hand, if the judgment turns on an incomplete or otherwise inaccurate view of these effects, including, of course, a view of the situation in which they operate, it may properly be termed incorrect or invalid, because it is not what the judger supposes it to be.

Observation verifies this analysis. Our study of the causes that lead to the diversities in moral judgments has shown that a leading cause is difference of opinion as to what the consequences of the act will be. And in the majority of instances when John Smith begins to doubt the correctness of one of his past judgments, it is upon the consequences believed to be involved that his decision turns. Under such and such circumstances is a man justified in lying? in breaking a promise or a contract? in helping himself to someone else's property? in giving a dose of poison to a hopeless invalid? in making a true statement injurious to the reputation of a neighbor? in giving money to a street beggar? Whatever decision is reached turns fundamentally upon what are believed to be the good or evil consequences involved.

If, then, we are to conform to the implications of everyday usage in applying the predicates right and wrong to the effects of volitions, we must know what these effects are. Now, knowledge is of two kinds; or, if you prefer, it has two levels. Using Professor James's terminology, one is acquaintance with; the other, knowledge about. The former is given in immediate experience, whether in the world of sense or in the inner world of pleasure, pain, emotion, or desire. It may be re-created, when past, in those persons who are fortunate enough to possess the capacity for full and vivid imagery. We may call this "realization." The second kind, or level, reveals reality through the instrumentality of concepts. Now, the concept is an abstract idea, such as "length" or "walking" or "very." It represents one or a group of aspects torn from the concrete objects that make up the real world and held before the mind in more or less complete isolation from such objects.

The ability to form and use concepts is the most powerful instrument in the possession of the human mind. Among other things, as a constituent of desire it determines the direction of every voluntary action we perform. But, like everything else in the world, the concept has its limitations. In its very nature as an abstraction, it reveals only a part, usually only a very small part, of the object at which it points. It may report truth but never the whole truth. In this respect it is like a map. Show a map of Switzerland to a person who has never been away from a North Dakota prairie or even seen a picture of a mountain. Compare the knowledge thus gained with that of a Swiss who has spent his vacations for many years exploring his native country. Or, again, let some one of us who has never come in contact with death and has never had to carry crushing financial burdens read in the newspaper that some stranger, formerly a clerk in a certain grocery store, died yesterday after a painful and lingering illness; he was thirty-five years old; a widow and three children survive him. How small a fraction of the grim realities at which these words hint would enter our consciousness!

Quite apart from poverty of detail, conceptual thought, again like a map, has another limitation. It reveals relations but can never reveal the things related. In other words, thought at its best, conceptual thought, merely performs the functions of a mathematical formula. It is a commonplace that a person born blind may know all the laws of light and yet have no acquaintance with color.

Thus, notwithstanding its marvelous range, conceptual thought is a very inadequate substitute for "acquaintance with" as a revelation of reality. There is only one road to genuine acquaintance with the world outside the consciousness of the moment, and it is through imagery, the power to realize. If, then, a moral judgment is to be valid, it must be either a judgment based upon a complete acquaintance with the whole situation in all its relevant details or, since this is rarely or perhaps never attainable, such a judgment as would result from an acquaintance with the whole situation.

The influence of realization upon the processes of moral judgment exhibits itself frequently in those pseudo-moral judgments in which the predicates right and wrong follow the judger's personal interests, and a vivid sense of his own gain or loss eclipses the vague concept of the loss or gain of the other part. Let the other side of the case come home to him and the victim's plight be fully realized, he "changes his mind," thereby bringing his judgment into conformity with his new insight. This phenomenon has been abundantly illustrated in this chapter.

The definition emerging from the preceding analysis is the following: When John Smith calls an action "right," he means that complete acquaintance with its results would evoke impersonal approval. Exchanging the negative term "impersonal" for a positive one, "right" characterizes the kind of action he would want all human beings to perform under the given conditions if he had a complete acquaintance with all the relevant consequences. The evidence for the correctness of this analysis is that when John Smith discovers that he has failed to meet some one of these conditions, he recognizes that his judgment calls for reconsideration.

QUESTIONS

1. Does Sharp think the ordinary man can give a correct answer to the question of what he means by "is right" or "is wrong"? Can he give better answers about what he means by "is probable" or "x caused y"?
2. How does Sharp think we should go about discovering what the plain man does mean by "is right"?

3. Does Sharp think it correct to say that an act is wrong if it arouses our dis-approbation? What does he mean by "disapprobation"?
4. What does Sharp mean in saying that it is an "analytic" proposition that "What is right for one is right for everyone else under the same conditions"? Does this view about the proposition in question seem to you correct?
5. In what way, according to Sharp, is "an impersonal standpoint" involved in a correct moral judgment? What does he mean by "an impersonal standpoint"?
6. In what way, according to Sharp, is awareness of all the relevant facts involved in a correct moral judgment? How is one to decide whether a fact is "relevant"?
7. In what sense does he think such awareness must be vivid and not merely abstract? Do you agree with Sharp that a capacity for vivid imagination is re-quired for subtle moral judgment?

Ralph Barton Perry   (1876-1957)

THE INTEREST THEORY

Ralph Barton Perry graduated from Princeton University and received a Ph.D. degree from Harvard University. He taught philosophy briefly at Williams College and at Smith College be-fore returning to Harvard, where he remained until his retire-ment. Perry was by no means merely an ivory-tower philosopher: an active advocate of democratic ideals, he was active and influ-ential on the political scene during both World Wars I and II. As a pure philosopher he was distinguished as a leader in the neorealist movement in epistemology, and he won the Pulitzer Prize in 1936 for his biography of William James. His most im-portant philosophical book, however, was *The General Theory of Value* (1926). His *Realms of Value* (1954), from which the following selection is drawn, summarizes and develops the theory of the earlier book. It was originally delivered as Gifford Lectures.

Perry has been the most influential ethical naturalist of the present century, at least in the United States. Nevertheless it is not easy to say what exactly are the general outlines of his theory. He does not, like some other advocates of an "interest theory," claim that his definitions of moral words in terms of human interests are just reports of their actual meanings or em-ployment; he rather says he is proposing good or proper mean-ings for these words. As a result, we are bound to be puzzled about two things: (1) the way in which evidence is supposed to support his definitions and just which argument is supposed to be such supporting evidence, and (2) the reason why he felt a need to offer arguments in support of his moral first principles, since these are true by definition, once his definitions are accepted. It is not here suggested that a satisfactory defense of Perry's general approach cannot be provided; but Perry himself did not throw it in the clearest possible light.

We may not be quite convinced by his theory just as it stands; but it may well be that only minor adjustments are needed to render it highly plausible.

Reprinted by permission of the publishers from Ralph Barton Perry. *Realms of Value: A Critique of Human Civilization.* Cambridge, Mass.: Harvard University Press. Copyright, 1954, by The President and Fellows of Harvard College.

REALMS OF VALUE

[The definition of "value"] *

The question, "What does 'value' mean?" is not the same as the question "What things have value?" Though the two questions are often confused, the difference is evident when attention is called to it. The statement that "a sphere is a body of space bounded by one surface all points of which are equally distant from a point within called its center" is different from the statement that "the earth is (or is not) a sphere." The statement that peace is a condition in which societies abstain from the use of violence in settling their disputes, is different from the statement that the world is (or is not) now at peace. And similarly, a statement, such as is proposed below, of what value is, differs from the statement that peace is valuable.

If the second of each of these pairs of statements is to be definitive and accurate it is clearly advisable to have in mind the first. If, in other words, one is to know whether peace is or is not valuable, it is well to know what 'valuable' is: in other words, to know what it is that is stated about peace when it is stated that it is valuable. But while the question raised by the second statement depends on an answer to the question raised by the first, the two questions are not the same question. And it is the first question with which the present inquiry is primarily concerned. In other words, theory of value ascribes value to things only in the light of what 'value' means.

Some philosophers, unfortunately, put the question concerning value in the form "What *is* meant by 'value'?" or "What *does* one mean by 'value'?" as though that meaning were already determined, and it was only necessary to call attention to it. Those who approach the matter in this way are accustomed to challenge a proposed definition of value by saying, "But this is not what is meant by 'value'" or "This is not what one means by

* The italicized headings are interpolations by the editor.

'value.'" The fact is, however, that there is no such established and universal meaning. Different people mean different things in different contexts. The problem is not to discover a present meaning — there are only too many meanings.

The problem is not solved, however, by simply enumerating these many meanings. This job is already done by the unabridged dictionaries which list, in fine print, all the varieties of meaning which appear in literature and ordinary speech. Theory of value is in search of a preferred meaning. The problem is to define, that is, *give* a meaning to the term, either by selecting from its existing meanings, or by creating a new meaning.

But one must not then leap to the conclusion that this giving of a meaning to the term 'value' is an arbitrary matter, dictated by the caprice, or mere personal convenience, of the author. One can, it is true, make the term mean "anything one likes," but this would not advance knowledge, or be of the slightest importance, or be capable either of proof or of disproof. The man who said "When I say 'value' I mean a purple cow" would not even be listened to, unless by a psychiatrist or a kindergarten teacher. There must, in other words, be a control or set of criteria, by which the definition is justified or rejected.

According to the definition of value here proposed, *a thing — any thing — has value, or is valuable, in the original and generic sense when it is the object of an interest — any interest.* Or, *whatever is object of interest is ipso facto valuable.* Thus the valuableness of peace is the characteristic conferred on peace by the interest which is taken in it, for what it is, or for any of its attributes, effects, or implications.

Value is thus defined in terms of interest, and its meaning thus depends on another definition, namely, a definition of interest. The following is here proposed: interest is *a train of events determined by expectation of its outcome.* Or, *a thing is an object of interest when its being expected induces actions looking to its realization or non-realization.* Thus peace is an object of interest when acts believed to be conducive to peace, or preventive of peace, are performed on that account, or when events are selected or rejected because peace is expected of them.

Both of these definitions require clarification and elaboration; but these summary statements will suffice for the present purpose of indicating the criterion by which the definitions are to be justified. These criteria are three in number, namely, *linguistic, formal,* and *empirical.* When the definition is challenged it must defend itself on three grounds: its use of words; the clarity, definiteness, tenability, and fruitfulness of the concepts which it employs; and its capacity to describe certain facts of life, to which it refers, and by which it is verified. . . .

[*The nature of interests*]

Psychology of diverse schools, and especially in its most recent developments, recognizes the existence of action systems which, when released or evoked, impel the individual to conduct himself in a certain specific manner. There are various general names for these action systems — 'drive,' 'driving adjustment,' 'need,' 'purpose,' 'motor attitude,' 'set,' 'governing propensity,' 'determining tendency,' — of which 'drive' is here selected both because of its dynamic suggestiveness, and because of prevailing usage in the literature of the subject.

The drive involves several factors. There is a neuro-muscular prearrangement or coördination, which is provided with stored energy. It is this motor equipment which distinguishes the drive from the skill. A drive, in other words, is not a mere apparatus, but a force, capable of motion and work. It contains, furthermore, not only a capacity and readiness to operate, but a tendency to operate. The drive is both a capacity and an impulse.

Corresponding to the prearrangement there is an exciting occasion by which the prearrangement is brought into operation. Both the prearrangement and the exciter are specific; the specific prearrangement is called into play by the specific exciter, and the exciter calls the specific prearrangement into play. The prearrangement is internal to the organism, while the exciter may be either internal or external. When the prearrangement is excited it usually takes command of the total organism, diverting its available energies from other possible uses, and thus requiring an adjustment and subordination of rival demands. The drive, as distinguished from the mere "reflex" is variable and modifiable, in respect of the intermediate phases through which it passes on its way to its more or less distant goal. Driving *toward* a goal, it learns *how* to reach it.

Social and personality psychologists recognize certain common drives by which to explain the conduct of individuals and groups. Animal psychologists, engaged in the study of learning, recognize the necessity of assuming impulsions, such as hunger and pain-avoidance, which underly the process of trial and error — without which the animal would not try, and without which success could not be distinguished from error. Freud's concern was not with the comparatively simple behavior of animals in an artificial maze, but with the complexities of human behavior in the labyrinth of life. The Freudian "wish," with all its variants, which impels to action, which conflicts with other wishes, which, when unable to execute itself overtly, goes underground and finds indirect or disguised modes of expression in dreams, wit, and slips of the tongue, which may so far ignore "reality" as to create hallucinations and incapacitate a person to live in his physical and social environment — the wish, which plays this dramatic role, is essentially the same thing as the drive recognized by the social and animal psychologists.

The current psychology of drives raises, and leaves unsettled, several questions affecting the nature of interests. There is, in the first place, both indefiniteness and disagreement as to what, and how many, drives there are. The recent history of the subject began with William McDougall's conception of "instincts" or forms of striving. His list, in which each instinct was accompanied by an emotion, comprised flight-fear, repulsion-disgust, curiosity-wonder, pugnacity-anger, self-abasement–self-assertion, parental love and tenderness, and others, major and minor. After McDougall, the study of "learning" had the effect of casting doubt on all such lists of innate drives. Learning was invoked to explain, and remained to explain away, until nothing was left except several dubious reflexes such as the grasping and withdrawal reflexes of the infant. But since it was evident that learning itself could not be explained without drives, the pendulum swung back again, and new lists appeared.

Thus E. C. Tolman enumerated "appetites" of thirst, hunger, sex, play, "avoidance" of cold, heat, and obstruction, and "social" drives, such as gregariousness. Tolman, be it noted, is primarily a student of animal behavior. Robert R. Sears, a child psychologist, named "hunger, sex, sleep and fatigue, elimination" as the "major primary drives." There would appear, in other words, to be some relation between the list of drives and the special field examined by the psychologist. Thus McDougall takes his cue from the adult human; Tolman from the rat; Sears from the infant.

The second question which is left in doubt is that of innateness. Often a drive is taken to be innate by definition. But, the child psychologist quoted above speaks of "major primary drives" and "major secondary drives." The minor drives are not enumerated, but appear to provide a sort of "et cetera" — lest otherwise the list appear too rigid. The primary drives are original, and the secondary are derived from the primary by "social interaction." The secondary drives (aggression, dependency, independence, status striving) presumably provide their own motivation once they are created. E. C. Tolman, on the other hand, adopts a division into "Biological Drives" and "Social Drives," and then goes on to state explicitly that: "The basic energy comes from the Biological Drives. The Social Drives or techniques are secondary motives which are derived from the Biological. . . ."

In this context the Atavistic Fallacy consists in supposing that the Biological Drives continue to provide the driving power which the Social Drives merely canalize. This would mean that the original drives are the only independent drives; meaning that if they ceased to operate the wheels of action would cease to turn. This is plainly contrary to the fact of development. Or it would mean that a present drive can be explained only as the repetition of a past success.

This last interpretation is, on the face of it, paradoxical, since it seems to say that doing something new consists only in doing something old, but doing it as well or better; which does not account for the genesis of new drives or of ways of meeting new situations. The principle of the conditioned reflex helps to explain *some* new drives, but there is no reason to suppose that it is the only explanation or a sufficient explanation. Imitation, random activity, imagination, and, above all, the total personality (whether internally unified or conflicting) constitute drives and generate them. As to ways of meeting new situations, surely thought, and learning by example or precept to *avoid* error, play a role not less important than trial *and* error.

Fortunately theory of value need not await a final verdict on these controversial topics. It is important for theory of value, and for the art of control in the sphere of human institutions, to know what drives can be assumed to be comparatively universal. But universality does not depend on origin. It is important, for example, to recognize that all men are impelled by the drives of hunger and pain avoidance; but if these were *learned* by all men in infancy as a result of conditions common to all living organisms, they would for all practical purposes *be* as universal as if they were innate.

It is also important to know what drives are the most powerful and deep-seated; but this, again, does not depend on innateness. Indeed it is characteristic of man that many of his most powerful drives, such as patriotism, ambition, and love of money, are clearly acquired. Drives may *become* deep-seated, in the sense of perseverance and mastery. Hence it is not in the least prejudicial to man's higher or more idealistic purposes that they should have been developed rather than original. Human interests can rise above their source. Indeed it might be said to be the very essence of man that both phylogenetically and ontogenetically he *does* rise above his source. . . .

[The nature of morality]

Morality is man's endeavor to harmonize conflicting interests: to prevent conflict when it threatens, to remove conflict when it occurs, and to advance from the negative harmony of non-conflict to the positive harmony of coöperation. Morality is the solution of the problem created by conflict — conflict among the interests of the same or of different persons. The solution of the personal problem lies in the substitution for a condition of warring and mutually destructive impulses a condition in which each impulse, being assigned a limited place, may be innocent and contributory. For the weakness of inner discord it substitutes the strength of a unified life in which the several interests of an individual make common cause together. The same description applies to the morality of a social group, all along the line from the domestic family to the family of nations.

Such a moralization of life takes place, insofar as it does take place, through organization — personal and social. This crucial idea of organization must not be conceived loosely, or identified with organism. In organism, as in a work of art, the part serves the whole; in moral organization the whole serves the parts, or the whole only for the sake of the parts. The parts are interests, and they are organized in order that they, the constituent interests themselves, may be saved and fulfilled.

When interests are thus organized there emerges an interest of the totality, or moral interest, whose superiority lies in its being greater than any of its parts — greater by the principle of inclusiveness. It is authorized to speak for all of the component interests when its voice is their joint voice. The height of any claim in the moral scale is proportional to the breadth of its representation. What suits all of a person's interests is exalted above what merely suits a fraction; what suits everybody is exalted above what merely suits somebody. . . .

Morality conceived as the harmonization of interests for the sake of the interests harmonized can be described as a cult of freedom. It does not force interests into a procrustean bed, but gives interests space and air in which to be more abundantly themselves. Its purpose is to provide room. And ideally the benefits of morality are extended to all interests. Hence moral progress takes the double form, of liberalizing the existing organization, and of extending it to interests hitherto excluded. Both of these principles have important applications to the "dynamics" of morality, or to the moral force in human history. The extension of moral organization is made possible by increase of contact and interaction, which, however, then multiplies the possibilities of conflict. Hence the peculiar destiny of man, whose ascent is rendered possible by the same conditions which make possible his fall. There can be no development of a unified personality or society without the risk of inner tensions; no neighborhood, nation, or society of all mankind, without the risk of war.

Morality as progressive achievement requires the integration of interests. They cannot be simply added together. If they are to compose a harmonious will that represents them all, they must be brought into line. At the same time, if such a will is truly to embrace them, which is the ground of its higher claim, they must themselves accept the realignment. Morality is an integration of interests, in which they are rendered harmonious without losing their identity. The procedure by which this is effected is the method of *reflective agreement*, appearing in the personal will, and in the social will.

[*The integration of interests: personal and social*]

Interests are integrated by reflection. In the creation of the personal will there occurs a thinking over, in which the several interests of the same person are reviewed, and invited to present their claims. Reflection overcomes the effects of forgetfulness and disassociation. It corrects the perspectives of time and immediacy, anticipating the interests of tomorrow, and giving consideration to the interests which at the moment are cold or remote. It brings to light the causal relations between one interest and another. From reflection there emerge decisions which fulfill, in some measure, the purpose of harmony: plans, schedules, quotas, substitutions, and other arrangements by which the several interests avoid collision and achieve mutual reinforcement.

The personal will which emerges from reflection is not, as has some-times been held, merely the strongest among existing interests, prevailing after a struggle of opposing forces. It is not a mere survivor, other con-testants having been eliminated. It does not intervene on one side or the other, but takes a line down the middle, analogous to the resultant or vector in a field of forces. It makes its own choices, and sets its own pre-cedents. Its accumulated decisions, having become permanent dispositions, form a character, or unwritten personal constitution. . . .

The similarity between the personal and social forms of the moral will must not be allowed to obscure their profound difference. It is true that as the personal will emerges from reflection so the social will emerges from communication and discussion. In both cases the emergent will represents a totality of interests, and achieves by organization a substitution of har-mony for conflict. The difference lies in the fact that whereas the personal will is composed of sub-personal interests, the social will is composed of persons.

But while the social moral will is a will of persons, society is not a person. Excluding fictitious persons, corporate persons, legal persons, and every metaphorical or figurative use of the term, the only real person is that being which is capable of reflecting, choosing, relating means to ends, making decisions, and subordinating particular interests to an overruling pur-pose. It follows that there can be no moral will on the social level except as composed of several personal wills which are peculiarly modified and in-terrelated.

The ramifications of this fact pervade the whole domain of morality and moral institutions. It is echoed in all of those doctrines which exalt the person as an end in himself. It gives meaning to fraternity as the ac-knowledgment of person by fellow-persons. It gives to the individual man that "dignity" of which we hear so much. It provides for that unique role of the person as thinker, judge, and chooser, which lies at the basis of all representative institutions, and determines the moral priority of individuals to society.

The creation of a social moral will out of personal wills depends on benevolence, that is, one person's positive interest in another person's in-terest. To be benevolent here means not that I treat you well so far as it happens to suit my existing interests to do so; my concern for your inter-ests is an independent interest. Taking your desires and aversions, your hopes and fears, your pleasures and pains, in short, the interests by which you are actually moved, I act as though these interests were my own. Though I cannot, strictly speaking, *feel* your interests, I can acknowledge them, wish them well, and allow for them in addition to the interests which are already embraced within me. When you are at the same time benevolently disposed to my interests, we then have the same problem of reconciling the same interests, except that my original interests form the content of your benevolence and your original interests the content of mine.

In this pooling of interests I am ordinarily concerned that your benevolence shall actually embrace my original interests; and you are similarly concerned to accent yours. Each of us assumes that the other can safely be trusted to look out for his own. Assuming that each will be biased in favor of his own interests, the bias of each will tend to correct the bias of the other. Each will be the special pleader of his own interests, and his insistence on them will reinforce the other's weaker benevolence.

There will be a further difference. Your interests are best and most immediately served by you, and mine by me. I can for the most part serve you best by letting you serve yourself. The greater part of my benevolence, therefore, will take a permissive form. I will sometimes help you, but more often will abstain from hurting you; or will so follow my own inclinations as to make it possible for you also to follow yours; or accept your inclinations as setting a limit to mine.

No will is here introduced over and above the wills of the two persons, but since the two wills now represent the same interests, they will have achieved a community of end and a coöperative relation of means. In each person the new socialized purpose will have become dominant over his original interests. Neither will have become the mere means to the other since the common end is now each person's governing end. Each can speak with equal authority for that end, and may legitimately use the pronouns 'we' and 'our' in behalf of both. Each, speaking for the common end, can approve or disapprove the other's conduct without arrogance or impertinence.

The social form of the moral will is an agreement of personal wills of which independent benevolence is the essential condition. There are many other factors which conduce to such agreement, and which in their totality make up the method or art of agreement. The first prerequisite of agreement is a desire to agree, rather than to "get the better" of the other party. To induce this attitude it is necessary that both parties should be conscious of the wastefulness of conflict, and the gains, even if they be selfish gains, of peace. The Quaker idea of achieving unanimity, or a "sense of the meeting," which leaves no slumbering grievances and seeds of fresh dispute, is precisely the moral norm which is here defined. The further Quaker idea of periods of silence may or may not be taken to imply a religious doctrine of "inner light"; it may be taken to mean only that an interval of meditation will serve to cool the temper of acrimony. . . .

Morality may be illustrated by the actual complexities of social life arranged in spheres of expanding inclusiveness. In the more intimate family or local circle there are several persons within the range of familiar acquaintance, each with interests of his own. Through communication and benevolence each adopts as his own the interest of father, mother, son, daughter, brother, sister, friend, neighbor; integrates them, speaks for the family or local group as a whole, and himself accepts this voice as authoritative over his original interests.

When representatives of capital and labor sit around a table and engage in what is called "collective bargaining," and insofar as this is a *moral* transaction which achieves a "right" solution of the problem of conflict, the process is similar except that the interests are represented, instead of being immediately present "in person." Each representative enters the conference as the advocate of one of the conflicting economic interests, and he is expected to advocate it. But he is also expected to take the view of the opposing advocate. He must listen to him, be impressed, concede his point, acknowledge his claims. In proportion as there is this exchange of interests, both parties tend to be actuated by both interests. Their two attitudes tend to converge and to approximate that of a third party, such as "the representative of the public," the judge, or the arbitrator, whose role it is to be equally considerate of both interests, and the partisan advocate of neither.

The procedures that are proper to collective bargaining are those which enable each finally to decide for all. The first step is the desire for agreement. Other proper procedures would include the discovery and amplification of the facts relevant to any of the interests represented; the invention of methods by which interests at present conflicting can both be fulfilled; the recognition of partial agreements already existing and of the commitments which these imply. Actually, other factors come into play — stubbornness, a war of nerves, the relative strength of war chests, endurance, threats, lung power, scowling eyebrows, appeals to the galleries. Undoubtedly the decision is forced and premature, and may have some day to be reopened. But when we speak of a solution of industrial problems which is better than brute force, or say that capital and labor should be partners rather than enemies, or praise the participants as more or less "fair," or judge the outcome to be more or less "just," it is this ideal solution that is appealed to as a standard. Each party makes a personal decision in the light of the interests represented by both, and the decisions tend to agree. . . .

Such is the principle of reflective agreement. No claim is here made for the frequency or success of its application. But it means something, it is humanly possible, and it is successfully applied in some measure. If reflective inter-personal agreement be the moral principle, one must be prepared to admit that there is not always a moral solution of a problem of conflict. There is, however, a *way* to such a solution — a *line of effort.* Morality is a *pursuit*, not an infallible recipe. The conflicting parties may not try at all, or they may try and fail. All that moral philosophy can do is to define the moral goal; all that moral prophets can do is to exhort men to aim at the goal; all that moral sages can do is to cite the experience of those who have been successful. If the conflicting parties do not look for agreement, there is no moral solution; if they do not succeed in reaching agreement, there is no moral solution. In case of unwillingness to agree, or in case of failure to agree, the action of the parties in question must take other grounds — partisanship, egoism, passion, whatever it be. . . .

[The interpretation of moral concepts]

There are certain terms of discourse, such as 'good,' 'right,' 'duty,' 'responsibility,' and 'virtue,' which are commonly recognized as having to do with morality, and to which a theory of morals must assign definite meanings. . . .

An object is *good* in the generic sense when it is the object of a positive interest; it is *morally good* in the special sense when the interest which makes it good satisfies the requirement of harmony, that is, innocence and coöperation. This requirement may be met in one or both of two ways. In the first place, it may qualify any interest when that interest is governed by a concern for other interests. Thus the object of a person's sensuous enjoyment acquires a moral character when it is governed by his concern for his health or practical achievements; and a person's ambition acquires a moral character when it is governed by his concern for the interests of other persons. Or, in the second place, the moral requirement may qualify a special interest — the moral interest — by having harmony as its object.

In other words, one may state of any object of interest that it is morally good when the interest is endorsed by other interests; and one may state that a total life in which all interests endorse one another is morally good when it is the object of the moral will.

The "good life," morally speaking, may be described as a condition of *harmonious happiness* — a condition in which, through the increase and coöperation of its members, all interests tend to be positive. This description throws light on the meaning of the familiar but obscure idea of "happiness," and on the traditional claim of happiness to rank as the supreme moral end.

Happiness is attributed to a person as a whole, as distinguished from his momentary or partial interests. He is happy insofar as every outlook is auspicious; he can face many prospects and face them all cheerfully. His present interest is accompanied by a sense of the applause of all his other interests, brought into consciousness by imagination and reflection. . . .

In common discourse, and in the moral theory known as 'utilitarianism,' happiness is identified with pleasure. This identification reflects a careless use of the term 'pleasure.' If pleasure is taken to be a bodily sensation, then it is a part of happiness only because pleasure is liked and enjoyed. If, on the other hand, pleasure or 'pleasantness' is taken to mean the individual's awareness of his own positive interest, then his happiness differs from his pleasure only in its pervading and qualifying the totality of his life. Similarly unhappiness will consist not in the sensation of pain, but in the feelings which reflect the negative quality of his interests.

This analysis must not be taken to imply the unimportance of *sensations* of pleasure and pain for happiness. Because pleasure is normally liked and pain disliked, the presence of these sensations is a constant factor in happiness and unhappiness. The sensation of pain will interrupt any form of enjoyment or prosperous achievement and substitute negative for positive interest. Sensation of pleasure, on the other hand, may substitute positive for negative interest, or reinforce a positive interest which already exists. The internal environment of the organism is carried into every external environment; wherever, whenever, with whomsoever and with whatsoever, a man lives, he must live with his own body. Its pleasures and pains, its health or malaise, will affect the tone of every interest and of life as a whole.

As happiness reflects a harmony of interests, so unhappiness is an effect of conflict, as when a man is said to be "at war with himself." Insofar as this condition prevails, each interest sees the others as its enemies, and is moved to defeat them. Each positive interest — each enjoyment or prosperous achievement — then begets a negative interest on behalf of the other interests which it jeopardizes.

The application of similar principles to inter-personal relations gives meaning to such expressions as 'the general good.' The happiness of a society or a family, or nation, or mankind, is morally good insofar as its personal members live together as friends, so that each regards the others' interests as harmless or helpful to his own. The interests of the several members are so happily attuned that each person in willing his own happiness wills also the happiness of his fellows. The happiness enjoyed is the happiness of each; its sociality lies in the fact that the several happinesses are conditioned by benevolence. The happy society is a society of happy men, who derive happiness from one another's happiness.

It is generally conceded that as the personal good is morally better than the good of one of its constituent interests, so the social good is morally better than the personal; and the good of mankind than that of any narrower human group. Interpreted in terms of harmonious happiness and the standard of inclusion, this means that the greater harmonies must include the lesser harmonies. There must be a harmony of harmonies. . . .

According to the theory here proposed, 'right' means conduciveness to moral good, and 'wrong' means conduciveness to moral evil: the one to harmony, and the other to conflict. So construed, right and wrong are dependent and instrumental values. That which is right or wrong may, however, like all objects of dependent interests, come to be loved or hated for its own sake, and thus acquire *intrinsic* value. . . .

An act is right when it conduces to the moral good, that is, to harmonious happiness; and it is wrong when it conduces to disharmony. The right may conduce to the good as antecedent cause to subsequent effect, as when a humane act leads to the happiness of the other party; or as part to whole, as when a man's humane act is embraced within his happiness, or when a man best serves a happy society by being happy himself. In both cases, whether the act "makes for," or "goes into the making of," its rightness consists in its *contributing to* harmonious happiness. This is the root meaning of 'right' and 'wrong.' . . .

The full meaning of substantive "rights" can be understood only in the context of polity and law, in which this idea plays a fundamental role. It is, however, a basic moral concept, and should receive its initial interpretation here.

Rights are sometimes considered axiomatic, but in a consequential theory such as is here proposed they must be explained by their conduciveness to the good life. Harmonious happiness is justified by its provision for the several interests which it harmonizes. The claim which *each* of these interests has upon the bounty of the whole is its "right." Harmonious happiness is achieved by organization, and it sets limits to the interests for which it provides. A right is therefore not the unrestricted demand of the component interest but a *right* demand — a demand the fulfillment of which is consistent with the fulfillment of other demands. Each interest is entitled to an area within which it enjoys liberty to follow its own inclination; but it is a limited area, bounded by the areas of other interests within a system which provides for all interests. . . .

There is a basic idea common to 'ought,' 'duty,' 'moral obligation,' and 'moral imperative.' To clarify the subject it is necessary not only to provide such a basic meaning, but also to account for various shades of meaning and meaninglessness.

On the level of everyday discourse what ought to be done is what is called for by some end; it is the converse of the right. The moral ought is what is called for by the end of the moral good, that is, by harmonious happiness. The act which ought to be performed may or may not be a necessary or sufficient condition of the good. The obligatory act may or may not be a unique act; in any given situation there may be many acts which satisfy the condition of conducing to the good, one of which ought to be performed.

The term 'duty' is applied primarily to the moral agent, and only secondarily to acts which are "in the line of duty." It is a stronger term than 'ought' since it is associated with an implied promise by which the agent has bound himself. When it is said that every right has its associated duty, it is meant that in claiming his benefit as a moral right he has committed himself to allotting some equivalent benefit on the other party. If he does not fulfill his part, not only as beneficiary but as benefactor, he incurs the charge of inconsistency, as well as the justifiable resentment of the other beneficiary. There are as many duties as there are rights, and there are as many rights as there are moral systems with delimited spheres and mutual engagements. There are duties as well as rights associated with every role in organized society — the parent, the neighbor, the soldier, the employer and worker, or the citizen.

When it is said that an act "ought" to be performed, it is meant that the act is called for by some good to which the act is conducive. In this basic sense the ought is sufficiently determined by the good, the act, and the circumstances. This analysis provides for "real obligation" and "real duty," as distinguished from, and antecedent to, the mere "feeling of obligation" or "sense of duty."

This distinction is plain and explicit in the case of contractual obligation. Whether a man does or does not really owe another man a sum of money is quite distinct from the question of his subjective attitude. He may blithely ignore his obligation, but he is not released on that account. His obligation is *there*, in the past undertakings and present relationships, whether he acknowledges it or not. But precisely the same holds of all moral obligation. It is implied in the total situation: a man has it, or does not have it, whether or not he experiences its compulsion. If this were not so it would be meaningless to call a man's attention to his obligations, or adduce proofs in their support, or to instill a consciousness of obligation where it does not already exist. When expecting "every man to do his duty," England was not creating the duties, but calling attention to them and demanding their performance. The latest example of this is afforded by the extension of morality to the interrelations of all mankind. When the nations of the earth are exhorted to take account of one another's interests this does not mean that they are to acquire new duties, but a new acknowledgment of old duties hitherto ignored. . . .

According to the view here adopted, ought, obligation, and duty, are not moral ultimates but are proved by the good. The influence of Kant among philosophers, and the influence on popular thought of the "stern" or "rigorous" school of morals, have conspired to create a presumption in favor of the view that the moral ought is "categorical" or "unconditional," rather than "hypothetical" or "conditional." . . .

Ignorance and unconscious assumption are not the only causes of this uncompromising aspect of the moral ought. It often expresses the pressure of the social conscience. The sentiment of the community speaks peremptorily to the individual, and will listen to no excuses. He then speaks the truth because he desires the esteem of his contemporaries. Or the ought may express what the individual person demands of himself. A person cannot "bear to think of himself" as a liar; he has acquired an ideal of himself which forbids it. This does not argue against the social beneficence of truth-speaking, but only that this appeal is reinforced by another appeal, namely, self-approval. A man has to live with himself as well as with others.

In an earlier chapter some attention was given to the theory that the words of the moral vocabulary have an "emotional," as distinguished from an "objective," meaning. While this theory was rejected in its sweeping application, it was acknowledged that although these words do have an objective meaning they may be, and frequently are, used with a merely emotive intent; that is, to express an attitude and to induce a like attitude in the person to whom they are addressed. This is peculiarly true of the word 'ought.' When a person is told that he "ought to speak the truth" this is often in order that he may feel impelled to speak the truth; and insofar as this is the case the ought is not arguable. The imperative is then categorical in the sense that it is uttered categorically, and demands unconditional obedience.

The uncompromising demands of conscience, whether personal or social, while they may be first in the order of psychological motivation, are not first in the order of justification. When an obligation is imputed to a moral agent, no reasons being given, or when he is exhorted to do as he ought, or appeal is made to his sentiment of self-esteem, or to his regard for the approving or disapproving attitudes of others, it is always appropriate for the agent to ask, "Why ought I?" and it is the answer to this question, the ultimate *why* of the obligation, which reveals the fundamental meaning of the concept.

Objection to any theory which makes moral obligation conditional or hypothetical is largely due to the supposition that it is then translated into terms of egoism. It is true that the theory may be, and commonly is, presented in this form. It is then taken to mean that the duty of any person is conditional on *his* existing interests. Thus the full meaning of 'this is your duty' would be 'this is your duty if such and such is your aim.' You would then escape the duty if such and such were not your aim.

This is not the view here proposed. Duty is derived from the good, and the good is relative to interests, but not merely to the interests of the agent whose duty is in question. The good result which determines the duty may relate to the interest of another, or to all interests concerned; even when they are not sympathetically felt, or even acknowledged, by the performer of the act. My duty is conditional on *the* purpose of harmonious happiness, not on *my* purpose. When so construed, duty possesses a certain unconditional character relatively to any given person. It cannot be escaped by his ignorance, inattention, indifference, or selfishness. This interpretation is consequential or teleological, but it is universalistic and not egoistic. . . .

[The proof of moral knowledge]

The moral good has been defined as harmonious happiness, or as that organization of interests in which each enjoys the non-interference and support of the others, whether within the personal life or the life of society. This becomes the moral "first principle." It sets the standard by which objects are deemed morally good or bad, and is the premise from which right, duty, and virtue are to be derived. It provides the most general predicate of moral judgment and the basic concept of moral knowledge. How is it to be proved? The moral philosopher is compelled not only to produce evidence, but to decide what kind of evidence may properly be demanded. . . .

Moral knowledge possesses the same general characteristics, and is subject to the same discipline, as all knowledge. It is true or false according to the evidence. It must avoid contradiction. It must invent and verify hypotheses. It must be faithful to the specific purpose of knowing, despite all temptations to the contrary. It must be self-denying, and accept the verdict pronounced by the facts or necessities of its subject matter. It must define its terms. These and all other formal criteria, or maxims, which are applicable to knowledge in general, are applicable to moral knowledge in particular, and in the same sense.

Subject to these generalities which characterize all knowledge, there are two kinds of moral knowledge, derivative and basic. When an act of homicide is judged to be wrong it is ordinarily sufficient to call it 'murder.' That is deemed sufficient, since it is assumed that murder is wrong. This judgment may be subsumed under some other accepted generalization, such as the right to life, or the goodness of security and order. But if one follows this line from premise to premise, and if one avoids circularity, one arrives eventually at an ultimate premise or first premise which cannot be similarly deduced.

The application to the standard of harmonious happiness is evident. It is judged that things are morally right and wrong, good and bad, obligatory and forbidden, judged by the standard of harmonious happiness. There are two judgments, the judgment which adopts the standard, and the judgment which applies it. The fundamental question of moral knowledge is the question of the proof of the first or basic judgment. It is a judgment about a standard, and to the effect that a specific standard, such as harmonious happiness, occupies a peculiar place among standards, and is entitled to be designated as "the moral standard." This is not a moral judgment in the sense of assigning such predicates as 'good,' 'right,' and 'ought.' Moral theory, whether it asserts that the ultimate moral standard is happiness, or that the moral right or good is indefinable, or that duty is obedience to God, or that the right is the reasonable, stands outside the whole circle of such judgments, and makes non-moral statements about them.

The first condition which such a theory must satisfy is that the proposed standard should be in fact a standard, or qualified to be a standard. If harmonious happiness can be truly affirmed to be the moral standard, it must so agree with human nature and the circumstances of human life that men can adopt it by education, persuasion, and choice; and, having adopted it, can govern their conduct in accordance with its requirements. It must be qualified to serve as a criterion by which human interests, acts, characters, and organizations can be classified and ranked. The evidence that it satisfied these requirements will be found in the fact that it is so adopted and employed.

If, however, harmonious happiness is to be proved to be *the* moral standard, to the exclusion of other standards for which a similar claim is made, it must possess further and unique qualifications. Otherwise it will be merely one standard among many, differing only historically. There would be no ground of persuasion by which the adherent of another standard could be converted to this standard. It could be judged *in terms of* this standard, but there could be no judgment *between* them. The standard of harmonious happiness would have no *theoretical* precedence. . . .

[There are] arguments to be advanced in its support — arguments which, though they may not satisfy everybody, at least have the merit of being appropriate to the thesis which is to be proved.

In the first place, the standard of harmonious happiness is *capable* of being agreed on — both theoretically and practically. It satisfies the requirement of cognitive universality and objectivity; that is, it is the same for all knowers who address themselves to the subject. Since the norm of harmonious happiness acknowledges all interests, its affirmation is free from the so-called "personal equation." As the astronomer recognizes all stellar facts regardless of the accidents of the observer's history, and thus overcomes the geocentricism which has led men to affirm that the heavens move about a stationary earth, so the theory of harmonious happiness overcomes that egocentricism which has led moral observers to subordinate all interests to their own, or to those of their neighborhood, class, or nation. It embraces human perspectives within a total system of relationships. It places itself in all points of view, and fits them together. It discovers alien and remote interests, and makes allowance for the ignorance which it cannot wholly dispel. It is impartial. It says, in effect, that since it is interest as such which generates good, and a harmonious relation of interests which constitutes moral good, to him who makes the judgment *his* interest is just one among the rest. Since the principle of harmonious happiness deals with the nature of interest in general, and with its types of relationship, it is applicable to all interests and persons.

But while the theoretical proof of the moral principle is obliged only to satisfy the knower as *knower*, the principle here proposed will tend also to appeal to each knower's will. The good of harmonious happiness, since it embraces all interests, is *to some extent* to everybody's interest, and thereby obtains a breadth of support exceeding that of any other good. Every person, including the person to whom the argument is addressed, has some stake in it.

The extent to which the harmonious happiness of all men will reward any given man will vary widely. In the absence of propinquity, interaction, and communication, and so long as this condition prevails, it may not reward him at all. When this aloofness is diminished, its reward will depend on how his particular personal happiness is constituted. All men, no doubt, have some spark of humanity, and are affected by the happiness or misery of others — but some men more than other men, and some men scarcely at all. The same is true of the extent to which men's means and ends reinforce one another. This varies with men's vocations, all the way from the recluse who is interested in solitude to the man of business whose affairs are complexly intertwined in a network of employers, workers, buyers, sellers, producers, consumers, and bankers, which now extends around the earth.

The norm of harmonious happiness, furthermore, is the only norm which is capable of appealing to all men not only severally but jointly. It is the only norm which promises benefits to each interest *together with* all other interests. It does not rob Peter to pay Paul, but limits Peter in order to pay both Peter and Paul. . . .

Making due allowance for the possibility of error in general, and for the degree of its probability in any particular field of inquiry, it may properly be argued for any theory that it agrees with widespread opinion. Opinion concerning the physical world is trustworthy in proportion as it can be attributed to observation. The relation between the sun and the earth, for example, reflects the observation of the alternation of day and night. This opinion has to be corrected to take account of the place of the observer, and the influence of the religious dogma which made the earth the scene of the drama of salvation. But whether the sun moves about the earth, or the earth about the sun, or the two move relatively to one another, the empirical fact of the periodic rising and setting remains undisturbed. And so with moral opinion. It has to be corrected to take account of non-evidential influences; not only such general influences as also affect physical opinion, but the peculiar pressures which arise from the fact that moral opinion is so closely connected with action as to be of special concern to society. These non-evidential influences being discounted, there remains an "experience of life" which has taught men the consequences of action and the ways to live prosperously together.

Again and again, in all spheres of life, and in all the ages of man, it has been observed that there are certain procedures by which the destructiveness of conflicting interests can be mitigated, and by which they can enjoy the benefits of peace and coöperation. Overlaid as it is by prejudices of many sorts, this lesson has been repeatedly learned, extended to new situations, and transmitted to future generations.

In spite of the marked differences of moral opinion which appear in different social groups and historical epochs there is nevertheless a notable amount of agreement. The disagreement is notable only because there was once an expectation of perfect agreement, and because of the shocked surprise with which the unfamiliar is always greeted. Language provides an analogy. The first stage is the assumption that all people speak the same language; the second stage is the discovery that there are strange, absurd, and unintelligible languages; the third stage is the discovery that all men use language, and that all languages have their common laws and meanings. In the matter of moral opinion the extreme relativists are those who have reached only the second of these stages.

If morality is taken as that organization of life by which conflict is escaped and by which coöperation is achieved, then the moral problem is universal; and it is, after all, not surprising that amidst all historic, ethnic, social, economic, and evolutionary aberrations there should emerge a broad knowledge of the points of the moral compass. This knowledge appears in generally accepted maxims, precepts, and virtues.

The theory here proposed reaffirms the standard virtues of antiquity — courage, temperance, wisdom, and justice. The good of harmonious happiness requires, like any end, a brave will that is not dismayed by obstacles, and effort sustained without complaint through long stretches of time. It requires a moderation of appetites lest in their excessive indulgence they should rob one another. It requires enlightened mediating judgments, that is, a true representation of ends and an intelligent choice of means. It requires a distribution of goods to each interest in accordance with a judgment which represents all interest. Christianity did not reject these virtues, but added faith, hope, and love; and these, also, are endorsed by the present theory. Harmonious happiness is an ideal and if an ideal is to be pursued there must be a steadfast belief in its attainability by means that lie beyond present knowledge, and a confidence in its actual attainment in the future. The pursuit of the harmonious happiness of all requires a sympathetic concern for one's fellow men — a sensitiveness to their pains or frustrations and an impulse to help.

Other funded moral wisdom falls into line. The most generally accepted of all maxims, the Golden Rule, is justified because the harmonious happiness of all requires that each man shall put himself in the place of other men, and recognize their interests, however cold and remote, as of the same coin with those warm and intimate interests which he calls his own. Veracity signifies the need of communication as the condition of all human intercourse. Honesty is that keeping of agreements which is essential to security and to concerted plans. Selfishness is that preoccupation with the narrower interests of self, family, class, or nation which obstructs the longer and wider vistas demanded by universal happiness.

These maxims and virtues are not invariably accepted. They are sometimes defied and they are frequently ignored. It cannot, however, be said that they are peculiar to Western Europe, or to capitalistic societies, or to Christianity, or to the modern world. They cross all such divisions, and when, as today, life is organized on a wider scale, to include all nations, all dependent and backward groups, and all hitherto unprivileged presons and classes, it is to this body of moral opinion that men appeal. Equally significant is the fact that when men differ as to the specific applications of moral opinion it is to the standard of harmonious happiness that they look for common ground. And it is by this standard that men criticize and justify their major social institutions — conscience itself, polity, law, economy — and by which they define the places in human society that are to be allotted to art, science, education, and religion.

QUESTIONS

1. What is Perry's proposal about a wise way to use "valuable" or "desirable"?
2. What is an "interest"? How is this term related to the psychologists' talk of "drives"? Mention some examples of objects of interests of yours.

3. Does Perry think that whether interests are innate or learned makes a difference to morality or the theory of values?

4. What does Perry think is the aim or job of morality as a cultural or institutional phenomenon?

5. Compare Perry's conception of the proper procedure for determining whether an individual want should be provided for in a person's schedule for living, with his conception of the proper procedure for deciding the proper place for a given interest of an individual in a society's schedule. In what sense would he say that reasonable democratic decisions presuppose benevolence?

6. How does Perry propose to define "morally good," "right," "wrong," "human rights," "moral obligation," and "duty"?

7. How close is Perry to utilitarianism?

8. What reasons does Perry give for his moral first principle?

9. Do you think Perry would defend his definitions of all these terms at least partly by the argument that they do serve to make true by definition moral propositions which there are strong reasons — emotional or otherwise — for accepting?

Alfred Cyril Ewing (1899-   )

A CRITIQUE OF NATURALISM

A. C. Ewing is a graduate of University College, Oxford; he has received the D.Phil. degree from Oxford University and the L.H.D. degree from Cambridge University. He is a fellow of the British Academy. He has taught philosophy at Cambridge University since 1931, and is now Reader in Philosophy; and he has taught at Northwestern University, the University of Michigan, and Princeton University in the United States. He has been the leading advocate of the nonnaturalist view and during the past twenty years has been the most prolific writer on ethics in the Anglo-American world. He is the author of ten books on philosophy, including *The Morality of Punishment* (1929), *Idealism, a Critical Survey* (1934), *The Individual, the State, and World Government* (1947), *The Definition of Good* (1947), *Ethics* (1953), and *Second Thoughts on Moral Philosophy* (1959).

The following selection is typical of criticisms he has raised not only against all forms of naturalism but against supernaturalism as well. The reader should note his lucid summary of several naturalist definitions different from those represented in this chapter. Ewing does not discuss a view exactly like Sharp's, and possibly his objection to the "impartial approval" theory is not an adequate refutation of Sharp's proposal. R. B. Perry's definition is construed as a proposal about the actual meanings of ethical words, and therefore the criticism of it may not be valid against the position Perry would most want to defend.

Ewing's criticisms of naturalism and supernaturalism would probably be seconded not only by most nonnaturalists but by most noncognitivists as well, although philosophers of the latter persuasion might well wish to put them somewhat differently.

The selection from A. C. Ewing, *Ethics.* Copyright 1953 by The Macmillan Company, and used with their permission. Also published by The English Universities Press, Ltd., London, and reprinted with their permission.

ETHICS

ATTEMPTS TO DEFINE ''GOOD'' AND ''OUGHT''

. . . The . . . question [what the words good and ought (or duty) mean] has also been very much debated by moral philosophers. Clearly we could not discuss ethical questions at all or make the ethical judgements we all make in ordinary life if we had not some idea of the meaning of terms such as good, bad, duty, etc., but it is very clear on the other hand that we do not prior to study understand the terms with the precision required by a philosopher, and a great deal of effort has accordingly been exercised to find definitions for them. That the question of definition is not merely a verbal one but is of great importance for our whole outlook on Ethics will soon be clear from what follows.

The problem of definition is complicated by the fact that the terms we seek to define are liable to be used in several different senses, and this is particularly the case with the chief ethical terms, *good* and *ought,* but I cannot possibly go into all the complications involved. However, a fundamental sense of "good" is the sense in which the word stands for what is intrinsically good or good as an end in itself as distinguished in particular from what is good only as a means, i.e. as an instrument for producing other things which are good in the more fundamental sense of the term. It is round this sense that the controversy has centered. Now in a very important book, *Principia Ethica* (1903), the Cambridge philosopher, G. E. Moore, maintained that the correct answer to the question is that good in this sense has no definition. This will seem at first sight a very unsatisfactory answer, but when we realize just what he means by "definition," I think we shall see that some terms must be indefinable if anything is to be defined at all. For he uses "definable" as equivalent to "analysable," and it is clear that we cannot go on analysing *ad infinitum.* If we ask what something, A, is and are then told that it is BCD, this will not help us unless we know what B, C, and D are. If we are then told that B consists of FGH, C of I, etc., the same question will arise once again. We cannot understand a definition of anything unless we understand certain terms, themselves not defined, of which the definition is composed. But how can we do this? We cannot understand them by knowing their definition, because they have none, so the only answer is — by direct experience. We have experience of certain characteristics and thus know what they are like, as we could not do without having experienced them. To take an example, we are acquainted with various colours directly by experience, and this is how we know what is meant by, e.g. "red." We cannot propound any definition of a colour that will enable a colour-blind man to know what it is like, but those who are not colour-blind certainly do know. The absence of a definition is in no way an obstacle to the possession of such knowledge. Similarly it may be contended that we know sufficiently what good is by the experience of apprehending good things. Goodness is of course a very different kind of characteristic from a colour, but they might still well resemble each other in being immediately apprehended and in being indefinable. We see some things (at least experiences) directly to be good, and to do this involves at the same time seeing what goodness is like, as to see a red rose is also to see what redness is like. This would not prevent good being definable in some other sense. If, e.g., we could discover some characteristic which always accompanied goodness and never occurred unless goodness were present, we might define good in terms of that characteristic, as the physicist defines a colour in terms of the light-waves which accompany or cause its perception. But such a definition would not tell us what the quality good is like any more than the physicist's definitions of colours in terms of wave-lengths will tell a colour-blind man what the colours are like.

The distinction between the two senses of "definition" may be brought out by this illustration. Suppose a future physiologist to discover a modification of the brain which accompanied every good experience and action and never occurred without being accompanied by a good experience or action, and suppose (which seems plausible) that the only intrinsically good things are experiences and actions or analysable in terms of experiences and actions. The brain-modifications would then be co-present with goodness whenever it occurred, but it would not follow in the least that "good" just *meant* "accompanied by this brain-modification" or that good was *identical* with the property of being accompanied by it. It would assuredly not provide a definition in Moore's sense of the term. Now it is Moore's sense of definition which will give the essential nature of what is to be defined as opposed to its accompaniments. To maintain that good is indefinable is not to maintain that we cannot know what it is like or that we cannot say anything about it but only that it is not reducible to anything else. Some properties are complex, and these can be defined in terms of the elements which make them up, but Moore insists that good is simple and therefore cannot be thus defined. . . .

It would now generally be admitted, not least by Moore himself, that the arguments in *Principia Ethica* which purported to give a knock-down proof that good is indefinable do not achieve this end. But his doctrine is plausible. The issue will be clearer when we have considered what the alternative is to something like Moore's view. What will happen if the fundamental concepts of ethics turn out to be all definable in Moore's sense? Of course one ethical concept may be defined in terms of other ethical concepts, but they cannot all be so defined without a vicious circle. If you define A in terms of B and B in terms of A, you will not have given an account which could explain adequately what either term means. Consequently, if all ethical concepts are to be definable, some must be defined in terms of non-ethical concepts, and these will be the fundamental ones. (Those which are definable in terms of other ethical concepts will be not fundamental but derivative from the latter.) But since all ethical concepts must be definable in terms of the fundamental ones, this will reduce the whole content of ethics to something non-ethical. And this is what some of the people whom Moore was criticizing and who have opposed him later have really been doing, whether intentionally or unintentionally.

Let us now consider some of the attempts to define good. For a certain type of mind, very common today, the only tolerable course seems to be to make ethics "scientific" by defining its concepts in terms of the empirical concepts of a natural science. Such definitions were described by Moore as naturalistic,[1] and this term has now been generally adopted. In opposition to it a view like Moore's is described as non-naturalist, but one must not regard a non-naturalist view as implying that no senses of "good" can be defined naturalistically. A man might well hold that, when he says "the strawberries are good," he does not mean anything more than that he likes them or possibly that most people would (naturalistic definitions in terms of concepts of psychology), and yet be a non-naturalist because he held that the sense of "good" I have mentioned, the fundamental ethical sense, is not naturalistically definable. Non-naturalism in Ethics must in any case be distinguished from supernaturalism. In denying naturalism Moore did not at all mean to imply that we cannot explain ethics without the introduction of supernatural beings such as a deity. He merely meant to point out the difference between good and the concepts belonging to psychology or any other natural science to which it was sought to reduce good.

Now for the purpose of defining good it is quite obvious at first sight that not every natural science would do. I cannot conceive that anybody in their senses would define the fundamental concepts of ethics in terms of chemistry, geology, botany or astronomy. But there is one science at least in terms of which it is much less unplausible to define ethical concepts, that

---

[1] This is not Moore's definition, but it represents approximately the way in which the term has been used by him and others.

is, psychology, the science of the human mind, and various attempts have been made to define them in psychological terms.

One proposed way of definition is in terms of approval, by which is meant the unique emotion or emotional attitude that we have when our attention is called to something ethically worthy or admirable. Thus it has been suggested that to say that something is right or good is to say that it is of such a kind as to evoke the approval of most people. But this view is surely open to objections of a very obvious kind. If it were true, it would be self-contradictory to say that a minority who felt disapproval of what most people approved could ever be in the right, and this is surely not so. We cannot possibly say that the majority and not the minority are necessarily right about any particular issue unless we have first considered the issue in question. And how are we to determine what constitutes a majority? It would obviously be arbitrary to confine oneself to people alive at the present time. Why should their ethical sentiments have this supreme authority in determining what is right or good and those of their late parents or grandparents none at all? But, if we took into account everybody who has ever lived, we should have a queer ethics indeed for, taking into account all ages, crude and savage far outnumber tolerably civilized men. And if we included also all future generations, which seems the only consistent course, this would make it impossible save by a miraculous prophecy to determine what is good or right at all. The Earth may continue to be inhabited by men for millions of years, and how are we to tell what the people who inhabit it in those far distant ages will approve or disapprove? Again the mere fact that people disapprove of what I do may make me feel uncomfortable, and if their sentiments are strong enough it may make it highly prudent to change my conduct provided I can do so without going against my conscience, but it could not of itself make it my moral duty to do so. The motive — Seek the approval of others — is not specifically moral: on the contrary it has been recognized by the greatest moral teachers as a major obstacle to true morality. My argument may be put like this — It is obvious that we ought to seek what is intrinsically good or right, just because it is good or right, as the only moral end-in-itself. But it is certainly not the case that we ought to seek what most people approve as the only moral end-in-itself just because they feel approval of it. Therefore "good" or "right" cannot mean the same as "approved by most people." And I cannot see what point there could possibly be in doing what others would approve if they knew what I have done when in fact they will not know it, unless there is some other reason besides the approval; yet, if something is my duty, I clearly ought to do it whether others know of it or not. If the approval theory were true, all obligations would be removed by secrecy. But in fact the good man will not value approval except as a sign that he has done something objectively good or right.

Others have attempted a definition in terms not of the approval of most people but of the speaker's own approval, and have maintained that

"This is good" or "This is right" means just that the person who uses these words has or tends to have a feeling or attitude of a certain kind about what he pronounces right or good. This view again is open to many objections. Firstly, if this definition were correct, it would follow that a man could never be wrong in an ethical judgement unless he had made a mistake about his own psychology. Again, two people would never mean the same thing when they pronounced an action right or wrong, since either would just mean "It is approved (disapproved) by *me*." Indeed the same person would never mean the same thing by an ethical judgement on two different occasions, since each time he would mean "I *now* feel (or tend to feel) approval of this." Nor, if A pronounced the same action right as B pronounced wrong, would they ever really be in disagreement, for what A would mean is — I (A) feel approval, which is quite compatible with B feeling disapproval at the same time of the same act. Further, when I condemned, e.g. Stalin, I should not be talking about Stalin but only about my own feelings. These consequences would follow if the theory under discussion were true, and they surely constitute a conclusive *reductio ad absurdum* of the theory. And why do I feel approval or disapproval of anything? Surely, normally, because I take it as good or bad, right or wrong independently of my feelings. Also if ethical judgements are simply about our own actual feelings or attitudes, why should we use to support them, as we constantly do, evidence, e.g. about their likely consequences for others, which is certainly not evidence about our own attitudes or feelings?

It has been suggested that ethical concepts should be defined not in terms of people's actual approval but of that of an impartial spectator. But what can "impartial" mean here? Only one who is not influenced in his approvals and disapprovals by circumstances other than those relevant to the real goodness or badness, rightness or wrongness, of what he approves or disapproves. As a definition of an ethical term this is obviously circular. It is equivalent to saying that something is good or right when it is approved by somebody who only approves what is really good or right.

Another psychological concept in terms of which good is sometimes analysed is that of desire or interest (the latter being a wider term used to cover also enjoyment and liking). Thus the important American philosopher, R. B. Perry, has defined good as "object of interest to someone." The reader may be inclined to dismiss this view at once merely on the ground that people sometimes desire evil things, but its defenders would reply that wrongdoing is to be explained not by a man desiring evil for its own sake but by his sacrificing a greater good for a lesser. A thief is not in the wrong because he attaches some value to money, but because he allows his interest in the money to override concern for the rights of others. So it is sometimes argued that all desires are for what is good *per se* and are only bad in so far as they interfere with a greater good. But I cannot see how one can deal in this fashion with the desire for revenge (to inflict pain on another). It may be argued that what the revengeful man really wants is not the pain of his enemy but the pleasure he expects to derive himself from the pain or from the thought of it, but that seems to be committing the fallacy of hedonistic psychology. However, in any case we may object that, if good = desired, better must = desired more, so that the degree of goodness is in proportion to the degree of desire, and this is obviously not so. We all desire the welfare and continued life of those near and dear to us much more than that of people equally worthy, of whom we have just read in the newspaper, and it is certainly not true that most people desire virtue quite as much as they ought to in comparison with other things, e.g. their own happiness or even material welfare. This is just what makes living the good life very difficult for us, and not only intellectually difficult. To say that "good" means "what most people desire" is also open to most of the same type of objections as I have brought against the corresponding theory in terms of approval; and to say that it means what I, the speaker, desire would be to commit oneself to a completely egoistic theory of ethics. Nor can we derive obligation from desire: they are fundamentally different concepts, as we feel when we are convinced that we ought not to do something and yet strongly desire to do it and believe that even its remoter results will be such that we desire them more than those of the action we regard it as our duty to do.

An allied view is that which defines "good" not as "what is actually desired" but as "such as to satisfy our desires in the long run." This again raises difficulties as to degrees of goodness. "The better" would have to be that which satisfies more, and this would practically commit one to hedonism, a view which we have already seen good reason to reject and which is even less satisfactory as a definition of good than as a theory of ethics. If this were the definition, it would be not only false but actually self-contradictory to say that anything could be good except in proportion to the pleasure it gave. A further objection is this. Supposing the definition is understood as referring only to the desires of the individual who pronounces something good, "good" becomes "what will satisfy me," and we are again committed to a completely egoistic theory of ethics; if on the other hand the reference is to the desires of people in general, what reason is there for me to seek to satisfy these except in so far as I desire to, unless we introduce the further concept of obligation which cannot be analysed in terms of desire? "I ought to do so-and-so" cannot be identified with "so-and-so is an efficient means towards the general satisfaction of people's desires," for it is certainly not a self-contradictory position for a man to be convinced that he ought to do something and yet doubt whether it is a more efficient means to this than some alternative action which he thinks he ought not to do. E.g. it is not self-contradictory to hold both that I should satisfy more people's desires more fully if I did not pay my debts but did something else with the money and yet hold that I ought to pay my debts. Many desires of others we indeed ought not to try to satisfy, and that most human desires could not be in this position certainly cannot be deduced from a mere definition of good or ought.

In view of the fact that people desire many things which they would not desire if they knew what the attainment of them would involve, it has been suggested that "good" means, not what is actually desired, but what all men would desire if they knew its true nature.[2] However, it is by no means a certainty that all men would desire what is good in proportion to its goodness even if they knew the true nature of the good things in question, but on the contrary at best a highly conjectural proposition. It is by no means certain that Hitler would have desired happiness for Jews as much as for equally worthy Aryans even if he had known how much they suffered through being confined in concentration camps and what was their exact psychological nature. Yet that he would must follow verbally if the definition be correct and we grant that their happiness is of equal value. We may go further and say that none of us would even with the fullest knowledge always desire what was good in proportion to its goodness, since we all inevitably desire the welfare of those we know and love more than that of those who are little more than names to us, though this need not necessarily lead to our sacrificing the latter to the former since we can control our desires for the sake of what is right. This statement about desire surely applies even to the greatest saints. For a man to desire the good of all other men fully as much as an equivalent amount of good for himself or those closest to him it would be necessary, not only that he should know all the circumstances including the state of their feelings, but that his emotional nature should be completely different from ours so that human love as we know it either did not exist in him at all or was extended equally to everybody. And if we imagine our nature thus completely and superhumanly or inhumanly altered, we can no longer have any foundation for saying what we should desire. In any case it is surely obvious that to call anything good is not to say what would happen if some quite impossible psychological revolution were effected in us.

I have said that of naturalistic definitions of the fundamental ethical concepts psychological are the least unplausible, but definitions in terms of biology and sociology have also been attempted, though these are clearly at the best definitions of instrumental rather than of intrinsic good. Thus biologists or people much influenced by biology have sometimes defined the good or the right as what tends to further human survival. But in ethics we do not aim only at mere life, and though some virtues and vices are likely appreciably to affect the duration of life or the number of descendants produced this is not the case with most. It would follow from the definition that it did not matter how miserable one made anybody else, provided only the misery did not actually shorten his life or diminish the number of his descendants or the chance of his having descendants. It would be better, both hedonistically and morally, not to live at all than to live in the way in

2 v. Field, *Moral Theory*, Chap. XI.

which many people have lived. Life in itself is valueless, whether it is good or evil depends on the specific nature of the life in question.

Another biological definition proffered of good or right is "in conformity with evolutionary development." This at once raises difficulties about defining evolution or development. For it may be retorted that everything that happens, good or bad, is in accord with evolutionary development, otherwise it could not happen at all. If, on the other hand, we define evolutionary development as change for the better, as one is tempted to do, the definition of good proposed will constitute a vicious circle. "Good" cannot be defined as "what is in conformity with good development." What is commonly meant seems to be that the good is what is in accordance with the main actual trends in the past and will conduce to similar developments in the future. This avoids the charge that the definition makes everything good, for we can recognize a distinction between the main trends and exceptions which are not characteristic of or actually hinder the predominant line of change. But to say that such and such is in accord with the main trend of development and to say that it is good is surely to say two quite different things. That things should change on the whole in such and such a way is quite compatible with the change being evil and not good. One of the main trends in human development has been that people have shown more and more efficiency in destroying each other in war. Does it follow that it would be good for this process to continue? The same type of consideration applies to other interpretations of the evolutionary definition of good. "Evolved" might mean just "later in time," in which case the definition would involve the unfounded and unreasonable dogma that all change is progress. Or it might mean "more complex," but we surely do not need any argument to determine that goodness is not the same as complexity.

Similar objections apply to the sociological definitions of "good" or "right" as "what furthers the development of society" or "what makes for social stability." What furthered the development of Nazi society and made for its stability was not good but bad. We can only defend the former definition if we already include good in the notion of development thus committing a vicious circle, and the latter if we are prepared to maintain that there is never any value in change and the right course is always simply to maintain the existing form of society.

To each of these naturalist theories there are, as we have seen, very serious specific objections, but there are also general arguments which can be used to rule out on principle any naturalist definition whatever. I mention three. (1) Any naturalist definition would have the effect of reducing ethics to a branch of an empirical science, whether psychology or some other, and this is indeed a great attraction at the present day when "scientific" and "rational" are commonly regarded as synonyms. Yet there is a logical consequence which few would really be prepared to swallow. If ethics is an empirical science, its method must be that of empirical generalization, i.e. as the logician calls it, induction. In order to establish ethical conclusions all that is needed will be to provide, in the case of theories which define ethical concepts in terms of the psychology of the speaker, a few introspections, and in the case of other naturalist theories a set of statistics about the actual feelings or desires of human beings, and these will *ipso facto* settle what is good or right beyond the possibility of contradiction. But this is not at all the method we follow in order to arrive at ethical conclusions, on the contrary it strikes us as in itself completely irrelevant to these. The mere fact that people actually feel in a certain way does not by itself convince us of the truth of anything in ethics, though it may well be a premiss which sometimes together with others leads to a true and reasonable ethical conclusion. No set of statistics by itself, it is surely obvious, can prove an ethical conclusion. We may go even further in our criticism: not only would it follow from naturalism that the truth of ethical propositions was always completely determinable by observations of oneself or sets of statistics about others, it would follow, at least from the forms of naturalism which do not equate ethical propositions with propositions merely about the psychology of the speaker, that all ethical propositions were themselves merely vague propositions about statistics. For the only difference between the proposition "Most people do . . ." and the proposition "91.7% do" is that the former is a very vague and the latter a more precise proposition about statistics. Yet it is surely not true that ethical propositions are propositions about statistics at all, whether precise or vague.

(2) When a definition BC is offered of A, it is plainly a fatal refutation of the definition if we can point to something of which it would be true to say that it is A but false to say that it is BC or vice versa, and I have used objections of this kind against the naturalist theories. But it is an important logical point that in order to refute a definition it is not necessary to show this much. If we can show it to be even possible that it might be true of something that it was A but false that it was BC or vice versa, it is enough to overthrow the definition. For, if BC really were what A meant, it would be self-contradictory to suggest even that A could possibly apply to something and BC not or vice versa, as it would be self-contradictory to suggest that a man could be a father (except in a metaphorical sense) without being a male parent. Thus, even if it were a fact that we always desire what is good and what is good alone, the corresponding definition of good in terms of desire could still be refuted by pointing out that, even if this be in fact true, there would be no contradiction in supposing it false. Even if it be a fact, it must still be admitted that it is just an empirical fact about human nature which might for anything we can see have been quite different, and not something which follows verbally from a knowledge of the way in which we use the term "good." An argument of this type is advanced against all naturalist definitions of "good." With any one we can on inspection see that the property given in the definition might without any contradiction be supposed to belong to some-

thing that was not good, and that therefore it cannot be an adequate definition. It is probably this point which Moore had mainly in mind in his attack on naturalism in *Principia Ethica*, and fundamentally it seems to me justified, though his way of putting his case is, as he would be the first to admit, open to criticism. Whatever empirical property is put forward as constituting a definition of "good" (or, for that matter, "obligatory" or "right") it seems clear that the question whether everything that is good (or obligatory or right) has that property or vice versa is not a question of definition at all, and therefore the alleged definition must each time be dismissed as untenable.

(3) A general defect in all naturalist theories is that they do not leave any room for the concept of ought as distinct from what in fact is the case. They all analyse ethical propositions in a way which has reference solely to what is, but what is is very different from what ought to be. And the sharp transition from the is to the ought they in no wise explain. This objection, used by the philosopher Hume against a very different type of theory, namely, that which deduced ethics from metaphysics, may equally be turned against the naturalism to which Hume himself was inclined. At least a very important feature appertaining to the characteristic of goodness is that it puts people under obligations. If something is good and there is no stronger counterobligation, we *ought* to promote or at least not destroy it. But not one of the characteristics I have mentioned as equated by various naturalists with goodness seems of itself to carry with it this power to put people under an obligation. If so, none of them can be equated with the characteristic of goodness, which does carry with it this power. No doubt we ought to satisfy the desires of other people, but only in so far as these desires are good; no doubt we ought to do what others approve of our doing, but only in so far as they approve what is right. On no view will the better object always coincide with what I desire more at the time, and even if it did, this would only make it prudent to pursue it rather than the worse, not obligatory; so the question arises why I ought to pursue it, unless it is seen to be self-evident that I ought to pursue the better rather than the worse, as is claimed by the non-naturalist. But if "good" means merely what most people desire or approve, it is by no means self-evident that we ought to pursue it, unless we make it verbally so by defining "I ought to do B" as meaning something like "B is of all actions open to me at the time the best fitted to satisfy men's desires or win their approval," and in that case we are open to the objection that it is impossible to see how we can reduce the notion of ought to what is merely a factual causal connection. A proposition affirming ethical obligation surely cannot merely state that such and such a case produces in fact such and such effects. That is a totally different proposition. These objections apply to all naturalistic theories of ethics.

It indeed seems to me that the non-naturalist is in a stronger position against his opponent if he makes his defence centre on the notion of an indefinable "ought" than if he like Moore makes it centre on an indefinable "good." Grave doubts have been expressed as to whether we really are aware of this alleged indefinable quality of goodness, and I myself share these doubts, but it is much more difficult to doubt that we are aware of obligation and that obligation is not reducible to any empirical quality or relation. Once we have admitted an indefinable ought, we may define "good" in its specifically ethical senses by means of this notion. We can then say that to assert something to be intrinsically good is to say that it is "such that we ought to have a favourable attitude towards it, i.e. choose, desire, pursue, further, welcome or admire it, for its own sake," and define a good man (morally) as "one who does what he ought." It is therefore wrong to suppose that the doctrine that good is indefinable is the only alternative to naturalism. We may maintain instead the indefinability of ought. There are indeed three alternatives. (a) We may make good indefinable and define ought in terms of it, i.e. we may say that "I ought to do A" means something such as "of the acts in my power at the time A would produce the greatest good." (b) We may hold that good and ought are both indefinable. (c) We may regard ought as indefinable and define good in terms of ought.[3] Moore took the first view in *Principia Ethica*, but the second in his later work *Ethics*, and the second view is now I think the most common among non-naturalists. Moore's arguments do not seem to be even directed to showing that good is the only indefinable ethical concept, or that good cannot be given a non-naturalist definition in terms of another concept of ethics.

It is a very sound rule, especially in philosophy, that we should, when confronted with a view which seems to us thoroughly unplausible and unreasonable, ask why it seemed plausible to anybody, and I had better ask this now about naturalism in Ethics. It seems to me that the following reasons largely explain why philosophers have often been tempted to adopt it. (1) It makes ethics into an empirical science, and empirical science has been so immensely successful in providing us with knowledge about the nature of things that it is plausible to suppose that it could be used to discover everything that may be discovered by us at all. But it may be objected that it does not follow that the methods which have been so successful in determining questions of empirical fact will be suitable for answering the, at least *prima facie*, very different questions of ethics.

(2) A non-naturalist view involves the introduction of a quality (good) or a relation (obligation) which is radically different from any other quality or relation and certainly from any which occur in our ordinary empirical knowledge. It was therefore tempting to try to explain away these concepts by analysing them in terms of qualities or relations of a more ordinary type. But, though it is tempting to reduce all knowledge to one type, we have no right to assume dogmatically that it really is of one type. We

---

[3] It is not of much significance whether "right" or "ought" is used for this purpose.

cannot tell in advance of trying whether the attempt so to reduce it will succeed or fail, and we have no right for the sake of a simplicity, which we do not know to be possible, to explain away real differences. We can always make things simpler by ignoring inconvenient facts, but it is the reverse of scientific to ignore facts. We must be empirically minded, but our ethical experience is just as much experience as is our perception of physical things.

(3) There is a tendency to make the assumption that some definition is needed of our ethical concepts. But, as I have shown, it is clear that everything cannot be defined in the sense of being reduced to something else, and if any concepts are indefinable at all it is only reasonable to suppose that the fundamental concepts of ethics will be so, since otherwise ethics will be reduced without residuum to what is not ethical. We must remember that to say they are indefinable is merely to say that they cannot be reduced to anything else, not that nothing more can be said about them.

(4) It is argued that, if there really were an indefinable quality of goodness perceivable by us, it is incredible that there should be so much dispute about it. Almost everybody would, it might be expected, know what it was, as everybody (except the colour-blind) knows what yellow is. But there are equal difficulties about seeing how, if the term is really definable, there can be such wide divergencies as to the definition or as to whether there is a definition. Of the naturalists themselves two are rarely agreed on the same definition. Yet a correct definition should give us what we mean, and how is it that there should be such widely different views not only as to what is true but as to what we mean by some of the most common terms? This is a difficulty, not as yet completely solved, that arises with all philosophical definition of common terms, and not only in ethics, but at any rate it seems to hit both sides equally. I must add that it seems to me much easier to be sure that we have a clear idea of obligation distinct from desire, fear, emotion or any other psychological terms than that we have a clear idea of an indefinable quality of goodness. . . .

The naturalist has, however, a further line of defence on which he can fall back. He may admit that a naturalistic analysis of what we mean by our ethical terms has been shown to be impossible, but take this as proving only that our ethical judgements, because not susceptible of such an analysis, are all mistaken, and that the task of the moral philosopher is to substitute for these mistaken judgements new ones couched exclusively in naturalistic terms like desire, which, because they have eliminated any trace of an "ought" or "good" that cannot be reduced to the concept of a natural science, in other words, everything specifically ethical, may claim to be true. This sceptical view about ethics is hard to refute conclusively, but harder still to believe. I cannot possibly help believing that I am not mistaken in holding that it would be ethically wrong of me to hire a gang of toughs in order to beat up the first critic who expressed disagreement with my views, and I suspect that, if I did this, he also, however sceptical in theory in his Ethics, would find it very hard to believe that my action was not ethically wrong. Hence naturalism would be much more plausible and attractive if it could be maintained that it gave an account of what we actually mean in our ethical judgements. In that case we could avoid being sceptics in ethics and yet be naturalists, for we could then still say that the judgements of common-sense ethics are often true. But if, as I have tried to show, any naturalistic account of what we assert in our ethical judgements is mistaken, we must choose between being ethical sceptics and giving up naturalism. . . .

Before going on . . . , I have a word to say about a quite different way of defining ethical concepts, that is, in terms of metaphysics. A metaphysical definition is a definition by reference to the ultimate nature of the real as distinguished from the less ultimate aspect in which reality is conceived as appearing for natural science. Of metaphysical definitions we need only trouble about one here, which is by far the clearest and the best known. I refer to the attempt to define ethical concepts in terms of religion by maintaining that to say something is good or right is to say that it is commanded by God. At first sight it may well seem that such a theory is refuted at once by the mere fact that agnostics and atheists can make rational judgements in ethics, but it will be replied that what even the atheist really has in mind when he thinks of obligation is some confused idea of a command, and that a command implies a commander and a perfect moral law a perfectly good commander on whose mind the whole moral law depends, so that the atheist is inconsistent in affirming the validity of the moral law and yet denying the existence of God. It may be doubted whether this argument, if valid, would make the theological statement an analysis of what the man meant and not rather of the logical consequences of what he meant, but there are other objections to such a definition.

(a) If "right" and "good" are themselves defined in terms of the commands of God, God cannot command anything because it is right or good, since this would only mean that He commanded it because He commanded it, and therefore there is no reason whatever for His commands, which become purely arbitrary. It would follow that God might just as rationally will that our whole duty should consist in cheating, torturing and killing people to the best of our ability, and that in that case it would be our duty to act in this fashion.

(b) And why are we to obey God's commands? Because we ought to do so? Since "we ought to do A" is held to mean "God commands us to do A," this can only mean that we are commanded by God to obey God's commands, which supplies no further reason. Because we love God? But this involves the assumptions that we ought to obey God if we love Him, and that we ought to love Him. So it again presupposes ethical propositions which cannot without a vicious circle be validated by once more referring to God's commands. Because God is good? This could only mean that God carries out His own commands. Because God will punish us if we do not obey Him? This might be a very good reason from the point of view of self-interest, but self-interest cannot, as we have seen, be an adequate basis for ethics. Without a prior conception of God being good or His commands being right God would have no more claim on our obedience than Hitler except that He would have more power to make things uncomfortable for us if we disobeyed Him than Hitler ever had, and that is not an ethical reason. A moral obligation cannot be created by mere power and threat of punishment. No doubt if we first grant the fundamental concepts of ethics, the existence of God may put us under certain obligations which we otherwise would not have had, e.g. that of thinking of God, as the existence of a man's parents puts him under certain obligations under which he would not stand if they were dead, but we cannot possibly derive all obligations in this fashion from the concept of God. No doubt, if God is perfectly good, we ought to obey His will, but how can we know what His will for us is in a particular case without first knowing what we ought to do?

What I have said of course constitutes no objection to the belief in God or even to the view that we can have a valid argument from ethics to the existence of God, but these views can be held without holding that our ethical terms have to be defined in terms of God. It has been held that the existence of anything implies the existence of God, but it would not therefore be concluded that the meaning of all our words includes a reference to God. Nor is what I have said meant to imply that religion can have no important bearing on ethics, but I think its influence should lie more in helping people to bring themselves to do what would be their duty in any case and in influencing the general spirit in which it is done than in prescribing what our duty is. While it is quite contrary to fact to suggest that an agnostic or atheist cannot be a good man, the influence in the former respects of religious belief, whether true or false, cannot be denied to have been exceedingly strong.

Metaphysical definitions, like naturalistic, err in trying to reduce the "ought" to the "is." Like them they would destroy what Kant calls the autonomy of ethics by refusing to recognize the uniqueness of its fundamental concepts and trying to reduce it to a mere branch of another study, in this case not a natural science but metaphysics or theology. The theological definition is more ethical than naturalism only in so far as it covertly reintroduces the notion of obligation or goodness thus involving a vicious circle. Indeed it is only plausible because God is already conceived as good. Apart from this it would make duty consist just in obeying the stronger, for if you once exclude the specifically ethical element from the conception of the Deity, God has no claim on us except that of mere power. But it cannot be *morally* obligatory to obey some being just because he is powerful.

QUESTIONS

1. In what sense have some philosophers (e.g., Moore and Ewing) claimed that ethical words cannot be defined? Is there some sense in which they concede ethical terms can be defined?
2. Does Ewing think that "good" is indefinable in all its various senses? Which sense of "good" does he think is not definable?
3. Make a list of the various definitions Ewing discusses, and pick out the one which strikes you as most plausible.
4. Is Ewing's criticism of Perry's view a conclusive refutation of it?
5. State carefully and assess the three objections which Ewing says appear to apply to naturalism in all its forms.
6. Does it seem to you Ewing is right in proposing that "good" can be defined in terms of "ought"?
7. What reasons does he offer for doubting whether ethical terms like "ought" can be defined theologically, that is, in terms of the concept "commanded by God"?

Plato (427-347 B.C.)

A CRITIQUE OF THEOLOGICAL ETHICS

Plato, a pupil of Socrates, spent most of his life teaching philosophy in Athens, where he founded a school called the Academy. The dialogues he composed, all of which (as far as is known) have been preserved for us, have had unsurpassed influence on human thought. Plato either invented or illuminated practically every philosophical problem.

The dialogue presented here — the *Euthyphro* — gives little clue to Plato's positive views about the questions of ethics, although it illustrates his method of reasoning in a delightful way. The student interested in Plato's constructive proposals should turn to the *Republic, Protagoras, Apology, Crito, Gorgias, Meno, Philebus,* and the *Laws.* On most points his normative ethics is similar to that of Aristotle. Hedonism, Plato thought, is too simple. The good life is one in which each part of the self performs its proper function, just as in a good society each group performs the tasks for which it is fitted; the good life is one in which reason, physical drives, and psychological wants are in proper balance — a life which shows wisdom, temperance or self-control, courage, and justice. Plato's metaethical view is that ethical truth may be attained partly by examining various theories and eliminating those with contradictions and obscurities, and partly by direct insight into the necessary truth of some ethical propositions.

At first sight the *Euthyphro* seems concerned with ethics only in a secondary way. It is asking what is the nature of religion, or of piety, or of the holy. But on second thought we can see that it is raising a larger issue, whether actions are made right or obligatory — although the emphasis is on religious obligations — simply by the commandment, approval, or desire of the gods. Plato finds it difficult to believe they are so.

Plato, *Euthyphro*, in Plato, *Plato on the Trial and Death of Socrates*, trans. by Lane Cooper, published by Cornell University Press, Ithaca, N. Y., 1941, and reprinted by their permission.

EUTHYPHRO

EUTHYPHRO   This, Socrates, is something new? What has taken you from your haunts in the Lyceum, and makes you spend your time at the Royal porch? You surely cannot have a case at law, as I have, before the Archon-King.

SOCRATES   My business, Euthyphro, is not what is known at Athens as a case at law; it is a criminal prosecution.

EUTHYPHRO   How is that? You mean that somebody is prosecuting you? I never would believe that you were prosecuting anybody else.

SOCRATES   No indeed.

EUTHYPHRO   Then somebody is prosecuting you?

SOCRATES   Most certainly.

EUTHYPHRO   Who is it?

SOCRATES   I am not too clear about the man myself, Euthyphro. He appears to me to be a young man, and unknown. I think, however, that they call him Meletus; and his deme is Pitthos, if you happen to know any one named Meletus of that deme, a hook-nosed man with long straight hair, and not much beard.

EUTHYPHRO   I don't recall him, Socrates. But tell me, of what does he accuse you?

SOCRATES   His accusation? It is no mean charge. For a man of his age it is no small thing to have settled a question of so much importance. He says, in fact, that he knows the method by which young people are corrupted, and knows who the persons are that do it. He is, quite possibly, a wise man, and, observing that my ignorance has led me to corrupt his generation, comes like a child to his mother to accuse me to the City. And to me he appears to be the only one who begins his political activity aright; for the right way to begin is to pay attention to the young, and make them just as good as possible; precisely as the able farmer will give his attention to the young plants first, and afterwards care for the rest. And so Meletus no doubt begins by clearing us away, the ones who ruin, as he says, the tender shoots of the young; that done, he obviously will care for the older generation, and will thus become the cause, in the highest and widest measure, of benefit to the State. With such a notable beginning, his chances of success look good.

EUTHYPHRO I hope so, Socrates; but I'm very much afraid it will go the other way. When he starts to injure you, it simply looks to me like beginning at the hearth to hurt the State. But tell me what he says you do to corrupt the young.

SOCRATES It sounds very queer, my friend, when first you hear it. He says I am a maker of gods; he charges me with making new gods, and not believing in the old ones. These are his grounds for prosecuting me, he says.

EUTHYPHRO I see it, Socrates. It is because you say that ever and anon you have the spiritual sign! So he charges you in this indictment with introducing novelties in religion, and that is the reason why he comes to court with this slanderous complaint, well knowing how easily such matters can be misrepresented to the crowd. For my own part, when I speak in the assembly about matters of religion, and tell them in advance what will occur, they laugh at me as if I were a madman; and yet I never have made a prediction that did not come true. But the truth is, they are jealous of all such people as ourselves. No, we must not worry over them, but go to meet them.

SOCRATES Dear Euthyphro, if we were only laughed at, it would be no serious matter. The Athenians, as it seems to me, are not very much disturbed if they think that So-and-so is clever, so long as he does not impart his knowledge to anybody else. But the moment they suspect that he is giving his ability to others, they get angry, whether out of jealousy, as you say, or, it may be, for some other reason.

EUTHYPHRO With regard to that, I am not very eager to test their attitude to me.

SOCRATES Quite possibly you strike them as a man who is chary of himself, and is unwilling to impart his wisdom; as for me, I fear I am so kindly they will think that I pour out all I have to every one; and not merely without pay — nay, rather, glad to offer something if it would induce some one to hear me. Well then, as I said just now, if they were going to laugh at me, as you say they do at you, it wouldn't be at all unpleasant to spend the time laughing and joking in court. But if they take the matter seriously, then there is no knowing how it will turn out. Only you prophets can tell!

EUTHYPHRO Well, Socrates, perhaps no harm will come of it at all, but you will carry your case as you desire, and I think that I shall carry mine.

SOCRATES   Your case, Euthyphro? What is it? Are you prosecuting, or defending?

EUTHYPHRO   Prosecuting.

SOCRATES   Whom?

EUTHYPHRO   One whom I am thought a maniac to be attacking.

SOCRATES   How so? Is it some one who has wings to fly away with?

EUTHYPHRO   He is far from being able to do that; he happens to be old, a very old man.

SOCRATES   Who is it, then?

EUTHYPHRO   It is my father.

SOCRATES   Your father, my good friend?

EUTHYPHRO   Just so.

SOCRATES   What is the complaint? Of what do you accuse him?

EUTHYPHRO   Of murder, Socrates.

SOCRATES   Good heavens, Euthyphro! Surely the crowd is ignorant of the way things ought to go. I fancy it is not correct for any ordinary person to do that [to prosecute his father on this charge], but only for a man already far advanced in point of wisdom.

EUTHYPHRO   Yes, Socrates, by Heaven! far advanced!

SOCRATES   And the man your father killed, was he a relative of yours? Of course he was? You never would prosecute your father, would you, for the death of anybody who was not related to you?

EUTHYPHRO   You amuse me, Socrates. You think it makes a difference whether the victim was a member of the family, or not related, when the only thing to watch is whether it was right or not for the man who did the deed to kill him. If he was justified, then let him go; if not, you have to prosecute him, no matter if the man who killed him shares your hearth, and sits at table with you. The pollution is the same if, knowingly, you associate with such a man, and do not cleanse yourself, and him as well, by bringing him to justice. The victim in this case was a laborer of mine, and when we were cultivating land in Naxos, we employed him on our farm. One day he had been drinking, and became enraged at one of our domestics, and cut his throat; whereupon my father bound him hand and foot, and threw him into a ditch. Then he sent a man to Athens to find out from the seer what ought to be done; meanwhile paying no attention to the man who had been bound, neglecting him because he was a murderer and it would be no great matter even if he died. And that was just what happened. Hunger, cold, and the shackles, finished him before the messenger got back from visiting the seer. That is why my father and my other kin are bitter at me when I prosecute my father as a murderer. They say he did not kill the man, and had he actually done it, the victim was himself a murderer, and for such a man one need have no consideration. They say that for a son to prosecute his father as a murderer is unholy.

How ill they know divinity in its relation, Socrates, to what is holy or unholy!

SOCRATES   But you, by Heaven! Euthyphro, you think that you have such an accurate knowledge of things divine, and what is holy and unholy, that, in circumstances such as you describe, you can accuse your father? You are not afraid that you yourself are doing an unholy deed?

EUTHYPHRO   Why, Socrates, if I did not have an accurate knowledge of all that, I should be good for nothing, and Euthyphro would be no different from the general run of men.

SOCRATES   Well then, admirable Euthyphro, the best thing I can do is to become your pupil, and challenge Meletus before the trial comes on. Let me tell him that in the past I have considered it of great importance to know about things divine; and that now, when he asserts that I erroneously put forward my own notions and inventions on this head, I have become your pupil. I could say: 'Come, Meletus, if you agree that Euthyphro has wisdom in such matters, you must admit as well that I hold the true belief, and must not prosecute. If you do not, you must lodge your complaint, not against me, but against my aforesaid master; accuse him of corrupting the elder generation, me and his own father; me by his instruction, his father by correcting and chastising him.' And if he would not yield, would neither quit the suit nor yet indict you rather than myself, then I would say the same in court as when I challenged him!

EUTHYPHRO   Yes, Socrates, by Heaven! if he undertook to bring me into court, I guess I would find out his rotten spot, and our talk there would concern him sooner by a long shot than ever it would me!

SOCRATES   Yes, my dear friend, that I know, and so I wish to be your pupil. This Meletus, I perceive, along presumably with everybody else, appears to overlook you, but sees into me so easily and keenly that he has attacked me for impiety. So, in the name of Heaven, tell me now about the matter you just felt sure you knew quite thoroughly. State what you take piety and impiety to be with reference to murder and all other cases. Is not the holy always one and the same thing in every action, and, again, is not the unholy always opposite to the holy, and like itself? And as unholiness does it not always have its one essential form, which will be found in everything that is unholy?

EUTHYPHRO   Yes, surely, Socrates.

SOCRATES   Then tell me. How do you define the holy and the unholy?

EUTHYPHRO   Well then, I say that the holy is what I am now doing, prosecuting the wrongdoer who commits a murder or a sacrilegious robbery, or sins in any other point like that, whether it be your father, or your mother, or whoever it may be. And not to prosecute would be unholy. And, Socrates, observe what a decisive proof I will give you that such is the law. It is one I have already given to others; I tell them that the right procedure must be not to tolerate the impious man, no matter who. Do not mankind believe that Zeus is the most excellent and just among the gods? And these same men admit that Zeus shackled his own father [Cronus] for swallowing his [other] sons unjustly; and that Cronus in turn had gelded his father [Uranus] for like reasons. But now they are enraged at me when I proceed against my father for wrongdoing; and so they contradict themselves in what they say about the gods and what they say of me.

SOCRATES   There, Euthyphro, you have the reason why the charge is brought against me. It is because, whenever people tell such stories about the gods, I am prone to take it ill; and, so it seems, that is why they will maintain that I am sinful. Well, now, if you who are so well versed in matters of the sort entertain the same beliefs, then necessarily, it would seem, I must give in; for what could we urge who admit that, for our own part, we are quite ignorant about these matters? But, in the name of friendship, tell me! Do you actually believe that these things happened so?

EUTHYPHRO   Yes, Socrates, and things even more amazing, of which the multitude do not know.

SOCRATES   And you actually believe that war occurred among the gods, and there were dreadful hatreds, battles, and all sorts of fearful things like that? Such things as the poets tell of, and good artists represent in sacred places; yes, and at the great Panathenaic festival the robe that is carried up to the Acropolis is all inwrought with such embellishments? What is our position, Euthyphro? Do we say that these things are true?

EUTHYPHRO   Not these things only, Socrates, but, as I just now said, I will, if you wish, relate to you many other stories about the gods, which I am certain will astonish you when you hear them.

SOCRATES   I shouldn't wonder. You shall tell me all about them when we have the leisure at some other time. At present try to tell me more clearly what I asked you a little while ago; for, my friend, you were not explicit enough before when I put the question, What is holiness? You merely said that what you are now doing is a holy deed — namely, prosecuting your father on a charge of murder.

EUTHYPHRO   And, Socrates, I told the truth.

SOCRATES   Possibly. But, Euthyphro, there are many other things that you will say are holy.

EUTHYPHRO   Because they are.

SOCRATES   Well, bear in mind that what I asked of you was not to tell me one or two out of all the numerous actions that are holy; I wanted you to tell me what is the essential form of holiness which makes all holy actions holy. I believe you held that there is one ideal form by which unholy things are all unholy, and by which all holy things are holy. Do you remember that?

EUTHYPHRO   I do.

SOCRATES   Well then, show me what, precisely, this ideal is, so that, with my eye on it, and using it as a standard, I can say that any action done by you or anybody else is holy if it resembles this ideal, or, if it does not, can deny that it is holy.

EUTHYPHRO   Well, Socrates, if that is what you want, I certainly can tell you.

SOCRATES   It is precisely what I want.

EUTHYPHRO   Well then, what is pleasing to the gods is holy, and what is not pleasing to them is unholy.

SOCRATES   Perfect, Euthyphro! Now you give me just the answer that I asked for. Meanwhile, whether it is right I do not know; but obviously you will go on to prove your statement true.

EUTHYPHRO   Indeed I will.

SOCRATES   Come now, let us scrutinize what we are saying. What is pleasing to the gods, and the man that pleases them, are holy; what is hateful to the gods, and the man they hate, unholy. But the holy and unholy are not the same; the holy is directly opposite to the unholy. Isn't it so?

EUTHYPHRO   It is.

SOCRATES   And the matter clearly was well stated.

EUTHYPHRO   I accept it, Socrates; that was stated.

SOCRATES   Was it not also stated, Euthyphro, that the gods revolt and differ with each other, and that hatreds come between them?

EUTHYPHRO   That was stated.

SOCRATES   Hatred and wrath, my friend — what kind of disagreement will produce them? Look at the matter thus. If you and I were to differ about numbers, on the question which of two was the greater, would a disagreement about that make us angry at each other, and make enemies of us? Should we not settle things by calculation, and so come to an agreement quickly on any point like that?

EUTHYPHRO   Yes, certainly.

SOCRATES   And similarly if we differed on a question of greater length or less, we would take a measurement, and quickly put an end to the dispute?

EUTHYPHRO   Just that.

SOCRATES   And so, I fancy, we should have recourse to scales, and settle any question about a heavier or lighter weight?

EUTHYPHRO   Of course.

SOCRATES   What sort of thing, then, is it about which we differ, till, unable to arrive at a decision, we might get angry and be enemies to one another? Perhaps you have no answer ready; but listen to me. See if it is not the following: right and wrong, the noble and the base, and good and bad. Are not these the things about which we differ, till, unable to arrive at a decision, we grow hostile (when we do grow hostile) to each other, you and I and everybody else?

EUTHYPHRO   Yes, Socrates, that is where we differ; on these subjects.

SOCRATES   What about the gods, then, Euthyphro? If, indeed, they have dissensions, must it not be on these subjects?

EUTHYPHRO   Quite necessarily.

SOCRATES   Accordingly, my noble Euthyphro, by your account some gods take one thing to be right, and others take another, and similarly with the honorable and the base, and good and bad. They would hardly be at variance with each other, if they did not differ on these questions. Would they?

EUTHYPHRO   You are right.

SOCRATES   And what each one of them thinks noble, good, and just, is what he loves, and the opposite is what he hates?

EUTHYPHRO   Yes, certainly.

SOCRATES   But it is the same things, so you say, that some of them think right, and others wrong; and through disputing about these they are at variance, and make war on one another. Is n't it so?

EUTHYPHRO   It is.

SOCRATES   Accordingly, so it would seem, the same things will be hated by the gods and loved by them; the same things would alike displease and please them.

EUTHYPHRO   It would seem so.

SOCRATES   And so, according to this argument, the same things, Euthyphro, will be holy and unholy.

EUTHYPHRO   That may be.

SOCRATES   In that case, admirable friend, you have not answered what I asked you. I did not ask you to tell me what at once is holy and unholy; but it seems that what is pleasing to the gods is also hateful to them. Thus, Euthyphro, it would not be strange at all if what you now are doing in punishing your father were pleasing to Zeus, but hateful to Cronus and Uranus, and welcome to Hephaestus, but odious to Hera, and if any other of the gods disagree about the matter, satisfactory to some of them, and odious to others.

EUTHYPHRO   But, Socrates, my notion is that, on this point, there is no difference of opinion among the gods; not one of them but thinks that if a person kills another wrongfully, he ought to pay for it.

SOCRATES   And what of men? Have you never heard a man contending that some one who has killed a person wrongfully, or done some other unjust deed, ought not to pay the penalty?

EUTHYPHRO   Why! there is never any end to their disputes about these matters; it goes on everywhere, above all in the courts. People do all kinds of wrong, and then there is nothing they will not do or say in order to escape the penalty.

SOCRATES   Do they admit wrongdoing, Euthyphro, and, while admitting it, deny that they ought to pay the penalty?

EUTHYPHRO   No, not that, by any means.

SOCRATES   Then they will not do and say quite everything. Unless I am mistaken, they dare not say or argue that if they do wrong they should not pay the penalty. No, I think that they deny wrongdoing. How about it?

EUTHYPHRO   It is true.

SOCRATES   Therefore they do not dispute that anybody who does wrong should pay the penalty. No, the thing that they dispute about is likely to be who is the wrongdoer, what he did, and when.

EUTHYPHRO   That is true.

SOCRATES   Well then, is n't that precisely what goes on among the gods, if they really do have quarrels about right and wrong, as you say they do? One set will hold that some others do wrong, and the other set deny it? For that other thing, my friend, I take it no one, whether god or man, will dare to say — that the wrongdoer should not pay the penalty!

EUTHYPHRO   Yes, Socrates, what you say is true — in the main.

SOCRATES   It is the individual act, I fancy, Euthyphro, that the disputants dispute about, both men and gods, if gods ever do dispute. They differ on a certain act; some hold that it was rightly done, the others that it was wrong. Isn't it so?

EUTHYPHRO   Yes, certainly.

SOCRATES   Then come, dear Euthyphro, teach me as well, and let me grow more wise. What proof have you that all the gods think that your servant died unjustly, your hireling who, when he had killed a man, was shackled by the master of the victim, and perished, dying because of his shackles before the man who shackled him could learn from the seers what ought to be done with him? What proof have you that for a man like him it is right for a son to prosecute his father, and indict him on a charge of murder? Come on. Try to make it clear to me beyond all doubt that under these conditions the gods must all consider this action to be right. If you can adequately prove it to me, I will never cease from praising you for your wisdom.

EUTHYPHRO   But, Socrates, that, very likely, would be no small task, although I could indeed make it very clear to you.

SOCRATES   I understand. You think that I am duller than the judges; obviously you will demonstrate to them that what your father did was wrong, and that the gods all hate such deeds.

EUTHYPHRO   I shall prove it absolutely, Socrates, if they will listen to me.

SOCRATES   They are sure to listen if they think that you speak well. But while you were talking, a notion came into my head, and I asked myself: Suppose that Euthyphro proved to me quite clearly that all the gods consider such a death unjust; would I have come one whit the nearer for him to knowing what the holy is, and what is the unholy? The act in question, seemingly, might be displeasing to the gods; but then we have just seen that you cannot define the holy and unholy in that way; for we have seen that a given thing may be displeasing, and also pleasing, to gods? So on this point, Euthyphro, I will let you off; if you like, the gods shall all consider the act unjust, and they all shall hate it. But suppose that we now correct our definition, and say that what the gods all hate is unholy, and what they love is holy, whereas what some of them love, and others hate, is either both or neither; are you willing that we now define the holy and unholy in this way?

EUTHYPHRO What is there to prevent us, Socrates?

SOCRATES Nothing to prevent me, Euthyphro. As for you, see whether when you take this definition you can quite readily instruct me, as you promised.

EUTHYPHRO Yes, I would indeed affirm that holiness is what the gods all love, and its opposite is what the gods all hate, unholiness.

SOCRATES Are we to examine this position also, Euthyphro, to see if it is sound? Or shall we let it through, and thus accept our own and others' statement, and agree to an assertion simply when somebody says that a thing is so? Must we not look into what the speaker says?

EUTHYPHRO We must. And yet, for my part, I regard the present statement as correct.

SOCRATES We shall soon know better about that, my friend. Now think of this. Is what is holy holy because the gods approve it, or do they approve it because it is holy?

EUTHYPHRO I do not get your meaning.

SOCRATES Well, I will try to make it clear. We speak of what is carried and the carrier, do we not, of led and leader, of the seen and that which sees? And you understand that in all such cases the things are different, and how they differ?

EUTHYPHRO Yes, I think I understand.

SOCRATES In the same way what is loved is one thing, and what loves is another?

EUTHYPHRO Of course.

SOCRATES Tell me now, is what is carried 'carried' because something carries it, or is it for some other reason?

EUTHYPHRO No, but for that reason.

SOCRATES And what is led, because something leads it? And what is seen, because something sees it?

EUTHYPHRO Yes, certainly.

SOCRATES Then it is not because a thing is seen that something sees it; but just the opposite: because something sees it, therefore it is seen. Nor because it is led, that something leads it; but because something leads it, therefore it is led. Nor because it is carried, that something carries it; but because something carries it, therefore it is carried. Do you see what I wish to say, Euthyphro? It is this: whenever an effect occurs, or something is effected, it is not the thing effected that gives rise to the effect; no, there is a cause, and then comes this effect. Nor is it because a thing is acted on that there is this effect; no, there is a cause for what it undergoes, and then comes this effect. Don't you agree?

EUTHYPHRO   I do.

SOCRATES   Well then, when a thing is loved, is it not in process of becoming something, or of undergoing something, by some other thing?

EUTHYPHRO   Yes, certainly.

SOCRATES   Then the same is true here as in the previous cases. It is not because a thing is loved that they who love it love it, but it is loved because they love it.

EUTHYPHRO   Necessarily.

SOCRATES   Then what are we to say about the holy, Euthyphro? According to your argument, is it not loved by all the gods?

EUTHYPHRO   Yes.

SOCRATES   Because it is holy, or for some other reason?

EUTHYPHRO   No, it is for that reason.

SOCRATES   And so it is because it is holy that it is loved; it is not holy because it is loved.

EUTHYPHRO   So it seems.

SOCRATES   On the other hand, it is beloved and pleasing to the gods just because they love it?

EUTHYPHRO   No doubt of that.

SOCRATES   So what is pleasing to the gods is not the same as what is holy, Euthyphro; nor, according to your statement, is the holy the same as what is pleasing to the gods; they are two different things.

EUTHYPHRO   How may that be, Socrates?

SOCRATES   Because we are agreed that the holy is loved because it is holy, and is not holy because it is loved. Isn't it so?

EUTHYPHRO   Yes.

SOCRATES   Whereas what is pleasing to the gods is pleasing to them just because they love it, such being its nature and its cause. Its being loved of the gods is not the reason of its being loved.

EUTHYPHRO   You are right.

SOCRATES   But suppose, dear Euthyphro, that what is pleasing to the gods and what is holy were not two separate things. In that case if holiness were loved because it was holy, then also what was pleasing to the gods would be loved because it pleased them; and, on the other hand, if what was pleasing to them pleased because they loved it, then also the holy would be holy because they loved it. But now you see that it is just the opposite, because the two are absolutely different from each other; for the one [what is pleasing to the gods] is of a sort to be loved because it is loved, whereas the other [what is holy] is loved because it is of a sort to be loved. Consequently, Euthyphro, it looks as if you had not given me my answer; as if when you were asked to tell the nature of the holy, you did not wish to explain the essence of it; you merely tell an attribute of it, namely, that it appertains to holiness to be loved by all the gods. What it *is*, as yet you have not said. So, if you please, do not conceal this from me; no, begin again. Say what the holy is, and never mind if gods do love it, nor if it has some other attribute; on that we shall not split. Come, speak out. Explain the nature of the holy and unholy.

EUTHYPHRO Now, Socrates, I simply don't know how to tell you what I think. Somehow everything that we put forward keeps moving about us in a circle, and nothing will stay where we put it.

SOCRATES Your statements, Euthyphro, look like the work of Daedalus, founder of my line. If I had made them, and they were my positions, no doubt you would poke fun at me, and say that, being in his line, the figures I construct in words run off, as did his statues, and will not stay where they are put. Meanwhile, since they are your definitions, we need some other jest; for in fact, as you see yourself, they will not stand still.

EUTHYPHRO But, Socrates, it seems to me that the jest is quite to the point. This tendency in our statements to go in a circle, and not to stay in one place, it is not I who put it there. To my mind, it is you who are the Daedalus; so far as I am concerned, they would have held their place.

SOCRATES If so, my friend, I must be more expert in his art than he, in that he merely made his own works capable of moving, whereas I give this power not merely to my own, but, seemingly, to the works of other men as well. And the rarest thing about my talent is that I am an unwilling artist; since I would rather see our arguments stand fast and hold their ground than have the art of Daedalus plus all the wealth of Tantalus to boot. But enough of this. And since, to my mind, you are languid, I will myself make bold with you to show how you might teach me about holiness. Do not weaken. See if you do not think that of necessity all that is holy is just.

EUTHYPHRO Yes, I do.

SOCRATES Well then, is all justice holy too? Or, granted that all holiness is just, is justice not all holy, but some part of it is holy, and some part of it is not?

EUTHYPHRO I do not follow, Socrates.

SOCRATES And yet you surpass me in your wisdom not less than by your youth. I repeat, you are languid through your affluence in wisdom. Come, lucky friend, exert yourself! What I have to say is not so hard to grasp. I mean the very opposite of what the poet [Stasinus] wrote:

> Zeus, who brought that all to pass, and made it all to grow,
> You will not name; for where fear is, there too is reverence.

On that I differ from the poet. Shall I tell you why?

EUTHYPHRO   By all means.

SOCRATES   I do not think that 'where fear is, there too is reverence'; for it seems to me that there are many who fear sickness, poverty, and all the like, and so are afraid, but have no reverence whatever for the things they are afraid of. Does it not seem so to you?

EUTHYPHRO   Yes, certainly.

SOCRATES   Where, however, you have reverence, there you have fear as well. Is there anybody who has reverence and a sense of shame about an act, and does not at the same time dread and fear an evil reputation?

EUTHYPHRO   Yes, he will be afraid of it.

SOCRATES   So it is not right to say that 'where fear is, there too is reverence.' No, you may say that where reverence is, there too is fear; not, however, that where fear is, there always you have reverence. Fear, I think, is wider in extent than reverence. Reverence is a part of fear, as the uneven is a part of number; thus you do not have the odd wherever you have number, but where you have the odd you must have number. I take it you are following me now?

EUTHYPHRO   Yes, indeed.

SOCRATES   Well then, what I asked you was like that. I asked you if wherever justice is, there is holiness as well; or, granted that wherever there is holiness, there is justice too, if where justice is, the holy is not always to be found. Thus holiness would be a part of justice. Shall we say so, or have you a different view?

EUTHYPHRO   No, that is my opinion; I think that you are clearly right.

SOCRATES   Then see what follows. If holiness is a part of justice, it seems to me that we must find out what part of justice it is. Suppose, for instance, in our case just now, you had asked me what part of number is the even, and which the even number is; I would have said it is the one that corresponds to the isosceles, and not to the scalene. Does it not seem so to you?

EUTHYPHRO   It does.

SOCRATES   Then try to show me in this way what part of the just is holiness, so that we may tell Meletus to cease from wronging me, and to give up prosecuting me for irreligion, because we have adequately learned from you of piety and holiness, and the reverse.

EUTHYPHRO   Well then, Socrates, I think that the part of justice which is religious and is holy is the part that has to do with the service of the gods; the remainder is the part of justice that has to do with the service of mankind.

SOCRATES   And what you say there, Euthyphro, to me seems excellent. There is one little point, however, on which I need more light. I am not yet quite clear about the thing which you call 'service.' I suppose you do not mean the sort of care we give to other things. The 'service' of the gods is not like that — the sort of thing we have in mind when we assert that it is not everybody who knows how to care for horses. It is the horseman that knows, is it not?

EUTHYPHRO   Yes, certainly.

SOCRATES   I suppose it is the special care that appertains to horses?

EUTHYPHRO   Yes.

SOCRATES   In the same way, it is not every one who knows about the care of dogs; it is the huntsman.

EUTHYPHRO   True.

SOCRATES   The art of the huntsman is the care of dogs.

EUTHYPHRO   Yes.

SOCRATES   And that of the herdsman is the care of cattle.

EUTHYPHRO   Yes, certainly.

SOCRATES   And in the same way, Euthyphro, holiness and piety mean caring for the gods? Do you say so?

EUTHYPHRO   I do.

SOCRATES   And so the aim of all this care and service is the same? I mean it thus. The care is given for the good and welfare of the object that is served. You see, for instance, how the horses that are cared for by the horseman's art are benefited and made better. Don't you think so?

EUTHYPHRO   Yes, I do.

SOCRATES   And so no doubt the dogs by the art of the huntsman, the cattle by that of the herdsman, and in like manner all the rest. Unless, perhaps, you think that the care may tend to injure the object that is cared for?

EUTHYPHRO   By Heaven, not I!

SOCRATES   The care aims at its benefit?

EUTHYPHRO   Most certainly.

SOCRATES   Then holiness, which is the service of the gods, must likewise aim to benefit the gods and make them better? Are you prepared to say that when you do a holy thing you make some deity better?

EUTHYPHRO   By Heaven, not I!

SOCRATES   Nor do I fancy, Euthyphro, that you mean it so; far from it. No, it was on this account that I asked just what you meant by service of the gods, supposing that, in fact, you did not mean that sort of care.

EUTHYPHRO   And, Socrates, you were right. I do not mean it so.

SOCRATES   Good. And now what kind of service of the gods will holiness be?

EUTHYPHRO   Socrates, it is the kind that slaves give to their masters.

SOCRATES   I understand. It seems to be a kind of waiting on the gods.

EUTHYPHRO   Just that.

SOCRATES   See if you can tell me this. The art which serves physicians, what result does it serve to produce? Don't you think that it is health?

EUTHYPHRO   I do.

SOCRATES   Further, what about the art that serves the shipwrights? What result does it serve to produce?

EUTHYPHRO   Obviously, Socrates, the making of a ship.

SOCRATES   And that which serves the builders serves the building of a house?

EUTHYPHRO   Yes.

SOCRATES   Now tell me, best of friends, about the service of the gods. What result will this art serve to produce? You obviously know, since you profess to be the best-informed among mankind on things divine!

EUTHYPHRO   Yes, Socrates, I say so, and I tell the truth.

SOCRATES   Then tell me, I adjure you, what is that supreme result which the gods produce when they employ our services?

EUTHYPHRO   They do many things and noble, Socrates.

SOCRATES   Just as the generals do, my friend. All the same you would have no trouble in summing up what they produce, by saying it is victory in war. Is n't it so?

EUTHYPHRO   Of course.

SOCRATES   And the farmers too, I take it, produce many fine results, but the net result of their production is the food they get from the earth.

EUTHYPHRO   Yes, surely.

SOCRATES   Well now, of the many fine and noble things which the gods produce, what is the sum of their production?

EUTHYPHRO   Just a little while ago I told you, Socrates, that the task is not a light one to learn precisely how all these matters stand. I will, however, simply tell you this. If any one knows how to say and do things pleasing to the gods in prayer and sacrifice, that is holiness, and such behavior saves the family in private life together with the common interests of the State. To do the opposite of things pleasing to the gods is impious, and this it is that upsets all and ruins everything.

SOCRATES   Surely, Euthyphro, if you had wished, you could have summed up what I asked for much more briefly. But the fact is that you are not eager to instruct me. That is clear. But a moment since, you were on the very point of telling me — and you slipped away. Had you given the answer, I would now have learnt from you what holiness is, and would be content. As it is — for perforce the lover must follow the loved one wherever he leads the way — once more, how do you define the holy, and what is holiness? Don't you say that it is a science of sacrifice and prayer?

EUTHYPHRO   I do.

SOCRATES   Well, and is not sacrifice a giving to the gods, and prayer an asking them to give?

EUTHYPHRO   Precisely, Socrates.

SOCRATES   By this reasoning, holiness would be the science of asking from the gods and giving to them.

EUTHYPHRO   Quite right, Socrates; you have caught my meaning perfectly.

SOCRATES   Yes, my friend, for I have my heart set on your wisdom, and give my mind to it, so that nothing you say shall be lost. No, tell me, what is this service to the gods? You say it is to ask of them and give to them?

EUTHYPHRO   I do.

SOCRATES   And hence to ask aright will be to ask them for those things of which we stand in need from them?

EUTHYPHRO   What else?

SOCRATES   And, on the other hand, to give aright will be to give them in return those things which they may need to receive from us? I take it there would be no art in offering any one a gift of something that he did not need.

EUTHYPHRO   True, Socrates.

SOCRATES   And therefore, Euthyphro, holiness will be a mutual art of commerce between gods and men.

EUTHYPHRO   An art of commerce, if you like to call it so.

SOCRATES   Well, I do not like it if it is not so. But tell me, what advantage would come to the gods from the gifts which they receive from us? Everybody sees what they give us. No good that we possess but is given by them. What advantage can they gain by what they get from us? Have we so much the better of them in this commerce that we get all good things from them, and they get nothing from us?

EUTHYPHRO   What! Socrates. Do you suppose that the gods gain anything by what they get from us?

SOCRATES   If not, then what would be the meaning, Euthyphro, of these gifts to the gods from us?

EUTHYPHRO   What do you think they ought to mean but worship, honor, and, as I just now said, good will?

SOCRATES   So, Euthyphro, the holy is what pleases them, not what is useful to them, nor yet what the gods love?

EUTHYPHRO   I believe that what gives them pleasure is precisely what they love.

SOCRATES   And so once more, apparently the holy is that which the gods love.

EUTHYPHRO   Most certainly.

SOCRATES   After that, will you be amazed to find your statements walking off, and not staying where you put them? And will you accuse me as the Daedalus who makes them move, when you are yourself far more expert than Daedalus, and make them go round in a circle? Don't you see that our argument has come full circle to the point where it began? Surely you have not forgotten how in what was said before we found that holiness and what is pleasing to the gods were not the same, but different from each other. Do you not remember?

EUTHYPHRO   I do.

SOCRATES   And are you not aware now that you say that what the gods love is holy? But is not what the gods love just the same as what is pleasing to the gods?

EUTHYPHRO Yes, certainly.

SOCRATES Well then, either we were wrong in our recent conclusion, or if that was right, our position now is wrong.

EUTHYPHRO So it seems.

SOCRATES And so we must go back again, and start from the beginning to find out what the holy is. As for me, I never will give up until I know. Ah! do not spurn me, but give your mind with all your might now at length to tell me the absolute truth; for if anybody knows, of all mankind, it is you, and one must not let go of you, you Proteus, until you tell. If you did not know precisely what is holy and unholy, it is unthinkable that for a simple hireling you ever would have moved to prosecute your aged sire on a charge of murder. No, you would have feared to risk the wrath of the gods on the chance that you were not doing right, and would have been afraid of the talk of men. But now I am sure that you think you know exactly what is holy and what is not. So tell me, peerless Euthyphro, and do not hide from me what you judge it to be.

EUTHYPHRO Another time, then, Socrates, for I am in a hurry, and must be off this minute.

SOCRATES What are you doing, my friend? Will you leave, and dash me down from the mighty expectation I had of learning from you what is holy and what is not, and so escaping from Meletus' indictment? I counted upon showing him that now I had gained wisdom about things divine from Euthyphro, and no longer out of ignorance made rash assertions and forged innovations with regard to them, but would lead a better life in future.

QUESTIONS

1. If a person is a theist, does he have moral obligations which unbelievers do not have? Is fulfillment of any moral obligation at the same time fulfillment of a religious obligation in some sense? How would Socrates have answered these questions?

2. A theist presumably need not worry about the question whether some gods may be pleased with an action and others displeased by it. But do we have more knowledge today about divine approval and commandments than the Greeks had?

3. Does Socrates succeed in proving that if the gods approve or command something, it must be because it is good or holy, and not that it is good or holy because the gods approve or command?

4. If we know the general sorts of things the gods approve or command, are we yet in a position to say what they will approve or command in all particular situations?

5. Would Socrates ask how we can have obligations to the gods if our actions cannot benefit them in any way? What does he think is the right answer to this question?

SUGGESTIONS FOR FURTHER READING

Dickinson, G. L. *Plato and His Dialogues*. New York: Norton, 1932.
Field, G. C. *The Philosophy of Plato*. New York: Oxford Univ. Press, 1949.
Friedlander, Paul. *Plato*. New York: Pantheon Books, 1958.
Grube, G. M. *Plato's Thought*. London: Methuen, 1935.
Jaeger, W. W. *Paideia, The Ideals of Greek Culture*. New York: Oxford Univ. Press, 1944. 3 vols., Vol. 3.
Joseph, H. W. B. *Knowledge and the Good in Plato's Republic*. New York: Oxford Univ. Press, 1949.
Levinson, R. B. *In Defense of Plato*. Cambridge: Harvard Univ. Press, 1953.
Lodge, R. C. *Plato's Theory of Ethics*. New York: Harcourt, Brace, 1928.
Nettleship, R. L. *Lectures on the Republic of Plato*. New York: Macmillan, 1937.
Pater, Walter. *Plato and Platonism*. New York: Macmillan, 1910.
Shorey, Paul. *What Plato Said*. Chicago: Univ. of Chicago Press, 1933.
Taylor, A. E. *Plato: The Man and His Work*. New York: Meridian Books, 1956.
Wild, John. *Plato's Theory of Man*. Cambridge: Harvard Univ. Press, 1953.
Woodbridge, F. J. E. *The Son of Apollo*. Boston: Houghton Mifflin, 1929.

George Finger Thomas   (1899-   )

REASON AND REVELATION
IN ETHICS

Many philosophers today suppose that theology is irrelevant for the determination of valid or defensible ethical first principles, while conceding that theological knowledge may help in the correct application of these principles by making clear the kind of world or situation in which we live. This view is not, however, shared by writers such as Emil Brunner (discussed below). Quite on the contrary, his proposal is that knowing God, God's activity, and God's revelation is central to the business of ascertaining what is good or right. Some persons defend views somewhere in between these two positions. One of these is George Thomas, a writer who has taught both religion and philosophy for many years.

Thomas received his undergraduate education at Southern Methodist University, studied at Oxford as a Rhodes Scholar, and received his Ph.D. degree from Harvard University. He has taught at Southern Methodist University, Swarthmore College, Dartmouth College, and the University of North Carolina; at present he is chairman of the Department of Religion at Princeton University.

CHRISTIAN ETHICS AND MORAL PHILOSOPHY

Is moral philosophy, then, an adequate basis for the good life? Many moral philosophers have thought so, especially in our secular age. But there are *limitations* of moral philosophy which have always prevented most men, even educated men, from regarding it as by itself sufficient. What are these limitations?

First, moral philosophers are concerned with the discovery of what is good for men and right for them to do, but they have seldom been able to awaken in men a love of the good or to stimulate their wills to do the right. This is the familiar problem of moral *incentive* or *motive*. It may be admitted, with Sidgwick, that there is a desire in man to do that which is right and reasonable. But that desire, by itself, is not strong enough in most men to overcome the natural passions and social forces which are opposed to the right and reasonable. It is not enough to appeal to the reason; the will and the affections must somehow be brought into line with the dictates of reason. Plato realized the importance of moral education through associating pleasure with the good and pain with the evil, and Aristotle emphasized the necessity of forming right habits. But philosophers have seldom probed this problem very deeply. They have tended to assume that if we know our true good we will seek it and if we know our duty we will do it. Therefore, they have thought that when they have defined the good and the right, their task is over. But man's will is divided and he cannot love his true good with all his heart. Again and again, he finds himself in the tragic situation of St. Paul: he knows what is good but he chooses the evil. He is powerless by himself to acquire the virtues or perform the duties which are required of him by moral philosophy. If he is to attain true goodness, he must be radically transformed. His desires must be redirected and his affections fixed firmly upon the good.

Second, man's effort to attain virtue by himself is often a source of *moral dangers*. Although the greatest moral philosophers insist upon a disinterested devotion to the good, the realization of higher values often leads to moral pride and complacency. Man's self-centeredness even perverts his virtues and turns them into means of furthering his own interests. Without faith and love, the attempt to attain virtue and do good works often leads to self-righteousness. Apart from this tendency of natural egoism to corrupt the achievements of the moral will, the excessive dependence upon moral striving is accompanied by serious dangers. It sometimes produces inner tension and anxiety concerning the success of one's efforts. Moralism in the sense of strenuous effort by the will to "live up to" high ethical ideals without the power to do so may be the cause of inner conflict and failure. The result may be psychological frustration or even breakdown. More often moralism leads to a stern, unlovely character with strength but without graciousness and spontaneity. Some of the finest moral qualities cannot be attained by conscious willing at all but must come from the unconscious influence of other persons and from participation in the life of a moral community.

Third, there is no *imaginative vision* in moral philosophy capable of inspiring spontaneous love and devotion. The principles of moral philosophy are expressed in concepts rather than images. This is necessary for the sake of clarity and precision; but it prevents most moral philosophers from moving the heart and stimulating the will. One of the reasons Bergson does not recognize the morality of philosophers as a third type of morality along with "closed" and "open" morality is that its concepts seem to him to have little power over the will.[1] His tendency to anti-intellectualism leads him to minimize unduly the function of reason in morality, for reason can survey the various ends sought by men and organize them into a unified ideal. But it is a timely warning against the opposite tendency to neglect the non-rational factors in the moral life. What is there in moral philosophy which can stimulate aspiration like the Christian vision of a universal community based upon love of God as Father and love of all men as brothers?

Fourth, the ideals of moral philosophers also lack the appeal that comes from the *incarnation* of a way of life in a living person and the inspiration that is derived from *imitation* of him. One of the greatest sources of appeal in Platonism, which is close to religious morality in many ways, is the embodiment of its ideal in Socrates. The power of Buddhist ethics is due largely to the fact that the followers of the Buddha are called upon to "take refuge" in *him* as well as in his *teachings*. Certainly, the reason Christian ethics has been able to transform the lives of men is to be found not only in the teachings of Christ but also in his life and in union with him. While a moral philosophy presents men with an *ideal* to be followed, it seldom offers them the *example* of one who has followed it. Nor is its ideal embodied in the way of life of a *community* or *church*, whose members strengthen and encourage one another in their efforts to realize it. Is this the reason why the greatest rival of Christian ethics in our time is not philosophical ethics but the secularized religious ethics of Communism, with its imaginative vision of a classless society embracing all men, the embodiment of its ideal in great leaders like Lenin, and its dependence upon an organized party to make its vision come true?

[1] Bergson, H., *The Two Sources of Morality and Religion*, New York, Holt, 1935, p. 57.

While moral philosophy has undoubtedly been one of the major sources of the ethical tradition of the Western world, these limitations force us to raise the question whether the attempt of many modern philosophers to separate moral philosophy from Christian ethics is not a fatal mistake. Should not moral philosophy and Christian ethics be regarded as complementary rather than mutually exclusive? May not the limitations of moral philosophy be overcome and its insights made more effective by the acceptance of Christian faith and love? May not Christians be aided by the insights of moral philosophy to obey God and serve their neighbors more wisely? The purpose of this chapter is to suggest that these questions should be answered in the affirmative, and to indicate a way in which the breach between Christian ethics and moral philosophy can be overcome.

THE AUTHORITY OF REVELATION AND THE AUTONOMY OF REASON

In carrying out this purpose, however, we shall be confronted with *objections* from moral philosophers and Christian theologians. Some moral philosophers repudiate Christian ethics on the ground that it is based on revelation rather than reason and consequently is "authoritarian." Some Christian theologians refuse to accept any of the theories of moral philosophers on the ground that they are useless and unnecessary for men of faith. It is essential to deal with these two objections before we attempt to show how Christian ethics and moral philosophy should be related to each other. We shall begin with the objection of secular moral philosophers that Christian ethics is "authoritarian."

With respect to the source of authority, Christian ethics and moral philosophy seem at first sight to be in absolute opposition to one another. Christian ethics derives its principles from the revelation recorded in the Bible. Liberal as well as orthodox Christians insist upon the authority of this revelation. In contrast, secular moral philosophers seem to reject every authority but that of reason. Moral philosophy, they insist, must be "autonomous"; the moralist must depend upon no source of truth beyond reason. This raises several important questions: In what sense does Christian ethics rest upon the authority of revelation? Insofar as it does so, is it necessarily "authoritarian"? Again, what do moral philosophers mean by the "autonomy" of the reason? Is this autonomy absolute or limited? Finally, is it possible to accept the "authority" of revelation without sacrificing the legitimate "autonomy" of the reason?

First, in what sense does Christian ethics assert the *authority of revelation?* Christians differ in their answer to this question. In Protestantism, Christian ethics is based upon the authority not of the Church but of the Bible. Since the Bible is the record of a divine revelation in history, this means that Christian ethics is ultimately based upon the authority of that revelation. However, the revelation cannot be simply identified with the words of the Bible in which it is expressed; the "Word" of God is not the same as the words in Hebrew and Greek by which it is mediated to us. Moreover, as Temple has said, it does not consist of dogmas and commandments stated in propositional form. It is a revelation of God and His redemptive activity, not of dogmas about God; of new life in love, not rules of conduct. For it is a revelation in historical events as interpreted by prophets and apostles, and the full meaning of historical events can never be exhausted by the words of any of its interpreters.[2] If so, the responsibility for interpreting the meaning of the revelation belongs to the individual person as a member of the Christian community. Does not God address men in the Biblical revelation as beings who can listen, understand, raise questions, and judge for themselves?

When understood in this way, the authority of revelation is wholly inconsistent with religious "authoritarianism." Religious "authoritarianism" is usually based upon belief in a visible authority, e.g., Church or Bible, as the source of dogmas which must be believed and rules which must be obeyed. Moreover, the pronouncements of this authority are unquestioned. They are felt to be binding whether or not they are approved by the reason and conscience of the individual. The free acceptance of revelation, as we have described it, is incompatible with this authoritarianism. According to our view, the acceptance of the authority of revelation by a Christian not only permits but demands that he use his reason fully in determining its meaning and its implications for his life.

This brings us to the question, what is the meaning of *"autonomy"* in moral philosophy? Positively, it asserts that man should determine his moral conduct by laws or principles approved by his own reason. Negatively, it denies the dependence of the rational will upon any external authority such as a church or state. According to Kant, it is "the property of the will to be a law to itself,"[3] and "the will possesses this property because it belongs to the intelligible world, under laws which, being independent of nature, have their foundation not in experience but in reason alone."[4] This view of the "autonomy" of the reason seems to assert that the reason lays down moral laws in complete independence of moral experience. However, Kant argued that his fundamental ethical principle was only a precise formulation of what is presupposed in the common moral consciousness. In any case, the usual method of philosophical ethics is to develop its principles through an examination of the moral experience of men as reflected in their moral judgments. Thus, "autonomy" means only that reason should not passively submit to an external authority, but should derive its ethical principles from reflection upon moral experience. If "autonomy" is interpreted in this way, reason may and should take into ac-

---

[2] Temple, William, *Nature, Man and God*, London, Macmillan, 1940, Lecture 12.
[3] Kant, I., *The Metaphysics of Morals*, tr. by T. K. Abbott in *Kant's Theory of Ethics*, London, Longmans, Green, 1909, p. 66.
[4] Ibid., p. 72.

count every kind of moral experience, including that of religious men, in formulating its ethical principles.

When the "authority" of revelation and the "autonomy" of reason are interpreted in this way, the absolute opposition between Christian ethics and moral philosophy is seen to be unnecessary. On the one hand, the Biblical revelation of moral truth was not imparted to men whose minds and consciences were passive, but was mediated to them through their moral experience. Moreover, it continues to be accepted by Christians because it seems to be confirmed by their own moral experience. Thus, there is nothing arbitrary or irrational about it. On the other hand, the moral philosopher depends upon the facts of moral experience, and since the value of his conclusions is determined largely by the depth and breadth of the moral experience from which he derives them, it is reasonable for him to take seriously the moral experience recorded in the Bible.

In fact, however, there is a fundamental *difference* between Christian ethics and secular moral philosophy in their interpretation of moral experience. Christian ethics is inseparable from the Christian faith that God has revealed His will in Christ. A philosopher who does not share this faith cannot accept Christian ethics as a whole, although he may incorporate into his own thinking certain ideas derived from it. Consequently, he cannot give the moral experience recorded in the Bible a "privileged position" in his examination of the facts of the moral consciousness. He may acknowledge that important and valid ethical ideas originated in this moral experience, but he cannot acknowledge their primacy in his ethical thinking.

Thus, while there is no logical necessity for an absolute opposition between Christian ethics and moral philosophy *as such*, there is a radical difference between Christian ethics and a *secular* moral philosophy. However, the Christian moralist can do much to bridge the gap. Although the secular moral philosopher refuses to give primacy to ethical insights derived from the Christian moral experience, the Christian moralist should acknowledge the truth of some of the ethical insights of moral philosophers and adapt them for the use of Christians. We shall indicate later in this chapter why he should do so and how he can do so in the most fruitful way.

In addition, he can seek to remove a common misconception from the minds of moral philosophers which stands in the way of their acceptance of the Christian faith and ethic. This is the idea that, while Christian ethics is based upon the moral experience of a particular people in the past, moral philosophy is a product of universal reason reflecting impartially upon the moral experience of all humanity. Because of this supposed difference between them, the secular moral philosopher believes that his method and conclusions are superior to those of the Christian moralist. But is his examination of moral experience as all-inclusive and impartial as he thinks? Does he actually analyze the moral judgments of *all* peoples of every time and place? Does he analyze moral judgments from the perspective of an *impartial* reason unconditioned by his own time and place?

The moral philosopher is incapable of such an analysis. The limitations of his knowledge and the effect of his culture upon him cannot be overcome. In his analysis he usually limits himself to the moral judgments of his own people or civilization. Even when he deals with the moral judgments of other peoples and other times, he is naturally influenced more deeply by those of his own. The ethical theories of Plato and Aristotle would have been impossible in any country except ancient Greece, and Kant's ethics is clearly a product of the Age of Reason. Thus, the perspective of the moral philosopher is not that of universal reason reflecting impartially upon the *general* moral experience of mankind; it is that of his own reason conditioned by the *particular* moral experience of his time and place. In reality, he accords a "privileged position" to the particular moral experience of ancient Greeks or modern Europeans, as the Christian moralist accords such a position to the experience of Hebrew prophets and Christian apostles.

If so, the moral philosopher should not claim superiority for his method. Like the Christian moralist, he gives the "privileged position" to those whom he believes to have been the wisest and best; and if he is pressed for the reason why he believes them to be so, it will be seen that his belief really rests upon metaphysical and ethical assumptions which he cannot demonstrate but accepts by a kind of faith. In brief, there is no such thing as an ethic which has been developed by pure reason without the aid of presuppositions. The difference between Christian ethics and secular moral philosophy is not that the former has presuppositions while the latter is free from them; it is that they derive their presuppositions from different sources. Can the moral philosopher prove that his presuppositions or the sources from which he draws them are superior to those of the Christian moralist? If the test of ethical presuppositions is their fruitfulness in ethical theory and their value as a guide in moral decisions, Christian ethics has stood this test successfully during many centuries. Can more be said of the ethical presuppositions of any philosopher?

FAITH AND REASON

The preceding argument concerning the relation of Christian ethics to moral philosophy presupposes a certain view of the nature of the Christian faith and its relation to reason. We must now make this view more explicit. Some philosophers suppose that faith has no cognitive value but is a wholly irrational act which springs from the will or the feelings. Now, it is certainly true that faith is not only intellectual assent; it is also a response of the whole self, including the will and heart, to the reality of God. But this does not destroy its *cognitive value*. For faith involves an apprehension of the reality and goodness of God as He has revealed Himself. It is not a blind faith, but a response to God as He has confronted man in his experience. It differs from reason when the latter is conceived as the faculty of discursive thinking. Faith *affirms* the reality and goodness of God as He is experienced and it leads to a commitment to Him. Reason, on the other hand, critically *examines* a judgment to determine whether there are adequate grounds for asserting it and it frequently leads to a refusal of commitment. Thus, faith is more adventurous than reason, reason more cautious than faith. But while faith goes beyond reason, it need not contradict any knowledge which has been definitely established by reason. And reason, which has a constructive as well as a critical task, cannot complete its task unless it is willing to accept premises or presuppositions which it cannot demonstrate. Thus, while faith without reason is uncritical, reason without faith is uncreative.

Of course, reason can attain to knowledge of certain kinds without the aid of faith. In the form of common sense, it can enable men to cope with problems of everyday life. In the form of science, it can describe natural phenomena, make predictions about future events, and design machines for exploiting natural resources. But it cannot attain to wisdom about the world as a whole or the highest good of man without *presuppositions* derived from faith.

The mind can understand reality, says Niebuhr, "only by making faith the presupposition of its understanding." [5] This is the Augustinian view of the relation between faith and understanding. "Credo ut intelligam," "I believe in order that I may understand." Since every world view rests upon presuppositions which cannot be rationally demonstrated, each of us must face the problem as to whether he is to start with presuppositions derived, at least in part, from the religious experience of God as transcendent Reality and Good. If we try to avoid the problem by denying the possibility of a world view and contenting ourselves with the description of relations between natural phenomena, as in Positivism, we refuse to heed the highest demand of reason and to meet the deepest need of life itself. If we try to find the meaning of the whole of reality in some aspect of nature, e.g., matter or life, we are merely explaining the whole by one of its finite parts to which we have arbitrarily accorded a privileged position over other finite parts. But if we have had a vital religious experience, we can never be satisfied with anything less than a religious world view based upon an affirmation of faith in God as transcendent Reality and Good.

Of course, in laying hold of God by faith, man's "reach exceeds his grasp." Though God has revealed Himself in religious experience, He remains hidden in His transcendent otherness. Nevertheless, faith ventures out beyond the world of finite and contingent things and affirms an infinite and supersensible Being as the Ground of its existence, its nature, and its value.

[5] Niebuhr, R., *The Nature and Destiny of Man*, New York, Scribners, 1941, I, p. 158.

Thus faith is a *source of truth* about reality, not a subjective fancy. As such, it involves, not only an act of trust, but also an intellectual act, an act of insight. That is why it is the source not only of religion but also of any philosophy which does justice to the transcendent element in experience. Every world view, irreligious as well as religious, is based upon a principle of meaning, a vision of truth, which is accepted by a kind of faith as the key to reality as a whole. In the words of Bradley, "metaphysics is the finding of bad reasons for what we believe on instinct." [6] A religious world view differs from naturalistic world views in that the principle of meaning upon which it rests is a transcendent principle, God. The fact that it is transcendent, however, does not mean that it is irrelevant to our understanding of the finite and contingent things of the world in which we live and to our life in that world. Indeed, finite and contingent things, especially the life and spirit of man, find their meaning and explanation only in relation to it and apart from it they become unintelligible.

This is not a mere dogmatic assertion of religion alone; it can be confirmed by reference to other spiritual activities and values also. Plato points out in the "Symposium" how the experience of beautiful faces and forms leads on to the experience of beautiful souls and finally to the experience of Beauty itself as the transcendent principle which is invisible but is present in all visible things of beauty and is the ultimate source of their beauty. One does not have to accept the Platonic theory of Ideas as universal Forms which subsist in a realm of their own to see that he is describing the experience of all those who love beauty as something more than the "aesthetic surface" of a physical object. The sense of frustration of every great artist because he cannot capture perfectly the vision that hovers before him points in the same direction. Similarly, all moral striving seems to presuppose an absolute and perfect goodness that is never fully realized in men's conduct but that haunts them and beckons them on. Thus, the aesthetic and moral experience of man, like his religious experience, points to a transcendent Reality and Good beyond the natural world. But since religious faith apprehends directly this Reality and Good, it is the source of the highest knowledge. Without faith, all knowledge of finite reality through common sense or science becomes distorted and loses its crown of wisdom.

This is the theoretical significance of faith; its *moral significance* is equally important. Without faith the will of man is directed towards values that are near and immediately accessible because they belong to the world of actuality. He finds it hard, if not impossible, to conceive of a life radically different from his own or values radically different from those of the society in which he lives. But the man of faith has caught a vision of possibilities that go far beyond anything in the world of actuality, of a new life and other values which are richer and more blessed than those he knows

[6] Bradley, F. H., *Appearance and Reality*, New York, Macmillan, 1893, p. XIV.

around him. Thus, it is faith in the Christian sense which envisages a universal, "open" community in the place of the exclusive, "closed" societies in which men actually live. It sees the possibility of a more perfect love than that of even the best men. Moreover, it trusts in the mercy and power of God to bring into reality that universal community and that perfect love in the lives of men. In this way, faith transforms the moral will by setting before it higher and broader purposes than those of the self or the group and strengthening it in its efforts to realize those purposes. By subjecting the self to the will of God, faith rescues it from its self-centeredness and self-love. It frees the self from its fears and anxieties about itself and enables it to give itself in love to others. Thus, faith not only apprehends God as the transcendent Reality who gives meaning to all existence, but also awakens devotion to Him as the absolute Good which is the source of all the higher values of the moral life. . . .

THE REPUDIATION OF MORAL PHILOSOPHY: EMIL BRUNNER

If this is true, the objection of secular moral philosophers that Christian ethics is authoritarian and that Christian faith is incompatible with reason is unwarranted. But we must also consider the objection of some *Christian theologians* against any attempt of Christian moralists to appropriate the conclusions of moral philosophers. This objection arises in large part out of a reaction against the tendency to accommodate Christian truth to secular thought or to form a synthesis between them.

The reaction against these tendencies in recent Protestant theology has led to a virtual *repudiation of philosophy* by some Christian theologians. Like Tertullian, they ask, "What has Athens to do with Jerusalem?" Perhaps the best example of this attitude in Christian ethics is to be found in Emil Brunner's *The Divine Imperative*. Since Brunner has usually shown himself more hospitable than Barth to secular thought, it might be supposed that he would be sympathetic with the efforts of moral philosophers to deal with problems of conduct. But his conclusions with respect to "philosophical ethics" are almost entirely negative. After a very brief survey of a few systems of "philosophical ethics," he concludes that each system has its values but also its defects and that any kind of "synthetic ethics" is also unsatisfactory.[7] All "natural morality," he says, necessarily leads to contradictions because of the cleavage of human life due to sin. When man makes himself independent of God, God becomes to him an alien power and His commands seem external and arbitrary. Therefore, he tries to free himself from them by means of a purely rational morality of universal laws and falls into ethical legalism. Or he develops an ethic of happiness which

[7] *The Divine Imperative*, copyright, 1947, by W. L. Jenkins, The Westminster Press, p. 43.

regards life as good in itself apart from God. In both cases, "natural morality" is a product of man's sinful rebellion against God's will. Though there are "fragments" of truth in it, each fragment "by its isolation from the whole, is itself twisted, distorted into a caricature of the original," so that "the picture presented by natural ethics is a heap of ruins." [8] Thus, philosophical ethics is virtually useless to the Christian. But this does not matter, since Christian ethics needs no help from any other source. Its own answer to the questions raised by morality is all-sufficient. "Does the Christian faith," Brunner asks, "give *the* answer, the *only* answer, and the *whole* answer to the ethical problem?" [9] His reply is an uncompromising "Yes."

This negative attitude towards "philosophical ethics" is determined, in part, by Brunner's conception of Christian ethics. Obedience to God's will, he holds, requires only one thing: love of God as expressed in love of one's neighbor. But how are we to determine what *duties* love of our neighbor requires? Brunner replies that we cannot be guided by any "principle" in deciding what the divine command of love requires in a situation. In this sense, Christian ethics has no "content." Its "content" must be discovered anew in each situation by listening to the voice of the Spirit. . . . [10]

Now, the real question for the Christian is not whether moral philosophy has the whole truth but whether it has important insights that must be included in the truth. As we have said, secular philosophers have often made exaggerated claims for moral philosophy, insisting that reason can discover the highest good without the aid of faith. Christians must reject these claims. But this does not justify the conclusion that, because moral philosophy does not have *all* the truth, it has *none* of the truth. Although Brunner has pointed out defects or weaknesses in a number of ethical theories, it hardly justifies him in rejecting them altogether. It is also true that there are serious contradictions between different ethical theories. There is a contradiction, for example, between the Hedonist's view that pleasure is the only good and Kant's view that the good will is both a good and the only unconditional good. But when we are faced by such a contradiction between two theories are we simply to throw up our hands and refuse to think further about the question? Or are we to try our best to decide whether one theory is right and the other wrong, or whether both are wrong, or whether, as is often the case, one is right in a certain respect and the other is right in another respect? If we take the former course and stop thinking about the problem, we shall never arrive at or even come closer to the truth, for the road to truth lies through the patient and critical examination of opposing views. If we take the latter course, we shall find ourselves involved in philosophical reflection with all its difficulties as

[8] *Ibid.*, p. 67.

[9] *Ibid.*, p. 51.

[10] *Ibid.*, p. 111.

well as its rewards. Anyone, Christian or otherwise, may refuse to become involved in it if he wishes, but if he does refuse he has no right to an opinion on the question whether the difficulties can be solved.

Thus, Brunner's criticisms of the weaknesses and contradictions in moral philosophy are not so much false as irrelevant. Like all branches of philosophy, ethics is a continuous, cumulative intellectual enterprise, and those who engage in that enterprise may hope to broaden their understanding of moral truth even if they do not arrive at final solutions of moral problems. The fact that there is error along with truth, chaff among the wheat, does not change this fact. Indeed, not the least fruitful part of philosophical reflection is that which consists in discriminating between error and truth. . . .

We have seen that Brunner's conception of moral philosophy is unjust. What are we to say of the adequacy of his *interpretation of Christian ethics?* His ethical insights are often so penetrating and his statement of them is so persuasive that a serious defect of his interpretation as a whole has not been sufficiently noticed. The divine command of love, he says, should not be regarded as a "principle" and what it requires in each situation cannot in any way be determined "beforehand" but must be discovered in the situation itself. He holds that if we come to a particular situation with a "principle" in our minds, we will not be sensitive to the claims of our neighbor and will not listen to the divine command coming to us in that unique situation. The "principle," like a "law" or "rule," will stand between us and our neighbor as an impersonal barrier and prevent a fully personal relation with him. Consequently, we will be in danger of sacrificing his welfare to our "principle."

Now, there is undoubtedly a danger of this kind in acting from *principle.* It is well known that "men of principle" are often too calculating and that they sometimes lack sensitiveness to the unique elements in a particular situation. But this is due to the way in which they conceive and apply a principle. If a principle is conceived in a narrow and rigid way, as specifying a certain type of act without regard to the needs of the particular situation, it becomes nothing more than a rule to be applied mechanically and without study of the situation. But a principle should not be conceived and applied in this wooden, unimaginative fashion. It should be defined in broader and more general terms than a specific rule. For it is meant to tell us the general direction we are to go, not the specific road we are to take. Thus, the command to love our neighbor should always be conceived as a principle rather than a rule. It does not specify a certain kind of act; it requires many different kinds of acts appropriate to the needs of different situations and leaves us free to determine what it requires of us in each situation. Thus, it is not true, as Brunner implies, that we must determine our duty *either* by reference to a principle *or* by considering the needs of our neighbor in the concrete situation; we must bring together *both* factors, general principle and particular needs, in reaching our decision.

In reality, Brunner himself treats as principles the idea that the Christian should perform the duties of his "calling" and the idea that he should accept but improve the "created orders" of society. In a sense, therefore, his repudiation of the guidance of moral decisions by "principles" is only a verbal matter. But it is also more than that. Time and again, he speaks of each situation as if it were essentially different from every other situation and must be approached without any presuppositions. This nominalistic tendency to stress the particular at the expense of the universal aspects of moral situations leads Brunner perilously close to the abyss of irrationalism. For the discernment of one's duty he seems to depend upon the guidance of the Holy Spirit alone, without the aid of rational principles of any kind. This seems to be due to his profound distrust of reason. As we have said, he is not consistent in the matter. He insists that, in arriving at political decisions, reason should be fully employed. But he seems to imply that in personal relationships the task of reason is over when it has considered the needs of one's neighbor in the situation. The decision itself is made under the guidance of the Holy Spirit without the aid of reason.

Since the time of Aristotle moral philosophers have recognized that there is an intuitive element in moral decision. Each must apprehend by a kind of "knack" or "insight" the act which is suitable to the particular situation and the manner in which it should be performed. But only extreme ethical Intuitionists have believed that intuition could be trusted to function without control by rational principles. Again, Christian moralists have always insisted that the illumination of our minds by the Spirit is necessary for the discernment of duty. But, here again, everything depends upon the way we conceive of that illumination. Does it replace the application of principles by reason to a particular situation, or does it make the work of reason more effective? The danger of the former conception is not only that it may deprive man of responsibility for his own decisions but also that it may emphasize spontaneous activity at the cost of deliberation and lead to the fanaticism which identifies absolutely man's interpretation of his duty with God's will for him.

Apart from the dangers of irrationalism, however, the crucial question that must be addressed to Brunner is, how can one determine one's *duty* without the help of principles? In the presence of conflicting claims from many different persons in a situation one cannot possibly meet all of them. It is not enough to say that one must open oneself to all of these claims and then listen for the command of God. He must also have principles that will help him to determine which claims are primary and how different claims can be reconciled. These principles must be derived from an analysis of the various kinds of human needs and relationships and the best methods of dealing with them. After all, if the command to love one's neighbor means that one is to serve his needs, one must use all the knowledge of his needs that is available from any source. . . .

Thus, Brunner's interpretation of Christian ethics, though it contains many penetrating insights, is inadequate. A Christian, like anyone else, must have *principles* to guide him in the determination of his duty and in the realization of value. If he refuses to make use of reason to discover and apply such principles, his obedience to the command of love, however sincere, will be irrational. In his search for these principles, the Christian moralist must get whatever help from moral philosophy he can. *Reason should be the ally, not the rival, of love.*

THE CHRISTIAN'S NEED FOR MORAL PHILOSOPHY

We have attempted to show that the repudiation of "philosophical ethics" by theologians like Brunner is unjustified and that it is necessary for Christian moralists to appropriate valid insights of moral philosophers concerning duty and value if their interpretation of Christian ethics is to be adequate. "But," it may be asked, "are not Christian faith and love sufficient? If we say that they must be supplemented with principles derived from non-Christian moralists, do we not admit that Christian ethics is imperfect?"

While Christian faith and love are an adequate *basis* for all morality, they do not by themselves provide the whole *content* of morality. This does not imply that Christian ethics is imperfect. Christian ethics was never intended to be an "ethical theory" which would solve in a systematic and comprehensive manner all the problems of morality, as it was not intended to be a new code of laws specifying what men should or should not do in every kind of situation. It is part of the Gospel, and the Gospel came into the world as a religion, not a theory. Unlike Judaism and Hinduism, which are religious cultures, the Gospel was concerned almost exclusively with the relation between man and God and between man and his neighbor in the Kingdom of God. Consequently, its ethic was purely religious and had little or nothing to say about the social institutions, civic virtues, and values of culture. As we have seen, this has been the source of many difficulties and disagreements among Christians who have had to concern themselves with problems of society. If they were not to withdraw from the world, they could not avoid these problems, and yet they could find no solutions of them in the Gospel. Therefore, they were forced to look for solutions wherever they could find them. It was no accident that from the second century they went to the best social and political philosophy which was available to them and that they have continued to do so ever since.

In short, since Christian ethics defines the right relationship between man and God and between man and his neighbor, it provides the *adequate foundation* of any morality which is to stand the test of life. To hear Jesus' words and to follow him is to have one's house built upon a rock. But Christians have the *responsibility of building* upon this foundation the best and fullest lives they can, using the materials of human nature and shaping them with the help of reason and experience. In this process of building, moral philosophy, like literature and history, is indispensable to them because it contains the wisdom of serious and thoughtful men during more than two thousand years.

At what specific points can the Christian moralist hope to derive valuable help from moral philosophers? We shall attempt to answer this question in some detail in the following chapters. One of the problems with which moral philosophers have concerned themselves from the beginning has been the problem of the nature and conditions of *happiness*. We shall find that certain moral philosophers have contributed much to man's understanding of this problem. Christians may also derive much help from moral philosophers in defining principles of *value*. The New Testament does not attempt to analyze, differentiate, and rank the major values which enrich life. Since its interest is in the attainment of the Highest Good, the blessedness of the Kingdom of God, it says little about values such as truth and beauty. On the other hand, philosophers since the time of Plato have devoted much attention to the analysis of different types of value and their relations to one another. It would be strange if they should have nothing to tell Christians about the values which contribute most to the good life. Finally, Christians can derive help from moral philosophy in formulating principles for the determination of their *duties* to their neighbors and in defining the *virtues* which constitute character.

QUESTIONS

1. Why does Thomas think that a sound moral philosophy needs supplement? If he is right, should the moral philosopher in some sense accept the Christian faith?
2. What conception of "revelation" does Thomas propose in order to show that the Christian tradition in ethics is not authoritarian? How should we discover God's will, according to Thomas?
3. What is the difference between secular moral philosophy and Christian ethics, according to him? Does he think that moral philosophy is more "presuppositionless" than the Christian faith? What does he think is the test of the validity of ethical "presuppositions"?
4. What does he think is the importance of faith for moral philosophy?
5. Does he think Brunner assesses correctly the proper role of principles in moral thinking? Explain.

6. What benefit does Thomas think the Christian may derive from the study of moral philosophy?

Richard Price (1723-91)

NONNATURAL PROPERTIES ARE KNOWN BY REASON

Richard Price, a British philosopher, became well known for political pamphlets which he wrote in defense of American independence and of the French Revolution. His most important work philosophically, however, was A *Review of the Principal Questions in Morals* (1757).

Price's statement and defense of the nonnaturalist view is as lucid and forceful as any that has been written. He was not, of course, familiar with some forms of naturalism which were invented only after his death; had he known of them, presumably he would have criticized them much as Ewing does and much as he himself criticizes supernaturalism. Price did not think that the meaning of ethical statements is such that we can sensibly claim to verify them by observation and the methods of science. The theory he was most concerned to combat was one that had been propounded by Francis Hutcheson, one like some of the "approval" theories criticized by Ewing, but also very like some of the forms of noncognitivism represented below. According to this view, moral statements are reports or expressions of the moral approval or disapproval elicited in the speaker by knowledge of a situation or action; such qualities as rightness and wrongness are not objective properties of situations about which we can have true or false beliefs. Price, in contrast, asserts that there is good reason for thinking that rightness and wrongness are as much objective properties of acts or situations as are properties like solidity and mass. Price concedes that these properties cannot be known about by observation, but he thinks his claim is no worse for this fact. The human understanding, he thinks, is quite competent to know such facts, and there are many other types of facts, which no sensible person would doubt we really do know, which are known about in exactly the same way. There are, then, unobservable moral facts (and in saying they are unobservable he is at odds with many forms of naturalism), which are known by understanding, "intuition," or direct awareness.

From Richard Price, A *Review of the Principal Questions in Morals*, ed. by D. Daiches Raphael, published by The Clarendon Press, Oxford, 1948, and reprinted with their permission.

A REVIEW OF THE PRINCIPAL QUESTIONS IN MORALS

THE QUESTIONS STATED CONCERNING THE FOUNDATION OF MORALS

Some actions we all feel ourselves irresistibly determined to approve, and others to disapprove. Some actions we cannot but think *right*, and others *wrong*, and of all actions we are led to form some opinion, as either *fit* to be performed or *unfit*; or neither fit nor unfit to be performed; that is, *indifferent*. What the power within us is, which thus determines, is the question to be considered.

A late very distinguished writer, Dr. *Hutcheson*, deduces our moral ideas from a *moral sense*; meaning by this *sense*, a power within us, different from reason, which renders certain actions pleasing and others displeasing to us. As we are so made that certain impressions on our bodily organs shall excite certain ideas in our minds, and that certain outward forms, when presented to us, shall be the necessary occasions of pleasure or pain. In like manner, according to Dr. *Hutcheson*, we are so made that certain affections and actions of moral agents shall be the necessary occasions of agreeable or disagreeable sensations in us, and procure our love or dislike of them. He has indeed well shewn that we have a faculty determining us *immediately* to approve or disapprove actions, abstracted from all views of private advantage; and that the highest pleasures of life depend upon this faculty. Had he proceeded no farther, and intended nothing more by the *moral sense*, than our *moral faculty* in general, little room would have been left for any objections: But then he would have meant by it nothing *new*, and he could not have been considered as the *discoverer* of it. From the term *sense*, which he applies to it, from his rejection of all the arguments that have been used to prove it to be an intellectual power, and from the whole of his language on this subject; it is evident, he considered it as the effect of a *positive constitution* of our minds, or as an *implanted* and *arbitrary* principle by which a *relish* is given us for certain moral objects and forms and aversion to others, similar to the relishes and aversions created by any of our other senses. In other words, our ideas of morality, if this account is right, have the same origin with our ideas of the sensible qualities of bodies, the harmony of sounds, or the beauties of painting or sculpture; that is, the mere good pleasure of our Maker adapting the mind and its organs in a particular manner to certain objects. Virtue (as those who embrace this scheme say) is an affair of taste. Moral right and wrong signify nothing *in the objects themselves* to which they are applied, any more than agreeable and harsh; sweet and bitter; pleasant and painful; but only *certain effects in us.* Our perception of *right,* or moral good, in actions, is that agreeable *emotion,* or feeling, which certain actions produce in us; and of *wrong,* or moral evil, the contrary. They are particular modifications of our minds, or impressions which they are made to receive from the contemplation of certain actions, which the contrary actions *might* have occasioned, had the Author of nature so pleased; and which to suppose to belong to these actions themselves is as absurd as to ascribe the pleasure or uneasiness, which the observation of a particular form gives us, to the form itself. 'Tis therefore, by this account, improper to say of an action, that it *is right,* in much the same sense that it is improper to say of an object of taste, that it is *sweet;* or of *pain,* that it is *in* fire.

The present enquiry therefore is: Whether this be a true account of virtue or not; whether it *has* or has *not* a foundation in the *nature* of its object; whether *right* and *wrong* are real characters of *actions,* or only qualities of our *minds;* whether, in short, they denote what actions *are,* or only *sensations* derived from the particular frame and structure of our natures.

I am persuaded, all attentive persons, who have not before considered this question, will wonder that it should be a subject of dispute, and think I am going to undertake a very needless work. I have given the naked and just state of it. And it is worth our attention, as we go along, that it is the *only* question about the foundation of morals, which can rationally and properly be made a subject of debate. For, granting that we have perceptions of *moral right* and *wrong,* they must denote either what the actions, to which we apply them, *are,* or only our *feelings;* and the *power* of perceiving them must be either that power whose object is truth, or some *implanted power* or *sense.* If the former is true, then is *morality* equally unchangeable with *all truth:* If, on the contrary, the latter is true, then is it that only which, according to the different constitutions of the *senses* of beings, it *appears* to be to them?

As to the schemes which found morality on self-love, on positive laws and compacts, or the Divine will; they must either mean that moral good and evil are only other words for *advantageous* and *disadvantageous, willed* and *forbidden.* Or they relate to a very different question; that is, not to the question, what is the nature and true *account* of virtue; but, what is the *subject-matter* of it.

As far as the former may be the intention of the schemes I have mentioned, they afford little room for controversy. Right and wrong when applied to actions which are commanded or forbidden by the will of God, or that produce good or harm, do not signify merely, that such actions are commanded or forbidden, or that they are useful or hurtful, but a *senti-*

ment[1] concerning them and our consequent approbation or disapprobation of the performance of them. Were not this true, it would be palpably absurd in any case to ask whether it is *right* to obey a command, or *wrong* to disobey it; and the propositions, *obeying a command is right,* or *producing happiness is right,* would be most trifling, as expressing no more than that obeying a command is obeying a command, or producing happiness is producing happiness. Besides, on the supposition that right and wrong denote only the relations of actions to will and law, or to happiness and misery, there could be no dispute about the faculty that perceives right and wrong, since it must be owned by all that these relations are objects of the investigations of *reason.*

Happiness requires something in its own nature, or in ours, to give it influence, and to determine our desire of it and approbation of pursuing it. In like manner, all laws, will, and compacts suppose *antecedent right* to give them effect; and, instead of being the *constituents* of right, they owe their whole force and obligation to it.

Having premised these observations, the question now returns — What is the power within us that perceives the distinctions of *right* and *wrong?*

My answer is: The UNDERSTANDING.

In order to prove this, it is necessary to enter into a particular enquiry into the origin of our ideas in general, and the distinct provinces of the *understanding* and of *sense.*

OF THE ORIGIN OF OUR IDEAS IN GENERAL

SENSATION and REFLECTION have been commonly reckoned the sources of all our ideas: and Mr. *Locke* has taken no small pains to prove this. How much soever, on the whole, I admire his excellent *Essay,* I cannot think him sufficiently clear or explicit on this subject. It is hard to determine exactly what he meant by *sensation* and *reflection.* If by the former we understand, the effects arising from the impressions made on our minds by external objects; and by the latter, the notice the mind takes of its own operations; it will be impossible to derive some of the most important of our ideas from them. This is the explanation Mr. *Locke* gives of them in the beginning of his *Essay.* But it seems probable that what he chiefly meant was that all our ideas are either derived *immediately* from these two sources, or ultimately *grounded* upon ideas so derived; or, in other words, that they furnish us with all the subjects, materials, and occasions of knowledge, comparison, and internal perception. This, however, by no means renders them, in any proper sense, the sources of all our ideas: Nor indeed does it appear, notwithstanding all he has said of the operations of the mind about its ideas, that he thought we had any faculty different from sensation and reflection which could give rise to any *simple ideas;* or that was capable of more than compounding, dividing, abstracting, or en-

[1] [Price uses the word "sentiment" to mean opinion, not feeling. — D. D. Raphael]

larging ideas previously in the mind. But be this as it may, what I am going to observe, will, I believe, be found true.

The power, I assert, that *understands*, or the faculty within us that discerns *truth*, and that compares all the objects of thought, and *judges* of them, is a spring of new ideas.[2]

As, perhaps, this has not been enough attended to, and as the question to be discussed is, whether our *moral ideas* are derived from the *understanding* or from a *sense*; it will be necessary to state distinctly the different natures and provinces of sense and reason.

To this purpose we may observe, first, that the power which judges of the perceptions of the senses, and contradicts their decisions; which discovers the nature of the sensible qualities of objects, enquires into their causes, and distinguishes between what is real and what is not real in them, must be a power within us which is superior to sense.

Again, it is plain that one sense cannot judge of the objects of another; the eye, for instance, of harmony, or the ear of colours. The faculty, therefore, which views and compares the objects of *all* the senses, cannot be sense. When, for instance, we consider sound and colour together, we observe in them *essence, number, identity, diversity,* etc., and determine their reality to consist, not in being properties of *external substances*, but in being modifications of *our souls*. The power which takes cognizance of all this, and gives rise to these notions, must be a power capable of subjecting all things alike to its inspection, and of acquainting itself with necessary truth and existence.

Sense consists in the obtruding of certain impressions upon us, independently of our wills; but it cannot perceive what they are, or whence they are derived. It lies prostrate under its object, and is only a capacity in the soul of having its own state altered by the influence of particular causes. It must therefore remain a stranger to the objects and causes affecting it.

Were not *sense* and *knowledge* entirely different, we should rest satisfied with sensible impressions, such as light, colours, and sounds, and enquire no farther about them, at least when the impressions are strong and vigorous: Whereas, on the contrary, we necessarily desire some farther acquaintance

---

2 The reader is desired to remember that by *ideas*, I mean here almost constantly *simple ideas*, or original and uncompounded perceptions of the mind. That our ideas of right and wrong are of this sort will be particularly observed hereafter. It may also be right to take notice that I all along speak of the understanding, in the most confined and proper sense of it. What gives occasion for observing this is the division which has been made by some writers, of all the powers of the soul into understanding and will; the former comprehending under it all the powers of external and internal sensation, as well as those of judging and reasoning; and the latter, all the affections of the mind, as well as the power of acting and determining.

There may be further some occasion for observing that the two acts of the understanding being intuition and deduction, I have in view the former. 'Tis plain, on the contrary, that those writers, who argue against referring our moral ideas to reason, have generally the latter only in view.

with them, and can never be satisfied till we have subjected them to the survey of reason. Sense presents *particular* forms to the mind; but cannot rise to any *general* ideas. It is the intellect that examines and compares the presented forms, that rises above individuals to universal and abstract ideas; and thus looks downward upon objects, takes in at one view an infinity of particulars, and is capable of discovering general truths. Sense sees only the *outside* of things; reason acquaints itself with their *natures*. Sensation is only a mode of feeling in the mind; but knowledge implies an active and vital energy of the mind. Feeling pain, for example, is the effect of sense; but the understanding is employed when pain itself is made an object of the mind's reflexion, or held up before it, in order to discover its nature and causes. Mere sense can perceive nothing in the most exquisite work of art, suppose a plant or the body of an animal, but what is painted in the eye or what might be described on paper. It is the intellect that must perceive in it order and proportion; variety and regularity; design, connection, art, and power; aptitudes, dependencies, correspondencies, and adjustment of parts so as to subserve an end, and compose one perfect whole; things which can never be represented on a sensible organ, and the ideas of which cannot be passively communicated, or stamped on the mind by the operation of external objects. Sense cannot perceive any of the modes of thinking beings; these can be discovered only by the mind's survey of itself.

In a word, it appears that *sense* and *understanding* are faculties of the soul totally different: The one being conversant only about *particulars*; the other about *universals*: The one not *discerning*, but *suffering*; the other not *suffering*, but *discerning*; and signifying the soul's *Power* of surveying and examining all things, in order to judge of them; which *Power*, perhaps, can hardly be better defined, than by calling it, in *Plato's* language, the power in the soul to which belongs the apprehension of TRUTH. . . .

OF THE ORIGIN OF OUR IDEAS OF MORAL RIGHT AND WRONG

Let us now return to our first enquiry, and apply the foregoing observations to our ideas of *right* and *wrong* in particular.

'Tis a very necessary previous observation, that our ideas of *right* and *wrong* are simple ideas, and must therefore be ascribed to some power of *immediate* perception in the human mind. He that doubts this need only try to give definitions of them, which shall amount to more than synonymous expressions. Most of the confusion in which the question concerning the foundation of morals has been involved has proceeded from inattention to this remark. There are, undoubtedly, some actions that are *ultimately* approved, and for justifying which no reason can be assigned; as there are some ends, which are *ultimately* desired, and for chusing which no reason can be given. Were not this true, there would be an infinite progression of reasons and ends, and therefore nothing could be at all approved or desired.

Supposing, then, that we have a power *immediately* perceiving right and wrong: the point I am now to endeavour to prove, is that this power is the *Understanding*, agreeably to the assertion at the end of the *first* section. I cannot but flatter myself, that the main obstacle to the acknowledgment of this has been already removed, by the observations made in the preceding section, to shew that the understanding is a power of immediate perception, which gives rise to new original ideas; nor do I think it possible that there should have been many disputes on this subject had this been properly considered.

But, in order more explicitly and distinctly to evince what I have asserted (in the only way the nature of the question seems capable of) let me.

First, Observe that it implies no absurdity, but evidently *may* be true. It is undeniable that many of our ideas are derived from our INTUITION of truth, or the discernment of the natures of things by the understanding. This therefore *may* be the source of our moral ideas. It is at least *possible* that *right* and *wrong* may denote what we *understand* and *know* concerning certain objects, in like manner with proportion and disproportion, connexion and repugnancy, contingency and necessity. I will add that nothing has been offered which has any tendency to prove the contrary. All that can appear, from the objections and reasonings of the Author [3] of the *Enquiry into the original of our ideas of beauty and virtue,* is only what has been already observed, and what does not in the least affect the point in debate: Namely, that the words *right* and *wrong*, *fit* and *unfit*, express simple and undeniable ideas. But that the power perceiving them is properly a *sense* and not *reason*; that these ideas denote nothing *true* of actions, nothing in the *nature* of actions; this, he has left entirely without proof. He appears, indeed, to have taken for granted that if virtue and vice are *immediately* perceived, they must be perceptions of an *implanted* sense. But no conclusion could have been more hasty. For will any one take upon him to say that all powers of immediate perception must be arbitrary and implanted; or that there can be no simple ideas denoting any thing besides the qualities and passions of the mind? In short: Whatever some writers have said to the contrary, it is certainly a point not yet decided, that virtue is wholly factitious, and to be *felt* not *understood*.

As there are some propositions, which, when attended to, necessarily determine all minds to *believe* them: And as there are some ends, whose natures are such, that, when perceived, all beings immediately and necessarily *desire* them: So it is very credible that, in like manner, there are some actions whose natures are such, that, when observed, all rational beings immediately and necessarily *approve* them.

I do not at all care what follows from Mr. *Hume's* assertion, that all our ideas are either *impressions, or copies of impressions*: or from Mr. *Locke's* assertion that they are all *deducible from* SENSATION *and* REFLECTION.

---

[3] [*Hutcheson.* — D. D. Raphael]

The first of these assertions is, I think, destitute of all proof; it supposes, when applied in this as well as many other cases, the point in question; and, when pursued to its consequences, ends in the destruction of all truth and the subversion of our intellectual faculties. The other wants much explication to render it consistent with any tolerable account of the original of our moral ideas: Nor does there seem to be any thing necessary to convince a person, that all our ideas are not deducible from sensation and reflexion, except taken in a very large and comprehensive sense, besides considering how Mr. *Locke* derives from them our *moral ideas.* He places them among our ideas of relations, and represents *rectitude* as signifying the conformity of actions to some rules or laws; which rules or laws, he says, are either the *will of God,* the *decrees of the magistrate,* or the *fashion of the country:* From whence it follows, that it is an absurdity to apply *rectitude* to rules and laws themselves; to suppose the *divine* will to be directed by it; or to consider it as *itself* a rule and law. But, it is undoubted, that this great man would have detested these consequences; and, indeed, it is sufficiently evident that he was strangely embarrassed in his notions on this, as well as some other subjects. But,

Secondly, I know of no better way of determining this point, than by referring those who doubt it to common sense, and putting them upon considering the nature of their own perceptions. Could we suppose a person, who, when he perceived an external object, was at a loss to determine whether he perceived it by means of his organs of sight or touch; what better method could be taken to satisfy him? There is no possibility of doubting in any such cases. And it seems not more difficult to determine in the present case.

Were the question, what that perception is, which we have of number, diversity, causation or proportion; and whether our ideas of them signify truth and reality perceived by the understanding, or impressions made by the objects to which we ascribe them, on our minds; were, I say, this the question, would it not be sufficient to appeal to every man's consciousness? These perceptions seem to me to have no greater pretence to be denominated perceptions of the understanding, than *right* and *wrong.*

It is true, some impressions of pleasure or pain, satisfaction or disgust, generally attend our perceptions of virtue and vice. But these are merely their effects and concomitants, and not the perceptions themselves, which ought no more to be confounded with them, than a particular truth (like that for which *Pythagoras* offered a Hecatomb) ought to be confounded with the pleasure that may attend the discovery of it. Some emotion or other accompanies, perhaps, all our perceptions; but more remarkably our perceptions of right and wrong. And this is what has led to the mistake of making them to signify nothing but impressions, which error some have extended to all objects of knowledge; and thus have been led into an extravagant and monstrous scepticism.

But to return; let any one compare the ideas arising from our *powers of sensation,* with those arising from our *intuition of the natures of things,* and enquire which of them his ideas of right and wrong most resemble. On the issue of such a comparison may we safely rest this question. It is scarcely conceivable that any one can impartially attend to the nature of his own perceptions, and determine that, when he thinks gratitude or beneficence to be *right*, he perceives nothing *true* of them, and *understands* nothing, but only receives an impression from a *sense*. Was it possible for a person to question whether his idea of *equality* was gained from sense or intelligence, he might soon be convinced, by considering whether he is not sure that certain lines or figures are *really* equal, and that their equality must be perceived by all minds, as soon as the objects themselves are perceived. In the same manner may we satisfy ourselves concerning the origin of the idea of *right*: For have we not a like consciousness, that we discern the one, as well as the other, *in* certain objects? Upon what possible grounds can we pronounce the one to be *sense*, and the other *reason*? Would not a Being purely intelligent, having happiness within his reach, *approve* of securing it for himself? Would not he *think* this right; and would it not *be* right? When we contemplate the happiness of a species, or of a world, and pronounce concerning the actions of reasonable beings which promote it, that they are *right*; is this judging erroneously? Or is it no determination of judgment at all, but a species of mental taste? Are not such actions *really right*? Or is every apprehension of rectitude in them false and delusive, just as the like apprehension is concerning the effects of external and internal sensation, when taken to belong to the causes producing them?

It seems, beyond contradiction, certain that every being must *desire* happiness for himself; and can those natures of things, from which the *desire* of happiness and *aversion* to misery necessarily arise, leave, at the same time, a rational nature totally indifferent as to any *approbation* of actions procuring the one, or preventing the other? Is there nothing that any *understanding* can perceive to be amiss in a creature's bringing upon himself, or others, calamities and ruin? Is there nothing truly wrong in the absolute and eternal misery of an innocent being? — "It *appears* wrong to us."— And what reason can you have for doubting, whether it appears what *it is?* Should a being, after being flattered with hopes of bliss, and having his expectations raised by encouragements and promises, find himself, without reason, plunged into irretrievable torments; would he not *justly* complain? Would he want a *sense* to cause the idea of *wrong* to arise in his mind? Can goodness, gratitude, and veracity, appear to any mind under the same characters, with cruelty, ingratitude, and treachery? Darkness may as soon appear to be light.

It would, I doubt, be to little purpose to plead further here, the natural and universal apprehensions of mankind, that our ideas of right and wrong belong to the understanding, and denote real characters of actions; because it will be easy to reply that they have a like opinion of the *sensible qualities* of bodies; and that nothing is more common than for men to mistake their own sensations for the properties of the objects producing them, or to apply, to the object itself, what they find always accompanying it, whenever observed. Let it therefore be observed,

Thirdly, That if right and wrong denote effects of sensation, it must imply the greatest absurdity to suppose them applicable to actions: That is, the ideas of *right* and *wrong,* and of *action,* must in this case be incompatible; as much so, as the idea of pleasure and a regular form, or of pain and the collisions of bodies. All sensations, as such, are modes of consciousness, or feelings of a sentient being, which must be of a nature totally different from the particular causes which produce them. A *coloured body,* if we speak accurately, is the same absurdity with a *square sound.* We need no experiments to prove that heat, cold, colours, tastes, etc., are not real qualities of bodies; because the ideas of matter and of these qualities, are incompatible. But is there indeed any such incompatibility between *actions* and *right?* Or any such absurdity in affirming the one of the other? Are the ideas of them as different as the idea of a sensation, and its cause?

On the contrary; the more we enquire, the more indisputable, I imagine, it will appear to us that we express necessary truth, when we say of some actions, they are right; and of others, they are wrong. Some of the most careful enquirers think thus, and find it out of their power not to be persuaded that these are real distinctions belonging to the natures of actions. Can it be so difficult to distinguish between the ideas of sensibility and reason; between the *intuitions of truth* and the *passions of the mind?* Is that a scheme of morals we can be very fond of, which makes our perceptions of moral good and evil in actions and manners to be all vision and fancy? Who can help seeing that right and wrong are as absolutely unintelligible, and void of sense and meaning, when supposed to signify nothing true of actions, no essential, inherent difference between them; as the perceptions of the external and internal senses are, when thought to be properties of the objects that produce them?

How strange would it be to maintain that there is no possibility of *mistaking* with respect to right and wrong; that the apprehensions of all beings, on this subject, are alike just, since all sensation must be alike *true* sensation? Is there a greater absurdity, than to suppose that the *moral rectitude* of an action is nothing absolute and unvarying; but capable, like all the modifications of pleasure and pain, of being intended and remitted, of increasing and lessening, of rising and sinking with the force and liveliness of our feelings? Would it be less ridiculous to suppose this of the relations between given quantities, of the equality of numbers, or the figure of bodies?

In the last place, let it be considered that all actions, undoubtedly, have a *nature.* That is, *some character* certainly belongs to them, and somewhat there is to be *truly* affirmed of them. This may be that some of them are right, others wrong. But if this is not allowed; if no actions are, *in themselves,* either right or wrong, or any thing of a moral and obligatory nature, which can be an object to the understanding; it follows that, in themselves, they *are* all indifferent. This is what is essentially true of them, and this is what all understandings, that perceive right, must perceive them to be. But are we not conscious that we perceive the contrary? And have we not as much reason to believe the contrary, as to believe or trust at all our own discernment?

In other words, every thing having a *nature* or *essence*, from whence such and such truths concerning it necessarily result, and which it is the proper province of the understanding to perceive; it follows that nothing whatever can be exempted from its inspection and sentence, and that of every thought, sentiment, and subject, it is the natural and ultimate judge. *Actions*, therefore, *ends* and *events* are within its province. Of these, as well as all other objects, it belongs to it to judge. What is this judgment? One would think it impossible for any person, without some hesitation and reluctance, to reply that the judgment he forms of them is this: that they are all essentially *indifferent*, and that there is no one thing fitter to be done than another. If this is judging truly, how obvious is it to infer that it signifies not what we do; and that the determination to think otherwise is an imposition upon rational creatures? Why then should they not labour to suppress in themselves this determination, and to extirpate from their natures all the delusive ideas of morality, worth, and virtue? What though the ruin of the world should follow? There would be nothing *really* wrong in this.

A rational agent void of all moral judgment, incapable of perceiving a difference, in respect of fitness and unfitness to be performed, between actions, and acting from blind propensions without any sentiments concerning what he does, is not possible to be imagined. And, do what we will, we shall find it out of our power, in earnest to persuade ourselves, that reason can have no concern in judging of and directing our conduct; or to exclude from our minds all notions of right and wrong in actions.

But what deserves particular consideration here is this. If all actions and all dispositions of beings are in *themselves indifferent*, the all-perfect understanding of the Deity, without doubt, perceives this; and therefore he cannot *approve*, or *disapprove* of any of his own actions, or of the actions of his creatures: The end he pursues, and the manner in which he treats his creatures must appear to him what it *is* — *indifferent*. What foundation then is left for his moral perfections? How can we conceive him to pursue universal happiness as his end, when, at the same time, we suppose nothing *in* the nature of that end to engage the choice of any being? Is it no diminution of his perfect character, to suppose him guided by mere unintelligent inclination, without any direction from reason, or any *moral approbation*?

In short, it seems sufficient to overthrow any scheme, that such consequences, as the following, should arise from it: That no one being can judge one end to be better than another, or believe a real moral difference between actions, without giving his assent to an impossibility; without mistaking the *affections of his own mind for truth*, and *sensation* for *knowledge*. That there being nothing intrinsically proper or improper, just or unjust;

there is nothing *obligatory;* but all beings enjoy, from the reasons of things and the nature of actions, liberty to act as they will.

The following important corollary arises from these arguments:

That morality is *eternal and immutable.*

Right and wrong, it appears, denote what actions *are.* Now whatever any thing *is,* that it is, not by will, or decree, or power, but by *nature and necessity.* Whatever a triangle or circle is, that it is unchangeably and eternally. It depends upon no will or power, whether the three angles of a triangle and two right ones shall be *equal;* whether the periphery of a circle and its diameter shall be *incommensurable;* or whether matter shall be *divisible, movable, passive,* and *inert.* Every object of the understanding has an indivisible and invariable essence; from whence arise its properties, and numberless truths concerning it. Omnipotence does not consist in a power to alter the nature of things, and to destroy necessary truth (for this is contradictory, and would infer the destruction of all wisdom, and knowledge) but in an absolute command over all *particular, external* existences, to create or destroy them, or produce any possible changes among them. The natures of things, then, being immutable, whatever we suppose the natures of actions to be, they must be immutably. If they are indifferent, this indifference is itself immutable, and there neither is nor can be any one thing that, *in reality,* we *ought* to do rather than another. The same is to be said of right and wrong, of moral good and evil, as far as they express *real characters* of actions. They must immutably and necessarily belong to those actions of which they are *truly* affirmed.

No will, therefore, can render *any thing* good and obligatory, which was not so antecedently, and from eternity; or any action right, that is not so in itself; meaning by *action,* not the bare external effect produced, but the ultimate principle of conduct, or the determination of a reasonable being, considered as arising from the perception of some motives and reasons and intended for some end. According to this sense of the word *action,* whenever the principle from which we act is different, the action is different, though the external effects produced, may be the same. If we attend to this, the meaning and truth of what I have just observed, will be easily seen. Put the case of any action, the performance of which is *indifferent,* or attended with no circumstances of the agent that render it better or fitter to be done than omitted. Is it not plain that, *while all things continue the same,* it is as impossible for any will or power to make acting obligatory here, as it is for them to make two equal things unequal without producing any change in either? It is true, the doing of any indifferent thing may become obligatory, in consequence of a command from a being possessed of rightful authority over us: But it is obvious that, in this case, the command produces a change in the circumstances of the agent, and that what, in consequence of it, becomes obligatory, is not the same with what *before* was indifferent. The external effect, that is, the *matter of the action* is indeed the same; but nothing is plainer than that actions, in this sense the same, may in a moral view be totally different according to the ends aimed at by them, and the principles of morality under which they fall.

When an action, otherwise indifferent, becomes obligatory, by being made the subject of a *promise*; we are not to imagine that our own will or breath alters the nature of things by making what is indifferent not so. But what was indifferent *before* the promise is still so; and it cannot be supposed that, *after* the promise, it becomes obligatory, without a contradiction. All that the promise does is to alter the connexion of a particular effect; or to cause that to be an *instance* of right conduct which was not so before. There are no effects producible by us, which may not, in this manner, fall under different principles of morality; acquire connexions sometimes with happiness, and sometimes with misery; and thus stand in different relations to the eternal rules of duty.

The objection, therefore, to what is here asserted, taken from the effects of positive laws and promises, has no weight. It appears that when an obligation to particular indifferent actions arises from the command of the Deity, or positive laws, it is by no means to be inferred from hence, that obligation is the creature of will, or that the nature of what is indifferent is changed: Nothing then becoming obligatory, which was not so from eternity; that is, *obeying the divine will, and just authority*. And had there been nothing right in this, had there been no reason from the natures of things for obeying God's will; it is certain, it could have induced no obligation, nor at all influenced an intellectual nature as such. Will and laws signify nothing, abstracted from something previous to them, in the character of the lawgiver and the relations of beings to one another, to give them force and render disobedience a crime. If mere will ever obliged, what reason can be given why the will of one being should oblige, and of another not; why it should not oblige alike to every thing it requires; and why there should be any difference between *power* and *authority?* It is truth and reason, then, that, in all cases, oblige, and not mere will. So far, we see, is it from being possible that any will or laws should *create* right; that they can have no effect, but in virtue of natural and antecedent right.

Thus, then, is morality fixed on an immovable *basis*, and appears not to be, in any sense, *factitious*; or the *arbitrary production* of any power human or divine; but *equally everlasting* and *necessary* with all *truth* and *reason*. And this we find to be as evident, as that right and wrong signify a *reality* in what is so denominated.

QUESTIONS

1. Price represents Hutcheson as holding that our moral opinions are the result of "an implanted and arbitrary principle by which a relish is given us for certain moral objects . . . and aversion to others," and Price infers that Hutcheson is committed to thinking that "moral right and wrong signify nothing in the objects themselves." Is this inference correct?

2. Why does Price say that "is wrong" cannot mean "is forbidden by God"?
3. What does it mean to say it is the "understanding" which perceives the differences of right and wrong?
4. It has been held, by Locke and others, that if a person has a *simple* concept, there must have been an example of it in the content of his sense experience. Explain what this means by some examples, and cite some instances which Price adduces as evidence that this thesis is not true.
5. Does Price believe that there are instances, outside of ethics, where there is knowledge, by the understanding, of propositions involving these simple concepts, which could not be known by observation? Cite an example.
6. Price represents Hutcheson as saying that since virtue and vice are immediately perceived, they must be perceptions of an "implanted sense." Explain this reasoning in your own words. How does Price's view enable him to avoid the inference?
7. What inferences does Price think are properly drawn from the fact that emotions are often present when moral judgments are made?
8. Which one of Price's arguments to establish that moral judgments are intellectual insights into necessary truth do you find most convincing?
9. Does Price's view have the consequence that moral principles are objective, valid for all rational beings?
10. Suppose two individuals of equal intelligence and moral insight have conflicting ethical beliefs. Would this fact be a difficulty for Price? Does his theory tell us any way to decide which of such beliefs is correct?

Sir William David Ross (1877-   )

CONTEMPORARY RATIONALISM IN ETHICS

W. D. Ross, whose work we have discussed before (p. 119), is a contemporary philosopher whose metaethical views are very similar to those of Price. Ross is by no means the only one. G. E. Moore, C. D. Broad, E. F. Carritt, A. C. Ewing, and, with some qualifications, N. Hartmann are included among other distinguished philosophers who subscribe essentially to the nonnaturalist theory. Hastings Rashdall and above all Henry Sidgwick should also be named as very distinguished philosophers of a slightly earlier period whose theories were the same. Altogether the roster of nonnaturalists is very impressive.

The following selection from Ross does not differ markedly from Price in any way. With Price, Ross believes that ethical properties are unobservable and ethical judgments not capable of being confirmed by the methods of natural science; and he thinks that there is, nevertheless, ethical knowledge. What this selec-

tion adds is some interesting suggestions about ethical knowledge — about whether we see the truth of general principles
first and then draw inferences about particular cases or whether
it is the other way about. There are other points of comparable
subtlety. Not all of the philosophers of the same general persuasion would agree with him on all the points he makes.

From W. D. Ross, *Foundations of Ethics*, published by The
Clarendon Press, Oxford, 1939, and reprinted with their permission.

THE FOUNDATION OF ETHICS

THE KNOWLEDGE OF WHAT IS RIGHT

I turn next to the epistemological questions connected with
duty. Can we be said to *know* our duty? And if we can, how do we acquire
this knowledge? I will start with a simple case. I am walking along the
street, and I see a blind man at a loss to get across the street through the
stream of traffic. I probably do not ask myself what I ought to do, but more
or less instinctively take him by the arm and pilot him across. But if afterwards I stop to ask whether I have done what I ought, I shall almost
certainly say 'Yes'; and if for any reason I ask myself, before doing the act,
whether I ought to do it, I shall give the same answer. Now it is clear that
it is in virtue of my thinking the act to have some other character that I think
I ought to do it. Rightness is always a resultant attribute, an attribute
that an act has because it has another attribute. It is not an attribute that
its subject is just directly perceived in experience to have, as I perceive
a particular extended patch to be yellow, or a particular noise to be loud.
No doubt there are causes which cause this patch to be yellow, or that noise
to be loud; but I can perceive the one to be yellow, or the other to be
loud, without knowing anything of the causes that account for this. I see
the attributes in question to attach to the subjects merely as these subjects,
not as subjects of such and such a character. On the other hand, it is only
by knowing or thinking my act to have a particular character, out of the
many that it in fact has, that I know or think it to be right. It is, among other
things, the directing of a physical body in a certain direction, but I never
dream that it is right in consequence of that. I think that it is right because it
is the relieving of a human being from distress. Now it seems at first sight to
follow from this that our perception of the particular duty follows from the
perception of a general duty to relieve human beings in distress. And,
generalizing, we might feel inclined to say that our perception of particular
duties is always an act of inference, in which the major premiss is some
general moral principle. And no doubt my grasp of the principle that I
should relieve human beings in distress precedes my grasp of the fact that
I should relieve this blind man, since up to this moment I may not have
known of the existence of this man, and certainly did not know of his

desire to cross this particular street; while I certainly had at least a latent awareness of the general principle, an awareness which the occurrence of *any* instance falling under the principle might call into activity — just as I have a latent knowledge of the laws of arithmetic or of English grammar before I proceed to make up my accounts or to write a letter.

Yet it will not do to make our perception of particular duties essentially inference from general principles. For it may, I suppose, be taken for granted that man was a practical being before he became a theoretical one, and that in particular he answered somehow the question how he ought to behave in particular circumstances, before he engaged in general speculation on the principles of duty. No doubt there was an earlier stage still, when men in fact did right acts without ever asking whether they were right, when, for instance, they helped one another in distress without thinking of any duty to do so. We see disinterested help being given by men to one another every day, without any thought of duty. Aristotle puts the point simply:

Parent seems by nature to feel friendship for offspring and offspring for parent, not only among men but among birds and among most animals; it is felt mutually by members of the same race, and especially by men. . . . We may see even in our travels how near and dear every man is to every other.[1]

Butler puts the matter more eloquently:

There is such a natural principle of attraction in man towards man, that having trod the same tract of land, having breathed in the same climate, barely having been born in the same artificial district or division, becomes the occasion of contracting acquaintances and familiarities many years after: for any thing may serve the purpose. Thus relations merely nominal are sought and invented, not by governors, but by the lowest of the people; which are found sufficient to hold mankind together in little fraternities and copartnerships: weak ties indeed, and what may afford fund enough for ridicule, if they are absurdly considered as the real principles of that union: but they are in truth merely the occasions, as any thing may be of any thing, upon which our nature carries us on according to its own previous bent and bias; which occasions therefore would be nothing at all, were there not this prior disposition and bias of nature.[2]

Aristotle's reference is perhaps the more interesting, in two respects. In the first place, it takes the practice of disinterested aid further back in time, by asserting its existence not merely among men, but among animals. He opens up the vista of the development of disinterested action, as it exists in man, from the instinctive co-operation of the members of an animal community. And secondly, he points to what is much the most striking and universal example of disinterested action, the operation of parental love, from which perhaps all disinterested action may be supposed to have developed.

In such action, in its earliest form, there was no thought of duty. We

[1] *Eth. Nic.* 1155 a 16-22.
[2] Sermon I (Gladstone's ed.), 38-9.

must suppose that when a certain degree of mental maturity had been reached, and a certain amount of attention had been, for whatever reason, focused on acts which had hitherto been done without any thought of their rightness, they came to be recognized, first rather vaguely as *suitable* to the situation, and then, with more urgency, as *called for* by the situation. *Thus* first, as belonging to particular acts in virtue of a particular character they possessed, was rightness recognized. Their rightness was not deduced from any general principle; rather the general principle was later recognized by intuitive induction as being implied in the judgements already passed on particular acts.

The question may, however, be asked: 'Once the general principles have been reached, are particular acts recognized as right by deduction from general principles, or by direct reflection on the acts as particular acts having a certain character?' Do we, without seeing directly that the particular act is right, read off its rightness from the general principle, or do we directly see its rightness? Either would be a possible account of what happens. But when I reflect on my own attitude towards particular acts, I seem to find that it is not by deduction but by direct insight that I see them to be right, or wrong. I never seem to be in the position of not seeing directly the rightness of a particular act of kindness, for instance, and of having to read this off from a general principle — 'all acts of kindness are right, and therefore this must be, though I cannot see its rightness directly.'

It appears to me that we apprehend individual facts by deduction from general principles in two kinds of situation, and in no more. (1) We may have no real insight that the attribute A implies the presence of the attribute B. But we may have accepted on what we believe to be good grounds the *belief* that A always implies B, and we then may say to ourselves, 'This is an instance of A, and therefore it must be an instance of B; I cannot see it for myself to be so, but I think it must be, because of a general principle which I have for good reason accepted.' Or (2) the general principle may be one that is not self-evident, but known as the consequence of a proof; and we may remember the principle while we have forgotten the proof. There again, we shall not see with self-evidence that the particular A is also a B, but we shall read this conclusion off from the remembered general principle 'all A is B.'

Both these situations actually occur in morals. (1) In most people's lives there is a stage at which they accept some moral principle on authority before they have really come to recognize its truth for themselves; and in such a case the rightness or wrongness of the particular act is not apprehended on its own merits but read off from the general principle. The suggestion is indeed sometimes made that we never pass beyond this stage of acceptance of moral principles on authority to a fresh original recognition of them. But the difficulty at once arises, that the reference to authority either lands us in an infinite regress, or leads back to *some one* who recognized the principle for himself. A may believe it because B said it was true, and *B* because *C* said it was true, but sooner or later we come to some one who believed it on its merits. Further, I think we can by careful introspection distinguish the acceptance of a moral principle on authority from its acceptance on its own merits, as we can distinguish the stage at which we accepted mathematical principles on our teacher's authority from that at which we came to recognize their truth for ourselves. It is probably the case that many people all through their lives remain in the condition of accepting most of their moral principles on authority, but we can hardly fail to recognize in the best and most enlightened of men an absolutely original and direct insight into moral principles, and in many others the power of seeing for themselves the truth of moral principles when these are pointed out to them. There is really no more reason to doubt this than to doubt that there are people who can grasp mathematical principles and proofs for themselves.

(2) The other situation in which we read off the rightness of particular acts from some general principle also arises. The general principle may have been accepted not on authority but on its merits, but it may have involved for its recognition a fairly elaborate consideration of the probable consequences of a certain type of act; this would be true of such a principle as the principle that indiscriminate charity is wrong. In such a case the rightness or wrongness of an individual act falling under such a description is by no means self-evident. It would involve for its recognition a tracing out of the probable consequences, which we in fact do not perform; but we remember the general principle, while we have forgotten, or do not take the time to recollect, the arguments for it; and so we read off the rightness or wrongness of the particular act from it.

Our insight into the basic principles of morality is not of this order. When we consider a particular act as a lie, or as the breaking of a promise, or as a gratuitous infliction of pain, we do not need to, and do not, fall back on a remembered general principle; we see the individual act to be by its very nature wrong.

QUESTIONS

1. Why does Ross call rightness a "resultant attribute"? Why does this fact make it a temptation to say that we perceive our particular obligations by inference from general moral principles?
2. Why does he reject the view that we *always* know our particular obligations by such inference? In which special types of case does he think we do know them by inference?
3. Is there any sense in which, according to Ross, there is evidence for the general principles of morals?

Peter F. Strawson (1919-)
PUZZLES FOR INTUITIONISTS

Nonnaturalists, of the kinds represented by the preceding selections, were the dominant party among moral philosophers in the first decades of the present century. However, the party has long been a target of fire from naturalist quarters, and after the middle 1930's the criticism became more intense when a new philosophical group — the noncognitivists — appeared and joined the naturalists in attack on the common enemy. As a result, nonnaturalists today, rightly or wrongly, appear to feel very much on the defensive.

One of the most persuasive among recent critics is P. F. Strawson, a fellow of University College, Oxford. Strawson is the author of an influential book on logic, *Introduction to Logical Theory* (1952), and of a book on metaphysics, *Individuals* (1959).

P. F. Strawson, "Ethical Intuitionism," *Philosophy*, Vol. 24, No. 88 (January, 1949) pp. 23-33. Reprinted by kind permission of the author and of the editor of *Philosophy*.

ETHICAL INTUITIONISM

NORTH What is the trouble about moral facts? When someone denies that there is an objective moral order, or asserts that ethical propositions are pseudo-propositions, cannot I refute him (rather as Moore refuted those who denied the existence of the external world) by saying: "You know very well that Brown did wrong in beating his wife. You know very well that you ought to keep promises. You know very well that human affection is good and cruelty bad, that many actions are wrong and some are right"?

WEST Isn't the trouble about moral facts another case of trouble about knowing, about learning? We find out facts about the external world by looking and listening; about ourselves, by feeling; about other people, by looking and listening *and* feeling. When this is noticed, there arises a wish to say that the facts *are* what is seen, what is heard, what is felt; and, consequently, that moral facts fall into one of these classes. So those who have denied that there are "objective moral characteristics" have not wanted to deny that Brown's action was wrong or that keeping promises is right. They have wanted to point out that rightness and wrongness are a matter of what is felt in the heart, not of what is seen with the eyes or heard with the ears. They have wanted to emphasize the way in which "Promise-keeping is right" resembles "Going abroad is exciting," "Stories about mothers-in-law are comic," "Bombs are terrifying"; and differs from "Roses are red" and "Sea-water is salt." This does not prevent you from talking about the moral order, or the moral world, if you want to; but it warns you not to forget that the only access to the moral world is through remorse and approval and so on; just as the only access to the world of comedy is through laughter; and the only access to the coward's world is through fear.

NORTH   I agree, of course, that we cannot see the goodness of something as we see its colour, or identify rightness by the sense of touch; though I think you should add that the senses are indispensable as a means of our becoming aware of those characteristics upon which moral characteristics depend. You may be partly right, too, in saying that access to the moral world is obtained through experience of the moral emotions; for it may be that only when our moral feelings have been strongly stirred do we first become clearly aware of the characteristics which evoke these feelings. But these feelings are not identical with that awareness. "Goodness" does not stand to "feeling approval," "guilt" to "feeling guilty," "obligation" to "feeling bound," as "excitingness" stands to "being excited" and "humorousness" to "feeling amused." To use the jargon for a moment: moral characteristics and relations are non-empirical, and awareness of them is neither sensory nor introspectual. It is a different kind of awareness, which the specialists call "intuition": and it is only empiricist prejudice which prevents your acknowledging its existence. Once acknowledged, it solves our problems: and we see that while "Promise-keeping is right" differs from "The sea is salt," this is not because it resembles "Detective-stories are exciting"; it differs from *both* in being the report neither of a sensible nor an introspectible experience, but of an intuition. We may, perhaps, know some moral characteristics mediately, through others. ("Obligation" is, perhaps, definable in terms of "goodness.") But at least one such characteristic — rightness or goodness — is unanalysable, and known by intuition alone. The fundamental cognitive situation in morals is that in which we intuit the rightness of a particular action or the goodness of a particular state of affairs. We see this moral characteristic as present in virtue of some other characteristics, themselves capable of being described in empirical terms, which the action or state of affairs possesses. (This is why I said that sense-perception is a necessary, though not a sufficient, condition of obtaining information about the moral order.) Our intuition, then, is not a bare intuition of the moral characteristic, but also the intuition of its dependence on some others: so that this fundamental situation yields us, by intuitive induction, knowledge of moral rules, generalizations regarding the right and the good, which we can apply in other cases, even when an actual intuition is lacking. So much do these rules become taken for granted, a part of our habitual moral life, that most of our everyday moral judgments involve merely an implicit reference to them [1]: a reference which becomes explicit only if the judgment is challenged or queried. Moral emotions, too, assume the character of habitual reactions. But emotions and judgments alike are grounded upon intuitions. Emotion may be the gatekeeper to the moral world; but intuition is the gate.

WEST   Not so fast. I understand you to say that at least one fundamental moral characteristic — rightness or goodness — is unanalysable. Perhaps both are. The experts are divided. In any case, the fundamental characteristic (or characteristics) can be known only by intuitive awareness of its presence in some particular contemplated action or state of affairs. There is, then, a kind of analogy between the word "right" (or "good") and the name of some simple sensible characteristic such as "red." [2] Just as everybody who understands the word "red" has seen some red things, so everybody who understands the word "right" or the word "good" has intuited the character, rightness, in some actions, or the character, goodness, in some states of affairs; and nobody who has not intuited these characters understands the words "right" or "good." But this is not quite enough, is it? In order for me to know *now* the meaning of an indefinable word, it is not enough that a certain perceptual or intuitional event should have occurred at some particular point in my history; for I might not only have forgotten the details of that event; I might have forgotten what *kind* of an event it was; I might not know *now* what it would be like for such an event to occur. If the word "red" expresses an indefinable visual concept, then it is self-contradictory to say: "I know what the word 'red' means, but I can't remember ever *seeing* red and I don't know what it would be *like* to see red." Similarly, if the word "right," or the word "good," expresses an indefinable intuitive concept, then it is self-contradictory to say: "I know what the word 'right' or the word 'good' means, but I can't remember ever *intuiting* rightness or goodness, and I don't know what it would be *like* to intuit rightness or goodness." If your theory is true, then this statement is a contradiction.

But it is not at all obvious to me that it is a contradiction. I should be quite prepared to assert that I understood the words "right" and "good," but that I couldn't remember ever intuiting rightness or goodness and that I couldn't imagine what it would be like to do so. And I think it is quite certain that I am not alone in this, but that there are a large number of people who are to be presumed capable of accurate reporting of their own cognitive experience, and who would find nothing self-contradictory in saying what I say. And if this is so, you are presented with a choice of two possibilities. The first is that the words "right" and "good" have quite a different meaning for one set of people from the meaning which they have

---

[1] Cf. D. Daiches Raphael, *The Moral Sense*, Chapters V and VI.
[2] Cf. G. E. Moore, *Principia Ethica*, p. 7 *et seq.*

for another set. But neither of us believes this. The second is that the intuitionist theory is a mistake; that the phrase "intuitional event having a moral characteristic as its object (or a part of its object)" is a phrase which describes nothing at all; or describes misleadingly the kind of emotional experience we both admit. There is no third possibility. It is no good saying: "All people who succeed in learning the meaning of moral words do as a matter of fact have moral intuitions, but unfortunately many people are inclined to forget them, to be quite unable to remember what they are like." True, there would be nothing self-contradictory in saying this: but it would simply be a variant of the first possibility; for I cannot be said to know *now* the meaning of a word expressing an intuitive concept unless I know now what it would be like to intuit the characteristic of which it is a concept. The trouble with your intuitionist theory is that, if true, it should be a truism. There should be no doubt about the occurrence of the distinctive experience of intuiting rightness (or goodness), and about its being the only way to learn the meaning of the primary moral words; just as there is no doubt about the occurrence of seeing red (or blue), and about this being the only way to learn the meaning of the primary colour words. But there *is* doubt; and over against this doubt there rises a certainty: the certainty that we all know what it is to *feel* guilty, to *feel* bound, to *feel* approving.

NORTH What I have said *is* a truism; and that is its strength. It is not I who am inventing a mythical faculty, but you, irritated, perhaps, by the language of intuitionism, who are denying the obvious. When you said that you couldn't *imagine* what it would be like to have moral intuitions, isn't it clear that you wanted "intuiting a moral characteristic" to be like seeing a colour or hearing a sound? Naturally you couldn't *imagine* anything of the sort. But I have already pointed out that moral characteristics are dependent on others of which the presence *is* ascertainable by looking and listening. You do not intuit rightness or goodness independently of the other features of the situation. You intuit *that* an action is (or would be) right, a state of affairs good, *because* it has (or would have) certain other empirically ascertainable qualities. The total content of your intuition includes the "because" clause. Of course, our ordinary moral judgments register unreflective reactions. Nevertheless "This act is right (or this state of affairs is good) because it has P, Q, R" — where "P, Q, R" stand for such empirically ascertainable qualities — expresses the type of fundamental cognitive situation in ethics, of which our normal judgments are copies, mediated by habit, but ready, if challenged, to become explicit as their original. Consider what happens when someone dissents from your opinion. You produce reasons. And this is not a matter of accounting for an emotional condition; but of bringing evidence in support of a verdict.

WEST When the jury brings in a verdict of guilty on a charge of murder, they do so because the facts adduced in evidence are of the kind covered by the definition of "murder." When the chemical analyst concludes that the material submitted for analysis is a salt, he does so because it exhibits the defining properties of a salt. The evidence is the sort of thing that is *meant* by "murder," by "salt." But the fundamental moral word, or words, you say, cannot be defined; their concepts are unanalysable. So it cannot be in this way that the "because" clause of your ethical sentence functions as evidence. "X is a right action because it is a case of promise-keeping" does not work like "X is a salt because it is a compound of basic and acid radicals"; for, if "right" is indefinable, "X is right" does not *mean* "X is an act of promise-keeping or of relieving distress or of telling the truth or . . ."

When I say "It will be fine in the morning; for the evening sky is red," the evidence is of a different sort. For I might observe the fine morning without having noticed the state of the evening sky. But you have rightly stressed the point that there is no *independent* awareness of *moral* qualities: that they are always "seen" as dependent on those other features mentioned in the "because" clause. So it is not in this way, either, that the "because" clause of your ethical sentence functions as evidence. And there is no other way. Generally, we may say that whenever q is evidence for p, *either* q is the sort of thing we mean by "p" ("p" is definable in terms of "q") *or* we can have knowledge of the state of affairs described by "p" independently of knowledge of the state of affairs described by "q." But neither of these conditions is satisfied by the q, the "because" clause, of your ethical sentence.

The "because" clause, then, does not, as you said it did, constitute evidence for the ethical judgment. And this, it seems to me, should be a serious matter for you. For where is such evidence to be found? It is no good saying that, after all, the ethical judgments of other people (or your own at other times) may corroborate your own present judgment. They may agree with it: but their agreement strengthens the probability of your judgment only on the assumption that their moral intuitions tend on the whole to be correct. But the only possible evidence for the existence of a *tendency* to have correct intuitions is the correctness of *actual* intuitions. And it is precisely the correctness of actual intuitions for which we are seeking evidence, and failing to find it.

And evidence you must have, if your account of the matter is correct. You will scarcely say that ethical intuitions are infallible; for ethical disagreements may survive the resolution of factual disagreements. (You might, of course, say that *genuine* intuitions were infallible: then the problem becomes one of finding a criterion for distinguishing between the genuine ones and those false claimants that carry the same inner conviction.) So your use of the language of "unanalysable predicates ascribed in moral judgment to particular actions and states of affairs" leads to contradiction. For to call such a judgment "non-infallible" would be meaningless unless there were some way of checking it; of confirming or confuting it, by producing evidence for or against it. But I have just shown that your account of these judgments is incompatible with the possibility of producing evidence for or against them. So, if your account is true, these judgments are both corrigible and incorrigible; and this is absurd.

But the absurdity points to the solution. Of course these judgments are corrigible: but not in the way in which the diagnosis of a doctor is corrigible; rather in the way in which the musical taste of a child is corrigible. Correcting them is not a matter of *producing evidence* for them or their contraries, though it is (partly) a matter of *giving reasons* for them or their contraries. We say, warningly, that ethical judgments are corrigible, because ethical disagreement sometimes survives the resolution of factual disagreement. We say, encouragingly, that ethical judgments are corrigible, because the resolution of factual disagreement sometimes leads to the resolution of ethical disagreement. But the one kind of agreement leads (when it *does* lead) to the other, not in the way in which agreed evidence leads to an agreed conclusion, but in the way in which common experience leads to sympathy. The two kinds of agreement, the two kinds of judgment, are as different as chalk from cheese. Ordinary language can accommodate the difference without strain: it is the pseudo-precise philosophical use of "judgment" which slurs over the difference and raises the difficulty. Is it not clear, then, what people have meant when they said that ethical disagreements were like disagreements in taste, in choice, in practical attitude? [3] Of course, as you said, when we produce our reasons, we are not often simply giving the causes of our emotional condition. But neither are we producing evidence for a verdict, for a moral diagnosis. We are using the facts to back our attitudes, to appeal to the capacity of others to feel as we feel, to respond as we respond.

NORTH   I think I see now what you have been leaving out all the time. First, you accused me of inventing a mythical faculty to give us ethical knowledge. Then, when I pointed out that ethical qualities are not intuited out of all relation to other empirically ascertainable features of actions and states of affairs, but are intuited as dependent upon these, you twisted this dependence out of all recognition. You wanted to make it like the causal dependence of a psychological disposition upon some empirical feature of its object: as a child's fondness for strawberries depends upon their sweetness. But the connection between wrongness and giving pain to others is not an accident of our constitution; nor does its perception require any special faculty—but *simply that which we use in all our reasoning.* From the fact that an action involves inflicting needless pain upon others, *it follows* necessarily that the action is wrong, just as, from the fact that a triangle is equilateral, it follows necessarily that its angles are equal. This is the kind of dependence that we intuit; not an analytic dependence, but a synthetic

---

[3] Cf. Charles Stevenson, *Ethics and Language,* Chapter 1.

entailment; and this is why the "because" clause of my ethical sentence does, after all, constitute evidence for the ascription of the moral characteristic.

I can anticipate the obvious objection. No moral rule, you will say, no moral generalization concerning the rightness of acts or the goodness of conditions, holds without exception. It is always possible to envisage circumstances in which the generalization breaks down. Or, if the generalization is so wide that no counter-example can be found, if it can be so interpreted as to cover every case, then it has become too wide: it has become tautologous, like "It is always right to do that which will have the best results on the whole," or intolerably vague, like "It is always right to treat people as ends in themselves" or "The greatest good is the greatest general welfare." It is plainly not with the help of such recipes as these that we find out what is right, what is good, in a particular case. There are no criteria for the meaning of "treating a man as an end," for "the greatest general welfare," which do not presuppose the narrower criteria of rightness and goodness of which I spoke and which seem always to have exceptions. All this is true. But it calls only for a trifling amendment to those narrower criteria. We cannot, for example, assert, as a necessary synthetic proposition, "All acts of promise-keeping are right" or "All states of aesthetic enjoyment are good." But we *can* assert, as a necessary synthetic proposition, "All acts of promise-keeping *tend as such* to be right (or have *prima facie* rightness)" [4] or "All states of aesthetic enjoyment *tend as such* to be good." And we derive our knowledge of such general necessary connections from seeing, in particular cases, that the rightness of an action, the goodness of a state, *follows from* its being an action or state of a certain kind.

WEST   Your "trifling amendment" is a destructive one. When we say of swans that they tend to be white, we are not ascribing a certain quality, namely "tending to be white," to each individual swan. We are saying that the number of swans which are white exceeds the number of those which are not, that if anything is a swan, the chances are that it will be white. When we say "Welshmen tend to be good singers," we mean that most Welshmen sing well; and when we say, of an *individual* Welshman, that *he* tends to sing well, we mean that he sings well more often than not. In all such cases, we are talking of a *class* of things or occasions or events; and saying, not that *all* members of the class have the property of *tending-to-have* a certain characteristic, but that *most* members of the class do in fact have that characteristic. Nobody would accept the claim that a sentence of the form "*Most* As are Bs" expresses a necessary proposition. Is the claim made more plausible by re-writing the proposition in the form "*All* As *tend to be* Bs"?

But, waiving this point, there remains the difficulty that the need for

[4] Ross, *Foundations of Ethics*, pp. 83-86; Broad, "Some of the Main Problems of Ethics," *Philosophy*, 1946, p. 117.

such an amendment to our moral generalizations is incompatible with the account you gave of the way in which we come to know both the moral characteristics of individual actions and states, and the moral generalizations themselves. You said that we intuited the moral characteristic as *following from* some empirically ascertainable features of the action or state. True, if we did so, we should have implicitly learnt a moral generalization: but it would be one asserting *without qualification* the entailment of the moral characteristic by these other features of the case. In other words, and to take your instance, if it *ever* follows, from the fact that an act has the empirically ascertainable features described by the phrase "being an act of promise-keeping," that the act is right, then it *always* follows, from the fact that an act is of this kind, that it has this moral quality. If, then, it is true that we intuit moral characteristics as thus "following from" others, it is false that the implied generalizations require the "trifling amendment"; and if it is true that they require the amendment, it is false that we so intuit moral characteristics.[5]

And this is all that need be said of that rationalist superstition according to which a quasi-logical necessity binds moral predicates to others. "Le coeur a ses raisons, que la raison ne connaît pas": this is the whole truth of the matter: but your attention was so riveted to the first half of it that you forgot the second.

Looking for a logical nexus where there was none to be found, you overlooked the logical relations of the ethical words among themselves. And so you forgot what has often enough been pointed out: that for every expression containing the words "right" or "good," used in their ethical senses, it is always possible to find an expression with the same meaning, but containing, instead of these, the word "ought." The equivalences are various, and the variations subtle; but they are always to be found. For one to say, for example, "I know where the good lies, I know what the right course is; but I don't know the end I *ought* to aim at, the course I *ought* to follow" would be self-contradictory. "Right"-sentences, "good"-sentences are shorthand for "ought"-sentences. And this is enough in itself to explode the myth of unanalysable characteristics designated by the indefinable predicates,

---

[5] One desperate expedient might occur to North. He might say that it is not the bare presence of the promise-keeping feature that entails the rightness of the act, but the presence of this feature, coupled with the absence of any features which would entail its wrongness. His general rules would then be, not of the form " 'x has ϕ' entails 'x is right,' " but of the form " 'x has ϕ and x has no Ψ such that "x has Ψ" entails "x is wrong" ' entails 'x is right.' " But the suggestion is inadmissible, since (i) the establishment of the general proposition "x has no Ψ, etc." would require the enumeration of all those features which would make it wrong to keep a promise, and (ii) any rule of the form " 'x has Ψ entails 'x is wrong' " would require expansion in exactly the same way as the "right-making" rule; which would involve an infinite regress of such expansions. Besides having this *theoretical* defect, the suggested model is, of course, *practically* absurd.

"right" and "good." For "ought" is a *relational* word; whereas "right" and "good" are *predicative*. The simplest sentences containing "ought" are syntactically more complicated than the simplest sentences containing "right" or "good." And hence, since the equivalences of meaning hold, the various ethical usages of "right" and "good" *are all definable*: variously definable in terms of "ought."

Of course this last consideration alone is not decisive against intuitionism. If this were all, you could still re-form the ranks: taking your stand on an intuited unanalysable non-natural *relation* of obligation, and admitting the definability of the ethical predicates in terms of this relation. But the objections I have already raised apply with equal force against this modified position; and, in other ways, its weakness is more obvious.[6]

NORTH   Well, then, suppose we agree to bury intuitionism. What have you to offer in its place? Has any analysis of moral judgments in terms of feeling ever been suggested which was not monstrously paradoxical or artificial? Even the simplest ethical sentence obstinately resists translation: and not in the way in which "Life, like a dome of many-coloured glass, Stains the white radiance of eternity" resists translation. For the ethical language is not the language of the poets, but the language of all the world. Somehow justice must be done both to this irreducible element of significance in ethical sentences, and to the community of knowledge of their correct, their appropriate, use. Intuitionism, at any rate, was a way of attempting to do this.

WEST   Yes, intuitionism was a way of attempting to do this. It started from the fact that thousands and thousands of people can say, with perfect propriety: "I know that this is right, that is good"; and ended, as we have seen, by making it inexplicable how anybody could ever say such a thing. This was because of a failure to notice that the whole sentence, including

---

[6] E.g. There was a certain plausibility in saying "My feeling morally obliged to pursue such a course (or end) presupposes my believing that it is right (or good)," and thence concluding that this belief cannot be "reduced to" the feeling which it arouses. (For examples of this sort of argument, see Ross, *op. cit.*, pp. 261-262, and Broad, *op. cit.*, p. 115.) But the weakness of the reasoning is more clearly exposed when the sentence is re-written as "My feeling morally obliged to pursue such a course presupposes my believing that I *am* morally obliged to pursue it." The point is that "presupposes" and "believing" are both ambiguous. If "presupposes" means "causally requires" and "believing" is used in its ordinary sense, then it is obviously false that the beliefs which *occasion* such a feeling invariably include some belief which would be correctly described in these terms. (Compare: "My feeling frightened presupposes my believing that I am frightened.") But the argument begins to have weight against the "analysability" of beliefs correctly so described only if they are invariably present as occasioning factors. If, on the other hand, "presupposes" means "logically requires," then "believing" might be used in a queer sense such that the sentence is *tautologically* true. But this result is secured only by defining "believing" (used in this sense) in terms of feeling (compare the sense in which "thinking x funny" means "being amused by x"): and this was precisely the result which North sought to avoid.

the "I know," and not just the last word in the subordinate clause, is a unit of the ethical language; and, following upon this failure, a feverish ransacking of the drawers of a Theory of Knowledge for an "I know" which would fit. (Do I, perhaps, work it out like the answer to a sum?)

The man who attempts to provide a translation sees more than this. He sees, at any rate, that the sentence must be treated as a unit. His error is to think that he can find a substitute, in a different language, which will serve the same purpose. So long as he confines himself to describing how, in what sort of circumstances, the sentence is used, he does valuable work. He errs when he talks as if to say how a sentence is used is the same as to use it. The man who says he can translate ethical sentences into feeling sentences makes the same sort of mistake as some who said they could (if they had time) translate material-object sentences into sentences about actual and possible sense-experiences. What they *mean* — the commentary they are making on the use of the ethical language or the material-object language — is correct. And it is precisely because the commentary would be incorrect as a translation that it is useful as a commentary. For it brings out the fact that the irreducibility of these languages arises from the systematic vagueness of the notation they use in comparison with that of the commentary-languages, and not from their being used to talk of, to describe, different things from those of which the commentary-languages talk. This descriptive vagueness is no defect: it is what makes these languages useful for the kinds of communication (and persuasion) for which they are severally required. But by being mistaken for something more than it is, it leads to one kind of metaphysics: the metaphysics of substance (the thing-in-itself), or of intuited unanalysable ethical characteristics. And by being ignored altogether, it leads to another kind of metaphysics: the tough metaphysics of translation, the brutal suggestion that we could get along just as well without the ethical language. Neither metaphysics — neither the tender metaphysics of ultimacy, nor the tough metaphysics of reduction [7] — does justice to the facts: but the latter does them less injustice; for it doesn't seek to supplement them with a fairy-tale.

And so the alternative to intuitionism is not the provision of translations. For the communication and sharing of our moral experience, we must use the tools, the ethical language, we have. No sentences provided by the philosopher will take their place. His task is not to supply a new set of tools, but to describe what it is that is communicated and shared, and how the tools are used to do the work. And though the experience he describes is emotional experience, his descriptions are not like those of the psychologist. The psychologist is concerned with the relation of these experiences to others of a different sort; the philosopher is concerned with their relation to the ordinary use of ethical language. Of course, then, it would be

[7] Cf. Wisdom, "Metaphysics and Verification," *Mind*, 1938.

absurd for the philosopher to deny that some actions are right (fair, legit-imate, etc.) and others wrong (unfair, illegitimate, etc.), and that we know this; and absurd to claim that we can say what such sentences say without using such words. For this *is* the language we use in sharing and shaping our moral experience; and the occurrence of experience so shared, so shaped, is not brought into question.

We are in the position of the careful phenomenalist; who, for all his emphasis on sense-experience, neither denies that there is a table in the dining-room, nor claims to be able to assert this without using such words as "dining-room" and "table." A phenomenalism as careful as this has been said to forfeit the right to be called a "philosophical doctrine." [8] Then let the title be reserved for the productions of those who rest in myth or par-adox, and fail to complete that journey, from the familiar to the familiar, [9] which is philosophical analysis.

QUESTIONS

1. Why would some people be dissatisfied with saying that we know that promise-keeping is right in much the way in which we know that going abroad is exciting and that promise-keeping and going abroad are the same kind of facts? How would nonnaturalists say that knowing a moral fact differs from knowing that going abroad is exciting?
2. Why does Strawson conclude that the nonnaturalist must, in consistency, say that a person can know the meaning of "right" (and other ethical terms) only if he remembers what it is like to be aware of the rightness of something? Do you remember intuiting the rightness of an action?
3. Is Strawson right in suggesting that the meaning of such terms as "right" is tied to experiences of feeling guilty, feeling bound, feeling approval?
4. Strawson says that the nonnaturalist account of moral insight is incompatible with the possibility of supporting a moral judgment by evidence, even though he admits we might in some sense support "You ought to do so-and-so" by saying "Because you promised." How is this? Is it because "having promised" doesn't have the logical relation to "you ought to" which evidence bears to conclusions in logic or science?
5. Is his suggestion plausible that the "evidence" in morals supports the con-clusion only in the way in which "common experience leads to sympathy" — as an appeal to the capacity of others to feel as we feel?
6. How may the nonnaturalist avoid these inferences by his conception of syn-thetic entailment — by comparing moral insight to insight that anything that is red is colored or extended in space? Why is it a difficulty for this answer that *not every* instance of promise-keeping, for example, is right?
7. Strawson says that ethical language is used to communicate and share our

[8] Hardie, "The Paradox of Phenomenalism," *Proceedings of the Aristotelian Society*, 1945-46, p. 150.
[9] Wisdom.

moral experience and that the philosopher's job is to describe what is communicated and shared and the way the tools are used to do this job. Where, then, does he think both naturalist and nonnaturalist are mistaken?

Alfred Jules Ayer (1910-   )

A PURELY EMOTIVE THEORY

A. J. Ayer was a student of Christchurch College, Oxford, and received his B.A. from Oxford University in 1932. Immediately thereafter he was appointed fellow and lecturer in philosophy at Christchurch. In 1946 he became professor of philosophy at the University of London, a post he resigned in 1959 to accept a professorship at Oxford. His books have included *Language, Truth and Logic* (1936), *Foundations of Empirical Knowledge* (1940), *Philosophical Essays* (1954), and *The Problem of Knowledge* (1956).

Ayer advocated vigorously, in his first book, the view that ethical statements are neither true nor false and that their function is to express the attitudes of the speaker, like exclamations, and to arouse feelings and stimulate action in auditors, like commands. Ayer's proposal was not the first of this type in the present century. But, because Ayer writes with extraordinary lucidity and force, and because the discussion appeared in the context of a defense of "logical empiricism" in general, and because the whole book was in a crusading spirit with an optimistic "let's finally set things straight in philosophy" tone, his proposal attracted a vast amount of attention.

The reader should pay particular attention to the reasoning which purports to dispose of naturalism and nonnaturalism; he should also note that Ayer's positive theory is by no means the only possible view if both naturalism and nonnaturalism are false. The selections that follow represent other possible forms of noncognitivist theory.

From *Language, Truth and Logic* by A. J. Ayer. Reprinted by permission of Dover Publications, Inc., New York 14, New York. Also published by Victor Gollancz, London, 1936, and reprinted with their permission.

LANGUAGE, TRUTH AND LOGIC

CRITIQUE OF ETHICS

There is still one objection to be met before we can claim to have justified our view that all synthetic propositions are empirical hypotheses. This objection is based on the common supposition that our speculative knowledge is of two distinct kinds — that which relates to questions of empirical fact, and that which relates to questions of value. It will be said that "statements of value" are genuine synthetic propositions, but that they cannot with any show of justice be represented as hypotheses, which are used to predict the course of our sensations; and, accordingly, that the existence of ethics and æsthetics as branches of speculative knowledge presents an insuperable objection to our radical empiricist thesis.

In face of this objection, it is our business to give an account of "judgements of value" which is both satisfactory in itself and consistent with our general empiricist principles. We shall set ourselves to show that in so far as statements of value are significant, they are ordinary "scientific" statements; and that in so far as they are not scientific, they are not in the literal sense significant, but are simply expressions of emotion which can be neither true nor false. In maintaining this view, we may confine ourselves for the present to the case of ethical statements. What is said about them will be found to apply, *mutatis mutandis*, to the case of æsthetic statements also.

The ordinary system of ethics, as elaborated in the works of ethical philosophers, is very far from being a homogeneous whole. Not only is it apt to contain pieces of metaphysics, and analyses of non-ethical concepts: its actual ethical contents are themselves of very different kinds. We may divide them, indeed, into four main classes. There are, first of all, propositions which express definitions of ethical terms, or judgements about the legitimacy or possibility of certain definitions. Secondly, there are propositions describing the phenomena of moral experience, and their causes. Thirdly, there are exhortations to moral virtue. And, lastly, there are actual ethical judgements. It is unfortunately the case that the distinction between these four classes, plain as it is, is commonly ignored by ethical philosophers; with the result that it is often very difficult to tell from their works what it is that they are seeking to discover or prove.

In fact, it is easy to see that only the first of our four classes, namely that which comprises the propositions relating to the definitions of ethical terms, can be said to constitute ethical philosophy. The propositions which describe the phenomena of moral experience, and their causes, must be assigned to the science of psychology, or sociology. The exhortations to moral virtue are not propositions at all, but ejaculations or commands which are designed to provoke the reader to action of a certain sort. Accordingly, they do not belong to any branch of philosophy or science. As for the expressions of ethical judgements, we have not yet determined how they should be classified. But inasmuch as they are certainly neither definitions nor comments upon definitions, nor quotations, we may say decisively that they do not belong to ethical philosophy. A strictly philosophical treatise on ethics should therefore make no ethical pronouncements. But it should, by giving an analysis of ethical terms, show what is the category to which all such pronouncements belong. And this is what we are now about to do.

A question which is often discussed by ethical philosophers is whether it is possible to find definitions which would reduce all ethical terms to one or two fundamental terms. But this question, though it undeniably belongs to ethical philosophy, is not relevant to our present enquiry. We are not now concerned to discover which term, within the sphere of ethical terms, is to be taken as fundamental; whether, for example, "good" can be defined in terms of "right" or "right" in terms of "good," or both in terms of "value." What we are interested in is the possibility of reducing the whole sphere of ethical terms to non-ethical terms. We are enquiring whether statements of ethical value can be translated into statements of empirical fact.

That they can be so translated is the contention of those ethical philosophers who are commonly called subjectivists, and of those who are known as utilitarians. For the utilitarian defines the rightness of actions, and the goodness of ends, in terms of the pleasure, or happiness, or satisfaction, to which they give rise; the subjectivist, in terms of the feelings of approval which a certain person, or group of people, has towards them. Each of these types of definition makes moral judgements into a sub-class of psychological or sociological judgements; and for this reason they are very attractive to us. For, if either was correct, it would follow that ethical assertions were not generically different from the factual assertions which are ordinarily contrasted with them; and the account which we have already given of empirical hypotheses would apply to them also.

Nevertheless we shall not adopt either a subjectivist or a utilitarian analysis of ethical terms. We reject the subjectivist view that to call an action right, or a thing good, is to say that it is generally approved of, because it is not self-contradictory to assert that some actions which are generally approved of are not right, or that some things which are generally approved of are not good. And we reject the alternative subjectivist view that a man who asserts that a certain action is right, or that a certain thing is good, is saying that he himself approves of it, on the ground that a man who confessed that he sometimes approved of what was bad or wrong would not be contradicting himself. And a similar argument is fatal to utilitarianism. We cannot agree that to call an action right is to say that of all the actions possible in the circumstances it would cause, or be likely to cause, the greatest happiness, or the greatest balance of pleasure over pain, or the greatest balance of satisfied over unsatisfied desire, because we find that it is not self-contradictory to say that it is sometimes wrong to perform the action which would actually or probably cause the greatest happiness, or the greatest balance of pleasure over pain, or of satisfied over unsatisfied desire. And since it is not self-contradictory to say that some pleasant things are not good, or that some bad things are desired, it cannot be the case that the sentence "x is good" is equivalent to "x is pleasant," or to "x is desired." And to every other variant of utilitarianism with which I am acquainted the same objection can be made. And therefore we should, I think, conclude that the validity of ethical judgements is not determined by the felicific tendencies of actions, any more than by the nature of people's feelings; but that it must be regarded as "absolute" or "intrinsic," and not empirically calculable.

If we say this, we are not, of course, denying that it is possible to invent a language in which all ethical symbols are definable in non-ethical terms, or even that it is desirable to invent such a language and adopt it in place of our own; what we are denying is that the suggested reduction of ethical to non-ethical statements is consistent with the conventions of our actual language. That is, we reject utilitarianism and subjectivism, not as proposals to replace our existing ethical notions by new ones, but as analyses of our existing ethical notions. Our contention is simply that, in our language, sentences which contain normative ethical symbols are not equivalent to sentences which express psychological propositions, or indeed empirical propositions of any kind.

It is advisable here to make it plain that it is only normative ethical symbols, and not descriptive ethical symbols, that are held by us to be indefinable in factual terms. There is a danger of confusing these two types of symbols, because they are commonly constituted by signs of the same sensible form. Thus a complex sign of the form "x is wrong" may constitute a sentence which expresses a moral judgement concerning a certain type of conduct, or it may constitute a sentence which states that a certain type of conduct is repugnant to the moral sense of a particular society. In the latter case, the symbol "wrong" is a descriptive ethical symbol, and the sentence in which it occurs expresses an ordinary sociological proposition; in the former case, the symbol "wrong" is a normative ethical symbol, and the sentence in which it occurs does not, we maintain, express an empirical proposition at all. It is only with normative ethics that we are at present concerned; so that whenever ethical symbols are used in the course of this argument without qualification, they are always to be interpreted as symbols of the normative type.

In admitting that normative ethical concepts are irreducible to empirical concepts, we seem to be leaving the way clear for the "absolutist" view of ethics — that is, the view that statements of value are not controlled by observation, as ordinary empirical propositions are, but only by a mysterious "intellectual intuition." A feature of this theory, which is seldom recognized by its advocates, is that it makes statements of value unverifiable. For it is notorious that what seems intuitively certain to one person may seem doubtful, or even false, to another. So that unless it is possible to provide some criterion by which one may decide between conflicting intuitions, a mere appeal to intuition is worthless as a test of a proposition's validity. But in the case of moral judgements, no such criterion can be given. Some moralists claim to settle the matter by saying that they "know" that their own moral judgements are correct. But such an assertion is of purely psychological interest, and has not the slightest tendency to prove the validity of any moral judgement. For dissentient moralists may equally well "know" that their ethical views are correct. And, as far as subjective certainty goes, there will be nothing to choose between them. When such differences of opinion arise in connection with an ordinary empirical proposition, one may attempt to resolve them by referring to, or actually carrying out, some relevant empirical test. But with regard to ethical statements, there is, on the "absolutist" or "intuitionist" theory, no relevant empirical test. We are therefore justified in saying that on this theory ethical statements are held to be unverifiable. They are, of course, also held to be genuine synthetic propositions.

Considering the use which we have made of the principle that a synthetic proposition is significant only if it is empirically verifiable, it is clear that the acceptance of an "absolutist" theory of ethics would undermine the whole of our main argument. And as we have already rejected the "naturalistic" theories which are commonly supposed to provide the only alternative to "absolutism" in ethics, we seem to have reached a difficult position. We shall meet the difficulty by showing that the correct treatment of ethical statements is afforded by a third theory, which is wholly compatible with our radical empiricism.

We begin by admitting that the fundamental ethical concepts are unanalysable, inasmuch as there is no criterion by which one can test the validity of the judgements in which they occur. So far we are in agreement with the absolutists. But, unlike the absolutists, we are able to give an explanation of this fact about ethical concepts. We say that the reason why they are unanalysable is that they are mere pseudo-concepts. The presence of an ethical symbol in a proposition adds nothing to its factual content. Thus if I say to someone, "You acted wrongly in stealing that money," I am not stating anything more than if I had simply said, "You stole that money." In adding that this action is wrong I am not making any further statement about it. I am simply evincing my moral disapproval of it. It is as if I had said, "You stole that money," in a peculiar tone of horror, or written it with the addition of some special exclamation marks. The tone, or the exclamation marks, adds nothing to the literal meaning of the sentence. It merely serves to show that the expression of it is attended by certain feelings in the speaker.

If now I generalise my previous statement and say, "Stealing money is wrong," I produce a sentence which has no factual meaning — that is, expresses no proposition which can be either true or false. It is as if I had written "Stealing money!!" — where the shape and thickness of the exclamation marks show, by a suitable convention, that a special sort of moral disapproval is the feeling which is being expressed. It is clear that there is nothing said here which can be true or false. Another man may disagree with me about the wrongness of stealing, in the sense that he may not have the same feelings about stealing as I have, and he may quarrel with me on account of my moral sentiments. But he cannot, strictly speaking, contradict me. For in saying that a certain type of action is right or wrong, I am not making any factual statement, not even a statement about my own state of mind. I am merely expressing certain moral sentiments. And the man who is ostensibly contradicting me is merely expressing his moral sentiments. So that there is plainly no sense in asking which of us is in the right. For neither of us is asserting a genuine proposition.

What we have just been saying about the symbol "wrong" applies to all normative ethical symbols. Sometimes they occur in sentences which record ordinary empirical facts besides expressing ethical feeling about those facts: sometimes they occur in sentences which simply express ethical feeling about a certain type of action, or situation, without making any statement of fact. But in every case in which one would commonly be said to be making an ethical judgement, the function of the relevant ethical word is purely "emotive." It is used to express feeling about certain objects, but not to make any assertion about them.

It is worth mentioning that ethical terms do not serve only to express feeling. They are calculated also to arouse feeling, and so to stimulate action. Indeed some of them are used in such a way as to give the sentences in which they occur the effect of commands. Thus the sentence "It is your duty to tell the truth" may be regarded both as the expression of a certain sort of ethical feeling about truthfulness and as the expression of the command "Tell the truth." The sentence "You ought to tell the truth" also involves the command "Tell the truth," but here the tone of the command is less emphatic. In the sentence "It is good to tell the truth" the command has become little more than a suggestion. And thus the "meaning" of the word "good," in its ethical usage, is differentiated from that of the word "duty" or the word "ought." In fact we may define the meaning of the various ethical words in terms both of the different feelings they are ordinarily taken to express, and also the different responses which they are calculated to provoke.

We can now see why it is impossible to find a criterion for determining the validity of ethical judgements. It is not because they have an "absolute" validity which is mysteriously independent of ordinary sense-experience, but because they have no objective validity whatsoever. If a sentence makes no statement at all, there is obviously no sense in asking whether what it says is true or false. And we have seen that sentences which simply express moral judgements do not say anything. They are pure expressions of feeling and as such do not come under the category of truth and falsehood. They are unverifiable for the same reason as a cry of pain or a word of command is unverifiable — because they do not express genuine propositions.

Thus, although our theory of ethics might fairly be said to be radically subjectivist, it differs in a very important respect from the orthodox subjectivist theory. For the orthodox subjectivist does not deny, as we do, that the sentences of a moralizer express genuine propositions. All he denies is that they express propositions of a unique non-empirical character. His own view is that they express propositions about the speaker's feelings. If this were so, ethical judgements clearly would be capable of being true or false. They would be true if the speaker had the relevant feelings, and false if he had not. And this is a matter which is, in principle, empirically verifiable. Furthermore they could be significantly contradicted. For if I say, "Tolerance is a virtue," and someone answers, "You don't approve of it," he would, on the ordinary subjectivist theory, be contradicting me. On our theory, he would not be contradicting me, because, in saying that tolerance was a virtue, I should not be making any statement about my own feelings or about anything else. I should simply be evincing my feelings, which is not at all the same thing as saying that I have them.

The distinction between the expression of feeling and the assertion of feeling is complicated by the fact that the assertion that one has a certain feeling often accompanies the expression of that feeling, and is then, indeed, a factor in the expression of that feeling. Thus I may simultaneously express boredom and say that I am bored, and in that case my utterance of the words, "I am bored," is one of the circumstances which make it true to say that I am expressing or evincing boredom. But I can express boredom without actually saying that I am bored. I can express it by my tone and gestures, while making a statement about something wholly unconnected with it, or by an ejaculation, or without uttering any words at all. So that even if the assertion that one has a certain feeling always involves the expression of that feeling, the expression of a feeling assuredly does not always involve the assertion that one has it. And this is the important point to grasp in considering the distinction between our theory and the ordinary subjectivist theory. For whereas the subjectivist holds that ethical statements actually assert the existence of certain feelings, we hold that ethical statements are expressions and excitants of feeling which do not necessarily involve any assertions.

We have already remarked that the main objection to the ordinary subjectivist theory is that the validity of ethical judgements is not determined by the nature of their author's feelings. And this is an objection which our theory escapes. For it does not imply that the existence of any feelings is a necessary and sufficient condition of the validity of an ethical judgement. It implies, on the contrary, that ethical judgements have no validity.

There is, however, a celebrated argument against subjectivist theories which our theory does not escape. It has been pointed out by Moore that if ethical statements were simply statements about the speaker's feelings, it would be impossible to argue about questions of value.[1] To take a typical example: if a man said that thrift was a virtue, and another replied that it was a vice, they would not, on this theory, be disputing with one another. One would be saying that he approved of thrift, and the other that *he* didn't; and there is no reason why both these statements should not be true. Now Moore held it to be obvious that we do dispute about questions of value, and accordingly concluded that the particular form of subjectivism which he was discussing was false.

It is plain that the conclusion that it is impossible to dispute about questions of value follows from our theory also. For as we hold that such sentences as "Thrift is a virtue" and "Thrift is a vice" do not express propositions at all, we clearly cannot hold that they express incompatible propositions. We must therefore admit that if Moore's argument really refutes the ordinary subjectivist theory, it also refutes ours. But, in fact, we deny that it does refute even the ordinary subjectivist theory. For we hold that one really never does dispute about questions of value.

This may seem, at first sight, to be a very paradoxical assertion. For we certainly do engage in disputes which are ordinarily regarded as disputes about questions of value. But, in all such cases, we find, if we consider the matter closely, that the dispute is not really about a question of value, but about a question of fact. When someone disagrees with us about the moral value of a certain action or type of action, we do admittedly resort to argument in order to win him over to our way of thinking. But we do not attempt to show by our arguments that he has the "wrong" ethical feeling towards a situation whose nature he has correctly apprehended. What we attempt to show is that he is mistaken about the facts of the case. We argue that he has misconceived the agent's motive: or that he has misjudged the effects of the action, or its probable effects in view of the agent's knowledge; or that he has failed to take into account the special circumstances in which the agent was placed. Or else we employ more general arguments about the effects which actions of a certain type tend to produce, or the qualities which are usually manifested in their performance. We do this in the hope that we have only to get our opponent to agree with us about the nature of the empirical facts for him to adopt the same moral attitude towards them as we do. And as the people with whom we argue have generally received the same moral education as ourselves, and live in the same social order, our expectation is usually justified. But if our opponent happens to have undergone a different process of moral "conditioning" from ourselves, so that, even when he acknowledges all the facts, he still disagrees with us about the moral value of the actions under discussion, then we abandon the attempt to convince him by argument. We

---

[1] Cf. *Philosophical Studies*, "The Nature of Moral Philosophy."

say that it is impossible to argue with him because he has a distorted or undeveloped moral sense; which signifies merely that he employs a different set of values from our own. We feel that our own system of values is superior, and therefore speak in such derogatory terms of his. But we cannot bring forward any arguments to show that our system is superior. For our judgement that it is so is itself a judgement of value, and accordingly outside the scope of argument. It is because argument fails us when we come to deal with pure questions of value, as distinct from questions of fact, that we finally resort to mere abuse.

In short, we find that argument is possible on moral questions only if some system of values is presupposed. If our opponent concurs with us in expressing moral disapproval of all actions of a given type *t*, then we may get him to condemn a particular action A, by bringing forward arguments to show that A is of type *t*. For the question whether A does or does not belong to that type is a plain question of fact. Given that a man has certain moral principles, we argue that he must, in order to be consistent, react morally to certain things in a certain way. What we do not and cannot argue about is the validity of these moral principles. We merely praise or condemn them in the light of our own feelings.

If anyone doubts the accuracy of this account of moral disputes, let him try to construct even an imaginary argument on a question of value which does not reduce itself to an argument about a question of logic or about an empirical matter of fact. I am confident that he will not succeed in producing a single example. And if that is the case, he must allow that its involving the impossibility of purely ethical arguments is not, as Moore thought, a ground of objection to our theory, but rather a point in favour of it.

Having upheld our theory against the only criticism which appeared to threaten it, we may now use it to define the nature of all ethical enquiries. We find that ethical philosophy consists simply in saying that ethical concepts are pseudo-concepts and therefore unanalysable. The further task of describing the different feelings that the different ethical terms are used to express, and the different reactions that they customarily provoke, is a task for the psychologist. There cannot be such a thing as ethical science, if by ethical science one means the elaboration of a "true" system of morals. For we have seen that, as ethical judgements are mere expressions of feeling, there can be no way of determining the validity of any ethical system, and, indeed, no sense in asking whether any such system is true. All that one may legitimately enquire in this connection is, What are the moral habits of a given person or group of people, and what causes them to have precisely those habits and feelings? And this enquiry falls wholly within the scope of the existing social sciences.

It appears, then, that ethics, as a branch of knowledge, is nothing more than a department of psychology and sociology. And in case anyone thinks that we are overlooking the existence of casuistry, we may remark that casuistry is not a science, but is a purely analytical investigation of the structure of a given moral system. In other words, it is an exercise in formal logic.

When one comes to pursue the psychological enquiries which constitute ethical science, one is immediately enabled to account for the Kantian and hedonistic theories of morals. For one finds that one of the chief causes of moral behaviour is fear, both conscious and unconscious, of a god's displeasure, and fear of the enmity of society. And this, indeed, is the reason why moral precepts present themselves to some people as "categorical" commands. And one finds, also, that the moral code of a society is partly determined by the beliefs of that society concerning the conditions of its own happiness — or, in other words, that a society tends to encourage or discourage a given type of conduct by the use of moral sanctions according as it appears to promote or detract from the contentment of the society as a whole. And this is the reason why altruism is recommended in most moral codes and egotism condemned. It is from the observation of this connection between morality and happiness that hedonistic or eudæmonistic theories of morals ultimately spring, just as the moral theory of Kant is based on the fact, previously explained, that moral precepts have for some people the force of inexorable commands. As each of these theories ignores the fact which lies at the root of the other, both may be criticized as being onesided; but this is not the main objection to either of them. Their essential defect is that they treat propositions which refer to the causes and attributes of our ethical feelings as if they were definitions of ethical concepts. And thus they fail to recognise that ethical concepts are pseudo-concepts and consequently indefinable.

As we have already said, our conclusions about the nature of ethics apply to æsthetics also. Æsthetic terms are used in exactly the same way as ethical terms. Such æsthetic words as "beautiful" and "hideous" are employed, as ethical words are employed, not to make statements of fact, but simply to express certain feelings and evoke a certain response. It follows, as in ethics, that there is no sense in attributing objective validity to æsthetic judgements, and no possibility of arguing about questions of value in æsthetics, but only about questions of fact. A scientific treatment of æsthetics would show us what in general were the causes of æsthetic feeling, why various societies produced and admired the works of art they did, why taste varies as it does within a given society, and so forth. And these are ordinary psychological or sociological questions. They have, of course, little or nothing to do with æsthetic criticism as we understand it. But that is because the purpose of æsthetic criticism is not so much to give knowledge as to communicate emotion. The critic, by calling attention to certain features of the work under review, and expressing his own feelings about them, endeavours to make us share his attitude towards the work as a whole. The only relevant propositions that he formulates are propositions describing the nature of the work. And these are plain records of fact. We conclude, therefore, that there is nothing in æsthetics, any more than there is in ethics, to justify the view that it embodies a unique type of knowledge.

QUESTIONS

1. What might one infer, from Ayer's first two paragraphs, is the general "empiricist" thesis of his book?
2. Of Ayer's four classes of material into which ordinary ethical discussions fall, which one corresponds to what we have called "normative ethics" and which to "metaethics"?
3. By what argument does Ayer refute utilitarian and subjectivist definitions of ethical terms? Does he give any clue how one is to decide whether one is contradicting one's self? Is Ayer's thesis necessarily contradictory to Perry's view (pp. 277-81)?
4. What distinction does Ayer draw between "normative" and "descriptive" ethical symbols?
5. Why does he reject intuitionist (or rationalist) nonnaturalism?
6. In what sense does "That's right" fail to contradict "That's not right," according to Ayer?
7. In what sense do ethical statements "express" feelings, according to him? What else do they do?
8. What does he say is the difference between "good" and "duty"?
9. Why does he think his theory superior to that form of subjectivism which says ethical statements make assertions about the feelings of the speaker?
10. In defending his view that ethical statements do not strictly contradict each other, do you think Ayer need go on to affirm that people do not "dispute" questions of value? Is he right in saying that we never aim to show, in an ethical discussion, that the other party has the "wrong" ethical feeling toward a situation? Would he be better off merely to claim that empirical evidence can never establish any such conclusion?

Charles Leslie Stevenson   (1908-   )

DISAGREEMENT IN ATTITUDE
CENTRAL TO ETHICS

C. L. Stevenson received his undergraduate education at Yale University. He then went to Cambridge University, where he took a second B.A. degree, with specialized work in philosophy; later he was granted a Ph.D. degree by Harvard. He has taught at Harvard, Yale, and the University of Michigan, where he is now professor of philosophy.

Stevenson developed in great detail a theory somewhat similar to Ayer's and is generally regarded as the leading figure among those defending some form of "emotive theory" in ethics. His major work on ethics is *Ethics and Language* (1944).

Stevenson's theory differs from Ayer's partly in being much more careful about details and partly in being qualified in such a way as to avoid some obvious objections; but it also differs in having another focus. The central idea of the theory is that there are disagreements in attitude — such as liking opposing disliking, or admiration opposing contempt — and that these disagreements are central to ethical disagreements. Indeed, having an ethical opinion is essentially just having an attitude toward something, according to him. In consequence, ethical opinions cannot be supported by evidence in the manner in which this support is possible in science; hence "ethical reasoning" is not giving evidence but offering "supporting" facts in the looser sense of considerations which tend to make people change their attitudes — ; such "reasoning" may be nothing more than emotionally charged rhetoric or prestige-suggestion. Stevenson's view of ethical language is that it is a tool which we use to express our attitudes and which can be used to mold the attitudes of others because of its emotional associations. He concedes to naturalists that their definitions may be right for some uses of some people; but this fact does not make it possible to resolve ethical disagreements definitively by observation and the methods of science; for people can always change their meanings, and in any case the cognitive meanings of ethical words tend to differ from one person to another. Since the central element in an ethical disagreement is disagreement in attitude, what you must really do, in order to get an opponent to agree with you ethically, is change his attitudes; nothing short of this measure really terminates an ethical controversy.

C. L. Stevenson, "The Nature of Ethical Disagreement," *Sigma*, Vols. 1-2, Nos. 8-9 (1947-48). Reprinted by the kind permission of the author and of the Centro di Metodologia, Milan, Italy, the publishers.

THE NATURE OF ETHICAL DISAGREEMENT

When people disagree about the value of something — one saying that it is good or right, and another that it is bad or wrong — by what methods of argument or inquiry can their disagreement be resolved? Can it be resolved by the methods of science, or does it require methods of some other kind, or is it open to no rational solution at all?

The question must be clarified before it can be answered. And the word that is particularly in need of clarification, as we shall see, is the word "disagreement."

Let us begin by noting that "disagreement" has two broad senses: In the first sense it refers to what I shall call "disagreement in belief." This occurs when Mr. A believes *p*, when Mr. B believes *not-p*, or something incompatible with *p*, and when neither is content to let the belief of the other remain unchallenged. Thus doctors may disagree in belief about the causes of an illness; and friends may disagree in belief about the exact date on which they last met.

In the second sense, the word refers to what I shall call "disagreement in attitude." This occurs when Mr. A has a favorable attitude to something, when Mr. B has an unfavorable or less favorable attitude to it, and when neither is content to let the other's attitude remain unchanged. The term "attitude" is here used in much the same sense that R. B. Perry uses "interest"; it designates any psychological disposition of being *for* or *against* something. Hence love and hate are relatively specific kinds of attitudes, as are approval and disapproval, and so on.

This second sense can be illustrated in this way: Two men are planning to have dinner together. One is particularly anxious to eat at a certain restaurant, but the other doesn't like it. Temporarily, then, the men cannot "agree" on where to dine. Their argument may be trivial, and perhaps only half serious; but in any case it represents a disagreement *in attitude*. The men have divergent preferences, and each is trying to redirect the preference of the other.

Further examples are readily found. Mrs. Smith wishes to cultivate only the four hundred; Mr. Smith is loyal to his old poker-playing friends. They accordingly disagree, in attitude, about whom to invite to their party. The progressive mayor wants modern school-buildings and large parks; the older citizens are against these "newfangled" ways; so they disagree on civic policy. These cases differ from the one about the restaurant only in that the clash of attitudes is more serious, and may lead to more vigorous argument.

The difference between the two senses of "disagreement" is essentially this: the first involves an opposition of beliefs, both of which cannot be true, and the second involves an opposition of attitudes, both of which cannot be satisfied.

Let us apply this distinction to a case that will sharpen it. Mr. A believes that most voters will favor a proposed tax, and Mr. B disagrees with him. The disagreement concerns attitudes — those of the voters — but note that A and B are *not* disagreeing in attitude. Their disagreement is *in belief about* attitudes. It is simply a special kind of disagreement in belief, differing from disagreement in belief about head colds only with regard to subject matter. It implies not an opposition of the actual attitudes of the speakers, but only of their beliefs about certain attitudes. Disagreement *in* attitude, on the other hand, implies that the very attitudes of the speakers are opposed. A and B may have opposed beliefs about attitudes without having opposed attitudes, just as they may have opposed beliefs about head colds without having opposed head colds. Hence we must not, from the fact that an argument is concerned with attitudes, infer that it necessarily involves disagreement *in* attitude.

We may now turn more directly to disagreement about values, with particular reference to normative ethics. When people argue about what is good, do they disagree in belief, or do they disagree in attitude? A long tradition of ethical theorists strongly suggest, whether they always intend to or not, that the disagreement is one *in belief*. Naturalistic theorists, for instance, identify an ethical judgment with some sort of scientific statement, and so make normative ethics a branch of science. Now a scientific argument typically exemplifies disagreement in belief, and if an ethical argument is simply a scientific one, then it too exemplifies disagreement in belief. The usual naturalistic theories of ethics that stress attitudes — such as those of Hume, Westermarck, Perry, Richards, and so many others — stress disagreement in belief no less than the rest. They imply, of course, that disagreement about what is good is disagreement *in belief* about attitudes; but we have seen that that is simply one sort of disagreement in belief, and by no means the same as disagreement *in* attitude. Analyses that stress disagreement *in* attitude are extremely rare.

If ethical arguments, as we encounter them in everyday life, involved disagreement in belief exclusively — whether the beliefs were about attitudes or about something else — then I should have no quarrel with the ordinary sort of naturalistic analysis. Normative judgments could be taken as scientific statements, and amenable to the usual scientific proof. But a moment's attention will readily show that disagreement in belief has not the exclusive role that theory has so repeatedly ascribed to it. It must be readily granted that ethical arguments usually involve disagreement in belief; but they *also* involve disagreement in attitude. And the conspicuous role of disagreement in attitude is what we usually take, whether we realize it or not, as the distinguishing feature of ethical arguments. For example:

Suppose that the representative of a union urges that the wage level in a given company ought to be higher — that it is only right that the workers receive more pay. The company representative urges in reply that the workers ought to receive no more than they get. Such an argument clearly represents a disagreement in attitude. The union is *for* higher wages; the company is *against* them, and neither is content to let the other's attitude remain unchanged. *In addition* to this disagreement in attitude, of course, the argument may represent no little disagreement in belief. Perhaps the parties disagree about how much the cost of living has risen, and how much the workers are suffering under the present wage scale. Or perhaps they disagree about the company's earnings, and the extent to which the company could raise wages and still operate at a profit. Like any typical ethical argument, then, this argument involves both disagreement in attitude and disagreement in belief.

It is easy to see, however, that the disagreement in attitude plays a unifying and predominating rôle in the argument. This is so in two ways:

In the first place, disagreement in attitude determines what beliefs are *relevant* to the argument. Suppose that the company affirms that the wage scale of fifty years ago was far lower than it is now. The union will immediately urge that this contention, even though true, is irrelevant. And it is irrelevant simply because information about the wage level of fifty years ago, maintained under totally different circumstances, is not likely to affect the present attitudes of either party. To be relevant, any belief that is introduced into the argument must be one that is likely to lead one side or the other to have a different attitude, and so reconcile disagreement in attitude. Attitudes are often functions of beliefs. We often change our attitudes to something when we change our beliefs about it; just as a child ceases to *want* to touch a live coal when he comes to *believe* that it will burn him. Thus in the present argument, any beliefs that are at all likely to alter attitudes, such as those about the increasing cost of living or the financial state of the company, will be considered by both sides to be relevant to the argument. Agreement in belief on these matters may lead to agreement in attitude toward the wage scale. But beliefs that are likely to alter the attitudes of neither side will be declared irrelevant. They will have no bearing on the disagreement in attitude, with which both parties are primarily concerned.

In the second place, ethical argument usually terminates when disagreement in attitude terminates, even though a certain amount of disagreement in belief remains. Suppose, for instance, that the company and the union continue to disagree in belief about the increasing cost of living, but that the company, even so, ends by favoring the higher wage scale. The union will then be content to end the argument, and will cease to press its point about living costs. It may bring up that point again, in some future argument of the same sort, or in urging the righteousness of its victory to the newspaper columnists; but for the moment the fact that the company has agreed in attitude is sufficient to terminate the argument. On the other hand: suppose that both parties agreed on all beliefs that were introduced into the argument, but even so continued to disagree in attitude. In that case neither party would feel that their dispute had been successfully terminated. They might look for other beliefs that could be introduced into the argument. They might use words to play on each other's emotions. They might agree (in attitude) to submit the case to arbitration, both feeling that a decision, even if strongly adverse to one party or the other, would be preferable to a continued impasse. Or, perhaps, they might abandon hope of settling their dispute by any peaceable means.

In many other cases, of course, men discuss ethical topics without having the strong, uncompromising attitudes that the present example has illustrated. They are often as much concerned with redirecting their own attitudes, in the light of greater knowledge, as with redirecting the attitudes of others. And the attitudes involved are often altruistic, rather than selfish. Yet the above example will serve, so long as that is understood, to suggest the nature of ethical disagreement. Both disagreement in attitude and disagreement in belief are involved, but the former predominates in that (1) it determines what sort of disagreement in belief is relevantly disputed in a given ethical argument, and (2) it determines, by its continued presence or its resolution, whether or not the argument has been settled. We may see further how intimately the two sorts of disagreement are related: since attitudes are often functions of beliefs, an agreement in belief may lead people, as a matter of psychological fact, to agree in attitude.

Having discussed disagreement, we may turn to the broad question that was first mentioned, namely: By what methods or argument or inquiry may disagreement about matters of value be resolved?

It will be obvious that to whatever extent an argument involves disagreement in belief, it is open to the usual methods of the sciences. If these methods are the *only* rational methods for supporting beliefs — as I believe to be so, but cannot now take time to discuss — then scientific methods are the only rational methods for resolving the disagreement in *belief* that arguments about values may include.

But if science is granted an undisputed sway in reconciling beliefs, it does not thereby acquire, without qualification, an undisputed sway in reconciling attitudes. We have seen that arguments about values include disagreement in attitude, no less than disagreement in belief, and that in certain ways the disagreement in attitude predominates. By what methods shall the latter sort of disagreement be resolved?

The methods of science are still available for that purpose, but only in an indirect way. Initially, these methods have only to do with establishing agreement in belief. If they serve further to establish agreement in attitude, that will be due simply to the psychological fact that altered beliefs may cause altered attitudes. Hence scientific methods are conclusive in ending arguments about values only to the extent that their success in obtaining agreement in belief will in turn lead to agreement in attitude.

In other words: the extent to which scientific methods can bring about agreement on values depends on the extent to which a commonly accepted body of scientific beliefs would cause us to have a commonly accepted set of attitudes.

How much is the development of science likely to achieve, then, with regard to values? To what extent *would* common beliefs lead to common attitudes? It is, perhaps, a pardonable enthusiasm to *hope* that science will do everything — to hope that in some rosy future, when all men know the consequences of their acts, they will all have common aspirations, and live peaceably in complete moral accord. But if we speak not from our enthusiastic hopes, but from our present knowledge, the answer must be far less exciting. We usually *do not know*, at the beginning of any argument about values, whether an agreement in belief, scientifically established, will lead to an agreement in attitude or not. It is logically possible, at least, that two men should continue to disagree in attitude even though they had all their beliefs in common, and even though neither had made any logical or inductive error, or omitted any relevant evidence. Differences in temperament, or in early training, or in social status, might make the men retain different attitudes even though both were possessed of the complete scientific truth. Whether this logical possibility is an empirical likelihood I shall not presume to say; but it is unquestionably a possibility that must not be left out of account.

To say that science can always settle arguments about value, we have seen, is to make this assumption: Agreement in attitude will always be consequent upon complete agreement in belief, and science can always bring about the latter. Taken as purely heuristic, this assumption has its usefulness. It leads people to discover the discrepancies in their beliefs, and to prolong enlightening argument that *may* lead, as a matter of fact, from commonly accepted beliefs to commonly accepted attitudes. It leads people to reconcile their attitudes in a rational, permanent way, rather than by rhapsody or exhortation. But the assumption is *nothing more*, for present knowledge, than a heuristic maxim. It is wholly without any proper foundation of probability. I conclude, therefore, that scientific methods cannot be guaranteed the definite rôle in the so-called "normative sciences" that they may have in the natural sciences. Apart from a heuristic assumption to the contrary, it is possible that the growth of scientific knowledge may leave many disputes about values permanently unsolved. Should these disputes persist, there are non-rational methods for dealing with them, of course, such as impassioned, moving oratory. But the purely intellectual methods of science, and, indeed, *all* methods of reasoning, may be insufficient to settle disputes about values, even though they may greatly help to do so.

For the same reasons, I conclude that normative ethics is not a branch of any science. It deliberately deals with a type of disagreement that science deliberately avoids. Ethics is not psychology, for instance; for although psychologists may, of course, agree or disagree in belief about attitudes, they need not, as psychologists, be concerned with whether they agree or disagree with one another *in* attitude. Insofar as normative ethics draws from the sciences, in order to change attitudes *via* changing people's beliefs, it *draws* from *all* the sciences; but a moralist's peculiar aim — that of *redirecting* attitudes — is a type of activity, rather than knowledge, and falls within no science. Science may study that activity, and may help indirectly to forward it; but it is not *identical* with that activity.

I have only a moment to explain why the ethical terms, such as "good," "wrong," "ought," and so on, are so habitually used to deal with disagreement in attitude. On account of their repeated occurrence in emotional situations they have acquired a strong emotive meaning. This emotive meaning makes them serviceable in initiating changes in a hearer's attitudes. Sheer emotive impact is not likely, under many circumstances, to change attitudes in any permanent way; but it *begins* a process that can then be supported by other means.

There is no occasion for saying that the meaning of ethical terms is *purely* emotive, like that of "alas" or "hurrah." We have seen that ethical *arguments* include many expressions of *belief*; and the rough rules of ordinary language permit us to say that some of these beliefs are expressed by an ethical judgment itself. But the beliefs so expressed are by no means always the same. Ethical terms are notable for their ambiguity, and opponents in an argument may use them in different senses. Sometimes this leads to artificial issues; but it usually does not. So long as one person says "This is good" with emotive praise, and another says "No, it is bad," with emotive condemnation, a disagreement in attitude is manifest. Whether or not the beliefs that these statements express are logically incompatible may not be discovered until later in the argument; but even if they are actually compatible, disagreement in attitude will be preserved by emotive meaning; and this disagreement, so central to ethics, may lead to an argument that is certainly not artificial in its issues, so long as it is taken for what it is.

The many theorists who have refused to identify ethical statements with scientific ones have much to be said in their favor. They have seen that ethical judgments mold or alter attitudes, rather than describe them, and they have seen that ethical judgments can be guaranteed no definitive scientific support. But one need not, on that account, provide ethics with any extramundane, sui generis *subject matter*. The distinguishing features of an ethical judgment can be preserved by a recognition of emotive meaning and disagreement in attitude, rather than by some non-natural quality — and with far greater intelligibility. If an unique subject matter is *postulated*, as it usually is, to preserve the important distinction between normative ethics and science, it serves no purpose that is not served by the very simple analysis I have here suggested. Unless non-natural qualities can be defended by positive arguments, rather than as an "only resort" from the acknowledged weakness of ordinary forms of naturalism, they would seem nothing more than the invisible shadows cast by emotive meaning.

QUESTIONS

1. What does Stevenson think is the difference between disagreements in belief and disagreements in attitude? Is he correct in thinking that there are two types of "disagreement" roughly to be distinguished in this way?
2. Which kind of disagreement do naturalists think is ordinarily involved in ethical disputes? May a naturalist hold that disagreement in attitude can arise out of disagreement in belief, so that *both* kinds of disagreement are normally present in debates about values?

3. What reasons does Stevenson offer for saying that disagreement in attitude "plays a unifying and predominating role" in ethical arguments? When, according to him, do we usually regard a consideration as "relevant" to a given ethical dispute? Is this correct? Is he right in his view about the stage when we consider an ethical disagreement to be terminated?

4. What is the proper role of scientific reasoning in ethical discussions, according to Stevenson? Does he think that a developing body of generally accepted scientific beliefs will assure agreement about ethical issues?

5. Why does he think use of ethical language is helpful in dealing with disagreements in attitude?

6. Does he hold that the meaning of ethical terms is "purely emotive"? How far does he agree, and disagree, with the naturalist about how these terms should be analyzed?

7. What is his view of the status of nonnaturalism?

Bertrand Russell (1872-   )

THE GOOD AS THE OBJECT OF
MY UNIVERSALIZED DESIRE

Bertrand Russell is one of the leading figures of the twentieth-century intellectual world. He was elected a fellow of Trinity College, Cambridge, in 1895, and he was lecturer in philosophy at Cambridge University from 1910 to 1916. A bibliography of his writings from 1895 through 1945 fills 44 printed pages. Among his most important works have been *The Philosophy of Leibniz* (1900); *The Principles of Mathematics* (1903); *Principia Mathematica*, 3 volumes (with A. N. Whitehead, 1910, 1912, 1913); *The Problems of Philosophy* (1912); *Our Knowledge of the External World* (1914); *Mysticism and Logic* (1918); *The Analysis of Mind* (1921); *The Analysis of Matter* (1927); *An Outline of Philosophy* (1927); *An Inquiry into Meaning and Truth* (1940); and *Human Knowledge* (1948).

Russell has frequently written on topics in the field of ethics. At various times he has defended forms of naturalism, nonnaturalism, and noncognitivism — always sanely and skillfully, although sometimes not in great detail. The following essay is his most lucid exposition of a noncognitivist point of view. Russell differs from Ayer and Stevenson in thinking that "is good" is used to express not just any desires or attitudes of the speaker but the special wish that everybody desire something. In other words, "x is good in itself" means "Would that everybody desired this!" In this respect Russell's view is more similar to that of David Hume (below) than to the theories of Ayer and Stevenson.

Religion and Science, by Bertrand Russell, published by Oxford University Press, London and New York, 1935, and reprinted with their permission.

RELIGION AND SCIENCE

SCIENCE AND ETHICS

Those who maintain the insufficiency of science . . . appeal to the fact that science has nothing to say about "values." This I admit; but when it is inferred that ethics contains truths which cannot be proved or disproved by science, I disagree. The matter is one on which it is not altogether easy to think clearly, and my own views on it are quite different from what they were thirty years ago. But it is necessary to be clear about it if we are to appraise such arguments as those in support of Cosmic Purpose. As there is no consensus of opinion about ethics, it must be understood that what follows is my personal belief, not the dictum of science.

The study of ethics, traditionally, consists of two parts, one concerned with moral rules, the other with what is good on its own account. Rules of conduct, many of which have a ritual origin, play a great part in the lives of savages and primitive peoples. It is forbidden to eat out of the chief's dish, or to seethe the kid in its mother's milk; it is commanded to offer sacrifices to the gods, which, at a certain stage of development, are thought most acceptable if they are human beings. Other moral rules, such as the prohibition of murder and theft, have a more obvious social utility, and survive the decay of the primitive theological systems with which they were originally associated. But as men grow more reflective there is a tendency to lay less stress on rules and more on states of mind. This comes from two sources — philosophy and mystical religion. We are all familiar with passages in the prophets and the gospels, in which purity of heart is set above meticulous observance of the Law; and St. Paul's famous praise of charity, or love, teaches the same principle. The same thing will be found in all great mystics, Christian and non-Christian: what they value is a state of mind, out of which, as they hold, right conduct must ensue; rules seem to them external, and insufficiently adaptable to circumstances.

One of the ways in which the need of appealing to external rules of conduct has been avoided has been the belief in "conscience," which has been especially important in Protestant ethics. It has been supposed that God reveals to each human heart what is right and what is wrong, so that, in order to avoid sin, we have only to listen to the inner voice. There are, however, two difficulties in this theory: first, that conscience says different things to different people; secondly, that the study of the unconscious has given us an understanding of the mundane causes of conscientious feelings.

As to the different deliverances of conscience: George III's conscience told him that he must not grant Catholic Emancipation, as, if he did, he would have committed perjury in taking the Coronation Oath, but later monarchs have had no such scruples. Conscience leads some to condemn the spoliation of the rich by the poor, as advocated by communists; and others to condemn exploitation of the poor by the rich, as practised by capitalists. It tells one man that he ought to defend his country in case of invasion, while it tells another that all participation in warfare is wicked. During the War, the authorities, few of whom had studied ethics, found conscience very puzzling, and were led to some curious decisions, such as that a man might have conscientious scruples against fighting himself, but not against working on the fields so as to make possible the conscription of another man. They held also that, while conscience might disapprove of all war, it could not, failing that extreme position, disapprove of the war then in progress. Those who, for whatever reason, thought it wrong to fight, were compelled to state their position in terms of this somewhat primitive and unscientific conception of "conscience."

The diversity in the deliverances of conscience is what is to be expected when its origin is understood. In early youth, certain classes of acts meet with approval, and others with disapproval; and by the normal process of association, pleasure and discomfort gradually attach themselves to the acts, and not merely to the approval and disapproval respectively produced by them. As time goes on, we may forget all about our early moral training, but we shall still feel uncomfortable about certain kinds of actions, while others will give us a glow of virtue. To introspection, these feelings are mysterious, since we no longer remember the circumstances which originally caused them; and therefore it is natural to attribute them to the voice of God in the heart. But in fact conscience is a product of education, and can be trained to approve or disapprove, in the great majority of mankind, as educators may see fit. While, therefore, it is right to wish to liberate ethics from external moral rules, this can hardly be satisfactorily achieved by means of the notion of "conscience."

Philosophers, by a different road, have arrived at a different position in which, also, moral rules of conduct have a subordinate place. They have framed the concept of the Good, by which they mean (roughly speaking) that which, in itself and apart from its consequences, we should wish to see existing — or, if they are theists, that which is pleasing to God. Most people would agree that happiness is preferable to unhappiness, friendliness to unfriendliness, and so on. Moral rules, according to this view, are justified if they promote the existence of what is good on its own account, but not otherwise. The prohibition of murder, in the vast majority of cases, can be justified by its effects, but the practice of burning widows on their husband's funeral pyre cannot The former rule, therefore, should be retained, but not the latter. Even the best moral rules, however, will have *some* exceptions, since no class of actions *always* has bad results. We have thus three different senses in which an act may be ethically commendable: (1) it may be in accordance with the received moral code; (2) it may be sincerely intended to have good effects; (3) it may in fact have good effects. The third sense, however, is generally considered inadmissible in morals. According to orthodox theology, Judas Iscariot's act of betrayal had good consequences, since it was necessary for the Atonement; but it was not on this account laudable.

Different philosophers have formed different conceptions of the Good. Some hold that it consists in the knowledge and love of God; others in universal love; others in the enjoyment of beauty; and yet others in pleasure. The Good once defined, the rest of ethics follows: we ought to act in the way we believe most likely to create as much good as possible, and as little as possible of its correlative evil. The framing of moral rules, so long as the ultimate Good is supposed known, is matter for science. For example: should capital punishment be inflicted for theft, or only for murder, or not at all? Jeremy Bentham, who considered pleasure to be the Good, devoted himself to working out what criminal code would most promote pleasure, and concluded that it ought to be much less severe than that prevailing in his day. All this, except the proposition that pleasure is the Good, comes within the sphere of science.

But when we try to be definite as to what we mean when we say that this or that is "the Good," we find ourselves involved in very great difficulties. Bentham's creed that pleasure is the Good roused furious opposition, and was said to be a pig's philosophy. Neither he nor his opponents could advance any argument. In a scientific question, evidence can be adduced on both sides, and in the end one side is seen to have the better case — or, if this does not happen, the question is left undecided. But in a question as to whether this or that is the ultimate Good, there is no evidence either way; each disputant can only appeal to his own emotions, and employ such rhetorical devices as shall rouse similar emotions in others.

Take, for example, a question which has come to be important in practical politics. Bentham held that one man's pleasure has the same ethical importance as another man's, provided the quantities are equal; and on this ground he was led to advocate democracy. Nietzsche, on the contrary, held that only the great man can be regarded as important on his own account, and that the bulk of mankind are only means to his well-being. He viewed ordinary men as many people view animals: he thought it justifiable to make use of them, not for their own good, but for that of the superman, and this view has since been adopted to justify the abandonment of democracy. We have here a sharp disagreement of great practical importance, but we have absolutely no means, of a scientific or intellectual kind, by which to persuade either party that the other is in the right.

There are, it is true, ways of altering men's opinions on such subjects, but they are all emotional, not intellectual.

Questions as to "values" — that is to say, as to what is good or bad on its own account, independently of its effects — lie outside the domain of science, as the defenders of religion emphatically assert. I think that in this they are right, but I draw the further conclusion, which they do not draw, that questions as to "values" lie wholly outside the domain of knowledge. That is to say, when we assert that this or that has "value," we are giving expression to our own emotions, not to a fact which would still be true if our personal feelings were different. To make this clear, we must try to analyse the conception of the Good.

It is obvious, to begin with, that the whole idea of good and bad has some connection with *desire*. *Prima facie*, anything that we all desire is "good," and anything that we all dread is "bad." If we all agreed in our desires, the matter could be left there, but unfortunately our desires conflict. If I say "what I want is good," my neighbour will say "No, what *I* want." Ethics is an attempt — though not, I think, a successful one — to escape from this subjectivity. I shall naturally try to show, in my dispute with my neighbour, that my desires have some quality which makes them more worthy of respect than his. If I want to preserve a right of way, I shall appeal to the landless inhabitants of the district; but he, on his side, will appeal to the landowners. I shall say: "What use is the beauty of the countryside if no one sees it?" He will retort: "What beauty will be left if trippers are allowed to spread devastation?" Each tries to enlist allies by showing that his own desires harmonize with those of other people. When this is obviously impossible, as in the case of a burglar, the man is condemned by public opinion, and his ethical status is that of a sinner.

Ethics is thus closely related to politics: it is an attempt to bring the collective desires of a group to bear upon individuals; or, conversely, it is an attempt by an individual to cause his desires to become those of his group. This latter is, of course, only possible if his desires are not too obviously opposed to the general interest: the burglar will hardly attempt to persuade people that he is doing them good, though plutocrats make similar attempts, and often succeed. When our desires are for things which all can enjoy in common, it seems not unreasonable to hope that others may concur; thus the philosopher who values Truth, Goodness and Beauty seems, to himself, to be not merely expressing his own desires, but pointing the way to the welfare of all mankind. Unlike the burglar, he is able to believe that his desires are for something that has value in an impersonal sense.

Ethics is an attempt to give universal, and not merely personal, importance to certain of our desires. I say "certain" of our desires, because in regard to some of them this is obviously impossible, as we saw in the case of the burglar. The man who makes money on the Stock Exchange by means of some secret knowledge does not wish others to be equally well informed: Truth (in so far as he values it) is for him a private possession, not the general human good that it is for the philosopher. The philosopher may, it is true, sink to the level of the stock-jobber, as when he claims priority for a discovery. But this is a lapse: in his purely philosophic capacity, he wants only to enjoy the contemplation of Truth, in doing which he in no way interferes with others who wish to do likewise.

To seem to give universal importance to our desires — which is the business of ethics — may be attempted from two points of view, that of the legislator, and that of the preacher. Let us take the legislator first.

I will assume, for the sake of argument, that the legislator is personally disinterested. That is to say, when he recognizes one of his desires as being concerned only with his own welfare, he does not let it influence him in framing the laws; for example, his code is not designed to increase his personal fortune. But he has other desires which seem to him impersonal. He may believe in an ordered hierarchy from king to peasant, or from mine-owner to black indentured labourer. He may believe that women should be submissive to men. He may hold that the spread of knowledge in the lower classes is dangerous. And so on and so on. He will then, if he can, so construct his code that conduct promoting the ends which he values shall, as far as possible, be in accordance with individual self-interest; and he will establish a system of moral instruction which will, where it succeeds, make men feel wicked if they pursue other purposes than his.[1] Thus "virtue" will come to be in fact, though not in subjective estimation, subservience to the desires of the legislator, in so far as he himself considers these desires worthy to be universalized.

The standpoint and method of the preacher are necessarily somewhat different, because he does not control the machinery of the State, and therefore cannot produce an artificial harmony between his desires and those of others. His only method is to try to rouse in others the same desires that he feels himself, and for this purpose his appeal must be to the emotions. Thus Ruskin caused people to like Gothic architecture, not by argument, but by the moving effect of rhythmical prose. *Uncle Tom's Cabin* helped to make people think slavery an evil by causing them to imagine themselves as slaves. Every attempt to persuade people that something is good (or bad) in itself, and not merely in its effects, depends upon the art of rousing feelings, not upon an appeal to evidence. In every case the preacher's skill consists in creating in others emotions similar to his own — or dissimilar, if he is a hypocrite. I am not saying this as a criticism of the preacher, but as an analysis of the essential character of his activity.

[1] Compare the following advice by a contemporary of Aristotle (Chinese, not Greek): "A ruler should not listen to those who believe in people having opinions of their own and in the importance of the individual. Such teachings cause men to withdraw to quiet places and hide away in caves or on mountains, there to rail at the prevailing government, sneer at those in authority, belittle the importance of rank and emoluments, and despise all who hold official posts." Waley, *The Way and Its Power*, p. 37.

When a man says "this is good in itself," he *seems* to be making a statement, just as much as if he said "this is square" or "this is sweet." I believe this to be a mistake. I think that what the man really means is: "I wish everybody to desire this," or rather "Would that everybody desired this." If what he says is interpreted as a statement, it is merely an affirmation of his own personal wish; if, on the other hand, it is interpreted in a general way, it states nothing, but merely desires something. The wish, as an occurrence, is personal, but what it desires is universal. It is, I think, this curious interlocking of the particular and the universal which has caused so much confusion in ethics.

The matter may perhaps become clearer by contrasting an ethical sentence with one which makes a statement. If I say "all Chinese are Buddhists," I can be refuted by the production of a Chinese Christian or Mohammedan. If I say "I believe that all Chinese are Buddhists," I cannot be refuted by any evidence from China, but only by evidence that I do not believe what I say; for what I am asserting is only something about my own state of mind. If, now, a philosopher says "Beauty is good," I may interpret him as meaning either "Would that everybody loved the beautiful" (which corresponds to "all Chinese are Buddhists") or "I wish that everybody loved the beautiful" (which corresponds to "I believe that all Chinese are Buddhists"). The first of these makes no assertion, but expresses a wish; since it affirms nothing, it is logically impossible that there should be evidence for or against it, or for it to possess either truth or falsehood. The second sentence, instead of being merely optative, does make a statement, but it is one about the philosopher's state of mind, and it could only be refuted by evidence that he does not have the wish that he says he has. This second sentence does not belong to ethics, but to psychology or biography. The first sentence, which does belong to ethics, expresses a desire for something, but asserts nothing.

Ethics, if the above analysis is correct, contains no statements, whether true or false, but consists of desires of a certain general kind, namely such as are concerned with the desires of mankind in general — and of gods, angels, and devils, if they exist. Science can discuss the causes of desires, and the means for realizing them, but it cannot contain any genuinely ethical sentences, because it is concerned with what is true or false.

The theory which I have been advocating is a form of the doctrine which is called the "subjectivity" of values. This doctrine consists in maintaining that, if two men differ about values, there is not a disagreement as to any kind of truth, but a difference of taste. If one man says "oysters are good" and another says "I think they are bad," we recognize that there is nothing to argue about. The theory in question holds that all differences as to values are of this sort, although we do not naturally think them so when we are dealing with matters that seem to us more exalted than oysters. The chief ground for adopting this view is the complete impossibility of finding any arguments to prove that this or that has intrinsic value. If we all agreed, we might hold that we know values by intuition. We cannot *prove*, to a colour-blind man, that grass is green and not red. But there are various ways of proving to him that he lacks a power of discrimination which most men possess, whereas in the case of values there are no such ways, and disagreements are much more frequent than in the case of colours. Since no way can be even imagined for deciding a difference as to values, the conclusion is forced upon us that the difference is one of tastes, not one as to any objective truth.

The consequences of this doctrine are considerable. In the first place, there can be no such thing as "sin" in any absolute sense; what one man calls "sin" another may call "virtue" and though they may dislike each other on account of this difference, neither can convict the other of intellectual error. Punishment cannot be justified on the ground that the criminal is "wicked," but only on the ground that he has behaved in a way which others wish to discourage. Hell, as a place of punishment for sinners, becomes quite irrational.

In the second place, it is impossible to uphold the way of speaking about values which is common among those who believe in Cosmic Purpose. Their argument is that certain things which have been evolved are "good," and therefore the world must have had a purpose which was ethically admirable. In the language of subjective values, this argument becomes: "Some things in the world are to our liking, and therefore they must have been created by a Being with our tastes, Whom, therefore, we also like, and Who, consequently, is good." Now it seems fairly evident that, if creatures having likes and dislikes were to exist at all, they were pretty sure to like *some* things in their environment, since otherwise they would find life intolerable. Our values have been evolved along with the rest of our constitution, and nothing as to any original purpose can be inferred from the fact that they are what they are.

Those who believe in "objective" values often contend that the view which I have been advocating has immoral consequences. This seems to me to be due to faulty reasoning. There are, as has already been said, certain ethical consequences of the doctrine of subjective values, of which the most important is the rejection of vindictive punishment and the notion of "sin." But the more general consequences which are feared, such as the decay of all sense of moral obligation, are not to be logically deduced. Moral obligation, if it is to influence conduct, must consist not merely of a belief, but of a desire. The desire, I may be told, is the desire to be "good" in a sense which I no longer allow. But when we analyse the desire to be "good" it generally resolves itself into a desire to be approved, or, alternatively, to act so as to bring about certain general consequences which we desire. We have wishes which are not purely personal, and, if we had not, no amount of ethical teaching would influence our conduct except through fear of disapproval. The sort of life that most of us admire is one which is guided by large impersonal desires; now such desires can, no doubt, be encouraged by example, education, and knowledge, but they can hardly be created by the mere abstract belief that they are good, nor discouraged by an analysis of what is meant by the word "good."

When we contemplate the human race, we may desire that it should be happy, or healthy, or intelligent, or warlike, and so on. Any one of these desires, if it is strong, will produce its own morality; but if we have no such general desires, our conduct, whatever our ethic may be, will only serve social purposes in so far as self-interest and the interests of society are in harmony. It is the business of wise institutions to create such harmony as far as possible, and for the rest, whatever may be our theoretical definition of value, we must depend upon the existence of impersonal desires. When you meet a man with whom you have a fundamental ethical disagreement — for example, if you think that all men count equally, while he selects a class as alone important — you will find yourself no better able to cope with him if you believe in objective values than if you do not. In either case, you can only influence his conduct through influencing his desires: if you succeed in that, his ethic will change, and if not, not.

Some people feel that if a general desire, say for the happiness of mankind, has not the sanction of absolute good, it is in some way irrational. This is due to a lingering belief in objective values. A desire cannot, in itself, be either rational or irrational. It may conflict with other desires, and therefore lead to unhappiness; it may rouse opposition in others, and therefore be incapable of gratification. But it cannot be considered "irrational" merely because no reason can be given for feeling it. We may desire A because it is a means to B, but in the end, when we have done with mere means, we must come to something which we desire for no reason, but not on that account "irrationally." All systems of ethics embody the desires of those who advocate them, but this fact is concealed in a mist of words. Our desires are, in fact, more general and less purely selfish than many moralists imagine; if it were not so, no theory of ethics would make moral improvement possible. It is, in fact, not by ethical theory, but by the cultivation of large and generous desires through intelligence, happiness, and freedom from fear, that men can be brought to act more than they do at present in a manner that is consistent with the general happiness of mankind. Whatever our definition of the "Good," and whether we believe it to be subjective or objective, those who do not desire the happiness of mankind will not endeavour to further it, while those who do desire it will do what they can to bring it about.

I conclude that, while it is true that science cannot decide questions of value, that is because they cannot be intellectually decided at all, and lie outside the realm of truth and falsehood. Whatever knowledge is attainable, must be attained by scientific methods; and what science cannot discover, mankind cannot know.

QUESTIONS

1. Why does Russell think that "conscience" is not a reliable source of knowledge about what is objectively right? Is his proposal about the genesis of conscience coherent with modern psychological knowledge as far as you know?
2. Is Russell's preferred method of liberating "ethics from external moral rules" anything different from act-utilitarianism or rule-utilitarianism?
3. Why does he think that, granted information about what is intrinsically good, science can tell us the right answers to ethical questions?
4. Does Russell think an opinion about what is ultimately good can be supported by evidence? How then may it be supported?
5. Explain what he means by saying that "ethics is an attempt to give universal, and not merely personal, importance to certain of our desires."
6. Explain what he means by saying: "The wish, as an occurrence, is personal, but what it desires is universal."
7. What is the difference between Russell's view and that of the naturalist who says "x is good" means "I desire x"? What does he mean by calling himself a "subjectivist" about values?
8. What does Russell say is the "chief reason" for adopting this view?
9. What does he affirm are logical consequences of his view? Do you think these really are implications of his theory?
10. Would Russell agree that the noncognitivist view tends to undermine serious concern to do what is right? Why? Does he think there is practical value in belief in "objective values"?

David Hume (1711-76)

THE IMPARTIAL SPECTATOR THEORY

At the age of twenty-six Hume had completed the greatest single work of British philosophy, his *Treatise of Human Nature*. In the present century his ideas have had more influence than those of any of the other historical figures in British philosophy, by far, and perhaps influence at least equal to that of any other philosopher.

Hume was born in Edinburgh, of a family of moderate means. He tried the legal profession and the career of a merchant, both unsuccessfully. As a philosopher, he was entirely self-educated. In addition to the *Treatise*, his important philosophical works included *Essays on Moral and Political Subjects* (1741), *Enquiry Concerning the Human Understanding* (1748),

Enquiry Concerning the Principles of Morals (1751), and the posthumous *Dialogues on Natural Religion* (1779). In his day Hume's reputation (and income) depended far more on his *History of England* (1754-62) than on his philosophical writings.

Hume believed that the fundamental principles of morals cannot be known by pure reason or intuition, and he adduces many arguments to prove his belief — although most of them would hardly touch a sophisticated nonnaturalist (and we must remember nonnaturalism had not received a convincing statement in his time). His view was that we make the moral judgments we do on account of our feelings or sentiments. A great deal of Hume's theory is concerned with determining how we come to have the feelings on which moral judgments are based — essentially a psychology of moral emotions. Hume's conclusion is that we all "sympathize" with others, that we take an altruistic interest in their welfare. It is on account of this sympathy that we disapprove of hurtful actions or traits of character and that we approve of beneficent ones.

So far it might seem as if Hume's view is just another emotive theory, fitted out with a psychological explanation of approval or disapproval of actions. But this appearance is misleading. The reason is that he thinks that moral terms ("right," "morally good," "morally bad," "reprehensible") have come to be reserved for a very special function — for the expression of impersonal feelings which are proportioned to an ideally vivid awareness of the situation which elicits them. Indeed, there is much in Hume to encourage interpreting him as holding an ideal observer theory like Sharp's — as saying that "is morally bad" means "I would disapprove if my feelings were impersonal and based on a vivid awareness of the situation." If he is a noncognitivist, his view is still one which recognizes such things as moral error and objective validity in moral opinions.

Hume's view of metaethics leads naturally to a utilitarian normative ethics.

The following selection, which consists of three parts, is concerned with his own positive theory, not with his criticisms of rationalist philosophers.

From David Hume, *Treatise of Human Nature*. Many editions, Bk. 3, Pt. 1, Section 2 and Bk. 3, Pt. 3, Section 1. Also, D. Hume. *Enquiry Concerning the Principles of Morals*. Many editions, Section 9 ["Conclusion" in this selection].

TREATISE OF HUMAN NATURE

MORAL DISTINCTIONS DERIVED
FROM A MORAL SENSE

Thus the course of the argument leads us to conclude that since vice and virtue are not discoverable merely by reason, or the comparison of ideas, it must be by means of some impression or sentiment they occasion, that we are able to mark the difference betwixt them. Our decisions concerning moral rectitude and depravity are evidently perceptions; and as all perceptions are either impressions or ideas, the exclusion of the one is a convincing argument for the other. Morality, therefore, is more properly felt than judged of; though this feeling or sentiment is commonly so soft and gentle that we are apt to confound it with an idea, according to our common custom of taking all things for the same which have any near resemblance to each other.

The next question is of what nature are these impressions, and after what manner do they operate upon us? Here we cannot remain long in suspense, but must pronounce the impression arising from virtue to be agreeable, and that proceeding from vice to be uneasy. Every moment's experience must convince us of this. There is no spectacle so fair and beautiful as a noble and generous action; nor any which gives us more abhorrence than one that is cruel and treacherous. No enjoyment equals the satisfaction we receive from the company of those we love and esteem; as the greatest of all punishments is to be obliged to pass our lives with those we hate or contemn. A very play or romance may afford us instances of this pleasure which virtue conveys to us; and pain which arises from vice.

Now, since the distinguishing impressions by which moral good or evil is known are nothing but *particular* pains or pleasures, it follows that in all inquiries concerning these moral distinctions it will be sufficient to show the principles which make us feel a satisfaction or uneasiness from the survey of any character, in order to satisfy us why the character is laudable or blameable. An action, or sentiment, or character, is virtuous or vicious; why? because its view causes a pleasure or uneasiness of a particular kind. In giving a reason, therefore, for the pleasure or uneasiness, we sufficiently explain the vice or virtue. To have the sense of virtue is nothing but to *feel* a satisfaction of a particular kind from the contemplation of a character. The very *feeling* constitutes our praise or admiration. We go no further; nor do we inquire into the cause of the satisfaction. We do not infer a character to be virtuous because it pleases; but in feeling that it pleases after such a particular manner we in effect feel that it is virtuous. The case is the same as in our judgments concerning all kinds of beauty, and tastes, and sensations. Our approbation is implied in the immediate pleasure they convey to us.

I have objected to the system which establishes eternal rational measures of right and wrong, that it is impossible to show in the actions of reasonable creatures any relations which are not found in external objects; and therefore, if morality always attended these relations, it were possible for inanimate matter to become virtuous or vicious. Now it may, in like manner, be objected to the present system, that if virtue and vice be determined by pleasure and pain, these qualities must in every case arise from the sensations; and consequently any object, whether animate or inanimate, rational or irrational, might become morally good or evil, provided it can excite a satisfaction or uneasiness. But though this objection seems to be the very same, it has by no means the same force in the one case as in the other. For . . . it is evident that under the term *pleasure* we comprehend sensations which are very different from each other, and which have only such a distant resemblance as is requisite to make them be expressed by the same abstract term. A good composition of music and a bottle of good wine equally produce pleasure; and, what is more, their goodness is determined merely by the pleasure. But shall we say, upon that account, that the wine is harmonious, or the music of a good flavour? In like manner, an inanimate object and the character or sentiments of any person may, both of them, give satisfaction; but, as the satisfaction is different, this keeps our sentiments concerning them from being confounded, and makes us ascribe virtue to the one and not to the other. Nor is every sentiment of pleasure or pain, which arises from characters and actions, of that *peculiar* kind which makes us praise or condemn. The good qualities of an enemy are hurtful to us, but may still command our esteem and respect. It is only when a character is considered in general, without reference to our particular interest, that it causes such a feeling or sentiment as denominates it morally good or evil. It is true, those sentiments from interest and morals are apt to be confounded, and naturally run into one another. It seldom happens that we do not think an enemy vicious, and can distinguish betwixt his opposition to our interest and real villainy or baseness. But this hinders not but that the sentiments are in themselves distinct, and a man of temper and judgment may preserve himself from these illusions. In like manner, though it is certain a musical voice is nothing but one that naturally gives a *particular* kind of pleasure, yet it is difficult for a man to be sensible that the voice of an enemy is agreeable, or to allow it to be musical. But a person of a fine ear, who has the command of himself, can separate these feelings and give praise to what deserves it. . . .

It may now be asked *in general* concerning this pain or pleasure that distinguishes moral good and evil, *from what principle is it derived, and whence does it arise in the human mind?* To this I reply, *first,* that it is absurd to imagine that, in every particular instance, these sentiments are produced by an *original* quality and *primary* constitution. For as the number of our duties is in a manner infinite, it is impossible that our original instincts should extend to each of them, and from our very first infancy impress on the human mind all that multitude of precepts which are contained in the completest system of ethics. Such a method of proceeding is not conformable to the usual maxims by which nature is conducted, where a few principles produce all that variety we observe in the universe, and everything is carried on in the easiest and most simple manner. It is necessary, therefore, to abridge these primary impulses and find some more general principles upon which all our notions of morals are founded.

But, in the *second* place, should it be asked, whether we ought to search for these principles in *nature*, or whether we must look for them in some other origin? I would reply that our answer to this question depends upon the definition of the word *nature*, than which there is none more ambiguous and equivocal. If *nature* be opposed to miracles, not only the distinction betwixt vice and virtue is natural, but also every event which has ever happened in the world, *excepting those miracles on which our religion is founded*. In saying, then, that the sentiments of vice and virtue are natural in this sense, we make no very extraordinary discovery.

But *nature* may also be opposed to rare and unusual; and in this sense of the word, which is the common one, there may often arise disputes concerning what is natural or unnatural; and one may in general affirm that we are not possessed of any very precise standard by which these disputes can be decided. Frequent and rare depend upon the number of examples we have observed; and as this number may gradually increase or diminish, it will be impossible to fix any exact boundaries betwixt them. We may only affirm on this head that if ever there was anything which could be called natural in this sense, the sentiments of morality certainly may; since there never was any nation of the world, nor any single person in any nation, who was utterly deprived of them, and who never, in any instance, showed the least approbation or dislike of manners. These sentiments are so rooted in our constitution and temper that, without entirely confounding the human mind by disease or madness, it is impossible to extirpate and destroy them.

But *nature* may also be opposed to artifice as well as to what is rare and unusual; and in this sense it may be disputed whether the notions of virtue be natural or not. We readily forget that the designs, and projects, and views of men are principles as necessary in their operation as heat and cold, moist and dry; but, taking them to be free and entirely our own, it is usual for us to set them in opposition to the other principles of nature. Should it therefore be demanded whether the sense of virtue be natural or artificial, I am of opinion that it is impossible for me at present to give any precise answer to this question. Perhaps it will appear afterwards that our sense of some virtues is artificial, and that of others natural. The discussion of this question will be more proper, when we enter upon an exact detail of each particular vice and virtue.[1]

---

[1] In the following discourse, *natural* is also opposed sometimes to *civil*, sometimes to *moral*. The opposition will always discover the sense in which it is taken.

Meanwhile, it may not be amiss to observe from these definitions of *natural* and *unnatural* that nothing can be more unphilosophical than those systems which assert that virtue is the same with what is natural, and vice with what is unnatural. For in the first sense of the word "nature," as opposed to miracles, both vice and virtue are equally natural; and in the second sense, as opposed to what is unusual, perhaps virtue will be found to be the most unnatural. At least it must be owned that heroic virtue, being as unusual, is as little natural as the most brutal barbarity. As to the third sense of the word, it is certain that both vice and virtue are equally artificial and out of nature. For, however it may be disputed whether the notion of a merit or demerit in certain actions be natural or artificial, it is evident that the actions themselves are artificial, and performed with a certain design and intention; otherwise they could never be ranked under any of these denominations. It is impossible, therefore, that the character of natural and unnatural can ever, in any sense, mark the boundaries of vice and virtue.

Thus we are still brought back to our first position that virtue is distinguished by the pleasure, and vice by the pain, that any action, sentiment, or character, gives us by the mere view and contemplation. This decision is very commodious; because it reduces us to this simple question, *why any action or sentiment, upon the general view or survey, gives a certain satisfaction or uneasiness,* in order to show the origin of its moral rectitude or depravity, without looking for any incomprehensible relations and qualities which never did exist in nature, nor even in our imagination, by any clear and distinct conception? I flatter myself I have executed a great part of my present design by a state of the question which appears to me so free from ambiguity and obscurity. . . .

OF THE ORIGIN OF THE NATURAL VIRTUES AND VICES

We come now to the examination of such virtues and vices as are entirely natural, and have no dependence on the artifice and contrivance of men. The examination of these will conclude this system of morals.

The chief spring or actuating principle of the human mind is pleasure or pain; and when these sensations are removed, both from our thought and feeling, we are in a great measure incapable of passion or action, of desire or violition. The most immediate effects of pleasure and pain are the propense and averse motions of the mind; which are diversified into volition, into desire and aversion, grief and joy, hope and fear, according as the pleasure or pain changes its situation and becomes probable or improbable, certain or uncertain, or is considered as out of our power for the present moment. But when, along with this, the objects that cause pleasure or pain acquire a relation to ourselves or others, they still continue to excite desire and aversion, grief and joy; but cause at the same time the indirect passions of pride or humility, love or hatred, which in this case have a double relation of impressions and ideas to the pain or pleasure.

We have already observed that moral distinctions depend entirely on certain peculiar sentiments of pain and pleasure, and that whatever mental quality in ourselves or others gives us a satisfaction by the survey or reflection is of course virtuous; as everything of this nature that gives uneasiness is vicious. Now, since every quality in ourselves or others which gives pleasure always causes pride or love, as every one that produces uneasiness excites humility or hatred, it follows that these two particulars are to be considered as equivalent with regard to our mental qualities; *virtue* and the power of producing love or pride; *vice* and the power of producing humility or hatred. In every case, therefore, we must judge of the one by the other, and may pronounce any *quality* of the mind virtuous which causes love or pride, and any one vicious which causes hatred or humility.

If any *action* be either virtuous or vicious, it is only as a sign of some quality or character. It must depend upon durable principles of the mind which extend over the whole conduct and enter into the personal character. Actions themselves, not proceeding from any constant principle, have no influence on love or hatred, pride or humility; and consequently are never considered in morality.

This reflection is self-evident and deserves to be attended to as being of the utmost importance in the present subject. We are never to consider any single action in our inquiries concerning the origin of morals, but only the quality or character from which the action proceeded. These alone are *durable* enough to affect our sentiments concerning the person. Actions are indeed better indications of a character than words, or even wishes and sentiments; but it is only so far as they are such indications that they are attended with love or hatred, praise or blame.

To discover the true origin of morals, and of that love or hatred which arises from mental qualities, we must take the matter pretty deep and compare some principles which have been already examined and explained.

We may begin with considering anew the nature and force of *sympathy*. The minds of all men are similar in their feelings and operations; nor can any one be actuated by any affection of which all others are not in some degree susceptible. As in strings equally wound up the motion of one communicates itself to the rest, so all the affections readily pass from one person to another, and beget correspondent movements in every human creature. When I see the *effects* of passion in the voice and gesture of any person, my mind immediately passes from these effects to their causes, and forms such a lively idea of the passion as is presently converted into the passion itself. In like manner, when I perceive the *causes* of any emotion, my mind is conveyed to the effects, and is actuated with a like emotion. Were I present at any of the more terrible operations of surgery, it is certain that, even before it begun, the preparation of the instruments, the laying of the bandages in order, the heating of the irons, with all the signs of anxiety and concern in the patient and assistants, would have a great effect upon my mind, and excite the strongest sentiments of pity and terror. No passion of another discovers itself immediately to the mind. We are only sensible of its causes or effects. From *these* we infer the passion; and consequently, *these* give rise to our sympathy.

Our sense of beauty depends very much on this principle; and where any object has a tendency to produce pleasure in its possessor, it is always regarded as beautiful; as every object that has a tendency to produce pain is disagreeable and deformed. Thus the convenience of a house, the fertility of a field, the strength of a horse, the capacity, security, and swift-sailing of a vessel, form the principal beauty of these several objects. Here the object, which is denominated *beautiful*, pleases only by its tendency to produce a certain effect. That effect is the pleasure or advantage of some other person. Now, the pleasure of a stranger for whom we have no friendship pleases us only by sympathy. To this principle, therefore, is owing the beauty which we find in everything that is useful. How considerable a part this is of beauty will easily appear upon reflection. Wherever an object has a tendency to produce pleasure in the possessor, or, in other words, is the proper *cause* of pleasure, it is sure to please the spectator by a delicate sympathy with the possessor. Most of the works of art are esteemed beautiful in proportion to their fitness for the use of man; and even many of the productions of nature derive their beauty from that source. Handsome and beautiful, on most occasions, is not an absolute but a relative quality, and pleases us by nothing but its tendency to produce an end that is agreeable.[2]

The same principle produces in many instances our sentiments of morals as well as those of beauty. No virtue is more esteemed than justice, and no vice more detested than injustice; nor are there any qualities which go further to the fixing the character, either as amiable or odious. Now, justice is a moral virtue, merely because it has that tendency to the good of mankind, and indeed is nothing but an artificial invention to that purpose. The same may be said of allegiance, of the laws of nations, of modesty, and of good manners. All these are mere human contrivances for the interest of society. And since there is a very strong sentiment of morals, which in all nations and all ages has attended them, we must allow that the reflecting on the tendency of characters and mental qualities is sufficient to give us the sentiments of approbation and blame. Now, as the means to an end can only be agreeable where the end is agreeable, and as the good of society, where our own interest is not concerned or that of our friends, pleases only by sympathy, it follows that sympathy is the source of the esteem which we pay to all the artificial virtues.

Thus it appears that *sympathy* is a very powerful principle in human nature, that it has a great influence on our taste of beauty, and that it pro-

---

[2] Decentior equus cujus astricta sunt ilia; sed idem velocior. Pulcher aspectu sit athleta, cujus lacertos exercitatio expressit; idem certamini paratior. Nunquam vero *species* ab *utilitate* dividitur. Sed hoc quidem discernere, modici judicii est. — *Quinct.* lib. 8.

duces our sentiment of morals in all the artificial virtues. From thence we may presume that it also gives rise to many of the other virtues, and that qualities acquire our approbation because of their tendency to the good of mankind. This presumption must become a certainty, when we find that most of those qualities which we *naturally* approve of have actually that tendency and render a man a proper member of society; while the qualities which we *naturally* disapprove of have a contrary tendency and render any intercourse with the person dangerous or disagreeable. For having found that such tendencies have force enough to produce the strongest sentiment of morals, we can never reasonably, in these cases, look for any other cause of approbation or blame; it being an inviolable maxim in philosophy that where any particular cause is sufficient for an effect, we ought to rest satisfied with it, and ought not to multiply causes without necessity. We have happily attained experiments in the artificial virtues, where the tendency of qualities to the good of society is the *sole* cause of our approbation, without any suspicion of the concurrence of another principle. From thence we learn the force of that principle. And where that principle may take place, and the quality approved of is really beneficial to society, a true philosopher will never require any other principle to account for the strongest approbation and esteem.

That many of the natural virtues have this tendency to the good of society, no one can doubt of. Meekness, beneficence, charity, generosity, clemency, moderation, equity, bear the greatest figure among the moral qualities, and are commonly denominated the *social* virtues, to mark their tendency to the good of society. This goes so far that some philosophers have represented all moral distinctions as the effect of artifice and education, when skilful politicians endeavoured to restrain the turbulent passions of men, and make them operate to the public good, by the notions of honour and shame. This system, however, is not consistent with experience. For, *first*, there are other virtues and vices beside those which have this tendency to the public advantage and loss. *Secondly*, had not men a natural sentiment of approbation and blame, it could never be excited by politicians; nor would the words *laudable* and *praiseworthy*, *blamable* and *odious*, be any more intelligible than if they were a language perfectly unknown to us, as we have already observed. But though this system be erroneous, it may teach us that moral distinctions arise in a great measure from the tendency of qualities and characters to the interests of society, and that it is our concern for that interest which makes us approve or disapprove of them. Now, we have no such extensive concern for society but from sympathy; and consequently it is that principle which takes us so far out of ourselves as to give us the same pleasure or uneasiness in the characters of others, as if they had a tendency to our own advantage or loss.

The only difference betwixt the natural virtues and justice lies in this, that the good which results from the former rises from every single act, and is the object of some natural passion; whereas a single act of justice, considered in itself, may often be contrary to the public good; and it is only the concurrence of mankind in a general scheme or system of action which is advantageous. When I relieve persons in distress, my natural humanity is my motive; and so far as my succour extends, so far have I promoted the happiness of my fellow creatures. But if we examine all the questions that come before any tribunal of justice, we shall find that, considering each case apart, it would as often be an instance of humanity to decide contrary to the laws of justice as conformable to them. Judges take from a poor man to give to a rich; they bestow on the dissolute the labour of the industrious; and put into the hands of the vicious the means of harming both themselves and others. The whole scheme, however, of law and justice is advantageous to the society; and it was with a view to this advantage that men, by their voluntary conventions, established it. After it is once established by these conventions, it is *naturally* attended with a strong sentiment of morals which can proceed from nothing but our sympathy with the interests of society. We need no other explication of that esteem which attends such of the natural virtues as have a tendency to the public good.

I must further add that there are several circumstances which render this hypothesis much more probable with regard to the natural than the artificial virtues. It is certain that the imagination is more affected by what is particular than by what is general; and that the sentiments are always moved with difficulty, where their objects are in any degree loose and undetermined. Now, every particular act of justice is not beneficial to society, but the whole scheme or system; and it may not perhaps be any individual person for whom we are concerned, who receives benefit from justice, but the whole society alike. On the contrary, every particular act of generosity or relief of the industrious and indigent is beneficial, and is beneficial to a particular person who is not undeserving of it. It is more natural, therefore, to think that the tendencies of the latter virtue will affect our sentiments and command our approbation than those of the former; and therefore, since we find that the approbation of the former arises from their tendencies, we may ascribe, with better reason, the same cause to the approbation of the latter. In any number of similar effects, if a cause can be discovered for one, we ought to extend that cause to all the other effects which can be accounted for by it; but much more, if these other effects be attended with peculiar circumstances which facilitate the operation of that cause.

Before I proceed further, I must observe two remarkable circumstances in this affair which may seem objections to the present system. The first may be thus explained. When any quality or character has a tendency to the good of mankind, we are pleased with it and approve of it because it presents the lively idea of pleasure; which idea affects us by sympathy, and is itself a kind of pleasure. But as this sympathy is very variable, it may

be thought that our sentiments of morals must admit of all the same variations. We sympathize more with persons contiguous to us than with persons remote from us; with our acquaintance, than with strangers; with our
countrymen, than with foreigners. But notwithstanding this variation of our
sympathy, we give the same approbation to the same moral qualities in
China as in England. They appear equally virtuous and recommend themselves equally to the esteem of a judicious spectator. The sympathy varies
without a variation in our esteem. Our esteem, therefore, proceeds not from
sympathy.

To this I answer, the approbation of moral qualities most certainly
is not derived from reason or any comparison of ideas; but proceeds entirely from a moral taste and from certain sentiments of pleasure or disgust which arise upon the contemplation and view of particular qualities
or characters. Now, it is evident that those sentiments, whencever they are
derived, must vary according to the distance or contiguity of the objects;
nor can I feel the same lively pleasure from the virtues of a person who
lived in Greece two thousand years ago that I feel from the virtues of a
familiar friend and acquaintance. Yet I do not say that I esteem the one
more than the other; and therefore, if the variation of the sentiment without a variation of the esteem be an objection, it must have equal force
against every other system, as against that of sympathy. But to consider
the matter aright, it has no force at all; and it is the easiest matter in the
world to account for it. Our situation with regard both to persons and
things is in continual fluctuation; and a man that lies at a distance from
us may in a little time become a familiar acquaintance. Besides, every particular man has a peculiar position with regard to others; and it is impossible we could ever converse together on any reasonable terms, were each
of us to consider characters and persons only as they appear from his peculiar point of view. In order, therefore, to prevent those continual *contradictions* and arrive at a more *stable* judgment of things, we fix on some
steady and *general* points of view, and always, in our thoughts, place ourselves in them, whatever may be our present situation. In like manner, external beauty is determined merely by pleasure; and it is evident a beautiful countenance cannot give so much pleasure when seen at a distance
of twenty paces as when it is brought nearer us. We say not, however, that
it appears to us less beautiful; because we know what effect it will have
in such a position, and by that reflection we correct its momentary appearance.

In general, all sentiments of blame or praise are variable, according to
our situation of nearness or remoteness with regard to the person blamed
or praised, and according to the present disposition of our mind. But these
variations we regard not in our general decisions, but still apply the terms
expressive of our liking or dislike in the same manner as if we remained
in one point of view. Experience soon teaches us this method of correcting our sentiments, or at least of correcting our language, where the sen-

timents are more stubborn and unalterable. Our servant, if diligent and faithful, may excite stronger sentiments of love and kindness than Marcus Brutus, as represented in history; but we say not upon that account that the former character is more laudable than the latter. We know that, were we to approach equally near to that renowned patriarch, he would command a much higher degree of affection and admiration. Such corrections are common with regard to all the senses; and, indeed, it were impossible we could ever make use of language or communicate our sentiments to one another, did we not correct the momentary appearances of things and overlook our present situation.

It is therefore from the influence of characters and qualities upon those who have an intercourse with any person that we blame or praise him. We consider not whether the persons affected by the qualities be our acquaintance or strangers, countrymen or foreigners. Nay, we overlook our own interest in those general judgments, and blame not a man for opposing us in any of our pretensions when his own interest is particularly concerned. We make allowance for a certain degree of selfishness in men because we know it to be inseparable from human nature and inherent in our frame and constitution. By this reflection we correct those sentiments of blame which so naturally arise upon any opposition.

But however the general principle of our blame or praise may be corrected by those other principles, it is certain they are not altogether efficacious, nor do our passions often correspond entirely to the present theory. It is seldom men heartily love what lies at a distance from them, and what no way redounds to their particular benefit; as it is no less rare to meet with persons who can pardon another any opposition he makes to their interest, however justifiable that opposition may be by the general rules of morality. Here we are contented with saying that reason requires such an impartial conduct, but that it is seldom we can bring ourselves to it, and that our passions do not readily follow the determination of our judgment. This language will be easily understood if we consider what we formerly said concerning that *reason* which is able to oppose our passion, and which we have found to be nothing but a general calm determination of the passions, founded on some distant view or reflection. When we form our judgments of persons merely from the tendency of their characters to our own benefit, or to that of our friends, we find so many contradictions to our sentiments in society and conversation, and such an uncertainty from the incessant changes of our situation, that we seek some other standard of merit and demerit which may not admit of so great variation. Being thus loosened from our first station, we cannot afterwards fix ourselves so commodiously by any means as by a sympathy with those who have any commerce with the person we consider. This is far from being as lively as when our own interest is concerned, or that of our particular friends; nor has it such an influence on our love and hatred; but being equally conformable to our calm and general principles, it is said to have an equal authority over our reason, and to command our judgment and opinion. We blame equally a bad action which we read of in history, with one performed in our neighbourhood the other day; the meaning of which is that we know from reflection that the former action would excite as strong sentiments of disapprobation as the latter, were it placed in the same position.

I now proceed to the *second* remarkable circumstance which I propose to take notice of. Where a person is possessed of a character that in its natural tendency is beneficial to society, we esteem him virtuous, and are delighted with the view of his character, even though particular accidents prevent its operation and incapacitate him from being serviceable to his friends and country. Virtue in rags is still virtue; and the love which it procures attends a man into a dungeon or desert, where the virtue can no longer be exerted in action and is lost to all the world. Now, this may be esteemed an objection to the present system. Sympathy interests us in the good of mankind; and if sympathy were the source of our esteem for virtue, that sentiment of approbation could only take place where the virtue actually attained its end and was beneficial to mankind. Where it fails of its end, it is only an imperfect means and, therefore, can never acquire any merit from that end. The goodness of an end can bestow a merit on such means alone as are complete and actually produce the end.

To this we may reply that, where any object, in all its parts, is fitted to attain any agreeable end, it naturally gives us pleasure and is esteemed beautiful, even though some external circumstances be wanting to render it altogether effectual. It is sufficient if everything be complete in the object itself. A house that is contrived with great judgment for all the commodities of life pleases us upon that account, though perhaps we are sensible that no one will ever dwell in it. A fertile soil and a happy climate delight us by a reflection on the happiness which they would afford the inhabitants, though at present the country be desert and uninhabited. A man whose limbs and shape promise strength and activity is esteemed handsome, though condemned to perpetual imprisonment. The imagination has a set of passions belonging to it upon which our sentiments of beauty much depend. These passions are moved by degrees of liveliness and strength, which are inferior to *belief*, and independent of the real existence of their objects. Where a character is in every respect fitted to be beneficial to society, the imagination passes easily from the cause to the effect, without considering that there are still some circumstances wanting to render the cause a complete one. *General rules* create a species of probability which sometimes influences the judgment, and always the imagination.

It is true, when the cause is complete and a good disposition is attended with good fortune which renders it really beneficial to society, it gives a stronger pleasure to the spectator, and is attended with a more lively sympathy. We are more affected by it; and yet we do not say that it is more virtuous, or that we esteem it more. We know that an alteration of fortune may render the benevolent disposition entirely impotent; and therefore we separate as much as possible the fortune from the disposition. The case is the same as when we correct the different sentiments of virtue which proceed from its different distances from ourselves. The passions do not always follow our corrections; but these corrections serve sufficiently to regulate our abstract notions, and are alone regarded when we pronounce in general concerning the degrees of vice and virtue. . . .

Upon these principles we may easily remove any contradiction which may appear to be betwixt the *extensive sympathy* on which our sentiments of virtue depend, and that *limited generosity* which I have frequently observed to be natural to men, and which justice and property suppose, according to the precedent reasoning. My sympathy with another may give me the sentiment of pain and disapprobation, when any object is presented that has a tendency to give him uneasiness, though I may not be willing to sacrifice anything of my own interest, or cross any of my passions for his satisfaction. A house may displease me by being ill-contrived for the convenience of the owner; and yet I may refuse to give a shilling towards the rebuilding of it. Sentiments must touch the heart to make them control our passions; but they need not extend beyond the imagination to make them influence our taste. When a building seems clumsy and tottering to the eye, it is ugly and disagreeable, though we may be fully assured of the solidity of the workmanship. It is a kind of fear which causes this sentiment of disapprobation; but the passion is not the same with that which we feel when obliged to stand under a wall that we really think tottering and insecure. The *seeming tendencies* of objects affect the mind; and the emotions they excite are of a like species with those which proceed from the *real consequences* of objects, but their feeling is different. Nay, these emotions are so different in their feeling that they may often be contrary, without destroying each other; as when the fortifications of a city belonging to an enemy are esteemed beautiful upon account of their strength, though we could wish that they were entirely destroyed. The imagination adheres to the *general* views of things, and distinguishes the feelings they produce from those which arise from our particular and momentary situation.

If we examine the panegyrics that are commonly made of great men, we shall find that most of the qualities which are attributed to them may be divided into two kinds, viz., such as make them perform their part in society; and such as render them serviceable to themselves and enable them to promote their own interest. Their *prudence, temperance, frugality, industry, assiduity, enterprise, dexterity,* are celebrated as well as their *generosity* and *humanity.* If we ever give an indulgence to any quality that disables a man from making a figure in life, it is to that of *indolence* which is not supposed to deprive one of his parts and capacity, but only suspends their exercise; and that without any inconvenience to the person himself, since it is, in some measure, from his own choice. Yet indolence is always allowed to be a fault, and a very great one if extreme: nor do a man's friends ever acknowledge him to be subject to it but in order to save his character in more material articles. He could make a figure, say they, if he pleased to give application. His understanding is sound, his conception quick, and his memory tenacious; but he hates business, and is indifferent about his fortune. And this a man sometimes may make even a subject of vanity, though with the air of confessing a fault; because he may think that this incapacity for business implies much more noble qualities, such as a philosophical spirit, a fine taste, a delicate wit, or a relish for pleasure and society. But take any other case: suppose a quality that, without being an indication of any other good qualities, incapacitates a man *always* for business, and is destructive to his interest; such as a blundering understanding and a wrong judgment of everything in life; inconstancy and irresolution; or a want of address in the management of men and business: these are all allowed to be imperfections in a character; and many men would rather acknowledge the greatest crimes than have it suspected that they are in any degree subject to them.

It is very happy, in our philosophical researches, when we find the same phenomenon diversified by a variety of circumstances, and, by discovering what is common among them, can the better assure ourselves of the truth of any hypothesis we may make use of to explain it. Were nothing esteemed virtue but what were beneficial to society, I am persuaded that the foregoing explication of the moral sense ought still to be received, and that upon sufficient evidence. But this evidence must grow upon us when we find other kinds of virtue which will not admit of any explication except from that hypothesis. Here is a man who is not remarkably defective in his social qualities; but what principally recommends him is his dexterity in business by which he has extricated himself from the greatest difficulties and conducted the most delicate affairs with a singular address and prudence. I find an esteem for him immediately to arise in me: his company is a satisfaction to me; and before I have any further acquaintance with him, I would rather do him a service than another whose character is in every other respect equal, but is deficient in that particular. In this case, the qualities that please me are all considered as useful to the person, and as having a tendency to promote his interest and satisfaction. They are only regarded as means to an end, and please me in proportion to their fitness for that end. The end, therefore, must be agreeable to me. But what makes the end agreeable? The person is a stranger: I am no way interested in him, nor lie under any obligation to him; his happiness concerns not me, further than the happiness of every human and indeed of every sensible creature; that is, it affects me only by sympathy. From that principle, whenever I discover his happiness and good, whether in its causes or effects, I enter so deeply into it that it gives me a sensible emotion. The appearance of qualities that have a *tendency* to promote it have an agreeable effect upon my imagination and command my love and esteem.

There have been many systems of morality advanced by philosophers in all ages; but if they are strictly examined, they may be reduced to two which alone merit our attention. Moral good and evil are certainly distinguished by our *sentiments*, not by *reason:* but these sentiments may arise either from the mere species or appearance of characters and passions, or from reflections on their tendency to the happiness of mankind and of particular persons. My opinion is that both these causes are intermixed in our judgments of morals, after the same manner as they are in our decisions concerning most kinds of external beauty: though I am also of opinion that reflections on the tendencies of actions have by far the greatest influence and determine all the great lines of our duty. There are, however, instances in cases of less moment, wherein this immediate taste or sentiment produces our approbation. Wit and a certain easy and disengaged behaviour are qualities *immediately agreeable* to others and command their love and esteem. Some of these qualities produce satisfaction in others by particular *original* principles of human nature, which cannot be accounted for: others may be resolved into principles which are more general. This will best appear upon a particular inquiry.

As some qualities acquire their merit from their being *immediately agreeable* to others, without any tendency to public interest, so some are denominated virtuous from their being *immediately agreeable* to the person himself who possesses them. Each of the passions and operations of the mind has a particular feeling, which must be either agreeable or disagreeable. The first is virtuous, the second vicious. This particular feeling constitutes the very nature of the passions, and therefore needs not be accounted for.

But however directly the distinction of vice and virtue may seem to flow from the immediate pleasure or uneasiness, which particular qualities cause to ourselves or others, it is easy to observe that it has also a considerable dependence on the principle of *sympathy* so often insisted on. We approve of a person who is possessed of qualities *immediately agreeable* to those with whom he has any commerce, though perhaps we ourselves never reaped any pleasure from them. We also approve of one who is possessed of qualities that are *immediately agreeable* to himself, though they be of no service to any mortal. To account for this, we must have recourse to the foregoing principles.

Thus to take a general review of the present hypothesis: Every quality of the mind is denominated virtuous which gives pleasure by the mere survey, as every quality which produces pain is called vicious. This pleasure and this pain may arise from four different sources. For we reap a pleasure from the view of a character which is naturally fitted to be useful to others or to the person himself, or which is agreeable to others or to the person himself. One may perhaps be surprised that amidst all these interests and pleasures we should forget our own which touch us so nearly on every other occasion. But we shall easily satisfy ourselves on this head when we consider that every particular person's pleasure and interest being different, it is impossible men could ever agree in their sentiments and judgments, unless they chose some common point of view from which they might survey their object, and which might cause it to appear the same to all of them. Now, in judging of characters, the only interest or pleasure which appears the same to every spectator is that of the person himself whose character is examined, or that of persons who have a connection with him. And though such interests and pleasures touch us more faintly than our own, yet, being more constant and universal, they counterbalance the latter even in practice and are alone admitted in speculation as the standard of virtue and morality. They alone produce that particular feeling or sentiment on which moral distinctions depend.

ENQUIRY CONCERNING THE PRINCIPLES OF MORALS

CONCLUSION

. . . It is sufficient for our present purpose, if it be allowed what surely without the greatest absurdity cannot be disputed, that there is some benevolence, however small, infused into our bosom, some spark of friendship for human kind, some particle of the dove kneaded into our frame, along with the elements of the wolf and serpent. Let these generous sentiments be supposed ever so weak, let them be insufficient to move even a hand or finger of our body, they must still direct the determinations of our mind and, where everything else is equal, produce a cool preference of what is useful and serviceable to mankind above what is pernicious and dangerous. A *moral distinction*, therefore, immediately arises; a general sentiment of blame and approbation; a tendency, however faint, to the objects of the one, and a proportionable aversion to those of the other. Nor will those reasoners who so earnestly maintain the predominant selfishness of human kind be any wise scandalized at hearing of the weak sentiments of virtue implanted in our nature. On the contrary, they are found as ready to maintain the one tenet as the other; and their spirit of satire — for such it appears, rather than of corruption — naturally gives rise to both opinions, which have, indeed, a great and almost an indissoluble connexion together.

Avarice, ambition, vanity, and all passions vulgarly, though improperly, comprised under the denomination of *self-love*, are here excluded from our theory concerning the origin of morals, not because they are too weak, but because they have not a proper direction for that purpose. The notion of morals implies some sentiment common to all mankind, which recommends the same object to general approbation, and makes every man, or most men, agree in the same opinion or decision concerning it. It also implies some sentiment so universal and comprehensive as to extend to all mankind and render the actions and conduct, even of the persons the most remote, an object of applause or censure, according as they agree or disagree with that rule of right which is established. These two requisite circumstances belong alone to the sentiment of humanity here insisted on. The other passions produce in every breast many strong sentiments of desire and aversion, affection and hatred; but these neither are felt so much in common nor are so comprehensive as to be the foundation of any general system and established theory of blame or approbation.

When a man denominates another his *enemy*, his *rival*, his *antagonist*, his *adversary*, he is understood to speak the language of self-love, and to express sentiments peculiar to himself and arising from his particular circumstances and situation. But when he bestows on any man the epithets of *vicious* or *odious* or *depraved*, he then speaks another language, and expresses sentiments in which he expects all his audience are to concur with him. He must here, therefore, depart from his private and particular situation and must choose a point of view common to him with others; he must move some universal principle of the human frame and touch a string to which all mankind have an accord and symphony. If he mean, therefore, to express that this man possesses qualities whose tendency is pernicious to society, he has chosen this common point of view and has touched the principle of humanity in which every man, in some degree, concurs. While the human heart is compounded of the same elements as at present, it will never be wholly indifferent to public good, nor entirely unaffected with the tendency of characters and manners. And though this affection of humanity may not generally be esteemed so strong as vanity or ambition, yet, being common to all men, it can alone be the foundation of morals or of any general system of blame or praise. One man's ambition is not another's ambition, nor will the same event or object satisfy both; but the humanity of one man is the humanity of every one, and the same object touches this passion in all human creatures.

But the sentiments which arise from humanity are not only the same in all human creatures, and produce the same approbation or censure, but they also comprehend all human creatures; nor is there any one whose conduct or character is not, by their means, an object to every one of censure or approbation. On the contrary, those other passions, commonly denominated selfish, both produce different sentiments in each individual, according to his particular situation, and also contemplate the greater part of mankind with the utmost indifference and unconcern. Whoever has a high regard and esteem for me flatters my vanity; whoever expresses contempt mortifies and displeases me; but as my name is known but to a small part of mankind, there are few who come within the sphere of this passion, or excite, on its account, either my affection or disgust. But if you represent a tyrannical, insolent, or barbarous behaviour, in any country or in any age of the world, I soon carry my eye to the pernicious tendency of such a conduct and feel the sentiment of repugnance and displeasure towards it. No character can be so remote as to be, in this light, wholly indifferent to me.

What is beneficial to society or to the person himself must still be preferred. And every quality or action of every human being must, by this means, be ranked under some class or denomination expressive of general censure or applause.

What more, therefore, can we ask to distinguish the sentiments dependent on humanity from those connected with any other passion, or to satisfy us why the former are the origin of morals, not the latter? Whatever conduct gains my approbation by touching my humanity procures also the applause of all mankind, by affecting the same principle in them; but what serves my avarice or ambition pleases these passions in me alone and affects not the avarice and ambition of the rest of mankind. There is no circumstance of conduct in any man, provided it have a beneficial tendency, that is not agreeable to my humanity, however remote the person; but every man, so far removed as neither to cross nor serve my avarice and ambition, is regarded as wholly indifferent by those passions. The distinction, therefore, between these species of sentiment being so great and evident, language must soon be moulded upon it and must invent a peculiar set of terms in order to express those universal sentiments of censure or approbation which arise from humanity or from views of general usefulness and its contrary. Virtue and Vice become then known; morals are recognized; certain general ideas are framed of human conduct and behaviour; such measures are expected from men in such situations. This action is determined to be conformable to our abstract rule; that other, contrary. And by such universal principles are the particular sentiments of self-love frequently controlled and limited.

QUESTIONS

1. In Hume's important first paragraph, what is the outline of his argument to prove that "morality is more properly felt than judged of"?
2. Do you think Hume is right in suggesting that our reaction to observing a virtuous deed is, at least generally, one of pleasure and that our reaction to observing vicious deeds is one of displeasure? Does this view commit Hume to saying that every time anything pleases us we, in effect, are feeling that it is morally good?
3. Explain how the following answers the preceding question: "It is only when a character is considered in general, without reference to our particular interest, that it causes such a feeling or sentiment as denominates it morally good or evil."
4. Does Hume think that for every kind of action we deem obligatory or wrong there is a separate innate tendency to feel pleasure or displeasure upon observation of it?
5. In what sense does Hume think that moral judgments, or feelings, are natural?
6. How does Hume infer from the foregoing considerations that it is proper to call a mind virtuous (morally good) if it excites (impersonal) love or

pride, and vicious (morally bad) if it excites (impersonal) hatred or humility?

7. Is Hume right in suggesting that we regard actions as morally good or bad only in so far as they manifest morally good or bad traits of character?

8. Does Hume's account of the psychology of sympathetic emotions imply that people are not entirely selfish?

9. How does Hume's conception of sympathy enable him to account for general approval of qualities of mind or conduct which are useful to mankind generally?

10. What is Hume's answer to the proposal that morality is an invention of politicians, for the sake of conforming human conduct to the requirements of social living?

11. What is the difference between the "natural virtues" and justice, according to Hume? Why does he admit that his theory applies more plausibly to the former (e.g., acts of generosity) than to the latter (e.g., giving money you find to a rich man to whom it belongs, rather than to a poor man who needs it)?

12. How does Hume answer the objection that we regard two similar acts as equally praiseworthy, although the one act done by a friend excites much more feeling in us than the other, similar act done by a stranger in a foreign country or in an earlier century?

13. Explain the meaning and importance of the following: "These variations we regard not in our general decisions, but still apply the terms expressive of our liking or dislike in the same manner as if we remained in one point of view. Experience soon teaches us this method of correcting our sentiments, or at least of correcting our language. . . . We blame equally a bad action which we read of in history, with one performed in our neighbourhood the other day; the meaning of which is that we know from reflection that the former action would excite as strong sentiments of disapprobation as the latter, were it placed in the same position."

14. How does Hume explain the fact that we deem a person's qualities morally good irrespective of whether he is an effectual person and of whether the qualities actually succeed in doing any good for mankind?

15. How does Hume explain our regarding indolence as a moral fault?

16. Is Hume's moral theory (a) a scientific hypothesis which explains how people feel and judge, (b) an analysis of the meaning and verifiability of moral judgments, or (c) both?

17. It has been objected to Hume's theory that it implies that moral questions can be settled by collecting statistics about how various people feel — whereas, fairly obviously, they cannot be settled in this way. Is the criticism a fair one?

SUGGESTIONS FOR FURTHER READING

Kydd, R. M. *Reason and Conduct in Hume's Treatise.* New York: Oxford Univ. Press, 1946.

Laird, John. *Hume's Philosophy of Human Nature.* London: Methuen, 1932.

MacNabb, D. G. C. *David Hume: His Theory of Knowledge and Morality.* New York: Longmans, Green, 1951.

Mossner, E. C. *The Life of David Hume*. Edinburgh: Nelson, 1954.
Passmore, J. A. *Hume's Intentions*. New York: Cambridge Univ. Press, 1952.
Smith, N. K. *The Philosophy of David Hume*. New York: Macmillan, 1941.

Patrick H. Nowell-Smith (1914-   )

MULTIFUNCTIONALISM

P. H. Nowell-Smith was an undergraduate at New College, Oxford. After service in the British army in the Middle East and in India, he was elected a fellow of Trinity College, Oxford. He is now professor of philosophy at the University of Leicester. The most important of his writings is *Ethics*, a book in the Pelican series published in 1954, which has excited a considerable amount of interest.

Nowell-Smith is critical of all the types of theory we have encountered thus far; each, he thinks, has had an important point to make, but each also has drawn mistaken inferences from its point and has otherwise overshot the mark. Nowell-Smith is one of a group of British philosophers who believe that very careful attention to the way in which words are used will serve to show that many prolonged controversies have been founded on confusions or oversimplifications about language and need not have occurred. In ethics in particular, he thinks, many have supposed that a given ethical word has only one job to do, and that it does this one job on all occasions; this supposition, he thinks, is a mistake — indeed words are often doing at least two jobs at once. (When words do this, he calls them Janus-words.) Again, he thinks moral philosophers have overlooked the richness of what is implied by certain words when used in certain contexts; equally they have had their eyes fixed so inflexibly on the questions about what moral statements assert and what feelings (if any) they express, that they have overlooked the many other things moral language does — such things as prescribe, praise, condemn, exhort, urge, advise. Once we take all these things into account, he suggests, we shall feel much less dissatisfied with our description of the working of ethical words than we tend to be with both naturalist accounts and the emotive theory. Nowell-Smith's own theory of ethics consists in large part of a detailed description of the jobs, meanings, and implications typical of moral words in different contexts; of the relations of different moral words to one another; of the role of moral discourse as a whole in society. Nowell-Smith's conclusion is in large part noncognitivist: he holds that the primary function of moral language is not often that of making an assertion which is true or false; usually the primary job is something like praising or advising — and in this case nothing true or false is asserted, although the use of moral language may be misleading if something implied by its use does not happen to be true.

By way of explanation of some terms in the early paragraphs below, it may be said that an "A-word" is one like "terrifying" in that it indicates that an object has properties which tend to arouse a certain emotion or range of emotions. A "G-word" is one, like "praiseworthy," which implies that an attitude or reaction ought to be aroused by a thing.

From Patrick H. Nowell-Smith, *Ethics*, published by Penguin Books, Baltimore, and Harmondsworth, Middlesex, 1954, and reprinted with their permission, Ch. 12.

ETHICS

'GOOD'

1

'GOOD' IN THE CONTEXT OF CHOICE   We have seen that when 'good' is used in the context of choice there can be no logical gap between deciding that something is the best or better than its rivals and choosing it. This does not imply that there can be no discrepancy between the decision which is, on the face of it, not a performance of any kind but a judgement, and the choice; but it does imply that if there is such a discrepancy a special reason must be given for it. And we must now consider the role of such expressions as 'because it is a good one' and 'because it is the best' when they are used to explain why a man chose the thing he did.

The answer to the question 'Why did you choose that car?' might be a statement of fact ('because it has more leg-room') or an A-sentence ('because it is more comfortable'); and I have already discussed the contextual background in which such answers can be given and taken as logically complete explanations. In each case the car must have some A-property and some ordinary, empirical properties on which its A-property depends. While the factual answer says what the empirical properties are and contextually implies an A-property without specifying what it is, the A-sentence does the reverse. And each answer implies a pro-attitude towards the A-property concerned; otherwise it would not be an answer to the question.

The answer 'because it is the best' functions in a similar way, but with certain important differences. In the first place it does not just imply a pro-attitude; it expresses it. But it does not only do this. If this were all I wanted to do I should have to say 'because I happen to like it more than the others.' It contextually implies that I have reasons for my choice; but it does not say what they are and therefore does not explain my choice.

We are tempted to say that it gives the best possible reason. After all, what better reason could there be for choosing a car than the fact that it was the best available or the best that I could afford? What better reason could there be for doing anything than the belief that it is the best thing to do?

The trouble is that the reason is *too* good. It is like saying that I was frightened because it was a terrifying experience; and, as an explanation, it operates in much the same way. Just as 'because it was terrifying' shows that my fear was not an unusual one and contextually implies that the object had certain unspecified properties by which people are usually frightened, so 'because it was the best' shows that my choice was no passing whim, that it was considered more or less carefully, that the object had certain unspecified 'good-making' properties, and that my choice was not a peculiar one. Any of these contextual implications could be expressly withdrawn, especially, as we shall see, the last; but in default of such withdrawal my audience would be entitled to assume them. Just as a G-sentence showed more plainly than an A-sentence that advice was being given but was less explicit about the reasons, so 'because it was the best' shows more plainly that I was choosing but says even less about the reasons.

In fact it says nothing about them at all; it only implies that I have reasons. The goodness of something is not one of the properties for which I choose it. If it were, it would make sense to ask why its superior goodness was a reason for choosing it. To ask a man who chose a car because it was faster or more economical or had more leg-room why he chose it is to display ignorance of people's purchasing habits; to say to him "I know you thought it the best car; but why did you choose it?" is logically odd.

The same logical ties that bind goodness so closely to choosing bind it also to activities that are akin to choosing. A man who says that he voted for a certain proposal because he thought it good has not explained why he voted for it; he has merely guarded himself against accusations of flippancy, irresponsibility or indulging in complicated machinations. And it is logically odd to say "I think it is an excellent proposal, but I shan't vote for it." As we saw, reasons could be given for this discrepancy, and the logical nexus between thinking good and voting comes out in the fact that we should feel entitled to infer that there must be a special reason. To call something good is, in a way, already to vote for it, to side with it, to let others know where I stand. But it does more than this; it implies that I have reasons for casting my vote as I do.

'GOOD' IN THE CONTEXT OF ADVICE   The considerations that apply to 'good' in the context of choice apply equally in the context of advice. And here again the subjectivist is right in connecting 'this is good' with the pro-attitude of the speaker. There is the same sort of absurdity in 'This is good, but I don't advise you to do it' as there is in 'This is the best course; but shall I take it?'. In the latter case the speaker both expresses a decision as to how he should act and in the same breath asks if he should; and in the former he gives advice and in the same breath retracts it. It would be equally odd if the hearer were to say "You have told me that it is the best course to take; but do you advise me to take it?".

The differences in the use of 'good' in advice and choice are due to the fact that the problem to be solved is now someone else's. The adviser is not making up his mind what to do, but helping someone else to make up his mind. And this difference brings with it another. The relevant pro-attitude is that of the audience. But in other respects the contextual implications are the same. To tell someone that something is the best thing for him to do is to advise him to do it, but not irresponsibly. The speaker implies that he has good reasons for his advice, that he knows what the problem is and that his advice is relevant. The same predictive and causal elements are present as in the case of A-sentences; and advice may, as before, be given disingenuously, improperly, mistakenly, or unfortunately if one or other of the contextual implications is absent.

2

OTHER USES OF 'GOOD'   I shall discuss the other uses of 'good' in the order in which they seem to diverge more and more from the fundamental use, which is to express or explain a preference.

(a) *Praising and Applauding.* Like choosing, these are performances, not statements; and, although in primary uses they do express the speaker's pro-attitude, they have other contextual implications which will be examined later. They can be done with or without words; but the gestures, hand-clapping and the like, which are used for praising have conventional, symbolic meanings. They mean what they do in the way that words mean, not in the way that clouds mean rain or cobras in the garden mean trouble. Virtue-words are words of praise; and relatively specific words like 'brave,' 'honest,' and 'generous' are also descriptive; for they describe a person's behaviour and predict the way in which he can be relied upon to behave in certain sorts of situation. They both praise and give the reason, what the praise is *for.* But 'good' does not do this. In cases where there are recognized standards that a man must reach to be worthy of praise they contextually imply that he has reached those standards; but they do not say what the standards are. 'Because it is a good one' does not explain why I praise something; but it does imply that the thing has certain unspecified properties for which I praise it. My praise was not casual or capricious.

(b) *Commending.* The verb 'to commend' is used in two ways. It may mean 'entrust to the care of'; but this sense is irrelevant, since 'good' is not used to commend in this sense. In the sense in which 'good' is used for commending it is akin to praising but has a more hortatory force. To commend something to someone is to advise him to choose it. The Oxford Dictionary, as we saw, calls 'good' "the most general adjective of commendation" in English; but it goes on to add "implying the existence in a high or at least satisfactory degree of characteristic qualities which are either admirable in themselves or useful for some purpose."

The form of this definition is interesting, since it brings out the difference between the job that the word is used for and the conditions limiting its use in a way that philosophers' definitions of 'good' never do. The writer of the dictionary sees clearly that the word is used to do a job which is not 'stating' but commending and that the elements of objective fact which some philosophers insist on treating as part of its meaning are really part of the contextual background of its use. In the uses which follow, this contextual background looms larger and larger, so that in some uses the word 'good' almost comes to be a descriptive word, though, as we shall see, it never quite does this and in moral contexts it can never wholly lose its gerundive force or its pro-force.

(c) *Verdicts and Appraisals*. In chapter 1 we saw that moral language is not only used for choosing and advising, but also making moral judgements, which are not decisions to do something but verdicts or appraisals of something or somebody. Now appraisals are *judgements*, not just expressions of a man's own taste or preference; and it is this point that the Consequential Property Theory tries to bring out, but in a misleading way. When we judge something to be good we always judge it to be good in respect of some property, and it is a question of empirical fact whether it has this property or not. Thus to judge a wine to be good is not just to express a preference for it — and we shall see that it need not be to do this at all —; the judgement must be backed by my belief that it has a certain bouquet, body, and flavour, and these are objective qualities, since a man who found that he disagreed markedly from all the experts on these points would admit himself to be wrong. It is an essential feature of judgements that they are made by reference to standards or criteria; but it is necessary to be extremely careful in discussing the way in which the criteria are related to the verdict or appraisal.

Let us assume for the moment that the criteria used by experts at wine-tastings, horse-shows, beauty contests, and school examinations are agreed to be the proper criteria, though this will have to be questioned later. We might be tempted to say that if the criteria for being a good X are that the X must have properties a, b, and c in some specifiable degree, then 'good X' simply means 'X which has the properties a, b, and c in the requisite degree.' But this will not do. For it is possible to understand what 'good X' means without knowing what the criteria are. Thus, if I do not know the criteria used at Crufts I could not tell a good dog (in this sense of 'good') from a bad one or pick out the best dog from a group. But this does not mean that I cannot understand what 'good dog' means in the way that I could not understand what 'mangy dog' meant if I did not know what 'mangy' meant. For I do know that if it is a good dog it must have in a fairly high degree those properties which are mentioned in the list of criteria for judging dogs, although I do not know what these properties are or to what degree a dog must have them to rate as 'good.'

The next two uses are special cases of the appraising use.

(d) *Efficiency*. When 'good' is predicated of any object (natural or artificial, animate or inanimate) that is used for a purpose it implies the presence in a relatively high degree of those properties that the object must have to do its job. But again it would be a mistake to say that 'good knife' just *means* 'knife that is sharp, easily handled, durable, etc.' The connexion between the properties which a knife must have to be efficient and its efficiency is an empirical one. We know from experience that a knife which has not got these properties at all just won't cut and that its relative efficiency at cutting depends on the degree to which it has these properties. Nor can we even say that 'good knife' means 'knife which cuts efficiently,' because we could understand what 'good' means in the expression 'good knife' without knowing what knives were for. But 'good knife' (in this sense of 'good') does mean 'Knife which has those properties (whatever they are) which a knife must have if it is to do its job efficiently (whatever that is).'

(e) *Skill*. When we call a man a good lawyer, scholar, cricketer or liar, the use is similar to the 'efficiency' use except for the fact that, since these are men, the purpose concerned is their purpose, not the purpose they are used for. Just as we could not use 'good' to imply efficiency unless we agreed about what the object concerned is for, so we could not use it to imply skill unless there was something that was agreed to constitute success at the activity concerned. But, just as we cannot say that 'good' means 'efficient' in the one sense, so we cannot say that it means 'successful' in the other. In activities involving skill there are rules for achieving success which are such that we know from experience that unless a man applies them he is unlikely to be successful. Thus, if we know the rules for success at bridge or cricket we can predict, in a very general way, what a good bridge-player or cricketer will do; and in calling a man 'good' we imply that he applies or follows the rules. This implication can, of course, be expressly withdrawn because we know that people sometimes achieve success in very unorthodox ways. But 'good' never quite loses its gerundive force and if we call a man a good cricketer without intending to imply that his methods ought to be imitated we mislead our audience.

(f) *The descriptive use*. Like most words, 'good' can be used to mean 'what most people would call good.' A man who uses it may not be choosing, advising, defending a choice or piece of advice, or appraising, but referring to an object which he or others would call good if they were doing one of these. Thus I may call a wine good even if I am not competent to apply the criteria, just because I have heard the experts praise it.

This use belongs to descriptive discourse because it is a question of historical fact whether people do or do not call the object good, and that is what is being asserted. It is necessarily a secondary use, since it would be impossible to use 'good' to mean 'what people call good' unless people called things good in primary ways. And 'good' is hardly ever used with this descriptive force alone. The speaker implies that he himself sides with those who call the thing good unless this implication is expressly withdrawn or obviously inadmissible in the context.

3

We must now consider the ways in which these uses of 'good' are connected with each other. It is clearly not an accident that the same word is used in all these different ways nor could this fact be explained in a purely historical or philological way. 'Good' is *the* Janus-word *par excellence*; it is often used to do more than one job on one occasion and the logical connexions between the various jobs are what they are because the facts are what they are. It is also most emphatically an ordinary, non-technical word and it is a consequence of this that the logic of its use reflects empirical truths that hold only for the most part and admit of exceptions. For ordinary language, unlike mathematics, is not deliberately constructed by men who have a keen eye for consistency and rigour; it is not deliberately constructed at all but grows and changes in an environment in which the exceptional case can be and must be ignored. The contextual implications of any use of 'good' are many and varied and, on occasion, any of them can be withdrawn, a point which should make us suspicious of counter-examples. It is impossible to understand the actual uses of 'good' by considering artificial and exceptional situations because the logic of ordinary language does not cater for such situations.

But there is one element which seems to be common to all cases. Although a man need have no comparisons in mind when he calls something 'good,' such comparisons are always implied. He must, if challenged, be able to produce examples of descriptively similar things that he would call not so good. For example, we always praise something with a certain degree of warmth which lies somewhere on a scale between mild commendation and hysterical adulation. The word 'good' can be used to express almost any degree of warmth, but it must be less than that expressed in the same context by 'excellent' or 'superb' and greater than that expressed by 'fair' or 'tolerable.'

It is not difficult to understand the connexions between the more obviously performatory uses, praising, applauding, and commending; nor is it difficult to appreciate their intimate connexion with preference and choice. To praise is not to choose; but it is connected with choosing in that it would be odd for a man to choose the thing he was prepared to praise less highly or not at all. He must have special reasons for this, modesty for example, a sense of unworthiness to possess the 'better' thing or a desire that someone else should have it. Again, if a man habitually praises one pianist more highly than another we expect to find him attending the recitals of the former more regularly and to be more annoyed when he is prevented from going. But he might have been told that the second is really a better pianist and be trying to cultivate a taste for his performance. Explanations can be given of discrepancies between praising and choice; but in default of an explanation the connexion is contextually implied.

If, on a particular occasion, I call a man brave it would be logically odd to ask if I was in favour of what he did; for 'brave' is a praising word and by using it I show that I am in favour. Similarly, if I call courage a 'virtue' I show that I am, in a general way, in favour of courage, although I might not always want to praise a brave deed. It is an empirical fact that men are, for the most part, in favour of the modes of conduct that they call (descriptively) brave, honest, or generous. But this pro-attitude is so widespread that these words are not pure descriptive words; they are terms of praise and imply a pro-attitude unless this is expressly withdrawn.

Now praising and applauding are activities which are often performed with the special purpose of encouraging the person concerned to continue in the same style, and hissing and booing are used with the opposite intention. Although the words and gestures employed in praising owe their encouraging force to convention, they have, granted the convention, a natural effect on the people praised. For it is an empirical fact that, except in special circumstances — for example, if the praise is considered impertinent — people enjoy being praised and are therefore likely to go on doing what they are praised for. Praising is logically tied to approval; for if we heard a man praise something we could not wonder whether he approved of it or not unless we suspected him of being disingenuous or ironical; and it is logically tied in the same way to encouraging. But, although it is an empirical fact that men tend to encourage and try to promote that of which they approve, we must, as always, assume that men on the whole intend the natural consequences of their actions and therefore do not praise that which they would prefer to be otherwise. And this assumption is reflected in the fact that praising implies both approval and encouragement.

The same logical ties bind praising to advising; it would be logically odd to praise one candidate more highly than another and to go on to say that one was advising against his being given the job or the prize. Odd, but not impossible; for there might, as always, be special reasons for this.

The "characteristic qualities" which, according to the dictionary, are implied by the use of 'good' may be "either admirable in themselves or useful for some purpose." In contexts involving efficiency or skill it is the latter that we have in mind. In such contexts there need be no direct connexion between the performatory uses, which are all variations of 'preferring' or 'being on the side of,' and the usefulness implied by 'good.' We may have no pro-attitude whatsoever towards the purpose for which something is used or the activity at which a man is skilful, as when we speak of a 'good cosh' or a 'good liar.' But there is still an indirect link with the pro-attitudes since 'good' in these contexts implies success, and 'success' is a pro-word. A man is not a good liar unless he fairly consistently achieves his aim.

PREFERENCE AND APPRAISAL   But it is the connexions between the performatory uses and the verdict-giving, judging, or appraising use when the qualities on which the verdict is based are thought to be "admirable in themselves" that are the most important and the most difficult. I shall substitute 'preferable' for 'admirable,' since admiration is itself a performance akin to praising and 'admirable' is therefore too narrow in scope to cover all appraisals other than those of efficiency or skill.

All the performatory uses contextually imply appraisal; for we have seen that it is improper to use 'good,' at least in an impersonal formula, to express or defend a preference unless the preference is a considered one, based on reasons and not unusual. And to say that the preference is 'based on reasons' is to say that the speaker applied criteria or standards. It is not necessary that he should have done this deliberately; he may have done it automatically; but he must be able to defend his choice by an appeal to the standards which justify it.

But, although the performatory uses imply appraisal, it is not so clear that the converse is true. Indeed it is not true in any direct sense; appraisals often imply preference only in a roundabout way. For when 'good' is used to give a verdict it need neither express nor imply a pro-attitude on the part of the speaker. In such cases what a man is primarily doing with the word 'good' is *applying* those standards which are only contextually implied in the more subjective uses. Since 'good' is a Janus-word, he may, of course, be expressing his preferences or advising as well; but he need not be. The embittered schoolmaster may have no interest in the work of the examination candidates at all; he may even prefer stupidity to intelligence or have a private belief that the usual criteria for intelligence are quite wrong. Nevertheless he may still apply the grading words 'good,' 'fair,' 'poor,' and so on in accordance with the accepted criteria either from conscientiousness or from habit or from fear of losing his job.

In the same way a professional taster of wine may dislike all wine or prefer the less good to the better; his judgement is based solely on the presence of those "characteristic qualities" which, as an expert, he is able to detect and knows to be among the criteria for 'good wine.' But even in these cases there is an indirect reference to choosing and advising which comes out when we turn from the question "What are the criteria in fact used for grading Xs?" to the question "Why do we have the criteria that we do?" Professional wine-tasters are, after all, business men or the employees of business men and, though their job may be to taste wine, they only have this job because wine is to be bought and sold. It is no accident that the criteria for 'good Xs' are connected with the Xs that people pre-fer or approve of more highly. The professional wine-taster may not *like* Chateau Laffitte; but he uses criteria for judging wine under which it gets high marks because people are prepared to pay highly for wine which rates highly under these criteria, and they do this because they like it. . . .

5

NON-PRACTICAL APPRAISALS   We often make appraisals in contexts where there is clearly no question of choosing or advising, for example moral judgements about historical or fictional characters. And this seems to involve a difficulty for theories which make appraisals logically dependent on pro-attitudes. Hutcheson and Hume, for example, tried to reduce moral judgements to expressions of feeling. They were not guilty of the Naturalistic Fallacy, since they were prepared to allow that moral approval and sympathy are special, moral feelings distinct from other types of feeling. But even this concession to the peculiarity of the moral use of language does not save them from an important objection that seems at first sight fatal to their case. Sentiments, as Hume noticed, seem to vary in rough proportion to the pro-pinquity of their objects. We are not moved by the iniquity of remote his-torical characters as we are by those closer to us; and we feel more approval for and sympathy with those near to us than with those who are more re-mote. Yet our moral judgements do not vary in the same way. "We read Cicero now without emotion, yet we can still judge Verres to be a villain. According to Hume's theory our judgement must change as do our feelings. I do not feel indignation as strongly now about the German invasion of Czechoslovakia as I did at the time it happened; yet I do not judge the action to be less wrong than I did then, or the agents less criminal. . . . It is but a weak subterfuge to say we transport ourselves by the force of imagi-nation into distant ages and countries, and consider the passions which we should have felt on contemplating these characters had we been contem-poraries and had commerce with the persons. . . . I now feel completely in-different to Verres, and know it. Yet, Hume tells me, when I judge Verres to have been a villain, I am so deceived by my imagination that I talk as if I felt a strong feeling of anger." [1]

Dr. Raphael's criticism is fatal to the theory that a man who makes a moral appraisal is always expressing a feeling; and a similar criticism could also be made of any theory which says that to appraise is always to praise, advise, commend, etc. On some occasions a man may be simply *applying* the criteria that he and others customarily use for these purposes. To call Verres a villain is to pass a verdict on him, to condemn him. Now the Moral Sense School were, I think, mistaken in construing moral approval and disapproval as *feelings*, since this suggests too strongly the analogy with

[1] D. D. Raphael: *The Moral Sense*, pp. 88 and 91.

itches, aches, and tickles. But they were right to connect moral appraisals and verdicts with approval and disapproval. For although a man who passes a verdict need not be expressing a pro- or con- attitude, we have seen that the criteria he uses are directly or indirectly linked with these attitudes; and in the case of moral judgements they must be linked in a special way that may be absent in other cases.

I said earlier that, although in other cases 'good' might lose its gerundive force, it cannot wholly do so when used to make moral appraisals. The reason is that, whatever may be the case with other types of appraisal, moral appraisals must be universal. Anyone who makes a moral appraisal even of a remote character must be willing to apply the same criteria universally. And it follows from this that he must be willing to apply them in practical contexts. If I am not prepared to condemn anyone whose behaviour is like that of Verres in all relevant respects, then, in calling Verres a villain, I am not making a genuine moral judgement; and the relevant respects are all of an empirical, objective kind. It would, of course, be trivial to include among them an objective property of villainy or moral turpitude; all that is necessary is that I should be prepared to condemn anyone who did the sort of thing that Verres is called a villain for having done, anyone who oppressed the poor, robbed the rich, took bribes, and cheated the treasury, and all for his own personal profit.

Moral appraisals are therefore connected with choosing and advising in a way that non-moral appraisals need not be. It is not logically odd to say "This is the better wine, but I prefer that"; but it is logically odd to say "This is the (morally) better course; but I shall do that." [2] And a man cannot be making a genuine moral judgement about Verres if he would himself be prepared to act on the same principles on which Verres acted and prepared to exhort others to do so. In condemning Verres he is not expressing any emotion; but he is affirming his own moral principles.

6

OBJECTIVE-SUBJECTIVE   In chapter 6 I said that the distinction between "For what job is the word '. . .' used?" and "Under what conditions is it proper to use that word for that job?" throws light on the objective-subjective dispute.

As we should expect, both parties are right. Just as the subjectivists are right in denying that A-words stand for special properties and explaining them in terms of people's reactions, so they are also right in connecting 'good' and 'bad' with people's desires, tastes, interests, approvals, and disapprovals. There is a logical absurdity about calling a play 'amusing' if the speaker believes that it never has amused anyone and never will; and there is the same logical absurdity in calling something 'good' without any direct

---

[2] This may sound surprising. We all know what it is to take what we know to be the morally worse course. I shall try to remove the air of paradox in chapter 18.

or indirect reference to a pro-attitude. If the connexion between 'good' and the pro-attitude that is contextually relevant were not a logical one, a gap would emerge between calling something good on the one hand and deciding to choose it, choosing it or advising others to choose it on the other which would make these activities unintelligible. Moreover, the subjectivists are also right in connecting 'good' with the pro-attitudes of the speaker, at least in moral cases.

But the objectivists are also right. They are mistaken in denying the points made by the subjectivists above and in thinking that goodness must be a unique, non-natural property. It is sometimes argued that if there were no such property we could not account for the fact that we use the impersonal form 'this is good' rather than the personal form 'I approve of this,' and those who use this argument are inclined to forget that we have an impersonal form 'this is nice' as well as the personal form 'I like it,' so that niceness would have to be an objective property too.

It would indeed be puzzling to understand why we use these impersonal forms if we were just talking about or expressing our own approvals; but this argument does not show that we are talking about something else, still less that this must be a unique property. We can account for the objective formula, as we did in the case of 'nice,' by saying (a) that 'X is good' is not only used in the context of choice and (b) that, when it is so used, it implies a great deal that is not implied by 'I approve of X' and is expressly denied by 'I happen to approve of X.' It implies that my approval is not an unusual one and that I could give reasons for it. It implies also — what is a matter of objective fact — that the object conforms to certain standards which are generally accepted.

It is sometimes argued that 'this is good' cannot just mean 'I approve of this' on the ground that we can say "I approve of this because it is good." Approval must therefore be an intellectual emotion which arises in us only when we recognize something to have the objective property 'goodness.' But it has never been clear what the connexion between the approval and the recognition of the property is supposed to be. Is it logically necessary that anyone who recognizes the property should feel approval or is it just an empirical fact that people who notice the property, and only they, have the feeling? Each of these answers involves insuperable difficulties; but if neither is correct we must find some other way of explaining the 'because' in 'I approve of X because it is good.'

The need for such an explanation vanishes when we see that this is not a reason-giving 'because' like that in 'I approve of Jones because he is kind to children' but more like 'I like Jones because he is likeable.' It rebuts the suggestion that I just 'happen to' approve of X and it implies that X has certain properties which make it worthy of my approval and that it conforms to the known standards for Xs.

The objectivist is right in drawing attention to the factual background which makes impersonal appraisals possible; but the facts which it contains are ordinary, empirical facts, not special, non-natural facts. Unlike the subjectivist (who tends to ignore the background altogether), he tries to include the background in the meaning of the word; and this, combined with the mistake of confusing practical and descriptive discourse, leads him into the vain pursuit of a single ingredient to which we always refer when we call something good.

QUESTIONS

1. Is Nowell-Smith right in thinking that to say "It is the best one" expresses a pro-attitude, and therefore the person who says these words must give "a special reason" if he fails to choose the object so described? He suggests that the difference between "it is good" and "I happen to like it" is that the former implies that I have reasons for my choice, that my choice or attitude is a considered one and not peculiar, and that the object has certain unspecified "good-making" properties. Can you think of other differences? And do you think the ones he mentions are really differences?

2. Do you think "This is the best course, but shall I take it?" is a logically odd question? What does Nowell-Smith think "This is the best" implies about the attitudes of the auditor, when someone uses it in the context of advising the auditor?

3. He says that gestures and hand-clapping "mean what they do in the way that words mean, not in the way that clouds mean rain. . . ." What do you think he might mean by this explanation?

4. List the jobs Nowell-Smith suggests ethical phrases do, as distinct from describing or making statements. Do you think one might reasonably say that they do these jobs *by* making some statement — as a naturalist might say?

5. What does he think are the differences in implication between the use of "good" in contexts of advice and in contexts of praising, commending, and giving a verdict?

6. Why does he think "good" cannot be given a naturalistic definition when used in judgments of skill or efficiency? Why does he think the descriptive use is "secondary"?

7. Would Nowell-Smith concede that his generalization about an implication of "good" could be refuted by citing counter examples? What evidence would he accept?

8. What is his view about the relation between appraisive uses of "good" and the approval or attitudes of the speaker? Does Nowell-Smith think that *all* uses of "good" are appraisive, or at least that a favorable appraisal is implied by all?

9. How serious is the cited criticism of Hume (p. 414) by Raphael?

10. Why does Nowell-Smith say that moral appraisals are "connected with choosing and advising in a way that non-moral appraisals need not be"? Does he have a reason for saying that moral appraisals "must be universal"?

11. How does he establish (if he does) that there is a "logical absurdity" in calling something good without any "reference to a pro-attitude"?

Kurt Baier (1917-)

THE ESSENTIALS OF MORALITY

Kurt Baier (see headnote on p. 133) is not a noncognitivist. Moreover, the selection that follows does not adequately represent what he thinks unless it is read along with some other pages (supra, pp. 136-40). Nevertheless some philosophers who are non-cognitivists welcome a proposal like the following. For it opens up the possibility that, even if we do not say that ethical judgments are ever true or false or known, we *can* say that certain ones (and *not* certain others) are *moral* judgments. It opens up the possibility of distinguishing *moral* from personal attitudes. And it opens up the possibility of saying that a judgment, action, or attitude is *morally justified* — required by, or at least compatible with, acceptance of the core of morality. This means, for example, that while we cannot say that a moral judgment is true, we can say that it is moral or morally justified, and that *this latter judgment is true.* Another way of putting the matter is to say that Baier's discussion may be construed as a conceptual analysis of "morality" or "moral judgment" or "morally justified" or "moral attitude"; and it might be argued that his analysis of these terms, although a "naturalist" one, is an acceptable analysis, whereas naturalistic definitions of words like "wrong" and "desirable" and "reprehensible" are not acceptable.

We might, then, adopt a noncognitivist view of the meaning and function of ethical words — say Stevenson's or Russell's or Nowell-Smith's — ; and we might supplement it with Baier's chapter and say that a judgment is "morally justified" if it, or the attitude it expresses, is coherent with the moral point of view. Baier himself speaks of a moral conviction being "true" under certain conditions; we might, however, prefer to say instead that moral convictions are "morally justified" under these conditions.

From Kurt Baier, *The Moral Point of View: a Rational Basis of Ethics.* Copyright 1958 by Cornell University, published by Cornell University Press, Ithaca, N. Y., and reprinted with their permission.

THE MORAL POINT OF VIEW

What, then, is the test (if any) which a moral conviction must pass in order to be called true? Many philosophers have held that there is not and cannot be such a test. They would perhaps admit that we may reduce our moral convictions to a few basic moral principles, or perhaps even only one, from which all others can be derived, but they would hold that at least one such principle must simply be selected as we please. Such basic principles are matters for deciding, not for finding out.

I shall argue, on the contrary, that our moral convictions are true if they can be seen to be required or acceptable *from the moral point of view*. It is indeed true that a person must adopt the moral point of view if he is to be moral. But it is not true that this is an arbitrary decision. On the contrary, I shall show, in Chapter Twelve [supra, pp. 136-40], that there are the very best reasons for adopting this point of view.

Answers to practical questions can be arrived at by reference to a point of view, which may be defined by a principle. When we adopt a certain point of view, we adopt its defining principle. To look at practical problems from that point of view is to be prepared to answer practical questions of the form 'What shall I do?' 'What should be done?' by reference to its defining principle.

Suppose the problem under discussion is whether or not a certain traffic roundabout should be erected at a certain intersection. I can look at this from various points of view, that of a pedestrian or a motorist, a local politician or a manufacturer of roundabouts, and so on. In cases such as these, we have in mind the point of view of self-interest as applied to certain special positions or jobs or functions in a society. To look at our problem from the point of view of a motorist is to ask whether the erection of a roundabout at this intersection is in the interest of a motorist. For different points of view there may, of course, be different, even opposing, answers to the same practical questions. The roundabout may be in the interest of a motorist but not of a pedestrian, in the interest of a manufacturer of roundabouts but not of a local politician who depends for his votes on the poorer section (the pedestrians) of the population.

However, a point of view is not necessarily defined by the principle of self-interest or its more specific application to a particular position in society. We can, for instance, look at this problem from the point of view of town planners or traffic experts, who may favor the roundabout because their special task is to solve traffic problems. Their point of view is defined by the principle 'Favor anything that keeps the traffic flowing; oppose anything that is likely to cause traffic holdups.' But the erection of the roundabout can hardly be said to be *in their interest*. They do not derive any personal advantage or benefit from the scheme. There are many such disinterested points of view, for example, the point of view of a social worker, a social reformer, an advocate of public health schemes, a missionary. . . .

Clearly, our central problem is to define the moral point of view.

1   SELF-INTEREST AND MORALITY

Throughout the history of philosophy, by far the most popular candidate for the position of the moral point of view has been self-interest. There are obvious parallels between these two standpoints. Both aim at the good. Both are rational. Both involve deliberation, the surveying and weighing of reasons. The adoption of either yields statements containing the word 'ought.' Both involve the notion of self-mastery and control over the desires. It is, moreover, plausible to hold that a person could not have a reason for doing anything whatsoever unless his behavior was designed to promote his own good. Hence, if morality is to have the support of reason, moral reasons must be self-interested, hence the point of view of morality and self-interest must be the same. On the other hand, it seems equally obvious that morality and self-interest are very frequently opposed. Morality often requires us to refrain from doing what self-interest recommends or to do what self-interest forbids. Hence morality and self-interest cannot be the same points of view.

Can we save the doctrine that the moral point of view is that of self-interest? One way of circumventing the difficulty just mentioned is to draw a distinction between two senses of 'self-interest,' shortsighted and enlightened. The shortsighted egoist always follows his short-range interest without taking into consideration how this will affect others and how their reactions will affect him. The enlightened egoist, on the other hand, knows that he cannot get the most out of life unless he pays attention to the needs of others on whose good will he depends. On this view, the standpoint of (immoral) egoism differs from that of morality in that it fails to consider the interests of others even when this costs little or nothing or when the long-range benefits to oneself are likely to be greater than the short-range sacrifices.

This view can be made more plausible still if we distinguish between those egoists who consider each course of action on its own merits and those who, for convenience, adopt certain rules of thumb which they have found will promote their long-range interest. Slogans such as 'Honesty is the best policy,' 'Give to charity rather than to the Department of Internal Revenue,' 'Always give a penny to a beggar when you are likely to be watched by your acquaintances,' 'Treat your servants kindly and they will work for you like slaves,' 'Never be arrogant to anyone — you may need his services one day,' are maxims of this sort. They embody the 'wisdom' of a given society. The enlightened long-range egoist may adopt these as rules of thumb, that is, as *prima-facie* maxims, as rules which he will observe unless he has good evidence that departing from them will pay him better than abiding by them. It is obvious that the rules of behavior adopted by the enlightened egoist will be very similar to those of a man who rigidly follows our own moral code.

. . . No 'intuition' is required to see that this is not the point of view of morality, even though it can be universally adopted without self-contradiction. In the first place, a consistent egoist adopts for all occasions the principle 'everyone for himself' which we allow (at most) only in conditions of chaos, when the normal moral order breaks down. Its adoption marks the return to the law of the jungle, the state of nature, in which the 'softer,' 'more chivalrous' ways of morality have no place.

This point can be made more strictly. It can be shown that those who adopt consistent egoism cannot make moral judgments. Moral talk is impossible for consistent egoists. But this amounts to a *reductio ad absurdum* of consistent egoism.

Let B and K be candidates for the presidency of a certain country and let it be granted that it is in the interest of either to be elected, but that only one can succeed. It would then be in the interest of B but against the interest of K if B were elected, and vice versa, and therefore in the interest of B but against the interest of K if K were liquidated, and vice versa. But from this it would follow that B ought to liquidate K, that it is wrong for B not to do so, that B has not 'done his duty' until he has liquidated K; and vice versa. Similarly K, knowing that his own liquidation is in the interest of B and therefore anticipating B's attempts to secure it, ought to take steps to foil B's endeavors. It would be wrong for him not to do so. He would 'not have done his duty' until he had made sure of stopping B. It follows that if K prevents B from liquidating him, his act must be said to be both wrong and not wrong — wrong because it is the prevention of what B ought to do, his duty, and wrong for B not to do it; not wrong because it is what K ought to do, his duty, and wrong for K not to do it. But one and the same act (logically) cannot be both morally wrong and not morally wrong. Hence in cases like these morality does not apply.

This is obviously absurd. For morality is designed to apply in just such cases, namely, those where interests conflict. But if the point of view of morality were that of self-interest, then there could *never* be moral solutions of conflicts of interest. However, when there are conflicts of interest, we always look for a 'higher' point of view, one from which such conflicts can be settled. Consistent egoism makes everyone's private interest the 'highest court of appeal.' But by 'the moral point of view' we *mean* a point of view which is a court of appeal for conflicts of interest. Hence it cannot (logically) be identical with the point of view of self-interest. . . . That it is not can be seen in the same way in which we can 'see' that the Court of Petty Sessions is not the Supreme Court.

2   MORALITY INVOLVES DOING THINGS
       ON PRINCIPLE

Another feature of consistent egoism is that the rules by which a consistent egoist abides are merely rules of thumb. A consistent egoist has only one supreme principle, to do whatever is necessary for the realization of his one aim, the promotion of his interest. He does not have *principles*, he has only an aim. If one has adopted the moral point of view, then one acts on principle and not merely on rules of thumb designed to promote one's aim. This involves conforming to the rules whether or not doing so favors one's own or anyone else's aim.

Kant grasped this point even if only obscurely. He saw that adopting the moral point of view involves acting on principle. It involves conforming to rules even when doing so is unpleasant, painful, costly, or ruinous to oneself. Kant, furthermore, argued rightly that, since moral action is action on principle (and not merely in accordance with rules of thumb), a moral agent ought not to make exceptions in his own favor, and he interpreted this to mean that moral rules are absolutely inflexible and without exceptions. Accordingly he concluded that if 'Thou shalt not kill' states a moral rule, then any and every act correctly describable as an act of killing someone must be said to be morally wrong.

Kant also saw that this view required him to reject some of our deepest moral convictions; we certainly think that the killing of a man in self-defense or by the hangman is not morally wrong. Kant was prepared to say that our moral convictions are wrong on this point. Can we salvage these moral convictions? The only alternative, to say that acting on principle does not require us not to make exceptions in our own favor, seems to be equally untenable.

It is therefore not surprising that many philosophers have abandoned Kant's (and the commonsense) view that the moral rightness of an act is its property of being in accordance with a moral rule or principle. Thus, the deontologists claim that rightness is a simple property which we can 'see' or 'intuit' in an act, and the utilitarians, that rightness is a complex property, namely, the tendency of an act to promote the greatest happiness of the greatest number. But, as is well known, these accounts are not plausible and lead to considerable difficulties.

However, this whole problem arises only because of a confusion, the confusion of the expression 'making an exception to a rule' with the expression 'a rule has an exception.' As soon as this muddle is cleared away, it can be seen that Kant is right in saying that acting on principle implies making no exception in anyone's favor, but wrong in thinking that therefore all moral rules must be absolutely without exception.

'No parking in the city' has a number of recognized exceptions which are part of the rule itself, for example, 'except in the official parking areas,' 'except in front of a parking meter,' 'except on Saturday mornings and after 8 P.M. every day.' A person who does not know the recognized exceptions does not completely know the rule, for these exceptions more precisely define its range of application. A policeman who is not booking a motorist parking in front of a parking meter is not granting exemption to (making an exception in favor of) this motorist. On the contrary, he is administering the rule correctly. If he did apply the no-parking rule to the motorist, *he* would be applying it where *it* does not apply, because this is one of the recognized exceptions which are *part of* the rule. On the other hand, a policeman who does not book a motorist parking his vehicle in a prohibited area at peak hour on a busy day is making an exception in the motorist's favor. If he does so because the man is his friend, he illegitimately grants an exemption. If he does so because the motorist is a doctor who has been called to attend to a man lying unconscious on the pavement, this is a 'deserving case' and he grants the exemption legitimately. . . .

When we say, therefore, that a person who has killed a burglar in self-defense has not done anything wrong, we are not making an exception in the housewoner's favor. It is much nearer the truth to say that, in our morality, the rule 'Thou shalt not kill' *has several recognized exceptions*, among them 'in self-defense.' We can say that a man does not know fully our moral rule 'Thou shalt not kill' if he does not know that it has, among others, this exception.

Like other rules of reason, our moral convictions are so only *presumptively*. Killing is wrong *unless* it is killing in self-defense, killing by the hangman, killing of an enemy in wartime, accidental killing, and possibly mercy killing. If it is one of these types of killing, then it is *not* wrong.

Even if it is one of the wrongful acts of killing, it is so only *prima facie*, other things being equal. For there may have been an overriding moral reason in favor of killing the man, for example, that he is about to blow up a train and that this is the only way of stopping him. . . .

All this follows from the very nature of moral principles. They are binding on everyone alike quite irrespective of what are the goals or purposes of the person in question. Hence self-interest cannot be the moral point of view, for it sets every individual one supreme goal, his own interest, which overrules all his other maxims.

3   MORAL RULES ARE MEANT FOR EVERYBODY

The point of view of morality is inadequately characterized by saying that *I* have adopted it if *I* act on principles, that is, on rules to which I do not make exceptions whenever acting on them would frustrate one or the other of my purposes or desires. It is characterized by greater universality than that. It must be thought of as a standpoint from which principles are considered as being acted on *by everyone*. Moral principles are not merely principles on which a person must always act without making exceptions, but they are principles *meant for everybody*.

It follows from this that the teaching of morality must be completely universal and open. Morality is meant to be taught to all members of the group in such a way that everyone can and ought always to act in accordance with these rules. It is not the preserve of an oppressed or privileged class or individual. People are neglecting their duties if they do not teach the moral rules to their children. Children are removed from the homes of criminals because they are not likely to be taught the moral rules there. Furthermore, moral rules must be taught quite openly and to everybody without discrimination. An esoteric code, a set of precepts known only to the initiated and perhaps jealously concealed from outsiders, can at best be a religion, not a morality. 'Thou shalt not eat beans and this is a secret' or 'Always leave the third button of your waistcoat undone, but don't tell anyone except the initiated members' may be part of an esoteric religion, but not of a morality. 'Thou shalt not kill, but it is a strict secret' is absurd. 'Esoteric morality' is a contradiction in terms.

The condition of universal teachability yields . . . other criteria of moral rules. They must not, in the first place, be 'self-frustrating.' They are so if their purpose is frustrated as soon as everybody acts on them, if they have a point only when a good many people act on the opposite principle. Someone might, for instance, act on the maxim 'When you are in need, ask for help, but never help another man when he is in need.' If everybody adopted this principle, then their adoption of the second half would frustrate what obviously is the point of the adoption of the first half, namely, to get help when one is in need. Although such a principle is not self-contradictory — for anybody could consistently adopt it — it is nevertheless objectionable from the moral point of view, for it could not be taught openly to everyone. It would then lose its point. It is a parasitic principle, useful to anyone only if many people act on its opposite.

The same is true of 'self-defeating' and 'morally impossible' rules. A principle is self-defeating if its point is defeated as soon as a person lets it be known that he has adopted it, for example, the principle 'Give a promise even when you know or think that you can never keep it, or when you don't intend to keep it.' The very point of giving promises is to reassure and furnish a guarantee to the promisee. Hence any remark that throws doubt on the sincerity of the promiser will defeat the purpose of making a promise. And clearly to *let it be known* that one gives promises even when one knows or thinks one cannot, or when one does not intend to keep them, is to raise such doubts. And to say that one acts on the above principle is to imply that one may well give promises in these cases. Hence to reveal that one acts on this principle will tend to defeat one's own purpose.

It has already been said that moral rules must be capable of being taught openly, but this rule is self-defeating when taught openly, for then everyone would be known to act on it. Hence it cannot belong to the morality of any group. . . .

4   MORAL RULES MUST BE FOR THE GOOD OF EVERYONE ALIKE

The conditions so far mentioned are merely formal. They exclude certain sorts of rule as not coming up to the formal requirements. But moral rules should also have a certain sort of content. Observation of these rules should be *for the good of everyone alike*. Thrasymachus' view that justice is the advantage of the stronger, if true of the societies of his day, is an indictment of their legal systems from the moral point of view. It shows that what goes by the name of morality in these societies is no more than a set of rules and laws which enrich the ruling class at the expense of the masses. But this is wrong because unjust, however much the rules satisfy the formal criteria. For given certain initial social conditions, formal equality before the law may favor certain groups and exploit others.

There is one obvious way in which a rule may be for the good of everyone alike, namely, if it furthers the common good. When I am promoted and my salary is raised, this is to my advantage. It will also be to the advantage of my wife and my family and possibly of a few other people — it will not be to the advantage of my colleague who had hoped for promotion but is now excluded. It may even be to his detriment if his reputation suffers as a result. If the coal miners obtain an increase in their wages, then this is to the advantage of coal miners. It is for their common good. But it may not be to the advantage of anyone else. On the other hand, if production is raised and with it everyone's living standard, that is literally to everyone's advantage. The rule 'Work harder,' if it has these consequences, is for the common good of all.

Very few rules, if any, will be for the common good of everyone. But a rule may be in the interest of everyone alike, even though the results of the observation of the rule are not for the common good in the sense explained. Rules such as 'Thou shalt not kill,' 'Thou shalt not be cruel,' 'Thou shalt not lie' are obviously, in some other sense, for the good of everyone alike. What is this sense? It becomes clear if we look at these rules from the moral point of view, that is, that of an independent, unbiased, impartial, objective, dispassionate, disinterested observer. Taking such a God's-eye point of view, we can see that it is in the interest of everyone alike that everyone should abide by the rule 'Thou shalt not kill.' From the moral point of view, it is clear that it is in the interest of everyone alike if everyone alike should be allowed to pursue his own interest provided this does not adversely affect someone else's interests. Killing someone in the pursuit of my interests would interfere with his.

There can be no doubt that such a God's-eye point of view is involved in the moral standpoint. The most elementary teaching is based on it. The negative version of the so-called Golden Rule sums it up: 'Don't do unto others as you would not have them do unto you.' When we teach children the moral point of view, we try to explain it to them by getting them to put themselves in another person's place: 'How would you like to have that done to you!' 'Don't do evil,' the most readily accepted moral rule of all, is simply the most general form of stating this prohibition. For doing evil is the opposite of doing good. Doing good is doing for another person what, if he were following (self-interested) reason, he would do for himself. Doing evil is doing to another person what it would be contrary to reason for him to do to himself. Harming another, hurting another, doing to another what he dislikes having done to him are the specific forms this takes. Killing, cruelty, inflicting pain, maiming, torturing, deceiving, cheating, rape, adultery are instances of this sort of behavior. They all violate the condition of 'reversibility,' that is, that the behavior in question must be acceptable to a person whether he is at the 'giving' or 'receiving' end of it.

It is important to see just what is established by this condition of being for the good of everyone alike. In the first place, anyone is doing wrong who engages in nonreversible behavior. It is irrelevant whether he knows that it is wrong or not, whether the morality of his group recognizes it or not. Such behavior is 'wrong in itself,' irrespective of individual or social recognition, irrespective of the consequences it has. Moreover, every single act of such behavior is wrong. We need not consider the whole group or the whole of humanity engaging in this sort of behavior, but only a single case. Hence we can say that all nonreversible behavior is morally wrong; hence that anyone engaging in it is doing what, *prima facie*, he ought not to do. We need not consider whether this sort of behavior has harmful consequences, whether it is forbidden by the morality of the man's group, or whether he himself thinks it wrong.

The principle of reversibility does not merely impose certain prohibitions on a moral agent, but also certain positive injunctions. It is, for instance, wrong — an omission — not to help another person when he is in need and when we are in a position to help him. The story of the Good Samaritan makes this point. The positive version of the Golden Rule makes the same point more generally: 'Do unto others as you would have them do unto you.' Note that it is wrong — not merely not meritorious — to omit to help others when they are in need and when you are in a position to help them. It does not follow from this, however, that it is wrong not to promote the greatest good of the greatest number, or not to promote the greatest amount of good in the world. Deontologists and utilitarians alike make the mistake of thinking that it is one, or the only one, of our moral duties to 'do the optimific act.' Nothing could be further from the truth. We do not have a duty to do good to others or to ourselves, or to others and/or to ourselves in a judicious mixture such that it produces the greatest possible amount of good in the world. We are morally required to do good only to those who are actually in need of our assistance. The view that we always ought to do the optimific act, or whenever we have no more stringent duty to perform, would have the absurd result that we are doing wrong whenever we are relaxing, since on those occasions there will always be opportunities to produce greater good than we can by relaxing. For the relief of suffering is always a greater good than mere enjoyment. Yet it is quite plain that the worker who, after a tiring day, puts on his slippers and listens to the wireless is not doing anything he ought not to, is not neglecting any of his duties, even though it may be perfectly true that there are things he might do which produce more good in the world, even for himself, than merely relaxing by the fireside. . . .

6   SOCIAL MORALITY

We have so far considered absolute morality only. As we have noted, the moral point of view is characterized by a formal and a material condition. The formal condition is this: a man cannot be said to have adopted the moral point of view unless he is prepared to treat the moral rules as principles rather than mere rules of thumb, that is, to do things *on principle* rather than merely to act purposively, merely to aim at a certain end. And, furthermore, he must act on rules which are meant for everybody, and not merely for himself or some favored group. The material condition is this: the rules must be for the good of everyone alike. This does not mean that they must be for the common good of all human beings, past, present, and future, for such a condition would be impossible to satisfy. Its meaning can be elucidated by setting forth the criteria of saying that a rule is for the good of everyone alike. As far as absolute morality is concerned, only one condition must be satisfied, namely, that these rules should be 'reversible,' that is, not merely for the good of the agent, but at least not detrimental to the persons who are affected by the agent's behavior.

An examination of social conditions will yield some further criteria of 'being for the good of everyone alike.' A society is more than just a number of individuals living in a certain area and behaving in ways directly affecting others, such as killing, maiming, and robbing. Life in society involves a social framework which multiplies the points of contact between individuals and which can transform the effects of a man's behavior on his fellow men. Within a given social framework, behavior may be harmful which is not, from its nature, the infliction of harm on another. It may be harmful only if and because a great many people in that society engage in it. No harm is done if one person walks across the lawn. But the lawn is ruined if everyone does. No harm is done if one person uses the gas. But if everyone uses it during peak hours, then the gas supply may break down, and everyone will be adversely affected.

That such behavior is morally objectionable is widely recognized. We acknowledge that it is, by the well-known formula 'You can't do that; what if everyone did the same!' Kant thought of it as the core of his categorical imperative, 'Act only on that maxim whereby thou canst at the same time will that it should become a universal law.' This is precisely what we 'cannot will' in the cases in question. Although it is not true that, as Kant put it, a will willing such a maxim to become a universal law would, literally, contradict itself, nevertheless, in making such a maxim *a universal law*, one would enjoin people to do evil, and such a law would obviously be wrong.

It is, however, important to distinguish behavior which is 'nonuniversalizable' from behavior that is 'nonreversible.' The latter can be seen to be *wrong in itself*, irrespective of the consequences and of how many people engage in it. This is not so in the case of nonuniversalizable behavior. There we have to consider the consequences, and not merely of a single act but of a great many of them. There is nothing wrong in itself with putting one straw on the camel's back, but one of them will be the last.

What exactly does this prove? That no one is allowed to lay even one straw on the camel's back? That every act of this kind is wrong? Surely not. Before we can say that any act of this sort is wrong, a number of conditions must be satisfied.

In the first place, all concerned must be *equally entitled* to behave in the nonuniversalizable way. It would, for instance, be most undesirable if everyone had dinner at 6:30 P.M., for all the nation's service would then come to a standstill at that time. But it cannot follow from this that eating at 6:30 P.M. is wrong for everyone. It cannot follow because the argument applies equally for any time, and it must be all right to eat at *some* time. Of course, there is no serious problem here. Not everyone is equally entitled to have his dinner at 6:30 P.M. Those who are on duty at that time must have it before or after or while they are attending to their duties.

There are further conditions. If everyone were celibate all his life, mankind would die out, or, at any rate, the number would soon be so seriously reduced as to make life unbearable. Those who do not find the prospect of the end of the human race upsetting will have to admit that the return to primitive conditions is undesirable. Again, if everyone suddenly stopped smoking, drinking, gambling, and going to the pictures, some states might go bankrupt and this would be undesirable. All the same, it can hardly be true that abstinence in matters of sex, smoking, drinking, gambling, and visits to the cinema can be wrong in any and every case, even though we are surely all equally entitled to refrain from these ways of spending our time.

There must, therefore, be a further condition. Everyone must not only be equally entitled to engage in these forms of activity, but people must also be inclined to do so. There would have to be a real danger that, unless they are stopped somehow, many will engage in this sort of behavior. People are lazy, so they will not go to the polling booth or make the detour round the newly planted lawn. People like picking flowers, so they will destroy the rare wild flowers. People want to heat their rooms, so they will want to use their radiators during peak hours. But there is no great danger that they will all go celibate, or give up smoking and drinking.

This point, by the way, shows that nonuniversalizability cannot be adduced to show that suicide is wrong. Suicide is no more wrong than celibacy and for the same reason. People are less keen on suicide even than on celibacy. There is no danger of the race dying out. In fact, all over the world people are so keen on procreation that the suicide rate could go up a long way before anyone need be alarmed. Of course if, one day, life and sex were to become burdens to all of us and if, nevertheless, it really is desirable that the race should go on, then reckless suicide or slothful celibacy might become morally wrongful types of conduct. Until then, those weary of life and sex need not have a bad conscience about their uncommon indulgences.

There is one further point in this. To say that it is wrong to walk across the lawn or switch on the gas during peak hours, provided (a) it would have undesirable consequences *if* everyone did it, (b) we are all equally entitled to do it, and (c) doing it is an indulgence, not a sacrifice, amounts to saying that since refraining from doing these things is a sacrifice such a sacrifice for the common good should not be demanded of one or a few only, but equally of all, even if a universal sacrifice is not needed. Since no one is more entitled than anyone else to indulge himself and since *all* cannot do so without the undesirable consequences which no one wants, *no one* should be allowed to indulge himself.

Now the conditions are complete. If the behavior in question is such that (i) the consequences would be undesirable if everyone did it, (ii) all are equally entitled to engage in it, and (iii) engaging in this sort of behavior is an indulgence, not a sacrifice, then such behavior *should be prohibited by the morality of the group.*

But now suppose that it is not prohibited. Is it wrong all the same? Kant certainly thought so. I think he is mistaken. For since, by indulging in the behavior in question, I am not actually doing any harm, my behavior is not wrong in itself, but only when taken in conjunction with that of others. I cannot prevent the evil by refraining. Others must refrain too. In the case of nonreversible behavior, *my action alone* is the cause of the evil. I can avoid the evil if I refrain. In the case under discussion, however, if I have reason to suppose that the others will not refrain, I surely have reason not to refrain either, as my only reason for refraining is my desire to avoid causing the evil consequences. If these cannot be avoided, I have no reason not to indulge myself. If the grass is not going to grow anyway, why should I make the detour? . . .

QUESTIONS

1. Why does Baier think that the point of view of selfish interest is not the point of view of morality? Is he right in saying that "by 'the moral point of view' we *mean* a point of view which is a court of appeal for conflicts of interest."?
2. Baier says, "It is never right to make an exception to a moral rule in anyone's favor." Does this mean that moral rules have no exceptions? In what sense?
3. Is it part of our concept of "morality" that its rules should be openly teachable, that they should not be self-frustrating or self-defeating?
4. The requirement that moral rules should be for the good of everyone alike appears to imply that a utilitarian test for moral rules is part of our very concept of "morality." Is this correct? What is "reversibility"?

5. What is the difference between "nonreversible" behavior and "nonuniversalizable" behavior?
6. Is behavior immoral, as being nonuniversalizable, if it would have bad consequences for everyone to do that sort of thing? Or must further conditions be met, before the behavior is immoral?
7. Can you think of any rules which are clearly moral rules, which fail to meet Baier's prescriptions? or any rules which meet them, which you feel quite sure do not state any real moral obligations?

CHAPTER 3   SUGGESTIONS FOR FURTHER READING

Baier, Kurt. *The Moral Point of View.* Ithaca, N. Y.: Cornell Univ. Press, 1958. Another attempt to show that ethical conduct has a rational basis.

Bourke, V. J. *Ethics.* New York: Macmillan, 1951. A widely used Catholic, and Thomist, text on ethics.

Brandt, Richard B. *Ethical Theory.* Englewood Cliffs, N. J.: Prentice-Hall, 1959, Chs. 4, 7-10. Discussion of all the metaethical theories.

Edwards, Paul. *The Logic of Moral Discourse.* Chicago: Free Press, 1955. Criticism of naturalism and nonnaturalism; a defense of noncognitivism.

Ewing, A. C. *The Definition of Good.* New York: Macmillan, 1947. The most complete statement of the nonnaturalist position.

Falk, W. D. "Guiding and Goading," *Mind,* Vol. 62 (1953), pp. 145-69. A critique of some noncognitivist assumptions.

Findlay, J. N. "Morality by Convention," *Mind,* Vol. 53 (1944), pp. 142-69. An attempt to combine noncognitivism with naturalism.

Firth, Roderick. "Ethical Absolutism and the Ideal Observer," *Philosophy and Phenomenological Research,* Vol. 12 (1952), pp. 317-45. Lucid statement and defense of ideal observer theory.

Hare, R. M. *The Language of Morals.* New York: Oxford Univ. Press, 1952. An influential noncognitive theory.

Harrison, J. "Can Ethics Do Without Propositions?" *Mind,* Vol. 59 (1950), pp. 358-71. An appraisal of the noncognitive theory.

———— "Empiricism in Ethics." *Philosophical Quarterly,* Vol. 2 (1952), pp. 289-306. Reply to some traditional criticisms of naturalism.

Hartmann, Nicolai. *Ethics,* New York: Macmillan, 1932. 3 vols., Vol. 1, Chs. 14 and 16. A different conception of ethical knowledge; nonnaturalism.

Moore, G. E. *Principia Ethica.* New York: Cambridge Univ. Press, 1959 (also paper), pp. 1-21. Historically influential criticism of naturalism.

Mortimer, R. C. *Christian Ethics.* London: Hutchinson, 1950. Near-supernaturalism, by an Anglican bishop; elementary level.

Nowell-Smith, Patrick. *Ethics.* Baltimore: Penguin Books, 1954. Another widely read noncognitivist statement.

Rashdall, Hastings. *Conscience and Christ.* London: Duckworth, 1933. Discussion of what a rational Christian will think about the ethical teaching of Jesus.

Rawls, John. "Outline of a Decision Procedure for Ethics." *Philosophical Review,* Vol. 60 (1951), pp. 177-97. Another attempt to find a rational basis for ethics short of a return to naturalism.

Spinoza, Benedict de. *Ethics*. Many editions, Bk. 1, Appendix; Bk. 3, Prop. 9, Note. A classic statement of naturalism.

Stevenson, C. L. *Ethics and Language*. New Haven: Yale Univ. Press, 1944, Chs. 1, 2, 4-7, 9. Historically the most important noncognitive theory.

Toulmin, S. E. *An Examination of the Place of Reason in Ethics*. New York: Cambridge Univ. Press, 1951, pp. 67-72, 82-85, Chs. 9-11. A recent attempt to find objective standards despite everything.

4   ETHICAL RELATIVISM

The term "ethical relativism" has become a familiar one in recent years. Moreover, many people — particularly social scientists but also many members of the educated public generally — have come to count themselves as ethical relativists in some sense or other. The view deserves our attention as a popular phenomenon irrespective of its intrinsic merits.

As understood by contemporary social scientists, ethical relativism roughly consists of three proposals, advocated as early as the fifth century B.C. by a Greek philosopher named Protagoras. These are as follows. (1) The ethical judgments supported by different individuals or groups are often different and conflicting in a very fundamental way. (2) When the judgments of different individuals or groups disagree, there is not always any way of establishing some one of them as correct; on the contrary, sometimes conflicting principles are equally valid or correct. (3) People ought to live, or try to live, according to the moral principles they themselves espouse. Thus Protagoras might say, corresponding to (1), that Athenians think it is wrong to expose unwanted infants, whereas Spartans think infanticide is right. Next, he might go on to say that neither view can really be established as valid or correct and that both Spartans and Athenians can properly claim that their own evaluation is as well justified as a moral principle can be expected to be. Finally, Protagoras would go on to advise each group to follow its own standard.

There has been a great deal of confusion and misunderstanding about this theory, and we need to be on our guard and careful to sort out the issues. One misunderstanding which leads to unwary acceptance of the theory is the supposition that the alternative to it is either some kind of dogmatic and unreasoned position, or at least one committed to advocating, as true absolutely without exception, simple moral principles like "One must never lie" or "One must never steal." This supposition is a complete mistake.

There is also misunderstanding about the third principle. Practically everyone today advocates "tolerance" for the values of other persons, in some sense. But in what sense? First, surely it is agreed that if a person has a moral conviction which is not a result of rationalizing in his own favor but rather the product of sincere soul-searching, then he ought not (except in some extreme cases) to be condemned or blamed morally for living in accordance with it. Second, surely it is agreed that a man with a strong conviction that it is his duty to do something is — unless what he thinks he should do would be quite harmful — properly encouraged to follow his conviction; and we should think rather less of him if he didn't. (If a pacifist asks us what to do, we shall tell him he must follow his convictions — what else, as a moral man, can he do? — even if we think his pacifism is mistaken.) In these senses we should be "tolerant" of another's values. But, at the same time, it is clear that we think a person may be quite mistaken in his moral views; he may think to be his duty some action which in fact is clearly wrong. For instance, a misinformed parent may think it his duty to discipline his child severely, when actually such discipline would have most unfortunate consequences on the mental condition of the child. Therefore, it seems we may think a person's conduct is *objectively wrong,* even though we think we should not blame him for it and might, if asked, tell him he should follow his conscience. Further, in some cases it may be our duty to prevent a man from doing what he regards as his duty, to send him to jail if he does it, and to advise him steadfastly and continuously not to do it, whatever he may think. For instance, at the turn of the present century the Philippine Ifugaos were headhunters. Perhaps we should not blame them morally for their headhunting. But not blaming them is quite consistent with advising them to desist, with preventing them from getting arms, and with promulgating a law with severe penalties, which prohibits headhunting. (It may be that we do not feel we are justified in such interference unless we believe that they would have changed their own minds if they had been clear about the actual facts, but we need not go into this.)

The third principle of ethical relativism — that people ought to try to live according to their own beliefs —, then, is unobjectionable and uncontroversial if construed in a cautious way. But if the principle is construed as the view that it is objectively right to do whatever one thinks is objectively right, the principle is extremely implausible. It is hard to believe that anyone who thought about the matter carefully would agree to this construction. We shall henceforth, therefore, ignore this third principle and concentrate on the first two principles.

It is important to see that the first two principles are distinct. Failure to see this distinction has been one of the confusions which have beset discussions of the subject. In order to make sure that they are distinguished, it is helpful to assign separate names. We shall call a person who accepts the first principle a *cultural relativist.* In contrast, we shall reserve the term *ethical relativism* for the view that *both* the first and second principles are true. According to our terminology, then, a man is not an ethical relativist unless he is also a cultural relativist; but he may well be a cultural relativist without being an ethical relativist.

1. *The thesis of cultural relativism*

The principle of cultural relativism, we have said, is that the moral principles of different individuals (or groups) are often different and conflicting *in a very fundamental way*. What exactly does this statement mean?

Everybody knows that the moral opinions of individuals and groups sometimes conflict; for instance, the Romans and the Spartans did not condemn infanticide, whereas in our view this practice is highly objectionable. If cultural relativism asserts only that there are different moral traditions in this sense, it is a true, but uninteresting, theory. If this were all it said, it would not be asserting that there is conflict of moral principle "in a very fundamental way." In order to give content to this last phrase, and to give the theory some teeth, let us construe the theory as asserting that there is sometimes conflict of *basic moral axioms* of different people or groups. This concept needs explanation.

Let us say that two individuals or groups differ in their "basic moral axioms" if they make conflicting appraisals of the *same things*, that is, of events or actions or situations which are the same in the sense of having the *same meaning* for both parties. Let me illustrate. On the one hand, the Romans believed very strongly that it is reprehensible to murder one's father, and they reserved the most horrible punishment for a person who committed this worst offense. The Romans would certainly say, "It is wrong to kill one's father." On the other hand, in some primitive groups, sons have killed their fathers as a matter of filial duty. Suppose, then, we talk with some resident of the South Pacific, in whose group it is customary for the son to bury his father alive on his sixtieth birthday, irrespective of the father's state of health. Presumably he would say, "It is right to kill one's father." Now, let us ask, is there here a difference of basic moral axioms? Well, perhaps; but not necessarily. Certainly there are conflicting appraisals of killing one's father. But does the act of killing one's father have the *same meaning* for both? Not quite. The man from the South Pacific may well think that his father's body in the next life will be exactly like the one he has just before departing this life, and hence it may be advisable to depart this life before feebleness sets in; whereas the Roman may not have these beliefs about the future life, or he may think there is no future life at all. So the man from the South Pacific is talking about burying alive a father who will exist in the next world in a certain kind of body; the Roman is not. In this situation, it seems only confusing to say that the Roman and the South Pacific islander have conflicting *basic* moral axioms; for their moral appraisals are not really about the same action, an action with meaning identical for both parties.

When, then, *shall* we say that a conflict of ethical appraisal is a conflict of basic ethical axioms? Suppose Mr. A and Mr. B disagree ethically about some event or action. Let us say that their disagreement is one of *basic* ethical axiom if all their more or less conscious factual beliefs about the event or action — or rather those of these beliefs which affect their ethical appraisal to some extent — are *identical*. When the meaning of an event appraised is the same in this sense, then ethical disagreement is a disagreement of basic ethical axiom.

The cultural relativist, then, is a person who thinks that the basic ethical axioms of different individuals or groups are conflicting, in this sense of "basic ethical axioms." This contention, I think it is agreed, is by no means a truism, and it is exceedingly important. An obvious reason for the importance of the theory is this: if ethical disagreements are *not* matters of basic ethical disagreement in this sense, then they can be resolved by more knowledge, by bringing disputants closer together in their understanding of the facts of a case. For, if there is not basic disagreement, identity of understanding of the facts of a case will guarantee ethical agreement. But if there is disagreement about basic axioms, then ethical disputes may well persist even when there is complete agreement about the facts, simply because the disputants are applying different ethical principles to the facts, in determining what ought to be done.

The truth of cultural relativism, as defined, is not easy to document. Suppose, as Americans, we ask ourselves: "Are there conflicts of basic ethical axiom between the Russians and ourselves?" This is not easy to say. It seems obvious that the Russians think some actions right which we think wrong; but it is another matter to show that the two parties are appraising the same thing — actions or events with the same meaning in the sense defined. Textbooks of sociology and anthropology are full of examples of conflicting values of different peoples, but for the most part the examples tell us nothing about whether there is conflict of basic ethical axioms. Usually the reporters of strange ethical beliefs have not investigated the factual suppositions behind the ethical standard being reported.

Of the four selections which follow, the first two advocate cultural relativism. The third advocates a limited form of it — limited in the sense that it is proposed that conflicts of basic values occur only in some areas, not in all, because the requirements of human living, either biological or social, simply have not permitted certain types of valuation to develop. The fourth selection, that by S. E. Asch, questions very severely whether cultural relativism has been established. It is doubtful whether the writers of the first two selections had as clearly in mind as might be desired exactly what needed to be established, that is, had in mind that it is difference of *basic* ethical axioms which is important. Whether they make out a case for cultural relativism as defined, the reader must decide for himself.

There are two ways of establishing the thesis of cultural relativism. One is by the use of examples. One may find a case of disagreement on an ethical point and then show that in fact there is an identical understanding of the facts of the case by both parties. Unfortunately, it is very difficult to make cross-cultural comparisons of this sort; usually two cultures are so different that a given form of behavior has a somewhat different meaning in one from what it has in the other. Nevertheless, it is possible that good examples may be found. The writer has argued elsewhere * that appraisals of cruelty to animals are sometimes different in a basic way.

The second way is by an appeal to theory. One may either show that the psychology of learning moral values is such that we should expect basic disagreements — for instance, because children simply learn whatever values are taught them (if this is really so). Or one may show that the mechanism of social change is such that a moral standard is relatively independent of beliefs about the behavior which it regulates. Both these types of theory, however, have not developed far beyond a state of infancy. Particularly is this true of the theory of the dynamics of social change. Moreover, in social psychology there is considerable controversy. Gestalt psychologists are inclined to think that, just as the psychological laws of perception are invariant from one social group to another, so the fundamental ethical commitments of social groups are universal and not a result of specific teaching or conditioning process. This is the view of Asch. In contrast, Freudians and behaviorists are inclined to emphasize the role of conditioning, of passive absorption of the ideals of other persons by prestige-suggestion or identification — the behavorist viewing the moral principles or value standards of a person as just another result of conditioning, and the Freudian viewing them as just another result of imitation of persons with whom the learner in some sense identifies.

Probably the preponderance of opinion among social scientists today is that there are *some differences* in the basic ethical axioms of individuals and social groups, although not by any means an unlimited amount of difference. As the selection from Linton shows, social scientists have generally ceased to support the view that difference of standards is the rule and have come to emphasize the similarity of the value judgments of different societies. This present emphasis — less extreme than the views of Sumner and Benedict, as stated below — is probably a result of attention that has been given to the functioning of social systems and to the analysis of institutions in terms of their capacity to minister to essential human wants and the maintenance of the social group as a continuing entity.

2. *The thesis of ethical relativism*

Suppose cultural relativism is true. Does its truth establish ethical relativism as well?

Certainly the truth of ethical relativism does not *follow*. It is consistent to believe that different peoples subscribe to conflicting basic ethical princi-

---

* *Hopi Ethics: A Theoretical Analysis* (Chicago: University of Chicago Press, 1954), pp. 213-15, 243-46; *Ethical Theory* (Englewood Cliffs, N. J.: Prentice-Hall, 1959), pp. 102-03.

ples and yet to assert that one and only one of these is justified, valid, or true. Perhaps, in view of what ethical principles are, a nonrelativist view is untenable; but the sheer existence of basic ethical disagreements does not by itself imply that no single one of the conflicting principles is uniquely justified or true. Notice that we should hardly infer, from the fact that different peoples subscribe to quite different views about the natural world — for instance, to the belief that the natural world is animate and controllable by magic as contrasted with the belief that nature is orderly and cannot be controlled by incantations —, that modern physics and astronomy do not deserve our confidence. Why need we think matters are different in ethics? The fact of disagreement, in general, does not prove that no one view is right or that it cannot be known to be right.

Incidentally, ethical *agreement* does not necessarily establish correctness or validity. For instance, at least most peoples prohibit marriage among members of the primary family group. But this prohibition does not prove that incestuous marriage is really wrong; obviously it may equally well point merely to universal prejudice or preconception.

How, then, may the ethical relativist's proposal about the equal validity of conflicting ethical principles be appraised by the reader? Perhaps obviously, by reviewing the conclusions he has reached from his study of the preceding chapter. But first let us reformulate the relativist thesis.

Let us begin by stipulating a meaning for the words "correct" or "valid" as applied to an ethical statement. As preparation for this stipulation, we might ask ourselves what we mean by saying that a scientific principle or theory is "well warranted." I suggest we mean two things. First, to say that a scientific principle is warranted is to say that there is some justified "scientific method" for assessing theories — a method which we are justified in following in the sense that reasons can be given for following it, reasons that are persuasive to thoughtful people in view of the purposes of scientific investigation and of the alternative "methods" for choosing beliefs which may be suggested. In other words, to say that a scientific principle is warranted is in part to say that there is a justified or "rational" method for assessing theories. But second, to say that a scientific principle is well warranted is to say that this justified or "rational" method approves of the principle in question, in view of the observational evidence. In other words, then, to say that a theory in science is well warranted is to say that there is a rational method for assessing theories and that the given theory stands up to assessment by this method.

It is helpful to define the words "valid" or "correct" in ethics in a parallel way. The proposal is, then, that we say that an ethical statement is "valid" or "correct" if we believe two things: first, that there is some method for assessing moral principles which can be justified in the sense that reasons can be given for using it, reasons that are persuasive in view of the purposes of moral principles and of alternative methods for assessing moral principles which might be put forward; and second, that the given principle stands up to assessment by this method. Of course, the "rational" method in ethics might be identical with the method of science; this is the view of naturalists. But it need not be. One might be a noncognitivist, say, like Hume, and still hold that a given ethical principle is valid or correct because there is a proper method for assessing it, perhaps by inquiry whether the attitude it expresses is based on a full view of the facts and is an impartial one. It is important to see that both cognitivists and noncognitivists (at least in some forms) can agree that an ethical principle is "valid" in this sense.

It is possible, of course, to hold that there is *no* justified or rational method for appraising ethical principles. It is convenient to call one who maintains this position an "ethical skeptic" or a "methodological relativist."

We can now explain the position of the ethical relativist more exactly. The relativist holds both that cultural relativism is true and also that some conflicting moral principles held by different people are *equally valid*. Saying such principles are equally valid may be either saying that the concept of validity in the above sense doesn't apply in ethics at all (so that the relativist is a skeptic), or else saying that when the "rational" method of appraising ethical principles is applied, even in ideal circumstances and with ideally complete information, the conflicting principles stand up to the assessment equally well. In other words, one might say that two ethical principles are "equally valid" just because no ethical statements are valid at all; this is the view of the skeptic or of the methodological relativist. Or one might say that, even with the best possible evidence available, the justified procedure for testing ethical principles fails to show that one of two conflicting principles is preferable to the other. Either of these views is a form of ethical relativism.

Evidently no anthropological or sociological or psychological facts will by themselves establish ethical relativism. For the thesis of the relativist asserts something about whether there is a rational method for testing ethical statements or else what can be done with such a rational method. Obviously cultural relativism tells us nothing about this matter. For light we must turn to the metaethical views that we have considered: naturalism, nonnaturalism, supernaturalism, and noncognitivism. Only after we have settled accounts with these theories are we in a position to appraise ethical relativism. We need not estimate what the rational reader will believe about this question; it will be enough to suggest that if the reader is convinced by cultural relativism and by one of the more extreme forms of noncognitive theory, probably he must in consistency adopt at least a mild form of ethical relativism.

Sumner and Benedict, in the readings that follow, advocate not only cultural relativism but also ethical relativism. The argument by which they support the latter view (we leave the assessment of the argument for the former to the reader) is, however, exceedingly frail. Both writers assume without argument that what it *means* to say that something is wrong is simply that the thing is not customary, or that it is contrary to the mores.

If this assumption is made, then it follows at once, from the truth of cultural relativism, that there are some societies in which an act is right (the one customary there), and other societies in which the same act is wrong (since it will be contrary to custom, or the mores, there). Their proposal about the meaning of ethical terms, however, is an extraordinarily implausible one. Their logical move from cultural relativism to ethical relativism must therefore be dismissed as quite ungrounded. To make this statement, however, is not to say that ethical relativism is untrue or to say that it cannot be supported by some more formidable kind of argument.

We have seen that some cultural relativists hold a "moderate" view, in the sense that they assert that basic disagreements of an ethical sort are limited to certain areas. Ethical relativism may similarly be "moderate": it may be supposed that some conflicting ethical principles are equally valid or correct but that such situations are infrequent and perhaps unimportant. A relativist might hold, for instance, that there is no ground for preferring some sets of regulations of sexual behavior to some others, but he might believe that there always is good and sufficient ground for permitting homicide only in very few and specifiable kinds of situation.

William Graham Sumner (1840-1910)

THE DEVELOPMENT OF
MORAL STANDARDS

W. G. Sumner was a learned and bold thinker who strongly influenced several generations of sociologists and anthropologists. Graduated by Yale University in 1863, after study at universities in Göttingen and Oxford he returned to Yale, where he taught from 1866 to 1909. His writings include six books in addition to his most important work, *Folkways* (1907) and his most immediately influential, *What the Social Classes Owe Each Other* (1883). Unlike most professors, Sumner was well known to the general public, and his ideas were familiar to a very substantial proportion of educated people.

Sumner was a cultural relativist about moral standards: he believed that moral standards are a product of folkways, which are themselves a result of historical interactions between men and their several environments, man's imitation of his fellows, accidents, and similar causes. In consequence, in his view, the tradition of one society may forbid the very same behavior for which the tradition of another society prescribes praise. But Sumner was also an ethical relativist, although not quite a consistent one. For, according to him, what it means to say that an action is "right" is that it conforms with the folkways of the agent's group; there is no standard outside the folkways by which they can be tested. Philosophers who think they can appraise folkways, he said, are only giving expression to the preconceptions of their own social group. Yet Sumner himself evidently regarded one set of folkways as better if it served human needs more efficiently than another set; in so far he was a kind of utilitarian in spite of himself.

To assess Sumner's cultural relativism we must turn to the social sciences. The reader is, however, in a position to appraise Sumner's ethical relativism without specialized scientific knowledge.

FOLKWAYS

1. DEFINITION AND MODE OF ORIGIN OF THE FOLKWAYS   If we put together all that we have learned from anthropology and ethnography about primitive men and primitive society, we perceive that the first task of life is to live. Men begin with acts, not with thoughts. Every moment brings necessities which must be satisfied at once. Need was the first experience, and it was followed at once by a blundering effort to satisfy it. It is generally taken for granted that men inherited some guiding instincts from their beast ancestry, and it may be true, although it has never been proved. If there were such inheritances, they controlled and aided the first efforts to satisfy needs. Analogy makes it easy to assume that the ways of beasts had produced channels of habit and predisposition along which dexterities and other psychophysical activities would run easily. Experiments with newborn animals show that in the absence of any experience of the relation of means to ends, efforts to satisfy needs are clumsy and blundering. The method is that of trial and failure, which produces repeated pain, loss, and disappointments. Nevertheless, it is a method of rude experiment and selection. The earliest efforts of men were of this kind. Need was the impelling force. Pleasure and pain on the one side, and on the other were the rude constraints which defined the line on which efforts must proceed. The ability to distinguish between pleasure and pain is the only physical power which is to be assumed. Thus ways of doing things were selected, which were expedient. They answered the purpose better than other ways, or with less toil and pain. Along the course on which efforts were compelled to go, habit, routine, and skill were developed. The struggle to maintain existence was carried on, not individually, but in groups. Each profited by the other's experience; hence there was concurrence towards that which proved to be most expedient. All at last adopted the same way for the same purpose; hence the ways turned into customs and became mass phenomena. Instincts were developed in connection with them. In this way folkways arise. The young learn them by tradition, imitation, and authority. The folkways, at a time, provide for all the needs of life then and there. They are uniform, universal in the group, imperative, and invariable. As time goes on, the folkways become more and more arbitrary, positive, and imperative. If asked why they act in a certain way in certain cases, primitive people always answer that it is because they and their ancestors always have done so. A sanction also arises from ghost fear. The ghosts of ancestors would be angry if the living should change the ancient folkways.

2. THE FOLKWAYS ARE A SOCIETAL FORCE   The operation by which folkways are produced consists in the frequent repetition of petty acts, often by great numbers acting in concert or, at least, acting in the same way when

face to face with the same need. The immediate motive is interest. It produces habit in the individual and custom in the group. It is, therefore, in the highest degree original and primitive. By habit and custom it exerts a strain on every individual within its range; therefore it rises to a societal force to which great classes of societal phenomena are due. Its earliest stages, its course, and laws may be studied; also its influence on individuals and their reaction on it. It is our present purpose so to study it. We have to recognize it as one of the chief forces by which a society is made to be what it is. Out of the unconscious experiment which every repetition of the ways includes, there issues pleasure or pain, and then, so far as the men are capable of reflection, convictions that the ways are conducive to societal welfare. These two experiences are not the same. The most uncivilized men, both in the food quest and in war, do things which are painful, but which have been found to be expedient. Perhaps these cases teach the sense of social welfare better than those which are pleasurable and favorable to welfare. The former cases call for some intelligent reflection on experience. When this conviction as to the relation to welfare is added to the folkways they are converted into mores, and, by virtue of the philosophical and ethical element added to them, they win utility and importance and become the source of the science and the art of living.

3. FOLKWAYS ARE MADE UNCONSCIOUSLY It is of the first importance to notice that, from the first acts by which men try to satisfy needs, each act stands by itself, and looks no further than the immediate satisfaction. From recurrent needs arise habits for the individual and customs for the group, but these results are consequences which were never conscious, and never foreseen or intended. They are not noticed until they have long existed, and it is still longer before they are appreciated. Another long time must pass, and a higher stage of mental development must be reached, before they can be used as a basis from which to deduce rules for meeting, in the future, problems whose pressure can be foreseen. The folkways, therefore, are not creations of human purpose and wit. They are like products of natural forces which men unconsciously set in operation, or they are like the instinctive ways of animals, which are developed out of experience, which reach a final form of maximum adaptation to an interest, which are handed down by tradition and admit of no exception or variation, yet change to meet new conditions, still within the same limited methods, and without rational reflection or purpose. From this it results that all the life of human beings, in all ages and stages of culture, is primarily controlled by a vast mass of folkways handed down from the earliest existence of the race, having the nature of the ways of other animals, only the topmost layers of which are subject to change and control, and have been somewhat modified by human philosophy, ethics, and religion, or by other acts of intelligent reflection. . . .

5. THE STRAIN OF IMPROVEMENT AND CONSISTENCY   The folkways, being ways of satisfying needs, have succeeded more or less well, and therefore have produced more or less pleasure or pain. Their quality always consisted in their adaptation to the purpose. If they were imperfectly adapted and unsuccessful, they produced pain, which drove men on to learn better. The folkways are, therefore, (1) subject to a strain of improvement towards better adaptation of means to ends, as long as the adaptation is so imperfect that pain is produced. They are also (2) subject to a strain of consistency with each other, because they all answer their several purposes with less friction and antagonism when they coöperate and support each other. The forms of industry, the forms of the family, the notions of property, the constructions of rights, and the types of religion show the strain of consistency with each other through the whole history of civilization. The two great cultural divisions of the human race are the oriental and the occidental. Each is consistent throughout; each has its own philosophy and spirit; they are separated from top to bottom by different mores, different standpoints, different ways, and different notions of what societal arrangements are advantageous. In their contrast they keep before our minds the possible range of divergence in the solution of the great problems of human life, and in the views of earthly existence by which life policy may be controlled. If two planets were joined in one, their inhabitants could not differ more widely as to what things are best worth seeking, or what ways are most expedient for well living.

7. ALL ORIGINS ARE LOST IN MYSTERY   No objection can lie against this postulate about the way in which folkways began, on account of the element of inference in it. All origins are lost in mystery, and it seems vain to hope that from any origin the veil of mystery will ever be raised. We go up the stream of history to the utmost point for which we have evidence of its course. Then we are forced to reach out into the darkness upon the line of direction marked by the remotest course of the historic stream. This is the way in which we have to act in regard to the origin of capital, language, the family, the state, religion, and rights. We never can hope to see the beginning of any one of these things. Use and wont are products and results. They had antecedents. We never can find or see the first member of the series. It is only by analysis and inference that we can form any conception of the "beginning" which we are always so eager to find.

12. TRADITION AND ITS RESTRAINTS   It is evident that the "ways" of the older and more experienced members of a society deserve great authority in any primitive group. We find that this rational authority leads to customs of deference and to etiquette in favor of the old. The old in turn cling stubbornly to tradition and to the example of their own predecessors. Thus tradition and custom become intertwined and are a strong

coercion which directs the society upon fixed lines, and strangles liberty. Children see their parents always yield to the same custom and obey the same persons. They see that the elders are allowed to do all the talking, and that if an outsider enters, he is saluted by those who are at home according to rank and in fixed order. All this becomes rule for children, and helps to give to all primitive customs their stereotyped formality. . . .

22. HUNGER, LOVE, VANITY, AND FEAR   There are four great motives of human action which come into play when some number of human beings are in juxtaposition under the same life conditions. These are hunger, sex passion, vanity, and fear (of ghosts and spirits). Under each of these motives there are interests. Life consists in satisfying interests, for "life," in a society, is a career of action and effort expended on both the material and social environment. However great the errors and misconceptions may be which are included in the efforts, the purpose always is advantage and expediency. The efforts fall into parallel lines, because the conditions and the interests are the same. It is now the accepted opinion, and it may be correct, that men inherited from their beast ancestors psychophysical traits, instincts, and dexterities, or at least predispositions, which give them aid in solving the problems of food supply, sex commerce, and vanity. The result is mass phenomena; currents of similarity, concurrence, and mutual contribution; and these produce folkways. The folkways are unconscious, spontaneous, uncoördinated. It is never known who led in devising them, although we must believe that talent exerted its leadership at all times. Folkways come into existence now all the time. There were folkways in stage coach times, which were fitted to that mode of travel. Street cars have produced ways which are suited to that mode of transportation in cities. The telephone has produced ways which have not been invented and imposed by anybody, but which are devised to satisfy conveniently the interests which are at stake in the use of that instrument.

23. PROCESS OF MAKING FOLKWAYS   Although we may see the process of making folkways going on all the time, the analysis of the process is very difficult. It appears as if there was a "mind" in the crowd which was different from the minds of the individuals which compose it. Indeed some have adopted such a doctrine. By autosuggestion the stronger minds produce ideas which when set afloat pass by suggestion from mind to mind. Acts which are consonant with the ideas are imitated. There is a give and take between man and man. This process is one of development. New suggestions come in at point after point. They are carried out. They combine with what existed already. Every new step increases the number of points upon which other minds may seize. It seems to be by this process that great inventions are produced. Knowledge has been won and extended by it. It seems as if the crowd had a mystic power in it greater than the sum of the powers of its members. . . .

30. HOW "TRUE" AND "RIGHT" ARE FOUND   If a savage puts his hand too near the fire, he suffers pain and draws it back. He knows nothing of the laws of the radiation of heat, but his instinctive action conforms to that law as if he did know it. If he wants to catch an animal for food, he must study its habits and prepare a device adjusted to those habits. If it fails, he must try again, until his observation is "true" and his device is "right." All the practical and direct element in the folkways seems to be due to common sense, natural reason, intuition, or some other original mental endowment. It seems rational (or rationalistic) and utilitarian. Often in the mythologies this ultimate rational element was ascribed to the teaching of a god or a culture hero. In modern mythology it is accounted for as "natural."

Although the ways adopted must always be really "true" and "right" in relation to facts, for otherwise they could not answer their purpose, such is not the primitive notion of true and right.

31. THE FOLKWAYS ARE "RIGHT." RIGHTS. MORALS   The folkways are the "right" ways to satisfy all interests, because they are traditional, and exist in fact. They extend over the whole of life. There is a right way to catch game, to win a wife, to make one's self appear, to cure disease, to honor ghosts, to treat comrades or strangers, to behave when a child is born, on the warpath, in council, and so on in all cases which can arise. The ways are defined on the negative side, that is, by taboos. The "right" way is the way which the ancestors used and which has been handed down. The tradition is its own warrant. It is not held subject to verification by experience. The notion of right is in the folkways. It is not outside of them, of independent origin, and brought to them to test them. In the folkways, whatever is, is right. This is because they are traditional, and therefore contain in themselves the authority of the ancestral ghosts. When we come to the folkways we are at the end of our analysis. The notion of right and ought is the same in regard to all the folkways, but the degree of it varies with the importance of the interest at stake. The obligation of conformable and coöperative action is far greater under ghost fear and war than in other matters, and the social sanctions are severer, because group interests are supposed to be at stake. Some usages contain only a slight element of right and ought. It may well be believed that notions of right and duty, and of social welfare, were first developed in connection with ghost fear and other-worldliness, and therefore that, in that field also, folkways were first raised to mores. "Rights" are the rules of mutual give and take in the competition of life which are imposed on comrades in the in-group, in order that the peace may prevail there which is essential to the group strength. Therefore rights can never be "natural" or "God-given," or absolute in any sense. The morality of a group at a time is the sum of the taboos and prescriptions in the folkways by which right conduct is defined. Therefore

morals can never be intuitive. They are historical, institutional, and empirical.

World philosophy, life policy, right, rights, and morality are all products of the folkways. They are reflections on, and generalizations from, the experience of pleasure and pain which is won in efforts to carry on the struggle for existence under actual life conditions. The generalizations are very crude and vague in their germinal forms. They are all embodied in folklore, and all our philosophy and science have been developed out of them.

32. THE FOLKWAYS ARE "TRUE" The folkways are necessarily "true" with respect to some world philosophy. Pain forced men to think. The ills of life imposed reflection and taught forethought. Mental processes were irksome and were not undertaken until painful experience made them unavoidable. With great unanimity all over the globe primitive men followed the same line of thought. The dead were believed to live on as ghosts in another world just like this one. The ghosts had just the same needs, tastes, passions, etc., as the living men had had. These transcendental notions were the beginning of the mental outfit of mankind. They are articles of faith, not rational convictions. The living had duties to the ghosts, and the ghosts had rights; they also had power to enforce their rights. It behooved the living therefore to learn how to deal with ghosts. Here we have a complete world philosophy and a life policy deduced from it. When pain, loss, and ill were experienced and the question was provoked, Who did this to us? the world philosophy furnished the answer. When the painful experience forced the question, Why are the ghosts angry and what must we do to appease them? the "right" answer was the one which fitted into the philosophy of ghost fear. All acts were therefore constrained and trained into the forms of the world philosophy by ghost fear, ancestral authority, taboos, and habit. The habits and customs created a practical philosophy of welfare, and they confirmed and developed the religious theories of goblinism.

34. DEFINITION OF THE MORES When the elements of truth and right are developed into doctrines of welfare, the folkways are raised to another plane. They then become capable of producing inferences, developing into new forms, and extending their constructive influence over men and society. Then we call them the mores. The mores are the folkways, including the philosophical and ethical generalizations as to societal welfare which are suggested by them, and inherent in them, as they grow.

35. TABOOS The mores necessarily consist, in a large part, of taboos, which indicate the things which must not be done. In part these are dictated by mystic dread of ghosts who might be offended by certain acts, but they also include such acts as have been found by experience to produce unwelcome results, especially in the food quest, in war, in health, or in increase or decrease of population. These taboos always contain a

greater element of philosophy than the positive rules, because the taboos contain reference to a reason, as, for instance, that the act would displease the ghosts. The primitive taboos correspond to the fact that the life of man is environed by perils. His food quest must be limited by shunning poisonous plants. His appetite must be restrained from excess. His physical strength and health must be guarded from dangers. The taboos carry on the accumulated wisdom of generations, which has almost always been purchased by pain, loss, disease, and death. Other taboos contain inhibitions of what will be injurious to the group. The laws about the sexes, about property, about war, and about ghosts, have this character. They always include some social philosophy. They are both mystic and utilitarian, or compounded of the two.

Taboos may be divided into two classes, (1) protective and (2) destructive. Some of them aim to protect and secure, while others aim to repress or exterminate. Women are subject to some taboos which are directed against them as sources of possible harm or danger to men, and they are subject to other taboos which put them outside of the duties or risks of men. On account of this difference in taboos, taboos act selectively, and thus affect the course of civilization. They contain judgments as to societal welfare.

41. INTEGRATION OF THE MORES OF A GROUP OR AGE . . . Changes in history are primarily due to changes in life conditions. Then the folkways change. Then new philosophies and ethical rules are invented to try to justify the new ways. The whole vast body of modern mores has thus been developed out of the philosophy and ethics of the Middle Ages. So the mores which have been developed to suit the system of great secular states, world commerce, credit institutions, contract wages and rent, emigration to outlying continents, etc., have become the norm for the whole body of usages, manners, ideas, faiths, customs, and institutions which embrace the whole life of a society and characterize an historical epoch. Thus India, Chaldea, Assyria, Egypt, Greece, Rome, the Middle Ages, Modern Times, are cases in which the integration of the mores upon different life conditions produced societal states of complete and distinct individuality (ethos). Within any such societal status the great reason for any phenomenon is that it conforms to the mores of the time and place. Historians have always recognized incidentally the operation of such a determining force. What is now maintained is that it is not incidental or subordinate. It is supreme and controlling. Therefore the scientific discussion of a usage, custom, or institution consists in tracing its relation to the mores, and the discussion of societal crises and changes consists in showing their connection with changes in the life conditions, or with the readjustment of the mores to changes in those conditions.

232. MORES AND MORALS; SOCIAL CODE   For every one the mores give the notion of what ought to be. This includes the notion of what

ought to be done, for all should coöperate to bring to pass, in the order of life, what ought to be. All notions of propriety, decency, chastity, politeness, order, duty, right, rights, discipline, respect, reverence, coöperation, and fellowship, especially all things in regard to which good and ill depend entirely on the point at which the line is drawn, are in the mores. The mores can make things seem right and good to one group or one age which to another seem antagonistic to every instinct of human nature. The thirteenth century bred in every heart such a sentiment in regard to heretics that inquisitors had no more misgivings in their proceedings than men would have now if they should attempt to exterminate rattlesnakes. The sixteenth century gave to all such notions about witches that witch persecutors thought they were waging war on enemies of God and man. Of course the inquisitors and witch persecutors constantly developed the notions of heretics and witches. They exaggerated the notions and then gave them back again to the mores, in their expanded form, to inflame the hearts of men with terror and hate and to acquire, in the next stage, so much more fantastic and ferocious motives. Such is the reaction between the mores and the acts of the living generation. The world philosophy of the age is never anything but the reflection on the mental horizon, which is formed out of the mores, of the ruling ideas which are in the mores themselves. It is from a failure to recognize the to and fro in this reaction that the current notion arises that mores are produced by doctrines. The "morals" of an age are never anything but the consonance between what is done and what the mores of the age require. The whole revolves on itself, in the relation of the specific to the general, within the horizon formed by the mores. Every attempt to win an outside standpoint from which to reduce the whole to an absolute philosophy of truth and right, based on an unalterable principle, is a delusion. New elements are brought in only by new conquests of nature through science and art. The new conquests change the conditions of life and the interests of the members of the society. Then the mores change by adaptation to new conditions and interests. The philosophy and ethics then follow to account for and justify the changes in the mores; often, also, to claim that they have caused the changes. They never do anything but draw new lines of bearing between the parts of the mores and the horizon of thought within which they are inclosed, and which is a deduction from the mores. The horizon is widened by more knowledge, but for one age it is just as much a generalization from the mores as for another. It is always unreal. It is only a product of thought. The ethical philosophers select points on this horizon from which to take their bearings, and they think that they have won some authority for their systems when they travel back again from the generalization to the specific custom out of which it was deduced. The cases of the inquisitors and witch persecutors who toiled arduously and continually for their chosen ends, for little or no reward, show us the relation between mores on the one side and philosophy, ethics, and religion on the other. . . .

494. HONOR, SEEMLINESS, COMMON SENSE, CONSCIENCE Honor, common sense, seemliness, and conscience seem to belong to the individual domain. They are reactions produced in the individual by the societal environment. Honor is the sentiment of what one owes to one's self. It is an individual prerogative, and an ultimate individual standard. Seemliness is conduct which befits one's character and standards. Common sense, in the current view, is a natural gift and universal outfit. As to honor and seemliness, the popular view seems to be that each one has a fountain of inspiration in himself to furnish him with guidance. Conscience might be added as another natural or supernatural "voice," intuition, and part of the original outfit of all human beings as such. If these notions could be verified, and if they proved true, no discussion of them would be in place here, but as to honor it is a well-known and undisputed fact that societies have set codes of honor and standards of it which were arbitrary, irrational, and both individually and socially inexpedient, as ample experiment has proved. These codes have been and are imperative, and they have been accepted and obeyed by great groups of men who, in their own judgment, did not believe them sound. Those codes came out of the folkways of the time and place. Then comes the question whether it is not always so. Is honor, in any case, anything but the code of one's duty to himself which he has accepted from the group in which he was educated? Family, class, religious sect, school, occupation, enter into the social environment. In every environment there is a standard of honor. When a man thinks that he is acting most independently, on his personal prerogative, he is at best only balancing against each other the different codes in which he has been educated, e.g. that of the trades union against that of the Sunday school, or of the school against that of the family. What we think "natural" and universal, and to which we attribute an objective reality, is the sum of traits whose origin is so remote, and which we share with so many, that we do not know when or how we took them up, and we can remember no rational selection by which we adopted them. The same is true of common sense. It is the stock of ways of looking at things which we acquired unconsciously by suggestion from the environment in which we grew up. Some have more common sense than others, because they are more docile to suggestion, or have been taught to make judgments by people who were strong and wise. Conscience also seems best explained as a sum of principles of action which have in one's character the most original, remote, undisputed, and authoritative position, and to which questions of doubt are habitually referred. If these views are accepted, we have in honor, common sense, and conscience other phenomena of the folkways, and the notions of eternal truths of philosophy or ethics, derived from somewhere outside of men and their struggles to live well under the conditions of earth, must be abandoned as myths.

QUESTIONS

1. What does Sumner think are the parts played by need, pleasure, pain, and experience in the development of customs?
2. What is a "folkway"? How does Sumner think it is passed on from one generation to the next? Do primitive people, according to him, think their ways make for social welfare? Is their regard for folkways supported by any other considerations?
3. What forces does Sumner think tend to modify folkways? Do these forces tend to bring about an internal coherence among the folkways of each social group? What forces tend to keep the folkways rigid, irresponsive to changes in conditions?
4. Name some examples of recently developed "folkways."
5. Does Sumner think that what people mean by "right" and "ought" is just "is useful"? According to him, which types of conduct are apt to be thought more obligatory than others?
6. What is the relation between morality and fear of ghosts, according to Sumner?
7. What is the difference between "folkways," "mores," and "taboos"?
8. Does Sumner think it is possible for there to be rational criticism of the mores? Does he think that philosophical criticism of the mores ever has any effect? What does he think is the status of "natural" or "self-evident" principles of ethics?
9. Would a naturalist like Perry or Sharp agree that Sumner has shown that there is no possible objective criticism of moral codes? Why?
10. Suppose one set of folkways meets best the needs of one social group and a different set meets best the needs of a second social group; and suppose each set of folkways is accepted by the group whose needs it meets well. Does this situation prove that there are no universally valid basic moral principles?
11. State what you think Sumner succeeds in showing about the objective justification of moral principles and about traditional answers to the question of what is right or intrinsically good.

Ruth Fulton Benedict   (1887-1948)

RELATIVISM AND PATTERNS OF CULTURE

Ruth Benedict was educated at Vassar and at Columbia University and taught at Columbia from 1923 to 1948. She was the author of *Patterns of Culture* (1934), *Zuni Mythology* (1935), *Race, Science, and Politics* (1940), and *The Chrysanthemum and the Sword* (1946).

Miss Benedict, partly as a result of reading the work of Oswald Spengler, viewed culture systems as systems of ideas and practices, which through long development had been rendered coherent as a result of "social choices" dominated by basic preferences or values of the society. Cultures develop, she thought, like a style in art; once having begun with a certain emphasis, congenial elements are assimilated and uncongenial ones rejected until a whole is fashioned which is the expression of the basic "spirit" or value. The final wholes differ from one another markedly. But Benedict denied that they differ in validity or justification; in her view all these different patterns of culture are "equally valid." But each society, she held, elevates its own pattern to the status of a norm, a standard for behavior; it regards conformity to its code as morally good. Indeed, she, like Sumner, thought that "morally good" just means "habitual" or "customary." She was, then, like Sumner, both a cultural relativist and an ethical relativist.

From Ruth Fulton Benedict, "Anthropology and the Abnormal," *Journal of General Psychology*, Vol. 10 (1934), pp. 59-80. Reprinted by permission of the Journal Press, Provincetown, Mass.

ANTHROPOLOGY AND THE ABNORMAL

Modern social anthropology has become more and more a study of the varieties and common elements of cultural environment and the consequences of these in human behavior. For such a study of diverse social orders primitive peoples fortunately provide a laboratory not yet entirely vitiated by the spread of a standardized worldwide civilization. Dyaks and Hopis, Fijians and Yakuts are significant for psychological and sociological study because only among these simpler peoples has there been sufficient isolation to give opportunity for the development of localized social forms. In the higher cultures the standardization of custom and belief over a couple of continents has given a false sense of the inevitability of the particular forms that have gained currency, and we need to turn to a wider survey in order to check the conclusions we hastily base upon this near-universality of familiar customs. Most of the simpler cultures did not gain the wide currency of the one which, out of our experience, we identify with human nature, but this was for various historical reasons, and certainly not for any that gives us as its carriers a monopoly of social good or of social sanity. Modern civilization, from this point of view, becomes not a necessary pinnacle of human achievement but one entry in a long series of possible adjustments.

These adjustments, whether they are in mannerisms like the ways of showing anger, or joy, or grief in any society, or in major human drives like those of sex, prove to be far more variable than experience in any one culture would suggest. In certain fields, such as that of religion or of formal marriage arrangements, these wide limits of variability are well known and can be fairly described. In others it is not yet possible to give a generalized account, but that does not absolve us of the task of indicating the significance of the work that has been done and of the problems that have arisen.

One of these problems relates to the customary modern normal-abnormal categories and our conclusions regarding them. In how far are such categories culturally determined, or in how far can we with assurance regard them as absolute? In how far can we regard inability to function socially as diagnostic of abnormality, or in how far is it necessary to regard this as a function of the culture? . . .

The most spectacular illustrations of the extent to which normality may be culturally defined are those cultures where an abnormality of our culture is the cornerstone of their social structure. It is not possible to do justice to these possibilities in a short discussion. A recent study of an island of northwest Melanesia by Fortune describes a society built upon traits which we regard as beyond the border of paranoia. In this tribe the exogamic groups look upon each other as prime manipulators of black magic, so that one marries always into an enemy group which remains for life one's deadly and unappeasable foes. They look upon a good garden crop as a confession of theft, for everyone is engaged in making magic to induce into his garden the productiveness of his neighbors'; therefore no secrecy in the island is so rigidly insisted upon as the secrecy of a man's harvesting of his yams. Their polite phrase at the acceptance of a gift is, "And if you now poison me, how shall I repay you this present?" Their preoccupation with poisoning is constant; no woman ever leaves her cooking pot for a moment untended. Even the great affinal economic exchanges that are characteristic of this Melanesian culture area are quite altered in Dobu since they are incompatible with this fear and distrust that pervades the culture. . . . They go farther and people the whole world outside their own quarters with such malignant spirits that all-night feasts and ceremonials simply do not occur here. They have even rigorous religiously enforced customs that forbid the sharing of seed even in one family group. Anyone else's food is deadly poison to you, so that communality of stores is out of the question. For some months before harvest the whole society is on the verge of starvation, but if one falls to the temptation and eats up one's seed yams, one is an outcast and a beachcomber for life. There is no coming back. It involves, as a matter of course, divorce and the breaking of all social ties.

Now in this society where no one may work with another and no one may share with another, Fortune describes the individual who was regarded by all his fellows as crazy. He was not one of those who periodically ran amok and, beside himself and frothing at the mouth, fell with a knife upon

anyone he could reach. Such behavior they did not regard as putting anyone outside the pale. They did not even put the individuals who were
known to be liable to these attacks under any kind of control. They merely
fled when they saw the attack coming on and kept out of the way. "He
would be all right tomorrow." But there was one man of sunny, kindly
disposition who liked work and liked to be helpful. The compulsion was
too strong for him to repress it in favor of the opposite tendencies of his
culture. Men and women never spoke of him without laughing; he was
silly and simple and definitely crazy. Nevertheless, to the ethnologist used
to a culture that has, in Christianity, made his type the model of all virtue, he seemed a pleasant fellow.

An even more extreme example, because it is of a culture that has
built itself upon a more complex abnormality, is that of the North Pacific
Coast of North America. The civilization of the Kwakiutl, at the time
when it was first recorded in the last decades of the nineteenth century,
was one of the most vigorous in North America. It was built up on an
ample economic supply of goods, the fish which furnished their food staple
being practically inexhaustible and obtainable with comparatively small labor, and the wood which furnished the material for their houses, their fur-
nishings, and their arts being, with however much labor, always procurable.
They lived in coastal villages that compared favorably in size with those
of any other American Indians and they kept up constant communication
by means of sea-going dug-out canoes.

It was one of the most vigorous and zestful of the aboriginal cultures of North America, with complex crafts and ceremonials, and elaborate
and striking arts. It certainly had none of the earmarks of a sick civilization. The tribes of the Northwest Coast had wealth, and exactly in our
terms. That is, they had not only a surplus of economic goods, but they
made a game of the manipulation of wealth. It was by no means a mere
direct transcription of economic needs and the filling of those needs. It
involved the idea of capital, of interest, and of conspicuous waste. It was
a game with all the binding rules of a game, and a person entered it as a
child. His father distributed wealth for him, according to his ability, at a
small feast or potlatch, and each gift the receiver was obliged to accept
and to return after a short interval with interest that ran to about 100
per cent a year. By the time the child was grown, therefore, he was well
launched, a larger potlatch had been given for him on various occasions
of exploit or initiation, and he had wealth either out at usury or in his
own possession. Nothing in the civilization could be enjoyed without validating it by the distribution of this wealth. Everything that was valued,
names and songs as well as material objects were passed down in family
lines, but they were always publicly assumed with accompanying sufficient
distributions of property. It was the game of validating and exercising all
the privileges one could accumulate from one's various forebears, or by gift,
or by marriage, that made the chief interest of the culture. Everyone in

his degree took part in it, but many, of course, mainly as spectators. In its highest form it was played out between rival chiefs representing not only themselves and their family lines but their communities, and the object of the contest was to glorify oneself and to humiliate one's opponent. On this level of greatness the property involved was no longer represented by blankets, so many thousand of them to a potlatch, but by higher units of value. These higher units were like our bank notes. They were incised copper tablets, each of them named, and having a value that depended upon their illustrious history. This was as high as ten thousand blankets, and to possess one of them, still more to enhance its value at a great potlatch, was one of the greatest glories within the compass of the chiefs of the Northwest Coast. . . .

Every contingency of life was dealt with in . . . two traditional ways. To them the two were equivalent. Whether one fought with weapons or "fought with property," as they say, the same idea was at the bottom of both. In the olden times, they say, they fought with spears, but now they fight with property. One overcomes one's opponents in equivalent fashion in both, matching forces and seeing that one comes out ahead, and one can thumb one's nose at the vanquished rather more satisfactorily at a potlatch than on a battle field. Every occasion in life was noticed, not in its own terms, as a stage in the sex life of the individual or as a climax of joy or of grief, but as furthering this drama of consolidating one's own prestige and bringing shame to one's guests. Whether it was the occasion of the birth of a child, or a daughter's adolescence, or of the marriage of one's son, they were all equivalent raw material for the culture to use for this one traditionally selected end. They were all to raise one's own personal status and to entrench oneself by the humiliation of one's fellows. A girl's adolescence among the Nootka was an event for which her father gathered property from the time she was first able to run about. When she was adolescent he would demonstrate his greatness by an unheard of distribution of these goods, and put down all his rivals. It was not as a fact of the girl's sex life that it figured in their culture, but as the occasion for a major move in the great game of vindicating one's own greatness and humiliating one's associates.

In their behavior at great bereavements this set of the culture comes out most strongly. Among the Kwakiutl it did not matter whether a relative had died in bed of disease, or by the hand of an enemy; in either case death was an affront to be wiped out by the death of another person. The fact that one had been caused to mourn was proof that one had been put upon. A chief's sister and her daughter had gone up to Victoria, and either because they drank bad whiskey or because their boat capsized they never came back. The chief called together his warriors. "Now, I ask you, tribes, who shall wail? Shall I do it or shall another?" The spokesman answered, of course, "Not you, Chief. Let some other of the tribes." Immediately they set up the war pole to announce their intention of wiping out the injury, and gathered a war party. They set out, and found seven men and two children asleep and killed them. "Then they felt good when they arrived at Sebaa in the evening."

The point which is of interest to us is that in our society those who on that occasion would feel good when they arrived at Sebaa that evening would be the definitely abnormal. There would be some, even in our society, but it is not a recognized and approved mood under the circumstances. On the Northwest Coast those are favored and fortunate to whom that mood under those circumstances is congenial, and those to whom it is repugnant are unlucky. This latter minority can register in their own culture only by doing violence to their congenial responses and acquiring others that are difficult for them. The person, for instance, who, like a Plains Indian whose wife has been taken from him, is too proud to fight, can deal with the Northwest Coast civilization only by ignoring its strongest bents. If he cannot achieve it, he is the deviant in that culture, their instance of abnormality.

This head-hunting that takes place on the Northwest Coast after a death is no matter of blood revenge or of organized vengeance. There is no effort to tie up the subsequent killing with any responsibility on the part of the victim for the death of the person who is being mourned. A chief whose son has died goes visiting wherever his fancy dictates, and he says to his host, "My prince has died today, and you go with him." Then he kills him. In this, according to their interpretation, he acts nobly because he has not been downed. He has thrust back in return. The whole procedure is meaningless without the fundamental paranoid reading of bereavement. Death, like all the other untoward accidents of existence, confounds man's pride and can only be handled in the category of insults. . . .

These illustrations, which it has been possible to indicate only in the briefest manner, force upon us the fact that normality is culturally defined. An adult shaped to the drives and standards of either of these cultures, if he were transported into our civilization, would fall into our categories of abnormality. He would be faced with the psychic dilemmas of the socially unavailable. In his own culture, however, he is the pillar of society, the end result of socially inculcated mores, and the problem of personal instability in his case simply does not arise.

No one civilization can possibly utilize in its mores the whole potential range of human behavior. Just as there are great numbers of possible phonetic articulations, and the possibility of language depends on a selection and standardization of a few of these in order that speech communication may be possible at all, so the possibility of organized behavior of every sort, from the fashions of local dress and houses to the dicta of a people's ethics and religion, depends upon a similar selection among the possible behavior traits. In the field of recognized economic obligations or sex tabus this selection is as non-rational and subconscious a process as it is in the field of phonetics. It is a process which goes on in the group for long periods of time and is historically conditioned by innumerable accidents of isolation or of contact of peoples. In any comprehensive study of psychology, the selection that different cultures have made in the course of history within the great circumference of potential behavior is of great significance.

Every society, beginning with some slight inclination in one direction or another, carries its preference farther and farther, integrating itself more and more completely upon its chosen basis, and discarding those types of behavior that are uncongenial. Most of those organizations of personality that seem to us most incontrovertibly abnormal have been used by different civilizations in the very foundations of their institutional life. Conversely the most valued traits of our normal individuals have been looked on in differently organized cultures as aberrant. Normality, in short, within a very wide range, is culturally defined. It is primarily a term for the socially elaborated segment of human behavior in any culture; and abnormality, a term for the segment that that particular civilization does not use. The very eyes with which we see the problem are conditioned by the long traditional habits of our own society.

It is a point that has been made more often in relation to ethics than in relation to psychiatry. We do not any longer make the mistake of deriving the morality of our own locality and decade directly from the inevitable constitution of human nature. We do not elevate it to the dignity of a first principle. We recognize that morality differs in every society, and is a convenient term for socially approved habits. Mankind has always preferred to say, "It is a morally good," rather than "It is habitual," and the fact of this preference is matter enough for a critical science of ethics. But historically the two phrases are synonymous.

The concept of the normal is properly a variant of the concept of the good. It is that which society has approved. A normal action is one which falls well within the limits of expected behavior for a particular society. Its variability among different peoples is essentially a function of the variability of the behavior patterns that different societies have created for themselves, and can never be wholly divorced from a consideration of culturally institutionalized types of behavior.

Each culture is a more or less elaborate working-out of the potentialities of the segment it has chosen. In so far as a civilization is well integrated and consistent within itself, it will tend to carry farther and farther, according to its nature, its initial impulse toward a particular type of action, and from the point of view of any other culture those elaborations will include more and more extreme and aberrant traits.

Each of these traits, in proportion as it reinforces the chosen behavior patterns of that culture, is for that culture normal. Those individuals to whom it is congenial either congenitally, or as the result of childhood sets, are accorded prestige in that culture, and are not visited with the social contempt or disapproval which their traits would call down upon them in a society that was differently organized. On the other hand, those individuals whose characteristics are not congenial to the selected type of human behavior in that community are the deviants, no matter how valued their personality traits may be in a contrasted civilization. . . .

The problem of understanding abnormal human behavior in any absolute sense independent of cultural factors is still far in the future. The categories of borderline behavior which we derive from the study of the neuroses and psychoses of our civilization are categories of prevailing local types of instability. They give much information about the stresses and strains of Western civilization, but no final picture of inevitable human behavior. Any conclusions about such behavior must await the collection by trained observers of psychiatric data from other cultures. Since no adequate work of the kind has been done at the present time, it is impossible to say what core of definition of abnormality may be found valid from the comparative material. It is as it is in ethics; all our local conventions of moral behavior and of immoral are without absolute validity, and yet it is quite possible that a modicum of what is considered right and what wrong could be disentangled that is shared by the whole human race. When data are available in psychiatry, this minimum definition of abnormal human tendencies will be probably quite unlike our culturally conditioned, highly elaborated psychoses such as those that are described, for instance, under the terms of schizophrenia and manic-depressive.

QUESTIONS

1. Give a brief profile of the character or personality of the "normal" person among the Dobuans and among the Kwakiutl, as it is depicted by Benedict. Which features of each would be condemned or disparaged in our society?
2. Explain Benedict's view of the development of the mores of societies, making use of such key phrases as "selection," "subconscious," "non-rational," "conditioned by accidents of isolation or contact," "development of preferences," "integration upon its chosen basis."
3. Does Benedict offer any reasoning in support of her dictum that "morality" is a "convenient term for socially approved habits"? Do you think this position is sound? Explain. Is the "concept of the normal" a "variant of the concept of the good"?
4. In what ways do you think Benedict's account of the forces involved in the development of values or standards differs from that of Sumner?
5. Do you detect any difference between the kind of ethical relativism supported by Sumner and that supported by Benedict, or between the supporting reasons offered by them?

Ralph Linton (1893-1953)

UNIVERSAL VALUES AND
SOCIAL FUNCTIONS

In the early decades of the present century, anthropologists stressed the variety among cultural systems. Sumner and Benedict illustrate this emphasis. Several factors have more recently produced a counteremphasis: the "functional" theory of cultures, according to which every element in a culture system somehow serves the needs of the social group, and none can be viewed as purely an historical accident; the development of social psychology and depth psychology, with a consequent interest in a psychological understanding of cultural values; and World War II, with its challenge for a new assessment of the bases of international understanding. Most social scientists today would say that the cultural relativism of Sumner and Benedict is an extreme and oversimplified view.

The following essay by Ralph Linton represents this new line of thought. Essays with very similar purport have been written recently by other leading anthropologists, such as Clyde Kluckhohn and Robert Redfield. Here Linton tries to show that many values are universal and that many are necessary because of the biological needs of man or the requirements of tolerable social organization. His view is that an understanding of the fact that many values have this status can be the basis for intercultural cooperation and tolerance of the means used to achieve these ends.

Linton does not question the partial truth of the cultural relativist position; he does deny the view that cultural relativism represents the whole truth about values — that a culture's values are all accidents of its history and might well have been otherwise.

In this essay Linton does not consider the status of ethical relativism. Very likely he would adopt a moderate form of relativism, but he has not concerned himself with this issue.

Linton received his education at Swarthmore, Columbia, the University of Pennsylvania, and Harvard. He held positions at the Bishop Museum, Honolulu, and at the Field Museum of Natural History; he taught at the University of Wisconsin, at

Columbia, and at Yale (from 1946 until his death). His major books were *The Study of Man* (1936), *Acculturation in Seven American Indian Tribes* (1940), *The Cultural Background of Personality* (1943), and *The Tree of Culture* (1955).

From Ralph Linton, "The Problem of Universal Values." From: *Method and Perspective in Anthropology: Papers in Honor of Wilson D. Wallis,* edited by Robert F. Spencer. University of Minnesota Press, Minneapolis. Copyright 1954 by the University of Minnesota, pp. 145-68.

THE PROBLEM OF UNIVERSAL VALUES

The study of values has assumed much more than academic interest for the modern world. With the rapid improvement in means of communication which has taken place during the last century and the resulting increase in cross-cultural contacts, the potentialities for conflict have become greater than ever before. It is obvious that unless the various nations which compose the modern world can come to some sort of agreement as to what things are important and desirable, we are headed for catastrophe. Moreover, the very ease of communication which may produce such a catastrophe ensures its inclusiveness. In the Dark Ages which would result from a world war of atomic bombs and bacteria there would be no region sufficiently isolated to escape destruction and carry on the torch of enlightenment. The peoples of the world must find common areas of understanding or die.

As students of human behavior in all its aspects, anthropologists might be expected to take a prominent part in solving the problems which the present situation has created. However, they have consistently avoided judgments regarding what things are universally desired or valued. Their principal contribution to date has been the development of the concept of cultural relativity. Through their comparative studies they have been able to demonstrate that different societies have successfully achieved the same ends by employing widely different means. From this they have concluded that the really scientific attitude toward cultural differences is the one summed up in the old saying: "Well, some do and some don't." While such tolerance is a necessary first step to international understanding, its contribution is essentially negative. Any sort of successful cooperation must be built on a realization that, no matter how various societies may go about it, all of them prize and desire certain things and should be willing to work together to get them.

No matter how much one may stress the right of every society to adhere to its own ways, the fact remains that some of the culturally approved practices of any society are likely to arouse strongly negative emotional reactions in the members of some other society. The European feels that the Muslim practice of eating with the fingers is repulsive, while the Muslim is equally revolted at the thought of using forks and spoons which may be cere-monially unclean. In spite of thorough training in cultural relativity, the present writer has never been able to observe the common Latin country practice of picking chickens alive with real equanimity. It is difficult to over-come such reactions and, the more of them the culture of another society arouses, the more difficult it is for the outsider to feel at home among its members. The assumption that continuous contact with the members of an-other society and increased familiarity with its culture will automatically result in increased liking is a victory of optimism over experience. Anyone who has had numerous cross-cultural contacts can testify that there are societies continued contact with which merely results in increasing dislike. If the world's societies are to reach a state of adjustment in which they can cooperate toward common ends, these ends must be so clearly defined that the societies' members can understand them and be willing to overcome some measure of mutual distaste in order to see them achieved. This, in turn, involves a recognition of universal values which can be used as a basis for determining which ends will be universally acceptable. Thanks to their long experience in comparative culture studies, the anthropologists should be able to make a real contribution toward this. They are in a particularly good position to recognize basic similarities as well as differences, and it is to be hoped that their current preoccupation with the latter is only a passing phase in the development of the science. . . . The first require-ment for a scientific approach to the problem of values in culture is some agreement as to what is meant by the term *value*. Like many other words in the English language, *value* carries multiple meanings depending upon its context. Even if we ignore its technical usages in such fields as economics, mathematics, and art, several meanings remain. The element common to these seems to be best expressed by the superficially humorous definition: "A value is anything of any value," i.e., anything regarded favorably. A value is thus anything capable of influencing the individual's decisions in choice situations or, going one step further back and as a necessary preliminary to such influence, anything capable of producing an emotional response. Under this definition there are, of course, individual values as well as those which are cultural, i.e., shared and transmitted by the members of a particular society. However, in a search for universals the individual values, insofar as they are individual, may be ignored. They are transitory, like the persons who hold them, and unless they come to be shared by other individuals, have little influence on the social-cultural continuum.

For our present purposes we will define a value as: *anything capable of producing similar choice responses in several of a society's members*. It may be noted that this fails to bring in the factor of favorable response implicit in the ordinary use of the term. However, any consideration of values as dynamic elements in culture soon reveals that there are, in all cultures, numerous acts, objects, and concepts toward which the members of the society have strong negative attitudes. These attitudes are frequently much stronger than one would anticipate from a mere antithesis between the thing toward which the attitude is held and its opposite. Thus in our own society at the present time the hysterical opposition to communism and the persecution of individuals in which it is reflected certainly are not matched by an equally strong emotional attachment to the liberties assured by our democratic system of government or by an equally intense respect and admiration for those who are attempting to maintain them in the face of the present attack upon them. . . .

To understand the relation of values to the operation of a society, one must recognize that values are an integral part of any society's culture and that, with regard to their origin, transmission, and integration, they follow the same rules as other culture elements. The normal society consists of an organized, self-perpetuating group of individuals which persists far beyond the life span of any one of its component members. Its persistence is made possible by the presence of a culture, i.e., an organized series of ideas and behavior patterns which are transmitted from generation to generation within the society. The culture as a whole provides techniques by which the members of the society can both satisfy their individual needs and co-operate toward common ends. The latter involves an elaborate system of specialized activities and reciprocal behaviors which together constitute the social system. The needs of individuals and of the society are shaped and the possible ways of satisfying them delimited by the milieu in which the society operates. At any given point in time this milieu is a product of the interaction of the society's external environment, both natural and social, and the content of its current culture.

All societies and cultures are not only continuums but continuums in a constant state of change and internal readjustment. The milieu is always unstable, presenting the society with new problems, and the culture itself is always changing under the pressure of internal as well as external forces. Individuals develop new solutions to old problems and new patterns are borrowed from other societies while each new element introduced into the culture produces disharmonies which take time to adjust. The only really stable factors in the cultural-social continuum are the needs of individuals as these stem from the physical-psychological qualities of our species and the social imperatives, i.e., the problems posed by organized group living per se, problems which must be solved if the society is to survive.

In this situation of constant flux, the society's main guide in meeting new problems and in deciding which of the new behavior patterns brought to its attention shall be accepted and integrated into the culture is its system of values. It is this system which guides its members' choices among the possible alternatives which are always present. From what we now know of psychological mechanisms we may assume that any pattern of behavior which is consistently effective, i.e., rewarded, will be given preference over other less consistently effective patterns in situations involving choice. It will also acquire the emotional associations which make it a value. However, human beings constantly generalize from one situation to another, while their use of language provides them with a highly effective tool for organizing such generalizations and expressing them as abstract concepts. Both behavior patterns and concepts are transmitted from individual to individual within the society and thus come to form part of the culture and to function as elements in the milieu within which culture change takes place.

Most value concepts find expression in more than one pattern of overt behavior, while, conversely, all but the simplest patterns of overt behavior involve more than one conceptual value. However, the number and the functional importance of the behavior patterns in which different values are involved vary greatly even within a single culture. Thus in our own society such a conceptual value as national survival is related to innumerable behavior patterns, while a conceptual value such as amusement is related to a much smaller number. The relative importance of the same conceptual value may also differ profoundly in different cultures. Thus the importance of esthetic activities relative to economic production was quite different in ancient Greek culture from what it is in modern America.

From the foregoing it can be seen that the values recognized by any society fall at once into two classes: *instrumental* and *conceptual*. The distinction can best be illustrated by an example. Nearly all societies have a conceptual value of modesty which is reflected in specific patterns of coverage for various parts of the body under various circumstances. Insistence that the genitals of both sexes should be kept covered in public is as nearly universal as any culturally determined pattern of behavior.[1] The objects used for this purpose vary greatly, ranging from *tanga* and pubic tassels to robes and trousers. However, the custom of wearing a garment of a particular type is always a focus for attitudes and emotions and constitutes in itself a value of the instrumental type. Thus some years ago the head of a great Christian denomination refused to receive the late Mahatma Gandhi because the latter insisted on wearing a loin cloth instead of trousers. Both the parties involved would certainly have agreed on the conceptual value of modesty, yet for each the behavior pattern by which this was instrumented in his own culture had acquired meanings and attitudes which made it a value in its own right. To the prelate, trousers were a symbol of both respect and respectability. To Gandhi, the loin cloth was less a garment than an expression of the struggle for Indian independence. Trousers, as the garb of the politically dominant European, had acquired strong negative associations. He no doubt felt that to don them for his reception would be an act of obeisance to the British Raj.

While instrumental values are, in nearly all cases, concise and easily recognizable, conceptual values are much less so. Some of those whose influence can be detected in the greatest variety of behavior patterns may not even be conscious or verbalized. They belong to what Kluckhohn has called

[1] Exceptions: African Nilotics, Amazonian Indians, and some Melanesians.

the implicit category of culture elements. Every culture includes a number of values which are so abstract and so generalized in their expression that they carry little emotional effect in themselves, although they lie at the base of the whole cultural structure. In general, the more concrete and conscious a value, the easier it is to attach emotion to it. For this reason the instrumental values of a society tend to carry higher emotional effect than the conceptual values. They constitute a sort of sensitive surface layer highly susceptible to external influences, and interference with them brings a more rapid response from the society's members than does the less obvious contravention of deeper-lying conceptual values.

Instrumental values are also much more susceptible to change than conceptual ones. In studying the history of particular societies, one is struck again and again by the persistence of particular conceptual value systems. Such systems not only determine what elements will be accepted or rejected in situations of free choice but also serve as guides in the reinterpretation of elements forced upon the society. This process of reinterpretation is nowhere better illustrated than in the modifications which various proselytizing religions have undergone in their diffusion. Originally pacifistic, Christianity became a warrior's creed in militaristic Europe. The simple, clear-cut creed of Islam was transformed in Persia into Sufi, mysticism, while Buddhism, after its initial denial of the efficacy of worship, became the most highly ritualized of all the great religions.

It is obvious that instrumental values are exceedingly variable. They constitute the area of value study to which the concept of cultural relativity is most completely applicable. If universal values exist, they must be sought for at the level of the deepest and most generalized conceptual values, those which stand in closest relation to the individual needs and social imperatives shared by the whole of mankind. A comparative study of cultures would seem to indicate that there are a considerable number of such values, but their identification is rendered difficult by their generality. Most of them are so fundamental and are taken so completely for granted by the people who accept them that they are likely to be overlooked.

In any attempt to list conceptual values, the mere order of precedence given to them in enumeration would seem to reflect judgments as to their relative importance, but the writer wishes to disown any such implications immediately. The values which seem to be universal are listed in a certain order only because it is impossible to present them in anything but a linear form.

Since in popular thinking the relation between values and religion is a particularly close one, supernatural values may be taken as the starting point in our search for universals. Practically all cultures believe in the existence of what we would call supernatural beings, entities which cannot be perceived by our senses at ordinary times, yet which are able in some way, usually undefined, to influence the course of nature and thus to aid or injure men. These entities are usually conceived of as essentially human in their motives and emotions, a quite natural projection of the worshiper's experience. . . .

Closely related to the belief in beings able to affect the lives of men is a belief in persistence after death. This belief is held by practically all societies and finds a rational explanation in the inability of the individual to imagine either himself or those who are closely associated with him as nonexistent. However, the concepts held by various societies regarding the after-life are fully as varied as their concepts of the supernatural in general. . . .

The behaviors enjoined by different societies for dealing with the supernatural are even more varied than the beliefs. It is obvious that the approach will differ according to whether the operator believes he is dealing with beings or with an impersonal force. In the former case, approaches are patterned upon the individual's experience with other individuals either more or less powerful than himself. In the latter, they are patterned upon his experience with the manipulation of familiar objects and forces and are correspondingly mechanistic. . . .

It should be noted that there are numerous societies in which the favor of supernatural beings is not to be gained by ethical behavior. This is not limited to those cases in which the supernatural being is dominated by the operator. Even where the being occupies a dominant position, the relation between him and his worshiper is frequently conceived of as something quite apart from the worshiper's relation with other human beings. So long as the worshiper performs the appropriate rites, and, so to speak, maintains his half of the reciprocal relation between himself and the being, his behavior in society is considered no concern of his supernatural vis-à-vis. In some cases this attitude reaches great lengths. Thus in Polynesia, in accordance with a generalized pattern of occupational specialization which extended even to supernatural beings, there were deities to whom one might appeal successfully for aid in each and every type of antisocial behavior. More familiar examples would be the classical Mercury, god of thieves, or Magdalene, the patron saint of medieval prostitutes.

It may be noted that until one reaches the level of monotheistic civilizations, the only category of supernatural beings who are uniformly insistent upon ethical behavior on the part of their worshipers is that of ancestral spirits. The individual's childhood experience of parents in their dual capacity of disciplinarians and protectors seems to carry over directly in so-called ancestor worship, and, while the shades feel a deep interest in the welfare of their descendants, they are also quick to censure and even punish deviations from good behavior.

The only universal features which can be derived from such a wide variety of beliefs are those of man's universal sense of inadequacy in the face of many situations and his belief that there are beings whose powers exceed his own and who will give him the aid which he so vitally needs, if he can learn the correct methods of approaching them. To this may be added the well-nigh universal belief that the individual's personality is not extinguished in death. . . .

The values associated with the operation and perpetuation of societies are more numerous than those associated with the supernatural and also show less variety. This is no doubt due to their more intimate connection with the physiological needs of human beings and the practical aspects of organizing groups of individuals for their mutual advantage. The problems presented by these are more numerous than those involved in dealing with the supernatural, but the possible solutions for each problem are much less numerous. Thus the possible methods for developing and controlling the exchange of products and services or for rearing children are strictly limited in number, while there seems to be no limit to the variety of beliefs and rituals which will serve to satisfy man's desire for help from supernatural powers and reassure him in time of crises.

Social values which are universally present are of the utmost interest, since societies rather than individuals are the units in the human struggle for survival. They also establish the limits within which many values are operative. Thus nearly all instrumental values which have to do with the interaction of individuals apply only to interaction with other members of the same society. At the primitive level the individual's tribe represents for him the limits of humanity and the same individual who will exert himself to any lengths in behalf of a fellow tribesman may regard the nontribesman as fair game to be exploited by any possible means, or even as a legitimate source of meat. . . .

Societies normally include a number of individuals of both sexes and at all age levels. This fact provides the starting point for differentiation of activities. Even the simplest societies distinguish between men's work and women's work, while the trend toward specialization culminates in modern mechanized society with its innumerable skilled occupations. The well-being of the society thus depends upon an exchange of goods produced by specialists and of services performed by them. As a result, all societies attach high value to reciprocity and to fair dealing. The latter statement may be questioned by those who have had uncomfortable experiences in our own system. However, in all societies, shrewdness and deceit are considered as legitimate in certain areas, usually those which are of not too vital importance for social well-being. The mutual recognition that the rule of caveat emptor holds in such areas endows dealing in them with a certain sporting element. Thus the old-time Yankee who deceived another man in a horse trade without resorting to a direct falsehood was admired by his society, while an attempt to pass a bad check would result in social ostracism.

The existence of reciprocity between different subsocieties within the larger unit, particularly by members of different classes, may be doubted by those trained in Marxist doctrines. However, one must recognize that even such a seemingly exploitive system as the feudal actually represented reciprocity on a large scale between noble and peasant. The feudal system emerged in a period of violence and confusion, when the trained soldier who became the feudal lord protected the peasant in return for his economic contribution. Indeed, without this contribution the soldier would have been unable to purchase the expensive equipment which the current military techniques entailed or to get the long practice required for its efficient use. In the same way, during the early phases of the capitalist system, the owner, who was normally also a manager, not only provided the capital required to obtain the machines which increased the workers' output, but also organized production processes and attended to the marketing of the product. That his returns were disproportionately large relative to his services cannot be doubted, but in the social-cultural continuum such inequalities tend to right themselves. A feudal system which has been outmoded by the growth of new technology and tactics is swept away by revolution, and we can see how, in the capitalist system, ownership is passing from single individuals or families to large numbers of stockholders, management is passing from owner to trained technician, while the relation between management and organized labor is shifting increasingly from exploitation to cooperation.

Management, in the sense of leadership and direction, is probably as old as social life. The differentiated activities of a simple society's members and a more or less equitable sharing of the advantages derived from them can be carried on without any formal type of direction or conscious techniques for enforcing reciprocity. However, most group activities, such as land-clearing, drive hunts, or seine fishing, require a high degree of co-ordinated effort, while the whole society needs leadership in emergencies. All societies recognize and obey leaders under certain conditions, although different individuals may assume the leadership in different situations. Thus many American Indian tribes had a war chief and a peace chief, the functions of each being clearly delimited.

The rewards which go with leadership differ greatly from one society to another and frequently do not involve economic advantage. Thus the head of a Plains Indian band levied no contributions upon his followers, though at the same time he was expected to keep open house and to maintain his followers' allegiance by frequent gifts. Even in medieval Europe a king was expected to meet his expenses from his personal estates, and any attempt to levy taxes on his feudal lords was hotly resented. That individuals are still eager to become leaders under such circumstances shows the efficacy of the psychological rewards to be derived from prestige and power.

The need for leadership and the universality of the power drive, no matter how it may be culturally camouflaged, are responsible for the fact that there are no genuinely equalitarian societies. Every human group recognizes that certain individuals or categories of individuals are socially more important than others. The so-called equalitarian societies are those in which the individual is able to find his own level in the prestige series without initial handicaps. However, in aristocratic societies the value of individual mobility involved in the democratic system is replaced and to some degree compensated for by values of social responsibility and skilled performance in the aristocratic role. Where the status of aristocrat is hereditary, it uniformly carries obligations both toward inferiors and toward the group as a whole, and involves elaborate patterns of behavior. One of the least desirable features of our own system is that which accords high status to the man of wealth, no matter how acquired, while imposing no social obligations upon him.

The values just discussed relate to the functioning of the society. However, the need for the society's preservation is even more vital. If the social-cultural continuum is to be perpetuated, there must be a constant increment of new individuals to replace those who drop out and, equally important, these individuals must be trained in the behaviors and indoctrinated in the attitudes necessary for the performance of particular roles in the operation of the society as a whole. The family is unquestionably the most efficient institution for meeting these social imperatives. It not only produces children but it trains them in the way that they should go. For this reason one finds that in all societies the family has become a focus for strong emotional attitudes.

Families are essentially of two types, conjugal and consanguine: those like our own (conjugal), in which the functional group is primarily the close, biologically determined unit of parents and offspring, and those in which the functional unit is primarily a group of siblings of the same sex and their offspring (consanguine), with their spouses always regarded as somewhat marginal. However, even in families of the latter type, the desirability of continuing matings, i.e., marriages, is recognized. Families of this type tend to be extensive and a constant turnover in spouses is as disconcerting and as injurious to efficiency as a constant turnover of labor in any other organized work group. Moreover, long before the days of modern psychology, it was recognized that the child needs affection and emotional security for its proper personality development. This is more likely to be provided by the child's own biological parents than by a succession of less emotionally involved caretakers.

The desire for permanence of matings has given rise to two quite distinct lines of approach, each with its own associated value system. In one of these, premarital chastity is valued, largely, it seems, from the anticipation that an individual who enters marriage without previous sex experience will be deterred by timidity from experimenting with other partners, the chance of new and disruptive attachments thus being reduced. This attitude is most frequently found in societies where marriages are arranged for the sons and daughters by the family elders. From this conceptual value has developed such rites as the tests of the bride's virginity, common in Muslim countries, or the idea held by our not very remote ancestors that a woman who had lost her virginity was permanently ruined and unfitted for marriage, even if she had been violated against her will. Where this particular configuration of values exists, it is usually supplemented by economic sanctions for marriage: such things as the dowry and the more widespread and frequently misunderstood bride-price. By giving both the partners and their affiliated kin groups an economic interest in the maintenance of the union, these sanctions act as a strong deterrent to separation.

In the other type, reliance for the continuity of the marriage rests primarily on the physical and emotional adjustment of the partners. Under these circumstances there may be strong insistence on postmarital faithfulness, but the attitude toward premarital experimentation is one of tolerance, if not actual encouragement. It is thought that partners are most likely to be faithful when they are sexually congenial and when their curiosity about other possible partners has been satisfied. Our own situation in this respect is a curious one, since our society reprehends premarital experimentation, the arrangement of marriage by elders, and economic sanctions — i.e., all the techniques for preserving marriage which have proved effective. Under the circumstances, it is not surprising that so many of our partnerships end up in the divorce courts.

The roles of individuals within the family are everywhere culturally prescribed. Parents, or in the case of strong consanguine family organization, members of the parents' generation in the kin group to which the child belongs, are expected to assume responsibility for the child's physical care and training. Conversely, the child is expected to render them respect and obedience, at least until it becomes adult, and to care for them in old age. The failure on either side to live up to these obligations is severely reprehended. Wives are, in general, expected to be submissive to husbands. In the marital relationship husbands are normally dominant, in spite of the claims made by certain earnest feminists. Needless to say, the exceptions to this rule fall into two groups: those in which a particular wife establishes dominance over a particular husband without cultural sanction, or those in which, owing to consanguine family organization, the husband is not regarded as a family member. In such cases the dominant role, both in respect to the woman and her children, is assumed by one of her brothers. The reasons for this are presumably to be found in physical factors, the male of our species being in general larger, stronger, and more active than the female, while the latter suffers from the additional disabilities connected with pregnancy and nursing. Each of the practices in which these factors of familial interaction are reflected becomes an instrumental value for the particular society, while such concepts as parental responsibility, filial obedience, and wifely submission are conceptual values which find incidental expression in great numbers of behavioral practices.

On the border line between the value systems which relate primarily to social imperatives and those which relate to individual needs lies the whole area of property concepts. It may be stated at once that no society has been able to maintain a completely communistic arrangement for more than a few generations. Moreover, the attempts to do so have not occurred among primitive peoples but among highly civilized ones where communities of disillusioned individuals have attempted to escape in this way from the conflicts and inequalities of an over inclusive system of individual ownership. The property concept probably originates in the sort of individual identification with particular places and objects which may be observed even in animals. Objects which the individual has made or which he uses consistently acquire a whole series of associations which give them values over and above those resulting from their practical potentialities. Among even the simplest and most primitive groups we find well-developed concepts of both personal and group property. Personal property is usually limited to tools and weapons, clothing, and similar objects of immediate utility. While there may be an easygoing attitude toward the loan of such objects, this in no way negates the fact of private ownership. Group property, aside from particular objects which acquire value from their function as symbols of the group, is mainly territorial. Each band or tribe has its range within which its members are free to hunt or exploit natural resources, but which is forbidden to members of other social units. This again is in line with the behavior of most gregarious animals.

Between the claims of the group as exemplified in these patterns of communal ownership and free exploitation and those of the individual as they may be extended over particular natural resources or means of production, there is an inevitable conflict which every society has had to solve. The solutions which various societies have chosen have depended upon whether priority was given to the interests of the entire group or to those of individuals. Where the groups involved are small enough and sufficiently localized so that there are frequent face-to-face contacts between members, the potential antisocial consequences of extreme extensions of individual ownership do not arise. They are neutralized by social pressures. The wealthy man finds it more rewarding to be admired and praised for his generosity than to continue hoarding, subjected to the disfavor of the group and to the spectacle of individuals suffering from want with whom he inevitably feels a considerable identification. Only the absentee landlord or slaveholder and the modern corporation manager are immune to these social pressures, and it is under them that the potential evils of private ownership have found fullest expression.

Another set of values, lying on the border line between the social and individual categories, comprises those which have to do with knowledge. Since organized social life depends upon individual learning, it is obvious that much knowledge has a primarily social function. No individual can operate successfully in any status unless he knows the associated roles. However, few people are content to cease learning at the point where their knowledge would suffice for adequate social integration. Curiosity and extreme teachability are characteristic of our species, and every individual tends to accumulate a quantity of information which is of no practical importance. The accumulation of this information and the drawing of conclusions from it become sources of emotional satisfaction not unlike that derived from skill in a game. They also may provide an escape from the immediate pressures of reality. Most readers have encountered persons who have followed some abstract line of study for sheer love of the intellectual exercise. Thus the writer has known a journeyman printer in Chicago who had taught himself to read and write the Malagasy language, an advertising man in a department store who had made himself one of the foremost American Tibetan scholars, and a bank clerk who was a nationally recognized authority on early American genealogies.

The attitudes of societies toward such accumulation of "unprofitable" knowledge vary profoundly. In general, the individuals who possess it are regarded with a mixture of admiration and contempt. The scholar is everywhere officially honored and unofficially starved. It is only in the few societies which support institutions of higher learning that he is able to use his accumulation of esoteric knowledge as a source of income. To these might perhaps be added Imperial China, where scholarship of a particular type was rewarded by official preferment and by assignment to political office. However, even here, pure scholarship brought no great financial reward. To be profitable, it had to be combined with good social connections and a considerable measure of shrewdness and political skill.

Impractical, "useless" knowledge of the sort just discussed is only one aspect of the need for escape from reality which underlies considerable areas of human behavior and which has not as yet been successfully explained by the behavioristic psychologists. There is no known society which does not have games of the sort in which the individual sets up purely artificial obstacles and gets satisfaction from overcoming them. Neither is there any known society which lacks literature, with its potentialities for emotional satisfaction through vicarious participation in the adventures of fictional characters. While this is only one of any literature's multiple functions, its importance is not to be discounted. Lastly, every known society has various forms of esthetic expression: music, the dance, and graphic arts. These serve to relieve the monotony of daily existence and to evoke pleasurable sensations, although why they should do the latter is still an unsolved problem.

The concrete expressions of the esthetic urge, if one may so term the human need to create beauty, are extraordinarily varied. In order to realize this, one need only contrast the music of different peoples, with its varied tonal scales and use of melody and rhythm, or the even more diverse expressions of graphic art. Whether there is some denominator common to all the expressions of a single type is one of the most important problems confronting the student of esthetics. It is obvious that appreciation of any particular art form is to some degree a result of learning and habituation. Thus, to a European, most African art is repulsive at first contact. It is only after he has become accustomed to the medium that he can appreciate its qualities and derive esthetic satisfaction from it. The real problem is whether behind such diverse objects as a Poro mask, the Venus de Milo, and a Peruvian jar there are common factors of form, dynamic interrelation of parts, harmony of color, and so forth, which may appear in different combinations but are responsible for the esthetic effect. It seems that we have here an area in which modern psychological techniques could be brought to bear on a problem which philosophers have discussed for centuries without coming to agreement.

This discussion of values has been of necessity brief and incomplete. Nevertheless, the writer hopes that the existence of universal values has been demonstrated and it has been made clear that these are to be found at the conceptual rather than at the instrumental level. When one turns from the discussion of such values in the abstract to a consideration of their possible utility as a basis for mutual understanding between societies, a number of new problems present themselves. It has already been noted that the conceptual values which have widest influence within a culture are frequently unverbalized. The emotional reactions to them are thus vague and diffuse. The values whose contravention brings the sharpest and most immediate response are those at the instrumental level. Thus two societies which share the same basic conceptual value may fail to realize the fact because of their different ways of implementing it. The best answer to situations of this sort would seem to be to bring the conceptual values into consciousness, a difficult task.

An even more serious difficulty arises from the varying degrees of importance which different societies attach to the same conceptual values. All societies arrange the values to which they subscribe in a hierarchy which determines the reactions of individuals and of the society as a whole in situations involving choice. Concepts like business honesty, truth, or chastity may stand high in the value hierarchy of one society and low in that of another. Such differences not only make for misunderstanding but also for mutual recriminations on moral grounds and for feelings of contempt and hostility. . . .

The values on which there is most complete agreement are those which have to do with the satisfaction of the primary needs of individuals. Whatever their other values may be, all men desire the three wishes of the Irish fairy tale, health, wealth, and happiness. To the people of the world's backward areas the first two are represented by an opportunity to acquire and put into effect the technological and scientific knowledge already available in America and Western Europe. That these do not necessarily produce happiness we have abundant evidence, but this is something which the backward people will have to find out for themselves.

QUESTIONS

1. What fact does Linton think must be recognized as a basis for successful international cooperation? Why?
2. What does he mean by "value"?
3. Linton says that values are an integral part of culture and that they follow the same rules as other cultural elements in respect of "origin, transmission, and integration." What are some of these rules?
4. What psychological mechanisms does he think are involved in the development of systems of values?
5. What is the difference between "conceptual" and "instrumental" values?
6. Why does he say the concept of cultural relativity is most applicable to the instrumental values? Where does he think universal values are to be found?
7. Make a list of the values which Linton regards as substantially universal. Then explain why they should be so, in view of human needs and the necessities of social living. How far do such considerations outline a framework for a social order for all societies?

Solomon E. Asch (1907-)

A CRITIQUE OF THE PSYCHOLOGY OF CULTURAL RELATIVISM

Cultural relativists usually take for granted a high degree of plasticity in the human mind. Human behavior is in large part, they think, a product of conditioning. Human valuations are no exception to this rule: they are conditioned responses to environmental stimuli, the results of training, of rewards and punishments. If only we train a child carefully, so they hold, we can bring him up to value anything we please; we can train him so that, for example, he will give his highest approval to cruelty and treachery.

In the following reading, S. E. Asch, a leading social psychologist, subjects this view to severe criticism. The conceptual apparatus of stimulus-response psychology, he urges, is wholly incompetent to explain the phenomena of moral experience. We have to assume, for this purpose, an unlearned concern about others. The typical relativist psychology of values, he thinks, simply takes for granted dubious and controversial psychological principles. Moreover, whereas psychologists have usually supposed that the variation of moral standards in different cultures supports the stimulus-response conception of moral valuations,

Asch points out that if we examine human valuations in their context — valuations as elicited by the total meaning of the situation at which they are directed —, we find it highly doubtful that there is variation at all. The appearance of relativism at a superficial level does not imply real variation at a deeper level, where context is taken into account.

Asch's argument, then, is a challenge to cultural relativism. Indirectly, since ethical relativists normally base their view on cultural relativism, it is also a challenge to ethical relativism.

Asch received his undergraduate education at the City College of New York, and has a Ph.D. degree from Columbia University. He has taught at Brooklyn College and at the New School in New York City; he has been visiting professor at Harvard University, and is now professor at Swarthmore College. He has been a member of the Institute for Advanced Study at Princeton and has been president of the Division of Personality and Social Psychology, American Psychological Association. He is associate editor of the *Psychological Review*. He has been a prolific contributor to technical psychological literature.

From Solomon E. Asch, *Social Psychology*. © 1952. Prentice-Hall, Inc., Englewood Cliffs, N. J. Reprinted by permission of the publisher.

SOCIAL PSYCHOLOGY

RULES AND VALUES

. . . Many of our daily actions, particularly those that pertain to human matters, possess for us the striking property of being just or unjust. We make such judgments and at times they affect what we do. Men differ in their judgments of right and wrong, but they invariably make such judgments. The sense that certain things should be done, that others should not be done, is universally known. It is part of the human minimum, as much so as our capacity to see and hear. It adds a quality of peculiar significance to our actions and experiences. It is not likely that we can go far in human psychology without taking this fact into account. We need therefore to ask: What are the properties of these inner commands that colour our world so deeply and of which few social experiences are wholly devoid? What are their sources? How do they form and change? What is their relation to other psychological forces? How closely do individuals and societies agree on judgments of right and wrong? How can we understand the agreements and the differences?

Although the facts of ethical judgment are problems for psychology, we hardly possess today a description of them, not to mention a theoretical explanation. Most current psychological theories have denied the authenticity of the facts of value, by attempting to reduce them to presumably simpler facts of motivation and learning, or to terms that lack the specific qualities of value-judgments. It is therefore well to look at the phenomena, and to ask how we experience obligation, or the sense that an action is right or wrong.

We may start with the simplest examples. A passerby sees a child crying and stops to find out what is the trouble. One sees an elderly person bending under a burden and helps him at a difficult crossing. Or one tells a stranger how to reach his destination. Though these examples are very simple, they illustrate that the situation of another person can become a matter of concern and exert a directed force. Even more pertinent are those instances where the felt necessity to act in a way we describe as right meets with opposition from other tendencies within ourselves. A physician, soon after he has accepted an appointment to a hospital, receives an offer that is far more attractive. One way of acting is then felt to be tempting, and the other binding. To act in accordance with this claim is attended by the sense of rightness; failure to observe it is felt as a violation, as wrong and improper. These peremptory experiences, which function as directed forces, contain the important ingredient of "should"; they are at the basis of the phenomena of duty and responsibility.

Do these experiences differ from other directed forces? To act in a given way because of the judgment that one should, or that it is right to do so, is to assert that it has become a motivational force. This is the reason that modern psychologies have assimilated the facts of which we speak to the general concepts of motivation, identifying the experience of "should" either with what we desire or are compelled to do. An examination of the facts throws doubt on this equivalence. First, we distinguish between personal preferences or aversions and right or wrong. It is one thing to desire an object and quite another to have the experience of should. One may enjoy detective stories, dancing, or chess, but no trace of obligation need attach to these desirable activities. On the other hand, it is by no means unusual to desire what one knows to be wrong, or to fail to desire what one knows to be right. In fact, the experiences of which we speak quite often take the form of an opposition between what we desire and what we judge we are called upon to do. Nor does it seem possible to reduce the experience of obligation to anticipation of punishment. There are acts that we feel we should do, although failure to comply does not involve painful consequences. There are times when we feel we have acted wrongly, although there is no prospect of punishment. The reverse is also the case; we may expect punishment from society without the slightest conviction of wrong.

These observations contradict the causal explanations of current behavioristic and psychoanalytic accounts which trace the genesis of obligation to dread of punishment. According to these accounts the human individual encounters rules and prohibitions that are wholly external to him and which are simply barriers to gratification. Right and wrong, it is asserted, have initially only one meaning: they are what adults reward and punish. Eventually these learned reactions are said to take deeper root; the child acts with the punishments of adults in mind even when they are not around. This is considered a crucial step in development, marking the formation of an "internalized inhibitory process" that anticipates future punishment. Indeed, many equate this result with becoming socialized, describing conscience as "anticipatory anxiety." The sign that this stage has been reached is the presence of guilt at the violation of a command, which is said to indicate the internalization of what was initially an external social pressure. All activities that possess the character of "should" are, according to this view, inhibitory operations, the derivatives of fear. There would be no sense of obligation without fear and no sense of guilt without the threat of punishment.

This reduction of ethical judgments to other, presumably more elementary functions lacking in normative character, cannot, it seems to me, be performed. The genetic accounts have, in the first place, not examined the facts they proposed to explain; we have seen that phenomenally right and wrong are not wholly identical with the generic experience of desire or aversion, or with anticipation of reward or punishment. From the functional standpoint too the reduction fails. It is understandable that rewards and punishments produce desire and fear, but there is no way of seeing how they can produce the experience of "should." Habit can produce strong connections; it can give rise to a feeling of familiarity and even to a sense of necessity; but there is no known way for an habitual connection to produce the specific experience of obligation. Authority can produce fear or anger; yet, however peremptory, it is as powerless to introduce into the human mind the distinction between a just and an unjust act as it is to establish a discrimination between red and green. Value experiences are connected in important ways with habit, but sheer uniformity often does not have the power to make acts appear right. They are connected with goals and motives, but they cannot be simply equated with what is desired. They have important relations to punishment and the anticipation of it, but they do not coincide with punishment. They are vitally connected with the pressure of social conditions, but the fact of social compulsion cannot transmute psychological functions into the experience of right and wrong. When we admire an act of courage or when we are shaken by deceit and treachery, when we are determined to tell the truth even if it is painful or when we dismiss a plan we consider unworthy, we are granting recognition to certain properties of action that are not described in the current categories of habit and desire. The reductionist interpretations fail us at the start; they cannot tell us by what alchemy the phenomena of which they speak give rise to the generic fact of value.

It is particularly necessary to stress that social compulsions or influences cannot produce the phenomena of value. Social forces are indeed a condition for the most significant ethical judgments, but society cannot import these categories into the individual. These are properties of individuals whose capacity to grasp the structure of social relations permits them to sense requirements. Children respond vividly with a sense of injustice when they are punished for an innocent act and are quick to notice that the parent does not observe the injunction he applies to them. They may repudiate the authority of the parent and pass a judgment upon the authority that is said to be the source of their values. At a given period of development the child is a being that feels the stresses, and handles the concepts, of right and wrong. He does so when he can comprehend the relation between a motive and an act and between an act and its consequence. Then he evaluates the worth of action and demands that others, including adults, observe the requirements he senses to be valid.

What are the sources of the vectors that we designate with the terms right and wrong? For a first step in explanation one need refer to what was said earlier concerning our objective orientation. The understanding of the situation of another, of his problems and tensions, has the power to produce in us a motive and emotion that refers directly to him. It can arouse in us tensions and goals that can be removed only by acting in a way relevant to the other's needs. Men can include within their view the structure of a situation and feel its tensions; when they do they are moved by the needs they sense in others. To become concerned for others, and to occupy ourselves with their fate, is a fundamental capacity of human beings. Gestalt theory has in this connection introduced the concept of "requiredness." The examples mentioned at the outset of this discussion all contain a gap or disjunction; a person was in need of help, or action was called for in a given case. The situation was in some sense incomplete; our apprehension of the facts and their relations, or of the need of the situation, laid a claim upon us to improve or to remedy it, to act in a manner fitting to it. Action that fits the requirements we judge to be appropriate or right; to fail to act appropriately we experience as violating a demand, or being unjust. This capacity reaches clearest expression in relations to persons; our grasp of their needs and requirements gives rise to the full-fledged experience of claims and responsibilities. This conclusion is in accord with the high phenomenal objectivity of our ethical judgments. We feel that we value as we do for reasons connected with the situation, not merely because we are personally inclined to do so. As one writer aptly put it: "We all feel that we value a thing because it has value and not that it has value because we value it." For this reason we regard the claims of certain situations to be binding on others as well as on ourselves. . . .

THE PSYCHOLOGICAL BASIS OF CULTURAL RELATIVISM

Cultural relativism finds a strict psychological foundation in the propositions of stimulus-response psychology about needs and learning. In particular they offer an apparently cogent explanation of the formation of different reactions to identical conditions. Stimulus-response theory asserts that one can at will attach to a given situation S_1 any of a number of acts, feelings, and evaluations, depending on the consequences that follow. To situation S_1 any of responses R_x, R_y, R_z are possible. Which of the responses will become connected to the situation S_1 depends on which response will be followed by reward. It follows that we can, by the manipulation of rewards and punishments, attach to the *same* situation either of two *opposed* responses. There are situations that approximate outwardly to this interpretation. A signal in a conditioning experiment can be connected with food or with shock; a word can designate one object or another wholly unlike it. In an earlier discussion, we questioned this interpretation and its general applicability. . . . Then we noted that the stimulus-response account presupposes a thoroughgoing relation of arbitrariness between situation and action and between action and consequence. Let us now see how this interpretation is applied to practices and convictions.

The extension is accomplished simply by the assertion that beliefs, customs, and values are also "responses," learned in precisely the same way as one learns the connection between a person and his name or between a person and his telephone number. We learn to believe that which rewards and to disbelieve that which incurs pain. Therefore the manipulation of rewards and punishments can determine us to judge the same action as good or bad, true or false. For an organism governed by rewards and punishments these are the only possible and necessary "proofs." The laws of learning grind out truth and falsehood indifferently; rewards and punishments are the sole content and criterion of right and wrong. It follows that our ideas of right and wrong, beautiful or ugly are decided by social sanctions and that identical actions can be made desirable or despicable. It is on this basis that we are said to learn that gangsters are bad and that democracy is desirable. These are standards that we have "accepted"; nothing in the nature of democracy and crime points to their value. Life in society is therefore likened to the running of a maze in which the paths are arbitrarily fixed and which one learns to run in the search for satisfaction and avoidance of pain. "Culture, as conceived by social scientists, is a statement of the design of the human maze, of the type of reward involved, and of what responses are to be rewarded. It is in this sense a recipe for learning." . . . When today we encounter the statement that culture is "learned" it often refers not only to the necessity of past experience but also to the arbitrary effect of experience described here.

Deeply embedded in this view is the assumption that aside from a few biological needs there are no factor forces or tendencies in men. All else is "plasticity," the capacity to be shaped in almost indefinitely different ways by rewards and punishments. The temper of this position was clearly expressed in the following well-known statement by J. B. Watson:

Give me a dozen healthy infants, well-formed, and my own specific world to bring them up in and I'll guarantee to take any one at random and train him to become any type of specialist I might select — doctor, lawyer, artist, merchant-chief, and yes, even beggar-man and thief, regardless of his talents, penchants, tendencies, abilities, vocations, and race of his ancestors. (*Behaviorism*. N. Y.: W. W. Norton, 1930.)

The core of the same thought has been expressed more recently in the following statement:

Man's biological nature is neither good nor bad, aggressive nor submissive, warlike nor peaceful, but neutral in these respects. He is capable of developing in either direction depending on what he is compelled to learn by his environment and by his culture. It is a mistake to assume that he can learn war more easily than peace. His learning machinery is not prejudiced, as is sometimes thought, toward the acquirement of bad habits. The bias is in his social environment. (M. A. May: A *Social Psychology of War and Peace*. New Haven: Yale University Press, 1944.)

This position presupposes a dynamically empty organism, lacking autonomous tendencies beyond primary needs and lacking directed forces toward nature or society, which can therefore be turned with equal ease in opposed directions. To be sure, men can learn. But the fact of learning has the peculiar property of not altering them in any way that is significant for a conception of their character, since the habits they form contain nothing of comprehension or insight. Stimulus-response theory excludes the direct perception of social necessities or the guidance of sociological events by conscious direction. The following may serve as an illustration. We find that people react in one way when they find that someone has been untruthful and in a quite different way when he has been truthful. How is this to be understood? The stimulus-response answer is that such actions have in the past been connected with different consequences. What is of interest about the answer is not that it emphasizes the results of action, but its disregard of the idea that truthfulness and untruthfulness are comprehended in terms of their structure — in terms of what they signify for the relation between one person and another — and that they are evaluated on that basis. Instead of concluding that the requirement of truthfulness grows out of a grasp of the causal relation between act and consequence, it treats of truthfulness as a habit that has survived in the course of a trial and error process. This view is responsible for the conclusion that human nature is like water, which takes on whatever shape is imparted to it.

It is not difficult to see how this starting point decides the general interpretation of social action. If convictions and decisions are exclusively the outcome of arbitrary forces upon people who believe what they are made to believe, then one must not deceive oneself into holding that they are other than an expression of bias. In the sense of cultural relativism your values are not yours; they are those of the *Times*, or the *Tribune*, or whatever source of special pleading has succeeded in gaining access to you. You are a mouthpiece with society pulling the strings. At the center of these formulations is a definite assumption about the kind of dependence that prevails between individuals and groups. A plastic individual meets an established social order; the relation is that of hammer and anvil. Such views recommend themselves to many because of their objectivistic character; they appear to assume so much less than other psychologies. It remains to be seen whether they do not contain large assumptions.

Earlier we noted some difficulties in this mode of thinking; here we may simply repeat them. (1) It fails to describe the concrete cognitive and emotional operations one encounters in the social setting. In the present context it simply ignores the fact that people make ethical discriminations and that they sense requirements, and assumes that they are initially blank as far as these distinctions are concerned. . . . It is in these terms that we have to understand the insistence that norms and values are first "external" to the individual and are then "internalized." In the context of the theory, "external" means action alien to the individual's character, tendencies, and capacities; "internal" refers to the blind adoption of these ways. The process of "socialization" is, according to this view, the uncritical adoption of beliefs and values. (2) The stimulus-response account of human needs and rewards is more restricted than observation leads us to conclude. Even if one could assume that the constructs "drive," "reward," "response," were adequate to the actions of infra-human organisms (from the observation of which they are largely derived), it would remain highly questionable whether they apply without modification to social action. In their first intention these terms refer to very particular phenomena, such as deprivation of food, turning a corner, avoiding a shock. It would seem necessary to show that they are relevant to social phenomena. But this is assumed, not proven. Therefore the assertions that society may be likened to a maze and that culture is learned are little more than reiterations of a belief that the rat's learning of a maze (or a particular interpretation of it) is all we need for the understanding of customs and institutions.

RELATIONAL DETERMINATION VERSUS RELATIVISM

The insufficiencies of an absolutist psychological theory * of ethical judgments are obvious. It has no means for dealing with cultural diversity (or, for that matter, with intra-individual diversity). On the other hand, although the observations to which relativism refers have greatly widened the horizon of the social sciences, the psychological interpretation

---

* EDITOR'S NOTE: Asch means by the "absolutist psychological theory" the view that human nature is such that everyone will approve or disapprove of the same things, irrespective of context, — such as deliberate misinforming of others (lying), fornication, sexual relations between members of the basic family group, unprovoked assault on other human beings, and appropriation of objects recognized as being the property of others.

they have received poses equally serious difficulties. It is often assumed that these positions are the sole alternatives. Is there not, however, a way to understand the diversities of human practices and convictions without at the same time denying the authentic role of ethical discrimination? We will attempt to show that there is an alternative that fits the facts more closely.

It is now necessary to consider a point about value-judgments that was only adumbrated in the preceding chapter. When we evaluate an act as right or wrong we do so with reference to its place and setting. We evaluate acts always as parts of given conditions. We consider it wrong to take food away from a hungry child, but not if he is overeating. We consider it right to fulfill a promise, but not if it is a promise to commit a crime. Each of these examples is evidence that requiredness is not a property that belongs to an action irrespective of its setting and relations. Every judgment of the value of an act takes into account the particular circumstances under which it occurs. There follows the important consequence that the *same* act may be evaluated as right because it is fitting under one set of conditions, and as wrong because it violates the requirements of another set of conditions. (Whether there are some acts that we evaluate as right or wrong under all circumstances is a difficult question that we may leave open in an elementary discussion.)

It has been customary to hold that diverse evaluations of the same act are automatic evidence for the presence of different principles of evaluation. The preceding examples point to an error in this interpretation and to the need for a distinction between relational determination and relativism. Indeed, an examination of the relational factors that determine the demands we sense may point to the operation of constant principles in situations that differ in concrete details. We shall explore now the bearing of the fact of relational determination upon the culturally determined diversities of evaluation.

The essential proposition of ethical relativism states that one can connect to the identical situation different and even opposed evaluations. Comparative observations of cultures seem to support this view abundantly. Infanticide, as we have seen, receives different evaluations, as do numerous other practices. It seems to follow that the content of our most basic convictions is variable and that there is hardly a principle that, cherished under one social climate, is not violated in another. These observations apparently contradict the conclusion that we sense the demands of conditions. Relativism asserts this contradiction, claiming that evaluations are subjective habits and preferences.

Some years ago Duncker and Wertheimer examined this problem and called attention to a fundamental oversight in the relativistic position. Duncker showed that the conclusion of relativism rests exclusively on the diverse connections observed between outer conditions and practices. But psychological analysis requires that we take cognizance of certain intermediate steps. We act toward a given situation in terms of its meaning — what we understand of it and what experience has taught us about it. On this basis we make evaluations and sense requirements that guide action. The terms of which we must take cognizance in the analysis of actions that have value-character are: (a) the externally given conditions; (b) the meaning they have for the actor; (c) the evaluations and requirements that available knowledge and understanding produce; and (d) the resulting actions. Now the thesis of relativism points to a lack of constancy in the relation between (a) and (d). It fails however to deal with the intervening terms. In particular, it does not consider the relation of evaluation (c) to the given cognitive conditions (b). But relativism, if it is to be psychologically valid, must assert that one can attach different evaluations to situations that have the same cognitive and emotional content. If, for example, we are to speak of relativism with reference to infanticide we must assume that the *same* action which is tolerated under one set of conditions is outlawed under other conditions. This assumption is as a rule dubious. The character of the object "infant" may not be the same under all conditions. In the first few days of life, an infant may be regarded as not yet human, in the way that many regard the embryo. (It should be noted that infanticide, when practiced, occurs only during the first few days following birth.) Therefore, the act of killing will not have the same meaning under all conditions. Precisely the same issue arises in connection with the killing of parents. In the society that follows this practice there prevails the belief that people continue to lead in the next world the same existence as in the present and that they maintain forever the condition of health and vigor they had at the time of death. It is therefore a filial duty of the son to dispatch his parents, an act that has the full endorsement of the parent and of the community.

Duncker suggests that different and apparently opposed practices and values are frequently not the consequence of diversity in ethical principles but of differences in the comprehension of a situation — differences in "situational meaning." The same external situation may possess quite varied meanings, depending upon the existing level of knowledge and upon other conditions. The resulting differences of action may therefore not be due to a diversity of principle. The meaning of a situation is usually a dependent part of a wider context. In a society in which supernatural beings are part of the cognitive scene, it will be plausible and convincing to impute illness to a purposeful, human-like agency. Consequently, the exorcising of illness by prayer and incantation will, under the given conditions, have a marked relevance. It will not signify that the persons in question are employing novel principles of causation or that they possess different modes of perceiving causation. Similarly, the concept of "stranger" may vary greatly; it may decide whether we shall slay him or treat him essentially like ourselves. The relativistic argument, by failing to take into account the psychological content of the situation, equates things that are psychologically different and only externally the same. It seeks for a mechanical regularity between external situation and action instead of a structural identity between the psychological content of a situation and the act. If we consider the psychological content, we have to conclude that the same action may represent psychologically different contents and that different actions may be functionally identical. To establish whether human beings actually possess contradictory values, it would be necessary to show that the relations between situational meanings and evaluation, or between the terms (b) and (c) above, can vary. This relativism has decidedly failed to do.

Implicit in the preceding discussion is the conclusion that the fact of cultural differences cannot be automatically converted into an argument for a relativism of values. . . . Cultural differences are compatible with identity in values. Indeed, the assumption of variance dictates the conclusion that practices will differ with circumstances. If action and experience are a function of given conditions, we must expect that the former will vary with the latter. To expect uniform practices among societies is as reasonable as to expect all those with poor eyesight to wear identical lenses or for a person to face all situations with the same emotion. This point is well understood when the facts of material culture are under discussion. We consider it reasonable that the Bantu do not build igloos and that Eskimos do not live in thatched huts. Instead of stating conclusions about the relativism of building practices we quite properly take into account the climate, the materials available, and the level of knowledge. The same mode of thinking is indicated when we speak of values, if we do not assume in advance that they are arbitrary. When an Eskimo family permits an old person to expose himself to death this must be viewed in relation to their situation, their problems, and the alternatives open to them. The act does not have the same meaning for them that it would have for us today; Eskimos do not have homes for the aged or retirement pensions. If we take the given circumstances into account the possibility is present for understanding diverse actions in terms of the same operations of valuing.

What can we say about the relation between "situational meaning" and evaluation? In general, anthropological evidence does not furnish proof of relativism in the relation between the meaning of situations and their evaluation. We do not know of societies in which bravery is despised and cowardice held up to honor, in which generosity is considered a vice and ingratitude a virtue. It seems rather, as Duncker proposed, that the relations between valuation and meaning are invariant. It is not usual to find groups placing a different valuation upon, or experiencing different obligations toward, a situation that they understand in an identical way. It seems rather that certain ethical discriminations are universally known. We still have to hear of a society to which modesty, courage, and hospitality are not known.

Throughout the preceding discussion we have assumed one far-reaching form of "relativism" to be present: that pertaining to knowledge and understanding. Historical conditions determine the extent and level of knowledge and therefore the content and evaluation of given conditions. We may illustrate the general fact with a simple instance. A need, such as hunger, does not innately refer to its adequate object. It is only when the hungry infant is fed that he can form a craving for milk or sweets and search for them subsequently. Obviously the object must be experienced (or heard about) if it is to become relevant to one's needs. One cannot crave an object one has not experienced. It will necessarily happen that in different societies there will be quite different food preferences. Here we have a concrete, if simple, instance of what many call relativism, although it is more properly an example of relational determination. What can it teach us? First, the variation is not unlimited; however different in quality and in adequacy, an article of food will generally become an object of craving because it has food-value. When two groups come in contact, each will continue to prefer its diet; here we have a difference that is to a degree arbitrary. But again we find that the differences are not as unlimited as a sketchy analysis suggests. To the extent that different diets are equally nutritious, a preference for the one that is familiar is a fact upon which one cannot place undue importance. It is more significant to ask about the changes in diet that follow increased knowledge. The answer is fairly obvious.

In the sense described there is a considerable relativism as a result of differences in level of knowledge. One cannot be intelligent about things one does not know; one cannot long for the sea or for mountains if one is not aware of their existence. One can have no desire for fame if one has no historical perspective; one cannot be fired with zeal to contribute to knowledge if science is unknown. Do not these facts commit us to a new relativism with the same practical consequences as the old? It seems to me that they do not. They demonstrate what no one questions — that knowledge and action change in accordance with material and social conditions.

A serious appraisal of the role of cognitive factors permits us to clarify an important problem about values. It may have seemed that to emphasize the probability of invariance between evaluation and action and the presence of certain universal ethical discriminations leaves no place for the growth or change of values. But it should be evident that changes of knowledge and understanding make necessary the evolution of values. When knowledge spreads that men have basic qualities in common, it becomes more difficult to oppress them. When we find that differences between races are chiefly socially determined, it becomes less easy to practice segregation and colonialism. When we learn that criminals have emotions and strong social tendencies we can no longer sustain a purely punitive attitude toward them. With an increased appreciation of the role of reflection and knowledge some come to feel the obligation to be intelligent. Increasing knowledge of human characteristics teaches us the value of the human person. As we learn more of the conditions that affect the development of persons we feel the obligation to improve the material conditions of mankind. In this way alone can we understand the more humane treatment of mental patients, the feeble-minded, and other disadvantaged groups. In this sense there can be a development in the notions of justice and the emergence of novel moral insight. There is reason to say that ideas have an immense effect on evaluation and action. . . .

What are the consequences of these ideas for understanding cultural differences in evaluation? Perhaps the main effect is to make the practices of peoples more comprehensible by divesting them, not of interest, but of bizarreness and grotesqueness. Once we abandon certain assumptions about the externality of man's relation to the surroundings, a wholly different view of cultural differences unfolds before us. These need no longer appear as responses to manipulation by social conditions or as the final signs of limitation and subjectivity. We can now see them also as the necessary consequence of permanent human tendencies coming to expression under particular conditions. It also becomes clear that the first step in understanding action or conviction is to establish the way in which it appears to the actor and the reason it appears to him to be right. This is the way to proceed if we take seriously human capacities for comprehension and for formulating explanations within the limitations of knowledge and experience. We need to establish the core of relevance that action or belief has for its practitioners; to do so we need to see action in its context.

Considered from the standpoint of method, relativism deals with social data in a piecemeal way. The impressiveness of its conclusions rests almost entirely on the divorce of data from their context. It lists the diversity of practices in response to the same external conditions, tearing them out of their context. In consequence it obscures their concrete content and dynamics. It should also be mentioned here that an adequate examination must include a reference to the repercussions that standards and values have upon those who are under their sway. The reactions to regulations, the problems they solve, and the conflicts they generate are as pertinent as is their existence and observance. Those views that stress the almost unlimited malleability of human character tend to overlook the inevitable concomitants of conditions, which it would be hard to understand relativistically. Unless we look at interrelations we remove the possibility of understanding either cultural differences or similarities.

QUESTIONS

1. Show by examples what, in Asch's opinion, is the central moral phenomenon the psychologist must explain. Does it differ in some way from personal desire?
2. Why does Asch deny that the experience of obligation is an "anticipatory anxiety" about punishment? Why does he think conditioning cannot produce

the "specific experience of obligation"? Do you think he has proved this point?

3. Suppose a child thinks it unjust that his parents should refuse him permission to go swimming when all other children have permission and there is no danger. Is his unfavorable judgment of the action of his parents to be explained by reference to the learning of their rules and by reward or punishment for misbehavior in the past?

4. Asch evidently believes that moral disapproval is somehow an unlearned response to situations. Describe his positive view. Do you think it differs markedly from the psychology of Hume (pp. 391 ff.)?

5. From Asch's account of it, formulate the main ideas of the psychological theory of values he aims to combat. What are his major criticisms of the theory?

6. Why does he think that the fact that we evaluate behavior only in a specific context constitutes an objection to "psychological absolutism" and to cultural relativism alike?

7. What is the thesis of "relational determination"? Why does he say that "the fact of cultural differences cannot be automatically converted into an argument for a relativism of values"? Why does he think it a criticism of cultural relativists that they consider anthropological facts "torn from their context"?

8. How far do the facts cited by Linton support Asch's theory? Do you think of any facts which suggest that Asch goes somewhat too far?

9. Does Asch's thesis imply that the basic moral principles of all peoples are the same?

CHAPTER 4 SUGGESTIONS FOR FURTHER READING

Aberle, D. F., and others. "The Functional Prerequisites of a Society." *Ethics*, Vol. 60 (1950), pp. 100-11. Rules necessary for a society.

Brandt, Richard B. *Ethical Theory*. Englewood Cliffs, N. J.: Prentice-Hall, 1959. Statement and defense of a mild relativist view.

Ginsberg, Morris. *Essays in Sociology and Social Philosophy*. Vol. 1, *On the Diversity of Morals*. New York: Macmillan, 1957. A philosophically trained sociologist's reflections.

Kluckhohn, Clyde. "Ethical Relativity." *Journal of Philosophy*, Vol. 52 (1955), pp. 663-77. An anthropologist's view.

Westermarck, Edvard Alexander. *The Origin and Development of the Moral Ideas*. New York: Macmillan, 1906, Vol. 1, Chs. 1-5. Historically important statement of a relativist position.

In a sense the question whether all human beings (and perhaps animals) have certain rights, and the question what such rights might be, is not a new topic. At least it isn't new if to say that someone has a right is to say that somebody or other (a different person or persons) ought to do something. For in Chapter 2 the major proposals about what people ought to do were canvassed; and if to talk about human rights is merely to raise this same question in different words, then we have already seen, by implication, what important things have been said about it.

Nevertheless, debates about human rights have played an important part in the thought of the past three hundred years. Therefore, even if, in a sense, questions about rights are not new questions, we should consider what such questions mean and what are the major possible answers to them which have been, or can be, put forward.

It can be questioned whether the term "rights," as it has occurred in historical "bills of rights," is an *ethical* or *moral* word at all, in the sense explained in Chapter 1. Some philosophers, notably T. H. Green, an important British writer of the last century, have at least come close to saying that it is not — they say that what it is to have a certain right is for some freedom, power, or privilege to be legally secured to one by the state (or at least for it to be recognized by society as a necessary condition for realizing the common good). In fact, the word "right" has actually been used by some people, at least in some places, in such a way that it would be queer to construe it as an ethical term. Thomas Hobbes, for instance, sometimes uses "right" in such a way that to say a sovereign has a right is, as it seems, to say no more and no less than that he has sufficient *power* to do a certain thing and that no other power or threat could reasonably deter him from exercising it if he wished.

The proposal that "right" (used as a noun) is not a moral term at all is a correct one if it refers only to *some* of our contemporary uses of the word. It is quite clear that sometimes we speak of a person's "rights," meaning to refer only to things he is *legally* entitled to. For example, we might ask our lawyer whether a person who has sold us a piece of real estate is within his rights if he insists on removing bulbs and bushes from the gardens after the sale has been consummated. When we ask this question, we are not at all raising an ethical issue; we are merely inquiring whether we are legally in a position to prevent him if we wish to do so. Again, suppose we say, "In Great Britain the right of free speech is a very broad one." We are commenting on what laws and courts do permit, not on what they should permit.

Nevertheless, the term "right" (used as a noun) is by no means always — and perhaps not even usually — employed for reference to legal powers. Certainly it is not so employed in "bills of rights." It is more plausible to say that bills of rights, like the United Nations Declaration below, are assertions that some things *ought* to be legal rights; but even this interpretation is too narrow. Note that it would not be a misuse of the word "right" for a student organization to draw up a "bill of rights for students" without any implication that the freedoms or privileges mentioned should be protected by the law of the land.

The third article of the United Nations Declaration, in saying that "Everyone has the right to life, liberty and security of person" seems clearly to be saying that something *ought* to be done in the moral sense, that someone or some group is acting wrongly if some things are not done. The assertion of the right seems to be an ethical statement. And most writers today seem to be in agreement on this matter.

If rights-claims are usually ethical statements, however, just what kind of ethical statement are they? How does "rights" tie in with other ethical words? Can we say the same as any rights-statement, but simply in different words, by some locution which makes use of "moral obligation" or "morally ought"? If so, what would this locution be? These questions are not easy ones, and philosophers who write on this subject are often very cautious in their statements. A. C. Ewing, in the passage reprinted below, however, ventures to say this: "The definition of 'rights of the individual' which I should suggest is 'powers or securities of a kind such that the individual can rightly demand of others that they should normally not interfere with them.'" This proposal will certainly do for a start. The reader will do well to brood over the text of the United Nations Declaration and frame a definition of his own that seems to suit the uses. Unfortunately, however, it seems that the word is not always used in quite the same sense in this document; hence probably the reader can at best hope to make his definition fit what seems the most important or central kind of use. It will be helpful, however, to notice two points about Ewing's proposal. First, Ewing's definition does not quite seem to fit, say, Article 23 of the United Nations Declaration. To say that "Everyone has the right to work . . . to just and favourable conditions of work and to protection against unemployment" is not just to say that he can demand that others "not interfere." Some more positive action is required. Ewing's definition may well cover all the rights-assertions that were made in the last century or before; but it seems not to cover what is apparently meant by some rights-claims made today. Second, Ewing's proposal is somewhat odd if it is intended to explain the use of "right" in a statement like "Animals have a right not to be treated cruelly." Perhaps you will think that animals have no rights and hence that we need not worry about this statement. But if you think they do have rights, it will seem odd to you to hear it said that what this statement means is that they "can rightly demand of others . . ." when in fact animals are not in a position to make demands at all. Presumably the reader will frame his definition so as not to fall into these traps.

Let us assume that the reader will concede that the meaning of "human rights" is such that rights-statements can be correctly paraphrased by a statement in which some word like "wrong" or "morally ought" or "is morally obligated to" plays an essential rôle (and in which "rights" has disappeared). Rights-statements, then, are tantamount to some kind of obligation-statement. If so, then two things follow. First, the metaethical theories which are plausible for obligation-statements — naturalism, supernaturalism, nonnaturalism, and noncognitivism — must all be plausible for rights-statements. Presumably the choice of theory we make for the former must be the same choice properly made for the latter. And second, the major normative theories which were represented in Chapter 2 for "right" or "obligation" are major possible alternative theories about rights; and presumably, again, the choice properly made among them for the case of "obligation" is the choice properly made for the case of rights. In a sense, then, all the reader need do for the case of rights, assuming that he is already convinced as to what is the right theory about obligations, is work out the logical implications of his prior commitments.

Actually, nothing like the amount of attention has been devoted to the meaning of "rights" in its noun use as has been devoted to "right" in its adjectival use. The reason for this difference is presumably that the word "right" as an adjective has more general application. But, if we look around carefully, we can find the major metaethical theories all represented in literature about rights. For instance, R. B. Perry (on p. 275) has proposed a naturalist definition of "rights." W. D. Ross and A. C. Ewing take a nonnaturalist view. If we look at defenses of the "divine right of kings" we shall find supernaturalist theories. And if we consult A. I. Melden's paper in the *American Philosophical Association, Eastern Division, Proceedings,* Vol. 1, 1952, we shall find a nice example of a noncognitivist explanation. Of the essays that appear below, it is difficult to say where Locke stands, since what little he has to say about metaethical questions is not contained in the book from which our passages are taken, and since in any event his relevant comments are obscure. J. S. Mill, too, while he uses the term "rights" freely throughout his essay, is not there concerned to explain it (he does so in the final chapter of *Utilitarianism,* the chapter on "justice," not reprinted in the present volume); if he were consistent with his statements about "obligation" and "right," we should rather be inclined to classify him as a noncognitivist.

Chapter 2 represented various normative theories about what is right or obligatory: egoism, formalism (Butler and Ross), act-utilitarianism, rule-utilitarianism, and a "natural law" theory (Aquinas). Theories of rights can be found corresponding to all of these. Among the authors represented below, J. S. Mill is best taken as a rule-utilitarian, John Locke as an intuitionist like Butler, and Ewing as something of a combination of a Ross-like intuitionist theory and a broad form of act-utilitarianism. Ralph Blake's "On Natural Rights" (*Ethics*, Vol. 36, pp. 86-96) is an unusually lucid and straightforward utilitarian proposal; and Jacques Maritain, in Chapter IV of *Man and the State* (Chicago: University of Chicago Press, 1951), offers a "natural law" theory of rights.

What rights, then, are there? Is the United Nations Declaration a document which stands up under careful examination, or must it be dismissed as a bit of unrealistic, if humanitarian, propaganda, an optimistic gesture of some sort? These questions are ones the reader of course must answer for himself, after examining what various writers have to say.

The United Nations Declaration

UNIVERSAL RIGHTS

Statements of ethical principles are seldom espoused or adopted by political organizations. It would be odd for hedonism or Kantianism to be proclaimed the "platform" of some social organization. In the case of rights, however, matters are different. Many such documents were produced in the eighteenth century; and we do not find it odd that the United Nations should have adopted one — or that such a document is embodied in the constitution of the Soviet Union.

The United Nations Declaration was carefully drawn by a group of thoughtful and enlightened people. Therefore we can use it for a comparison with earlier "bills of rights" or with the ideas of Locke and Mill in order to determine where modern thought has moved in relation to thought two or three centuries ago. And, if we find it necessary to criticize the United Nations document, we can feel that we are criticizing some of the best contemporary thinking. Moreover, presumably the document's employment of the word "rights" is representative of the usage of educated people today (at least of those who are not philosophers), and therefore the document provides us with a set of texts on which to try out what strike us as useful definitions of "rights," as well as evidence as to whether various distinctions made by philosophers are important and well taken.

The reader could hardly find a better exercise for his moral theory than that of determining which ones of the following principles are defensible.

UNIVERSAL DECLARATION OF HUMAN RIGHTS

Complete text adopted on December 10, 1948, by General Assembly of United Nations

PREAMBLE

Whereas recognition of the inherent dignity and of the equal and inalienable rights of all members of the human family is the foundation of freedom, justice and peace in the world,

Whereas disregard and contempt for human rights have resulted in barbarous acts which have outraged the conscience of mankind, and the advent of a world in which human beings shall enjoy freedom of speech and belief and freedom from fear and want has been proclaimed as the highest aspiration of the common people,

Whereas it is essential, if man is not to be compelled to have recourse, as a last resort, to rebellion against tyranny and oppression, that human rights should be protected by the rule of law,

Whereas it is essential to promote the development of friendly relations between nations,

Whereas the peoples of the United Nations have in the Charter reaffirmed their faith in fundamental human rights, in the dignity and worth of the human person and in the equal rights of men and women and have determined to promote social progress and better standards of life in larger freedom,

Whereas Member States have pledged themselves to achieve, in co-operation with the United Nations, the promotion of universal respect for and observance of human rights and fundamental freedoms,

Whereas a common understanding of these rights and freedoms is of the greatest importance for the full realization of this pledge,

Now, Therefore,

THE GENERAL ASSEMBLY PROCLAIMS

This universal declaration of human rights as a common standard of achievement for all peoples and all nations, to the end that every individual and every organ of society, keeping this Declaration constantly in mind, shall strive by teaching and education to promote respect for these rights and freedoms and by progressive measures, national and international, to secure their universal and effective recognition and observance, both among the peoples of Member States themselves and among the peoples of territories under their jurisdiction.

Article 1. All human beings are born free and equal in dignity and rights. They are endowed with reason and conscience and should act towards one another in a spirit of brotherhood.

Article 2. Everyone is entitled to all the rights and freedoms set forth in this Declaration, without distinction of any kind, such as race, colour, sex, language, religion, political or other opinion, national or social origin, property, birth or other status.

Furthermore, no distinction shall be made on the basis of the political, jurisdictional or international status of the country or territory to which a person belongs, whether it be independent, trust, non-self-governing or under any other limitation of sovereignty.

Article 3. Everyone has the right to life, liberty and security of person.

Article 4. No one shall be held in slavery or servitude; slavery and the slave trade shall be prohibited in all their forms.

Article 5. No one shall be subjected to torture or to cruel, inhuman or degrading treatment or punishment.

Article 6. Everyone has the right to recognition everywhere as a person before the law.

Article 7. All are equal before the law and are entitled without any discrimination to equal protection of the law. All are entitled to equal protection against any discrimination in violation of this Declaration and against any incitement to such discrimination.

Article 8. Everyone has the right to an effective remedy by the competent national tribunals for acts violating the fundamental rights granted him by the constitution or by law.

Article 9. No one shall be subjected to arbitrary arrest, detention or exile.

Article 10. Everyone is entitled in full equality to a fair and public hearing by an independent and impartial tribunal, in the determination of his rights and obligations and of any criminal charge against him.

Article 11. (1) Everyone charged with a penal offence has the right to be presumed innocent until proved guilty according to law in a public trial at which he has had all the guarantees necessary for his defence.

(2) No one shall be held guilty of any penal offence on account of any act or omission which did not constitute a penal offence, under national or international law, at the time when it was committed. Nor shall a heavier penalty be imposed than the one that was applicable at the time the penal offence was committed.

Article 12. No one shall be subjected to arbitrary interference with his privacy, family, home or correspondence, nor to attacks upon his honour and reputation. Everyone has the right to the protection of the law against such interference or attacks.

Article 13. (1) Everyone has the right to freedom of movement and residence within the borders of each state.

(2) Everyone has the right to leave any country, including his own, and to return to his country.

Article 14. (1) Everyone has the right to seek and to enjoy in other countries asylum from persecution.

(2) This right may not be invoked in the case of prosecutions genuinely arising from non-political crimes or from acts contrary to the purposes and principles of the United Nations.

Article 15. (1) Everyone has the right to a nationality.

(2) No one shall be arbitrarily deprived of his nationality nor denied the right to change his nationality.

Article 16. (1) Men and women of full age, without any limitation due to race, nationality or religion, have the right to marry and to found a family. They are entitled to equal rights as to marriage, during marriage and at its dissolution.

(2) Marriage shall be entered into only with the free and full consent of the intending spouses.

(3) The family is the natural and fundamental group unit of society and is entitled to protection by society and the State.

Article 17. (1) Everyone has the right to own property alone as well as in association with others.

(2) No one shall be arbitrarily deprived of his property.

Article 18. Everyone has the right to freedom of thought, conscience and religion; this right includes freedom to change his religion or belief, and freedom, either alone or in community with others and in public or private, to manifest his religion or belief in teaching, practice, worship and observance.

Article 19. Everyone has the right to freedom of opinion and expression; this right includes freedom to hold opinions without interference and to seek, receive and impart information and ideas through any media and regardless of frontiers.

Article 20. (1) Everyone has the right to freedom of peaceful assembly and association.

(2) No one may be compelled to belong to an association.

Article 21. (1) Everyone has the right to take part in the government of his country, directly or through freely chosen representatives.

(2) Everyone has the right of equal access to public service in his country.

(3) The will of the people shall be the basis of the authority of government; this will shall be expressed in periodic and genuine elections which shall be by universal and equal suffrage and shall be held by secret vote or by equivalent free voting procedures.

Article 22. Everyone, as a member of society, has the right to social security and is entitled to realization, through national effort and international co-operation and in accordance with the organization and resources of each State, of the economic, social and cultural rights indispensable for his dignity and the free development of his personality.

Article 23. (1) Everyone has the right to work, to free choice of employment, to just and favourable conditions of work and to protection against unemployment.

(2) Everyone, without any discrimination, has the right to equal pay for equal work.

(3) Everyone who works has the right to just and favourable remuneration ensuring for himself and his family an existence worthy of human dignity, and supplemented, if necessary, by other means of social protection.

(4) Everyone has the right to form and to join trade unions for the protection of his interests.

Article 24. Everyone has the right to rest and leisure, including reasonable limitation of working hours and periodic holidays with pay.

Article 25. (1) Everyone has the right to a standard of living adequate for the health and well-being of himself and of his family, including food, clothing, housing and medical care and necessary social services, and the right to security in the event of unemployment, sickness, disability, widowhood, old age or other lack of livelihood in circumstances beyond his control.

(2) Motherhood and childhood are entitled to special care and assistance. All children, whether born in or out of wedlock, shall enjoy the same social protection.

Article 26. (1) Everyone has the right to education. Education shall be free, at least in the elementary and fundamental stages. Elementary education shall be compulsory. Technical and professional education shall be made generally available and higher education shall be equally accessible to all on the basis of merit.

(2) Education shall be directed to the full development of the human personality and to the strengthening of respect for human rights and fundamental freedoms. It shall promote understanding, tolerance and friendship among all nations, racial or religious groups, and shall further the activities of the United Nations for the maintenance of peace.

(3) Parents have a prior right to choose the kind of education that shall be given to their children.

Article 27. (1) Everyone has the right freely to participate in the cultural life of the community, to enjoy the arts and to share in scientific advancement and its benefits.

(2) Everyone has the right to the protection of the moral and material interests resulting from any scientific, literary or artistic production of which he is the author.

Article 28. Everyone is entitled to a social and international order in which the rights and freedoms set forth in this Declaration can be fully realized.

Article 29. (1) Everyone has duties to the community in which alone the free and full development of his personality is possible.

(2) In the exercise of his rights and freedoms, everyone shall be subject only to such limitations as are determined by law solely for the purpose of securing due recognition and respect for the rights and freedoms of others and of meeting the just requirements of morality, public order and the general welfare in a democratic society.

(3) These rights and freedoms may in no case be exercised contrary to the purposes and principles of the United Nations.

Article 30. Nothing in this Declaration may be interpreted as implying for any State, group or person any right to engage in any activity or to perform any act aimed at the destruction of any of the rights and freedoms set forth herein.

QUESTIONS

1. Work out a definition of "rights" which, in your opinion, might be put in place of each occurrence of this word in the Preamble, without changing the meaning of anything said. Include other ethical terms in the definition if you find it necessary. As the word is here used, can a person have a right even if the fact is not recognized or protected by the law of his country?
2. Do you think there is any difference between the meaning of "rights" in Article 2, which says "Everyone is *entitled* to all the rights . . ." and Article 3 which says "Everyone *has* the right . . ."?
3. Make a classified list of all the rights asserted by the Declaration, according to such categories as economic, political, civil, cultural, or what you will.
4. Might a country in which it is customary for parents to choose a person's wife legitimately object to Article 16?
5. Does Article 17 underwrite capitalism?
6. Do you think Article 21 is reasonably applicable to underdeveloped countries, where the average citizen has only a very low degree of education?
7. Can it be argued that Articles 22, 24, and 25 are unrealistic, in view of the poverty of some nations? Can something be called "a right" which cannot possibly be provided?
8. Given the amount of unemployment in the United States, does this country secure the right formulated in Article 23?
9. Does Article 26 require a system of state-supported scholarships for higher education?
10. Does Article 30 sanction the outlawing of the Communist Party?

John Locke   (*1632-1704*)

NATURAL RIGHTS AND THE
AUTHORITY OF GOVERNMENTS

John Locke is another of the great figures in Western thought and is one of especial historical importance because of the influence of his ideas on the political thinking of the men who brought forth the United States, during the second half of the eighteenth century.

Locke's thought on politics was no mere intellectual exercise: his father fought in the Parliamentary army against Charles I, and Locke may himself have witnessed the execution of Charles I in 1649. He was educated at Oxford and later studied medicine. He held a post as family physician in the household of the Earl of Shaftesbury for some years. In later life Locke held various offices in the government. He was a virtual exile in France between 1684 and 1689, because of suspicions of complicity in the Monmouth rebellion.

The essential objects of Locke's political writing were destruction of the concept of the divine right of monarchs and establishment of the idea that the authority of government derives from a limited delegation of rights by the members of a community — authority which can properly be exercised only within the limits of the delegation and for the purposes on account of which the rights were delegated. Locke's theory naturally takes concrete form in a constitutional government which restricts the power of legislatures.

The logical foundation of his political theory, of course, lies in his general theory of right conduct and human rights. Unfortunately, however, Locke did not write a systematic treatise on ethics, and it is not clear what he thinks ethical statements mean or how they may be justified. Hence, although he says that the (moral) law of nature is "intelligible and plain to a rational creature," we cannot reconstruct the details of his metaethical theory — if indeed he did work it out in detail. What is clear is that Locke thought that a man has certain moral duties and correspondingly has certain rights quite universally and without exception, and that these moral rights are his just because he is a human being, and that they are altogether independent of recognition by the state and of membership in any society. If I meet a complete stranger in a lonely island over which no nation has sovereignty, this man has rights against me just by being a man. What are these rights? Primarily rights to life, health, property, and freedom of action except where action would infringe the like rights of others and except where there is other limitation by the (moral) law of nature.

Some of a man's rights he can transfer to another; and such a delegation of rights is the source of the authority of civil society. There are some rights society does not have because they cannot have been transferred to it; for instance, society has no right to take my life unless I have committed a crime, for I had no right to take my own life (my life belonging to God), and hence cannot have transferred it to the community.

Locke was a prolific writer. The most important of his works are the *Essay Concerning Human Understanding* (1690), three letters on tolerance (1689 and 1690), and *Two Treatises of Government* (1690).

From John Locke, *Two Treatises of Government*. Many editions.

TWO TREATISES OF GOVERNMENT

CHAPTER 2   OF THE STATE OF NATURE

4. To understand political power aright, and derive it from its original, we must consider what estate all men are naturally in, and that is, a state of perfect freedom to order their actions, and dispose of their possessions and persons as they think fit, within the bounds of the law of Nature, without asking leave or depending upon the will of any other man.

A state also of equality, wherein all the power and jurisdiction is reciprocal, no one having more than another, there being nothing more evident than that creatures of the same species and rank, promiscuously born to all the same advantages of Nature, and the use of the same faculties, should also be equal one amongst another, without subordination or subjection, unless the lord and master of them all should, by any manifest declaration of his will, set one above another, and confer on him, by an evident and clear appointment, an undoubted right to dominion and sovereignty.

6. But though this be a state of liberty, yet it is not a state of licence; though man in that state have an uncontrollable liberty to dispose of his person or possessions, yet he has not liberty to destroy himself, or so much as any creature in his possession, but where some nobler use than its bare preservation calls for it. The state of Nature has a law of Nature to govern it, which obliges every one, and reason, which is that law, teaches all man-

kind who will but consult it, that being all equal and independent, no one ought to harm another in his life, health, liberty or possessions; for men being all the workmanship of one omnipotent and infinitely wise Maker; all the servants of one sovereign Master, sent into the world by His order and about His business; they are His property, whose workmanship they are made to last during His, not one another's pleasure. And, being furnished with like faculties, sharing all in one community of Nature, there cannot be supposed any such subordination among us that may authorise us to destroy one another, as if we were made for one another's uses, as the inferior ranks of creatures are for ours. Every one as he is bound to preserve himself, and not to quit his station wilfully, so by the like reason, when his own preservation comes not in competition, ought he as much as he can to preserve the rest of mankind, and not unless it be to do justice on an offender, take away or impair the life, or what tends to the preservation of the life, the liberty, health, limb, or goods of another.

7. And that all men may be restrained from invading others' rights, and from doing hurt to one another, and the law of Nature be observed, which willeth the peace and preservation of all mankind, the execution of the law of Nature is in that state put into every man's hands, whereby every one has a right to punish the transgressors of that law to such a degree as may hinder its violation. For the law of Nature would, as all other laws that concern men in this world, be in vain if there were nobody that in the state of Nature had a power to execute that law, and thereby preserve the innocent and restrain offenders; and if any one in the state of Nature may punish another for any evil he has done, every one may do so. For in that state of perfect equality, where naturally there is no superiority or jurisdiction of one over another, what any may do in prosecution of that law, every one must needs have a right to do.

8. And thus, in the state of Nature, one man comes by a power over another, but yet no absolute or arbitrary power to use a criminal, when he has got him in his hands, according to the passionate heats or boundless extravagancy of his own will, but only to retribute to him so far as calm reason and conscience dictate, what is proportionate to his transgression, which is so much as may serve for reparation and restraint. For these two are the only reasons why one man may lawfully do harm to another, which is that we call punishment. In transgressing the law of Nature, the offender declares himself to live by another rule than that of reason and common equity, which is that measure God has set to the actions of men for their mutual security, and so he becomes dangerous to mankind; the tie which is to secure them from injury and violence being slighted and broken by him, which being a trespass against the whole species, and the peace and safety of it, provided for by the law of Nature, every man upon this score, by the right he hath to preserve mankind in general, may restrain, or where it is necessary, destroy things noxious to them, and so may bring such evil on any one who hath transgressed that law, as may make

him repent the doing of it, and thereby deter him, and, by his example, others from doing the like mischief. And in this case, and upon this ground, every man hath a right to punish the offender, and be executioner of the law of Nature.

9. I doubt not but this will seem a very strange doctrine to some men; but before they condemn it, I desire them to resolve me by what right any prince or state can put to death or punish an alien for any crime he commits in their country? It is certain their laws, by virtue of any sanction they receive from the promulgated will of the legislature, reach not a stranger. They speak not to him, nor, if they did, is he bound to hearken to them. The legislative authority by which they are in force over the subjects of that commonwealth hath no power over him. Those who have the supreme power of making laws in England, France, or Holland are, to an Indian, but like the rest of the world — men without authority. And therefore, if by the law of Nature every man hath not a power to punish offences against it, as he soberly judges the case to require, I see not how the magistrates of any community can punish an alien of another country, since, in reference to him, they can have no more power than what every man naturally may have over another.

10. Besides the crime which consists in violating the laws, and varying from the right rule of reason, whereby a man so far becomes degenerate, and declares himself to quit the principles of human nature and to be a noxious creature, there is commonly injury done, and some person or other, some other man, receives damage by his transgression; in which case, he who hath received any damage has (besides the right of punishment common to him, with other men) a particular right to seek reparation from him that hath done it. And any other person who finds it just may also join with him that is injured, and assist him in recovering from the offender so much as may make satisfaction for the harm he hath suffered.

11. From these two distinct rights (the one of punishing the crime, for restraint and preventing the like offence, which right of punishing is in everybody, the other of taking reparation, which belongs only to the injured party) comes it to pass that the magistrate, who by being magistrate hath the common right of punishing put into his hands, can often, where the public good demands not the execution of the law, remit the punishment of criminal offences by his own authority, but yet cannot remit the satisfaction due to any private man for the damage he has received. That he who hath suffered the damage has a right to demand in his own name, and he alone can remit. The damnified person has this power of appropriating to himself the goods or service of the offender by right of self-preservation, as every man has a power to punish the crime to prevent its being committed again, by the right he has of preserving all mankind, and doing all reasonable things he can in order to that end. And thus it is that every man in the state of Nature has a power to kill a murderer, both to deter others from doing the like injury (which no reparation can compensate) by

the example of the punishment that attends it from everybody, and also to secure men from the attempts of a criminal who, having renounced reason, the common rule and measure God hath given to mankind, hath, by the unjust violence and slaughter he hath committed upon one, declared war against all mankind, and therefore may be destroyed as a lion or a tiger, one of those wild savage beasts with whom men can have no society nor security. And upon this is grounded that great law of Nature, "Whoso sheddeth man's blood, by man shall his blood be shed." And Cain was so fully convinced that every one had a right to destroy such a criminal, that, after the murder of his brother, he cries out, "Every one that findeth me shall slay me," so plain was it writ in the hearts of all mankind.

12. By the same reason may a man in the state of Nature punish the lesser breaches of that law, it will, perhaps, be demanded, with death? I answer: Each transgression may be punished to that degree, and with so much severity, as will suffice to make it an ill bargain to the offender, give him cause to repent, and terrify others from doing the like. Every offence that can be committed in the state of Nature may, in the state of Nature, be also punished equally, and as far forth, as it may, in a commonwealth. For though it would be beside my present purpose to enter here into the particulars of the law of Nature, or its measures of punishment, yet it is certain there is such a law, and that too as intelligible and plain to a rational creature and a studier of that law as the positive laws of commonwealths, nay, possibly plainer; as much as reason is easier to be understood than the fancies and intricate contrivances of men, following contrary and hidden interests put into words; for truly so are a great part of the municipal laws of countries, which are only so far right as they are founded on the law of Nature, by which they are to be regulated and interpreted.

13. To this strange doctrine — viz., That in the state of Nature every one has the executive power of the law of Nature — I doubt not but it will be objected that it is unreasonable for men to be judges in their own cases, that self-love will make men partial to themselves and their friends; and, on the other side, ill-nature, passion, and revenge will carry them too far in punishing others, and hence nothing but confusion and disorder will follow, and that therefore God hath certainly appointed government to restrain the partiality and violence of men. I easily grant that civil government is the proper remedy for the inconveniences of the state of Nature, which must certainly be great where men may be judges in their own case, since it is easy to be imagined that he who was so unjust as to do his brother an injury will scarce be so just as to condemn himself for it. But I shall desire those who make this objection to remember that absolute monarchs are but men; and if government is to be the remedy of those evils which necessarily follow from men being judges in their own cases, and the state of Nature is therefore not to be endured, I desire to know what kind of government that is, and how much better it is than the state of Nature, where one man commanding a multitude has the liberty to be judge in

his own case, and may do to all his subjects whatever he pleases without the least question or control of those who execute his pleasure? and in whatsoever he doth, whether led by reason, mistake, or passion, must be submitted to? which men in the state of Nature are not bound to do one to another. And if he that judges, judges amiss in his own or any other case, he is answerable for it to the rest of mankind.

14. It is often asked as a mighty objection, where are, or ever were, there any men in such a state of Nature? To which it may suffice as an answer at present, that since all princes and rulers of "independent" governments all through the world are in a state of Nature, it is plain the world never was, nor never will be, without numbers of men in that state. I have named all governors of "independent" communities, whether they are, or are not, in league with others; for it is not every compact that puts an end to the state of Nature between men, but only this one of agreeing together mutually to enter into one community, and make one body politic; other promises and compacts men may make one with another, and yet still be in the state of Nature. The promises and bargains for truck, etc., between the two men in Soldania, in or between a Swiss and an Indian, in the woods of America, are binding to them, though they are perfectly in a state of Nature in reference to one another for truth, and keeping of faith belongs to men as men, and not as members of society.

15. To those that say there were never any men in the state of Nature, I will not only oppose the authority of the judicious Hooker (*Eccl. Pol.* i. 10), where he says, "the laws which have been hitherto mentioned"— *i.e.*, the laws of Nature —"do bind men absolutely, even as they are men, although they have never any settled fellowship, never any solemn agreement amongst themselves what to do or not to do; but for as much as we are not by our-selves sufficient to furnish ourselves with competent store of things needful for such a life as our Nature doth desire, a life fit for the dignity of man, therefore to supply those defects and imperfections which are in us, as living single and solely by ourselves, we are naturally induced to seek communion and fellowship with others; this was the cause of men uniting themselves as first in politic societies." But I, moreover, affirm that all men are naturally in that state, and remain so till, by their own consents, they make themselves members of some politic society, and I doubt not, in the sequel of this discourse, to make it very clear.

CHAPTER 7   OF POLITICAL OR CIVIL SOCIETY

. . . 87. Man being born, as has been proved, with a title to per-fect freedom and an uncontrolled enjoyment of all the rights and privileges of the law of Nature, equally with any other man, or number of men in the world, hath by nature a power not only to preserve his property — that is, his life, liberty, and estate, against the injuries and attempts of other men, but to judge of and punish the breaches of that law in others, as he is persuaded the offence deserves, even with death itself, in crimes where the heinousness of the fact, in his opinion, requires it. But because no political society can be, nor subsist, without having in itself the power to preserve the property, and in order thereunto punish the offences of all those of that society, there, and there only, is political society where every one of the members hath quitted this natural power, resigned it up into the hands of the community in all cases that exclude him not from appealing for protection to the law established by it. And thus all private judgment of every particular member being excluded, the community comes to be umpire, and by understanding indifferent rules and men authorised by the community for their execution, decides all the differences that may happen between any members of that society concerning any matter of right, and punishes those offences which any member hath committed against the society with such penalties as the law has established; whereby it is easy to discern who are, and are not, in political society together. Those who are united into one body, and have a common established law and judicature to appeal to, with authority to decide controversies between them and punish offenders, are in civil society one with another; but those who have no such common appeal, I mean on earth, are still in the state of Nature, each being where there is no other, judge for himself and executioner; which is, as I have before showed it, the perfect state of Nature.

88. And thus the commonwealth comes by a power to set down what punishment shall belong to the several transgressions they think worthy of it, committed amongst the members of that society (which is the power of making laws), as well as it has the power to punish any injury done unto any of its members by any one that is not of it (which is the power of war and peace); and all this for the preservation of the property of all the members of that society, as far as is possible. But though every man entered into society has quitted his power to punish offences against the law of Nature in prosecution of his own private judgment, yet with the judgment of offences which he has given up to the legislative, in all cases where he can appeal to the magistrate, he has given up a right to the commonwealth to employ his force for the execution of the judgments of the commonwealth whenever he shall be called to it, which, indeed, are his own judgments, they being made by himself or his representative. And herein we have the original of the legislative and executive power of civil society, which is to judge by standing laws how far offences are to be punished when committed within the commonwealth; and also by occasional judgments founded on the present circumstances of the fact, how far injuries from without are to be vindicated, and in both these to employ all the force of all the members when there shall be need.

89. Wherever, therefore, any number of men so unite into one society as to quit every one his executive power of the law of Nature, and to resign it to the public, there and there only is a political or civil society. And this is done wherever any number of men, in the state of Nature, enter into

society to make one people one body politic under one supreme government: or else when any one joins himself to, and incorporates with any government already made. For hereby he authorises the society, or which is all one, the legislative thereof, to make laws for him as the public good of the society shall require, to the execution whereof his own assistance (as to his own decrees) is due. And this puts men out of a state of Nature into that of a commonwealth, by setting up a judge on earth with authority to determine all the controversies and redress the injuries that may happen to any member of the commonwealth, which judge is the legislative or magistrates appointed by it. And wherever there are any number of men, however associated, that have no such decisive power to appeal to, there they are still in the state of Nature.

90. And hence it is evident that absolute monarchy, which by some men is counted for the only government in the world, is indeed inconsistent with civil society, and so can be no form of civil government at all. For the end of civil society being to avoid and remedy those inconveniences of the state of Nature which necessarily follow from every man's being judge in his own case, by setting up a known authority to which every one of that society may appeal upon any injury received, or controversy that may arise, and which every one of the society ought to obey. Wherever any persons are who have not such an authority to appeal to, and decide any difference between them there, those persons are still in the state of Nature. And so is every absolute prince in respect of those who are under his dominion.

CHAPTER 8   OF THE BEGINNING
OF POLITICAL SOCIETIES

95. Men being, as has been said, by nature all free, equal, and independent, no one can be put out of this estate and subjected to the political power of another without his own consent, which is done by agreeing with other men, to join and unite into a community for their comfortable, safe, and peaceable living, one amongst another, in a secure enjoyment of their properties, and a greater security against any that are not of it. This any number of men may do, because it injures not the freedom of the rest; they are left, as they were, in the liberty of the state of Nature. When any number of men have so consented to make one community or government, they are thereby presently incorporated, and make one body politic, wherein the majority have a right to act and conclude the rest.

96. For, when any number of men have, by the consent of every individual, made a community, they have thereby made that community one body, with a power to act as one body, which is only by the will and determination of the majority. For that which acts any community, being only the consent of the individuals of it, and it being one body, must move one way, it is necessary the body should move that way whither the greater

force carries it, which is the consent of the majority, or else it is impossible it should act or continue one body, one community, which the consent of every individual that united into it agreed that it should; and so every one is bound by that consent to be concluded by the majority. And therefore we see that in assemblies empowered to act by positive laws where no number is set by that positive law which empowers them, the act of the majority passes for the act of the whole, and of course determines as having, by the law of Nature and reason, the power of the whole.

97. And thus every man, by consenting with others to make one body politic under one government, puts himself under an obligation to every one of that society to submit to the determination of the majority, and to be concluded by it; or else this original compact, whereby he with others incorporates into one society, would signify nothing, and be no compact if he be left free and under no other ties than he was in before in the state of Nature. For what appearance would there be of any compact? What new engagement if he were no farther tied by any decrees of the society than he himself thought fit and did actually consent to? This would be still as great a liberty as he himself had before his compact, or any one else in the state of Nature, who may submit himself and consent to any acts of it if he thinks fit.

98. For if the consent of the majority shall not in reason be received as the act of the whole, and conclude every individual, nothing but the consent of every individual can make anything to be the act of the whole, which, considering the infirmities of health and avocations of business, which in a number though much less than that of a commonwealth, will necessarily keep many away from the public assembly; and the variety of opinions and contrariety of interests which unavoidably happen in all collections of men, it is next to impossible ever to be had. And, therefore, if coming into society be upon such terms, it will be only like Cato's coming into the theatre, *tantum ut exiret*. Such a constitution as this would make the mighty leviathan of a shorter duration than the feeblest creatures, and not let it outlast the day it was born in, which cannot be supposed till we can think that rational creatures should desire and constitute societies only to be dissolved. For where the majority cannot conclude the rest, there they cannot act as one body, and consequently will be immediately dissolved again.

99. Whosoever, therefore, out of a state of Nature unite into a community, must be understood to give up all the power necessary to the ends for which they unite into society to the majority of the community, unless they expressly agreed in any number greater than the majority. And this is done by barely agreeing to unite into one political society, which is all the compact that is, or needs be, between the individuals that enter into or make up a commonwealth. And thus, that which begins and actually constitutes any political society is nothing but the consent of any number of freemen capable of majority, to unite and incorporate into such a society. And

this is that, and that only, which did or could give beginning to any lawful government in the world. . . .

CHAPTER 11   OF THE EXTENT
OF THE LEGISLATIVE POWER

134. The great end of men's entering into society being the enjoyment of their properties in peace and safety, and the great instrument and means of that being the laws established in that society, the first and fundamental positive law of all commonwealths is the establishing of the legislative power, as the first and fundamental natural law which is to govern even the legislative. Itself is the preservation of the society and (as far as will consist with the public good) of every person in it. This legislative is not only the supreme power of the commonwealth, but sacred and unalterable in the hands where the community have once placed it. Nor can any edict of anybody else, in what form soever conceived, or by what power soever backed, have the force and obligation of a law which has not its sanction from that legislative which the public has chosen and appointed; for without this the law could not have that which is absolutely necessary to its being a law, the consent of the society, over whom nobody can have a power to make laws[1] but by their own consent and by authority received from them; and therefore all the obedience, which by the most solemn ties any one can be obliged to pay, ultimately terminates in this supreme power, and is directed by those laws which it enacts. Nor can any oaths to any foreign power whatsoever, or any domestic subordinate power, discharge any member of the society from his obedience to the legislative, acting pursuant to their trust, nor oblige him to any obedience contrary to the laws so enacted or farther than they do allow, it being ridiculous to imagine one can be tied ultimately to obey any power in the society which is not the supreme.

135. Though the legislative, whether placed in one or more, whether it be always in being or only by intervals, though it be the supreme power in every commonwealth, yet, first, it is not, nor can possibly be, absolutely arbitrary over the lives and fortunes of the people. For it being but the

---

[1] "The lawful power of making laws to command whole politic societies of men, belonging so properly unto the same entire societies, that for any prince or potentate, of what kind soever upon earth, to exercise the same of himself, and not by express commission immediately and personally received from God, or else by authority derived at the first from their consent, upon whose persons they impose laws, it is no better than mere tyranny. Laws they are not, therefore, which public approbation hath not made so." — Hooker (*Eccl. Pol.*, lib. i., s. 10). "Of this point, therefore, we are to note that such men naturally have no full and perfect power to command whole politic multitudes of men, therefore utterly without our consent we could in such sort be at no man's commandment living. And to be commanded, we do consent when that society, whereof we be a part, hath at any time before consented, without revoking the same after by the like universal agreement.

"Laws therefore human, of what kind soever, are available by consent." — Hooker (*Eccl. Pol.*).

joint power of every member of the society given up to that person or assembly which is legislator, it can be no more than those persons had in a state of Nature before they entered into society, and gave it up to the community. For nobody can transfer to another more power than he has in himself, and nobody has an absolute arbitrary power over himself, or over any other, to destroy his own life, or take away the life or property of another. A man, as has been proved, cannot subject himself to the arbitrary power of another; and having, in the state of Nature, no arbitrary power over the life, liberty, or possession of another, but only so much as the law of Nature gave him for the preservation of himself and the rest of mankind, this is all he doth, or can give up to the commonwealth, and by it to the legislative power, so that the legislative can have no more than this. Their power in the utmost bounds of it is limited to the public good of the society.[2] It is a power that hath no other end but preservation, and therefore can never have a right to destroy, enslave, or designedly to impoverish the subjects; the obligations of the law of Nature cease not in society, but only in many cases are drawn closer, and have, by human laws, known penalties annexed to them to enforce their observation. Thus the law of Nature stands as an eternal rule to all men, legislators as well as others. The rules that they make for other men's actions must, as well as their own and other men's actions, be conformable to the law of Nature — i.e., to the will of God, of which that is a declaration, and the fundamental law of Nature being the preservation of mankind, no human sanction can be good or valid against it.

136. Secondly, the legislative or supreme authority cannot assume to itself a power to rule by extemporary arbitrary decrees, but is bound to dispense justice and decide the rights of the subject by promulgated standing laws,[3] and known authorised judges. For the law of Nature being unwritten, and so nowhere to be found but in the minds of men, they who, through pas-

---

[2] "Two foundations there are which bear up public societies; the one a natural inclination whereby all men desire sociable life and fellowship; the other an order, expressly or secretly agreed upon, touching the manner of their union in living together. The latter is that which we call the law of a commonweal, the very soul of a politic body, the parts whereof are by law animated, held together, and set on work in such actions as the common good requireth. Laws politic, ordained for external order and regimen amongst men, are never framed as they should be, unless presuming the will of man to be inwardly obstinate, rebellious, and averse from all obedience to the sacred laws of his nature; in a word, unless presuming man to be in regard of his depraved mind little better than a wild beast, they do accordingly provide notwithstanding, so to frame his outward actions, that they be no hindrance unto the common good, for which societies are instituted. Unless they do this they are not perfect." — Hooker (*Eccl. Pol.*, lib. i., s. 10).

[3] "Human laws are measures in respect of men whose actions they must direct, howbeit such measures they are as have also their higher rules to be measured by, which rules are two — the law of God and the law of Nature; so that laws human must be made according to the general laws of Nature, and without contradiction to any positive law of Scripture, otherwise they are ill made." — Hooker (*Eccl. Pol.*, lib. iii., s. 9).

"To constrain men to anything inconvenient doth seem unreasonable." — (*Ibid.*, i., 10).

sion or interest, shall miscite or misapply it, cannot so easily be convinced of their mistake where there is no established judge; and so it serves not as it aught, to determine the rights and fence the properties of those that live under it, especially where every one is judge, interpreter, and executioner of it too, and that in his own case; and he that has right on his side, having ordinarily but his own single strength, hath not force enough to defend himself from injuries or punish delinquents. To avoid these inconveniencies which disorder men's properties in the state of Nature, men unite into societies that they may have the united strength of the whole society to secure and defend their properties, and may have standing rules to bound it by which every one may know what is his. To this end it is that men give up all their natural power to the society they enter into, and the community put the legislative power into such hands as they think fit, with this trust, that they shall be governed by declared laws, or else their peace, quiet, and property will still be at the same uncertainty as it was in the state of Nature.

137. Absolute arbitrary power, or governing without settled standing laws, can neither of them consist with the ends of society and government, which men would not quit the freedom of the state of Nature for, and tie themselves up under, were it not to preserve their lives, liberties, and fortunes, and by stated rules of right and property to secure their peace and quiet. It cannot be supposed that they should intend, had they a power so to do, to give any one or more an absolute arbitrary power over their persons and estates, and put a force into the magistrate's hand to execute his unlimited will arbitrarily upon them; this were to put themselves into a worse condition than the state of Nature, wherein they had a liberty to defend their right against the injuries of others, and were upon equal terms of force to maintain it, whether invaded by a single man or many in combination. Whereas by supposing they have given up themselves to the absolute arbitrary power and will of a legislator, they have disarmed themselves, and armed him to make a prey of them when he pleases; he being in a much worse condition that is exposed to the arbitrary power of one man who has the command of a hundred thousand than he that is exposed to the arbitrary power of a hundred thousand single men, nobody being secure, that his will who has such a command is better than that of other men, though his force be a hundred thousand times stronger. And, therefore, whatever form the commonwealth is under, the ruling power ought to govern by declared and received laws, and not by extemporary dictates and undetermined resolutions, for then mankind will be in a far worse condition than in the state of Nature if they shall have armed one or a few men with the joint power of a multitude, to force them to obey at pleasure the exorbitant and unlimited decrees of their sudden thoughts, or unrestrained, and till that moment, unknown wills, without having any measures set down which may guide and justify their actions. For all the power the government has, being only for the good of the society, as it ought not to be arbitrary and at pleasure, so it ought to be exercised by established and promulgated laws, that

both the people may know their duty, and be safe and secure within the limits of the law, and the rulers, too, kept within their due bounds, and not be tempted by the power they have in their hands to employ it to purposes, and by such measures as they would not have known, and own not willingly.

138. Thirdly, the supreme power cannot take from any man any part of his property without his own consent. For the preservation of property being the end of government, and that for which men enter into society, it necessarily supposes and requires that the people should have property, without which they must be supposed to lose that by entering into society which was the end for which they entered into it; too gross an absurdity for any man to own. Men, therefore, in society having property, they have such a right to the goods, which by the law of the community are theirs, that nobody hath a right to take them, or any part of them, from them without their own consent; without this they have no property at all. For I have truly no property in that which another can by right take from me when he pleases against my consent. Hence it is a mistake to think that the supreme or legislative power of any commonwealth can do what it will, and dispose of the estates of the subject arbitrarily, or take any part of them at pleasure. This is not much to be feared in governments where the legislative consists wholly or in part in assemblies which are variable, whose members upon the dissolution of the assembly are subjects under the common laws of their country, equally with the rest. But in governments where the legislative is in one lasting assembly, always in being, or in one man as in absolute monarchies, there is danger still, that they will think themselves to have a distinct interest from the rest of the community, and so will be apt to increase their own riches and power by taking what they think fit from the people. For a man's property is not at all secure, though there be good and equitable laws to set the bounds of it between him and his fellow-subjects, if he who commands those subjects have power to take from any private man what part he pleases of his property, and use and dispose of it as he thinks good.

139. But government, into whosoever hands it is put, being as I have before showed, entrusted with this condition, and for this end, that men might have and secure their properties, the prince or senate, however it may have power to make laws for the regulating of property between the subjects one amongst another, yet can never have a power to take to themselves the whole, or any part of the subjects' property, without their own consent; for this would be in effect to leave them no property at all. And to let us see that even absolute power, where it is necessary, is not arbitrary by being absolute, but is still limited by that reason, and confined to those ends which required it in some cases to be absolute, we need look no farther than the common practice of martial discipline. For the preservation of the army, and in it of the whole commonwealth, requires an absolute

obedience to the command of every superior officer, and it is justly death to disobey or dispute the most dangerous or unreasonable of them; but yet we see that neither the sergeant that could command a soldier to march up to the mouth of a cannon, or stand in a breach where he is almost sure to perish, can command that soldier to give him one penny of his money; nor the general that can condemn him to death for deserting his post, or not obeying the most desperate orders, cannot yet with all his absolute power of life and death dispose of one farthing of that soldier's estate, or seize one jot of his goods; whom yet he can command anything, and hang for the least disobedience. Because such a blind obedience is necessary to that end for which the commander has his power — viz., the preservation of the rest, but the disposing of his goods has nothing to do with it.

140. It is true governments cannot be supported without great charge, and it is fit every one who enjoys his share of the protection should pay out of his estate his proportion for the maintenance of it. But still it must be with his own consent — i.e., the consent of the majority, giving it either by themselves or their representatives chosen by them; for if any one shall claim a power to lay and levy taxes on the people by his own authority, and without such consent of the people, he thereby invades the fundamental law of property, and subverts the end of government. For what property have I in that which another may by right take when he pleases to himself?

141. Fourthly. The legislative cannot transfer the power of making laws to any other hands, for it being but a delegated power from the people, they who have it cannot pass it over to others. The people alone can appoint the form of the commonwealth, which is by constituting the legislative, and appointing in whose hands that shall be. And when the people have said, "We will submit, and be governed by laws made by such men, and in such forms," nobody else can say other men shall make laws for them; nor can they be bound by any laws but such as are enacted by those whom they have chosen and authorised to make laws for them.

142. These are the bounds which the trust that is put in them by the society and the law of God and Nature have set to the legislative power of every commonwealth, in all forms of government. First: They are to govern by promulgated established laws, not to be varied in particular cases, but to have one rule for rich and poor, for the favourite at Court, and the countryman at plough. Secondly: These laws also ought to be designed for no other end ultimately but the good of the people. Thirdly: They must not raise taxes on the property of the people without the consent of the people given by themselves or their deputies. And this properly concerns only such governments where the legislative is always in being, or at least where the people have not reserved any part of the legislative to deputies, to be from time to time chosen by themselves. Fourthly: Legislative neither must nor can transfer the power of making laws to anybody else, or place it anywhere but where the people have.

QUESTIONS

1. What fundamental right does Locke think all men "naturally" have? What moral principles, or "natural laws," restrict it? What does he mean by the "state of Nature"?
2. Suppose Locke had become a skeptic in his theology. In what respects must he have, in consistency, modified his views about the state of nature and man's rights and duties in it?
3. Who has police and judicial power in the state of nature? What principle, according to Locke, must one man use in deciding the punishment proper for a crime?
4. By what act are men removed from a state of nature and incorporated in a commonwealth? Why does Locke think that an absolute monarchy is no form of civil government at all?
5. Why does Locke think that a civil society must be governed by the decision of the majority?
6. Does Locke think any governmental official can have power superior to that of the legislature? Why?
7. Exactly what inherent limitations are there to the authority of the legislature?
8. Why must there be government by written laws and known, authorized judges?
9. How far may a government legitimately use its power of taxation, according to Locke? Do you think Locke would have approved of a graduated income tax or an inheritance tax?
10. Do you think Locke would approve support for the aged or payments for medical care out of public funds?

SUGGESTIONS FOR FURTHER READING

Locke, John. *Essays on the Law of Nature.* Ed. by W. von Leyden. New York: Oxford Univ. Press, 1954.

Aaron, R. I. *John Locke.* New York: Oxford Univ. Press, 1955.

Cranston, Maurice. *John Locke: a Biography.* New York: Macmillan, 1957.

Gough, J. W. *John Locke's Political Philosophy.* New York: Oxford Univ. Press, 1950.

Kendall, W. *John Locke and the Doctrine of Majority Rule.* Urbana: Univ. of Illinois Press, 1941.

O'Connor, D. J. *John Locke.* Harmondsworth, Middlesex: Penguin Books, 1952.

John Stuart Mill (1806-73)

A UTILITARIAN DEFENSE OF
FREEDOM OF ACTION

J. S. Mill, as we have seen (pp. 28-43), was a utilitarian but not a "pure" hedonistic one, since he believed that enjoyments might be more or less desirable on account of their "quality" as well as on account of their intensity. In his essay *On Liberty* Mill uses utilitarian, but by no means purely hedonist, reasoning to support the view that action which affects only the agent should be restricted neither by law nor by moral criticism.

A utilitarian may take a rather simple view about rights in general. Just as he may say that a given course of action is right if and only if performing it will maximize welfare, so he may say that people have a right to something if and only if the securing of it to them will maximize welfare. He *must* say this if he happens to think that what it *means* to say that somebody has a right to something is just that some person or persons will be acting wrongly if they do not secure him in this thing. Mill, however, is not here proposing any general theory of rights of this sort. Indeed, in this work he leaves obscure how he thinks the word "rights" is properly used. All Mill is here arguing for is that certain *freedoms* ought to be secured and not encroached upon; he is accenting the negative rights — the rights not to be interfered with — as contrasted with the positive rights to an education and to a decent wage. Nevertheless, Mill's argument illustrates the form a utilitarian theory of rights may take.

Mill writes forcibly, and his essay is justly famous. But his view has its difficulties. He is not arguing simply for restrictions on governmental interference or for institutional safeguards against behavior interfering with other persons; he is arguing that people should not even condemn certain kinds of behavior morally, as if moral condemnation were a kind of interference with freedom. Again, Mill's proposal that "other-regarding behavior" is properly subject to restrictions but that "self-regarding behavior" is not, seems simpler than it is; when we come to actual cases we find that more instructions are needed for making decisions.

From John Stuart Mill, *On Liberty*. London: Parker, 1859.

ON LIBERTY

CHAPTER 1   INTRODUCTORY

. . . The object of this Essay is to assert one very simple principle, as entitled to govern absolutely the dealings of society with the individual in the way of compulsion and control, whether the means used be physical force in the form of legal penalties, or the moral coercion of public opinion. That principle is, that the sole end for which mankind are warranted, individually or collectively, in interfering with the liberty of action of any of their number, is self-protection. That the only purpose for which power can be rightfully exercised over any member of a civilised community, against his will, is to prevent harm to others. His own good, either physical or moral, is not a sufficient warrant. He cannot rightfully be compelled to do or forbear because it will be better for him to do so, because it will make him happier, because, in the opinions of others, to do so would be wise, or even right. These are good reasons for remonstrating with him, or reasoning with him, or persuading him, or entreating him, but not for compelling him, or visiting him with any evil in case he do otherwise. To justify that, the conduct from which it is desired to deter him must be calculated to produce evil to some one else. The only part of the conduct of any one, for which he is amenable to society, is that which concerns others. In the part which merely concerns himself, his independence is, of right, absolute. Over himself, over his own body and mind, the individual is sovereign.

It is, perhaps, hardly necessary to say that this doctrine is meant to apply only to human beings in the maturity of their faculties. We are not speaking of children, or of young persons below the age which the law may fix as that of manhood or womanhood. Those who are still in a state to require being taken care of by others, must be protected against their own actions as well as against external injury. For the same reason, we may leave out of consideration those backward states of society in which the race itself may be considered as in its nonage. The early difficulties in the way of spontaneous progress are so great, that there is seldom any choice of means for overcoming them; and a ruler full of the spirit of improvement is warranted in the use of any expedients that will attain an end, perhaps otherwise unattainable. Despotism is a legitimate mode of government in dealing with barbarians, provided the end be their improvement, and the means justified by actually effecting that end. Liberty, as a principle, has no application to any state of things anterior to the time when mankind have become capable of being improved by free and equal discussion. Until then, there is nothing for them but implicit obedience to an Akbar or a Charlemagne, if they are so fortunate as to find one. But as soon as mankind have attained the capacity of being guided to their own improvement by conviction or persuasion (a period long since reached in all nations with whom we need here concern ourselves), compulsion, either in the direct form or in that of pains and penalties for non-compliance, is no longer admissible as a means to their own good, and justifiable only for the security of others.

It is proper to state that I forego any advantage which could be derived to my argument from the idea of abstract right, as a thing independent of utility. I regard utility as the ultimate appeal on all ethical questions; but it must be utility in the largest sense, grounded on the permanent interests of a man as a progressive being. Those interests, I contend, authorise the subjection of individual spontaneity to external control, only in respect to those actions of each, which concern the interest of other people. If any one does an act hurtful to others, there is a *prima facie* case for punishing him, by law, or, where legal penalties are not safely applicable, by general disapprobation. There are also many positive acts for the benefit of others, which he may rightfully be compelled to perform; such as to give evidence in a court of justice; to bear his fair share in the common defence, or in any other joint work necessary to the interest of the society of which he enjoys the protection; and to perform certain acts of individual beneficence, such as saving a fellow-creature's life, or interposing to protect the defenceless against ill-usage, things which whenever it is obviously a man's duty to do, he may rightfully be made responsible to society for not doing. A person may cause evil to others not only by his actions but by his inaction, and in either case he is justly accountable to them for the injury. The latter case, it is true, requires a much more cautious exercise of compulsion than the former. To make any one answerable for doing evil to others is the rule; to make him answerable for not preventing evil is, comparatively speaking, the exception. Yet there are many cases clear enough and grave enough to justify that exception. In all things which regard the external relations of the individual, he is *de jure* amenable to those whose interests are concerned, and, if need be, to society as their protector. There are often good reasons for not holding him to the responsibility; but these reasons must arise from the special expediencies of the case: either because it is a kind of case in which he is on the whole likely to act better, when left to his own discretion, than when controlled in any way in which society have it in their power to control him; or because the attempt to exercise control would produce other evils, greater than those which it would prevent. When such reasons as these preclude the enforcement of responsibility, the conscience of the agent himself should step into the vacant judgment seat, and protect those interests of others which have no external protection; judging himself all the more rigidly, because the case does not admit of his being made accountable to the judgment of his fellow-creatures.

But there is a sphere of action in which society, as distinguished from the individual, has, if any, only an indirect interest; comprehending all that portion of a person's life and conduct which affects only himself, or if it also affects others, only with their free, voluntary, and undeceived consent and participation. When I say only himself, I mean directly, and in the first instance; for whatever affects himself, may affect others through himself; and the objection which may be grounded on this contingency, will receive consideration in the sequel. This, then, is the appropriate region of human liberty. It comprises, first, the inward domain of consciousness; demanding liberty of conscience in the most comprehensive sense; liberty of thought and feeling; absolute freedom of opinion and sentiment on all subjects, practical or speculative, scientific, moral, or theological. The liberty of expressing and publishing opinions may seem to fall under a different principle, since it belongs to that part of the conduct of an individual which concerns other people; but, being almost of as much importance as the liberty of thought itself, and resting in great part on the same reasons, is practically inseparable from it. Secondly, the principle requires liberty of tastes and pursuits; of framing the plan of our life to suit our own character; of doing as we like, subject to such consequences as may follow: without impediment from our fellow-creatures, so long as what we do does not harm them, even though they should think our conduct foolish, perverse, or wrong. Thirdly, from this liberty of each individual, follows the liberty, within the same limits, of combination among individuals; freedom to unite, for any purpose not involving harm to others: the persons combining being supposed to be of full age, and not forced or deceived.

No society in which these liberties are not, on the whole, respected, is free, whatever may be its form of government; and none is completely free in which they do not exist absolute and unqualified. The only freedom which deserves the name, is that of pursuing our own good in our own way, so long as we do not attempt to deprive others of theirs, or impede their efforts to obtain it. Each is the proper guardian of his own health, whether bodily, or mental and spiritual. Mankind are greater gainers by suffering each other to live as seems good to themselves, than by compelling each to live as seems good to the rest. . . .

CHAPTER 2   OF THE LIBERTY OF THOUGHT AND DISCUSSION

The time, it is to be hoped, is gone by, when any defence would be necessary of the "liberty of the press" as one of the securities against corrupt or tyrannical government. No argument, we may suppose, can now be needed, against permitting a legislature or an executive, not identified in interest with the people, to prescribe opinions to them, and determine what doctrines or what arguments they shall be allowed to hear. This aspect of the question, besides, has been so often and so triumphantly enforced by preceding writers, that it needs not be specially insisted on in this place. Though the law of England, on the subject of the press, is as servile to this day as it was in the time of the Tudors, there is little danger of its being actually put in force against political discussion, except during some temporary panic, when fear of insurrection drives ministers and judges from their propriety; and, speaking generally, it is not, in constitutional countries, to be apprehended, that the government, whether completely responsible to the people or not, will often attempt to control the expression of opinion, except when in doing so it makes itself the organ of the general intolerance of the public. Let us suppose, therefore, that the government is entirely at one with the people, and never thinks of exerting any power of coercion unless in agreement with what it conceives to be their voice. But I deny the right of the people to exercise such coercion, either by themselves or by their government. The power itself is illegitimate. The best government has no more title to it than the worst. It is as noxious, or more noxious, when exerted in accordance with public opinion, than when in opposition to it. If all mankind minus one were of one opinion, and only one person were of the contrary opinion, mankind would be no more justified in silencing that one person, than he, if he had the power, would be justified in silencing mankind. Were an opinion a personal possession of no value except to the owner; if to be obstructed in the enjoyment of it were simply a private injury, it would make some difference whether the injury was inflicted only on a few persons or on many. But the peculiar evil of silencing the expression of an opinion is, that it is robbing the human race; posterity as well as the existing generation; those who dissent from the opinion, still more than those who hold it. If the opinion is right, they are deprived of the opportunity of exchanging error for truth: if wrong, they lose, what is almost as great a benefit, the clearer perception and livelier impression of truth, produced by its collision with error.

It is necessary to consider separately these two hypotheses, each of which has a distinct branch of the argument corresponding to it. We can never be sure that the opinion we are endeavouring to stifle is a false opinion; and if we were sure, stifling it would be an evil still.

First: the opinion which it is attempted to suppress by authority may possibly be true. Those who desire to suppress it, of course deny its truth; but they are not infallible. They have no authority to decide the question for all mankind, and exclude every other person from the means of judging. To refuse a hearing to an opinion, because they are sure that it is false, is to assume that *their* certainty is the same thing as *absolute* certainty. All silencing of discussion is an assumption of infallibility.

. . . There is the greatest difference between presuming an opinion to be true, because, with every opportunity for contesting it, it has not been refuted, and assuming its truth for the purpose of not permitting its refutation. Complete liberty of contradicting and disproving our opinion is the very condition which justifies us in assuming its truth for purposes of action; and on no other terms can a being with human faculties have any rational assurance of being right.

When we consider either the history of opinion, or the ordinary conduct of human life, to what is it to be ascribed that the one and the other are no worse than they are? Not certainly to the inherent force of the human understanding; for, on any matter not self-evident, there are ninety-nine persons totally incapable of judging of it for one who is capable; and the capacity of the hundredth person is only comparative; for the majority of the eminent men of every past generation held many opinions now known to be erroneous, and did or approved numerous things which no one will now justify. Why is it, then, that there is on the whole a preponderance among mankind of rational opinions and rational conduct? If there really is this preponderance — which there must be unless human affairs are, and have always been, in an almost desperate state — it is owing to a quality of the human mind, the source of everything respectable in man either as an intellectual or as a moral being, namely, that his errors are corrigible. He is capable of rectifying his mistakes, by discussion and experience. Not by experience alone. There must be discussion, to show how experience is to be interpreted. Wrong opinions and practices gradually yield to fact and argument; but facts and arguments, to produce any effect on the mind, must be brought before it. Very few facts are able to tell their own story, without comments to bring out their meaning. The whole strength and value, then, of human judgment, depending on the one property, that it can be set right when it is wrong, reliance can be placed on it only when the means of setting it right are kept constantly at hand. In the case of any person whose judgment is really deserving of confidence, how has it become so? Because he has kept his mind open to criticism of his opinions and conduct. Because it has been his practice to listen to all that could be said against him; to profit by as much of it as was just, and expound to himself, and upon occasion to others, the fallacy of what was fallacious. Because he has felt, that the only way in which a human being can make some approach to knowing the whole of a subject, is by hearing what can be said about it by persons of every variety of opinion, and studying all modes in which it can be looked at by every character of mind. No wise man ever acquired his wisdom in any mode but this; nor is it in the nature of human intellect to become wise in any other manner. . . .

Let us now pass to the second division of the argument, and dismissing the supposition that any of the received opinions may be false, let us assume them to be true, and examine into the worth of the manner in which they are likely to be held, when their truth is not freely and openly canvassed. However unwillingly a person who has a strong opinion may admit the possibility that his opinion may be false, he ought to be moved by the consideration that, however true it may be, if it is not fully, frequently, and fearlessly discussed, it will be held as a dead dogma, not a living truth.

There is a class of persons (happily not quite so numerous as formerly) who think it enough if a person assents undoubtingly to what they think true, though he has no knowledge whatever of the grounds of the opinion, and could not make a tenable defence of it against the most superficial objections. Such persons, if they can once get their creed taught from authority, naturally think that no good, and some harm, comes of its being allowed to be questioned. Where their influence prevails, they make it nearly impossible for the received opinion to be rejected wisely and considerately, though it may still be rejected rashly and ignorantly; for to shut out discussion entirely is seldom possible, and when it once gets in, beliefs not grounded on conviction are apt to give way before the slightest semblance of an argument. Waiving, however, this possibility — assuming that the true opinion abides in the mind, but abides as a prejudice, a belief independent of, and proof against, argument — this is not the way in which truth ought to be held by a rational being. This is not knowing the truth. Truth, thus held, is but one superstition the more, accidentally clinging to the words which enunciate a truth.

If the intellect and judgment of mankind ought to be cultivated, a thing which Protestants at least do not deny, on what can these faculties be more appropriately exercised by any one, than on the things which concern him so much that it is considered necessary for him to hold opinions on them? If the cultivation of the understanding consists in one thing more than in another, it is surely in learning the grounds of one's own opinions. Whatever people believe, on subjects on which it is of the first importance to believe rightly, they ought to be able to defend against at least the common objections. But, some one may say, "Let them be *taught* the grounds of their opinions. It does not follow that opinions must be merely parroted because they are never heard controverted. Persons who learn geometry do not simply commit the theorems to memory, but understand and learn likewise the demonstrations; and it would be absurd to say that they remain ignorant of the grounds of geometrical truths, because they never hear any one deny, and attempt to disprove them." Undoubtedly: and such teaching suffices on a subject like mathematics, where there is nothing at all to be said on the wrong side of the question. The peculiarity of the evidence of mathematical truths is that all the argument is on one side. There are no objections, and no answers to objections. But on every subject on which difference of opinion is possible, the truth depends on a balance to be struck between two sets of conflicting reasons. Even in natural philosophy, there is always some other explanation possible of the same facts; some geocentric theory instead of heliocentric, some phlogiston instead of oxygen; and it has to be shown why that other theory cannot be the true one: and until this is shown, and until we know how it is shown, we do not understand the grounds of our opinion. But when we turn to subjects infinitely more complicated, to morals, religion, politics, social relations, and the business of life, three-fourths of the arguments for every disputed opinion consist in dispelling the appearances which favour some opinion different from it. The greatest orator, save one, of antiquity, has left it on record that he always studied his adversary's case with as great, if not still greater, intensity than even his own. What Cicero practised as the means of forensic success requires to be imitated by all who study any subject in order to arrive at the truth. He who knows only his own side of the case, knows little of that. His reasons may be good, and no one may have been able to refute them. But if he is equally unable to refute the reasons on the opposite side; if he does not so much as know what they are, he has no ground for preferring either opinion. The rational position for him would be suspension of judgment, and unless he contents himself with that, he is either led by authority, or adopts, like the generality of the world, the side to which he feels most inclination. Nor is it enough that he should hear the arguments of adversaries from his own teachers, presented as they state them, and accompanied by what they offer as refutations. That is not the way to do justice to the arguments, or bring them into real contact with his own mind. He must be able to hear them from persons who actually believe them; who defend them in earnest, and do their very utmost for them. He must know them in their most plausible and persuasive form; he must feel the whole force of the difficulty which the true view of the subject has to encounter and dispose of; else he will never really possess himself of the portion of truth which meets and removes that difficulty. . . .

It still remains to speak of one of the principal causes which make diversity of opinion advantageous, and will continue to do so until mankind shall have entered a stage of intellectual advancement which at present seems at an incalculable distance. We have hitherto considered only two possibilities: that the received opinion may be false, and some other opinion, consequently, true; or that, the received opinion being true, a conflict with the opposite error is essential to a clear apprehension and deep feeling of its truth. But there is a commoner case than either of these; when the conflicting doctrines, instead of being one true and the other false, share the truth between them; and the nonconforming opinion is needed to supply the remainder of the truth, of which the received doctrine embodies only a part. Popular opinions, on subjects not palpable to sense, are often true, but seldom or never the whole truth. They are a part of the truth; sometimes a greater, sometimes a smaller part, but exaggerated, distorted, and disjointed from the truths by which they ought to be accompanied and limited. Heretical opinions, on the other hand, are generally some of these suppressed and neglected truths, bursting the bonds which kept them down, and either seeking reconciliation with the truth contained in the common opinion, or fronting it as enemies, and setting themselves up, with similar exclusiveness, as the whole truth. The latter case is hitherto the most frequent, as, in the human mind, one-sidedness has always been the rule, and many-sidedness the exception. Hence, even in revolutions of opinion, one part of the truth usually sets while another rises. Even progress, which ought to superadd, for the most part only substitutes, one partial and incomplete truth for another; improvement consisting chiefly in this, that the new fragment of truth is more wanted, more adapted to the needs of the time, than that which it displaces. Such being the partial character of prevailing opinions, even when resting on a true foundation, every opinion which embodies somewhat of the portion of truth which the common opinion omits, ought to be considered precious, with whatever amount of error and confusion that truth may be blended. No sober judge of human affairs will feel bound to be indignant because those who force on our notice truths which we should otherwise have overlooked, overlook some of those which we see. Rather, he will think that so long as popular truth is one-sided, it is more desirable than otherwise that unpopular truth should have one-sided assertors too; such being usually the most energetic, and the most likely to compel reluctant attention to the fragment of wisdom which they proclaim as if it were the whole. . . .

CHAPTER 3   OF INDIVIDUALITY, AS ONE OF THE ELEMENTS OF WELL-BEING

Such being the reasons which make it imperative that human beings should be free to form opinions, and to express their opinions without reserve; and such the baneful consequences to the intellectual, and through that to the moral nature of man, unless this liberty is either conceded, or asserted in spite of prohibition; let us next examine whether the same reasons do not require that men should be free to act upon their opinions — to carry these out in their lives, without hindrance, either physical or moral, from their fellow-men, so long as it is at their own risk and peril. This last proviso is of course indispensable. No one pretends that actions should be as free as opinions. On the contrary, even opinions lose their immunity when the circumstances in which they are expressed are such as to constitute their expression a positive instigation to some mischievous act. An opinion that corn-dealers are starvers of the poor, or that private property is robbery, ought to be unmolested when simply circulated through the press, but may justly incur punishment when delivered orally to an excited mob assembled before the house of a corn-dealer, or when handed about among the same mob in the form of a placard. Acts, of whatever kind, which, without justifiable cause, do harm to others, may be, and in the more important cases absolutely require to be, controlled by the unfavourable sentiments, and, when needful, by the active interference of mankind. The liberty of the individual must be thus far limited; he must not make himself a nuisance to other people. But if he refrains from molesting others in what concerns them, and merely acts according to his own inclination and judgment in things which concern himself, the same reasons which show that opinion should be free, prove also that he should be allowed, without molestation, to carry his opinions into practice at his own cost. That mankind are not infallible; that their truths, for the most part, are only half-truths; that unity of opinion, unless resulting from the fullest and freest comparison of opposite opinions, is not desirable, and diversity not an evil, but a good, until mankind are much more capable than at present of recognising all sides of the truth, are principles applicable to men's modes of action, not less than to their opinions. As it is useful that while mankind are imperfect there should be different opinions, so it is that there should be different experiments of living; that free scope should be given to varieties of character, short of injury to others; and that the worth of different modes of life should be proved practically, when any one thinks fit to try them. It is desirable, in short, that in things which do not primarily concern others, individuality should assert itself. Where, not the person's own character, but the traditions or customs of other people are the rule of conduct, there is wanting one of the principal ingredients of human happiness, and quite the chief ingredient of individual and social progress.

In maintaining this principle, the greatest difficulty to be encountered does not lie in the appreciation of means towards an acknowledged end, but in the indifference of persons in general to the end itself. If it were felt that the free development of individuality is one of the leading essentials of well-being; that it is not only a co-ordinate element with all that is designated by the terms civilisation, instruction, education, culture, but is itself a necessary part and condition of all those things; there would be no danger that liberty should be undervalued, and the adjustment of the boundaries between it and social control would present no extraordinary difficulty. But the evil is, the individual spontaneity is hardly recognised by the common modes of thinking as having any intrinsic worth, or deserving any regard on its own account. . . .

It is not by wearing down into uniformity all that is individual in themselves, but by cultivating it, and calling it forth, within the limits imposed by the rights and interests of others, that human beings become a noble and beautiful object of contemplation; and as the works partake the character of those who do them, by the same process human life also becomes rich, diversified, and animating, furnishing more abundant aliment to high thoughts and elevating feelings, and strengthening the tie which binds every individual to the race, by making the race infinitely better worth belonging to. In proportion to the development of his individuality, each person becomes more valuable to himself, and is therefore capable of being more valuable to others. There is a greater fulness of life about his own existence, and when there is more life in the units there is more in the mass which is composed of them. As much compression as is necessary to prevent the stronger specimens of human nature from encroaching on the rights of others cannot be dispensed with; but for this there is ample compensation even in the point of view of human development. The means of development which the individual loses by being prevented from gratifying his inclinations to the injury of others, are chiefly obtained at the expense of the development of other people. And even to himself there is a full equivalent in the better development of the social part of his nature, rendered possible by the restraint put upon the selfish part. To be held to rigid rules of justice for the sake of others, develops the feelings and capacities which have the good of others for their object. But to be restrained in things not affecting their good, by their mere displeasure, develops nothing valuable, except such force of character as may unfold itself in resisting the restraint. If acquiesced in, it dulls and blunts the whole nature. To give any fair play to the nature of each, it is essential that different persons should be allowed to lead different lives. In proportion as this latitude has been exercised in any age, has that age been noteworthy to posterity. Even despotism does not produce its worst effects, so long as individuality exists under it; and whatever crushes individuality is despotism, by whatever name it may be called, and whether it professes to be enforcing the will of God or the injunctions of men. . . .

CHAPTER 4   OF THE LIMITS TO THE
AUTHORITY OF SOCIETY
OVER THE INDIVIDUAL

What, then, is the rightful limit to the sovereignty of the individual over himself? Where does the authority of society begin? How much of human life should be assigned to individuality, and how much to society?

Each will receive its proper share, if each has that which more particularly concerns it. To individuality should belong the part of life in which it is chiefly the individual that is interested; to society, the part which chiefly interests society.

Though society is not founded on a contract, and though no good purpose is answered by inventing a contract in order to deduce social obligations from it, every one who receives the protection of society owes a return for the benefit, and the fact of living in society renders it indispensable that each should be bound to observe a certain line of conduct towards the rest. This conduct consists, first, in not injuring the interests of one another; or rather certain interests, which, either by express legal provision or by tacit understanding, ought to be considered as rights; and secondly, in each person's bearing his share (to be fixed on some equitable principle) of the labours and sacrifices incurred for defending the society or its members from injury and molestation. These conditions society is justified in enforcing, at all costs to those who endeavour to withhold fulfilment. Nor is this all that society may do. The acts of an individual may be hurtful to others, or wanting in due consideration for their welfare, without going to the length of violating any of their constituted rights. The offender may then be justly punished by opinion, though not by law. As soon as any part of a person's conduct affects prejudicially the interests of others, society has jurisdiction over it, and the question whether the general welfare will or will not be promoted by interfering with it, becomes open to discussion. But there is no room for entertaining any such question when a person's conduct affects the interests of no persons besides himself, or needs not affect them unless they like (all the persons concerned being of full age, and the ordinary amount of understanding). In all such cases, there should be perfect freedom, legal and social, to do the action and stand the consequences.

It would be a great misunderstanding of this doctrine to suppose that it is one of selfish indifference, which pretends that human beings have no business with each other's conduct in life, and that they should not concern themselves about the well-doing or well-being of one another, unless their own interest is involved. Instead of any diminution, there is need of a great increase of disinterested exertion to promote the good of others. But disinterested benevolence can find other instruments to persuade people to their good than whips and scourges, either of the literal or the metaphorical sort. I am the last person to undervalue the self-regarding virtues; they are only second in importance, if even second, to the social. It is equally the business of education to cultivate both. But even education works by conviction and persuasion as well as by compulsion, and it is by the former only that, when the period of education is passed, the self-regarding virtues should be inculcated. Human beings owe to each other help to distinguish the better from the worse, and encouragement to choose the former and avoid the latter. They should be for ever stimulating each other to increased exercise of their higher faculties, and increased direction of their feelings and aims towards wise instead of foolish, elevating instead of degrading, objects and contemplations. But neither one person, nor any number of persons, is warranted in saying to another human creature of ripe years, that he shall not do with his life for his own benefit what he chooses to do with it. He is the person most interested in his own well-being: the interest which any other person, except in cases of strong personal attachment, can have in it, is trifling, compared with that which he himself has; the interest which society has in him individually (except as to his conduct to others) is fractional, and altogether indirect; while with respect to his own feelings and circumstances, the most ordinary man or woman has means of knowledge immeasurably surpassing those that can be possessed by any one else. The interference of society to overrule his judgment and purposes in what only regards himself must be grounded on general presumptions; which may be altogether wrong, and even if right, are as likely as not to be misapplied to individual cases, by persons no better acquainted with the circumstances of such cases than those are who look at them merely from without. In this department, therefore, of human affairs, individuality has its proper field of action. In the conduct of human beings towards one another it is necessary that general rules should for the most part be observed, in order that people may know what they have to expect: but in each person's own concerns his individual spontaneity is entitled to free exercise. Considerations to aid his judgment, exhortations to strengthen his will, may be offered to him, even obtruded on him, by others: but he himself is the final judge. All errors which he is likely to commit against advice and warning are far outweighed by the evil of allowing others to constrain him to what they deem his good.

I do not mean that the feelings with which a person is regarded by others ought not to be in any way affected by his self-regarding qualities or deficiencies. This is neither possible nor desirable. If he is eminent in any of the qualities which conduce to his own good, he is, so far, a proper object of admiration. He is so much the nearer to the ideal perfection of human nature. If he is grossly deficient in those qualities, a sentiment the opposite of admiration will follow. There is a degree of folly, and a degree of what may be called (though the phrase is not unobjectionable) lowness or depravation of taste, which, though it cannot justify doing harm to the person who manifests it, renders him necessarily and properly a subject of distaste, or, in extreme cases, even of contempt: a person could not have the opposite qualities in due strength without entertaining these feelings. Though doing no wrong to any one, a person may so act as to compel us to judge him, and feel to him, as a fool, or as a being of an inferior order: and since this judgment and feeling are a fact which he would prefer to avoid, it is doing him a service to warn him of it beforehand, as of any other disagreeable consequence to which he exposes himself. It would be well, indeed, if this good office were much more freely rendered than the common notions of politeness at present permit, and if one person could honestly point out to another that he thinks him in fault, without being considered unmannerly or presuming. We have a right, also, in various ways, to act upon our unfavourable opinion of any one, not to the oppression of his individuality, but in the exercise of ours. We are not bound, for example, to seek his society; we have a right to avoid it (though not to parade the avoidance), for we have a right to choose the society most acceptable to us. We have a right, and it may be our duty, to caution others against him, if we think his example or conversation likely to have a pernicious effect on those with whom he associates. We may give others a preference over him in optional good offices, except those which tend to his improvement. In these various modes a person may suffer very severe penalties at the hands of others for faults which directly concern only himself; but he suffers these penalties only in so far as they are the natural and, as it were, the spontaneous consequences of the faults themselves, not because they are purposely inflicted on him for the sake of punishment. A person who shows rashness, obstinacy, self-conceit — who cannot live within moderate means — who cannot restrain himself from hurtful indulgences — who pursues animal pleasures at the expense of those of feeling and intellect — must expect to be lowered in the opinion of others, and to have a less share of their favourable sentiments; but of this he has no right to complain, unless he has merited their favour by special excellence in his social relations, and has thus established a title to their good offices, which is not affected by his demerits towards himself.

What I contend for is, that the inconveniences which are strictly inseparable from the unfavourable judgment of others, are the only ones to which a person should ever be subjected for that portion of his conduct and character which concerns his own good, but which does not affect the interest of others in their relations with him. Acts injurious to others require a totally different treatment. Encroachment on their rights; infliction on them of any loss or damage not justified by his own rights; falsehood or duplicity in dealing with them; unfair or ungenerous use of advantages over them; even selfish abstinence from defending them against injury — these are fit objects of moral reprobation, and, in grave cases, of moral retribution and punishment. And not only these acts, but the dispositions which lead to them, are properly immoral, and fit subjects of disapprobation which may rise to abhorrence. Cruelty of disposition; malice and ill-nature; that most anti-social and odious of all passions, envy; dissimulation and insincerity, irascibility on insufficient cause, and resentment disproportioned to the provocation; the love of domineering over others; the desire to engross more than one's share of advantages (the πλεονεξία of the Greeks); the pride which derives gratification from the abasement of others; the egotism which thinks self and its concerns more important than everything else, and decides all doubtful questions in its own favour; — these are moral vices, and constitute a bad and odious moral character: unlike the self-regarding faults previously mentioned, which are not properly immoralities, and to whatever pitch they may be carried, do not constitute wickedness. They may be proofs of any amount of folly, or want of personal dignity and self-respect; but they are only a subject of moral reprobation when they involve a breach of duty to others, for whose sake the individual is bound to have care for himself. What are called duties to ourselves are not socially obligatory, unless circumstances render them at the same time duties to others. The term duty to oneself, when it means anything more than prudence, means self-respect or self-development, and for none of these is any one accountable to his fellow creatures, because for none of them is it for the good of mankind that he be held accountable to them. . . .

The distinction here pointed out between the part of a person's life which concerns only himself, and that which concerns others, many persons will refuse to admit. How (it may be asked) can any part of the conduct of a member of society be a matter of indifference to the other members? No person is an entirely isolated being; it is impossible for a person to do anything seriously or permanently hurtful to himself, without mischief reaching at least to his near connections, and often far beyond them. If he injures his property, he does harm to those who directly or indirectly derived support from it, and usually diminishes, by a greater or less amount, the general resources of the community. If he deteriorates his bodily or mental faculties, he not only brings evil upon all who depended on him for any portion of their happiness, but disqualifies himself for rendering the services which he owes to his fellow-creatures generally; perhaps becomes a burthen on their affection or benevolence; and if such conduct were very frequent, hardly any offence that is committed would detract more from the general sum of good. Finally, if by his vices or follies a person does no direct harm to others, he is nevertheless (it may be said) injurious by his example; and ought to be compelled to control himself, for the sake of those whom the sight or knowledge of his conduct might corrupt or mislead.

And even (it will be added) if the consequences of misconduct could be confined to the vicious or thoughtless individual, ought society to abandon to their own guidance those who are manifestly unfit for it? If protection against themselves is confessedly due to children and persons under age, is not society equally bound to afford it to persons of mature years who are equally incapable of self-government? If gambling, or drunkenness, or incontinence, or idleness, or uncleanliness, are as injurious to happiness, and as great a hindrance to improvement, as many or most of the acts prohibited by law, why (it may be asked) should not law, so far as is consistent with practicability and social convenience, endeavour to repress these also? And as a supplement to the unavoidable imperfections of law, ought not opinion at least to organise a powerful police against these vices, and visit rigidly with social penalties those who are known to practise them? There is no question here (it may be said) about restricting individuality, or impeding the trial of new and original experiments in living. The only things it is sought to prevent are things which have been tried and condemned from the beginning of the world until now; things which experience has shown not to be useful or suitable to any person's individuality. There must be some length of time and amount of experience after which a moral or prudential truth may be regarded as established: and it is merely desired to prevent generation after generation from falling over the same precipice which has been fatal to their predecessors.

I fully admit that the mischief which a person does to himself may seriously affect, both through their sympathies and their interests, those nearly connected with him and, in a minor degree, society at large. When, by conduct of this sort, a person is led to violate a distinct and assignable obligation to any other person or persons, the case is taken out of the self-regarding class, and becomes amenable to moral disapprobation in the proper sense of the term. If, for example, a man, through intemperance or extravagance, becomes unable to pay his debts, or, having undertaken the moral responsibility of a family, becomes from the same cause incapable of supporting or educating them, he is deservedly reprobated, and might be justly punished; but it is for the breach of duty to his family or creditors, not for the extravagance. . . . In like manner, when a person disables himself, by conduct purely self-regarding, from the performance of some definite duty incumbent on him to the public, he is guilty of a social offence. No person ought to be punished simply for being drunk; but a soldier or a policeman should be punished for being drunk on duty. Whenever, in short, there is a definite damage, or a definite risk of damage, either to an individual or to the public, the case is taken out of the province of liberty, and placed in that of morality or law.

But with regard to the merely contingent, or, as it may be called, constructive injury which a person causes to society, by conduct which neither violates any specific duty to the public, nor occasions perceptible hurt to any assignable individual except himself; the inconvenience is one which society can afford to bear, for the sake of the greater good of human freedom. If grown persons are to be punished for not taking proper care of themselves, I would rather it were for their own sake, than under pretence of preventing them from impairing their capacity of rendering to society benefits which society does not pretend it has a right to exact. But I cannot consent to argue the point as if society had no means of bringing its weaker members up to its ordinary standard of rational conduct, except waiting till they do something irrational, and then punishing them, legally or morally, for it. Society has had absolute power over them during all the early portion of their existence: it has had the whole period of childhood and nonage in which to try whether it could make them capable of rational conduct in life. The existing generation is master both of the training and the entire circumstances of the generation to come; it cannot indeed make them perfectly wise and good, because it is itself so lamentably deficient in goodness and wisdom; and its best efforts are not always, in individual cases, its most successful ones; but it is perfectly well able to make the rising generation, as a whole, as good as, and a little better than, itself. If society lets any considerable number of its members grow up mere children, incapable of being acted on by rational consideration of distant motives, society has itself to blame for the consequences. Armed not only with all the powers of education, but with the ascendency which the authority of a received opinion always exercises over the minds who are least fitted to judge for themselves; and aided by the *natural* penalties which cannot be prevented from falling on those who incur the distaste or the contempt of those who know them; let not society pretend that it needs, besides all this, the power to issue commands and enforce obedience in the personal concerns of individuals, in which, on all principles of justice and policy, the decision ought to rest with those who are to abide the consequences. . . .

[An] important example of illegitimate interference with the rightful liberty of the individual, not simply threatened, but long since carried into triumphant effect, is Sabbatarian legislation. Without doubt, abstinence on one day in the week, so far as the exigencies of life permit, from the usual daily occupation, though in no respect religiously binding on any except Jews, is a highly beneficial custom. And inasmuch as this custom cannot be observed without a general consent to that effect among the industrious classes, therefore, in so far as some persons by working may impose the same necessity on others, it may be allowable and right that the law should guarantee to each the observance by others of the custom, by suspending the greater operations of industry on a particular day. But this justification, grounded on the direct interest which others have in each individual's observance of the practice, does not apply to the self-chosen occupations in which a person may think fit to employ his leisure; nor does it hold good, in the smallest degree, for legal restrictions on amusements. It is true that the amusement of some is the day's work of others; but the pleasure, not to say the useful recreation, of many, is worth the labour of a few, provided the occupation is freely chosen, and can be freely resigned. The operatives are perfectly right in thinking that if all worked on Sunday, seven days' work would have to be given for six days' wages; but so long as the great mass of employments are suspended, the small number who for the enjoyment of others must still work, obtain a proportional increase of earnings; and they are not obliged to follow those occupations if they prefer leisure to emolument. If a further remedy is sought, it might be found in the establishment by custom of a holiday on some other day of the week for those particular classes of persons. The only ground, therefore, on which restrictions on Sunday amusements can be defended, must be that they are religiously wrong; a motive of legislation which can never be too earnestly protested against. "Deorum injuriæ Diis Curæ." It remains to be proved that society or any of its officers holds a commission from on high to avenge any supposed offence to Omnipotence, which is not also a wrong to our fellow-creatures. The notion that it is one man's duty that another should be religious, was the foundation of all the religious persecutions ever perpetrated, and, if admitted, would fully justify them. Though the feeling which breaks out in the repeated attempts to stop railway travelling on Sunday, in the resistance to the opening of Museums, and the like, has not the cruelty of the old persecutors, the state of mind indicated by it is fundamentally the same. It is a determination not to tolerate others in doing what is permitted by their religion, because it is not permitted by the persecutor's religion. It is a belief that God not only abominates the act of the misbeliever, but will not hold us guiltless if we leave him unmolested.

QUESTIONS

1. What is the central theme of Mill's essay, according to him? Would Mill object to abrogation of the ordinary rights recognized in democratic countries, in a backward and underdeveloped society?
2. How would Mill apply his utilitarianism to justify his views about the proper scope and limitations of compulsion?
3. Which three kinds of freedom does Mill advocate?
4. What advantages does Mill see in permitting complete freedom of speech (except when such communication is likely to cause serious and immediate harm to other persons)?
5. Do these same advantages support the claim that people have a right to freedom of action? Is it consistent for Mill, as a utilitarian, to advocate a right to freedom of action as a means for encouraging development of individuality and spontaneity?
6. Does Mill think that an agent's self-regarding conduct, no matter what, should

affect our behavior toward him? Is it a "fit object of moral reprobation"? What is the difference between the "moral reprobation" to which Mill objects and the unreceptive behavior which he would permit? What is the difference, according to him, between moral vices and "self-regarding faults"?

7. Do you think Mill makes clear just how one is to decide whether conduct is "self-regarding" or "other-regarding"? In view of his examples, state as precisely as you can what the difference is.

Alfred Cyril Ewing (1899-   )

A CONTEMPORARY THEORY OF RIGHTS

In the following pages A. C. Ewing (see p. 282) attempts to arrive at a sound normative theory about human rights by comparing and criticizing some major traditional theories. He discusses five kinds of view. In discussing the first two, he has in mind the ideas of Locke and Hobbes. The third type of view has been most plausibly stated by T. H. Green, a British philosopher of last century. Ewing rejects all these theories and finds himself required to choose between the fourth theory, utilitarianism, and a fifth theory, corresponding to W. D. Ross's views about right actions (pp. 218-29). Ewing remains undecided between these two; a broad act-utilitarianism which accepts actions like that of keeping a promise as intrinsically good he finds not very different from a Ross-ian theory. The important points to notice in his paper are the reasons for rejecting the first three theories and the reasons why he is unmoved by various objections to the last two theories.

The selection from A. C. Ewing, *The Individual, the State, and World Government*. Copyright 1947 by The Macmillan Company and used with their permission

THE INDIVIDUAL, THE STATE, AND WORLD GOVERNMENT

GENERAL THEORIES OF RIGHTS

. . . The definition of "rights of the individual" which I should suggest is "powers or securities of a kind such that the individual can rightly demand of others that they should normally not interfere with them." A "right" must be distinguished from "what is right," for it may be right for me, and even my duty, to do things for the benefit of A, such as to give him presents, which A has no right to demand. Again a right of mine may still be a right to which I am entitled as against the state even though I am using it wrongly. This is because it is undesirable for the state to take away all liberty, and any liberty may be abused. To say that somebody has a right against the state to do so-and-so is to say that it is wrong or at least normally wrong for the state to interfere with his doing it and that he is justified in demanding non-interference from the state. This is not necessarily to say that he is acting rightly if he does it. It will be noted that I have defined "rights" in terms of "right." I think "right" is indefinable, but in any case its definition would fall not within political philosophy but within general ethics.

The rights of which I am to speak in this chapter are rights to do what one likes with one's life. The main types of view concerning them are these:

1. The view that according to the constitution of their nature or the will of God all individuals have certain definite rights which it is always wrong to violate.

2. The view that the state is based on a kind of contract and that therefore the individual retains those rights, and those only, which he could not be conceived as contracting away.

3. The view that the individual has no rights except those which the state gives him, rights being created by the recognition of the state.

4. The utilitarian view that what rights an individual possesses depend solely on the general good.

5. The view that the individual has natural rights which are not based merely on the general good, but that these rights are not absolute but only *prima facie*; that is, there is always a strong objection to violating them, over and above any evil consequences of the violation, and they should not be violated even for the sake of doing good unless the good is very great, but under exceptional circumstances they may rightly be violated if the good to be hereby secured is very great. (I have applied here to rights the phrase "prima facie" in the special sense in which Sir David Ross applied it to duties.[1])

The first and second views are not common among thinkers to-day, but both have exercised a big influence, especially on "liberalism" in the old-fashioned sense, though in the case of Hobbes the second view was used as a basis for totalitarianism. The fourth view has also exercised great influence in liberalism and is no doubt the dominant view to-day among the parties of the left from full-blooded red to faint pink. The third view is of course the view of the totalitarian, except that the Nazi prefers to talk about the nation (Volk) rather than about the state, while the Fascist prefers the latter phraseology, but it is hardly credible that such a view will

---

[1] *The Right and the Good*, p. 19; *Foundations of Ethics*, p. 84.

last long as a seriously held doctrine. I certainly think the fourth and fifth views greatly preferable to any of the first three.

Let us now discuss the rival views on their merits. The first and second have the great advantage and attraction of being able to provide definite unbreakable universal laws, which would be a great help in practice; but when we try to specify what the inviolable rights are, difficulties thicken. Is the right to property inviolable? If so there could be no social reform that would involve any sacrifice of wealth on the part of the rich unless all who had to make the sacrifice consented. Is the right to free speech inviolable? Then I ought not to be prosecuted for saying without a shred of evidence that my neighbour is a murderer or by false stories inciting people to kill him, who would be severely punished for the crime while I came off scot-free. Or the right to free assembly? Then the state ought not to prevent the holding of a public meeting under circumstances where it is practically certain that it will lead to a sanguinary riot. Or the right to behave as a man likes in his family relations provided the other members of his family agree? Then there must be an end of universal compulsory education. Or the right to think for oneself? It may be doubted whether the state can completely respect even that right as long as it has any control over education, since education affects or even largely determines what I shall believe; and even if the state does not interfere with education directly but leaves it to the parents, it is delegating to the latter the power to interfere with the right of free thought. It is somewhat more plausible to maintain that the right to life is inalienable, not in the sense that the individual must never for a good end sacrifice it but in the sense that the state ought never to take it from him against his will. But in order to maintain this one would have not only to oppose capital punishment and conscription in war but to deny a policeman the right to shoot a murderer who attacked him, even if that was the only way of saving his own life. It is therefore commonly held that it is impossible to draw up any list of concrete rights which hold in all circumstances, because the observance of the right of one man might at any time clash with the same or a different right in others; and certainly any plausible attempt to draw up such a list must make the bill of rights so complicated by the addition of reservations that it becomes unreasonable to say that we know intuitively as a definite *a priori* proposition or can prove metaphysically that the individual ought to have the rights in question. In general, it is contended, there is no right on the part of an individual the observance of which may not, at least conceivably, clash with equally or more important rights on the part of others, and therefore no right which may not on occasion have to be sacrificed. It is at any rate logically impossible that there could be more than one such right, yet advocates of the view I am discussing believe in a *variety* of rights. To maintain absolute rights in the sense indicated is to maintain that there are certain absolutely universal laws of conduct admitting of no conceivable exception, for we cannot have rights for an individual without obligations on the part of others, including the state, to observe these rights. Now the view that there are such universal laws is a view which when maintained in Kant's ethics is almost universally repudiated by philosophers. If the arguments against Kant's view are accepted, with this view must fall the doctrine of absolute rights.

The second main objection to the doctrine of absolute rights is that for an individual to claim any right quite independently of the good of society is immoral, and that when an individual has a right to anything, the right must be based not only on his own good or on his nature as an individual but mainly on the social good which is furthered by granting the right. The individual has no right to do or enjoy what it is not to the common good that he should do or enjoy, and if it is to the common good that he should do or enjoy it his right depends on this and is therefore not his as an individual. For, though an individual may have the right not to be forcibly stopped from doing some things which it is wrong to do, this can only be conceded on the ground that it is better, all things considered, that he should be given a freedom which involves the possibility of abuse; and therefore such a right would still be dependent on the common good and not merely on his individual nature as such irrespective of others. He can have no rights *against* the state, though he may have rights within the state to help him serve the state and may even have a right in exceptional circumstances to act against the state as an organisation because this may be the only way of serving the ultimate true interests of the state. This argument is important, and contains a valuable corrective of the individualist view, but it is dangerous if not carefully applied. It is, however, obviously true at any rate that an individual has no claim to rights irrespective of their effects on others.

Confronted with these objections, it may still be possible to maintain some absolutely universal rights by making them purely formal. Thus we can say that an individual from the nature of the case has always the inalienable right to be treated as well as is compatible with the general good and the principles of morality. Or we can say that every individual has an inalienable right to equal consideration, for that his own good should be treated as of equal importance with equally important goods of others; but it may doubted whether these statements are more than tautologies, though useful enough as a reminder to people who under the influence of prejudice violate the rights of some men for the supposed advantage of others. They apply even to animals, but this does not mean that an animal's good should be considered as much as a man's, because it is less important than a man's.[2] If we substitute for "equally important good" "equal good" the statement indeed ceases to be a tautology because it implies utilitarianism,

---

[2] I do not mean that the good of an animal ought to be treated as of less importance than the *equal* good of a man, but that a man is capable of much greater good than an animal and liable to much greater evils.

but becomes philosophically disputable. It is a controversial question among philosophers whether the quantity of good produced or likely to be produced is the only relevant ground for deciding what is right. But, even if this question is answered in the affirmative, the principle that a man's good must be treated as of equal importance with the equal good of any other man will not by itself give us any information as to what his concrete rights are.

Professor Hocking has laid down as the one and only fundamental right of the individual inalienable by any outside agency that he should be allowed to develop his powers, whatever they are,[3] or, as stated by Professor Robinson in his address to the International Congress of Philosophy in 1937, "the principle that every member of a cultural group capable of self-government has a right to the indispensable means to his development to the highest level of achievement within his own culture to which his native capacities will enable him to attain." [4] But surely a society in which there was not anybody who had for no fault of his own to spend any time in mechanical or relatively mechanical work which he might have spent in some other way more profitably for the development of his own capacities is so utopian as to be almost inconceivable, and that being so this right must be violated by any society of which we can think. It would be violated even in a society the mechanical work of which should be divided equally between all its members. The same amount of mechanical work which might be good for some would detrimentally affect the mental development of others. We may say that every individual has a right to a minimum of development, but what the minimum is cannot be fixed absolutely since it depends on social conditions and on the individual's own capacities. Nor has he a right to develop all his capacities; he has not a right to develop his capacity for burglary, and the state has a perfect right to prevent him from developing this capacity. In giving this fundamental principle Professor Hocking has indeed given the main ground which makes it obligatory to respect the subsidiary rights which ought to be respected, but he has not given a principle that holds without exception.

But there is one class of more concrete rights that might be described as absolute. The rule "Do not inflict pain" is not absolute, but the rule "Do not inflict pain for its own sake or for the sake of rejoicing in the pain" is absolute, and similarly I have an absolute and inviolable right not to have such pain inflicted on me. We cannot talk of the state as actuated by motives, but we can describe individual rights as having been violated by state or at least governmental action in cases where those in charge of the state allow individuals to be punished in a degree and manner determined by sadistic motives and not by considerations of the good of so-

---

[3] *Present Status of the Philosophy of Law and Right*, ch. 7, 8. Hocking admits, however, that "an individual can suspend and perhaps ultimately destroy his own right by his own free choice not to become what he is capable of becoming." (*ibid.*, pp. 74-5).

[4] *Traveaux du IXe Congrès International de Philosophie*, XI, p. 124.

ciety and the individual punished. The concentration camps of Germany were an appalling violation of individual rights, and would still have been so if all their inmates had been guilty of offences deserving some degree of punishment. It is true that we are in a sense not concerned with the motives of others as such, but the presence of motives like those mentioned will make itself felt also in external actions, as victims of concentration camps know to their cost. Similarly, the individual has a right not to be treated selfishly by the rulers; that is, not to be made the victim of actions on the part of the latter which are merely motived by the desires of the rulers for personal advantages for themselves. But these rights will not carry us very far; and there do not seem to be any absolute positive rights any more than there are absolutely universal positive duties. It is not an absolute positive duty to act from the moral motive, for this should not be the motive of all actions, it being better to do many out of love provided they are also in accordance with the moral law. And if it is not a duty always to act from the moral motive there is no motive from which it can be a duty always to act, since taken by itself, any other desire will sometimes lead to action inconsistent with morality.

The contract theory,[5] even if the "contract" is regarded not as historical but as metaphorical, is open to the same type of objections as is the doctrine of absolute natural rights, when the contract is taken as the complete explanation of all political obligation. No doubt the theory is not at fault in finding the essence of the state in some sort of implicit mutual understanding, but it is not the understanding itself but the good ends it subserves which must be regarded as at any rate the main basis of political obligation and the criterion for determining individual rights. Those who base the duty to obey and serve the state primarily on the notion of contract commit the error of tacitly assuming that an individual has a right to do whatever he likes unless he has explicitly or implicitly surrendered that right, an assumption for which there is not the slightest warrant. I should not like to say how far the main advocates of the contract theory were guilty of this error, but in so far as they were not they did not really base political obligation on the contract. A social contract is not needed to justify the claim of the state on the individual and the obligation of the individual to obey laws. The general good, for which some laws and some organisation by governmental action are obviously necessary, is sufficient to justify these. Further, important as the obligation to keep promises may be, it cannot be made the foundation of all other obligations to society. It is certain that we are also under an obligation to do good, whether we have promised to or not; even if all obligations cannot, as the utilitarians claim, be reduced to the obligation of doing good, at least it is an obligation and is an adequate reason for service of the state even without adding to it the

[5] V. Lewis, "Is there a Social Contract?" *Philosophy*, Vol. XV, no. 57, pp. 64ff, and no. 58, pp. 177ff.

supposition that we have implicitly contracted to serve the state. The most that can be admitted is that the facts that we have received and are receiving benefits from the state and that these benefits depend on the observance of laws by others increase any obligation we have to obey the same laws ourselves and generally to serve the state. (This additional source of obligation is not indeed present in all cases: an oppressed minority is not obliged to repay the state for benefits which it has not received, and its obligation to obey and serve the state, in so far as it has such an obligation at all, would therefore have to be based simply on utilitarian grounds, which might, however, be very strong in some cases, provided, though unjustly treated oneself, one felt the state was still fulfilling a useful function and realised the terrible slaughter and anarchy that might be caused by rebellion.) If the advocate of the contract theory replies that apart from his implicit consent to the contract it would be indeed wrong of the individual to act in a way detrimental to others but that the state would have no right to stop him, this is equivalent to the absurd proposition that if I act wrongly others ought never — without my implicit consent — to adopt the most effective means to stop me (for state action is usually a much more effective preventive of the grosser kinds of wrongs than individual action).

Let us turn then to the third view mentioned above, namely the view that the individual has no rights except those which the state gives him, rights being created by recognition of the state. Now if the assertion that the individual has no rights against the state means that whatever any state does to the individual is right it is obviously false. Any person who after reading selections from the list of abominations practised on individuals on behalf of states during the last few years can still seriously believe that the individual has no right against the state in this sense must be well nigh devoid of conscience and human sympathy. This view is, incidentally, not usually held even by a totalitarian about most states or about any states in most periods of their history. Even the most devoted Nazis or Fascists do not consistently carry it out, for they do not think what is done by the British state or by the Russian state is always right. For them it would certainly be a violation by the state of individual rights to imprison a man for being a Nazi. Clearly state actions may do harm or good, and if they cause unnecessary harm when they might do good they are wrong. No doubt there is a sense in which it may be right and even a duty to treat an individual in a certain way without his "having a right" to be treated in this way, as in the giving of presents, and so it may be wrong for him to be treated in a certain way without his "having a right" not to be treated in that way, but most at least of the wrong acts of states do not fall into this category. It must be admitted that a state does wrong and that its wrong acts are very commonly, if not always, of the kind which, if wrong at all, violate the rights of individuals in any ordinary ethical sense of the word "right." An individual has at least a right to be treated as well as is compatible with the general good and the principles of morality, and states do not always treat individuals in that way. Therefore they surely violate individual rights in a perfectly good, clear and usual sense of the term. The only person who could consistently contradict what I have said is the moral sceptic who is prepared to maintain that the distinction between right and wrong, good and bad is quite arbitrary or mistaken. I am not here arguing against such a person and, if I accepted his view, there would be no point in discussing any topic of political philosophy, since no one course could be better than any other except in so far as "better" meant merely that somebody thought or said it was better. But this is not the usual position of the totalitarian, for he believes that totalitarianism is better than other systems, and he insists that some individual acts, for example acts in favour of the Nazis, are better than others, such as acts directed against the Nazis. It seems to me sheer inexcusable inconsistency to apply the conceptions of better and worse to individual action but to refuse to apply them if the individuals are acting as state officials.

The totalitarian theory commits the same kind of error as the contractual theory of rights, only from a different angle, for, while the contract theory denies implicitly that the state has any right over the individual except what the individual has conceded by his explicit or implicit consent, the totalitarian theory denies that the individual has any right in relation to the state except what the state has conceded to the individual, provided it is the sort of state which the totalitarian approves. The totalitarian theory indeed goes further in the one direction than the contract theory does in the other, for, while the contract theory regards the cession of rights as irrevocable except in cases of extreme misgovernment, the totalitarian theory regards rights granted by the state as revocable at any moment; but either theory starts from the error of assuming that one party to the antithesis, individual *versus* state, has no obligation to the other not founded on its consent. It is therefore perhaps not so surprising as it might seem to find that the attempt to explain the obligation to the state in terms of a contract, since it is not founded on any appreciation of the real reason why individual rights should be respected, sometimes degenerates into a form of limited totalitarianism, as in Hobbes. . . . Rights are moral facts to be discovered, and to say that they are created by consent is like saying that Columbus created America by discovering the western continent.

The suggestion that the individual has no rights against the state, in so far as it was due to intellectual causes at all, seems to have largely originated from a confusion between legal and moral rights. Obviously a legal right depends on recognition by some constituted authority or by the legal code itself;[6] but it does not follow that a moral right does so, and once we have admitted the possibility of laws and governmental authorities be-

---

[6] I mean to include under this the case where a law implies but does not expressly state that a person has certain rights. In that case we might say that the person has a legal right even if nobody had yet recognized this implication, and even perhaps if judges wrongly refused to admit the implication.

ing mistaken it is surely quite out of the question to suppose that recognition by anybody could constitute a moral right or that non-recognition of his moral rights could deprive an individual of them. The fact that there may be no means of enforcing a duty cannot prevent it from being a duty unless we identify obligation with compulsion and say that I am not morally bound to pay my debts unless it is the case that I shall be sued and penalised if I do not pay them; and the same surely applies to a right, for to say that somebody has a right implies that others are under an obligation to respect the right. At least there is a very important sense of right and duty, "moral right," in which the above sentence is true, though there is another important sense, "legal right" and "legal duty," in which it may be doubted. And when men discuss the rights of the individual against the state in the context in which the present crisis provokes vital and passionate discussion of this question, it is not the actual legal position but the moral justification of it that they are discussing. The notions of legality and morality have tended to be more mixed together in the discussion of rights than in the discussion of duties, but it seems to me that in either case their admixture can cause nothing but confusion. . . .

[We come now to the theory of rights held by] . . . utilitarianism, meaning by this not necessarily hedonistic utilitarianism, according to which the only good is pleasure, but any theory which makes the rightness of an act dependent exclusively on the balance of good it produces or is likely to produce. I think that hedonism is much more nearly adequate as a criterion for political action than as a criterion for individual action, and I think that a consistent and rational policy of universalistic hedonism if pursued by states would produce vastly better results than any policy which has hitherto been carried out, but I cannot believe that hedonism represents the final truth about ethics. For it seems to me that some pleasant experiences are in themselves, quite apart from their consequences, less good than others equally pleasant. . . . I think indeed that an extended application of the hedonistic criterion in the sphere of politics, national and international, would be highly desirable, not because it is a perfect criterion but because it is very much better than the other muddled criteria such as "national honour" which are now so often employed and because it is easier for the state to aim directly at happiness with success than at other goods. The warning "pursue pleasure and it flies" applies to the individual pursuing it for himself and not to the state, while on the other hand the dangers of trying to produce good morality or good art by law are well known. Certainly, if a consistent hedonist policy were pursued by all states, it would mean the complete end of war and acute poverty, an education for all adequate to fill their increasing leisure with interest, and a vast improvement in physical health; but these consequences would follow equally from most ethical theories sponsored by thinkers provided they were only consistently applied. . . .

On the utilitarian view we must in judging the right of an individual consider his own good neither more nor less than the equal good of any other, and decide according to the amount of good secured compared to that secured by other alternatives. The good may be conceived either hedonistically or as including many other elements besides pleasure of greater value than pleasure. But in either case there is a difficulty. Whatever right we take, however fundamental, it is at least conceivable that it may conflict with the greater good of others, and if so according to this principle it ought to be sacrificed. Yet, if we admit so much, have we not set our feet on a slippery slope which leads to the utmost excesses of totalitarianism, and has not the difference between Hitler and ourselves become only a matter of degree and not of principle? He claimed for all his crimes the excuse that they were for the greatest good, and we have admitted that all rights have to be sacrificed to the greatest good. If there are no absolute individual rights may not the government, if it deems this a necessary means to the production of a greater good, suppress free speech, deceive the people by lies, condemn the innocent, put men to death without trial or torture them mercilessly in order to secure their compliance? True, a good utilitarian will not do these things nearly as readily or as often as Hitler did, but would he not have to admit that it might sometimes be right to do them and that if we do not do them it is only because it is better for the community as a whole that they should not be done? Is this not to make the individual a mere means to the good of society? And, if the individual has no absolute rights, who is to decide what rights he has but the state? Have we not fallen back to a form of totalitarianism which may indeed differ from the totalitarianism of Hitler and Mussolini in seeking good ends, but is still totalitarianism? Surely the rights of individuals are worth preserving even if we should in a given case thereby slightly lessen the amount of good produced?

Writers who reject utilitarianism, outside the Roman Catholic Church at any rate, now usually concede that no laws of action which we can formulate are absolutely binding in all conceivable circumstances, but some insist that besides the obligation to produce the greatest good we have other obligations which are not to be based on the good done by fulfilling them, as the obligation to keep promises or to make reparation for wrong done. If any two of these obligations conflict with each other in a given case or one of them conflicts with the obligation to produce the greatest good, which obligation we should fulfil is to be determined by a balancing of the two against each other, and the result of the balancing cannot be fixed by any universal rules but must depend on individual insight. For example, if it does a little more harm to us than it does good to others to make reparation for wrong done we still ought to make it, but not if it does very grave harm and bestows only a slight good. (Sir David Ross has set the fashion of calling these *"prima facie* obligations," meaning not that they are obligations in appearance only, but that they are obligations each of which holds not absolutely and unconditionally but only in the absence of a superior conflicting obligation.) Now the same conception that is applied to obligations can be applied to rights: indeed it must be, for an obligation implies a right on the part of those toward whom I have the obligation, at least in the case of obligations of "justice" as opposed to those of "charity." So, if we hold the view of ethics I have just described, we may admit that the individual possesses natural rights, which are not indeed absolute, but which must not be set aside except in very unusual circumstances and for very stringent reasons, and which need not be justified by a consideration of the general good, though they would have to be set aside if they conflicted too much with that good. Thus, it might be for the general good in a given case to condemn an innocent man and yet it might be wrong to do so because the violation of individual rights involved was such a serious violation of *prima facie* obligations as to outweigh the good produced. I do not wish to discuss here the general issue between this view and utilitarianism. That is a question which is exceedingly difficult to decide, since the utilitarian may meet all the more obvious objections by asserting that intrinsic goodness attaches not only to the consequences of (for example) keeping a promise or acting justly but to the action itself, or that intrinsic badness attaches to the action of refusing to behave in this way, and that this goodness (or badness) must be taken into account before we decide whether an action is right. He may also appeal to remote consequences and point out that experience shows that, even if we cannot point at the time to any particular evils which for instance a certain lie will produce, there is the gravest risk of even apparently innocuous lies producing unforeseen bad consequences. He may also argue that, when we can see that a law of conduct is in general beneficial, we ought to follow it even in many particular cases where it seems not to be beneficial, on the ground that it is so hard to calculate the consequences in particular cases that it is safer to keep to the general law. Again he may contend that it is better to base individual rights on the intrinsic goodness of individual life and liberty than on any abstract obligations not founded on the good. On the other hand Sir David Ross's account, though harder to accept as an ultimate explanation, seems to agree better with our actual thinking about ethical problems. But both views admit the possibility that any ethical law we can formulate is liable to exceptions and may have to be set aside if the consequences of keeping it are too bad. For, even if the consequences likely to be produced do not constitute the only relevant consideration, it is admitted that they at least constitute a highly relevant one, and one which, if the consequences are *sufficiently* good or bad, may outweigh any other. This is an admission which it is difficult to avoid and yet dangerous to make. Almost all the political crimes of history have been justified by their perpetrators as means to the greatest good, and if we once admit that there are no absolutely universal rules imposing obligations and conferring rights are we not giving an excuse for tyranny? Surely, it may be asked, the wickedness against which we fought in World War II and against which good men have always fought lies just in refusing to recognise any moral law as binding when its observance does not seem expedient? Is not the principle that the end justifies the means so that we may adopt evil means to a good end thoroughly immoral?

This is an objection with which I have great sympathy. But it is an objection that cannot well be made by any one who is not a thoroughgoing pacifist. For anybody who holds that war is ever justifiable, especially (though not only) the modern type of war, is most certainly admitting that it is right to use terribly evil means for the sake of attaining a good end. He is admitting that it may be right to kill, torture and deceive for a good end, and *a fortiori* it would seem that it might be justifiable to sacrifice for a good end the individual rights which make up a man's freedom. And on general principles, evil as such means are, it is always conceivable that if we do not adopt them there may result evils which are still greater. The present generation in many countries was strongly inclined to think that no evil could be greater than a modern war, but most of them would now admit that there is still a greater evil, domination of the larger part of the world by a government like Hitler's, and that war is justifiable if the only way of avoiding the latter evil is to incur the former. To this I cannot help giving a very reluctant assent. If we were a fully Christian people perhaps we could have found a better way than fighting, but human nature being what it is to-day I cannot help believing that in going to war rather than following a policy of non-resistance the United Nations adopted the least evil course that was open to them. However great the evil involved in certain means and however grave the obligations violated by their adoption, it is always at least theoretically possible that the evil resulting from failure to adopt them may be still greater and the obligations violated by their non-adoption still graver, and in that case surely it would be wrong not to adopt them.

QUESTIONS

1. What does Ewing think is the meaning of the noun "right" (as in "human rights")? How is it to be distinguished from the adjective "right" (as in "the right thing to do")?
2. Of the types of theory Ewing lists, are any metaethical theories or are all of them normative proposals? How far is the first theory kin to supernaturalism? Are there any similarities between the second and the fifth?
3. How far does Ewing go in saying there are no absolute rights? Is he right in thinking that his point is fatal to the first and second types of theory?
4. Do animals have rights? Would the view that they have be consistent with all the theories Ewing describes?
5. What do you understand by the "contract theory"? Do you think the contract theory might give a firmer justification for a democratic system of government than a utilitarian theory? Does the fact that we accept benefits from the state place us under an obligation to obey its laws?

6. Why does Ewing think the totalitarian or "recognition" theory of rights commits an error opposite to that of the contract theory?
7. Is a legal right the same thing as a moral right?
8. Should we recognize a distinction between an "act-utilitarian" and a "rule-utilitarian" theory of rights? If so, what do you think the difference would be? Which kind is Ewing describing? What is the danger of this kind of view?
9. What theory of rights is the complement of Ross's view of prima facie obligations (pp. 220-28)? Why does Ewing think a person who takes the latter view about obligation must take the former view of rights?
10. How far does this last view go toward the "absolute rights" theory? How far is it similar to utilitarianism of the two different types?

CHAPTER 5   SUGGESTIONS FOR FURTHER READING

Benn, S. I., and R. S. Peters. *Social Principles and the Democratic State*. London: Allen & Unwin, 1959, Ch. 4.

Blake, Ralph M. "On Natural Rights." *Ethics*, Vol. 36 (1925), pp. 89-96. A utilitarian view.

Brandt, Richard B. *Ethical Theory*. Englewood Cliffs, N. J.: Prentice-Hall, 1959, Ch. 17.

Carritt, E. F. *Ethical and Political Thinking*. New York: Oxford Univ. Press, 1947, Chs. 6 and 15.

Green, T. H. *Lectures on the Principles of Political Obligation*. New York: Longmans, Green, 1959, pp. 142-59.

Hart, H. L. A. "Are There Any Natural Rights?"; S. M. Brown, Jr. "Inalienable Rights." *Philosophical Review*, Vol. 64 (1955), pp. 175-232.

Hobbes, Thomas. *Leviathan*. Ed. by M. Oakeshott. Oxford: Blackwell (n.d.), Chs. 13-15, 17-19.

Maritain, Jacques. *Man and the State*. Chicago: Univ. of Chicago Press, 1951, Ch. 4. A natural law theory.

Melden, A. I., and W. K. Frankena. "Human Rights" (symposium). *American Philosophical Association, Eastern Division, Proceedings*, Vol. 1 (1952), pp. 167-207. Discussion of a noncognitivist view defended by Melden.

6

THE MORALITY
OF INSTITUTIONS

It would scarcely be possible to read most of the foregoing selections in this book without forming some conclusions about how to go about determining a rational or defensible answer to an ethical question. Perhaps you have found yourself a convert to some form of naturalism, or else you are convinced by some form of egoism or utilitarianism or natural-law theory. If so, you have committed yourself to a definite program for resolving ethical issues; you still have some balancing of values to do, but for the most part your theory tells you what the correct answer to any ethical question is, once you have the facts of the case in hand. You may not, however, have been persuaded by a type of theory with built-in substantive moral principles. Even so, presumably by this time you will have formed some ideas about how in general to go about resolving a moral issue. This is true even if you have decided that moral issues don't have answers in anything like the sense in which scientific questions have answers; in this case you will at least have come to the conclusion that all one need do, in order to have as reliable an answer to a moral question as possible, is to take a good look at the facts and see how one feels about them. With this preparation, then, it would seem that we are ready to look at some of the more important perennial moral issues: about the structure of the major institutions.

In the present chapter, then, we shall present readings on the questions of what is a fair distribution of economic goods, whether private ownership of property is justified, what form the family structure should have and whether it is permissible to own slaves, the moral merits of a representative government, and whether roughly our present system of criminal justice is defensible. In addition, the discussions of these matters will be preceded by a more general reading on the question of what conditions must be satisfied by any institution if it is to qualify as being just.

There are, of course, many other features of the structure of our society and culture which could be examined in this way: the system of education, corporations and labor unions and the practices of both, the church, tax laws, laws regulating marriage and divorce, social security arrangements and the care of the aged. Obviously it is possible to deal here only with a few.

It may not be clear that institutions are matters for ethical judgment at all. Many people are apt to say that economic institutions are the business of economists or business experts, not of moral philosophers and are not an object for moral judgment generally. Moral questions concerning them, it may be said, are out of place. It will be helpful to look into this matter.

In the first place, there seem to be two different questions which arise in connection with institutions. One question is whether the rules of a given institution can be justified, at least in the exact form they actually take. Quite another question is whether the existence of the institution affects moral obligations, and if so, how. For instance, we may ask whether the capitalist economic system is justifiable; or we may ask whether, in a capitalist country, one is morally bound not to appropriate property recognized as belonging to other persons. Or again, it is one thing whether a penal code providing capital punishment is defensible; it is another question whether a judge who has been elected and has sworn an oath of office in a country where such a penal code prevails, is morally bound to conduct proceedings in the spirit of this code without providing escapes for persons who might receive a capital sentence and in general to follow recognized practices for the conduct of judges. We might call the former type of question a question *about* the institution, and the latter type of question, a moral question which arises *within* the institution. Hardly anyone will doubt that moral questions of the latter sort do arise and are real questions; our concern, however, is with the former type.

What makes people hesitant to admit that there is any such thing as a moral question at all about at least some of the institutions I have mentioned? Primarily, I think, the assumption that somehow they are given in the nature of things, that there is no conceivable, or at any rate no remotely tolerable, alternative. It is true that, if you assume that monogamous marriage, the family, and the capitalist system always have been and are incapable of alteration, then at least there is *no point* in raising moral questions about them. But, as soon as we think about it, we can see that this assumption is just incorrect. Of course, one *can* have a noncapitalist economic system; one *can* abolish private ownership at least of the means of production; one *can* abolish marriage and the family, having community of wives and children (to some extent, Plato advocated precisely this arrangement). So there clearly *is* point in raising questions about them. Perhaps you will say there is still no point in raising the question because it is already so clear what the right answer is. But all the same, it is worthwhile raising such questions in order at least to be clear *why* the right answer is the right one.

There is a more vexing question that may be raised by one who doubts whether questions about institutions are really *moral* questions. "It is true," such a person may say, "that we can and should make comparative evaluations of different forms of institutions. We should consider whether monogamous marriage, with the present arrangements about the rights and responsibilities of parents with respect to the children, is the best system possible. But there is not a *moral* issue here, in the sense of an issue about what is right or wrong or obligatory to do. It is only a question of the comparative efficiency of means, of evaluation of some institutional framework as better or worse in the sense of more, or less, efficient at producing good results. Institutions raise questions of more and less desirable or good, but not questions of right and wrong and obligation. So they raise ethical questions in the broad sense, but not what we might call moral questions in the narrow sense."

This proposal seems mistaken. We have only to phrase some issues in order to see that it is. Is it not a moral question — a question of right and wrong and of our obligation as citizens in a position to take action — whether there is gross injustice in the economic system? whether a person is denied that amount of private property essential to his full development as a person? whether there are slaves, men treated wholly as the property of another? whether the marriage system is fundamentally frustrating in some cases, for instance in a society where no divorce is possible? whether the government is not accountable to its citizens in any way nor its policies capable of repudiation by a secret ballot? Why institutions raise moral questions, even in the narrow sense, is not difficult to fathom. The reason is that, at least in most cases, institutions touch on *human rights*: they bear in an important way, not just trivially, on human welfare and on matters of justice. Now, when human rights are violated, a moral question in the narrow sense is clearly raised, for it seems that all of us (this is what is meant by saying there is a "right") have at least some obligation to do what we can, according to our opportunities and capacities, to remedy the situation. The structure of human institutions touches on human rights, then; and for that reason it clearly raises moral questions.

There are "moral" questions about institutions in both the broad, ethical sense and in the narrower, moral sense, which it is worth one's while examining for the sake of a clearer view of one's obligations, of what one should support.

An examination of these issues is not of merely practical importance. It is relevant to theory. For attention to such issues is necessary for filling out, or at least for testing, the principles of our normative ethics. To some extent the same thing is true for our metaethics.

It may not be obvious how examining these questions can function to fill out or test our normative ethical theory. In order to make this relation clear, let us consider a special case. Suppose, for instance, you agree with W. D. Ross that there are many different prima facie obligations, about which you can know by intuition or rational insight. Your general agreement with Ross, however, does not carry with it any automatic identification of exactly what the prima facie obligations are. These you must discover, if your theory is to take on body, is not to be merely an abstract form. How can you give it body? How will you go about deciding what are at least some of the fundamental prima facie obligations? One way of deciding, and perhaps the only promising way, is to look at discussions of the morality of institutions and see what principles have historically been claimed relevant for morality. You can then examine these principles and consider "intuitively" whether their implications for concrete problems are plausible; then you may try out a modified set of principles and consider the plausibility of their implications. In the end you may arrive at a set of principles, with an implied solution for concrete institutional problems, which "intuitively" seems satisfactory. The scrutiny of the implications of proposed, abstract principles for concrete, institutional problems will have made clear, as nothing else does, whether you can live with the principles and what they commit you to.

It is true that the convinced utilitarian, or at least the convinced hedonistic utilitarian, will have much less use for this sort of an ethical examination of institutions. He has already decided what the basic ethical principles are and has no need of finding out what they are. But in his case an examination of institutions can have the function of putting his theory to the test, favorable or unfavorable. For it could well be that, on reflection, the implications of his theory for institutions might be so grossly discrepant with the judgments of thoughtful people that the utilitarian would be led to doubt his theory as a whole. Seeing the implications for such concrete contexts, then, can serve as a kind of confirming or disconfirming check.

The selections which follow represent various points of view: both different types of normative theory and different metaethical views. They therefore provide some idea how intelligent adherents of different, general ethical theories go about attacking, or applying their general theories to, more concrete problems. It may be well to review in advance where the authors of these selections stand on the more abstract issues we have discussed.

Two of the following selections represent a broadly utilitarian normative theory: Mill's evaluation of the institution of representative government and Michael and Wechsler's assessment of criminal justice. Kant appears on behalf of his own conceptual framework in his pages on criminal law. The natural-law theory has representation of a sort — which St. Thomas might well disavow — in Aristotle's discussion of slavery and the family. Butler's view that there are intuitively known moral principles binding without exception is at least very close to the view Locke is urging in his chapter on property (although we should be most cautious in making statements about Locke's general ethical views). Ross's conception that there are several different nonutilitarian prima facie obligations is represented by Raphael's argument that there is a prima facie right to equality of welfare, or a prima facie duty to bring about equality of welfare.

The readings are less illuminating as examples of metaethical theories, and perhaps this is as it should be, since the issues under consideration are normative ones. Locke at some points sounds rather like a supernaturalist, but we cannot safely classify him so. It is most reasonable, everything considered, to count Mill as a noncognitivist, but his chapter hardly illustrates this theory in a simple and straightforward way. Michael and Wechsler are naturalists; and of course Aristotle is a naturalist, if not a self-conscious one. Kant and Raphael are best assigned to the nonnaturalist or intuitionist camp, or at least regarded as strong sympathizers. Rawls's metaethical views are too complex for summary here.*

It is not suggested that all the normative conclusions of these writers are defensible. Since they sometimes contradict one another, it is impossible for all to be correct. And it is possible to find serious flaws: few people today will wish to underwrite Aristotle's defence of slavery or to make as strong claims for property rights as Locke was prepared to make. A point of interest in some of the discussions is whether or not, in view of the contrast with opinions of thoughtful persons today, what is said provides some evidence favoring the thesis of ethical relativism.

Since some of the selections are primarily attacks on the utilitarian view, it may be helpful to restate what the utilitarian is committed to in the matter of assessing institutions. The utilitarian view is that an institution, as a system of rules, is right or justified if, and only if, its rules work out in such a way as to maximize utility. The utilitarian recognizes no fundamental principle such as that a man has a right to the fruits of his own labor, or that a man should be punished if and only if he has trampled on the rights of others in a way prohibited by law, or that a man who has offended against others should be punished to a degree roughly corresponding with the magnitude of his offense, or that people have a right to equality of welfare. It is true that a utilitarian thinks that people should be treated equally when there is *no* utilitarian reason for treating them unequally; but on this theory a departure from equality, however great — as in a slave system — is justified if it does the best for human welfare in the long run. The utilitarian, of course, is very much alive to the values of a system in which no one has favored status: the values of the absence of snobbery and of the absence of the frustration which comes from a sense of unmerited inequality. But, on his view, if any of the above principles is a valid principle at all, it is a derivative one: it is true because, in the total circumstances, action in accordance with it will yield most welfare.

---

* See his "Outline of a Decision Procedure for Ethics," *Philosophical Review*, Vol. 60 (1951), pp. 177-97.

John Rawls (1921-)

THE JUSTICE OF INSTITUTIONS

About institutions one may ask two very general questions: In what circumstances does an institution qualify as morally acceptable, everything considered? and In what circumstances does an institution qualify as being *just?* It is useful to raise this second question, since it accents the fact that *every* institution potentially poses questions of justice — not only the systems of criminal and civil justice, but other institutions such as economic and political institutions, the organization of family life with its distribution of rights and duties, the system of education with its privileges.

Everyone agrees that the above two questions are distinct, that they are not the same in meaning. All the same, it is possible to doubt whether the difference between them is of much importance: partly because we hesitate to say a system is unjust if in the end it is morally acceptable, everything considered; and partly because the meanings of "just" and "unjust" are very elusive. Utilitarians, in particular, are apt to discount the import of the difference between the questions, while admitting there is a difference. For, according to them, the utility of a system of institutions is sufficient to make them both morally acceptable and just. According to J. S. Mill, for example, an act or institution is unjust if, and only if, it deprives someone of something, the having of which by everyone is so important for the collective welfare that possession of the something ought to be guaranteed to everyone by law, or at least by the moral code. An institution is just, then, if it does not deprive people of things which it is important for the collective welfare that they have. Justice and moral acceptability alike, then, belong to an institution which serves the public welfare best.

Nonutilitarians, however, may find the difference between the above two questions of more importance. In the first place, they think the utility of an act or institution is not the sole thing relevant to whether it is morally acceptable or right. There are other requirements the satisfaction of which by an act or institution may advance its claim to be morally acceptable or right — or even to be absolutely necessary conditions of being morally acceptable or right. Some of these requirements may naturally be identified as "requirements of justice." We might even see, on reflection, that what we *mean* by claiming that something is just is that it meets such "requirements of justice"— and that whether it meets these is a matter quite different from that of whether the act or institution is expedient and whether it is morally acceptable or right, everything considered. Both John Rawls and D. D. Raphael (in the reading which follows Rawls's) adopt this point of view. (Their point about nonutilitarian requirements for moral acceptability would still be important even if we are doubtful whether satisfaction of their nonutilitarian requirements is exactly what we *mean* by saying something is "just.")

In the following paper, Rawls affirms that the justice of an institution is one thing; its expediency and even its moral acceptability, everything considered, is another. That an institution makes for the general welfare, he holds, by no means secures that it is just. Then what requirement must an institution satisfy in order to be just? Rawls's answer to this question is very clear; he formulates two "principles of justice." Moreover, he does not concede that the authority of these principles is in any way derivative from utilitarian considerations; on the contrary, he suggests a sophisticated type of contract theory as an explanation of their authority.

John Rawls, "Justice as Fairness," *Philosophical Review*, Vol. 67 (1958), pp. 164-94. Reprinted by permission of the author and of the editors of *The Philosophical Review*.

JUSTICE AS FAIRNESS

1. . . . In this paper I wish to show that the fundamental idea in the concept of justice is fairness; and I wish to offer an analysis of the concept of justice from this point of view. To bring out the force of this claim, and the analysis based upon it, I shall then argue that it is this aspect of justice for which utilitarianism, in its classical form, is unable to account, but which is expressed, even if misleadingly, by the idea of the social contract.

To start with I shall develop a particular conception of justice by stating and commenting upon two principles which specify it, and by considering the circumstances and conditions under which they may be thought to arise. . . .

Throughout I consider justice only as a virtue of social institutions, or what I shall call practices. The principles of justice are regarded as formulating restrictions as to how practices may define positions and offices, and assign thereto powers and liabilities, rights and duties. Justice as a virtue of particular actions or of persons I do not take up at all. It is important to distinguish these various subjects of justice, since the meaning of the concept varies according to whether it is applied to practices, particular actions, or persons. These meanings are, indeed, connected, but they are not identical. I shall confine my discussion to the sense of justice as applied to practices, since this sense is the basic one. Once it is understood, the other senses should go quite easily.

Justice is to be understood in its customary sense as representing but *one* of the many virtues of social institutions, for these may be antiquated, inefficient, degrading, or any number of other things, without being unjust. Justice is not to be confused with an all-inclusive vision of a good society; it is only one part of any such conception. It is important, for example, to distinguish that sense of equality which is an aspect of the concept of justice from that sense of equality which belongs to a more comprehensive social ideal. There may well be inequalities which one concedes are just, or at least not unjust, but which, nevertheless, one wishes, on other grounds, to do away with. I shall focus attention, then, on the usual sense of justice in which it is essentially the elimination of arbitrary distinctions and the establishment, within the structure of a practice, of a proper balance between competing claims. . . .

2. The conception of justice which I want to develop may be stated in the form of two principles as follows: first, each person participating in a practice, or affected by it, has an equal right to the most extensive liberty compatible with a like liberty for all; and second, inequalities are arbitrary unless it is reasonable to expect that they will work out for everyone's advantage, and provided the positions and offices to which they attach, or from which they may be gained, are open to all. These principles express justice as a complex of three ideas: liberty, equality, and reward for services contributing to the common good.

The term "person" is to be construed variously depending on the circumstances. On some occasions it will mean human individuals, but in others it may refer to nations, provinces, business firms, churches, teams, and so on. The principles of justice apply in all these instances, although there is a certain logical priority to the case of human individuals. As I shall use the term "person," it will be ambiguous in the manner indicated.

The first principle holds, of course, only if other things are equal: that is, while there must always be a justification for departing from the initial position of equal liberty (which is defined by the pattern of rights and duties, powers and liabilities, established by a practice), and the burden of proof is placed on him who would depart from it, nevertheless, there can be, and often there is, a justification for doing so. Now, that similar particular cases, as defined by a practice, should be treated similarly as they arise, is part of the very concept of a practice; it is involved in the notion of an activity in accordance with rules. The first principle expresses an analogous conception, but as applied to the structure of practices themselves. It holds, for example, that there is a presumption against the distinctions and classifications made by legal systems and other practices to the extent that they infringe on the original and equal liberty of the persons participating in them. The second principle defines how this presumption may be rebutted.

It might be argued at this point that justice requires only an equal liberty. If, however, a greater liberty were possible for all without loss or conflict, then it would be irrational to settle on a lesser liberty. There is no reason for circumscribing rights unless their exercise would be incompatible, or would render the practice defining them less effective. Therefore no serious distortion of the concept of justice is likely to follow from including within it the concept of the greatest equal liberty.

The second principle defines what sorts of inequalities are permissible; it specifies how the presumption laid down by the first principle may be put aside. Now by inequalities it is best to understand not *any* differences between offices and positions, but differences in the benefits and burdens attached to them either directly or indirectly, such as prestige and wealth, or liability to taxation and compulsory services. Players in a game do not protest against there being different positions, such as batter, pitcher, catcher, and the like, nor to there being various privileges and powers as specified by the rules; nor do the citizens of a country object to there being the different offices of government such as president, senator, governor, judge, and so on, each with their special rights and duties. It is not differences of this kind that are normally thought of as inequalities, but differences in the resulting distribution established by a practice, or made possible by it, of the things men strive to attain or avoid. Thus they may complain about the pattern of honors and rewards set up by a practice (e.g., the privileges and salaries of government officials) or they may object to the distribution of power and wealth which results from the various ways in which men avail themselves of the opportunities allowed by it (e.g., the concentration of wealth which may develop in a free price system allowing large entrepreneurial or speculative gains).

It should be noted that the second principle holds that an inequality is allowed only if there is reason to believe that the practice with the inequality, or resulting in it, will work for the advantage of *every* party engaging in it. Here it is important to stress that *every* party must gain from the inequality. Since the principle applies to practices, it implies that the representative man in every office or position defined by a practice, when he views it as a going concern, must find it reasonable to prefer his condition and prospects with the inequality to what they would be under the practice without it. The principle excludes, therefore, the justification of inequalities on the grounds that the disadvantages of those in one position are outweighed by the greater advantages of those in another position. This rather simple restriction is the main modification I wish to make in the utilitarian principle as usually understood. When coupled with the notion of a practice, it is a restriction of consequence, and one which some utilitarians, e.g., Hume and Mill, have used in their discussions of justice without realizing apparently its significance, or at least without calling attention to it. Why it is a significant modification of principle, changing one's conception of justice entirely, the whole of my argument will show.

Further, it is also necessary that the various offices to which special benefits or burdens attach are open to all. It may be, for example, to the common advantage, as just defined, to attach special benefits to certain offices. Perhaps by doing so the requisite talent can be attracted to them and encouraged to give its best efforts. But any offices having special benefits must be won in a fair competition in which contestants are judged on their merits. If some offices were not open, those excluded would normally be justified in feeling unjustly treated, even if they benefited from the greater efforts of those who were allowed to compete for them. Now if one can assume that offices are open, it is necessary only to consider the design of practices themselves and how they jointly, as a system, work together. It will be a mistake to focus attention on the varying relative positions of particular persons, who may be known to us by their proper names, and to require that each such change, as a once for all transaction viewed in isolation, must be in itself just. It is the system of practices which is to be judged, and judged from a general point of view: unless one is prepared to criticize it from the standpoint of a representative man holding some particular office, one has no complaint against it.

3. Given these principles one might try to derive them from a priori principles of reason, or claim that they were known by intuition. These are familiar enough steps and, at least in the case of the first principle, might be made with some success. Usually, however, such arguments, made at this point, are unconvincing. They are not likely to lead to an understanding of the basis of the principles of justice, not at least as principles of justice. I wish, therefore, to look at the principles in a different way.

Imagine a society of persons amongst whom a certain system of practices is *already* well established. Now suppose that by and large they are mutually self-interested; their allegiance to their established practices is normally founded on the prospect of self-advantage. One need not assume that, in all senses of the term "person," the persons in this society are mutually self-interested. If the characterization as mutually self-interested applies when the line of division is the family, it may still be true that members of families are bound by ties of sentiment and affection and willingly acknowledge duties in contradiction to self-interest. Mutual self-interestedness in the relations between families, nations, churches, and the like, is commonly associated with intense loyalty and devotion on the part of individual members. Therefore, one can form a more realistic conception of this society if one thinks of it as consisting of mutually self-interested families, or some other association. Further, it is not necessary to suppose that these persons are mutually self-interested under all circumstances, but only in the usual situations in which they participate in their common practices.

Now suppose also that these persons are rational: they know their own interests more or less accurately; they are capable of tracing out the likely consequences of adopting one practice rather than another; they are capable of adhering to a course of action once they have decided upon it; they can resist present temptations and the enticements of immediate gain; and the bare knowledge or perception of the difference between their condition and that of others is not, within certain limits and in itself, a source of great dissatisfaction. Only the last point adds anything to the usual definition of rationality. This definition should allow, I think, for the idea that a rational man would not be greatly downcast from knowing, or seeing, that others are in a better position than himself, unless he thought their being so was the result of injustice, or the consequence of letting chance work itself out for no useful common purpose, and so on. So if these persons strike us as unpleasantly egoistic, they are at least free in some degree from the fault of envy.

Finally, assume that these persons have roughly similar needs and interests, or needs and interests in various ways complementary, so that fruitful cooperation amongst them is possible; and suppose that they are sufficiently equal in power and ability to guarantee that in normal circumstances none is able to dominate the others. This condition (as well as the others) may seem excessively vague; but in view of the conception of justice to which the argument leads, there seems no reason for making it more exact here.

Since these persons are conceived as engaging in their common practices, which are already established, there is no question of our supposing them to come together to deliberate as to how they will set these practices up for the first time. Yet we can imagine that from time to time they discuss with one another whether any of them has a legitimate complaint against their established institutions. Such discussions are perfectly natural in any normal society. Now suppose that they have settled on doing this in the following way. They first try to arrive at the principles by which complaints, and so practices themselves, are to be judged. Their procedure for this is to let each person propose the principles upon which he wishes his complaints to be tried with the understanding that, if acknowledged, the complaints of others will be similarly tried, and that no complaints will be heard at all until everyone is roughly of one mind as to how complaints are to be judged. They each understand further that the principles proposed and acknowledged on this occasion are binding on future occasions. Thus each will be wary of proposing a principle which would give him a peculiar advantage, in his present circumstances, supposing it to be accepted. Each person knows that he will be bound by it in future circumstances the peculiarities of which cannot be known, and which might well be such that the principle is then to his disadvantage. The idea is that everyone should be required to make *in advance* a firm commitment, which others also may reasonably be expected to make, and that no one be given the opportunity to tailor the canons of a legitimate complaint to fit his own special condition, and then to discard them when they no longer suit his purpose. Hence each person will propose principles of a general kind which will, to a large degree, gain their sense from the various applications to be made of them, the particular circumstances of which being as yet unknown. These principles will express the conditions in accordance with which each is the least unwilling to have his interests limited in the design of practices, given the competing interests of the others, on the supposition that the interests of others will be limited likewise. The restrictions which would so arise might be thought of as those a person would keep in mind if he were designing a practice in which his enemy were to assign him his place.

The two main parts of this conjectural account have a definite significance. The character and respective situations of the parties reflect the typical circumstances in which questions of justice arise. The procedure whereby principles are proposed and acknowledged represents constraints, analogous to those of having a morality, whereby rational and mutually self-interested persons are brought to act reasonably. Thus the first part reflects the fact that questions of justice arise when conflicting claims are made upon the design of a practice and where it is taken for granted that each person will insist, as far as possible, on what he considers his rights. It is typical of cases of justice to involve persons who are pressing on one another their claims, between which a fair balance or equilibrium must be found. On the other hand, as expressed by the second part, having a morality must at least imply the acknowledgment of principles as impartially applying to one's own conduct as well as to another's, and moreover principles which may constitute a constraint, or limitation, upon the pursuit of one's own interests. There are, of course, other aspects of having a morality: the acknowledgment of moral principles must show itself in accepting a reference to them as reasons for limiting one's claims, in acknowledging the burden of providing a special explanation, or excuse, when one acts contrary to them, or else in showing shame and remorse and a desire to make amends, and so on. It is sufficient to remark here that having a morality is analogous to having made a firm commitment in advance; for one must acknowledge the principles of morality even when to one's disadvantage. A man whose moral judgments always coincided with his interests could be suspected of having no morality at all.

Thus the two parts of the foregoing account are intended to mirror the kinds of circumstances in which questions of justice arise and the constraints which having a morality would impose upon persons so situated. In this way one can see how the acceptance of the principles of justice might come about, for given all these conditions as described, it would be natural if the two principles of justice were to be acknowledged. Since there is no way for anyone to win special advantages for himself, each might consider it reasonable to acknowledge equality as an initial principle. There is, however, no reason why they should regard this position as final; for if there are inequalities which satisfy the second principle, the immediate gain which equality would allow can be considered as intelligently invested in view of its future return. If, as is quite likely, these inequalities work as incentives to draw out better efforts, the members of this society may look upon them as concessions to human nature: they, like us, may think that people ideally should want to serve one another. But as they are mutually self-interested, their acceptance of these inequalities is merely the acceptance of the relations in which they actually stand, and a recognition of the motives which lead them to engage in their common practices. *They* have no title to complain of one another. And so provided that the conditions of the principle are met, there is no reason why they should not allow such inequalities. Indeed, it would be short-sighted of them to do so, and could result, in most cases, only from their being dejected by the bare knowledge, or perception, that others are better situated. Each person will, however, insist on an advantage to himself, and so on a common advantage, for none is willing to sacrifice anything for the others.

These remarks are not offered as a proof that persons so conceived and circumstanced would settle on the two principles, but only to show that these principles could have such a background, and so can be viewed as those principles which mutually self-interested and rational persons, when similarly situated and required to make in advance a firm commitment, could acknowledge as restrictions governing the assignment of rights and duties in their common practices, and thereby accept as limiting their rights against one another. The principles of justice may, then, be regarded as those principles which arise when the constraints of having a morality are imposed upon parties in the typical circumstances of justice. . . .

5. That the principles of justice may be regarded as arising in the manner described illustrates an important fact about them. Not only does it bring out the idea that justice is a primitive moral notion in that it arises once the concept of morality is imposed on mutually self-interested agents similarly circumstanced, but it emphasizes that, fundamental to justice, is the concept of fairness which relates to right dealing between persons who are cooperating with or competing against one another, as when one speaks of fair games, fair competition, and fair bargains. The question of fairness arises when free persons, who have no authority over one another, are engaging in a joint activity and amongst themselves settling or acknowledging the rules which define it and which determine the respective shares in its benefits and burdens. A practice will strike the parties as fair if none feels that, by participating in it, they or any of the others are taken advantage of, or forced to give in to claims which they do not regard as legitimate. This implies that each has a conception of legitimate claims which he thinks it reasonable for others as well as himself to acknowledge. If one thinks of the principles of justice as arising in the manner described,

then they do define this sort of conception. A practice is just or fair, then, when it satisfies the principles which those who participate in it could propose to one another for mutual acceptance under the afore-mentioned circumstances. Persons engaged in a just, or fair, practice can face one another openly and support their respective positions, should they appear questionable, by reference to principles which it is reasonable to expect each to accept.

It is this notion of the possibility of mutual acknowledgment of principles by free persons who have no authority over one another which makes the concept of fairness fundamental to justice. Only if such acknowledgment is possible can there be true community between persons in their common practices; otherwise their relations will appear to them as founded to some extent on force. If, in ordinary speech, fairness applies more particularly to practices in which there is a choice whether to engage or not (e.g., in games, business competition), and justice to practices in which there is no choice (e.g., in slavery), the element of necessity does not render the conception of mutual acknowledgment inapplicable, although it may make it much more urgent to change unjust than unfair institutions. For one activity in which one can always engage is that of proposing and acknowledging principles to one another supposing each to be similarly circumstanced; and to judge practices by the principles so arrived at is to apply the standard of fairness to them.

Now if the participants in a practice accept its rules as fair, and so have no complaint to lodge against it, there arises a prima facie duty (and a corresponding prima facie right) of the parties to each other to act in accordance with the practice when it falls upon them to comply. When any number of persons engage in a practice, or conduct a joint undertaking according to rules, and thus restrict their liberty, those who have submitted to these restrictions when required have the right to a similar acquiescence on the part of those who have benefited by their submission. These conditions will obtain if a practice is correctly acknowledged to be fair, for in this case all who participate in it will benefit from it. The rights and duties so arising are special rights and duties in that they depend on previous actions voluntarily undertaken, in this case on the parties having engaged in a common practice and knowingly accepted its benefits. It is not, however, an obligation which presupposes a deliberate performative act in the sense of a promise, or contract, and the like. An unfortunate mistake of proponents of the idea of the social contract was to suppose that political obligation does require some such act, or at least to use language which suggests it. It is sufficient that one has knowingly participated in and accepted the benefits of a practice acknowledged to be fair. This prima facie obligation may, of course, be overridden: it may happen, when it comes one's turn to follow a rule, that other considerations will justify not doing so. But one cannot, in general, be released from this obligation by denying the justice of the practice only when it falls on one to obey. If a person rejects a practice, he should, so far as possible, declare his intention in advance, and avoid participating in it or enjoying its benefits.

This duty I have called that of fair play, but it should be admitted that to refer to it in this way is, perhaps, to extend the ordinary notion of fairness. Usually acting unfairly is not so much the breaking of any particular rule, even if the infraction is difficult to detect (cheating), but taking advantage of loop-holes or ambiguities in rules, availing oneself of unexpected or special circumstances which make it impossible to enforce them, insisting that rules be enforced to one's advantage when they should be suspended, and more generally, acting contrary to the intention of a practice. It is for this reason that one speaks of the sense of fair play: acting fairly requires more than simply being able to follow rules; what is fair must often be felt, or perceived, one wants to say. It is not, however, an unnatural extension of the duty of fair play to have it include the obligation which participants who have knowingly accepted the benefits of their common practice owe to each other to act in accordance with it when their performance falls due; for it is usually considered unfair if someone accepts the benefits of a practice but refuses to do his part in maintaining it. Thus one might say of the tax-dodger that he violates the duty of fair play: he accepts the benefits of government but will not do his part in releasing resources to it; and members of labor unions often say that fellow workers who refuse to join are being unfair: they refer to them as "free riders," as persons who enjoy what are the supposed benefits of unionism, higher wages, shorter hours, job security, and the like, but who refuse to share in its burdens in the form of paying dues, and so on.

The duty of fair play stands beside other prima facie duties such as fidelity and gratitude as a basic moral notion; yet it is not to be confused with them. These duties are all clearly distinct, as would be obvious from their definitions. As with any moral duty, that of fair play implies a constraint on self-interest in particular cases; on occasion it enjoins conduct which a rational egoist strictly defined would not decide upon. So while justice does not require of anyone that he sacrifice his interests in that *general position* and procedure whereby the principles of justice are proposed and acknowledged, it may happen that in particular situations, arising in the context of engaging in a practice, the duty of fair play will often cross his interests in the sense that he will be required to forego particular advantages which the peculiarities of his circumstances might permit him to take. There is, of course, nothing surprising in this. It is simply the consequence of the firm commitment which the parties may be supposed to have made, or which they would make, in the general position, together with the fact that they have participated in and accepted the benefits of a practice which they regard as fair. . . .

The acceptance of the duty of fair play by participants in a common practice is a reflection in each person of the recognition of the aspirations and interests of the others to be realized by their joint activity. Failing a special explanation, their acceptance of it is a necessary part of the criterion for their recognizing one another as persons with similar interests and capacities, as the conception of their relations in the general position supposes them to be. Otherwise they would show no recognition of one another as persons with similar capacities and interests, and indeed, in some cases perhaps hypothetical, they would not recognize one another as persons at all, but as complicated objects involved in a complicated activity. To recognize another as a person one must respond to him and act towards him in certain ways; and these ways are intimately connected with the various prima facie duties. Acknowledging these duties in *some* degree, and so having the elements of morality, is not a matter of choice, or of intuiting moral qualities, or a matter of the expression of feelings or attitudes (the three interpretations between which philosophical opinion frequently oscillates); it is simply the possession of one of the forms of conduct in which the recognition of others as persons is manifested. . . .

6. The discussion so far has been excessively abstract. While this is perhaps unavoidable, I should now like to bring out some of the features of the conception of justice as fairness by comparing it with the conception of justice in classical utilitarianism as represented by Bentham and Sidgwick, and its counterpart in welfare economics. This conception assimilates justice to benevolence and the latter in turn to the most efficient design of institutions to promote the general welfare. Justice is a kind of efficiency.

Now it is said occasionally that this form of utilitarianism puts no restrictions on what might be a just assignment of rights and duties in that there might be circumstances which, on utilitarian grounds, would justify institutions highly offensive to our ordinary sense of justice. But the classical utilitarian conception is not totally unprepared for this objection. Beginning with the notion that the general happiness can be represented by a social utility function consisting of a sum of individual utility functions with identical weights (this being the meaning of the maxim that each counts for one and no more than one), it is commonly assumed that the utility functions of individuals are similar in all essential respects. Differences between individuals are ascribed to accidents of education and upbringing, and they should not be taken into account. This assumption, coupled with that of diminishing marginal utility, results in a prima facie case for equality, e.g., of equality in the distribution of income during any given period of time, laying aside indirect effects on the future. But even if utilitarianism is interpreted as having such restrictions built into the utility function, and even if it is supposed that these restrictions have in practice much the same result as the application of the principles of justice (and appear, perhaps, to be ways of expressing these principles in the language of mathematics and psychology), the fundamental idea is very different from the conception of justice as fairness. For one thing, that the principles of justice should be accepted is interpreted as the contingent result of a higher order administrative decision. The form of this decision is regarded as being similar to that of an entrepreneur deciding how much to produce of this or that commodity in view of its marginal revenue, or to that of someone distributing goods to needy persons according to the relative urgency of their wants. The choice between practices is thought of as being made on the basis of the allocation of benefits and burdens to individuals (these being measured by the present capitalized value of their utility over the full period of the practice's existence), which results from the distribution of rights and duties established by a practice.

Moreover, the individuals receiving these benefits are not conceived as being related in any way: they represent so many different directions in which limited resources may be allocated. The value of assigning resources to one direction rather than another depends solely on the preferences and interests of individuals as individuals. The satisfaction of desire has its value irrespective of the moral relations between persons, say as members of a joint undertaking, and of the claims which, in the name of these interests, they are prepared to make on one another; and it is this value which is to be taken into account by the (ideal) legislator who is conceived as adjusting the rules of the system from the center so as to maximize the value of the social utility function.

It is thought that the principles of justice will not be violated by a legal system so conceived provided these executive decisions are correctly made. In this fact the principles of justice are said to have their derivation and explanation; they simply express the most important general features of social institutions in which the administrative problem is solved in the best way. These principles have, indeed, a special urgency because, given the facts of human nature, so much depends on them; and this explains the peculiar quality of the moral feelings associated with justice. This assimilation of justice to a higher order executive decision, certainly a striking conception, is central to classical utilitarianism; and it also brings out its profound individualism, in one sense of this ambiguous word. It regards persons as so many *separate* directions in which benefits and burdens may be assigned; and the value of the satisfaction or dissatisfaction of desire is not thought to depend in any way on the moral relations in which individuals stand, or on the kinds of claims which they are willing, in the pursuit of their interests, to press on each other.

7. Many social decisions are, of course, of an administrative nature. Certainly this is so when it is a matter of social utility in what one may call its ordinary sense: that is, when it is a question of the efficient design of social institutions for the use of common means to achieve common ends. In this case either the benefits and burdens may be assumed to be impartially distributed, or the question of distribution is misplaced, as in the instance of maintaining public order and security or national defense. But as an interpretation of the basis of the principles of justice, classical utilitarianism is mistaken. It *permits* one to argue, for example, that slavery

is unjust on the grounds that the advantages to the slaveholder as slave-holder do not counterbalance the disadvantages to the slave and to society at large burdened by a comparatively inefficient system of labor. Now the conception of justice as fairness, when applied to the practice of slavery with its offices of slaveholder and slave, would not allow one to consider the advantages of the slaveholder in the first place. As that office is not in accord-ance with principles which could be mutually acknowledged, the gains ac-cruing to the slaveholder, assuming them to exist, cannot be counted as in *any* way mitigating the injustice of the practice. The question whether these gains outweigh the disadvantages to the slave and to society cannot arise, since in considering the justice of slavery these gains have no weight at all which requires that they be overridden. Where the conception of justice as fairness applies, slavery is *always* unjust.

I am not, of course, suggesting the absurdity that the classical utilitarians approved of slavery. I am only rejecting a type of argument which their view allows them to use in support of their disapproval of it. The conception of justice as derivative from efficiency implies that judging the justice of a practice is always, in principle at least, a matter of weighing up advantages and disadvantages, each having an intrinsic value or disvalue as the satisfac-tion of interests, irrespective of whether or not these interests necessarily in-volve acquiescence in principles which could not be mutually acknowledged. Utilitarianism cannot account for the fact that slavery is always unjust, nor for the fact that it would be recognized as irrelevant in defeating the accusation of injustice for one person to say to another, engaged with him in a common practice and debating its merits, that nevertheless it allowed of the greatest satisfaction of desire. The charge of injustice cannot be rebutted in this way. If justice were derivative from a higher order executive efficiency, this would not be so.

But now, even if it is taken as established that, so far as the ordinary conception of justice goes, slavery is always unjust (that is, slavery by defi-nition violates commonly recognized principles of justice), the classical utilitarian would surely reply that these principles, as other moral principles subordinate to that of utility, are only generally correct. It is simply for the most part true that slavery is less efficient than other institutions; and while common sense may define the concept of justice so that slavery is unjust, nevertheless, where slavery would lead to the greatest satisfaction of desire, it is not wrong. Indeed, it is then right, and for the very same reason that justice, as ordinarily understood, is usually right. If, as ordinarily understood, slavery is always unjust, to this extent the utilitarian conception of justice might be admitted to differ from that of common moral opinion. Still the utilitarian would want to hold that, as a matter of moral principle, his view is correct in giving no special weight to considerations of justice beyond that allowed for by the general presumption of effectiveness. And this, he claims, is as it should be. The every day opinion is morally in error, although, indeed, it is a useful error, since it protects rules of generally high utility.

The question, then, relates not simply to the analysis of the concept of justice as common sense defines it, but the analysis of it in the wider sense as to how much weight considerations of justice, as defined, are to have when laid against other kinds of moral considerations. Here again I wish to argue that reasons of justice have a *special* weight for which only the conception of justice as fairness can account. Moreover, it belongs to the concept of justice that they do have this special weight. While Mill recognized that this was so, he thought that it could be accounted for by the special urgency of the moral feelings which naturally support principles of such high utility. But it is a mistake to resort to the urgency of feeling; as with the appeal to intuition, it manifests a failure to pursue the question far enough. The special weight of considerations of justice can be explained from the conception of justice as fairness. It is only necessary to elaborate a bit what has already been said as follows.

If one examines the circumstances in which a certain tolerance of slavery is justified, or perhaps better, excused, it turns out that these are of a rather special sort. Perhaps slavery exists as an inheritance from the past and it proves necessary to dismantle it piece by piece; at times slavery may conceivably be an advance on previous institutions. Now while there may be some excuse for slavery in special conditions, it is never an excuse for it that it is sufficiently advantageous to the slaveholder to outweigh the disadvantages to the slave and to society. A person who argues in this way is not perhaps making a wildly irrelevant remark; but he is guilty of a moral fallacy. There is disorder in his conception of the ranking of moral principles. For the slaveholder, by his own admission, has no moral title to the advantages which he receives as a slaveholder. He is no more prepared than the slave to acknowledge the principle upon which is founded the respective positions in which they both stand. Since slavery does not accord with principles which they could mutually acknowledge, they each may be supposed to agree that it is unjust: it grants claims which it ought not to grant and in doing so denies claims which it ought not to deny. Amongst persons in a general position who are debating the form of their common practices, it cannot, therefore, be offered as a reason for a practice that, in conceding these very claims that ought to be denied, it nevertheless meets existing interests more effectively. By their very nature the satisfaction of these claims is without weight and cannot enter into any tabulation of advantages and disadvantages.

Furthermore, it follows from the concept of morality that, to the extent that the slaveholder recognizes his position vis-a-vis the slave to be unjust, he would not choose to press his claims. His not wanting to receive his special advantages is one of the ways in which he shows that he thinks slavery is unjust. It would be fallacious for the legislator to suppose, then, that it is a ground for having a practice that it brings advantages greater than disadvantages, if those for whom the practice is designed, and to whom the advantages flow, acknowledge that they have no moral title to them and do not wish to receive them.

For these reasons the principles of justice have a special weight; and with respect to the principle of the greatest satisfaction of desire, as cited in the general position amongst those discussing the merits of their common practices, the principles of justice have an absolute weight. In this sense they are not contingent; and this is why their force is greater than can be accounted for by the general presumption (assuming that there is one) of the effectiveness, in the utilitarian sense, of practices which in fact satisfy them.

If one wants to continue using the concepts of classical utilitarianism, one will have to say, to meet this criticism, that at least the individual or social utility functions must be so defined that no value is given to the satisfaction of interests the representative claims of which violate the principles of justice. In this way it is no doubt possible to include these principles within the form of the utilitarian conception; but to do so is, of course, to change its inspiration altogether as a moral conception. For it is to incorporate within it principles which cannot be understood on the basis of a higher order executive decision aiming at the greatest satisfaction of desire. . . .

8. By way of conclusion I should like to make two remarks: first, the original modification of the utilitarian principle (that it require of practices that the offices and positions defined by them be equal unless it is reasonable to suppose that the representative man in *every* office would find the inequality to his advantage), slight as it may appear at first sight, actually has a different conception of justice standing behind it. I have tried to show how this is so by developing the concept of justice as fairness and by indicating how this notion involves the mutual acceptance, from a general position, of the principles on which a practice is founded, and how this in turn requires the exclusion from consideration of claims violating the principles of justice. Thus the slight alteration of principle reveals another family of notions, another way of looking at the concept of justice.

Second, I should like to remark also that I have been dealing with the *concept* of justice. I have tried to set out the kinds of principles upon which judgments concerning the justice of practices may be said to stand. The analysis will be successful to the degree that it expresses the principles involved in these judgments when made by competent persons upon deliberation and reflection. Now every people may be supposed to have the concept of justice, since in the life of every society there must be at least some relations in which the parties consider themselves to be circumstanced and related as the concept of justice as fairness requires. Societies will differ from one another not in having or in failing to have this notion but in the range of cases to which they apply it and in the emphasis which they give to it as compared with other moral concepts. . . .

QUESTIONS

1. State Rawls's two "principles of fairness of institutions." Show how these principles might be applied to one of our institutions — capitalism or the division of labor between the sexes, for example — to test its fairness. Is the British monarchy a fair institution by his test?
2. What is the justification for saying Rawls offers a "contract theory" of these principles? What are the differences between Rawls's conception of the "social contract" and that of Locke?
3. Do you think an institution is just if, and only if, departures from equality make *everyone* better off? Would a slave system be justified if, in the circumstances, it were necessary to make *most* people *very much* better off? Is system A just if there is known to be a system B which serves the welfare of all equally well, but in which there is more equality than in A? Is the justification of an institution with inequalities dependent on comparison with *no* institutionalized framework in the area of behavior in question or on comparison with other possible institutional frameworks?
4. What is the duty of "fair play" according to Rawls? Is this duty a "fundamental moral notion" alongside fidelity and gratitude? Is acknowledgment of it involved in acknowledging others as persons?
5. Could a utilitarian justify these same principles? Explain. Wherein does Rawls think the utilitarian theory might arrive at an evaluation of a system of slavery different from that of his contract theory? In what way does he think the utilitarian argument surreptitiously borrows from the contract conception? Is this fair?

David Daiches Raphael (1916-   )

JUSTICE REQUIRES EQUALITY

The following essay, unlike Rawls's paper, does not attempt to formulate general criteria of "just institutions." It has a narrower aim in two respects: it is concerned with only a few institutions, preeminently the economic ones; and it is concerned only with a particular issue, whether equality in some sense is required by justice.

Raphael's conclusion is a criticism of the utilitarian view of the morality of institutions. For he thinks that society has an obligation to do something, in order to secure justice for the individual, which it would not be required to do if maximizing welfare were a sufficient condition of the morality and justice of institutions. There are special requirements, or principles, of justice, which are not implied by the principle of utility. A just society will prize highly and for their own sake two things (along with others): equality of satisfactions for its members and equality of opportunity for their self-development.

The claim that there are such special requirements of justice has obvious implications for what an economic system must be like if it is to be just and moral.

D. D. Raphael teaches at the University of Glasgow. His major works are *Moral Judgment* (1955) and *The Moral Sense* (1947).

From D. D. Raphael, "Justice and Liberty," *Proceedings of the Aristotelian Society*, N.S., Vol. 51 (1950-51), pp. 167-96. Reprinted by kind permission of the author and the editor of the *Proceedings of the Aristotelian Society*.

JUSTICE AND LIBERTY

I I

The notion of justice has traditionally been divided into (*a*) distributive and (*b*) retributive or corrective justice. . . . I take distributive justice to refer to a principle of equality in some sense. The difficulty is to specify that sense. Retributive or corrective justice I take to refer to the claims of reparation and of desert. "Reparation" here is used in a wider sense than the normal, to mean both the making good of injury (the ordinary sense of "reparation") and the readiness to requite benefits that is implied in the obligation of gratitude. "Desert" refers primarily to the merit of virtue and the demerit of vice, in consequence of which the first is thought to call for reward and the second for punishment; the ideas of "merit" and "reward" (but rarely those of "demerit" and "punishment") are also extended to express the praise accorded to certain non-moral qualities and activities and to the benefits that are accordingly regarded as their due. I have distinguished reparation from desert only in order to ignore the former in what follows. For social theory, and in particular for the relation of justice to liberty, the principles of justice that are relevant are those of equality and desert.

Theorists who deny or ignore the alleged claim to equality sometimes treat the claim of desert, i.e. the apportionment of happiness or the means to it in accordance with merit (or perhaps merit and capacity), as *distributive* justice, since such apportionment is, in their view, the one proper principle of distribution. . . . Since I shall argue that there is, in the moral thinking of our society at least, a claim to equality other than the so-called "proportionate equality," I retain the name of distributive justice for the claim to equality, and I subsume the requital of desert, whether by way of reward or by way of punishment, under retributive justice. If this diversity of usage is confusing, we may speak simply of the alleged principle or claim of equality and the alleged principle or claim of desert. By a "moral claim" I mean nothing other than a moral obligation, considered as *what* is owed to the person or persons towards whom the obligation is felt. . . .

I propose to consider first, whether the concept of merit can be reduced to that of social utility; and secondly, whether there is a positive claim to equality, and if so, in what sense. I shall argue that neither desert nor equality can be wholly reduced to considerations of social utility or absolutely rejected as valid moral claims. I shall maintain that both are, to a degree, independent moral claims in modern democratic thought. . . .

I V

I turn next to the principle of equality. Many people who would agree that the principle of desert may go hand in hand with the claims of liberty would deny that liberty is compatible with equality. The first difficulty is to decide whether there is any valid principle of equality. Nobody in his senses would say that the alleged claim to equality is a claim that all men *are* equal. The first of the "truths" that are "held to be self-evident" by the American Declaration of Independence is "that all men are born equal." Similarly the French Declaration of 1789 begins "Men are born free and equal." "Rubbish," retorts the realist who cannot recognize a metaphor when he sees one, "Ivan Ivanovitch is born with poor physique, poor brains, poor parents, and as a slave of Mr. Stalin; Henry Ford junior is born with good physique, good brains, a millionaire father, and as a free citizen of the free-enterprise U.S.A." Locke and Rousseau, the Pilgrim Fathers and the French Revolutionaries, the drafters and the signatories of the U.N.O. Declaration of Human Rights, all knew perfectly well that men are not born equal in endowments, possessions, or opportunities. What they and their declarations say is that men are equal in respect of their *rights*, i.e. that in some sense men have a claim to equality, not that they *are* equal.

It may be said that a claim to equality must depend on an existing equality. If men have a claim to be considered or treated equally, this can only be because they are already equal in some respect which involves an obligation to treat them equally in action affecting them. It is often held that the claim to equality depends on religious doctrine and is an illustration of the fact that the whole of morality does. The ideals of liberty, equality, and fraternity, that have made themselves felt in western civilization since the French Revolution, owe their origin, it is claimed, to Christianity and rest on Christian doctrine. That they originated with the religious doctrine I think we may admit. Whether they can logically be derived from it is more dubious. The justification for equal treatment despite natural inequality, it is said, is the fact that, in religious doctrine, we are all the children of God and are therefore brothers. But does this metaphor help? It says that I should treat every man as I treat my brothers, i.e. as love would prompt, and wishes to persuade me that this is my duty by affirming that, morally and religiously though not biologically, all men are my brothers; moral conduct towards other men, i.e. my duty to them, is therefore the same in content as my natural conduct to my natural brothers. But does a man always love each of his brothers *equally?* Or as much as he may love one or two of his friends, or his wife, or his children? His children — there, it might be said, is the point. God loves us all as his children, and he loves us equally. For if you ask a parent which of his children he loves best, he will tell you that he loves each of them equally. This is not always true; did not Jacob love Joseph best? But even if it is true, does it follow that because a father loves his children equally, they will love each other equally? No, it will be replied, but they *should.* The doctrine of the fatherhood of God and the consequent brotherhood of man, however, was meant to tell us *why* we should love each other equally. It was intended to do this by giving us reason to regard those who are not literally our brothers as if they were. But the use of the image does not necessarily convey with it the idea of equality. Where a group of people are literally of the same family, they may think that they *ought* to act with equal love to each of their brethren, but their kinship does not necessarily cause them to do so nor does it give them a reason why they ought to do so. A man may consider both that he has an obligation to treat his brothers equally and that he has an obligation to treat all men equally, but he may still ask why in *each* of the two cases. The fact that he and his brothers have a common parent who loves them equally seems irrelevant.

The religious doctrine so far considered, then, does not give a basis for the claim to equality. But perhaps we have not seized upon the crucial element in the doctrine. It may be argued that the principle of equality rests on the fact that all men are born equal as moral agents, as having the dignity of a moral being, i.e. of the capacity to be moral, and thus they are equal in the sight of God. Other theologians, I have been told, interpret "equality in the sight of God" as equality in sin; we are all born equally steeped in original sin. Whether or not we accept the latter interpretation of "equality in the sight of God," it is of course true that all men are potential moral agents and therefore have an equal "dignity" not possessed by beings incapable of morality. But this equality is not what an enslaved or downtrodden populace refers to in claiming equality of rights. The "rights" or claims of justice are claims to *happiness* (or the opportunity to pursue happiness, or the means to happiness). Nobody would say that the equality of all men as potential moral agents involves equal claims to happiness, and it is to be hoped that the upholders of original sin do not think that all men have equal claims to misery, that they are all *equally* damned. If we are to consider the relation between our *moral* natures and our claims to happiness, it seems more reasonable to say that moral achievement, not mere potentiality, is what counts in determining "rights" or claims; the non-egalitarian principle of desert supplies the connecting link.

It is for this reason that some moralists would deny the validity of any positive claim to equality. If men are equal only in moral potentiality, and if claims to happiness are determined by moral achievement, in which men are unequal, how can we say they have equal claims? Accordingly, it may be held, the principle of desert is the sole principle of "distributive justice" and there is no claim to equal distribution apart from this. "Distributive justice," the argument would run, following Aristotle, is a distribution according to merit; unequal shares to unequals, and equal shares to equals. Equal distribution is right only when there is equal merit.

To sustain this view, we must interpret "merit" widely. . . . Inequality, whether of liberty, wealth, opportunity, or other desirable things, may be justified by differences of moral merit, of economic "merit," or of natural "merit"; a man who has wilfully committed a crime "deserves" to be imprisoned; an enterprising manufacturer "deserves" the fruits of his success; a bright child "deserves" a good education. Taking "merit" in this wide sense, it may be claimed that just distribution is always in accordance with merit.

What, then, are we to say of claims to equality? That these, when justified, are always based on equal merit? This suggestion would cover only a proportion of the relevant instances. It may be held, however, that claims to equality are usually to be interpreted negatively as justified protests against particular inequalities, justified not because there is any positive claim to equality but because the inequality is not "deserved," i.e. has an improper ground. It is unjust that Aristides be selected for ostracism; that a businessman become rich by "profiteering," that is, by making large profits in circumstances in which the general interest is harmed by his "enterprise"; that a dull-witted Vere de Vere be selected for Eton in preference to a bright Smith. The ground of the particular inequality attacked is morally "irrelevant," while an existing "relevant" ground for differentiation is ignored. The objection is not to inequality as such but to the ground of differentiation. The unequal treatment has conflicted with merit, where "merit" can mean moral worth, social utility, or natural capacity. In these respects men are of unequal "worth," and their treatment or status, it may be held, should be in accordance with their different "worths." But throughout history unequal treatment has almost always far exceeded, or cut across, the differences of "worth." Some men are of lesser "worth" than others, but none are so much less valuable than others that they should be their serfs, still less their slaves or chattels. Even where those treated as of less account have not been serfs but just a lower class, the higher class has seldom consisted of those who are more "worthy" in virtue, utility, or capacity; usually, membership of the privileged class has been based on birth or similar accidents. Accordingly, the argument might conclude, the cry for equality is really a cry against unjustified inequality; but if, *per impossibile*, human affairs could be so arranged that men were treated in accordance with their natural inequalities, all would be well. To treat them equally, however, when they are naturally unequal, is just as wrong as to exaggerate or to run directly counter to their natural inequalities.

This view of course smacks of the "aristocrat," the "superior person," and therefore in these days many of us have a prejudice against it. But it cannot be easily dismissed, and the difficulty of justifying a positive claim to equality in the face of natural inequality tempts one to think that it must be true. Further, it need not in practice lead to aristocracy, for a modern exponent of the theory may agree that if, like Plato, we try to adjust our human affairs to the degree of inequality conferred on men by nature we shall be sure to make a mess of it. The advice that the theory might offer for practice is this: "We should neither try to secure equality nor try to adjust treatment to nature. Both are impracticable. What we should do, and what successful reformers have in fact done, is to protest against and remove unjustified inequality, inequality that clearly goes against the inequalities of nature. If we stick to this task, we shall have plenty to do, and shall not be led into extravagant and impracticable paths."

As practical advice, I think this is sensible; and the view does contain a great part of the truth about equality. Where the cry for equality has reference to the claims of "worth," i.e. of moral merit, natural capacity, or social utility, it is not based on a positive belief in equality but is a negative plea against unjustified inequality. To this extent the claim to equality is negative.

But the theory, as expounded so far, omits one of the justifying grounds for unequal treatment, and this ground, paradoxical though it appears at first sight, points to a limited positive claim to equality. Unequal treatment may be justified, not only on account of the different "worths" of the recipients, but also on account of their different needs. We think it right to make special provision for those affected by special needs, through natural disability, such as mental or physical weakness, or through the slings and arrows of outrageous fortune, through sickness, unemployment, or destitute old age. Here, it would seem, we go *against* nature, and think ourselves justified in doing so. The unequal treatment meted out is in *inverse* proportion to natural inequalities. We attempt to remedy, so far as we can, the inequality of nature. Though in the mere provision of aid, monetary or other, we seem at first sight to do more for the needy person than for the normal, to make an unequal discrimination in favour of the former, the inequality of treatment is an attempt to reduce the existing inequality, to bring the needy person up to the same level of advantages as the normal. We try to make up for the natural inequality and to give the handicapped, so far as possible, equal opportunities and equal satisfactions to those possessed by the nonhandicapped.

It is, however, an exaggeration to say, without qualification, that justice here is a matter of going against nature. For in dealing with the handicaps with which some people are born, we usually cannot provide them with fully equal opportunities to those possessed by normal people. We can try, as the theory we are considering bids us, to see that their handicap is not allowed, by the social arrangements of man, to extend beyond what it naturally must be. In the past, for example, handicapped children were neglected while normal children were, for reasons of utility, given opportunity for development. We think that we ought to remedy the neglect, to give the handicapped child such opportunities for development as his natural capacities allow. We try to ensure that the inequalities of nature are not exaggerated, but we cannot remove the natural inequalities themselves.

Yet it would be a mistake to think that, because some natural handicaps cannot be removed, there is no obligation to remove those which we can. If we can cure congenital blindness, we think we have an obligation to do so. We do not think that illness should simply be left to take its natural course; sometimes "leaving it to nature" is the best way to cure illness, sometimes not, and we think we ought to take the course, natural or not, which will be most likely to effect the cure. Where a person's peculiar disadvantages are due to external causes, such as an economic slump, an earthquake, or a flood, we certainly think that we should remedy them and, if possible, prevent them.

The claim of need, then, involves a distribution not in accordance with existing differences but contrary to them. People do of course differ in their needs, so that the provision of satisfaction for them will be an unequal one. But strictly, the potential needs and desires of people, even the most fortunate, are unlimited. Although I have not the special need of an invalid for eggs, I could do with quite a lot. Although normal children do not have the special need of the handicapped child for special educational equipment and personal supervision, they could quite well do with better educational equipment and more personal supervision than they now receive. How do we determine when a need is a "special" need? Our recognition of "special" needs is a recognition that some persons, by reasons of nature or accident, fall below the normal level of satisfactions, below the level which most people enjoy and which we regard as essential for decent living. Our attempt to meet these special needs is an attempt to bring such people up to the normal level of satisfactions, or as near to it as we can. When we do more for the handicapped child or the disabled man, this is a recognition that they are at present unequal to (below) most people in capacity to earn their living and have a reasonably happy life. Our unequal (greater) provision of care for them is an attempt to reduce the existing inequality; we want, so far as we can, to bring them to a level of equality with others in capacity to enjoy their lives. Thus the basis of the claim of special need is really a recognition of a claim to equality. It is a positive moral claim taking its place with others such as the claims of moral worth, utility, and capacity. For note that this claim of need remains even if there is no other moral claim. The permanently disabled, the aged, the insane, have, we think, a claim to be taken care of, to a reasonable measure of comfort and happiness, even though they are incapable of making any return.

V

Having established that there is a positive claim to equality, let us now consider more directly its content. To what precisely do we regard people as having an equal claim? Equality of what? Of consideration, of opportunity, of material goods, or of happiness? Certainly to equality of consideration; i.e. we recognize the right of *everyone* to have his various claims considered. But this is only a way of saying that everyone *has* claims; it does not involve any additional content as the claim of distributive justice. We also recognize a claim to equality of opportunity, that is, a claim of every man to an equal chance of developing his capacities and pursuing his interests. Is there also a claim to equal distribution? That is, when material means to happiness are available, should they, in the absence of other claims, be distributed equally? The question may be put alternatively thus: have men a claim to equal happiness, or only to an equal chance of pursuing happiness?

In fact, of course, equal happiness cannot be secured. If, for instance, everyone were given the same amount of money, the different tastes of different persons, and the different costs of satisfying their tastes, would mean that the same amount of money would provide more happiness for some than for others; if I like beer and you like whisky, I should be able to say "Nunc est bibendum" more often than you. Again, some would, by luck or greater ability, soon turn their standard income into a larger one, while others would soon be paupers. However, this practical impossibility of providing equal happiness does not affect the theoretical question. For many obligations cannot in practice be fully satisfied. If, for example, it be held that we have an obligation to increase the sum of happiness or good, or to distribute happiness in accordance with merit, this is in practice often impossible. The relevant obligation is really to try to aim at or approach the proposed ideal.

Let us first see what is involved in "equality of opportunity." I think that this is bound up with the idea of liberty. The idea of liberty is, primarily, a negative one, the removal of restraints upon doing what one wishes. Such restraints may be imposed by the actions of other persons or may be due to natural obstacles. Social liberty refers to the removal of restraints by other persons. The restraints of nature may be external or internal. The Firth of Clyde prevents me from walking to Bute, and if I wish to get to Bute a ferry must be provided. But besides such external obstacles to the satisfaction of our desires, there are also internal restraints. If I want to be a champion tennis-player, I am restrained by the weakness of my sight. Of internal restraints, some can be removed, others cannot. I have not the natural endowment to become a good tennis-player, but I have the natural endowment to become a fair chess-player. Natural endowments, however, cannot always be exercised by their possessor without training and suitable environment; in the absence of these, they remain unfulfilled potentialities. My potential capacity to become a fair chess-player is subject to the natural restraint that, if left to itself without training and practice, it cannot be actualized. Suitable training and practice are the removal of the natural restraint on the exercise of natural potentialities. Two children may have the potentiality of becoming good craftsmen. If one is given the necessary training and suitable environment to enable him to develop his potentialities so as to lead a satisfying life and to be socially useful, he thereby receives opportunity to make the most of his capacities. If the other is not given such training, he is denied the opportunity to make the most of his capacities. Equal opportunity means, ideally, maximum opportunity for all to develop the potentialities they have, and failing that, the maximum that is possible in the face of, e.g. economic difficulties. The opportunity is to be equally, i.e. impartially, spread in the sense that discrimination in the provision of a particular type of opportunity for some and not for others should depend on the potentialities that the prospective recipients have, instead of depending on "irrelevant" considerations such as birth or wealth.

Social liberty . . . is the absence of restraint by other persons. The provision of opportunity, however, involves, not the absence of action by other persons, but its presence in the form of aid and training in the development of capacities. Liberal political philosophy concentrated on social liberty. But the mere absence of interference by others does not give full opportunities to all to pursue happiness in accordance with their capacities, because many capacities do not develop of themselves but need assistance. When Mill rests the claim to liberty on the value of "the development of individuality," he implies an extension of the old Liberal idea of liberty. It would be generally agreed by thoughtful people to-day that men have a moral claim not only to social liberty but also to liberty in the further sense of maximum development of potentiality. Equal liberty for all will not result in equal happiness, for men differ in their potentialities so that some will be more able than others to achieve happiness for themselves by the exercise of their developed capacities.

Let us now turn to the other suggested principle of equal satisfactions. There seems to be some claim that all should be given equal satisfactions to the extent that this is within our power, e.g. in the provision of material means to happiness. This principle would conflict with the principle of maximum opportunity for all, if the latter were taken to imply not only that a man should be enabled to develop his potentialities to the fullest extent but also that he should be allowed to use his developed capacities as he wishes for his own maximum enjoyment. The second of these two implications is required by the principle of social liberty, and the two together by a combination of the principle of maximum opportunity with the principle of social liberty. The principle of opportunity alone, however,

need not necessarily be held to conflict with the principle of equal satisfactions, for a man might be enabled to develop his capacities but required
to devote the fruits of his capacities to the common good; that is to say,
he might be expected to retain or receive, for his own enjoyment, a roughly
equal amount of material means to satisfaction as others, while any surplus
material results of his exercise of capacity were distributed to others whose
own capacities did not allow them to effect as much. This is the egalitarian
position — from each according to his capacity, to each according to his
needs. The position conflicts with the principle of maximum social liberty,
but not with the principle of maximum opportunity.

In practice, however, neither the position of extreme Liberalism nor
the position of extreme egalitarianism is acceptable in isolation. The egalitarian has to give some weight to social liberty for the sake of utility, that
is, in order to provide incentives to production so that the needs which
can be satisfied may be at a maximum. There is in fact no limit to the
desires which can be satisfied, so that distribution "to each according to
his needs" must always be below what could be done. Accordingly, certain
desires, which are thought to be more fundamental than others, are distinguished by the name of "needs," and it is thought that these should
be satisfied for all equally before further desires are satisfied for any. "Bread
for all before there is jam for some." The jam, however, is not distributed
equally. On the other hand, the Liberal position is rarely carried to the
extreme conclusion, "each for himself and devil take the hindmost." Few
adherents of the position would be content to let the weak and the aged
starve to death. Some sort of basic minimum, ranging from the paltry assistance of the Poor Law to the ambitions of the "Beveridge Programme,"
is usually admitted, and this is a concession to the principle of equal satisfactions. Justice, then, is thought to require a basic minimum of equal
satisfactions, unrelated to utility or to capacity. Above that line, room is
left for individuals to do as they think fit. The position of the line is different in different societies and at different periods of history, depending
both on economic circumstances and on the level of social morality. That
it depends on economic circumstances is obvious enough. "A chicken in
every pot" is impossible if a country cannot afford to raise or buy enough
chickens. But it depends on the level of social morality too. Tom Paine
proposed in 1797 the establishment of a national fund, from which everyone should receive £15 at the age of 21 and £10 at the age of 50 "to enable them to live without wretchedness and go decently out of the world."
The country could have afforded this very limited scheme of "social security,"
depending as it did, like the Beveridge plan, on some redistribution of existing income, but most of the people who could influence social legislation
at the time would have thought it wildly utopian. On the other hand, many
people to-day would say that the Labour Government, in sticking to all the
benefits of the Welfare State irrespective of whether the country can af-

ford them at present, is allowing its moral fervour to outrun economic necessity.

Distributive justice, we have found, makes two claims of equality, first, equality of opportunity, that is, the greatest possible degree of opportunity for all impartially; and second, the provision of material means to satisfaction for all impartially, such provision in practice being limited, for utilitarian reasons, to a standard of basic needs.

The first of these principles depends partly on utility (since the development and exercise of a good many capacities is useful for the production of means to satisfaction for society at large), and partly on valuing self-development. This means that the development of capacity is regarded as a moral claim, reinforced by the claims of utility if the capacity is especially useful to society (as, e.g., technical skill or teaching ability is and the capacity for playing chess is not), and overridden by the claim of utility if the capacity is socially harmful (e.g. the capacity for burglary; we do not think we ought to provide schools of burglary for potentially successful burglars). Since people differ in capacities, and since some men are better endowed than others with a particular capacity, this claim for the development of capacity is not one for equality (except in the sense that it is a claim of everyone) but reflects the differences of nature. We speak of "*equal* opportunity" because in the past the opportunities provided for development have not been in accordance with the inequalities of nature but have either run counter to them for the private interests of some or else exaggerated them for the sake of general interest. Where opportunity was not confined to privilege, it depended on social utility; it was extended to those whose development would benefit society to an unusual degree. Thus there is no need to invoke justice in order to approve of the provision of free higher education for the gifted children of poor parents; social utility will require it no less. But the provision of equal opportunity for the handicapped, in mind or body, can often not be justified by utility.

The second element of distributive justice ensures that there is a basic minimum for all even if some of those affected could not achieve it by their own efforts. Here we "go against nature" in the sense that we rate basic needs above the capacity to satisfy them, and of course above social utility, for keeping alive the aged and the incurably sick is not economic. We think it is due to *them* as individuals.

The two principles of equality, like the principle of retributive justice, are chiefly concerned to protect the individual irrespective of general utility. One is a claim that each person be given such opportunity for development as his natural capacity allows, even though it may not always add to social utility (but we shall do still more for socially useful capacities because of their utility). The other is a claim for the satisfaction of basic needs (i.e. those regarded as essential for tolerable living) for each individual even though there may be no economic return. We think these two things are due to individuals as such, as being "ends-in-themselves." If, with

Mill, we hold that the most important element in the idea of liberty is not the negative factor of the absence of restraint but the positive factor of valuing individuality, then the essential point of justice and that of liberty are identical.

QUESTIONS

1. Does the proposition that all men have a right to equality of some sort *follow* from the religious man's assertion of the fatherhood of God and the brotherhood of all men? Explain. Does it follow from the fact that all men are potentially moral agents?
2. To what extent can the proposition that all men have a right to equality of some sort be derived from the proposition that people should be given what they "merit" or "deserve"? What does the thesis about "merit" come to when we think of the "worth" of a person as referring either to (a) moral merit, (b) natural capacity, or (c) social utility?
3. Is there an obligation to remove natural inequalities as far as possible? Can this obligation be viewed as an obligation to give to people in accordance with their "worth"?
4. Is there an obligation to give "equality of consideration"? What is this?
5. What might it mean to say that people ought to have "equality of opportunity"? Is there an obligation on the community to secure this equality for people as far as possible?
6. Explain what may be meant by the slogan: "From each according to his capacity, to each according to his needs." Why does Raphael think this program not quite practicable?
7. What more fundamental principles does Raphael think may be adduced in support of "equality of opportunity"?
8. What does it mean to advocate "Bread for all before there is jam for some"? Could a consistent utilitarian advocate this principle? Explain.

Aristotle (384-322 B.C.)

MARRIAGE, THE FAMILY, AND SLAVERY

Chapter 1 (pp. 58-85) contains Aristotle's description of what he takes to be the good life for man, as set forth in his *Nicomachean Ethics*. In the *Politics*, to which we now turn, the interest is in the details of the institutional structure which makes the good life possible. The book concentrates on forms of government, but the following selection is concerned rather with the household or family: with marriage, the proper relation of man to wife and to children, and the position of slaves.

Aristotle's reasoning, unlike Locke's, is throughout utilitarian in a broad sense: institutions are justified by an appeal to the way they contribute to the good life and an appeal to the disadvantages of other institutional arrangements. As a result, although the contemporary reader is certain to be repelled by some of Aristotle's conclusions, especially about slavery, it is not clear that the source of the disagreement with Aristotle is as much any fundamental ethical axioms as it is his factual assumptions about human beings and the working of alternative institutions.

Part of the interest of this passage from Aristotle derives from the fact that he is a Greek defending moral rules some of which are very different from ours. He is therefore a test case for the theses of relativists and their critics.

Aristotle, *Politics*. Trans. by Benjamin Jowett. Oxford: Clarendon Press, 1885, Bks. I, II, VII.

POLITICS

BOOK I

Family, village, state; authority; the morality of slavery *

Every state is a community of some kind, and every community is established with a view to some good; for mankind always act in order to obtain that which they think good. But, if all communities aim at some good, the state or political community, which is the highest of all, and which embraces all the rest, aims, and in a greater degree than any other, at the highest good.

Now there is an erroneous opinion [1] that a statesman, king, householder, and master are the same, and that they differ, not in kind, but only in the number of their subjects. For example, the ruler over a few is called a master; over more, the manager of a household; over a still larger number, a statesman or king, as if there were no difference between a great household and a small state. The distinction which is made between the king and the statesman is as follows: When the government is personal, the ruler is a king; when, according to the principles of the political science, the citizens rule and are ruled in turn, then he is called a statesman.

But all this is a mistake; for governments differ in kind, as will be evident to any one who considers the matter according to the method which has hitherto guided us. As in other departments of science, so in politics, the compound should always be resolved into the simple elements or least parts of the whole. We must therefore look at the elements of which the state is composed, in order that we may see in what they differ

---

* The italicized headings are interpolations by the present editor. The footnotes are by the translator.

[1] Cp. Plato, *Politicus*, 258 E foll.

from one another, and whether any scientific distinction can be drawn between the different kinds of rule.

He who thus considers things in their first growth and origin, whether a state or anything else, will obtain the clearest view of them. In the first place (1) there must be a union of those who cannot exist without each other; for example, of male and female, that the race may continue; and this is a union which is formed, not of deliberate purpose, but because, in common with other animals and with plants, mankind have a natural desire to leave behind them an image of themselves. And (2) there must be a union of natural ruler and subject, that both may be preserved. For he who can foresee with his mind is by nature intended to be lord and master, and he who can work with his body is a subject, and by nature a slave; hence master and slave have the same interest. Nature, however, has distinguished between the female and the slave. For she is not niggardly, like the smith who fashions the Delphian knife for many uses; she makes each thing for a single use, and every instrument is best made when intended for one and not for many uses. But among barbarians no distinction is made between women and slaves, because there is no natural ruler among them: they are a community of slaves, male and female. Wherefore the poets say, —

It is meet that Hellenes should rule over barbarians; [2]

as if they thought that the barbarian and the slave were by nature one.

Out of these two relationships between man and woman, master and slave, the family first arises, and Hesiod is right when he says, —

First house and wife and an ox for the plough

for the ox is the poor man's slave. The family is the association established by nature for the supply of men's every-day wants, and the members of it are called by Charondas 'companions of the cupboard' [ὁμοσιπύους], and by Epimenides the Cretan, 'companions of the manger' [ὁμοκάπους]. But when several families are united, and the association aims at something more than the supply of daily needs, then comes into existence the village. And the most natural form of the village appears to be that of a colony from the family, composed of the children and grandchildren, who are said to be 'suckled with the same milk.' . . .

When several villages are united in a single community, perfect and large enough to be nearly or quite self-sufficing, the state comes into existence, originating in the bare needs of life, and continuing in existence for the sake of a good life. And therefore, if the earlier forms of society are natural, so is the state, for it is the end of them, and the [completed] nature is the end. For what each thing is when fully developed, we call its nature, whether we are speaking of a man, a horse, or a family. Besides, the final cause and end of a thing is the best, and to be self-sufficing is the end and the best.

[2] Eurip. *Iphig. in Aulid.* 1400.

Hence it is evident that the state is a creation of nature, and that man is by nature a political animal. And he who by nature and not by mere accident is without a state, is either above humanity, or below it; he is the

> Tribeless, lawless, hearthless one,

whom Homer denounces — the outcast who is a lover of war; he may be compared to an unprotected piece in the game of draughts.

Now the reason why man is more of a political animal than bees or any other gregarious animals is evident. Nature, as we often say, makes nothing in vain, and man is the only animal whom she has endowed with the gift of speech. And whereas mere sound is but an indication of pleasure or pain, and is therefore found in other animals (for their nature attains to the perception of pleasure and pain and the intimation of them to one another, and no further), the power of speech is intended to set forth the expedient and inexpedient, and likewise the just and the unjust. And it is a characteristic of man that he alone has any sense of good and evil, of just and unjust, and the association of living beings who have this sense makes a family and a state.

Thus the state is by nature clearly prior to the family and to the individual, since the whole is of necessity prior to the part; for example, if the whole body be destroyed, there will be no foot or hand, except in an equivocal sense, as we might speak of a stone hand; for when destroyed the hand will be no better. But things are defined by their working and power; and we ought not to say that they are the same when they are no longer the same, but only that they have the same name. The proof that the state is a creation of nature and prior to the individual is that the individual, when isolated, is not self-sufficing; and therefore he is like a part in relation to the whole. But he who is unable to live in society, or who has no need because he is sufficient for himself, must be either a beast or a god: he is no part of a state. A social instinct is implanted in all men by nature, and yet he who first founded the state was the greatest of benefactors. For man, when perfected, is the best of animals, but, when separated from law and justice, he is the worst of all; since armed injustice is the more dangerous, and he is equipped at birth with the arms of intelligence and with moral qualities which he may use for the worst ends. Wherefore, if he have not virtue, he is the most unholy and the most savage of animals, and the most full of lust and gluttony. But justice is the bond of men in states, and the administration of justice, which is the determination of what is just, is the principle of order in political society.

Seeing then that the state is made up of households, before speaking of the state we must speak of the management of the household. The parts of the household are the persons who compose it, and a complete household consists of slaves and freemen. Now we should begin by examining everything in its least elements; and the first and least parts of a family are master and slave, husband and wife, father and children. We have therefore to consider what each of these three relations is and ought to be: — I mean the relation of master and servant, of husband and wife, and thirdly of parent and child. . . .

Let us first speak of master and slave, looking to the needs of practical life and also seeking to attain some better theory of their relation than exists at present. For some are of opinion that the rule of a master is a science, and that the management of a household, and the mastership of slaves, and the political and royal rule, as I was saying at the outset, are all the same. Others affirm that the rule of a master over slaves is contrary to nature, and that the distinction between slave and freeman exists by law only, and not by nature; and being an interference with nature is therefore unjust.

Property is a part of the household, and therefore the art of acquiring property is a part of the art of managing the household; for no man can live well, or indeed live at all, unless he be provided with necessaries. And as in the arts which have a definite sphere the workers must have their own proper instruments for the accomplishment of their work, so it is in the management of a household. Now, instruments are of various sorts; some are living, others lifeless; in the rudder, the pilot of a ship has a lifeless, in the look-out man, a living instrument; for in the arts the servant is a kind of instrument. Thus, too, a possession is an instrument for maintaining life. And so, in the arrangement of the family, a slave is a living possession, and property a number of such instruments; and the servant is himself an instrument, which takes precedence of all other instruments. . . . Hence we see what is the nature and office of a slave; he who is by nature not his own but another's and yet a man, is by nature a slave; and he may be said to belong to another who, being a human being, is also a possession. And a possession may be defined as an instrument of action, separable from the possessor.

But is there any one thus intended by nature to be a slave, and for whom such a condition is expedient and right, or rather is not all slavery a violation of nature?

There is no difficulty in answering this question, on grounds both of reason and of fact. For that some should rule and others be ruled is a thing, not only necessary, but expedient; from the hour of their birth, some are marked out for subjection, others for rule.

. . . It is clear that the rule of the soul over the body, and of the mind and the rational element over the passionate is natural and expedient; whereas the equality of the two or the rule of the inferior is always hurtful. The same holds good of animals as well as of men; for tame animals have a better nature than wild, and all tame animals are better off when they are ruled by man; for then they are preserved. Again, the male is by nature superior, and the female inferior; and the one rules, and the other is ruled; this principle, of necessity, extends to all mankind. Where then there is such a difference as that between soul and body, or between men and animals (as in the case of those whose business is to use their body, and who can do nothing better), the lower sort are by nature slaves, and it is better for them as for all inferiors that they should be under the rule of a master. For he who can be, and therefore is another's, and he who participates in reason enough to apprehend, but not to have, reason, is a slave by nature. Whereas the lower animals cannot even apprehend reason; they obey their instincts. And indeed the use made of slaves and of tame animals is not very different; for both with their bodies minister to the needs of life. Nature would like to distinguish between the bodies of freemen and slaves, making the one strong for servile labour, the other upright, and although useless for such services, useful for political life in the arts both of war and peace. But this does not hold universally: for some slaves have the souls and others have the bodies of freemen. And doubtless if men differed from one another in the mere forms of their bodies as much as the statues of the Gods do from men, all would acknowledge that the inferior class should be slaves of the superior. And if there is a difference in the body, how much more in the soul! But the beauty of the body is seen, whereas the beauty of the soul is not seen. It is clear, then, that some men are by nature free, and others slaves, and that for these latter slavery is both expedient and right.

But that those who take the opposite view have in a certain way right on their side, may be easily seen. For the words slavery and slave are used in two senses. There is a slave or slavery by law as well as by nature. The law of which I speak is a sort of convention, according to which whatever is taken in war is supposed to belong to the victors. But this right many jurists impeach, as they would an orator who brought forward an unconstitutional measure: they detest the notion that, because one man has the power of doing violence and is superior in brute strength, another shall be his slave and subject. . . . Some, clinging, as they think, to a principle of justice (for law and custom are a sort of justice), assume that slavery in war is justified by law, but they are not consistent. For what if the cause of the war be unjust? No one would ever say that he is a slave who is unworthy to be a slave. Were this the case, men of the highest rank would be slaves and the children of slaves if they or their parents chance to have been taken captive and sold. . . .

We see then that there is some foundation for this difference of opinion, and that some actual slaves and freemen are not so by nature, and also that there is in some cases a marked distinction between the two classes, rendering it expedient and right for the one to be slaves and the others to be masters: the one practising obedience, the others exercising the authority which nature intended them to have. The abuse of this authority is injurious to both; for the interests of part and whole, of body and soul, are the same, and the slave is a part of the master, a living but separated part of his bodily frame. Where the relation between them is natural they are friends and have a common interest, but where it rests merely on law and force the reverse is true.

The previous remarks are quite enough to show that the rule of a master is not a constitutional rule, and therefore that all the different kinds of rule are not, as some affirm, the same with each other. For there is one rule exercised over subjects who are by nature free, another over subjects who are by nature slaves. The rule of a household is a monarchy, for every house is under one head: whereas constitutional rule is a government of freemen and equals. The master is not called a master because he has science, but because he is of a certain character, and the same remark applies to the slave and the freeman. Still there may be a science for the master and a science for the slave. The science of the slave would be such as the man of Syracuse taught, who made money by instructing slaves in their ordinary duties. And such a knowledge may be carried further, so as to include cookery and similar menial arts. For some duties are of the more necessary, others of the more honourable sort; as the proverb says, 'slave before slave, master before master.' But all such branches of knowledge are servile. There is likewise a science of the master, which teaches the use of slaves; for the master as such is concerned, not with the acquisition, but with the use of them. Yet this so-called science is not anything great or wonderful; for the master need only know how to order that which the slave must know how to execute. Hence those who are in a position which places them above toil, have stewards who attend to their households while they occupy themselves with philosophy or with politics. . . .

Of household management we have seen that there are three parts — one is the rule of a master over slaves, which has been discussed already, another of a father, and the third of a husband. A husband and father rules over wife and children, both free, but the rule differs, the rule over his children being a royal, over his wife a constitutional rule. For although there may be exceptions to the order of nature, the male is by nature fitter for command than the female, just as the elder and full-grown is superior to the younger and more immature. But in most constitutional states the citizens rule and are ruled by turns, for the idea of a constitutional state implies that the natures of the citizens are equal, and do not differ at all. The relation of the male to the female is of this kind, but there the inequality is permanent. The rule of a father over his children is royal, for he receives both love and the respect due to age, exercising a kind of royal power. And therefore Homer has appropriately called Zeus 'father of Gods and men,' because he is the king of them all. For a king is the natural superior of his subjects, but he should be of the same kin or kind with them, and such is the relation of elder and younger, of father and son.

Thus it is clear that household management attends more to men than to the acquisition of inanimate things, and to human excellence more than to the excellence of property which we call wealth, and to the virtue of freemen more than to the virtue of slaves. A question may indeed be raised, whether there is any excellence at all in a slave beyond merely instrumental and ministerial qualities — whether he can have the virtues of temperance, courage, justice, and the like; or whether slaves possess only bodily and ministerial qualities. And, whichever way we answer the question, a difficulty arises; for, if they have virtue, in what will they differ from freemen? On the other hand, since they are men and share in reason, it seems absurd to say that they have no virtue. A similar question may be raised about women and children, whether they too have virtues: ought a woman to be temperate and brave and just, and is a child to be called temperate, and intemperate, or not? So in general we may ask about the natural ruler, and the natural subject, whether they have the same or different virtues. For a noble nature is equally required in both, but if so, why should one of them always rule, and the other always be ruled? Nor can we say that this is a question of degree, for the difference between ruler and subject is a difference of kind, and therefore not of degree; yet how strange is the supposition that the one ought, and that the other ought not, to have virtue! For if the ruler is intemperate and unjust, how can he rule well? if the subject, how can he obey well? If he be licentious and cowardly, he will certainly not do his duty. It is evident, therefore, that both of them must have a share of virtue, but varying according to their various natures. And this is at once indicated by the soul, in which one part naturally rules, and the other is subject, and the virtue of the ruler we maintain to be different from that of the subject; — the one being the virtue of the rational, and the other of the irrational part. Now, it is obvious that the same principle applies generally, and therefore almost all things rule and are ruled according to nature. But the kind of rule differs; — the freeman rules over the slave after another manner from that in which the male rules over the female, or the man over the child; although the parts of the soul are present in all of them, they are present in different degrees. For the slave has no deliberative faculty at all; the woman has, but it is without authority, and the child has, but it is immature. So it must necessarily be with the moral virtues also; all may be supposed to partake of them, but only in such manner and degree as is required by each for the fulfilment of his duty. Hence the ruler ought to have moral virtue in perfection, for his duty is entirely that of a master artificer, and the master artificer is reason; the subjects, on the other hand, require only that measure of virtue which is proper to each of them. Clearly, then, moral virtue belongs to all of them; but the temperance of a man and of a woman, or the courage and justice of a man and of a woman, are not, as Socrates maintained, the same; the courage of a man is shown in commanding, of a woman in obeying. And this holds of all other virtues, as will be more clearly seen if we look at them in detail, for those who say generally that virtue consists in a good disposition of the soul, or in doing rightly, or the like, only deceive themselves. Far better than such definitions is their mode of speaking, who, like Georgias, enumerate the virtues. All classes must be deemed to have their special attributes; as the poet says of women,

Silence is a woman's glory,[3]

but this is not equally the glory of man. . . .

BOOK II

Should there be community of wives, children, and property?

Our purpose is to consider what form of political community is best of all for those who are most able to realize their ideal of life. We must therefore examine not only this but other constitutions, both such as actually exist in well-governed states, and any theoretical forms which are held in esteem; that what is good and useful may be brought to light. And let no one suppose that in seeking for something beyond them we at all want to philosophize at the expense of truth; we only undertake this enquiry because all the constitutions with which we are acquainted are faulty.

We will begin with the natural beginning of the subject. Three alternatives are conceivable: The members of a state must either have (1) all things or (2) nothing in common, or (3) some things in common and some not. That they should have nothing in common is clearly impossible, for the state is a community, and must at any rate have a common place — one city will be in one place, and the citizens are those who share in that one city. But should a well-ordered state have all things, as far as may be, in common, or some only and not others? For the citizens might conceivably have wives and children and property in common, as Socrates proposes in the Republic of Plato. Which is better, our present condition, or the proposed new order of society?

There are many difficulties in the community of women. The principle on which Socrates rests the necessity of such an institution does not appear to be established by his arguments; and then again as a means to the end which he ascribes to the state, taken literally, it is impossible, and how we are to limit and qualify it is nowhere precisely stated. I am speaking of the premiss from which the argument of Socrates proceeds, 'that the greater the unity of the state the better.' Is it not obvious that a state may at length attain such a degree of unity as to be no longer a state? — since the nature of a state is to be a plurality, and in tending to greater unity, from being a state, it becomes a family, and from being a family, an individual; for the family may be said to be more one than the state, and the individual than the family. So that we ought not to attain this greatest unity even if we could, for it would be the destruction of the state. . . . And there is another objection to the proposal. For that which is common to the greatest number has the least care bestowed upon it. Every one thinks chiefly of his own, hardly at all of the common interest; and only when he is himself con-

[3] Soph. Aj. 293.

cerned as an individual. For besides other considerations, everybody is more inclined to neglect the duty which he expects another to fulfil; as in families many attendants are often less useful than a few. Each citizen will have a thousand sons who will not be his sons individually, but anybody will be equally the son of anybody, and will therefore be neglected by all alike. Further, upon this principle, every one will call another 'mine' or 'not mine' according as he is prosperous or the reverse; — however small a fraction he may be of the whole number, he will say of every individual of the thousand, or whatever be the number of the city, 'such a one is mine,' 'such a one his'; and even about this he will not be positive; for it is impossible to know who chanced to have a child, or whether, if one came into existence, it has survived. But which is better — to be able to say 'mine' about every one of the two thousand or the ten thousand citizens, or to use the word 'mine' in the ordinary and more restricted sense? For usually the same person is called by one man his son whom another calls his brother or cousin or kinsman or blood-relation or connexion by marriage either of himself or of some relation of his, and these relationships he distinguishes from the tie which binds him to his tribe or ward; and how much better is it to be the real cousin of somebody than to be a son after Plato's fashion! Nor is there any way of preventing brothers and children and fathers and mothers from sometimes recognizing one another; for children are born like their parents, and they will necessarily be finding indications of their relationship to one another. Geographers declare such to be the fact; they say that in Upper Libya, where the women are common, nevertheless the children who are born are assigned to their respective fathers on the ground of their likeness. And some women, like the females of other animals — for example mares and cows — have a strong tendency to produce offspring resembling their parents, as was the case with the Pharsalian mare called Dicaea (the Just).

Other evils, against which it is not easy for the authors of such a community to guard, will be assaults and homicides, voluntary as well as involuntary, quarrels and slanders, all which are most unholy acts when committed against fathers and mothers and near relations, but not equally unholy when there is no relationship. Moreover, they are much more likely to occur if the relationship is unknown, and, when they have occurred, the customary expiations of them cannot be made. Again, how strange it is that Socrates, after having made the children common, should hinder lovers from carnal intercourse only, but should permit familiarities between father and son or between brother and brother, than which nothing can be more unseemly, since even without them, love of this sort is improper. How strange, too, to forbid intercourse for no other reason than the violence of the pleasure, as though the relationship of father and son or of brothers with one another made no difference.

This community of wives and children seems better suited to the husbandmen than to the guardians, for if they have wives and children in common, they will be bound to one another by weaker ties, as a subject class should be, and they will remain obedient and not rebel. In a word, the result of such a law would be just the opposite of that which good laws ought to have, and the intention of Socrates in making these regulations about women and children would defeat itself. For friendship we believe to be the greatest good of states and the preservative of them against revolutions; neither is there anything which Socrates so greatly lauds as the unity of the state which he and all the world declare to be created by friendship. But the unity which he commends would be like that of the lovers in the Symposium, who, as Aristophanes says, desire to grow together in the excess of their affection, and from being two to become one, in which case one or both would certainly perish. Whereas [the very opposite will really happen;] in a state having women and children common, love will be watery; and the father will certainly not say 'my son,' or the son 'my father.' As a little sweet wine mingled with a great deal of water is imperceptible in the mixture, so, in this sort of community, the idea of relationship which is based upon these names will be lost; there is no reason why the so-called father should care about the son, or the son about the father, or brothers about one another. Of the two qualities which chiefly inspire regard and affection — that a thing is your own and that you love it — neither can exist in such a state as this.

Again, the transfer of children as soon as they are born from the rank of husbandmen or of artisans to that of guardians, and from the rank of guardians into a lower rank, will be very difficult to arrange; the givers or transferrers cannot but know whom they are giving and transferring, and to whom. And the previously mentioned evils, such as assaults, unlawful loves, homicides, will happen more often amongst those who are transferred to the lower classes, or who have a place assigned to them among the guardians; for they will no longer call the members of any other class brothers, and children, and fathers, and mothers, and will not, therefore, be afraid of committing any crimes by reason of consanguinity. Touching the the community of wives and children, let this be our conclusion. . . .

Again, if Socrates makes the women common, and retains private property, the men will see to the fields, but who will see to the house? And what will happen if the agricultural class have both their property and their wives in common? Once more; it is absurd to argue, from the analogy of the animals, that men and women should follow the same pursuits; for animals have not to manage a household.

BOOK VII

Some problems about marriage and procreation

. . . Since the legislator should begin by considering how the frames of the children whom he is rearing may be as good as possible, his first care will be about marriage — at what age should his citizens marry, and who are fit to marry? In legislating on this subject he ought to consider the persons and their relative ages, that there may be no disproportion in them, and that they may not differ in their bodily powers, as will be the case if the man is still able to beget children while the woman is unable to bear them, or the woman able to bear while the man is unable to beget, for from these causes arise quarrels and differences between married persons. Secondly, he must consider the time at which the children will succeed to their parents; there ought not to be too great an interval of age, for then the parents will be too old to derive any pleasure from their affection, or to be of any use to them. Nor ought they to be too nearly of an age; to youthful marriages there are many objections — the children will be wanting in respect to their parents, who will seem to be their contemporaries, and disputes will arise in the management of the household. Thirdly, and this is the point from which we digressed, the legislator must mould to his will the frames of newly-born children. Almost all these objects may be secured by attention to one point. Since the time of generation is commonly limited within the age of seventy years in the case of a man, and of fifty in the case of a woman, the commencement of the union should conform to these periods. The union of male and female when too young is bad for the procreation of children; in all other animals the offspring of the young are small and ill-developed, and generally of the female sex, and therefore also in man, as is proved by the fact that in those cities in which men and women are accustomed to marry young, the people are small and weak; in childbirth also younger women suffer more, and more of them die; some persons say that this was the meaning of the response once given to the Troezenians — ['Shear not the young field'] — the oracle really meant that many died because they married too young; it had nothing to do with the ingathering of the harvest. It also conduces to temperance not to marry too soon; for women who marry early are apt to be wanton; and in men too the bodily frame is stunted if they marry while they are growing (for there is a time when the growth of the body ceases). Women should marry when they are about eighteen years of age, and men at seven-and-thirty; then they are in the prime of life, and the decline in the powers of both will coincide. Further, the children, if their birth takes place at the time that may reasonably be expected, will succeed in their prime, when the fathers are already in the decline of life, and have nearly reached their term of three-score years and ten. . . .

What constitution in the parent is most advantageous to the offspring is a subject which we will hereafter consider when we speak of the education of children, and we will only make a few general remarks at present. The temperament of an athlete is not suited to the life of a citizen, or to health, or to the procreation of children, any more than the valetudinarian or exhausted constitution, but one which is in a mean between them. A man's constitution should be inured to labour, but not to labour which is excessive or of one sort only, such as is practised by athletes; he should be capable of all the actions of a freeman. These remarks apply equally to both parents. . . .

As to the exposure and rearing of children, let there be a law that no deformed child shall live, but where there are too many (for in our state population has a limit), when couples have children in excess, and the state of feeling is averse to the exposure of offspring, let abortion be procured before sense and life have begun; what may or may not be lawfully done in these cases depends on the question of life and sensation.

And now, having determined at what ages men and women are to begin their union, let us also determine how long they shall continue to beget and bear offspring for the state; men who are too old, like men who are too young, produce children who are defective in body and mind; the children of very old men are weakly. The limit, then, should be the age which is the prime of their intelligence, and this in most persons, according to the notion of some poets who measure life by periods of seven years, is about fifty; at four or five years later, they should cease from having families; and from that time forward only cohabit with one another for the sake of health, or for some similar reason.

As to adultery, let it be held disgraceful for any man or woman to be unfaithful when they are married, and called husband and wife. If during the time of bearing children anything of the sort occur, let the guilty person be punished with a loss of privileges in proportion to the offence.

QUESTIONS

1. What purpose or function underlies the institution of the family, according to Aristotle?
2. In what ways, according to Aristotle, do natural differences among persons correspond to differences of status and role in the organization of households?
3. What does Aristotle mean by saying that man is a "political animal"?
4. What is Aristotle's definition of a "slave"?
5. What reasons does he offer in justification of the institution of slavery? When is slavery unjust?
6. What kind of authority does a man have over his family, in Aristotle's view?
7. Why does he think that what is a virtue in some people is not a virtue in others in different stations or roles?
8. On what grounds does Aristotle prefer traditional marriage and family institutions to Plato's proposal of community of wives?
9. What is Aristotle's view on infanticide?

John Locke (1632-1704)

PRIVATE PROPERTY

Property is an institution everywhere; that is, everywhere there are some things over which some individual is recognized as having an absolute or at least an extensive right of disposal. No community fails to recognize such a right over at least some things such as clothing or tools. But there are great variations among societies as to the kinds of objects privately owned and as to the extent to which ownership confers a right of disposal. Among the Hopi Indians, for example, ownership of real estate does not entitle one to sell or to bequeath by testament.

The question for moral philosophers is, What fundamental, acceptable moral principles are relevant to this institution and what specific form or forms of this institution are morally justified? Utilitarians answer, of course, that any particular institution of property is justified for a given community provided its rules are ones which maximize welfare and that the principle of utility is the only valid, fundamental moral principle. Some critics of utilitarianism (e.g., Raphael and Rawls), we have seen, wish to modify this view in various ways; they insist there are other relevant, basic moral principles in addition to some kind of principle of utility, and they insist that a given institution of property is morally justified only if it conforms with these principles.

John Locke (see p. 497) is not an utilitarian and does not justify the institution of private property by appeal to the principle of utility. Nor does he mention as relevant the principles cited by Raphael and Rawls. But neither does Locke think ownership rights are wholly founded on compact or contract, although to some extent compact affects one's property rights. Quite on the contrary, Locke is anxious to say that the right to ownership is prior to the compact which he concedes is the source of the authority of government — because he wishes to justify the thesis that governments have a power to levy taxes only with the consent of the citizens or their representatives and only for certain purposes. Therefore, Locke claims that man has a right to the disposal of some things in a state of nature and that already prior to the formation of civil society it is wrong for one man to deprive another of his property. Indeed, Locke says that "the great end of men's entering into society" is "the enjoyment of their properties in peace and safety." As a result, the government's right to tax derives only from a presumed delegation to it of some of the citizens' natural right to their property. Of course, since the major point (in Locke's view) of civil society is peaceful enjoyment of property, it may not be supposed that men have assigned to governments the right to take away their property at its pleasure. Locke does not explicitly rule out the right to tax for welfare projects, but the spirit of his view is that there is an absolute right to property which may not be taxed except for those expenses of government incurred for the purpose of keeping order and preventing interference with other rights. It is interesting to note that when the men who prepared the constitution of the United States drew up a list of inalienable rights, they failed to mention a right to property; to have done so would have been to invite inferences to Lockean suggestions of an absolute right independent of the claims of human welfare.

How then does Locke establish a natural right to property? The answer is that Locke finds it self-evident that the individual has a right of disposal over his own person and labor (except as limited by natural law) and hence to what he mixes with his labor. Moreover, Locke argues that the worth of any object is primarily a consequence of the labor which has been mixed with it.

The reader should consider carefully whether the ethical principles Locke finds self-evident can even be stated precisely, whether they are plausible only on the assumption of conditions (e.g., of abundant unclaimed land) in Locke's day and not today, and whether indeed they are, when taken absolutely, plausible in any circumstances.

From John Locke, *Two Treatises of Government*. First published 1690. Many editions, Ch. 5.

TWO TREATISES OF GOVERNMENT

OF PROPERTY

24. Whether we consider natural reason, which tells us that men, being once born, have a right to their preservation, and consequently to meat and drink and such other things as Nature affords for their subsistence, or "revelation," which gives us an account of those grants God made of the world to Adam, and to Noah and his sons, it is very clear that God, as King David says (Psalm cxv. 16), "has given the earth to the children of men,"

given it to mankind in common. But, this being supposed, it seems to some a very great difficulty how any one should ever come to have a property in anything. I will not content myself to answer, that, if it be difficult to make out "property" upon a supposition that God gave the world to Adam and his posterity in common, it is impossible that any man but one universal monarch should have any "property" upon a supposition that God gave the world to Adam and his heirs in succession, exclusive of all the rest of his posterity; but I shall endeavour to show how men might come to have a property in several parts of that which God gave to mankind in common, and that without any express compact of all the commoners.

25. God, who hath given the world to men in common, hath also given them reason to make use of it to the best advantage of life and convenience. The earth and all that is therein is given to men for the support and comfort of their being. And though all the fruits it naturally produces, and beasts it feeds, belong to mankind in common, as they are produced by the spontaneous hand of Nature, and nobody has originally a private dominion exclusive of the rest of mankind in any of them, as they are thus in their natural state, yet being given for the use of men, there must of necessity be a means to appropriate them some way or other before they can be of any use, or at all beneficial, to any particular men. The fruit or venison which nourishes the wild Indian, who knows no enclosure, and is still a tenant in common, must be his, and so his — i.e., a part of him, that another can no longer have any right to it before it can do him any good for the support of his life.

26. Though the earth and all inferior creatures be common to all men, yet every man has a "property" in his own "person." This nobody has any right to but himself. The "labour" of his body and the "work" of his hands, we may say, are properly his. Whatsoever, then, he removes out of the state that Nature hath provided and left it in, he hath mixed his labour with it, and joined to it something that is his own, and thereby makes it his property. It being by him removed from the common state Nature placed it in, it hath by this labour something annexed to it that excludes the common right of other men. For this "labour" being the unquestionable property of the labourer, no man but he can have a right to what that is once joined to, at least where there is enough, and as good left in common for others.

27. He that is nourished by the acorns he picked up under an oak, or the apples he gathered from the trees in the wood, has certainly appropriated them to himself. Nobody can deny but the nourishment is his. I ask, then, when did they begin to be his? when he digested? or when he ate? or when he boiled? or when he brought them home? or when he picked them up? And it is plain, if the first gathering made them not his, nothing else could. That labour put a distinction between them and common. That added something to them more than Nature, the common mother of all, had done, and so they became his private right. And will any one say he had no right to those acorns or apples he thus appropriated because he had not the con-

sent of all mankind to make them his? Was it a robbery thus to assume to himself what belonged to all in common? If such a consent as that was necessary, man had starved, notwithstanding the plenty God had given him. We see in commons, which remain so by compact, that it is the taking any part of what is common, and removing it out of the state Nature leaves it in, which begins the property, without which the common is of no use. And the taking of this or that part does not depend on the express consent of all the commoners. Thus, the grass my horse has bit, the turfs my servant has cut, and the ore I have digged in any place, where I have a right to them in common with others, become my property without the assignation or consent of anybody. The labour that was mine, removing them out of that common state they were in, hath fixed my property in them.

28. By making an explicit consent of every commoner necessary to any one's appropriating to himself any part of what is given in common, children or servants could not cut the meat which their father or master had provided for them in common without assigning to every one his peculiar part. Though the water running in the fountain be every one's, yet who can doubt but that in the pitcher is his only who drew it out? His labour hath taken it out of the hands of Nature where it was common, and belonged equally to all her children, and hath thereby appropriated it to himself.

29. Thus this law of reason makes the deer that Indian's who hath killed it; it is allowed to be his goods who hath bestowed his labour upon it, though, before, it was the common right of every one. And amongst those who are counted the civilised part of mankind, who have made and multiplied positive laws to determine property, this original law of Nature for the beginning of property, in what was before common, still takes place, and by virtue thereof, what fish any one catches in the ocean, that great and still remaining common of mankind; or what ambergris any one takes up here is by the labour that removes it out of that common state Nature left it in, made his property who takes that pains about it. And even amongst us, the hare that any one is hunting is thought his who pursues her during the chase. For being a beast that is still looked upon as common, and no man's private possession, whoever has employed so much labour about any of that kind as to find and pursue her has thereby removed her from the state of Nature wherein she was common, and hath begun a property.

30. It will, perhaps, be objected to this, that if gathering the acorns or other fruits of the earth, etc., makes a right to them, then any one may engross as much as he will. To which I answer, Not so. The same law of Nature that does by this means give us property, does also bound that property too. "God has given us all things richly." Is the voice of reason confirmed by inspiration? But how far has He given it us —"to enjoy"? As much as any one can make use of to any advantage of life before it spoils, so much he may by his labour fix a property in. Whatever is beyond this is more than his share, and belongs to others. Nothing was made by God for man to spoil or destroy. And thus considering the plenty of natural

provisions there was a long time in the world, and the few spenders, and to how small a part of that provision the industry of one man could extend itself and engross it to the prejudice of others, especially keeping within the bounds set by reason of what might serve for his use, there could be then little room for quarrels or contentions about property so established.

31. But the chief matter of property being now not the fruits of the earth and the beasts that subsist on it, but the earth itself, as that which takes in and carries with it all the rest, I think it is plain that property in that too is acquired as the former. As much land as a man tills, plants, improves, cultivates, and can use the product of, so much is his property. He by his labour does, as it were, enclose it from the common. Nor will it invalidate his right to say everybody else has an equal title to it, and therefore he cannot appropriate, he cannot enclose, without the consent of all his fellow-commoners, all mankind. God, when He gave the world in common to all mankind, commanded man also to labour, and the penury of his condition required it of him. God and his reason commanded him to subdue the earth — *i.e.*, improve it for the benefit of life and therein lay out something upon it that was his own, his labour. He that, in obedience to this command of God, subdued, tilled, and sowed any part of it, thereby annexed to it something that was his property, which another had no title to, nor could without injury take from him.

32. Nor was this appropriation of any parcel of land, by improving it, any prejudice to any other man, since there was still enough and as good left, and more than the yet unprovided could use. So that, in effect, there was never the less left for others because of his enclosure for himself. For he that leaves as much as another can make use of does as good as take nothing at all. Nobody could think himself injured by the drinking of another man, though he took a good draught, who had a whole river of the same water left him to quench his thirst. And the case of land and water, where there is enough of both, is perfectly the same.

33. God gave the world to men in common, but since He gave it them for their benefit and the greatest conveniencies of life they were capable to draw from it, it cannot be supposed He meant it should always remain common and uncultivated. He gave it to the use of the industrious and rational (and labour was to be his title to it); not to the fancy or covetousness of the quarrelsome and contentious. He that had as good left for his improvement as was already taken up needed not complain, ought not to meddle with what was already improved by another's labour; if he did it is plain he desired the benefit of another's pains, which he had no right to, and not the ground which God had given him, in common with others, to labour on, and whereof there was as good left as that already possessed, and more than he knew what to do with, or his industry could reach to.

34. It is true, in land that is common in England or any other country, where there are plenty of people under government who have money and commerce, no one can enclose or appropriate any part without the consent

of all his fellow-commoners; because this is left common by compact — *i.e.*, by the law of the land, which is not to be violated. And, though it be common in respect of some men, it is not so to all mankind, but is the joint propriety of this country, or this parish. Besides, the remainder, after such enclosure, would not be as good to the rest of the commoners as the whole was, when they could all make use of the whole; whereas in the beginning and first peopling of the great common of the world it was quite otherwise. The law man was under was rather for appropriating. God commanded, and his wants forced him to labour. That was his property, which could not be taken from him wherever he had fixed it. And hence subduing or cultivating the earth and having dominion, we see, are joined together. The one gave title to the other. So that God, by commanding to subdue, gave authority so far to appropriate. And the condition of human life, which requires labour and materials to work on, necessarily introduces private possessions.

35. The measure of property Nature well set, by the extent of men's labour and the conveniency of life. No man's labour could subdue or appropriate all, nor could his enjoyment consume more than a small part; so that it was impossible for any man, this way, to entrench upon the right of another or acquire to himself a property to the prejudice of his neighbour, who would still have room for as good and as large a possession (after the other had taken out his) as before it was appropriated. Which measure did confine every man's possession to a very moderate proportion, and such as he might appropriate to himself without injury to anybody in the first ages of the world, when men were more in danger to be lost, by wandering from their company, in the then vast wilderness of the earth than to be straitened for want of room to plant in.

36. The same measure may be allowed still, without prejudice to anybody, full as the world seems. For, supposing a man or family, in the state they were at first, peopling of the world by the children of Adam or Noah, let him plant in some inland vacant places of America. We shall find that the possessions he could make himself, upon the measures we have given, would not be very large, nor, even to this day, prejudice the rest of mankind or give them reason to complain or think themselves injured by this man's encroachment, though the race of men have now spread themselves to all the corners of the world, and do infinitely exceed the small number that was at the beginning. Nay, the extent of ground is of so little value without labour that I have heard it affirmed that in Spain itself a man may be permitted to plough, sow, and reap, without being disturbed, upon land he has no other title to, but only his making use of it. But, on the contrary, the inhabitants think themselves beholden to him who, by his industry on neglected, and consequently waste land, has increased the stock of corn, which they wanted. But be this as it will, which I lay no stress on, this I dare boldly affirm, that the same rule of propriety — viz., that every man should have as much as

he could make use of, would hold still in the world, without straitening anybody, since there is land enough in the world to suffice double the inhabitants, had not the invention of money, and the tacit agreement of men to put a value on it, introduced (by consent) larger possessions and a right to them; which, how it has done, I shall by and by show more at large.

37. This is certain, that in the beginning, before the desire of having more than men needed had altered the intrinsic value of things, which depends only on their usefulness to the life of man, or had agreed that a little piece of yellow metal, which would keep without wasting or decay, should be worth a great piece of flesh or a whole heap of corn, though men had a right to appropriate by their labour, each one to himself, as much of the things of Nature as he could use, yet this could not be much, nor to the prejudice of others, where the same plenty was still left, to those who would use the same industry.

Before the appropriation of land, he who gathered as much of the wild fruit, killed, caught, or tamed as many of the beasts as he could — he that so employed his pains about any of the spontaneous products of Nature as any way to alter them from the state Nature put them in, by placing any of his labour on them, did thereby acquire a propriety in them; but if they perished in his possession without their due use — if the fruits rotted or the venison putrefied before he could spend it, he offended against the common law of Nature, and was liable to be punished: he invaded his neighbour's share, for he had no right farther than his use called for any of them, and they might serve to afford him conveniencies of life.

38. The same measures governed the possession of land, too. Whatsoever he tilled and reaped, laid up and made use of before it spoiled, that was his peculiar right; whatsoever he enclosed, and could feed and make use of, the cattle and product was also his. But if either the grass of his enclosure rotted on the ground, or the fruit of his planting perished without gathering and laying up, this part of the earth, notwithstanding his enclosure, was still to be looked on as waste, and might be the possession of any other. Thus, at the beginning, Cain might take as much ground as he could till and make it his own land, and yet leave enough to Abel's sheep to feed on: a few acres would serve for both their possessions. But as families increased and industry enlarged their stocks, their possessions enlarged with the need of them; but yet it was commonly without any fixed property in the ground they made use of till they incorporated, settled themselves together, and built cities, and then, by consent, they came in time to set out the bounds of their distinct territories and agree on limits between them and their neighbours, and by laws within themselves settled the properties of those of the same society. For we see that in that part of the world which was first inhabited, and therefore like to be best peopled, even as low down as Abraham's time, they wandered with their flocks and their herds, which was their substance, freely up and down — and this Abraham did in a country

where he was a stranger; whence it is plain that, at least, a great part of the land lay in common, that the inhabitants valued it not, nor claimed property in any more than they made use of; but when there was not room enough in the same place for their herds to feed together, they, by consent, as Abraham and Lot did (Gen. xiii. 5), separated and enlarged their pasture where it best liked them. And for the same reason, Esau went from his father and his brother, and planted in Mount Seir (Gen. xxxvi. 6).

39. And thus, without supposing any private dominion and property in Adam over all the world, exclusive of all other men, which can no way be proved, nor any one's property be made out from it, but supposing the world, given as it was to the children of men in common, we see how labour could make men distinct titles to several parcels of it for their private uses, wherein there could be no doubt of right, no room for quarrel.

40. Nor is it so strange as, perhaps, before consideration, it may appear, that the property of labour should be able to overbalance the community of land, for it is labour indeed that puts the difference of value on everything; and let any one consider what the difference is between an acre of land planted with tobacco or sugar, sown with wheat or barley, and an acre of the same land lying in common without any husbandry upon it, and he will find that the improvement of labour makes the far greater part of the value. I think it will be but a very modest computation to say, that of the products of the earth useful to the life of man, nine-tenths are the effects of labour. Nay, if we will rightly estimate things as they come to our use, and cast up the several expenses about them — what in them is purely owing to Nature and what to labour — we shall find that in most of them ninety-nine hundredths are wholly to be put on the account of labour.

41. There cannot be a clearer demonstration of anything than several nations of the Americans are of this, who are rich in land and poor in all the comforts of life; whom Nature, having furnished as liberally as any other people with the materials of plenty — i.e., a fruitful soil, apt to produce in abundance what might serve for food, raiment, and delight; yet, for want of improving it by labour, have not one hundredth part of the conveniencies we enjoy, and a king of a large and fruitful territory there feeds, lodges, and is clad worse than a day labourer in England.

42. To make this a little clearer, let us but trace some of the ordinary provisions of life, through their several progresses, before they come to our use, and see how much they receive of their value from human industry. Bread, wine, and cloth are things of daily use and great plenty; yet notwithstanding acorns, water, and leaves, or skins must be our bread, drink and clothing, did not labour furnish us with these more useful commodities. For whatever bread is more worth than acorns, wine than water, and cloth or silk than leaves, skins or moss, that is wholly owing to labour and industry. The one of these being the food and raiment which unassisted Nature furnishes us with; the other provisions which our industry and pains prepare

for us, which how much they exceed the other in value, when any one hath computed, he will then see how much labour makes the far greatest part of the value of things we enjoy in this world; and the ground which produces the materials is scarce to be reckoned in as any, or at most, but a very small part of it; so little, that even amongst us, land that is left wholly to nature, that hath no improvement of pasturage, tillage, or planting, is called, as indeed it is, waste; and we shall find the benefit of it amounts to little more than nothing.

43. An acre of land that bears here twenty bushels of wheat, and another in America, which, with the same husbandry, would do the like, are, without doubt, of the same natural, intrinsic value. But yet the benefit mankind receives from one in a year is worth five pounds, and the other possibly not worth a penny; if all the profit an Indian received from it were to be valued and sold here, at least I may truly say, not one thousandth. It is labour, then, which puts the greatest part of value upon land, without which it would scarcely be worth anything; it is to that we owe the greatest part of all its useful products; for all that the straw, bran, bread, of that acre of wheat, is more worth than the product of an acre of as good land which lies waste is all the effect of labour. For it is not barely the ploughman's pains, the reaper's and thresher's toil, and the baker's sweat, that is to be counted into the bread we eat; the labour of those who broke the oxen, who digged and wrought the iron and stones, who felled and framed the timber employed about the plough, mill, oven, or any other utensils, which are a vast number, requisite to this corn, from its sowing to its being made bread, must all be charged on the account of labour, and received as an effect of that; Nature and the earth furnished only the almost worthless materials as in themselves. It would be a strange catalogue of things that industry provided and made use of about every loaf of bread before it came to our use if we could trace them; iron, wood, leather, bark, timber, stone, bricks, coals, lime, cloth, dyeing-drugs, pitch, tar, masts, ropes, and all the materials made use of in the ship that brought any of the commodities made use of by any of the workmen, to any part of the work, all which it would be almost impossible, at least too long, to reckon up.

44. From all which it is evident, that though the things of Nature are given in common, man (by being master of himself, and proprietor of his own person, and the actions or labour of it) had still in himself the great foundation of property; and that which made up the great part of what he applied to the support or comfort of his being, when invention and 'arts had improved the conveniencies of life, was perfectly his own, and did not belong in common to others.

45. Thus labour, in the beginning, gave a right of property, wherever any one was pleased to employ it, upon what was common, which remained a long while, the far greater part, and is yet more than mankind makes use of. Men at first, for the most part, contented themselves with what

unassisted Nature offered to their necessities; and though afterwards, in some parts of the world, where the increase of people and stock, with the use of money, had made land scarce, and so of some value, the several communities settled the bounds of their distinct territories, and, by laws, within themselves, regulated the properties of the private men of their society, and so, by compact and agreement, settled the property which labour and industry began. And the leagues that have been made between several states and kingdoms, either expressly or tacitly disowning all claim and right to the land in the other's possession, have, by common consent, given up their pretences to their natural common right, which originally they had to those countries; and so have, by positive agreement, settled a property amongst themselves, in distinct parts of the world; yet there are still great tracts of ground to be found, which the inhabitants thereof, not having joined with the rest of mankind in the consent of the use of their common money, lie waste, and are more than the people who dwell on it, do, or can make use of, and so still lie in common; though this can scarce happen amongst that part of mankind that have consented to the use of money.

46. The greatest part of things really useful to the life of man, and such as the necessity of subsisting made the first commoners of the world look after — as it doth the Americans now — are generally things of short duration, such as — if they are not consumed by use — will decay and perish of themselves. Gold, silver, and diamonds are things that fancy or agreement hath put the value on, more than real use and the necessary support of life. Now of those good things which Nature hath provided in common, every one hath a right (as hath been said) to as much as he could use, and had a property in all he could effect with his labour; all that his industry could extend to, to alter from the state Nature had put it in, was his. He that gathered a hundred bushels of acorns or apples had thereby a property in them; they were his goods as soon as gathered. He was only to look that he used them before they spoiled, else he took more than his share, and robbed others. And, indeed, it was a foolish thing, as well as dishonest, to hoard up more than he could make use of. If he gave away a part to anybody else, so that it perished not uselessly in his possession, these he also made use of. And if he also bartered away plums that would have rotted in a week, for nuts that would last good for his eating a whole year, he did no injury; he wasted not the common stock; destroyed no part of the portion of goods that belonged to others, so long as nothing perished uselessly in his hands. Again, if he would give his nuts for a piece of metal, pleased with its colour, or exchange his sheep for shells, or wool for a sparkling pebble or a diamond, and keep those by him all his life, he invaded not the right of others; he might heap up as much of these durable things as he pleased; the exceeding of the bounds of his just property not lying in the largeness of his possession, but the perishing of anything uselessly in it.

47. And thus came in the use of money; some lasting thing that men might keep without spoiling, and that, by mutual consent, men would take in exchange for the truly useful but perishable supports of life.

48. And as different degrees of industry were apt to give men possessions in different proportions, so this invention of money gave them the opportunity to continue and enlarge them. For supposing an island, separate from all possible commerce with the rest of the world, wherein there were but a hundred families, but there were sheep, horses, and cows, with other useful animals, wholesome fruits, and land enough for corn for a hundred thousand times as many, but nothing in the island, either because of its commonness or perishableness, fit to supply the place of money. What reason could any one have there to enlarge his possessions beyond the use of his family, and a plentiful supply to its consumption, either in what their own industry produced, or they could barter for like perishable, useful commodities with others? Where there is not something both lasting and scarce, and so valuable to be hoarded up, there men will not be apt to enlarge their possessions of land, were it never so rich, never so free for them to take. For I ask, what would a man value ten thousand or an hundred thousand acres of excellent land, ready cultivated and well stocked, too, with cattle, in the middle of the inland parts of America, where he had no hopes of commerce with other parts of the world, to draw money to him by the sale of the product? It would not be worth the enclosing, and we should see him give up again to the wild common of Nature whatever was more than would supply the conveniencies of life, to be had there for him and his family.

49. Thus, in the beginning, all the world was America, and more so than that is now; for no such thing as money was anywhere known. Find out something that hath the use and value of money amongst his neighbours, you shall see the same man will begin presently to enlarge his possessions.

50. But since gold and silver, being little useful to the life of man, in proportion to food, raiment, and carriage, has its value only from the consent of men — whereof labour yet makes in great part the measure — it is plain that the consent of men have agreed to a disproportionate and unequal possession of the earth — I mean out of the bounds of society and compact; for in governments the laws regulate it; they having, by consent, found out and agreed in a way how a man may, rightfully and without injury, possess more than he himself can make use of by receiving gold and silver, which may continue long in a man's possession without decaying for the overplus, and agreeing those metals should have a value.

51. And thus, I think, it is very easy to conceive, without any difficulty, how labour could at first begin a title of property in the common things of Nature, and how the spending it upon our uses bounded it; so that there could then be no reason of quarrelling about title, nor any doubt about the largeness of possession it gave. Right and conveniency went together. For

as a man had a right to all he could employ his labour upon, so he had no temptation to labour for more than he could make use of. This left no room for controversy about the title, nor for encroachment on the right of others. What portion a man carved to himself was easily seen; and it was useless, as well as dishonest, to carve himself too much, or take more than he needed.

QUESTIONS

1. What theological beliefs are presupposed by Locke's theory of property rights?
2. Does Locke offer any further justification of his claim that a man has exclusive moral right to his person and the work of his hands? Can questions reasonably be raised about this point, say on the ground that in time of need others have a moral right to our labor?
3. How far does the doctrine that a man has a right to what he has "mixed his labor with" have application in modern society? How serious a qualification, today, is Locke's remark "at least where there is enough, and as good left in common for others"? Is Locke's doctrine suited primarily to an age when there are great unexplored tracts of arable land? Or does it suit our "Space Age" as well?
4. Do you think Locke is right at least in supposing that the consent of all is unnecessary for the appropriation of what no one has laid claim to?
5. Locke says we may appropriate only "as much as any one can make use of to any advantage of life before it spoils. . . . Whatever is beyond this is more than his share, and belongs to others." Such appropriation is necessarily modest, Locke thinks, and does not encroach on the rights of others. In what way does Locke concede that money and exchange modify this position? Does he think there is a justification for the modification?
6. Is Locke right that the value of anything depends almost entirely on the labor which has gone into it? How far does this fact, if it is a fact, serve to justify the view that mixing of labor with something confers ownership of it?
7. Explain the respective roles of the right arising from contract and of the right deriving from "mixing one's labor," in Locke's view of the morality of property.
8. Does Locke view these rights as absolute or as prima facie only (that is, rights that must stand aside when more pressing moral considerations demand it)?
9. Outline the kind of justification of rules of ownership you think would be offered by a utilitarian.
10. Since we are forced to pay taxes on real estate, and since there are all sorts of ordinances limiting the use of real estate, does a person really "own" his land today? What powers do you think properly mark ownership of something?
11. What does Locke's theory imply for the following issues: (a) whether the owner of a piece of real estate owns everything underneath it right down to the center of the Earth; (b) whether the owner of a piece of real estate owns the space above it and can sell pieces of it to different bidders; (c) whether the Soviet Union owns the moon if it is the first to land a human being on it? How do you think such questions should be adjudicated?

John Stuart Mill   (1806-73)

A UTILITARIAN DEFENSE OF
REPRESENTATIVE GOVERNMENT

Since the time of Socrates the justification of government and of specific forms of it has been one of the topics which has most tempted philosophers to take up their pens. By what right does the government give orders to its citizens, to the point of demanding their very lives? What moral principles, if any, bind the individual to obey the decisions of his government? What form of government is best suited to do well jobs the performance of which is the point of having governments? These are some of the questions which have agitated a great many people.

We have already examined one answer to these questions, that of John Locke (pp. 498-510). The rightful authority of government, he proposed, derives from a compact of the citizens, by which they transfer some of their natural rights to society (and indirectly to the government) for the purpose of receiving certain protections. The authority of government, then, originates in consent, in free delegation of certain rights by the citizens, a delegation which all of us continually reaffirm in our conduct. A different answer was given by Thomas Hobbes (pp. 142-49), who held that the right of the sovereign derives from — or is perhaps identical with — his power, which is ceded him by rational persons in preference to the alternative of living in a perpetual state of war with all other men. Still another answer was given by T. H. Green, a writer of last century, who argued that the rightful authority of government derives from the fact that it is a condition of an organized system of institutions, which again is a condition of a tolerable mode of existence for men; in good reason we must accept the authority of the state as being a condition of having anything and everything we want.

The answer of J. S. Mill (p. 28) is different from these. As a utilitarian, he thinks that a system of institutions is morally justified by its contribution to human welfare generally. Consent is not necessary; power does not give right; it is a fiction to say that in wanting anything, a man thereby in good reason wants a government with possibly highly unpleasant implications for himself. No: government rather is justified because life would not be worth living for the group if there were not a power which enforced laws, thereby giving order to human life. But *which* form of government is best justified? Mill cannot say that a representative government is the only one justified because it alone can claim consent of the governed, because it alone can claim that reasonable subjects would delegate to it the authority it has. His defense of representative government must be utilitarian; he must say that a representative government does best the jobs a government should do.

In the following reading Mill is attempting to justify representative government to its critics, along utilitarian lines. He does not say it is *always* the best form of government. But as a defense of representative government for a highly developed and civilized community his discussion stands out as one of the great defenses of democratic political institutions.

From John Stuart Mill, *Considerations on Representative Government*. First published 1861. Many editions, Chs. 2 and 3.

CONSIDERATIONS ON REPRESENTATIVE GOVERNMENT

CHAPTER 2 THE CRITERION OF A GOOD FORM OF GOVERNMENT

The form of government for any given country being (within certain definite conditions) amenable to choice, it is now to be considered by what test the choice should be directed; what are the distinctive characteristics of the form of government best fitted to promote the interests of any given society. . . .

If we ask ourselves on what causes and conditions good government in all its senses, from the humblest to the most exalted, depends, we find that the principal of them, the one which transcends all others, is the qualities of the human beings composing the society over which the government is exercised.

We may take, as a first instance, the administration of justice; with the more propriety, since there is no part of public business in which the mere machinery, the rules and contrivances for conducting the details of the operation, are of such vital consequence. Yet even these yield in importance to the qualities of the human agents employed. Of what efficacy are rules of procedure in securing the ends of justice, if the moral condition of the people is such that the witnesses generally lie, and the judges and their subordinates take bribes? Again, how can institutions provide a good municipal administration if there exists such indifference to the subject that those who would administer honestly and capably cannot be induced to serve, and the duties are left to those who undertake them because they have some private interest to be promoted? Of what avail is the most broadly popular representative system if the electors do not care to choose the best member of parliament, but choose him who will spend most money to be elected? How can a representative assembly work for good if its members can be bought, or if their excitability of temperament, uncorrected by public discipline or private self-control, makes them incapable of calm deliberation, and they resort to manual violence on the floor of the House, or shoot at one another with rifles? How, again, can government, or any joint concern, be carried on in a tolerable manner by people so envious that, if one among them seems likely to succeed in anything, those who ought to cooperate with him form a tacit combination to make him fail? Whenever the general disposition of the people is such that each individual regards those only of his interests which are selfish, and does not dwell on, or concern himself for, his share of the general interest, in such a state of things good government is impossible. The influence of defects of intelligence in obstructing all the elements of good government requires no illustration. Government consists of acts done by human beings; and if the agents, or those who choose the agents, or those to whom the agents are responsible, or the lookers-on whose opinion ought to influence and check all these, are mere masses of ignorance, stupidity, and baleful prejudice, every operation of government will go wrong; while, in proportion as the men rise above this standard, so will the government improve in quality; up to the point of excellence, attainable but nowhere attained, where the officers of government, themselves persons of superior virtue and intellect, are surrounded by the atmosphere of a virtuous and enlightened public opinion.

The first element of good government, therefore, being the virtue and intelligence of the human beings composing the community, the most important point of excellence which any form of government can possess is to promote the virtue and intelligence of the people themselves. The first question in respect to any political institutions is, how far they tend to foster in the members of the community the various desirable qualities, moral and intellectual; or rather (following Bentham's more complete classification) moral, intellectual, and active. The government which does this the best has every likelihood of being the best in all other respects, since it is on these qualities, so far as they exist in the people, that all possibility of goodness in the practical operations of the government depends.

We may consider, then, as one criterion of the goodness of a government, the degree in which it tends to increase the sum of good qualities in the governed, collectively and individually; since, besides that their well-being is the sole object of government, their good qualities supply the moving force which works the machinery. This leaves, as the other constituent element of the merit of a government, the quality of the machinery itself; that is, the degree in which it is adapted to take advantage of the amount of good qualities which may at any time exist, and make them instrumental to the right purposes. Let us again take the subject of judicature as an example and illustration. The judicial system being given, the goodness of the administration of justice is in the compound ratio of the worth of the men composing the tribunals, and the worth of the public opinion which influences or controls them. But all the difference between a good and a bad system of judicature lies in the contrivances adopted for bringing whatever moral and intellectual worth exists in the community to bear upon the administration of justice, and making it duly operative on the result. The arrangements for rendering the choice of the judges such as to obtain the highest average of virtue and intelligence; the salutary forms of procedure; the publicity which allows observation and criticism of whatever is amiss; the liberty of discussion and censure through the press; the mode of taking evidence, according as it is well or ill adapted to elicit truth; the facilities, whatever be their amount, for obtaining access to the tribunals; the arrangements for detecting crimes and apprehending offenders; — all these things are not the power, but the machinery for bringing the power into contact with the obstacle: and the machinery has no action of itself, but without it the power, let it be ever so ample, would be wasted and of no effect. A similar distinction exists in regard to the constitution of the executive departments of administration. Their machinery is good, when the proper tests are prescribed for the qualifications of officers, the proper rules for their promotion; when the business is conveniently distributed among those who are to transact it, a convenient and methodical order established for its transaction, a correct and intelligible record kept of it after being transacted; when each individual knows for what he is responsible, and is known to others as responsible for it; when the best-contrived checks are provided against negligence, favouritism, or jobbery, in any of the acts of the department. But political checks will no more act of themselves than a bridle will direct a horse without a rider. If the checking functionaries are as corrupt or as negligent as those whom they ought to check, and if the public, the mainspring of the whole checking machinery, are too ignorant, too passive, or too careless and inattentive, to do their part, little benefit will be derived from the best administrative apparatus. Yet a good apparatus is always preferable to a bad. It enables such insufficient moving or checking power as exists to act at the greatest advantage; and without it, no amount of moving or checking power would be sufficient. Publicity, for instance, is no impediment to evil nor stimulus to good if the public will not look at what is done; but without publicity, how could they either check or encourage what they were not permitted to see? The ideally perfect constitution of a public office is that in which the interest of the functionary is entirely coincident with his duty. No mere system will make it so, but still less can it be made so without a system, aptly devised for the purpose.

What we have said of the arrangements for the detailed administration of the government is still more evidently true of its general constitution. All government which aims at being good is an organisation of some part of the good qualities existing in the individual members of the community for the conduct of its collective affairs. A representative constitution is a means of bringing the general standard of intelligence and honesty existing in the community, and the individual intellect and virtue of its wisest members, more directly to bear upon the government, and investing them with greater influence in it, than they would in general have under any other mode of organisation; though, under any, such influence as they do have is the source of all good that there is in the government, and the hindrance of every evil that there is not. The greater the amount of these good qualities which the institutions of a country succeed in organising, and the better the mode of organisation, the better will be the government.

We have now, therefore, obtained a foundation for a twofold division of the merit which any set of political institutions can possess. It consists partly of the degree in which they promote the general mental advancement of the community, including under that phrase advancement in intellect, in virtue, and in practical activity and efficiency; and partly of the degree of perfection with which they organise the moral, intellectual, and active worth already existing, so as to operate with the greatest effect on public affairs. A government is to be judged by its action upon men, and by its action upon things; by what it makes of the citizens, and what it does with them; its tendency to improve or deteriorate the people themselves, and the goodness or badness of the work it performs for them, and by means of them. Government is at once a great influence acting on the human mind, and a set of organised arrangements for public business: in the first capacity its beneficial action is chiefly indirect, but not therefore less vital, while its mischievous action may be direct.

The difference between these two functions of a government is not a difference merely in degree, but in kind. We must not, however, suppose that they have no intimate connection with one another. The institutions which ensure the best management of public affairs practicable in the existing state of cultivation tend by this alone to the further improvement of that state. A people which had the most just laws, the purest and most efficient judicature, the most enlightened administration, the most equitable and least onerous system of finance, compatible with the stage it had attained in moral and intellectual advancement, would be in a fair way to pass rapidly into a higher stage. Nor is there any mode in which political institutions can contribute more effectually to the improvement of the people than by doing their more direct work well. And, reversely, if their machinery is so badly constructed that they do their own particular business ill, the effect is felt in a thousand ways in lowering the morality and deadening the intelligence and activity of the people. But the distinction is nevertheless real, because this is only one of the means by which political institutions improve or deteriorate the human mind, and the causes and modes of that beneficial or injurious influence remain a distinct and much wider subject of study.

Of the two modes of operation by which a form of government or set of political institutions affects the welfare of the community — its operation as an agency of national education, and its arrangements for conducting the collective affairs of the community in the state of education in which they already are; the last evidently varies much less, from difference of country and state of civilisation, than the first. It has also much less to do with the fundamental constitution of the government. The mode of conducting the practical business of government, which is best under a free constitution, would generally be best also in an absolute monarchy: only an absolute monarchy is not so likely to practise it. The laws of property, for example; the principles of evidence and judicial procedure; the system of taxation and of financial administration, need not necessarily be different in different forms of government. Each of these matters has principles and rules of its own, which are a subject of separate study. General jurisprudence, civil and penal legislation, financial and commercial policy, are sciences in themselves, or rather, separate members of the comprehensive science or art of government: and the most enlightened doctrines on all these subjects, though not equally likely to be understood or acted on under all forms of government, yet, if understood and acted on, would in general be equally beneficial under them all. It is true that these doctrines could not be applied without some modifications to all states of society and of the human mind: nevertheless, by far the greater number of them would require modifications solely of details, to adapt them to any state of society sufficiently advanced to possess rulers capable of understanding them. A government to which they would be wholly unsuitable must be one so bad in itself, or so opposed to public feeling, as to be unable to maintain itself in existence by honest means.

It is otherwise with that portion of the interests of the community which relate to the better or worse training of the people themselves. Considered as instrumental to this, institutions need to be radically different, according to the stage of advancement already reached. The recognition of this truth, though for the most part empirically rather than philosophically, may be regarded as the main point of superiority in the political theories of the present above those of the last age; in which it was customary to claim representative democracy for England or France by arguments which would equally have proved it the only fit form of government for Bedouins or Malays. The state of different communities, in point of culture and development, ranges downwards to a condition very little above the highest of the beasts. The upward range, too, is considerable, and the future possible extension vastly greater. A community can only be developed out of one of these states into a higher by a concourse of influences, among the principal of which is the government to which they are subject. In all states of human improvement ever yet attained, the nature and degree of authority exercised over individuals, the distribution of power, and the conditions of command and obedience, are the most powerful of the influences, except their religious belief, which make them what they are, and enable them to become what they can be. They may be stopped short at any point in their progress by defective adaptation of their government to that particular stage of advancement. And the one indispensable merit of a government, in favour of which it may be forgiven almost any amount of other demerit compatible with progress, is that its operation on the people is favourable, or not unfavourable, to the next step which it is necessary for them to take, in order to raise themselves to a higher level.

Thus (to repeat a former example), a people in a state of savage independence, in which every one lives for himself, exempt, unless by fits, from any external control, is practically incapable of making any progress in civilisation until it has learnt to obey. The indispensable virtue, therefore, in a government which establishes itself over a people of this' sort is, that it make itself obeyed. To enable it to do this, the constitution of the government must be nearly, or quite, despotic. A constitution in any degree popular, dependent on the voluntary surrender by the different members of the community of their individual freedom of action, would fail to enforce the first lesson which the pupils, in this stage of their progress, require. Accordingly, the civilisation of such tribes, when not the result of juxtaposition with others already civilised, is almost always the work of an absolute ruler, deriving his power either from religion or military prowess; very often from foreign arms.

Again, uncivilised races, and the bravest and most energetic still more than the rest, are averse to continuous labour of an unexciting kind. Yet all real civilisation is at this price; without such labour, neither can the mind be disciplined into the habits required by civilised society, nor the material world prepared to receive it. There needs a rare concurrence of circumstances, and for that reason often a vast length of time, to reconcile such a people to industry, unless they are for a while compelled to it. Hence even personal slavery, by giving a commencement to industrial life, and enforcing it as the exclusive occupation of the most numerous portion of the community, may accelerate the transition to a better freedom than that of fighting and rapine. It is almost needless to say that this excuse for slavery is only available in a very early state of society. A civilised people have far other means of imparting civilisation to those under their influence; and slavery is, in all its details, so repugnant to that government of law, which is the foundation of all modern life, and so corrupting to the master-class when they have once come under civilised influences, that its adoption under any circumstances whatever in modern society is a relapse into worse than barbarism.

At some period, however, of their history, almost every people, now civilised, have consisted, in majority, of slaves. A people in that condition require to raise them out of it a very different polity from a nation of savages. If they are energetic by nature, and especially if there be associated with them in the same community an industrious class who are neither slaves nor slaveowners (as was the case in Greece), they need, probably, no more to ensure their improvement than to make them free: when freed, they may often be fit, like Roman freedmen, to be admitted at once to the full rights of citizenship. This, however, is not the normal condition of slavery, and is generally a sign that it is becoming obsolete. A slave, properly so called, is a being who has not learnt to help himself. He is, no doubt, one step in advance of a savage. He has not the first lesson of political society still to acquire. He has learnt to obey. But what he obeys is only a direct command. It is the characteristic of *born* slaves to be incapable of conforming their conduct to a rule, or law. They can only do what they are ordered, and only when they are ordered to do it. If a man whom they fear is standing over them and threatening them with punishment, they obey; but when his back is turned, the work remains undone. The motive determining them must appeal not to their interests, but to their instincts; immediate hope or immediate terror. A despotism, which may tame the savage, will, in so far as it is a despotism, only confirm the slaves in their incapacities. Yet a government under their own control would be entirely unmanageable by them. Their improvement cannot come from themselves, but must be superinduced from without. The step which they have to take, and their only path to improvement, is to be raised from a government of will to one of law. They have to be taught self-government, and this, in its initial stage, means the capacity to act on general instructions. What they require is not a government of force, but one of guidance. Being, however, in too low a state to yield to the guidance of any but those to whom they look up as the possessors of force, the sort of government fittest for them is one which possesses force, but seldom uses it: a parental despotism or aristocracy, resembling the St. Simonian form of Socialism; maintaining a general superintendence over all the operations of society, so as to keep before each the sense of a present force sufficient to compel his obedience to the rule laid down, but which, owing to the impossibility of descending to regulate all the minutiæ of industry and life, necessarily leaves and induces individuals to do much of themselves. This, which may be termed the government of leading-strings, seems to be the one required to carry such a people the most rapidly through the next necessary step in social progress. Such appears to have been the idea of the government of the Incas of Peru; and such was that of the Jesuits of Paraguay. I need scarcely remark that leading-strings are only admissible as a means of gradually training the people to walk alone.

It would be out of place to carry the illustration further. To attempt to investigate what kind of government is suited to every known state of society would be to compose a treatise, not on representative government, but on political science at large. For our more limited purpose we borrow from political philosophy only its general principles. To determine the form of government most suited to any particular people, we must be able, among the defects and shortcomings which belong to that people, to distinguish those that are the immediate impediment to progress; to discover what it is which (as it were) stops the way. The best government for them is the one which tends most to give them that for want of which they cannot advance, or advance only in a lame and lopsided manner. We must not, however, forget the reservation necessary in all things which have for their object improvement, or Progress; namely, that in seeking the good which is needed, no damage, or as little as possible, be done to that already possessed. A people of savages should be taught obedience, but not in such a manner as to convert them into a people of slaves. And (to give the observation a higher generality) the form of government which is most effectual for carrying a people through the next stage of progress will still be very improper for them if it does this in such a manner as to obstruct, or positively unfit them for, the step next beyond. . . .

It is, then, impossible to understand the question of the adaptation of forms of government to states of society without taking into account not only the next step, but all the steps which society has yet to make; both those which can be foreseen, and the far wider indefinite range which is at present out of sight. It follows, that to judge of the merits of forms of government, an ideal must be constructed of the form of government most eligible in itself, that is, which, if the necessary conditions existed for giving effect to its beneficial tendencies, would, more than all others, favour and promote not some one improvement, but all forms and degrees of it. This having been done, we must consider what are the mental conditions of all sorts, necessary to enable this government to realise its tendencies, and what, therefore, are the various defects by which a people is made incapable of reaping its benefits. It would then be possible to construct a theorem of the circumstances in which that form of government may wisely be introduced; and also to judge, in cases in which it had better not be introduced, what inferior forms of polity will best carry those communities through the intermediate stages which they must traverse before they can become fit for the best form of government.

Of these inquiries, the last does not concern us here; but the first is an essential part of our subject: for we may, without rashness, at once enunciate a proposition, the proofs and illustrations of which will present themselves in the ensuing pages; that this ideally best form of government will be found in some one or other variety of the Representative System.

CHAPTER 3   THAT THE IDEALLY
BEST FORM OF GOVERNMENT IS
REPRESENTATIVE GOVERNMENT

. . . There is no difficulty in showing that the ideally best form of government is that in which the sovereignty, or supreme controlling power in the last resort, is vested in the entire aggregate of the community; every citizen not only having a voice in the exercise of that ultimate sovereignty, but being, at least occasionally, called on to take an actual part in the government, by the personal discharge of some public function, local or general.

To test this proposition, it has to be examined in reference to the two branches into which, as pointed out in the last chapter, the inquiry into the goodness of a government conveniently divides itself, namely, how far it promotes the good management of the affairs of society by means of the existing faculties, moral, intellectual, and active, of its various members, and what is its effect in improving or deteriorating those faculties.

The ideally best form of government, it is scarcely necessary to say, does not mean one which is practicable or eligible in all states of civilisation, but the one which, in the circumstances in which it is practicable and eligible, is attended with the greatest amount of beneficial consequences, immediate and prospective. A completely popular government is the only polity which can make out any claim to this character. It is pre-eminent in both the departments between which the excellence of a political constitution is divided. It is both more favourable to present good government, and promotes a better and higher form of national character, than any other polity whatsoever.

Its superiority in reference to present well-being rests upon two principles, of as universal truth and applicability as any general propositions which can be laid down respecting human affairs. The first is, that the rights and interests of every or any person are only secure from being disregarded when the person interested is himself able, and habitually disposed, to stand up for them. The second is, that the general prosperity attains a greater height, and is more widely diffused, in proportion to the amount and variety of the personal energies enlisted in promoting it.

Putting these two propositions into a shape more special to their present application; human beings are only secure from evil at the hands of others in proportion as they have the power of being, and are, self-*protecting*; and they only achieve a high degree of success in their struggle with Nature in proportion as they are self-*dependent*, relying on what they themselves can do, either separately or in concert, rather than on what others do for them.

The former proposition — that each is the only safe guardian of his own rights and interests — is one of those elementary maxims of prudence, which every person, capable of conducting his own affairs, implicitly acts upon, wherever he himself is interested. Many, indeed, have a great dislike to it as a political doctrine, and are fond of holding it up to obloquy, as a doctrine of universal selfishness. To which we may answer, that whenever it ceases to be true that mankind, as a rule, prefer themselves to others, and those nearest to them to those more remote, from that moment Communism is not only practicable, but the only defensible form of society;

and will, when that time arrives, be assuredly carried into effect. For my own part, not believing in universal selfishness, I have no difficulty in admitting that Communism would even now be practicable among the *élite* of mankind, and may become so among the rest. But as this opinion is anything but popular with those defenders of existing institutions who find fault with the doctrine of the general predominance of self-interest, I am inclined to think they do in reality believe that most men consider themselves before other people. It is not, however, necessary to affirm even thus much in order to support the claim of all to participate in the sovereign power. We need not suppose that when power resides in an exclusive class, that class will knowingly and deliberately sacrifice the other classes to themselves: it suffices that, in the absence of its natural defenders, the interest of the excluded is always in danger of being overlooked; and, when looked at, is seen with very different eyes from those of the persons whom it directly concerns. In this country, for example, what are called the working classes may be considered as excluded from all direct participation in the government. I do not believe that the classes who do participate in it have in general any intention of sacrificing the working classes to themselves. They once had that intention; witness the persevering attempts so long made to keep down wages by law. But in the present day their ordinary disposition is the very opposite: they willingly make considerable sacrifices, especially of their pecuniary interest, for the benefit of the working classes, and err rather by too lavish and indiscriminating beneficence; nor do I believe that any rulers in history have been actuated by a more sincere desire to do their duty towards the poorer portion of their countrymen. Yet does Parliament, or almost any of the members composing it, ever for an instant look at any question with the eyes of a working man? When a subject arises in which the labourers as such have an interest, is it regarded from any point of view but that of the employers of labour? I do not say that the working men's view of these questions is in general nearer to the truth than the other: but it is sometimes quite as near; and in any case it ought to be respectfully listened to, instead of being, as it is, not merely turned away from, but ignored. On the question of strikes, for instance, it is doubtful if there is so much as one among the leading members of either House who is not firmly convinced that the reason of the matter is unqualifiedly on the side of the masters, and that the men's view of it is simply absurd. Those who have studied the question know well how far this is from being the case; and in how different, and how infinitely less superficial a manner the point would have to be argued, if the classes who strike were able to make themselves heard in Parliament.

It is an adherent condition of human affairs that no intention, however sincere, of protecting the interests of others can make it safe or salutary to tie up their own hands. Still more obviously true is it, that by their own hands only can any positive and durable improvement of their circumstances in life be worked out. Through the joint influence of these two principles, all free communities have both been more exempt from social injustice and crime, and have attained more brilliant prosperity, than any others, or than they themselves after they lost their freedom. Contrast the free states of the world, while their freedom lasted, with the cotemporary subjects of monarchical or oligarchical despotism: the Greek cities with the Persian satrapies; the Italian republics and the free towns of Flanders and Germany, with the feudal monarchies of Europe; Switzerland, Holland, and England, with Austria or anterevolutionary France. Their superior prosperity was too obvious ever to have been gainsaid: while their superiority in good government and social relations is proved by the prosperity, and is manifest besides in every page of history. If we compare, not one age with another, but the different governments which co-existed in the same age, no amount of disorder which exaggeration itself can pretend to have existed amidst the publicity of the free states can be compared for a moment with the contemptuous trampling upon the mass of the people which pervaded the whole life of the monarchical countries, or the disgusting individual tyranny which was of more than daily occurrence under the systems of plunder which they called fiscal arrangements, and in the secrecy of their frightful courts of justice.

It must be acknowledged that the benefits of freedom, so far as they have hitherto been enjoyed, were obtained by the extension of its privileges to a part only of the community; and that a government in which they are extended impartially to all is a desideratum still unrealised. But though every approach to this has an independent value, and in many cases more than an approach could not, in the existing state of general improvement, be made, the participation of all in these benefits is the ideally perfect conception of free government. In proportion as any, no matter who, are excluded from it, the interests of the excluded are left without the guarantee accorded to the rest, and they themselves have less scope and encouragement than they might otherwise have to that exertion of their energies for the good of themselves and of the community, to which the general prosperity is always proportioned.

Thus stands the case as regards present well-being; the good management of the affairs of the existing generation. If we now pass to the influence of the form of government upon character, we shall find the superiority of popular government over every other to be, if possible, still more decided and indisputable.

This question really depends upon a still more fundamental one, viz., which of two common types of character, for the general good of humanity, it is most desirable should predominate — the active, or the passive type; that which struggles against evils, or that which endures them; that which bends to circumstances, or that which endeavours to make circumstances bend to itself.

The commonplaces of moralists, and the general sympathies of mankind, are in favour of the passive type. Energetic characters may be admired, but the acquiescent and submissive are those which most men personally prefer. The passiveness of our neighbours increases our sense of security, and plays into the hands of our wilfulness. Passive characters, if we do not happen to need their activity, seem an obstruction the less in our own path. A contented character is not a dangerous rival. Yet nothing is more certain than that improvement in human affairs is wholly the work of the uncontented characters; and, moreover, that it is much easier for an active mind to acquire the virtues of patience than for a passive one to assume those of energy.

Of the three varieties of mental excellence, intellectual, practical, and moral, there never could be any doubt in regard to the first two which side had the advantage. All intellectual superiority is the fruit of active effort. Enterprise, the desire to keep moving, to be trying and accomplishing new things for our own benefit or that of others, is the parent even of speculative, and much more of practical, talent. The intellectual culture compatible with the other type is of that feeble and vague description which belongs to a mind that stops at amusement, or at simple contemplation. The test of real and vigorous thinking, the thinking which ascertains truths instead of dreaming dreams, is successful application to practice. Where that purpose does not exist, to give definiteness, precision, and an intelligible meaning to thought, it generates nothing better than the mystical metaphysics of the Pythagoreans or the Vedas. With respect to practical improvement, the case is still more evident. The character which improves human life is that which struggles with natural powers and tendencies, not that which gives way to them. The self-benefiting qualities are all on the side of the active and energetic character: and the habits and conduct which promote the advantage of each individual member of the community must be at least a part of those which conduce most in the end to the advancement of the community as a whole.

The striving, go-ahead character of England and the United States is only a fit subject of disapproving criticism on account of the very secondary objects on which it commonly expends its strength. In itself it is the foundation of the best hopes for the general improvement of mankind. It has been acutely remarked that whenever anything goes amiss the habitual impulse of French people is to say, "Il faut de la patience"; and of English people, "What a shame." The people who think it a shame when anything goes wrong — who rush to the conclusion that the evil could and ought to have been prevented, are those who, in the long run, do most to make the world better. If the desires are low placed, if they extend to little beyond physical comfort, and the show of riches, the immediate results of the energy will not be much more than the continual extension of man's power over material objects; but even this makes room, and prepares the mechanical appliances, for the greatest intellectual and social achievements; and while the energy is there, some persons will apply it, and it will be applied more and more, to the perfecting not of outward circumstances alone, but of man's inward nature. Inactivity, unaspiringness, absence of desire, are a more fatal hindrance to improvement than any misdirection of energy; and are that through which alone, when existing in the mass, any very formidable mis-direction by an energetic few becomes possible. It is this, mainly, which re-tains in a savage or semi-savage state the great majority of the human race.

Now there can be no kind of doubt that the passive type of character is favoured by the government of one or a few, and the active self-helping type by that of the Many. Irresponsible rulers need the quiescence of the ruled more than they need any activity but that which they can compel. Submissiveness to the prescriptions of men as necessities of nature is the lesson inculcated by all governments upon those who are wholly without participation in them. The will of superiors, and the law as the will of supe-riors, must be passively yielded to. But no men are mere instruments or materials in the hands of their rulers who have will or spirit or a spring of internal activity in the rest of their proceedings: and any manifestation of these qualities, instead of receiving encouragement from despots, has to get itself forgiven by them. Even when irresponsible rulers are not suffi-ciently conscious of danger from the mental activity of their subjects to be desirous of repressing it, the position itself is a repression. Endeavour is even more effectually restrained by the certainty of its impotence than by any positive discouragement. Between subjection to the will of others, and the virtues of self-help and self-government, there is a natural incompatibility. This is more or less complete, according as the bondage is strained or relaxed. Rulers differ very much in the length to which they carry the control of the free agency of their subjects, or the supersession of it by managing their business for them. But the difference is in degree, not in principle; and the best despots often go the greatest lengths in chaining up the free agency of their subjects. A bad despot, when his own personal indulgences have been provided for, may sometimes be willing to let the people alone; but a good despot insists on doing them good, by making them do their own business in a better way than they themselves know of. The regulations which restricted to fixed processes all the leading branches of French manufactures were the work of the great Colbert.

Very different is the state of the human faculties where a human being feels himself under no other external restraint than the necessities of nature, or mandates of society which he has his share in imposing, and which it is open to him, if he thinks them wrong, publicly to dissent from, and exert himself actively to get altered. No doubt, under a government partially popu-lar, this freedom may be exercised even by those who are not partakers in the full privileges of citizenship. But it is a great additional stimulus to any one's self-help and self-reliance when he starts from even ground, and has not to feel that his success depends on the impression he can make upon the sentiments and dispositions of a body of whom he is not one. It is a great discouragement to an individual, and a still greater one to a class, to be left out of the constitution; to be reduced to plead from outside the door to the arbiters of their destiny, not taken into consultation within. The maximum of the invigorating effect of freedom upon the character is only obtained when the person acted on either is, or is looking forward to becoming, a citizen as fully privileged as any other. What is still more important than even this matter of feeling is the practical discipline which the character obtains from the occasional demand made upon the citizens to exercise, for a time and in their turn, some social function. It is not sufficiently considered how little there is in most men's ordinary life to give any largeness either to their conceptions or to their sentiments. Their work is a routine; not a labour of love, but of self-interest in the most elementary form, the satisfaction of daily wants; neither the thing done, nor the process of doing it, introduces the mind to thoughts or feelings extending beyond individuals; if instructive books are within their reach, there is no stimulus to read them; and in most cases the individual has no access to any person of cultivation much superior to his own. Giving him something to do for the public, supplies, in a measure, all these deficiences. If circumstances allow the amount of public duty assigned him to be considerable, it makes him an educated man. Notwithstanding the defects of the social system and moral ideas of antiquity, the practice of the dicastery and the ecclesia raised the intellectual standard of an average Athenian citizen far beyond anything of which there is yet an example in any other mass of men, ancient or modern. The proofs of this are apparent in every page of our great historian of Greece; but we need scarcely look further than to the high quality of the addresses which their great orators deemed best calculated to act with effect on their understanding and will. A benefit of the same kind, though far less in degree, is produced on Englishmen of the lower middle class by their liability to be placed on juries and to serve parish offices; which, though it does not occur to so many, nor is so continuous, nor introduces them to so great a variety of elevated considerations, as to admit of comparison with the public education which every citizen of Athens obtained from her democratic institutions, must make them nevertheless very different beings, in range of ideas and development of faculties, from those who have done nothing in their lives but drive a quill, or sell goods over a counter. Still more salutary is the moral part of the instruction afforded by the participation of the private citizen, if even rarely, in public functions. He is called upon, while so engaged, to weigh interests not his own; to be guided, in case of conflicting claims, by another rule than his private partialities; to apply, at every turn, principles and maxims which have for their reason of existence the common good: and he usually finds associated with him in the same work minds more familiarised than his own with these ideas and operations, whose study it will be to supply reasons to his understanding, and stimulation to his feeling for the general interest. He is made to feel himself one of the public, and whatever is for their benefit to be for his benefit. Where this school of public spirit does not exist, scarcely any sense is entertained that private persons, in no eminent social situation, owe any duties to society, except to obey the laws and submit to the government. There is no unselfish sentiment of identification with the public. Every thought or feeling, either of interest or of duty, is absorbed in the individual and in the family. The man never thinks of any collective interest, of any objects to be pursued jointly with others, but only in competition with them, and in some measure at their expense. A neighbour, not being an ally or an associate, since he is never engaged in any common undertaking for joint benefit, is therefore only a rival. Thus even private morality suffers, while public is actually extinct. Were this the universal and only possible state of things, the utmost aspirations of the lawgiver or the moralist could only stretch to make the bulk of the community a flock of sheep innocently nibbling the grass side by side.

From these accumulated considerations it is evident that the only government which can fully satisfy all the exigencies of the social state is one in which the whole people participate; that any participation, even in the smallest public function, is useful; that the participation should everywhere be as great as the general degree of improvement of the community will allow; and that nothing less can be ultimately desirable than the admission of all to a share in the sovereign power of the state. But since all cannot, in a community exceeding a single small town, participate personally in any but some very minor portions of the public business, it follows that the ideal type of a perfect government must be representative.

QUESTIONS

1. Why does Mill think that the type of human being a system of government tends to produce is a very important consideration for the evaluation of the system of government?
2. What other feature of government is important, according to Mill?
3. Does Mill think that a democracy is the best form of government for an underdeveloped country, whose citizens enjoy only a small amount of education? What form of government, for instance, would he probably advocate for Pakistan? for the Congo? for British Guiana? How sound is his view?
4. For what situations does he think democracy the best form of government?
5. List the main reasons he gives for preferring a democratic, or representative, form of government.

Immanuel Kant   (1724-1804)

A RETRIBUTIVE THEORY OF
CRIMINAL JUSTICE

Every society except some of the simplest has some institutional devices, which may be called "legal," for dealing with serious offenders against security of life, limb, property, and other things valued by the group. The institutional devices have been quite varied, however. For instance, in some societies a murder is punished merely by requiring a payment to the family of the victim. The Old Testament law, "An eye for an eye," is a sample of another type of system. Institutions of criminal law have varied in many other ways.

Philosophers have long been interested in identifying the sound moral principles relevant for the evaluation of such institutions and in determining which forms of this institution can stand up to moral criticism. One of these philosophers is Immanuel Kant (p. 190), who attacked the problems in lectures on the moral basis for legal institutions in general.

Consistently with his general theory of morals, Kant thought that if a law about the treatment of criminals is right at all, it must be one we are prepared to have applied to absolutely all cases. This assertion, however, leaves — although Kant did not emphasize and perhaps did not fully grasp the point — a great deal of latitude as to the content of the law. For a law is perfectly universal even if it is complex, provides for numerous types of exception, and permits a role for utilitarian considerations. (Kant himself appears to rely on utilitarian considerations for an exception discussed in the final paragraph below.) For instance, Kant could consistently advocate fixing sentences for a given offense in accordance with particular circumstances such as the health of the offender, the likelihood of his repeating his crime, the need of a stiff sentence for purposes of deterrence. (In fact, it is the practice of many judges in the United States to vary the severity of sentences on the basis of some such rule.) Kant's view, however, was that any rule for punishments except the Principle of Equality is wavering and uncertain. Hence his proposal was that, if a person has broken the law or more generally has trampled on the rights of others, he should be punished by society by the infliction on him of an amount of harm equal to that he has inflicted on others. Kant seems to have thought that the degree of harm inflicted corresponds with the degree of wickedness of the agent, presumably with the thought that the degree of turpitude of a person is a function of the amount of harm he is willing to cause, without moral excuse, to another person.

Kant's conclusion, then, is a form of the retributive theory of punishment, if we define "retributive theory" as the theory that a person who does wrong should always be punished with a severity corresponding with the "moral gravity" (in some sense) of his deed.

From Immanuel Kant, *The Philosophy of Law*. Trans. by W. Hastie. Edinburgh: T. and T. Clark, 1887, pp. 195-201.

THE PHILOSOPHY OF LAW

Judicial or Juridical Punishment (*pœna forensis*) is to be distinguished from Natural Punishment (*pœna naturalis*), in which Crime as Vice punishes itself, and does not as such come within the cognizance of the Legislator. Juridical Punishment can never be administered merely as a means for promoting another Good either with regard to the Criminal himself or to Civil Society, but must in all cases be imposed only because the individual on whom it is inflicted *has committed a Crime*. For one man ought never to be dealt with merely as a means subservient to the purpose of another, nor be mixed up with the subjects of Real Right. Against such treatment his Inborn Personality has a Right to protect him, even although he may be condemned to lose his Civil Personality. He must first be found guilty and *punishable*, before there can be any thought of drawing from his Punishment any benefit for himself or his fellow-citizens. The Penal Law is a Categorical Imperative; and woe to him who creeps through the serpent-windings of Utilitarianism to discover some advantage that may discharge him from the Justice of Punishment, or even from the due measure of it, according to the Pharisaic maxim: 'It is better that *one* man should die than that the whole people should perish.' For if Justice and Righteousness perish, human life would no longer have any value in the world. — What, then, is to be said of such a proposal as to keep a Criminal alive who has been condemned to death, on his being given to understand that if he agreed to certain dangerous experiments being performed upon him, he would be allowed to survive if he came happily through them? It is argued that Physicians might thus obtain new information that would be of value to the Commonweal. But a Court of Justice would repudiate with scorn any proposal of this kind if made to it by the Medical Faculty; for Justice would cease to be Justice, if it were bartered away for any consideration whatever.

But what is the mode and measure of Punishment which Public Justice takes as its Principle and Standard? It is just the Principle of Equality, by which the pointer of the Scale of Justice is made to incline no more to the one side than the other. It may be rendered by saying that the undeserved evil which any one commits on another, is to be regarded as perpetrated on himself. Hence it may be said: 'If you slander another, you slander yourself; if you steal from another, you steal from yourself; if you strike another, you strike yourself; if you kill another, you kill yourself.' This is the Right of RETALIATION (jus talionis); and properly understood, it is the only Principle which in regulating a Public Court, as distinguished from mere private judgment, can definitely assign both the quality and the quantity of a just penalty. All other standards are wavering and uncertain; and on account of other considerations involved in them, they contain no principle conformable to the sentence of pure and strict Justice. It may appear, however, that difference of social status would not admit the application of the Principle of Retaliation, which is that of 'Like with Like.' But although the application may not in all cases be possible according to the letter, yet as regards the effect it may always be attained in practice, by due regard being given to the disposition and sentiment of the parties in the higher social sphere. Thus a pecuniary penalty on account of a verbal injury, may have no direct proportion to the injustice of slander; for one who is wealthy may be able to indulge himself in this offence for his own gratification. Yet the attack committed on the honour of the party aggrieved may have its equivalent in the pain inflicted upon the pride of the aggressor, especially if he is condemned by the judgment of the Court, not only to retract and apologize, but to submit to some meaner ordeal, as kissing the hand of the injured person. In like manner, if a man of the highest rank has violently assaulted an innocent citizen of the lower orders, he may be condemned not only to apologize but to undergo a solitary and painful imprisonment, whereby, in addition to the discomfort endured, the vanity of the offender would be painfully affected, and the very shame of his position would constitute an adequate Retaliation after the principle of 'Like with Like.' But how then would we render the statement: 'If you *steal* from another, you steal from yourself'? In this way, that whoever steals anything makes the property of all insecure; he therefore robs himself of all security in property, according to the Right of Retaliation. Such a one has nothing, and can acquire nothing, but he has the Will to live; and this is only possible by others supporting him. But as the State should not do this gratuitously, he must for this purpose yield his powers to the State to be used in penal labour; and thus he falls for a time, or it may be for life, into a condition of slavery. — But whoever has committed Murder, must *die*. There is, in this case, no juridical substitute or surrogate, that can be given or taken for the satisfaction of Justice. There is no Likeness or proportion between Life, however painful, and Death; and therefore there is no Equality between the crime of Murder and the retaliation of it but what is judicially accomplished by the execution of the Criminal. His death, however, must be kept free from all maltreatment that would make the humanity suffering in his Person loathsome or abominable. Even if a Civil Society resolved to dissolve itself with the consent of all its members — as might be supposed in the case of a People inhabiting an island resolving to separate and scatter themselves throughout the whole world — the last Murderer lying in the prison ought to be executed before the resolution was carried out. This ought to be done in order that every one may realize the desert of his deeds, and that bloodguiltiness may not remain upon the people; for otherwise they might all be regarded as participators in the murder as a public violation of Justice.

The Equalization of Punishment with Crime, is therefore only possible by the cognition of the Judge extending even to the penalty of Death, according to the Right of Retaliation. This is manifest from the fact that it is only thus that a Sentence can be pronounced over all criminals proportionate to their internal *wickedness*; as may be seen by considering the case when the punishment of Death has to be inflicted, not on account of a murder, but on account of a political crime that can only be punished capitally. A hypothetical case, founded on history, will illustrate this. In the last Scottish Rebellion there were various participators in it — such as Balmerino and others — who believed that in taking part in the Rebellion they were only discharging their duty to the House of Stuart; but there were also others who were animated only by private motives and interests. Now, suppose that the Judgment of the Supreme Court regarding them had been this: that every one should have liberty to choose between the punishment of Death or Penal Servitude for life. In view of such an alternative, I say that the Man of Honour would choose Death, and the Knave would choose servitude. This would be the effect of their human nature as it is; for the honourable man values his Honour more highly than even Life itself, whereas a Knave regards a Life, although covered with shame, as better in his eyes than not to be. The former is, without gainsaying, less guilty than the other; and they can only be proportionately punished by death being inflicted equally upon them both; yet to the one it is a mild punishment when his nobler temperament is taken into account, whereas it is a hard punishment to the other in view of his baser temperament. But, on the other hand, were they all equally condemned to Penal Servitude for life, the honourable man would be too severely punished, while the other, on account of his baseness of nature, would be too mildly punished. In the judgment to be pronounced over a number of criminals united in such a conspiracy, the best Equalizer of Punishment and Crime in the form of public Justice is Death. And besides all this, it has never been heard of, that a Criminal condemned to death on account of a murder has complained that the Sentence inflicted on him was more than right and just; and any one would treat him with scorn if he expressed himself to this effect against it. Otherwise it would be necessary to admit that although wrong and injustice are not done to the Criminal by the law, yet the Legislative Power is not entitled to administer this mode of Punishment; and if it did so, it would be in contradiction with itself.

However many they may be who have committed a murder, or have even commanded it, or have been accessories in it, they ought all to suffer death; for so Justice wills it, in accordance with the Idea of the juridical Power as founded on the universal Laws of Reason. But the number of the Accomplices (*correi*) in such a deed might happen to be so great that the State, in resolving to be without such criminals, would be in danger of soon also being deprived of subjects. But it will not thus dissolve itself, neither must it return to the much worse condition of Nature, in which there would be no external Justice. Nor, above all, should it deaden the sensibilities of the People by the spectacle of Justice being exhibited in the mere carnage of a slaughtering bench. In such circumstances the Sovereign must always be allowed to have it in his power to take the part of the Judge upon himself as a case of Necessity,— and to deliver a Judgment which, instead of the penalty of death, shall assign some other punishment to the Criminals, and thereby preserve a multitude of the People. The penalty of Deportation is relevant in this connection. Such a form of Judgment cannot be carried out according to a public law, but only by an authoritative act of the royal Prerogative, and it may only be applied as an act of grace in individual cases.

QUESTIONS

1. Kant asserts that an innocent man may not be punished (hanged or imprisoned by the state) merely in order to do some good or avoid an evil however great. What reason does he give for this position? Does his reason work equally effectively as an objection to *remitting* a judicial penalty for the sake of some good purpose?
2. What do you think Kant may mean by saying "The Penal Law is a Categorical Imperative"? Does this statement necessarily exclude utilitarian considerations?
3. What does he mean by the "Principle of Equality" as a standard for affixing penalties for criminal behavior?
4. Kant also says that only adherence to the Principle of Equality will provide punishments for criminals "proportionate to their internal wickedness." Is there a tight connection between the kind of harm a man does and his blameworthiness in doing it? For instance, is an assassination from patriotic motives as wicked as planning and executing a murder in order to inherit the victim's property? What do you think of Kant's argument about the proper fate for participants in the Scottish Rebellion?
5. Is Kant consistent in allowing the exception he does in the final paragraph?

Jerome Michael   (1890-1953) and
Herbert Wechsler   (1909-   )

A UTILITARIAN THEORY OF
CRIMINAL JUSTICE

Many philosophers since very early times have thought that a broadly utilitarian justification is the only defensible justification of institutions for treatment of persons who perform antisocial acts; they have also thought that utilitarian considerations properly determine the particular form such institutions should take.

The following argument was written by two law professors of this persuasion, as part of the introductory chapter of an influential and learned treatise on criminal law, long used in the United States as a standard textbook in the law schools. Both authors were teachers at the Columbia University Law School at the time they were writing their book. Wechsler is now a professor at that institution.

The view represented by this chapter is representative of most, but not all, opinion of professors of criminal law in the United States.

We should notice that the authors are not in the least arguing that judges or prosecutors should do what, in the total circumstances of the moment, they think will have best consequences; they are not defending act-utilitarianism for judges. They are discussing what the proper penal code is and what the rules are that judges should follow in assigning penalties where they have discretion; the authors are advocating following utilitarian considerations in fixing these general principles, rules, and practices.

Criminal Law and Its Administration, by Jerome Michael and Herbert Wechsler, published by The Foundation Press, Inc., Brooklyn, N. Y. Reprinted by permission of the publisher, pp. 4-17.

CRIMINAL LAW AND ITS ADMINISTRATION

SECTION 2.   THE BASIC PROBLEMS
OF CRIMINAL LAW: ENDS AND MEANS°

I

It will not be denied that the nature and function of law require it to be evaluated as a means to an end, but it is well to make the point explicit at the start and to consider some of its implications. No one would contend that legislators and administrators should be given tremendous power over the lives and happiness of other men and be paid to exercise such power because legislation and administration are valuable for their own sake. If they are desirable at all, it is only because they are a means to the achievement of some valuable state of social affairs. Accordingly, the evaluation of a particular legal activity raises two questions: (1) what ends does the activity serve, i.e., what are its actual or probable results in society; and (2) are they ends which men should endeavor to achieve by law, i.e., are they desirable in themselves or as a means to ends desirable but more remote? Similarly, the determination of what kind of legal activity to undertake turns on the ends which ought to be served and the means which are well adapted to serving them.[1] Thus any question about what ought to be done in any of the branches of legal activity is different from and more complex than a question about what has been done, is being done or will be done in any of them.[2]

Questions about the character and results of a particular legal activity, or about the adaptation of particular means to particular ends, are questions of fact. They can be answered, if they are answerable at all, by the knowledge derived from common experience or from the special experience obtained by historical and sociological investigation. That life imprisonment is well adapted to rendering the persons subjected to it incapable of committing crimes outside of prison, is obviously indicated by common knowledge of what imprisonment involves. Investigation of what occurred during the prohibition era sustains the conclusion that national prohibition gave considerable impetus to the organization of professional criminals. That the severity of the penalties of the early nineteenth century criminal law was responsible for the refusal of many men to participate in their enforcement, is the inescapable finding of a somewhat more extensive historical investigation. But whether or not the incapacitation of persons convicted of crime,

---

° This discussion builds upon and incorporates extracts from Michael and Adler, *Crime, Law and Social Science* (1933); Wechsler and Michael, "A Rationale of the Law of Homicide" (1937) 37 *Col. L. Rev.* 701, 1261; Wechsler, "A Caveat on Crime Control" (1937) 27 *J. Crim. L.* 629.

[1] See Aristotle, *Ethics*, Bk. L, c. v; Michael and Adler, *Crime, Law and Social Science* (1933), c. II.

[2] See F. S. Cohen, *Ethical Systems and Legal Ideals* (1933) 1-112.

or the organization of professional criminals, or the nullification of penal laws, is desirable, undesirable, or more or less desirable than some alternative state of affairs is a question of value rather than of fact.[3] It is logically impossible to demonstrate that some state of social affairs is good or bad or better or worse than some other state of affairs by facts alone.[4] The syllogism requires a judgment about what is good or bad in social life. The assertion, evaluation, and exploration of such propositions is the province of politics and also of ethics, since what is good in social life cannot be considered apart from what is good in individual life. Both the lawmaker and his critic necessarily employ ethical and political ideas and the more civilized they are the more fully are they conscious that they are doing so.

While this much is clear, what is likely to be unclear is whether the ultimate propositions in ethics and politics, those which concern ends rather than means, can reasonably be asserted as anything more than a personal preference.[5] If they can only be asserted as a personal preference, it is impossible to evaluate law and legal activity on any other ground than their conformity to the personal desires of the individual who makes the judgment. Even in this event, however, judgments of preference may be better or worse in the sense that the individual's appraisal of his own lasting desires may be faulty. He may, for example, either fail to perceive or underestimate his own concern for the welfare of other people. If, on the other hand, the ultimate propositions of ethics and politics can be asserted on some broader basis than personal preference, the reason must be that it is possible, as we think it is, to achieve some grasp of the fundamental and permanent in human desires in general, the specifically human in the capacities of men. This is the groundwork upon which ethical and political thought must build in the articulation of ultimate ends and the ordering of more immediate ends and means.

In the ordering of means and ends one must obviously employ what-

[3] In the wealth of literature, see, in addition to that cited *supra* notes 1 and 2, M. R. Cohen, *Reason and Nature* (1931) 369-385, 401-412, and *Law and the Social Order* (1933) 188-192.

[4] "The fact that questions of value have to be dealt with by dialectical rather than statistical methods puts a limitation on the use of history for juristic purposes. History is undoubtedly a method of extending our experience. It helps to eliminate vicious rationalism, the tendency typified by Blackstone to find false reasons for actual legal rules. Yet, by itself, history cannot establish standards of value or of what is desirable in the law. In fact, the same sets of historical facts teach different lessons to those who have different biases as to what is desirable. It is customary to have historical introductions to all sorts of practical discussions; but generally they are like the chaplain's prayer that opens a political convention, graceful and altogether unexceptional, but hardly determinative of subsequent proceedings." (*Law and the Social Order*, 192).

[5] *Cf.* Sweezy, Book Review (1940) 53 *Harv. L. Rev.* 1064: "Underlying conceptions of good and evil, it has been frequently observed, do not constitute a fruitful subject of controversy. These are matters of taste which it is best to leave for the individual to work out for himself as best he can."

ever knowledge there is of the adaptation of particular means to particular ends, and the question of adaptation of means to end is, as we have said, a question of fact. That it is a question of fact does not mean, however, that it is easy to answer. To a very considerable degree knowledge of matters of fact, particularly of the crucial sociological and psychological facts of law, consists of opinions the relative validity of which it is difficult or impossible to measure. Hence, even when men agree about remote ends, they frequently disagree about the adaptation of means to these ends and, therefore, about the relative value of intermediate ends. This inadequacy in knowledge of matters of fact marks the limitations of the rôle of reason in the solution of practical problems, and nowhere are these limitations more apparent or more lamentable than in the field of the criminal law. An understanding of our limitations in this respect is, however, as much a condition of wisdom as an understanding of our rational power. Understanding of our limitations charts the path to decreasing them and guarantees a proper modesty in our expectations. It protects us against actions which are rash and gives us the fortitude to take risks in action which only a thoughtless conservatism decries. But more than this, it enables us to dismiss claims to goodness which can be shown to be unfounded or inferior to competing claims. This is as important a part of the rational process as the assertion of claims which can be shown to be well founded and, which, therefore, compel assent.

II

The major problems of the criminal law [6] are two: what behavior should be made criminal, and what should be done with persons who commit crimes. For reasons already stated, the analysis of these problems should begin with a consideration of ends; and the initial question properly concerns ultimate ends. In this dimension, it has been argued that the ultimate end of the criminal law should be retribution — the punishment of those who will to inflict undeserved evil on others by penalties proportioned to their offenses. This contention has far-reaching implications and its validity must be appraised.

That the retributive position is an ancient one cannot be doubted and it may be that, as Bradley has said, it represents the unstudied belief

[6] There are difficulties in defining precisely the scope of the criminal as opposed to the civil law. If we look at the law as it is, it is obviously difficult to maintain any of the traditional positions: that the criminal law deals with behavior which is offensive to society as a whole rather than that which is offensive only to individuals; that the criminal law deals with acts that involve great moral turpitude rather than those that involve slight moral turpitude or are morally indifferent; that the criminal law determines who shall be punished and the civil law who shall make restitution or pay damages; that the criminal law determines what proceedings shall be brought by the state rather than what proceedings may be instituted by private citizens at their option. See, in this connection, Kenny, *Outlines of Criminal Law* (15th ed., 1936), c. 1; M. R. Cohen, "On Absolutisms in Legal Thought" (1936) 84 *U. of Pa. L. Rev.* 681, 686-687, "Moral Aspects of the Criminal Law" (1940) 49 *Yale L.J.* 987, 988-990.

of most men.[7] Its first systematic development is, however, to be found in the ethical writings of Kant [8] and Hegel [9] and their followers, Stammler and Kohler. Kant argued that it is self-evident that the desert of crime is punishment; that justice requires that a man who has willed an unjust act [10] be punished by a penalty which is strictly proportional in nature and intensity to his crime; that a person who does such an act affirms that it is right that people be dealt with in that way and, therefore, he himself should be dealt with in the same way; that if society fails to punish a criminal, it sanctions his principles and thereby becomes *particeps criminis*. Kant denied that any other considerations are relevant; a world in which justice is sacrificed is not worth preserving on other grounds.[11] "Juridical punishment can never be administered merely as a means for promoting another good, either with regard to the criminal himself or to civil society, but must in all cases be imposed only because the individual on whom it is inflicted has committed a crime. For one man ought never to be dealt with merely as a means subservient to the purpose of another . . . Against such treatment his inborn personality has a right to protect him . . . The Penal Law is a Categorical Imperative; and woe to him who creeps through the serpent-windings of Utilitarianism to discover some advantage that may discharge him from the

[7] Bradley, *Ethical Studies* (2d ed., 1927) 1-41. "If there is any opinion to which the man of uncultivated morals is attached, it is the belief in the necessary connection of punishment and guilt. Punishment is punishment only where it is deserved. We pay the penalty, because we owe it, and for no other reason; and if punishment is inflicted for any other reason whatever than because it is merited by wrong, it is a gross immorality, a crying injustice, an abominable crime, and not what it pretends to be . . . Having once the right to punish, we may modify the punishment according to the useful and the pleasant; but these are external to the matter, they can not give us a right to punish, and nothing can do that but criminal desert. . . . Yes, in despite of sophistry, and in the face of sentimentalism with well nigh the whole body of our self-styled enlightenment against them, our people believe to this day that *punishment is inflicted for the sake of punishment*. . . ." Id. at pp. 26-27, 28. But *cf.* Holmes, *The Common Law* (1881) 45, quoted *infra* note 17: see also Sharp and Otto, "A Study of the Popular Attitude Toward Retributive Punishment" (1910) 20 *Int. J. of Ethics* 341, "Retribution and Deterrence in the Moral Judgments of Common Sense" *id.* at 438.

[8] See *The Science of Right*, Part 2, sec. 49; *Philosophy of Law* (Hastie tr., 1887) 194-204.

[9] *The Philosophy of Right* (Dyde tr., 1896) 90-103.

[10] What actions are unjust depends of course upon Kant's ethical analysis which we cannot examine in detail. It may be useful, however, to call attention to the following points in his ethical doctrine: (1) Men are rational and have freedom of will; (2) no action can be affirmed to be right or wrong unless it proceeds on a principle of conduct which can be affirmed to be right or wrong for all men in the given situation independent of their special inclinations; (3) no man should use another as a means to some desired end. For some elaboration of these points, see Broad, *Five Types of Ethical Theory* (1930), c. V; M. R. Cohen, "Moral Aspects of the Criminal Law" (1940) 49 *Yale L.J.* 987, 992-994, 1009-1012.

[11] *Philosophy of Law*, 196.

justice of punishment or even from the due measure of it . . ." [12] Hegel states the position somewhat differently. He agrees that punishment is just because it is deserved but, the justice of punishment having been thus established, he, apparently, would permit other factors than the culpability of the offense to be considered in determining the character of the punishment. Later writers introduce even further qualifications [13] while adhering to the basic point that the end of punishment should be retribution.[14]

The critics of the retributive position deny that it is self-evident that retribution is just, whether one believes in free will (in the sense that purposive behavior is uncaused by antecedent physical, mental and environmental conditions but is the product of the will which is itself a first cause) or in determinism (in the sense of the rule of cause and effect in the behavior of human beings).[15] They ask what intuitive necessity there is, apart from

[12] *Philosophy of Law*, 195. In two cases, however, Kant does not adhere to his own principle. He concedes that punishment may be mitigated if it would "deaden the sensibilities of the People by the spectacle of Justice being exhibited in the mere carnage of the slaughtering bench" and also, apparently, if it would result in an undue depopulation of the State.

[13] See, for example, Kohler, *Philosophy of Law* (Modern Legal Philosophy ed., 1914) 279 *et seq.*

[14] Can one who holds the retributive view define the criminal law unambiguously as the body of law, possible and actual, which ought to serve the end of retribution?

[15] Determinists have attacked the retributive theory on the ground that it presupposes a non-determinist view of human behavior. They have argued that the idea of personal guilt is incompatible with a recognition of the fact that the individual's will to do evil is itself a product of his heredity and environment; that the individual ought not to be held at fault for willing what antecedent conditions caused him to will; and that if there is any fault, it must rest with these antecedent conditions. See, for example, McConnell, *Criminal Responsibility and Social Constraint* (1912) 48 *et seq.* To the extent, and only to the extent, that one who holds the retributive view reasons from his belief in freedom of the will, or that the justice of retribution is, intuitively, dependent upon such freedom (*cf.* Kohler, *op. cit. supra* note 13, at 281), is this attack relevant. It is not decisive because if there is any basis, intuitively, for the justice of retribution, there is no logical reason why it may not remain even if determinism be admitted, why, in short, one may not intuit the justice of punishing those who have the capacity to deliberate and choose to do evil, even though one concede that their choices may be determined. The idea of determinism, of the reign of cause and effect in the whole physical order, does not deny the reality of deliberation in the psychological order. Thus Aquinas, following Aristotle, distinguishes between actions which are instinctive and those which follow upon deliberation; by freedom of the will he means only the capacity to deliberate. Yet he does not reject the conceptions of guilt and sin. Freedom is so defined that there is no conflict with determinism.

On the other hand, some believers in freedom of the will have argued against determinism on the ground that such a view renders punishment inappropriate because it destroys the conception of guilt and, in doing so, the basis of all morality. This argument is completely unfounded. Even were punishment rendered inappropriate by determinism, the truth of determinism would be unaffected; "we cannot prove the existence of anything by the argument that if it did not exist our policies would be unjustified." (M. R. Cohen, *Reason and Nature*, 327.) But, beyond this, once retribution is rejected, it is obvious that a concern for future actions, that evil be repaid with punishment rather than ignored. "If we give up all utilitarian ideas of social welfare, what necessity is there that the universe should be organized like a penitentiary on the basis of rewards and punishments?" [16] Holmes contended that "it will be seen on self-inspection, that this feeling of fitness [of punishment following wrongdoing] is absolute and unconditional only in the case of our neighbors" and that then it is "only vengeance in disguise." [17] Throughout the history of thought it has been argued in various ways that human punishment is a creature of human law and human law an instrument of the state; that the ultimate end of the state should be the welfare of its members and that both law and legal penalties should serve the same end; and that they are just precisely to the extent that they do serve that end. Since punishment consists in the infliction of pain it is, apart from its consequences, an evil; consequently, it is good and, therefore, just only if and to the degree that it serves the common good by advancing the welfare of the person punished or of the rest of the population. This is the position taken by Plato,[18] Aristotle,

punishment not only is appropriate in a deterministic world but that it is appropriate only in such a world. For, if retribution is rejected, the whole purpose of inflicting punishment is to control behavior by providing individuals with an additional motive for refraining from criminal conduct — the motive of avoiding punishment, just as the purpose of moral education is to provide them with other motives for right conduct. The basic assumption is that action is governed by motives, that character can be improved by individual effort, which can, in turn, be stimulated. See John Stuart Mill, *An Examination of Sir William Hamilton's Philosophy* (1866) ii, 291; M. R. Cohen, *op. cit. supra* at 326-330; Dewey, *Human Nature and Conduct* (1922) 18-19; *cf.* Saleilles, *The Individualization of Punishment* (Mod. Cr. Sci. ed., 1911), c. vi.

[16] M. R. Cohen, *Law and the Social Order*, 310.

[17] *The Common Law*, 45: "It does not seem to me that anyone who has satisfied himself that an act of his was wrong and that he will never do it again, would feel the least need or propriety, as between himself and an earthly punishing power alone, of his being made to suffer for what he has done, although when third persons were introduced, he might, as a philosopher, admit the necessity of hurting him to frighten others. But when our neighbors do wrong, we sometimes feel the fitness of making them smart for it, whether they have repented or not."

Cf. John Stuart Mill, *op. cit. supra* note 15, at 292-293. "Now, the primitive consciousness we are said to have, that we are accountable for our actions, and that if we violate the rule of right we shall deserve punishment, I contend is nothing else than our knowledge that punishment will be just; that by such conduct we shall place ourselves in the position in which our fellow-creatures, or the Deity, or both, will naturally, and may justly inflict punishment upon us . . . We are supposed capable of understanding that other people have rights, and all that follows from this. The mind which possesses this idea, if capable of placing itself at the point of view of another person, must recognize it as just that others should protect themselves against any disposition on his part to infringe their rights; and he will do so the more readily because he also has rights, and his rights continually require the same protection. This, I maintain, is our feeling of accountability, in so far as it can be separated from the prospect of being actually called to account."

[18] See Protagoras, 324: ". . . No one punishes the evil-doer under the notion, or for the reason, that he has done wrong, — only the unreasonable fury of a beast acts in that manner. But he who desires to inflict rational punishment does not retaliate for a past

Cicero, St. Thomas Aquinas, and the medieval Church,[19] as well as by Hobbes,[20] Beccaria,[21] Bentham,[22] and many others in more modern times.[23] According to this view retribution is itself unjust since it requires some human beings to inflict pain upon others, regardless of its effect upon them or upon the social welfare. In any event, it is urged, the retributive theory is incapable of practical application. How can men lacking omniscience measure degrees of guilt in individual cases and apportion pain thereto? How is it possible, moreover, to inflict pain upon the guilty without also inflicting pain upon their innocent relatives and friends? Since the retributive theory requires not only that the guilty be punished but also that the guiltless be not, how, as Ewing has asked, is it possible to avoid doing more retributive injustice than justice in any given case? [24]

These considerations seem to us not only to refute the retributive position but also to establish that the criminal law, like the rest of the law, should serve the end of promoting the common good; and that its specific capacity for serving this end inheres in its power to prevent or control socially undesirable behavior. The consequence of rejecting retribution as the ultimate end of the criminal law is that it does not constitute a valid criterion for the evaluation of particular legal provisions, that no legal provision can be justified merely because it calls for the punishment of the morally guilty

wrong which cannot be undone; he has regard to the future, and is desirous that the man who is punished, and he who sees him punished, may be deterred from doing wrong again. He punishes for the sake of prevention. . . ." See also *Gorgias*, 525; *Republic*, 380, 615; *Phaedo*, 113; *Laws*, 854, 862, 934, 957.

[19] See Michael and Adler, *op. cit. supra* note 1, at 342-352.

[20] *Leviathan* (1651), Part II, c. 30.

[21] *Crimes and Punishments* (1764), *passim*, especially cc. I, II, VII.

[22] "The general object which all laws have, or ought to have, in common, is to augment the total happiness of the community; and therefore in the first place, to exclude, as far as may be, everything that tends to subtract from that happiness; in other words, to exclude mischief . . . But all punishment is mischief; all punishment in itself is evil. Upon the principle of utility, if it ought at all to be admitted, it ought only to be admitted in as far as it promises to exclude some greater evil." *Principles of Morals and Legislation* (Oxford ed., 1879) 170.

[23] See, in addition to the works cited above, Ewing, *The Morality of Punishment* (1929) 13-45; Holmes, *The Common Law*, 42-46; Willoughby, *Social Justice* (1900) 316 *et seq.*; McConnell, *Criminal Responsibility and Social Constraint* (1912) 6-59; Saleilles *op. cit. supra* note 15; Aschaffenburg, *Crime and Its Repression* (Mod. Cr. Sci. ed., 1913) 250 *et seq.*; Oppenheimer, *The Rationale of Punishment* (1913) 234 *et seq.*

[24] Ewing, *op. cit. supra* note 23, at 39-40; see also Aschaffenburg, *loc. cit. supra* note 23. But *cf.* M. R. Cohen, *op. cit. supra* note 10, at 1007: "Few readers of the Bible, I imagine, have felt outraged at the fact that when Achan sins, his innocent children are also killed. . . . Furthermore, as a result of the last war, Germany was made to pay reparations, and the burden fell upon the innocent children who had no part and could in no way prevent the invasion of Belgium and all the destruction which it involved. Was this unjust? By no means, if we recognize collective responsibility. It is obvious that in many relations the family or the nation rather than the individual is regarded as the moral unit."

by penalties proportioned to their guilt, or criticised merely because it fails to do so. This does not mean that legal provisions which may have been instituted to serve the end of retribution are necessarily impolitic. Unless the retributive purpose is deemed to be authoritative for purposes of present administration,[25] the question remains whether the particular provision is well or poorly adapted to the prevention of socially undesirable behavior or to promoting the common good in other ways.[26]

III

The only means which the criminal law can employ to prevent socially undesirable behavior is the treatment of those persons who have engaged or are likely to engage in such behavior. There are many possible methods of treatment and they may serve the end of prevention in different ways. If a person has engaged in behavior of a sort which is undesirable and can be deterred, and if he is subjected to treatment which is generally regarded as unpleasant, other persons may be deterred from engaging in similar conduct by the fear that if they do so they will be similarly treated. Whatever the character of his past behavior, if the person subjected to treatment is himself likely to engage in undesirable behavior in the future, his treatment may serve to prevent him from doing so by incapacitating, intimidating or reforming him. Accordingly, the determination of the kinds of behavior to be made criminal involves three major problems: (1) What sorts of conduct is it both desirable and possible to deter; (2) what sorts indicate that persons who behave in those ways are dangerously likely to engage in socially undesirable behavior in the future; (3) will the attempt to prevent particular kinds of undesirable behavior by the criminal law do less good, as measured by the success of such efforts, than harm, as measured by their other and harmful results. The determination of methods of treating criminals also involves three major problems: (1) What methods are best adapted to the various ends of treatment; (2) to what extent do methods which serve one end of treatment also serve or disserve other ends; (3) if one end of treatment must be preferred over others, either because there are no methods of treatment well adapted to all of them, or for other reasons,

---

[25] This suggests an important historical problem, in connection with which see Goebel, *Felony and Misdemeanor* (1937), especially 62-122, 280-335, 399-440; Rusche and Kirchheimer, *Punishment and Social Structure* (1939); Holdsworth, *History of English Law* (3d ed., 1923), ii, 43-50; Pollock and Maitland, *History of English Law* (2d ed., 1923), ii, 466-476; Sayre, "Mens Rea" (1932) 45 *Harv. L. Rev.* 974; Phillipson, *Three Criminal Law Reformers* (1923), especially 27-32, 39, 85-99, 164-168, 170-179; Ives, *A History of Penal Methods* (1914).

[26] Is it possible for one who rejects the retributive view to define the criminal law unambiguously as the body of law, possible and actual, which ought to serve the end of preventing behavior incompatible with the common welfare? Is that not true of much of what is traditionally known as the civil law? See note 6 *supra*.

what should be the order of preference among them? [27] That there is an intimate relationship between these two sets of problems is clear, since the consequences, desirable and undesirable, of making behavior criminal will to a very considerable extent depend upon the character of the methods employed in the treatment of criminals [28] and since the choice of methods of treatment must depend in part, at least, upon the reasons for making the behavior criminal.[29]

In order to determine the kinds of behavior which it is desirable to deter, the probable results, both good and bad, of behavior of various sorts must be discovered and then estimated as being on the whole socially desirable or socially undesirable. In making behavior criminal three questions must therefore be answered: (1) What consequences of human activity are socially undesirable; (2) what sorts of behavior tend to produce such results; (3) which of the sorts having that tendency are nevertheless socially desirable because their socially beneficial potentialities are greater than their socially dangerous tendencies? It is therefore apparent that, in its broadest aspect, the determination of the behavior to be made criminal, is the problem of the kind of social order we ought to strive for; and that, with respect to particular kinds of conduct, it is the problem whether or not they are conducive to that kind of social order. Although we shall be concerned in this course with behavior which for the most part would be intolerable in any society, we cannot wholly avoid the problem in its broadest form. For even behavior which menaces life or fundamental interests in property may serve ends which are more desirable than the lives or property interests which it endangers.[30] This is especially true, as we shall see, when the threat is remote.

In order to determine the kinds of undesirable behavior which it is possible to deter, the probability that the desire to avoid punishment will be stronger than whatever desires move men to such conduct, must be estimated.[31] The determination of the kinds of behavior which indicate that the actors are dangerously likely to engage in socially undesirable behavior in the future, involves the even more difficult psychological problem of

[27] For a fuller development of the points made in the text, see Wechsler and Michael, "A Rationale of the Law of Homicide" (1937) 37 Col. L. Rev. 730-733, 752, 1261-1263, hereinafter cited as "A Rationale of the Law of Homicide"; M. R. Cohen, op. cit. supra note 10, at 1012 et seq.

[28] Consider, for example, the differences in the probable consequences of making it a crime to employ minors in industry, to possess a firearm, or to exceed a speed limit, according as the penalty is a small fine or a long term of imprisonment.

[29] Thus, if the primary reason for making particular behavior criminal is that it is deemed to be indicative of a dangerous personality, it is likely to be foolish to devote much attention to deterrence as an object of treatment.

[30] See "A Rationale of the Law of Homicide," 37 Col. L. Rev. 742-746; Wechsler, "A Caveat on Crime Control" (1937) 27 J. Crim. L. 629, 631-633; cf. Cardozo, The Paradoxes of Legal Science (1928) 72 et seq.

[31] See "A Rationale of the Law of Homicide," 37 Col. L. Rev. 752-757.

estimating the potentialities of men for good and evil conduct, of appraising their characters on the basis of their prior behavior.[32] Whatever the purpose of the inquiry, whether to discover what kinds of behavior can be deterred or to discover what kinds of behavior are indicative of bad character, it may be aided by a consideration of other factors than the nature of the behavior itself. What are the relevant factors? Is the knowledge or intention or motive with which a man engages in certain conduct, or the state of his emotions at the time, or his age, or his prior history, pertinent to either of these inquiries? The Anglo-American criminal law, as it now exists, makes some of these factors significant for legal purposes. Are the discriminations reflected in contemporary law justifiable if the purpose of the law is to prevent socially undesirable behavior or only, as some writers assert, if its end is retribution? And if the latter, what discriminations should be made in a system designed to serve non-retributive ends?

That behavior is of a sort which it is desirable and possible to deter or which is indicative of the dangerousness of individuals who engage in it, does not necessarily establish that it should be made criminal. The consequences of making it criminal may be more undesirable than the consequences of the behavior itself. We desire to prevent anti-social behavior in order to improve the conditions of social life; we must take care, therefore, that social life is not made worse by the medicine than by the disease.[33]

When we turn to the problems of treatment we find that they are no less complex or difficult. We can be reasonably certain that no methods of treatment can be devised which will deter all potential offenders or reform all actual offenders or, what is even more difficult, do both at once. We do know, of course, that death and life imprisonment are effective methods of incapacitation. We do not know and may never know with certainty what methods of treatment are most efficacious as deterrents or as reformatives or how efficacious any method of treatment is.[34] Common sense tells us that most men fear punishment to an indeterminate and inconstant degree and that the more certain and severe punishment is, the more intensely it is likely to be feared.[35] But the law must rely for its enforcement upon ordinary men acting as complainants, as witnesses, as jurors, and as officials. Common sense also warns us that to varying and uncertain degrees the widespread imposition of drastically severe penalties arouses in many such men a

---

[32] Id. at pp. 757-761, 1272-1273.

[33] See Bentham, *Principles of Morals and Legislation*, 175-177; Michael and Adler, *op. cit. supra* note 1, at 353; F. S. Cohen, *Ethical Systems and Legal Ideals*, 249-285.

[34] To be able to answer these questions with certainty, we should have to know the causes of crime; to know the causes of crime we need a complete etiology of human behavior. For an evaluation of the most important empirical studies of causation, treatment, and prevention, see Michael and Adler, *op. cit. supra* note 1, at 44-225.

[35] For Bentham's elaborate discussion of the implications of this point, see his *Principles of Penal Law*, Part II, Book I, c. III in *Works* (1843), i. Compare Von Hentig, "Punishment," *Encyc. Soc. Sci.*, xii, 712-715, "The Limits of Deterrence" (1938) 29 J. Crim. L. 555.

sympathy for the accused which leads them to refuse to participate in inflicting them. When this result occurs nullification ensues,[36] and the effect of the severity of punishment is greatly to magnify its uncertainty [37] and to provoke a general hatred of the law which in a democratic society must inevitably culminate in its change. Accordingly, penalties must be mitigated in most cases to avoid nullification.[38] Common sense further warns us that the infliction of severe punishment short of total incapacitation is likely to result in the return to society of men utterly unfit for a non-criminal life, embittered, and determined to exact their revenge.[39] It cautions us, too, that,

[36] See "A Rationale of the Law of Homicide," 37 *Col. L. Rev.* 1264-1265, and the material *infra* sec. 4, B, 1. Compare Ewing, *op. cit. supra* note 23, at 56-60; and see, in general, Ives, *A History of Penal Methods*; Phillipson, *Three Criminal Law Reformers*; O'Brien, *The Foundation of Australia* (1937); J. Hall, *Theft, Law and Society* (1935) 87 *et seq.*

[37] This was the situation in England in Romilly's time, produced primarily by the widespread applicability of the death penalty against which he and some of his contemporaries successfully protested. See *The Speeches* of Sir Samuel Romilly (1820), Vol. 1; Eden, *Principles of Penal Law* (1771) 13-14, 21-39; Bentham, *Works* (1843 ed.), i, 441 *et seq.*, 525 *et seq.* and the references *supra* note 36.

[38] For a short discussion of the development of criminal penalties in England, see Stephen, *A History of the Criminal Law of England* (1883), i, 457-490, hereinafter cited as "History of the Criminal Law."

[39] *Cf.* Alexander Paterson, *The Prison Problem of America* (Printed at H. M. Prison, Maidstone, for Private Circulation) 11-12: "Common sense suggests that if the prison administration is designed to protect society against its dangerous and mischievous elements, its first duty, after securing the safe custody of the offender, is to ensure that a man on emerging from prison is not more depraved than when he entered it. Within his cell he may degrade himself, within the wall he may be degraded by others. Prison can so easily become an unhealthy little cess-pool. It is unnatural that men should live apart from women and children, unnatural that they should be solitary for so many hours in so small a space, that their movements should be so confined and their daily doings so minutely routined. In such an artificial surrounding it is difficult for men to develop or retain a normal social habit and attitude of mind. They may well become more hardened and antisocial, and return to the freedom that must come some day firmly pledged to prey rather than co-operate.

"In some well-ordered prisons a more insidious process operates. The man who comes in as a criminal is made into a prisoner. All initiative and self-reliance are lost, obeying every order given to him he comes in time to wait for an order. He develops a desire to please, which makes him furtive and sycophantic. In the external show of order and cleanliness his conduct is model, but in the inner things that matter he is at heart still a thief and a waster, actually more useless and dangerous because he has cloaked his dishonesty with the paint and plaster of a well-behaved inmate of an Institution.

"Furthermore, prison may well do an infinity of harm to the casual beginner in crime by forcing him day after day into an association he cannot escape with men whose very speech is mud. It will not be long before he learns their slang, adopts their scale of values, and is infected with their attitude towards authority within and society without the walls. Once he is accepted as a member of a gang, only a miracle will regain him from their clutches.

"The prison administration, therefore, that hopes to reform its criminals, has to start well 'behind scratch'; it has a great deal to do before it can be reasonably sure that by the ordinary operation of cause and effect its men are not growing steadily worse every month

to some extent at least, cruelty or bloodshed inflicted in the name of the law is likely to have the same deleterious effect upon public morals as cruelty or bloodshed inflicted in the name of anything else.[40] Moreover, prisons are relatively few in number and expensive to build and maintain; the government of any considerable number of persons sentenced to life imprisonment is inordinately difficult; and it may be doubted whether any widespread extension of the death penalty would be politically feasible, even if it were wise. There is an additional reason for the mitigation of punishment whenever criminal behavior can be attributed to some grave injustice done the criminal either by some other person or by society as a whole as, for example, when many people are near starvation and men are driven to steal by hunger. As T. H. Green has pointed out,[41] the mitigation of penalties on that ground serves to direct attention to and to increase popular awareness of the original injustice and, thus, may lead to its correction.

On the other hand, while common sense may suggest that lenient or non-punitive methods of treatment are, in general, better adapted to reformation than severe methods, not all men are corrigible; and the separation of the corrigible from the incorrigible requires psychological judgments which are difficult or impossible to make with any assurance on the basis of the psychological knowledge that we now have; [42] reluctance to delegate to officials the power to make them may, accordingly, be wise. Moreover, the desire for revenge, the belief that retributive punishment is just, and the feeling that examples must be made of those guilty of shocking crimes are to a very considerable degree entrenched in the general population. Too lenient treatment of offenders, however well adapted to reforming them, may therefore lead to lynching, self-help or indifference about prosecution which may be far worse in their social consequences than the utilization of more severe methods of treatment which satisfy the popular desire for

they spend in prison." See also Bates, *Prisons and Beyond* (1936), *passim*, and the data assembled in Rusche and Kirchheimer, *op. cit. supra* note 25, especially 138 *et seq.*

On the relationship between deterrence and reformation and the implications of pursuing either end to the exclusion of the other, see "A Rationale of the Law of Homicide," 37 *Col. L. Rev.* 1313-1325; M. R. Cohen, *op. cit. supra* note 10, at 1012 *et seq.*; Ewing, *op. cit. supra* note 23, at 46-69, 73-125. Cf. Schopenhauer, *The World as Will and Idea* (Haldane and Kemp tr., 1886) 412: "The Penitentiary system also seeks not so much to punish the deed as the man, in order to reform him. It therefore sets aside the real aim of punishment, determent from the deed, in order to attain the very problematic end of reformation. But it is always a doubtful thing to attempt to attain two different ends by *one* means; how much more so, if the two are in any sense opposite ends. Education is a benefit, punishment ought to be an evil; the penitentiary prison is supposed to accomplish both at once."

[40] See the material *supra* note 36 and, in addition, Livingston's vigorous argument against the use of the death penalty, *Works* (1873 ed.), i, 194 *et seq.*

[41] *Lectures on the Principles of Political Obligation* (1927) 193-194.

[42] See note 34, *supra*; cf. Dession, "Psychiatry and The Conditioning of Criminal Justice" (1938) 47 *Yale L.J.* 319.

severity though they have no reformative efficacy. This may be what Stephen meant by his famous remark that the criminal law stands to the passion for vengeance in much the same relation as marriage to the sexual appetite.[43] But, on the other hand, it is urged that the desires for revenge and for retribution are themselves anti-social and, therefore, ought not to be encouraged by law;[44] that if the public mind is unprepared to view the problems of social control dispassionately, it ought to be educated to do so; and that the legal devices adopted by society can and ought to be employed to that end. Apart from these considerations, Bentham believed, and not without reason, that unless punishments are graded in proportion to the social harmfulness of behavior, there is no incentive to the potential offender to engage in less rather than more undesirable behavior.[45] And Beccaria insisted that it is important, not only for the prevention of crime but for social relations in general, that the community should properly evaluate the relative significance of anti-social conduct of various sorts, the degree to which various types of behavior are inimical to the general welfare; and that very lenient treatment of those who engage in exceedingly harmful behavior may lead the community to regard it as less harmful than it is.[46]

But more than this, the deterrence of potential offenders and the incapacitation and the reformation of actual offenders are not the only values which must be considered in determining the ends of treatment. Although criminals ought to be subjected to treatment for the sake of preventing crime and although the deterrence of potential offenders and the incapacitation and reformation of actual offenders are the proximate means to the prevention of crime by the criminal law, the methods employed in treating criminals may in their collateral consequences serve or disserve other social ends and

[43] *General View of the Criminal Law of England* (1863) 99; see also Holmes, *The Common Law*, 41-42; Ewing, *op. cit. supra* note 23, at 71.

[44] *Cf.* Holmes, *The Common Law*, 41-42: "If people would gratify the passion of revenge outside of the law, if the law did not help them, the law has no choice but to satisfy the craving itself, and thus avoid the greater evil of private retribution. At the same time, this passion is not one which we wish to encourage, either as private individuals or as law makers."

Consider, however, Tarde's hedonistic argument that since people as they are take pleasure in the infliction of pain upon those who have offended, the legal system ought to do its share to provide that pleasure as a means to the happiness of the citizen. *Penal Philosophy* (Howell tr., 1912) 34-36. See also Bentham, *op. cit. supra* note 22, 170-171, n. 1; Ewing, *op. cit. supra* note 23, at 69-71. Compare the following rigorous passages in Stephen, *History of the Criminal Law*, i, 478: "In cases which outrage the moral feelings of the community to a great degree, the feeling of indignation and desire for revenge which is excited in the minds of decent people is, I think, deserving of legitimate satisfaction;" and ii, 81-82: "I think it highly desirable that criminals should be hated, that the punishment inflicted on them should be so construed as to give expression to that hatred, and to justify it so far as the public provision of means for expressing and gratifying a healthy natural sentiment can justify and encourage it."

[45] See Bentham, *The Theory of Legislation, Principles of the Penal Code*, Part Third, c. ii.

[46] *Crimes and Punishments*, c. 23; *cf.* Ewing, *op. cit. supra* note 23, at 104.

their potentialities in these respects must also be taken into account. By the same token, the position of deterrence, incapacitation and reformation in relation to one another, as the ends of treatment, cannot be determined solely by reference to the crime preventive efficacy of a system derived from one ordering of these ends as opposed to another, even when their relative efficacy in this regard can be foretold. The extent to which other desirable ends — such, for example, as the proper expenditure of the national income — will be served or disserved by various alternative policies is an important element in the choice. No program for the determination of methods of treatment, no set of criteria for their evaluation, can ignore this obvious multiplicity of treatment ends.

QUESTIONS

1. What sort of general ethical theory do Michael and Wechsler propose to employ in their assessment of criminal law? It might appear that their utilitarian approach simply excludes a Kantian-type theory without discussion. How would the authors say their general framework could accommodate a retributive theory if there were good reasons for it?
2. Do you think the authors give an accurate account of Kant's theory? Is Kant's view overturned merely by throwing doubt on the self-evidence of the retributive position? Do you think the retributive theory is manifestly implausible if human actions are the product of heredity and training?
3. Are the authors right in their proposal that laws which inflict hardships are just only if they serve the collective welfare — or the welfare of the victim — in an important way?
4. If you were a utilitarian charged with setting up an ideal penal code, what major questions would you have to answer?
5. Do you think that, in view of the importance of the reformation of the criminal among the purposes of criminal law, the penalty for a crime should take into account the agent's knowledge, motives, state of emotions, age, prior history, and emotional condition at the time of the crime?
6. What problems are there in fixing on a scale of penalties for the purpose of maximal deterrence of prospective criminals?
7. What purposes other than deterrence, incapacitation, and reformation should be considered by the critic of codes of criminal law?

CHAPTER 6   SUGGESTIONS FOR FURTHER READING

Anshen, R. A., ed. *The Family: Its Function and Destiny*. New York: Harper, 1949.

Beaglehole, Ernest. *Property; a Study in Social Psychology*. New York: Macmillan, 1932.

Benn, S. I., and R. S. Peters. *Social Principles and the Democratic State*. London: Allen & Unwin, 1959, Chs. 5-8, 9, 10-15. An excellent discussion of justice, property, theory of punishment, the moral basis of the authority of the state, democracy, and freedom.

Brandt, Richard B. *Ethical Theory*. Englewood Cliffs, N. J.: Prentice-Hall, 1959, Chs. 16 and 19. The concept of justice; theories of justice, punishment.

Cherno, Melvin. "Locke on Property: a Reappraisal." *Ethics*, Vol. 68 (1957), pp. 51-55.

Cohen, Morris R. "Property and Sovereignty." In Cohen, M. R. *Law and the Social Order*. New York: Harcourt, Brace, 1933.

Coker, F. W., ed. *Democracy, Liberty, and Property*. New York: Macmillan, 1948. A collection of readings from American writers.

Dewey, John. *The Public and Its Problems*. Denver: Alan Swallow, 1957.

Ewing, A. C. *The Morality of Punishment*. London: Kegan Paul, Trench, Trubner, 1929, Chs. 1-5. A review of theories.

Greaves, H. R. G. *The Foundations of Political Theory*. London: Allen & Unwin, 1958.

Hall, L., and S. Glueck. *Cases on Criminal Law and Its Enforcement*. St. Paul, Minn.: West, 1958. A lively statement with many cases.

Lampman, R. J. "Recent Thought on Egalitarianism." *Quarterly Journal of Economics*, Vol. 71 (1957), pp. 234-66. Review of recent egalitarian thought by an economist.

Larkin, Paschal. *Property in the Eighteenth Century*. London: Longmans, Green, 1930.

Lindsay, A. D. *The Essentials of Democracy*. Philadelphia: Univ. of Pennsylvania Press, 1929.

McKeon, R. "The Development of the Concept of Property in Political Theory." *Ethics*, Vol. 48 (1938), pp. 302-66.

McPherson, C. B. "The Social Bearing of Locke's Political Theory." *Western Political Quarterly*, Vol. 7 (1954), pp. 1-22.

Mundle, C. W. K. "Punishment and Desert." *Philosophical Quarterly*, Vol. 4 (1954), pp. 216-28. Interesting restatement and criticism of the retributive theory.

Myrdal, Fru Alva. *Nation and Family: The Swedish Experiment in Democratic Family and Population Policy*. New York: Harper, 1941.

Pennock, J. R. *Liberal Democracy: Its Merits and Prospects*. New York: Rinehart, 1950. A judicious appraisal of democracy.

Ross, Alf. *Why Democracy?* Cambridge: Harvard Univ. Press, 1952.

Ross, Sir William David. *The Right and the Good*. New York: Oxford Univ. Press, 1930, pp. 56-64. A distinctive view of the justification for punishment.

Schlatter, R. B. *Private Property*. New Brunswick, N. J.: Rutgers Univ. Press, 1951.

Wooton, Barbara. *The Social Foundations of Wage Policy*. London: Allen & Unwin, 1955, Ch. 6. An economist writes on justice and wage policy.

7 MORAL RESPONSIBILITY AND FREE CHOICE

In our initial survey of the scope of ethical theory we distinguished three types of ethical question: about the desirable and the undesirable, about the right and the wrong, and about the praiseworthy and the blameworthy. Thus far our readings — except for the chapter on metaethics which concerned the meaning and justification of ethical statements generally — have concentrated on the first two of these types of question. We come now to the third.

1. Moral assessments and moral responsibility

This third type of question is marked by the occurrence of the phrases "morally blameworthy," "reprehensible," "morally praiseworthy," "morally admirable" or other expressions close to these in meaning. Any judgments of actions or persons in which such words occur may be called "moral assessments."

These words are not philosophers' technical terms; they are words which occur in ordinary conversation, although perhaps not very frequently. You may ask, "What are sample sentences in which they might appear?" As an answer to this query, we can recur to our earlier discussion (p. 2) of "reprehensible" and "morally blameworthy," in which it was pointed out that we should all regard it as one thing to ask whether a student is morally obligated to do something for another student, and quite another thing to ask whether his act is morally blameworthy if he does a certain thing — in view of his own conclusions about what he ought to do, the frame of mind he was in, the temptations to which he was subject. We are also familiar with people saying (whether rightly or wrongly we need not now decide) that a person is morally blameless, that is, not morally culpable or reprehensible, if he does whatever he himself sincerely believes to be right. Similarly, we understand perfectly — even if we don't agree — when someone says that the self-sacrificing behavior of a saint was morally praiseworthy or admirable, although not obligatory and perhaps not even to be recommended for everybody. Again, we understand what is being said when a defender of the retributive theory of punishment affirms that one deed ought to be punished by the state more severely than another if and only if the former deed is morally more reprehensible or blameworthy. We are, then, at least familiar with these perplexing terms of moral assessment.

What, however, is the meaning of these terms? We may begin with some contrasts. We have just seen that a person may be morally obligated to do something, although in some circumstances he will not be morally blameworthy if he fails to do it. It is clear, then, that "he is morally blameworthy" does not mean the same as "he failed to do what he was morally obligated to do." Similarly, "he is morally to blame for doing x" does not mean the same as "it was wrong for him to do x" — at least in some possible meanings of the latter expression. In order to see this distinction, let us take note of a case in which it is wrong to do something, yet the agent is nevertheless not morally blameworthy. Suppose an employer asks an employee a question about the political views of another employee. There are conceivable circumstances in which it would be wrong (let us suppose) for the employee to tell the truth. But obviously he may not be acting reprehensibly if he does. He may be an admirer of Kant and be convinced that a person ought never to lie. Or if he is fatigued and fails to grasp the situation readily, he may speak the truth before he realizes the consequences of doing so. In fact, his speaking the truth may mark him as a saint if he dislikes the employer thoroughly and if he knows that what he says will in the end work serious injury to himself or ones he cares about. The question whether an action is morally reprehensible, then, is different from the question whether the act is right or wrong.

There is another contrast that can be drawn. Moral reprehensibility of a deed is different from the question whether the action is desirable. It has sometimes been thought that "blameworthy act" means just the same as "act which is intrinsically undesirable," and that "praiseworthy act" means just the same as "act which is intrinsically desirable." But this proposal is mistaken. A person may believe firmly that an act is morally reprehensible or blameworthy, while being in a state of doubt as to whether it is intrinsically undesirable. Indeed, a person may be convinced, for example, that cruel actions are reprehensible, although he is equally strongly convinced — being a hedonist — that only unpleasant states of mind are intrinsically undesirable.

To draw these contrasts, however, is not to deny all connection between the various terms contrasted. In Chapter 2 (p. 129) we suggested that to say that an act is objectively wrong may be to say (or at least to imply) that the agent will be blameworthy if he does it without a valid *excuse*.

Is there nothing more positive that can be said? One thing that can be said is that various philosophers today think that "doing x was reprehensible" or "he is morally blameworthy for doing x" means, at least in part, that it would be *a good thing for the agent to be punished for doing x*, in view of the probable good effects of so doing, in one way or another. Not necessarily punished by the state, they would add, but by someone, perhaps one's schoolteacher; and some might even say, perhaps only by one's own conscience. Something like this view is adopted by Nowell-Smith in his essay below. But by no means all philosophers agree with this proposal, as will be clear from the essay by Campbell, which criticizes a view of the Nowell-Smith variety quite sharply. (If Nowell-Smith's view is well taken, "It is a good thing for people to be punished for their reprehensible deeds" is true by definition.)

If Nowell-Smith's proposal does not seem obviously true to you, perhaps what you should do is review your conclusion about the meanings of ethical terms, arrived at after reading Chapter 3. Perhaps "morally blameworthy" is an emotive term; perhaps what it does is express your annoyed resentment at an agent and nothing more. Or perhaps you can construe it along the lines suggested by Sharp's "ideal observer" theory: a person is morally reprehensible if an "ideal judge" would disapprove of him for his deed. We must leave the matter with these hints.

So far we have said nothing of the term "moral responsibility," which appears in the title of the present chapter. How is "being morally responsible" related to the assessment words we have been discussing?

This phrase is being used here in a sense wholly different from the sense "responsible" bears in the expression "is a responsible person," when the word means "can be relied upon." Quite clearly, also, to say that a person was "not responsible" for his action is different from saying that he didn't do it or that he was not the cause of whatever untoward effects are the source of our assessment of him. We may concede that a person told a lie but still deny that he should be held responsible for it. Again, to say that a person is responsible is not to say that he is *legally liable for damages;* there may be no damage, and we may say that a person is not morally responsible even when he is legally liable. We do come a bit closer when we say that "is responsible" means "answerable" in somewhat the way a British prime minister "is responsible" to Parliament, meaning that Parliament can remove him from office if he fails to satisfy it.

Philosophers are not altogether consistent in their use of the term "morally responsible." Nevertheless, what they generally mean when they say that a person's action was "responsible," or that the agent can be "held responsible," or that "moral responsibility" was present, is simply that it is permissible to make moral assessments, judgments of praise or blame, from other facts understood in the context. To deny that a person is morally responsible is to refuse to authorize such inferences and to deny their propriety. To say that a person who has killed another with a gun is not morally responsible is to say that an unfavorable moral assessment should not be made — that there is some consideration which *excuses* the person from moral condemnation and should protect him from punishment and condemnation. The excuse may be, for instance, illness or "not being himself," or it may be that the agent was acting under some misapprehension about the facts. Usually, we judge a man to be the deliberate author of what his behavior causes, and we make our moral assessments accordingly.

Denial of responsibility is a denial of the propriety of such inferences; affirmation of responsibility is an affirmation of their propriety.

Since to say that a person is not morally responsible is to say that he should be excused from condemnation and punishment, we shall, if we are rational, avoid legal penalties for actions which morally are excused — with some important exceptions we cannot here discuss. Therefore, a part of criminal law is concerned with the formulation of rules about excuses from punishment for persons who have acted in a way which the law forbids; and if you pick up a textbook on criminal law, you will find a section on this, possibly labeled "Criminal Responsibility." You will probably find chapters on the legal effects of innocent mistakes of fact on the part of the criminal, of his suffering from mental defects, of his being intoxicated, and so on. Such facts may operate to excuse a person from punishment, although he has acted in a forbidden way. When there is such an excuse, it is said that "criminal responsibility" is not present. The philosophical theory of responsibility attempts to make clear when and why people are not morally responsible for their deeds — and, of course, as a consequence, when and why they should not be held legally responsible for their deeds.

2. Theories about moral assessments and responsibility

A normative theory of moral *assessments*, then, is a set of proposals — with some kind of defense of them — in answer to the questions: When is a person morally praiseworthy or blameworthy? What factors influence a person's praiseworthiness or blameworthiness, and to just what extent? A normative theory of moral *responsibility* is a set of proposals — with some kind of defense — in answer to the questions: When is a person's conduct morally excused? Under what conditions is a person morally responsible for his conduct?

Evidently, on the one hand, the former theory comprehends the latter, since we can hardly answer the two questions of the first theory without thereby also answering the questions to which the theory of moral responsibility is addressed. On the other hand, the theory of assessments raises questions which the theory of responsibility does not. For to know about excuses is only to know when normal inferences to praiseworthiness or blameworthiness are *not* allowed; it is not yet knowing when a person is praiseworthy or blameworthy provided there is no excuse. So the wider theory also answers the question: When, excuses aside, are people morally praiseworthy or blameworthy? Or, much the same thing, the question: What considerations, other than excuses, tend to increase or decrease a person's praiseworthiness or blameworthiness? Incidentally, somewhere one must consider mitigating considerations, that is, considerations which reduce the praiseworthiness or blameworthiness of an agent without being excuses in the sense of ruling out such assessments altogether. Whether or not we should call such considerations "excuses" is a merely verbal issue.

All of these questions are questions of normative ethics. They are questions like What kinds of things are intrinsically desirable? and Which kinds of acts are morally obligatory? The kinds of argument properly used to justify some answer to these latter questions are the kinds of argument properly used to justify an answer to questions about moral assessments and responsibility.

What kinds of theories have been proposed? Unfortunately the proposals that have been made do not lend themselves to as simple a classification as those about the good and the right. At least, there is not the simple contrast of views that we can draw between hedonist and nonhedonist views about the good and among egoist, utilitarian, and formalist views about the right. Moreover, we can hardly say that one theory is a theory about moral assessments in general, another a theory just about moral responsibility: the two questions tend to fuse. As a result, the most helpful preparation for the readings to follow will be simply the formulation of some general propositions which have been offered as answers to our questions, with some commentary pointing out relations among them.

It is worth notice that one thing is universally agreed: a person is excused, is not morally responsible for his action or its consequences, if his act was not voluntary in the sense of being under his conscious control. Thus an action is excused if it is compelled — as when a stronger hand forces one to write or directs a knife. In fact, in such cases we hardly speak of a person as "having done" the thing at all. Moreover, it is agreed that a person is not responsible for his uncontrollable reflexes or for things done when sleepwalking or under hypnosis.

Let us turn now to some general theories:

A. One proposal, with a long tradition behind it, asserts that a person is responsible at all only if he initiates some change (or refrains from doing so) with a view to realizing some goal; and that his deed is praiseworthy or blameworthy according as his *initiation, with its intended result, would have been objectively right or wrong, if it had been as he conceived of it.* This view automatically excuses involuntary acts, since involuntary acts are not initiations of a change (or refraining) with a view to realizing a goal. Such a view also makes the morality of a deed depend not on the actual consequences but on those the agent expected or intended.

This proposal may be complicated by insisting that, to be responsible, the agent's act must be "free" in one of the senses discussed below.

B. Many people have been dissatisfied with the foregoing proposal primarily because they have thought a man ought always to follow his conscience, right or wrong. The foregoing principle accounts a man praiseworthy or blameworthy according as his action, if the facts about it were as the man supposes them to be, would be objectively right or wrong, irrespective of whether the agent thinks his act right or wrong. An amendment is therefore proposed: a deed is praiseworthy or blameworthy according as *the agent thinks* it is objectively right or wrong. According to this view, an action may be objectively right but still morally culpable if the agent is persuaded that what he has done is morally wrong.

Defenders of both of the foregoing principles have been disturbed by the fact that there is such a thing as blameworthy, or culpable, ignorance, both of facts and of moral principles. For instance, people sometimes do not take the trouble to find the facts or to think through moral issues; or else they avoid this effort because of a vague fear that things might not come out as they would like. In such cases, the ignorance itself is culpable. In view of this possibility, defenders of the above principles are sometimes prepared to say that it is no excuse for having performed an objectively wrong act, to say that one didn't know it would have such-and-such results, or didn't believe it was wrong, if the ignorance and belief were themselves blameworthy.

C. It has been thought that neither of the preceding proposals pays enough attention to motives. For instance, Kant urged that an act is praiseworthy only if it is *both* true that the act as the agent conceives it is one he would be willing to have done by everyone and *also* true that the act is done solely out of respect for the moral law, out of a sense of duty. Motives may also be conceived to make a difference in other ways, say, when an otherwise blameworthy act is done out of selfless affection for another person.

D. We come now to a quite different point. Many philosophers have thought that "freedom of choice" in a very special sense is a necessary condition for moral responsibility. That is, they believe that *every* act is excused unless, given the character and desires of the agent and the total situation just as they were, the agent could still have done something else — could have done his duty if in fact he failed, or could have failed to do it if in fact he did it.

This view is the source of the "free will" controversy, since it implies that all actions are excused if human conduct is caused by antecedent states of affairs or is always an instance of a causal law.

This proposal is probably an extension of two common-sense beliefs: the belief that a person is not properly blamed for failing to do the impossible, and the belief that moral condemnation should be reduced if a person's action can be traced to some congenital defect or to the influence of early misfortunes such as lack of education or a childhood spent in a broken family or on the streets of a slum area.

E. Other philosophers have thought that the condition of responsibility just stated is too strong. They agree that a person is morally responsible for an act only if it was "free" in a sense. But their proposal is that the act need only be free in the sense that the agent could or would have done something different *if his character and desires had been different*: an act is free if the agent's character and desires are the only obstacles to his doing something else. A "trait of character" is understood as some trait like selfishness or laziness (not one like stupidity), of a type which can usually be altered by punishment, praise, or blame. Such is the view adopted by

Nowell-Smith, in his essay. A view of this sort does not excuse a deed just because it had psychological causes; it does excuse a person if he is insane, acts from an "irresistible impulse" (as in kleptomania), or acts from passion in circumstances in which a man of principle would not be able to perform better.

The following selections represent the foregoing points of view or a combination of them.

The reader will do well to re-examine two readings which appeared earlier, which deal to some extent with our present topic: pages 191-94 by Kant, and pages 38-39 by John Stuart Mill.

Alfred Cyril Ewing (1899-)

WHAT MAKES ACTS BLAMEWORTHY: A CONTEMPORARY VIEW

The following selection by A. C. Ewing (p. 282) emphasizes points which have stood out in recent discussions: that the question whether an act is blameworthy or praiseworthy is a different one from whether it is objectively right or wrong; that whether a person follows the guidance of his own conscience has a great deal to do with whether his deed is to be assessed favorably or unfavorably from the moral point of view; that a person is wholly blameless for doing what is objectively wrong because of an unavoidable error in belief about facts; that a person's motives — at least if we mean by "motive" the goal on account of which a person performs an action — are very important for a moral evaluation of his behavior, although other things are also important. Ewing also has some things to say about the notion and relevance of subconscious motives.

The selection from A. C. Ewing, *Ethics*. Copyright 1953 by The Macmillan Company, and used with their permission. Also published by The English Universities Press, Ltd., London, and reprinted with their permission.

ETHICS

DESERTS AND RESPONSIBILITY

In discussing actions we have so far been discussing the principles according to which we decide which action it is best to choose to do in a given situation, i.e. which action is externally the right one. But there is another way, equally ethical, of looking at actions. We look at them in this second way when we consider whether the agent deserves praise or blame, and here we think of motives rather than effects, of the inner rather than the outer side. The contrast between the two aspects of an action appears most clearly when we consider the case of a man who does something wrong in all good faith because he mistakenly thinks it right. It is apparent to every thinking person in a war where people on both sides fight with a good conscience believing that they are doing what is right, or in any case where a person acts with good intentions but makes a terrible mistake as to the consequences to be anticipated from what he does. Confronted with such cases we do not blame the agent morally for acting as he did except in so far as we think him morally responsible for his beliefs, though of course we may still blame him intellectually, i.e. call him a fool. This distinction raises some difficulties. It is a recognized principle of ethics that it is always our duty to do what after proper consideration we think we ought to do, but suppose we are mistaken, then we by this principle ought to do something which is wrong and which therefore we ought not to do. Is not this a contradiction? It would be if we were not using two different senses of "ought" (and correspondingly of "right," "wrong," "duty"). Whether we are mistaken or not in our beliefs, there is clearly no morally permissible alternative to doing what we think we ought, provided we add a reservation, hard to define, about sufficient consideration. For, if we do not thus act, we cannot be acting out of moral motives but are on the contrary going against the moral principle in us, and so we ought to be blamed and not praised even if the action happens to be externally right, for that is only a matter of luck, since we did it not because it was right but thinking it wrong. Even if we accept the authority of somebody else, we do so on our own moral responsibility, and are only entitled to do so if we think him more likely to be right than ourselves. Yet the mere possibility of enquiring whether we ought to perform an action implies that there is a sense in which an action may still be wrong even if it is done with the best possible motives in the conviction that it is right. If what we thought right were automatically the right thing to do in all senses, there would be no point in devoting trouble and care to finding out what was right. We cannot answer the question what we ought to do in this other sense by pointing merely to our actual opinions and our motives. Granted that our motive is to do what is right, we still have to find out what is right. . . . Let us now turn to the question of moral blame.

Here one naturally starts by laying down the principle which I have already mentioned, namely, that we cannot be morally blamed if we do what we think right, "act in accordance with our conscience" as the phrase is. The question is not however quite so simply answered as it might seem. A man may think his conscience tells him to do the most outrageous things, as did many Nazis. Suppose Hitler believed that he was doing his duty when he inflicted appalling sufferings on the Jews and other unfortunate people and violated almost every canon of morals. Is he to escape all moral blame because he somehow deluded himself into thinking that all the abominable things he wanted to do were right or actually his duty? If he had this knack of deluding himself into believing that everything he did was right, does it follow that he was morally less blameworthy than are most people, who have a better ideal but constantly fall below it, as according to themselves have very many who would be accounted saints or almost saints? The reply would be made that Hitler was at any rate morally at fault in neglecting his duty of trying to consider properly what really was right before he acted as he did, but it is quite possible that it may not have occurred to him that he had not considered the question sufficiently, and then by the above principle he could not be blamed for neglecting that duty. But could he really escape all moral blame in this fashion? I am not therefore altogether satisfied with the above, usually accepted, principle.

But, even if we do accept it, it is important to recognize a distinction between two kinds of mistake which lead people to make wrong decisions as to what they ought to do. One kind of mistake relates to matters of fact, as when, e.g. a doctor through an error of judgement gives medicine that does harm rather than good, or a man breaks an agreement because he has genuinely misunderstood its import. Such an error is certainly not morally blameworthy unless due to negligence or avoidable prejudice, however much it may show lack of intelligence. But there is another kind of error which consists not in mistake as to matters of fact but in mistaken judgements of value. Such errors, whether morally blameworthy in the strict sense or not, at least disclose what we may call a moral defect in the person concerned. The latter is at any rate in a morally less desirable state than he would be in if he did not make such errors, whether it is "his fault" or not. An example of the first kind of error is given by a man who says something false because he thinks it true, of the second by a man who says something false because he underestimates the evil of lying or by one who attaches little value to any but "material" goods. Whether they could help it or not, it must be admitted that such men are in a lower state morally than they would be if they were free from these grave moral errors. Perhaps this is only because they are at an earlier stage of development or perhaps it is because they have knowingly done wrong in the past, but in any case they are in this state, however they got there.

For any action to have moral merit it is required not merely that it should be externally what the agent thinks right after due consideration, but that its motives should be good. What is a good and what a bad motive? There is no doubt that the desire to do one's duty because it is one's duty — I disagree with Kant in seeing no reason for not calling it a desire — is a good motive, but it is not the only one. Love for a particular person, benevolence, the desire for knowledge, the desire to create what is beautiful also can reasonably claim this title, and it is hard to refuse them it. Yet they may all lead us into evil courses on occasion if there is not at the back of our minds a moral consciousness which prevents this, so that the strictly moral motive, the desire to do what is right as such, though it need not and should not or indeed could not always be our motive, should always in a sense be present potentially. But whether a man has acted from the right motives or not on a particular occasion depends not only on the nature of the desires involved in themselves but on the context. Suppose as examiner I consciously gave a candidate a first-class mark out of love for him or out of a desire to give him pleasure (benevolence).

Now love and benevolence are as such good in themselves, but I certainly could not be said to have acted from the right motives, and consequently even if he deserved such a mark my action would be morally bad, though not so bad as if I had given a third-class mark to a candidate out of the evil desire to cause him pain. In either case the motive from which I acted ought to have had no influence at all in deciding the man's class. In other cases I might be blamed not because I acted from a motive which ought not to have influenced me at all, but because my action was not affected by other motives which ought also to have influenced me. This would be the case if I were motivated strongly by a desire for the welfare of a friend but indifferent to suffering brought on others by the way in which I sought to further that welfare. To say that a man's motive is wrong is therefore by no means necessarily to say that he is acting from a desire which is intrinsically evil. The only intrinsically evil desires are desires to produce things evil-in-themselves for their own sake, of which the most common (if not the only one) is the desire to inflict pain in anger or hatred on someone who has offended the agent. An action consciously and preventably influenced by such a desire is always blameworthy even if it be externally right, and even if it be also influenced by moral motives, as might well be the case with a person administering punishment. It is not equally clear that the desire to produce what is good in itself is always intrinsically good, for my pleasure is good in itself, yet the desire for pleasure for oneself does not seem to be intrinsically good. Reflections of this kind have suggested to some thinkers that pleasure itself is not intrinsically good in the sense in which other things are, especially moral value, but this is too complicated a topic to pursue here.

So there are various ways in which even an externally right act may be blameworthy because it is wrongly motivated. On the other hand we cannot say that moral blameworthiness depends only on motives, since a man may out of a good motive do something which he believes to be wrong, e.g. steal out of love. Further, the degree of blameworthiness for a wrong act depends also on the strength of the temptation to do it: a man would be blamed much less for killing another unjustifiably if he did it to save his own life than if he did it to steal from the other extra beer and tobacco money, and a man is less blameworthy if owing to peculiar psychological causes a desire which would be slight in most men has become intensely strong in him. Also, other things being equal, the degree of blameworthiness will increase in proportion to the clarity with which the culprit realizes his action to be wrong. Thus, if it is a necessary condition of moral blameworthiness in the fullest sense that the agent should be conscious that he is acting wrongly, the degree of blameworthiness will increase in proportion to the clarity of this consciousness and the unsuitability of the motive, while it will decrease in proportion to the strength of the temptation.

A difficulty that has not been discussed nearly enough by philosophers is raised by what psychologists tell us about the "sub-conscious." For the latter insist that we constantly have desires of which we are not conscious, and the question is raised whether we can be blamed for these. It seems to me that in this connection it is important to bear three things in mind. (1) We cannot be morally blamed merely for the presence of a desire, whether conscious or sub-conscious, except in so far as that desire is due to previous voluntary wrong actions or abstentions from action on our part. Soldiers in the past have often thought of fear itself as shameful, but this is a mistake. There is nothing wrong about feeling fear when shells are falling all round you, cowardice consists not in being afraid but in letting fear influence our actions when they ought not to be so influenced. On the other hand the presence of a morally unsatisfactory desire such as hatred of another man imposes on us a duty to take steps towards eliminating the desire, a process which however cannot reach its goal immediately. We cannot make ourselves feel immediately quite different about someone by a mere act of will: all we can do is to will to pay attention to ideas which will gradually lessen the desire, e.g. his good points and the Christian duty of forgiveness. (2) If a desire is, strictly speaking, unconscious, i.e. if we cannot be aware of it at all, we surely cannot be blamed for not taking steps to reduce or eliminate it, however undesirable it may be, since we do not know of its existence. At least we cannot be so blamed until we have inferred it from our actions or been credibly informed of its existence by a psycho-analyst. I am not even to blame if an act which I consciously seem to myself to do out of good motives is really due to unconscious bad ones, unless the presence of the latter is again due to previous voluntary wrong acts of my own. (3) But I strongly suspect that a very great many of the so-called cases of unconscious desire are really cases where the person concerned is or has been at times conscious in some degree of the desire but without being guilty of deliberate deceit conceived as such has voluntarily turned his attention from it and refused to admit it in words even to himself. This is certainly mistaken policy, and may well be morally wrong, but, if so, in a lesser degree because his consciousness of the situation is *ex hypothesi* not very clear. People commonly do not realize the harmfulness of thus deceiving themselves or exactly what they are doing in such cases at the time they do it, and certainly a very important factor in determining the degree of guilt is the degree of the agent's awareness of the wrongness of the act. It should be noted that a person who has thus refused to take cognizance of a desire may altogether forget about it later on, indeed almost immediately, and so be quite honest when he says he has never been aware of such a desire. We need not therefore be haunted by the anxiety that in addition to any conscious guilt we may feel we are also gravely guilty because of our sub-conscious. But psycho-analysis has at least shown that deceiving oneself as to one's desires is a very dangerous practice, even if it does not carry with it much moral guilt. Certainly it seems to have been a leading cause of a great many psychological break-downs, e.g. very many cases of "shell-shock" in the first world-war were due largely to the refusal to admit to oneself the presence of fear.

But it may be asked — are we after all to blame for anything? A negative answer to this question has sometimes been given on the ground that everything we do is determined by previous causes so that we could not have acted differently. . . .

QUESTIONS

1. Propose an example to show that the question whether a certain course of action was or would be objectively wrong is different from the question whether a deed is blameworthy or praiseworthy.
2. What do you think it means to say that an action was "blameworthy" or that a person is "blameworthy on account of his action"? What is it to hold a person "morally to blame"?
3. Why does Ewing think we always ought to do what we think is right? Why does he doubt whether a person is always morally blameless for doing what he thinks right? Is an act praiseworthy if the agent believes it to be right?
4. Is an act blameworthy if the agent does something wrong on account of mistake of fact? Suppose the mistake of fact was itself something for which he is morally to blame?
5. Why does Ewing think matters are somewhat different if the mistake is one about moral principle? Do you think a man is blameworthy if he does something wrong, thinking it right because of a mistake in his moral principles?
6. Ewing thinks an act which is objectively right may be blameworthy because it is done from wrong motives. Are there any examples which make this plausible? Is an act's motive being good enough to make it positively praiseworthy?
7. Is Ewing right, in your opinion, in saying that whether a motive is a good or a bad one depends on the context? Does he identify "having a bad motive" with "desiring something intrinsically bad"?
8. Do you think Ewing succeeds in showing that moral blameworthiness ever depends on other matters besides the motivation of an act? at least if we mean by "motivation" the *total* motivation revealed by his act — including the fact that some known consequences of his act did not repel him? What is the relation of "motive" and "strength of temptation"?
9. Does Ewing think it morally bad to have a subconscious hatred for one's father and a subconscious desire to see harm come to him?

Aristotle (384-322 B.C.)

WHAT MAKES ACTS BLAMEWORTHY:
A GREEK VIEW

Aristotle was the first philosopher to produce a systematic theory of moral assessments and moral responsibility. Despite being the first, his chapter has remained a classical — if not *the* classical — discussion of the subject. His conclusions were amazingly close to what we should want to say today.

Aristotle holds that a person can be blamed only for voluntary acts. An act is not voluntary, he says, if it is done under compulsion, or if it was done because of nonculpable ignorance of particular facts (as when a man kills someone while handling a gun which he thought, and had good reason to think, was unloaded). Ignorance of moral principle or of one's own true interests, however, he regards as no excuse; a moral man is supposed to know such things.

More positively, Aristotle holds that a man is properly praised or blamed not for what he does but for what he *intends*. That is, the moral judge is to consider what the agent was aiming to bring about, along with the means he chose to bring it about. If this goal-with-means, as he conceived it (or as he would have conceived it if he had known the facts it was his business to know, as a moral man), was in fact bad or wrong, then his action was blameworthy. Hence it is no excuse to say that you thought what you intended was good or right (when it wasn't), or to say that your passions overcame you, or to say that you couldn't have done differently because of your bad character (for, Aristotle says, a man is responsible for his own character). He is prepared, however, to excuse a man for an act when pressure put upon him is such as is "beyond human nature to resist and is such as no one could endure."

From Aristotle, *Ethics for English Readers*, trans. by H. Rackham, published by Basil Blackwell, Oxford, 1952, and reprinted with their permission.

NICOMACHEAN ETHICS

BOOK III

Voluntary action, intention, and responsibility *

Inasmuch as virtue is concerned with emotions and actions, and these meet with praise or blame when they are voluntary but are condoned and sometimes even pitied when they are involuntary, perhaps it is necessary in investigating the nature of virtue to define the meaning of the terms voluntary and involuntary. This will also be of service to guide legislators in awarding honours and punishments.

Now actions are thought to be involuntary when they are done under compulsion or owing to ignorance. They are compulsory when they originate from outside, and are of such a nature that the person acting or acted upon contributes nothing to them: for instance, if his ship is carried out of its course by an adverse wind, or if he is overpowered by a stronger party. But in the case of actions committed owing to fear of greater evils, or for some honourable motive,— for example if a man is ordered to do something disgraceful by a tyrant who has his parents and children in his power and will kill them if he refuses, in such circumstances it is open to question whether his actions are involuntary or voluntary. A somewhat similar situation arises when a ship's cargo is jettisoned in a storm at sea; except in certain circumstances nobody throws away his goods voluntarily, but every sensible person will do so when his own safety and that of all his companions is at stake. Actions of this sort are therefore of a mixed character, although they approximate rather to voluntary acts because at the time when they are committed the agent chooses to do them, and the object aimed at by an action corresponds with the occasion when the act is committed. Consequently the terms voluntary and involuntary must be used with reference to the time when the man commits the act; and he commits it voluntarily, because the movement of the parts of the body employed in such actions originates within him and an act initiated from within oneself is in one's power either to commit or not to commit. Therefore such acts are voluntary, although perhaps they are involuntary in the absolute sense of the term, because nobody would choose to do any of them for their own sake.

And sometimes people are actually praised for actions of this kind, when they endure disgrace or pain in order to secure important and honourable objects — although they are blamed when they do so with no such motive, because to endure very disgraceful treatment for no honourable or important reason is a mark of a base character. And in some cases an action although not praised is condoned, when the pressure put upon a man

---

* The italicized heading is an interpolation by the present editor. The footnotes are by the translator.

to do wrong is beyond human nature to resist and is such as no one could endure. No doubt however there are some things which a man cannot really be *compelled* [1] to do; and rather than commit these he ought to endure death preceded by the direst sufferings; the reason [2] that in the tragedy of Euripides 'compels' Alcmaeon to murder his mother seems merely ludicrous!

But sometimes it is difficult to decide what course ought to be adopted for the sake of what object, and what suffering endured in return for what recompense; and it is still more difficult to abide by one's decision, inasmuch as often the consequences in prospect are painful and the conduct forced upon us discreditable. This is why praise and blame are bestowed according as people were acting under compulsion or not.

What definition then can be given of the term compulsory? Perhaps we may say that without qualification an act is compulsory when its cause lies in external circumstances and when the agent contributes nothing; while actions that are in themselves involuntary but adopted in a given situation and for the sake of a given object, and that originate in the agent, are involuntary in themselves but in the given situation and in return for the objects obtained voluntary. But they approximate more to voluntary actions, because conduct is a matter of particular acts, and the particular acts in question are voluntary. However it is not easy to lay down rules as to what sort of actions should be chosen for the sake of securing what objects, since particular cases vary widely.

It may be maintained that acts done for pleasure or for honourable purposes are compulsory, because they impose an external constraint upon us. But on this showing all conduct would be compulsory, since pleasure and honour supply the motives of all the actions of everybody. Also acts done under compulsion and against one's will are painful, but persons doing things because they are pleasant or honourable enjoy doing them.

And it is absurd to put the responsibility on external circumstances and not on one's own susceptibility to inducements of this nature, or to credit oneself with one's honourable actions but put down one's base deeds to the attractions of pleasure.

It appears then that an action is compulsory if it originates from outside, the person who is compelled to do it contributing nothing.

Actions done owing to ignorance are in every case non-voluntary; but they are involuntary only when they are painful to do and are followed by repentance. If a man commits an act owing to ignorance but afterwards feels no regret at having done it, he has not acted voluntarily, as he was not aware of what he was doing, and yet he has not acted involuntarily, as he is not sorry for what he did. Consequently one who acts through ignorance, if he regrets it afterwards, appears to have been an involuntary

---

[1] I.e. some acts are so repulsive that no pressure put on a man could overcome his abhorrence of them, so that if he commits them he must be considered to have chosen to do so.

[2] The line has come down to us from a play now lost:

Here my chief motive was my sire's behest.

agent, but if he does not regret it, he may be distinguished by being called a 'non-voluntary' agent; as his case is different, it is better to give him a different name.

Also acting *owing to* ignorance seems to be a different thing from acting *in* ignorance; a man who is drunk or has lost his temper does not seem to act owing to ignorance but because of his intoxication or anger, yet he does not know what he is doing but is acting in ignorance. So while all wicked men are ignorant of what they ought to do and what to abstain from, and it is being mistaken about this that makes men dishonest and bad in every way, yet acting involuntarily does not really mean acting in ignorance of one's true interests, for it is not ignorance in forming one's intention which causes an involuntary act (that sort of ignorance constitutes vice) nor is it general ignorance (for that blame is awarded), but ignorance of the particular circumstances in which the action takes place and of the matters with which it is concerned. For these are the things that may justify compassion and forgiveness, since a man who acts in ignorance of one of these acts involuntarily.

It will then perhaps be well for us to define their nature and determine their number. The list includes the agent, the act done, the thing or person whom it concerns, and in some cases the instrument employed — for instance, a tool used in doing the act, and the purpose intended — for instance, to effect a rescue, and the manner in which the act was done — for instance, gently or violently. Now nobody could be ignorant of all these points unless he was out of his mind: obviously a man cannot fail to know who the agent is, as this is himself; but he may not know what he is doing — for instance, people say that they let a thing slip out in the course of conversation, or that they did not know it was a secret, as Aeschylus [3] said in reply to a charge of revealing religious mysteries; or that the thing went off while they were trying to show how it worked, like the man with the catapult; and someone might mistake his own son for one of the enemy, as Merope did,[4] or in fencing think there was a button on the point of his foil when there was not, or he might think that a stone he threw at somebody was only a lump of pumice-stone; or a doctor might give his patient a draught meant to cure him which actually killed him, or in a wrestling match in which only hand-holds were allowed a man in attempting to get a grip of his opponent might hit him a hard blow.

These are all circumstances about which the agent may be ignorant, and a man who has acted in ignorance of any of them is deemed to have acted unwillingly, especially in the case of the most important, and these are thought to be the nature of the act and the purpose intended. If then an action is pronounced involuntary on the ground of ignorance in these

---

[3] Aeschylus was indicted before the court of Areopagus on the charge of having violated the Mysteries of Demeter in one of his tragedies, but he was acquitted. A phrase which he seems to have used in his defence, 'It came to my lips,' became proverbial.

[4] In a play of Euripides now lost.

respects, there must also be the qualification that the agent was sorry for it and regretted it afterwards.

As what is done under compulsion or through ignorance is involuntary, it would seem that a voluntary action is one that originates in the agent himself when he knows the particular circumstances in which it takes place. For perhaps it is a mistake to say that actions prompted by passion or desire are involuntary, since in the first place that will mean that none of the lower animals ever acts voluntarily, nor children either; and in the second place are none of our actions that are due to desire or passion voluntary, or are the creditable ones voluntary and the discreditable ones involuntary? Would not that be absurd, when it is the same person who is responsible for both? It would surely be odd to call a thing we do from proper motives involuntary, and it is proper for us to be angry at some things and to desire some things — for instance, health and knowledge. Moreover, involuntary acts are thought to be painful and voluntary ones pleasant. And further, what is the difference in respect of involuntariness between mistakes due to miscalculation and mistakes due to passion? Both are to be avoided; but irrational emotions seem just as natural to mankind as rationality, so that actions prompted by passion or desire are a man's own actions. It would be odd then to class them as involuntary.

Now that we have defined the terms 'voluntary' and 'involuntary,' the next subject to discuss is the meaning of intention,[5] since this seems to have an extremely close connexion with virtue, and to be a better indication of a man's character than his actions are. Intentional acts are clearly voluntary, but the two terms are not synonymous. The power to act voluntarily is more widely distributed, as it is shared by children and animals, but these do not possess deliberate intention. Also we speak of actions done on the spur of the moment as being voluntary, but not as deliberately intended. And it seems to be a mistake to identify intention with desire or passion or wish, because irrational animals do not possess deliberate intention, but they have desires and passions. Also a man who lacks self-control acts from desire, but not with deliberate intention, while with the self-controlled man it is the other way about — his conduct is prompted by intention but not by desire. And desire and intention can conflict with one another, but you cannot feel two opposite desires at the same time. And desire takes account of what is pleasant and what painful, whereas intention has no connexion with either. Still less is deliberate intention the same thing as passion, as acts due to passion seem the least intentional of all.

Nor yet is an intention the same as a wish, although they appear to be closely related. Intention is not directed to objects that are impossible to attain, and a man would be thought a fool if he said he intended to do an impossibility, but people do wish for impossibilities, for instance, to live

[5] The term denotes deliberate choice of a course of conduct, and may in some cases be rendered 'will.'

for ever. Also a man may wish for a thing that does not depend upon himself to secure, for instance, an athlete wishes to win a race, or an actor a theatrical competition; but nobody forms a deliberate intention with regard to objects of this sort, but only about things that he thinks he can secure by his own efforts. Again, the object of a wish is rather an aim or end, but intention selects the means to an end — for instance, we wish to be healthy, but we form intentions about the means that will make us healthy; we wish for happiness, but to speak of intending to be happy would be a misuse of language. In general, intention seems to be concerned with things that depend on ourselves to bring about.

Nor yet can intention be the same thing as opinion. We seem to form opinions about everything in heaven and earth, and about impossibilities just as much as about things within our reach. Also opinions are true or false, not good or bad, but intentions are distinguished as good or bad rather than as true or false. So doubtless nobody maintains the view that intention is the same thing as opinion. But no more can it be identified with a particular kind of opinion.[6] What distinguishes our moral characters is the goodness or badness of the intentions we form, not the correctness or incorrectness of the opinions we hold.

Also we form intentions to obtain something good or to avoid something bad, but we form opinions as to what a thing is or what it is good for or how it can be got — we do not form an opinion to get it or avoid it. And an intention is commended for being directed to a proper object rather than for being correct, but an opinion for being correct in itself. And we form intentions about things that we positively know to be good, but we think things that we do not absolutely know to be true. And it does not appear that the people who form the best intentions are also those who hold the best opinions; some people seem to have satisfactory opinions but owing to defects of character to adopt wrong intentions. . . .

That the object wished for is an end has been stated, but as to what this end is there is a difference of opinion; some define it as the good, others as that which appears to be good.

Those who say that what is wished for is the good are faced with the consequence that what a person who chooses wrongly wishes is not wished at all, since if it were really wished it would *ex hypothesi* be good, but it may happen to be in fact something bad. Those on the other hand who say that it is what appears good that is wished for, imply that there is no natural object of wish at all, but that it is only what seems to be good to each individual; although different things, and it may happen exactly opposite things, seem good to different people.

If this is unsatisfactory, suppose we say that what is wished in the absolute and real sense is the good, but what is wished by each individual is the apparent good; and that consequently what the good man wishes is

---

6 I.e. the belief that a thing is good and attainable.

wished in the true sense of the term, but the bad man wishes for just anything (exactly as with our bodies, things truly wholesome are wholesome for people of sound constitution but quite different things are good for the health of those who are delicate; and so with taste and temperature etc.). The reason of this is that the good man judges everything correctly, and in every case he sees the truth. For every variety of character has its own idea of what is honourable and what is pleasant; and perhaps it is the special mark of a good man that in each of these fields he discerns the truth: he serves as a standard by which they can be measured. The mass of mankind appear to be led astray in their judgement by pleasure, which seems to be a good thing though it is not good really; so they choose what is pleasant as a good, and avoid pain as an evil.

Inasmuch then as our end is an object wished, while the means to our end are objects of deliberation and of intentional choice, it follows that actions connected with the means to our ends are intentional and voluntary. Consequently virtue also depends on ourselves. And the same is the case with vice; for where it is in our power to act, it is also in our power to abstain from action, and where we can say yes we can also say no; and consequently if it rests with us to act when action is honourable, it also rests with us not to act when action is disgraceful. And if committing disgraceful actions and likewise refraining from them rests with ourselves, and if (as was said) this is what constitutes goodness or badness of character, it follows that our morality or immorality rests with ourselves.

The saying

None would be base, and none would not be blessed [7]

seems to be half false and half true; no one is unwilling to be blessed by fortune, but baseness of character is not involuntary; or else we must dispute what was said just now, and assert that a man is not the origin and the begetter of his actions as he is of his children. And if this is clearly true and we are unable to trace back our actions to sources outside ourselves, actions whose sources are within us must be actions that depend upon ourselves and are voluntary.

This view appears to be confirmed both by the conduct of individuals and by the actual principles of our legislature. Punishment is inflicted on or satisfaction demanded from malefactors who were not acting under compulsion or in ignorance not due to their own negligence, and honour is given to those who do noble deeds, with the object of suppressing the former and encouraging the latter; yet nobody urges us to do things that do not depend upon ourselves and are not voluntary. It is no use trying to persuade us not to be hot or suffer pain or be hungry or anything else of that kind, as we shall experience those feelings all the same.

---

[7] In this proverbial verse (by some attributed to Solon) the term rendered 'base' originally denoted low station, not bad character.

Indeed the very fact that an offence was committed in ignorance is made a ground for punishment if the offender is held to have been responsible for his ignorance: for instance the penalty is doubled if he was under the influence of drink, because the situation originated in himself — he need not have got drunk, and it was being drunk that made him not know what he was doing. Also men are punished when they commit an offence in ignorance of some provision of the law which they ought to know and which is not difficult to understand; and similarly in other circumstances the offender's ignorance of which seems due to carelessness, as such ignorance might have been avoided, because he might have taken the trouble to ascertain the facts.

Perhaps he is the sort of man who does not attend to that kind of thing. But men are themselves responsible for getting slack about rules as a result of careless living, just as they are responsible for becoming dishonest or dissolute by acting unfairly or by passing their time in drinking and debauchery. It is a man's actions in various fields of conduct that make him what he is. This is shown by people training for some athletic contest or preparing for some profession: they constantly practice the actions that belong to the intended pursuit. Not to know that habits of character are formed by actually practising various activities denotes an utter lack of sense; but if a man knowingly acts in a way that will result in making him dishonest his dishonesty is voluntary.

Again, it is not reasonable to say that a man who acts dishonestly or dissolutely does not wish to be dishonest or dissolute; but this does not mean that he can stop being dishonest and become honest merely if he wishes to do so. An invalid cannot recover his health merely by wishing for it, yet his illness is voluntary if in fact it is due to extravagant living and neglect of the doctor's advice. At the beginning it was in his power not to be ill, but when he let himself go it was so no longer; when someone throws a stone he cannot afterwards bring it back again, but nevertheless he is responsible for having picked it up and thrown it. Similarly the dishonest or dissolute man might have originally avoided becoming what he is, and therefore he is what he is voluntarily, but having become dishonest or dissolute voluntarily, it is no longer open to him not to be so.

But not only are vices of the mind voluntary; sometimes defects of the body are so too, and we blame the persons in whom this is the case. Nobody blames people who are ugly by nature, but we blame those whose lack of good looks is due to want of exercise and to neglect of their persons. And similarly with regard to weakness and deformity — nobody would reproach a man who was born blind or had been blinded by a disease or by a blow — he would rather be pitied; but everybody would blame one who had lost his sight owing to drinking or debauchery. Blame then is attached to bodily defects for which we are ourselves responsible, though not to those for which we are not responsible. It follows therefore that we are responsible for moral blemishes to which blame is attached.

But suppose somebody were to say, 'All men seek what appears to them to be good, but they are not responsible for its so appearing; each individual's conception of his end corresponds to his particular character. If we assume that a man is in a sense responsible for his own character, he will be in a way responsible for his own conception of the good; but supposing this is not the case, then no man is responsible for his own wrongdoing: it is due to his ignorance of the right end, he thinks wrong-doing will bring him the greatest good, and the choice of the right end to aim at is not a matter of volition: a man needs to be born possessing a gift of vision which will enable him to judge correctly and to choose the true good. A man of good natural endowment is a man born with this insight well developed; for to be born in possession of what is the greatest and noblest of faculties, one which cannot be acquired from somebody else or learnt but which a man will continue to possess with the same quality that it had at his birth — this will be the perfection of good breeding in the true sense of the term.'

Now if this is true, how will virtue be voluntary any more than vice? Both the good man and the bad man alike have a fixed conception of the aim or end implanted in them by nature or acquired in some other way, and this conception they use as a standard for their subordinate aims in shaping their conduct whatever it may be. Whether therefore a man's conception of the end is not implanted in him by nature but is in some measure due to himself, or whether, although his view of the end is given him by nature, yet inasmuch as the subordinate steps are taken voluntarily virtue is a voluntary thing, it follows that vice also will be equally voluntary; for the bad man also possesses initiative in his actions even if not in his choice of an end. If it be true therefore that the virtues are voluntary because, even if the nature of the end we set before ourselves is an outcome of our characters, we are ourselves partly the cause of our own characters, it would follow that the vices are voluntary also, since the same consideration applies to them too.

We have now described in outline the virtues in general, stating the class to which they belong and showing that they render us capable of performing the same actions as the actions by which they were produced, and of performing them in the manner which right reason may prescribe; and that they depend upon ourselves and are voluntary.

But our dispositions are not voluntary in the same way as our actions are. We can control our actions from start to finish, being conscious of them at each step; but we can only control our dispositions at their beginning — the additions to them stage by stage are imperceptible, like the growth of bodily infirmities; but they are voluntary in that at the start it rested with ourselves to employ our faculties in the one way or in the other.

QUESTIONS

1. Presumably you will agree with Aristotle that an involuntary act is never blameworthy and that acts done under compulsion are involuntary. But is something done out of ignorance involuntary or merely unintentional? Probably you will say that unintentional acts too are blameless, at least in most instances?

2. Is throwing over the cargo in a storm in order to save the passengers in any sense an "involuntary" act, or is it rather one justified by the end it serves?

3. Do we excuse any act when the pressure "is beyond human nature to resist and is such as no one could endure"? Why?

4. Would Aristotle say that ignorance of moral principles excuses wrong behavior? If not, then what kind of ignorance does? Would Ewing agree with Aristotle at this point?

5. Does Aristotle make any distinction between mistake of fact, inadvertence, and accident, as excuses for a deed?

6. Would Aristotle regard anger or "irresistible impulse" as excuses from blameworthiness? Would he say that action on impulse is "intended"? Is this plausible? Is there a difference between acting intentionally and acting after deliberation or with premeditation? Would we say that a man who lacked self-control did not act with intention?

7. Is Aristotle correct in saying that "intention" includes the means selected for its ability to realize a desired end?

8. What does Aristotle mean by saying that what we wish is always for an "apparent" good?

9. Aristotle says that whether we act immorally depends on us. In what sense does he think it "depends on us"?

10. Does Aristotle think culpable ignorance is an excuse from blameworthiness? What is an example of such ignorance?

11. Aristotle says that his views of what is or is not a legitimate excuse corresponds with the practice of criminal justice in his day. As far as you know, does it correspond with practice at the present?

12. Does Aristotle think it a fair excuse to say that one could not have helped performing a wrong act because of one's bad character? Does not a bad character make it impossible for us to do what we ought? If so, why is the excuse not a good one? Is a man really responsible for his character, in the way Aristotle thinks?

13. Suppose I commit a murder because I have a bad character. Would it be fair to say that I should be punished, perhaps, for acquiring the bad character, but not for the murder, since, having the bad character, I really cannot help the murder?

14. Do you think Aristotle is right in thinking that men always seek what they think to be the good or the best end? Why, in his view, is it important for him to say that we are responsible for our (bad) moral principles?

15. Make a list of the properties an act must have, according to Aristotle, in order to be either blameworthy or praiseworthy, and of the properties of an

act which can affect how blameworthy or praiseworthy it is. How far would this list differ from a similar list based on Ewing's views?

Saint Thomas Aquinas (1225-74)

A CHRISTIAN GLOSS ON ARISTOTLE

St. Thomas Aquinas (p. 238) was a careful student and admirer of the work of Aristotle, and his views of the conditions of moral responsibility and blameworthiness are very similar to those of his predecessor. But there had been much discussion of this subject by the Christian Fathers including St. Augustine, with which St. Thomas was familiar and which he took into account. As a result his conclusions may be viewed as a Christian modification or interpretation of the Aristotelian framework.

It is by no means easy to be sure exactly where St. Thomas differs from Aristotle. On some points the difference is simply one of supplement — the consideration of distinctions, or types of situation, which Aristotle had overlooked. The most interesting question is whether St. Thomas differed from Aristotle about the moral bindingness of an agent's own conscience. In general St. Thomas seems to agree with Aristotle that when a man's act — in the sense of the goal he is aiming at, with the means he is taking to realize it, *as he believes them both to be* — is good and rational to do, the act is praiseworthy; and that when the act, in this same sense, is bad and something it is rational to avoid, then it is blameworthy. This view commits him to saying that one's actual performance with its actual consequences is not what determines whether one is praiseworthy or blameworthy; what determines this is one's intentions — except when culpable ignorance is the reason why one did not see that what did happen would happen. This view also commits him to saying that the agent's belief that what he was doing was right or wrong does not determine whether his act is praiseworthy or blameworthy; following conscience is not necessarily praiseworthy, and deviating from it is not necessarily blameworthy. Thus he says that mistakes of moral principle do not excuse because moral principles are matters one is bound to know, so that ignorance of them constitutes culpable negligence. (It is not clear whether logical mistakes in the application of true moral principles are culpable.) In other places, however, St. Thomas seems to take a more complex line: to hold that one is always blameworthy if one fails to follow conscience. One is to blame even if one's conscience is in error. If, for instance, conscience wrongly tells one, to use St. Thomas' example, that one should commit an act of fornication or disbelieve in Christ, one is blameworthy if one fails. As a result, his view as a whole appears to be that, when conscience errs, one is blameworthy if one deviates from conscience; but one is also blameworthy for following conscience, because a mistake in moral principle is no excuse. In other words, when conscience errs, at least on serious matters, it is impossible to avoid blame, no matter what one does. (If conscience tells you something is wrong which is not wrong at all, one is not blameworthy for following conscience.)

From *Basic Writings of St. Thomas Aquinas,* ed. by Anton C. Pegis. Copyright 1945 by Random House, Inc. Reprinted by permission. Also reprinted by permission of Burns & Oates Ltd., London.

SUMMA THEOLOGICA

FIRST PART OF THE SECOND PART

QUESTION 6

First Article: Whether there is anything voluntary in human acts?

. . . There must needs be something voluntary in human acts. In order to make this clear, we must take note that the principle of some acts is within the agent, or in that which is moved; whereas the principle of some movements is outside. For when a stone is moved upwards, the principle of this movement is outside the stone; whereas, when it is moved downwards, the principle of this movement is in the stone. Now of those things that are moved by an intrinsic principle, some move themselves, some not. For since every agent or thing moved acts or is moved for an end, . . . those are perfectly moved by an intrinsic principle whose intrinsic principle is one not only of movement but of movement for an end. Now in order that a thing be done for an end, some knowledge of the end is necessary. Therefore, whatever so acts or is so moved by an intrinsic principle that it has some knowledge of the end, has within itself the principle of its act, so that it not only acts, but acts for an end. On the other hand, if a thing has no knowledge of the end, even though it have an intrinsic principle of action or movement, nevertheless, the principle of acting or being moved for an end is not in that thing, but in something else, by which the principle of its action towards an end is imprinted on it. Therefore such things are not said to move themselves, but to be moved by others. But those things which have a knowledge of the end are said to move themselves because there is in them a principle by which they not only act but also act for an end. And, consequently, since both are from an intrinsic principle, *i.e.*, that they act and that they act for an end, the movements and acts of such things are said to be voluntary; for the term *voluntary* signifies that their movements and acts are from their own inclination. . . .

Second Article: Whether there is anything voluntary in irrational animals?

. . . Now knowledge of the end is twofold, perfect and imperfect. Perfect knowledge of the end consists in not only apprehending the thing which is the end, but also in knowing it under the aspect of end, and the relationship of the means to that end. And such a knowledge of the end belongs to none but the rational nature. — But imperfect knowledge of the end consists in a mere apprehension of the end, without knowing it under the aspect of end, or the relationship of an act to the end. Such a knowledge of the end is exercised by irrational animals, through their senses and their natural estimative power.

Consequently, perfect knowledge of the end is accompanied by the voluntary in its perfect nature, inasmuch as, having apprehended the end, a man can, from deliberating about the end and the means thereto, be moved, or not, to gain that end. . . . The will is the name of the rational appetite, and consequently it cannot be in beings devoid of reason. . . .

Sixth Article: Whether fear causes what is involuntary absolutely?

. . . Things done through fear and compulsion differ . . . in this, that the will does not consent, but is moved entirely counter to that which is done through compulsion; whereas what is done through fear becomes voluntary because the will is moved towards it, although not for its own sake, but because of something else, that is, in order to avoid an evil which is feared. For the conditions of a voluntary act are satisfied, if it be done because of something else voluntary; since the voluntary is not only what we will for its own sake as an end, but also what we will for the sake of something else as an end. It is clear therefore that in what is done from compulsion, the will does nothing inwardly, whereas in what is done through fear, the will does something. . . .

Seventh Article: Whether concupiscence causes involuntariness?

. . . Concupiscence does not cause involuntariness, but, on the contrary, makes something to be voluntary. For a thing is said to be voluntary from the fact that the will is moved to it. Now concupiscence inclines the will to desire the object of concupiscence. Therefore the effect of concupiscence is to make something to be voluntary rather than involuntary. . . . He who acts from fear retains the repugnance of the will to that which he does, considered in itself. But he that acts from concupiscence, *e.g.*, an incontinent man, does not retain his former will whereby he repudiated the object of his concupiscence; rather his will is changed so that he desires that which previously he repudiated. Accordingly, that which is done out of fear is involuntary to a certain extent, but that which is done from concupiscence is in no way involuntary. . . .

If concupiscence were to destroy knowledge altogether, as happens with those whom concupiscence has rendered mad, it would follow that concupiscence would take away voluntariness. And yet, properly speaking, it would not make the act involuntary, because in beings bereft of reason there is neither voluntary nor involuntary.

Eighth Article: Whether ignorance causes involuntariness?

If ignorance cause involuntariness, it is in so far as it deprives one of knowledge, which is a necessary condition of voluntariness, as was declared above. But it is not every ignorance that deprives one of this knowledge. Accordingly, we must take note that ignorance has a three-fold relationship to the act of the will: in one way, *concomitantly*; in another, *consequently*; in a third way, *antecedently*. Concomitantly, when there is ignorance of what is done, but so that even if it were known, it would be done. For then ignorance does not induce one to will this to be done, but it just happens that a thing is at the same time done and not known. Thus, in the example given, a man did indeed will to kill his foe, but killed him in ignorance, thinking to kill a stag. And ignorance of this kind, as the Philosopher states, does not cause involuntariness, since it is not the cause of anything that is repugnant to the will; but it causes *non-voluntariness*, since that which is unknown cannot be actually willed.

Ignorance is *consequent* to the act of the will, in so far as ignorance itself is voluntary; and this happens in two ways in accordance with the two aforesaid modes of the voluntary. First, because the act of the will is brought to bear on the ignorance, as when a man wills not to know, that he may have an excuse for sin, or that he may not be withheld from sin, according to Job 21:14: *We desire not the knowledge of Thy ways.* And this is called *affected ignorance.* — Secondly, ignorance is said to be voluntary, when it regards that which one can and ought to know, for in this sense *not to act* and *not to will* are said to be voluntary, as was stated above. And ignorance of this kind happens either when one does not actually consider what one can and ought to consider (this is called *ignorance of evil choice*, and arises from some passion or habit), or when one does not take the trouble to acquire the knowledge which one ought to have; in which sense, ignorance of the general principles of law, which one ought to know, is voluntary, as being due to negligence. . . .

Ignorance is *antecedent* to the act of the will when it is not voluntary, and yet is the cause of man's willing what he would not will otherwise. Thus a man may be ignorant of some circumstance of his act, which he was not bound to know, with the result that he does that which he would not do if he knew of that circumstance. For instance, a man, after taking proper precaution, may not know that someone is coming along the road, so that he shoots an arrow and slays a passer-by. Such ignorance causes what is involuntary absolutely.

QUESTION 19

First Article: Whether the goodness of the will depends on the object?

. . . Virtue is a habit through which men wish for good things. But a good will is one which is in accordance with virtue. Therefore the goodness of the will is from the fact that a man wills that which is good. . . . Good and evil are essential differences of the act of the will. For good and evil pertain essentially to the will; just as truth and falsehood pertain to the reason. . . . The specific difference in acts is according to objects. . . . Therefore good and evil in the acts of the will is derived properly from the objects. . . . The will is not always directed to what is truly good, but sometimes to the apparent good; and this has indeed some measure of good, but not of a good that is suitable absolutely to be desired. Hence it is that the act of the will is not always good, but sometimes evil.

Second Article: Whether the goodness of the will depends on the object alone?

. . . Given that the act of the will is fixed on some good, no circumstance can make that act evil. Consequently, when it is said that a man wills a good when he ought not, or where he ought not, this can be understood in two ways. First, so that this circumstance is referred to the thing willed. According to this, the act of the will is not fixed on something good, since to will to do something when it ought not to be done is not to will something good. Secondly, so that the circumstance is referred to the act of willing. According to this, it is impossible to will something good when one ought not to, because one ought always to will what is good; except, perhaps, accidentally, in so far as a man, by willing some particular good, is prevented from willing at the same time another good which he ought to will at that time. And then evil results, not from his willing that particular good, but from his not willing the other. The same applies to the other circumstances.

Third Article: Whether the goodness of the will depends on reason?

. . . The will's object is proposed to it by the reason. For the understood good is the proportioned object of the will, while the sensible or imaginary good is proportioned, not to the will, but to the sensitive appetite; for the will can tend to the universal good, which reason apprehends, whereas the sensitive appetite tends only to the particular good, apprehended by a sensitive power. Therefore the goodness of the will depends on the reason in the same way as it depends on its object.

Fifth Article: Whether the will is evil when it is at variance with erring reason?

. . . Since conscience is a kind of dictate of the reason (for it is an application of knowledge to action, as was stated in the First Part) to inquire whether the will is evil when it is at variance with erring reason is the same as to inquire whether an erring conscience binds. On this matter, some distinguished three kinds of acts; for some are good of their nature, some are indifferent, some are evil of their nature. And they say that if reason or conscience tell us to do something which is of its nature good, there is no error; and the same is true, if it tell us not to do something which is evil of its nature, since it is the same reason that prescribes what is good and forbids what is evil. On the other hand, if a man's reason or conscience tell him that he is bound by precept to do what is in itself evil or what is in itself good is forbidden, then his reason or conscience errs. In like manner, if a man's reason or conscience tell him that what is in itself indifferent, for instance, to lift a straw from the ground, is forbidden or commanded, his reason or conscience errs. They say, therefore, that reason or conscience, when erring in matters of indifference, either by commanding or by forbidding them, binds; so that the will which is at variance with that erring reason is evil and sinful. But when reason or conscience errs in commanding what is evil in itself, or in forbidding what is good in itself and necessary for salvation, it does not bind; and so in such cases the will which is at variance with erring reason or conscience is not evil.

But this is unreasonable. For in matters of indifference, the will that is at variance with erring reason or conscience is evil in some way because of the object on which the goodness or malice of the will depends; not indeed because of the object according as it is in its own nature, but according as it is accidentally apprehended by reason as something evil to do or to avoid. And since the object of the will is that which is proposed by the reason, as we have stated above, from the very fact that a thing is proposed by the reason as being evil, the will by tending thereto becomes evil. And this is the case not only in indifferent matters, but also in those that are good or evil in themselves. For it is not only indifferent matters that can receive the character of goodness or malice accidentally; but likewise that which is good can receive the character of evil, or that which is evil can receive the character of goodness, because of the reason apprehending it as such. For instance, to refrain from fornication is good, and yet the will does not tend to this good except in so far as it is proposed by the reason. If, therefore, the erring reason propose it as an evil, the will tends to it as to something evil. Consequently, the will is evil because it wills evil, not indeed that which is evil in itself, but that which is evil accidentally, through being apprehended as such by the reason. In like manner, to believe in Christ is good in itself, and necessary for salvation; but the will does not tend thereto, except inasmuch as it is proposed by the reason. Consequently, if it be proposed by the reason as something evil, the will tends to it as to something evil; not as if it were evil in itself, but because it is evil accidentally, through the apprehension of the reason. Hence the Philosopher says that, *properly speaking, the incontinent man is one who does not follow right reason; but accidentally, he is also one who does not follow false reason.* We must therefore conclude that, absolutely speaking, every will at variance with reason, whether right or erring, is always evil.

> *Sixth Article: Whether the will is good when it abides by erring reason?*

. . . Ignorance sometimes causes an act to be involuntary, and sometimes not. And since moral good and evil consist in an act in so far as it is voluntary, as was stated above, it is evident that when ignorance causes an act to be involuntary, it takes away the character of moral good and evil; but not, when it does not cause the act to be involuntary. Again, it has been stated above that when ignorance is in any way willed, either directly or indirectly, it does not cause the act to be involuntary. And I call that ignorance *directly* voluntary to which the act of the will tends, and that, *indirectly* voluntary, which is due to negligence, because a man does not wish to know what he ought to know, as we have stated above.

If, therefore, reason or conscience err with an error that is voluntary, either directly or through negligence, so that one errs about what one ought to know, then such an error of reason or conscience does not excuse the will, which abides by that erring reason or conscience, from being evil. But if the error arise from the ignorance of some circumstance, and without any negligence, so that it cause the act to be involuntary, then that error of reason or conscience excuses the will, which abides by that erring reason, from being evil. For instance, if erring reason tell a man that he should go to another man's wife, the will that abides by that erring reason is evil, since this error arises from ignorance of the divine law, which he is bound to know. But if a man's reason errs in mistaking another for his wife, and if he wish to give her her right when she asks for it, his will is excused from being evil; for this error arises from ignorance of a circumstance, which ignorance excuses, and causes the act to be involuntary.

QUESTION 20

Fifth Article: Whether the consequences of the external act increase its goodness or malice?

. . . The consequences do not make an act that was evil, to be good; nor one that was good, to be evil. For instance, if a man give an alms to a poor man who makes bad use of the alms by committing a sin, this does not undo the good done by the giver; and, in like manner, if a man bear patiently a wrong done to him, the wrongdoer is not thereby excused. Therefore the consequences of an act do not increase its goodness or malice. . . . The consequences of an act are either foreseen or not. If they are foreseen, it is evident that they increase the goodness or malice. For when a man foresees that many evils may follow from his act, and yet does not therefore desist from it, this shows his will to be all the more inordinate.

But if the consequences are not foreseen, we must make a distinction. For if they follow from the nature of the action, and in the majority of cases, in this respect the consequences increase the goodness or malice of that action; for it is evident that an action is of its nature better, if better results can follow from it, and of its nature worse, if it is of a nature to produce worse results. On the other hand, if the consequences follow by accident and seldom, then they do not increase the goodness or malice of the act; for we do not judge of a thing according to that which belongs to it by accident, but only according to that which belongs to it essentially.

QUESTION 21

First Article: Whether a human act is right or sinful in so far as it is good or evil?

. . . The goodness of a human act depends principally on the eternal law, and consequently its malice consists in its being in disaccord with the eternal law. But this is the very nature of sin, for Augustine says that *sin is a word, deed or desire in opposition to the eternal law.* Therefore a human action is sinful by reason of its being evil.

. . . Evil is more comprehensive than sin, as also is good than right. For every privation of good, in whatever subject, is an evil, whereas sin consists properly in an act done for a certain end, and lacking due order to that end. Now the due order to an end is measured by some rule. In things that act according to nature, this rule is the power itself of nature that inclines them to that end. When, therefore, an act proceeds from a natural power, in accord with the natural inclination to an end, then the act is said to be right; for the mean does not exceed its limits, viz., the action does not swerve from the order of its active principle to the end.

But when an act strays from this rectitude, it comes under the notion of sin.

Now in those things that are done by the will, the proximate rule is the human reason, while the supreme rule is the eternal law. When, therefore, a human act tends to the right according to the order of reason and of the eternal law, then that act is right; but when it turns aside from that rectitude, then it is said to be a sin. Now it is evident, from what has been said, that every voluntary act that turns aside from the order of reason and of the eternal law is evil, and that every good act is in accord with reason and the eternal law. Hence it follows that a human act is right or sinful by reason of its being good or evil.

QUESTIONS

1. In Chapter 2 the selection from St. Thomas (pp. 239-47) discussed what is good for man, what ought to be chosen, what it is right to do, what is in accordance with "natural law." In the foregoing reading he is concerned with something different: what kinds of action are morally blameworthy or praiseworthy. These new predicates apply to an action because of its intention, not because of what it is or accomplishes. Do you agree that a person can be blamed only for what he intends and not for what he accomplishes?
2. What does St. Thomas mean by a "voluntary" act? Are the acts of animals ever perfectly voluntary? Does he think people "intend" only what is their ultimate aim or goal or do they also intend the means they use?
3. Why does he think that acts done under compulsion are not voluntary, whereas acts done because of fear of bodily harm are at least partly voluntary and subject to moral blame?
4. Would he think a man can excuse his act by saying he desired to do it so much that he "couldn't help it"? Is this a case of involuntariness?
5. What kind of ignorance does St. Thomas regard as a proper excuse? Suppose a man is mistaken in his moral principles (not his application of true principles to a given case). Would St. Thomas regard this fact as a legitimate excuse? Is he right that erroneous moral beliefs reached by rationalization are no excuse? Is there anything a person can do to be sure he has correct moral principles?
6. St. Thomas thinks that a person always aims at what he supposes to be a good thing for him. How, then, can St. Thomas say that a man is sometimes morally blameworthy?
7. In Question 19, Article 5, St. Thomas appears to say that a man is blameworthy if he fails to do whatever his conscience tells him is his duty—even if his conscience tells him he must commit fornication or must disbelieve in Christ. Is this consistent with Article 6, or Question 6, Article 8, where he appears to hold that belief in wrong moral principles is no excuse?
8. In what circumstances may the consequences of an act affect the morality of a decision to do it, according to St. Thomas?
9. Should St. Thomas allow motives a larger role in determining which acts are blameworthy or praiseworthy — perhaps as Ewing does?

Patrick H. Nowell-Smith (1914-)

A UTILITARIAN CONCEPTION OF RESPONSIBILITY

Many philosophers have thought that all human actions are excused, are neither blameworthy nor praiseworthy, if human choices are not free. St. Thomas Aquinas wrote in his *Summa Contra Gentiles* (Chapter LXXIII): "If the will were deprived of liberty, many goods would be done away, for no praise would be given to human virtue, since virtue would be as nothing if man did not act freely; there would be no justice in rewarding or punishing, if man were not free in acting well or ill. . . ." But "free" in what sense? The "problem" of freedom arises when it is thought that actions are morally excused unless they are free in a sense which is incompatible with being caused.

"Determinists" about human actions believe that all human behavior, and especially decisions and actions, are examples of the operation of causal laws; usually Determinists do not think this fact affects whether people are responsible, say, for deliberate or premeditated misbehavior, although a few do believe that their view implies that terms like "wicked" and "reprehensible" have no sensible application. "Libertarians," on the other hand, think that human decisions and actions, at least when the agent thinks he has obligations which conflict with his inclinations, are *not* entirely examples of the operation of causal laws, and that it is always possible for a person to do what he thinks is his duty, despite his character and inclinations. Libertarians generally hold that, if one denies this position, one must drop terms like "reprehensible" from one's vocabulary, and that one cannot reasonably feel guilt or remorse, or indignation toward others.

Nowell-Smith sides with the Determinists in this controversy; Campbell (in the succeeding selection) with the Libertarians. Nowell-Smith thinks that the idea that the concept of blameworthiness must be dropped if human action and choices are caused rests on confusions and misunderstandings.

Since his paper is exceptionally difficult, it may be helpful to comment further on the structure of his argument.

Nowell-Smith opens his attack on the Libertarians by criticizing a common Libertarian belief that we can see that our choices are uncaused, simply by introspection. He next argues that the theoretical predictability of choices (which the Determinist usually grants is implied by his thesis about causation) is not incompatible with "free choice" in any ordinary sense; rather the predictability of nature and man is necessary if we are to be free to control our world effectively. He agrees that acts must be "free" in a sense if they are to be either praiseworthy or blameworthy; this freedom, however, is not *absence* of causation, but a presence of a *special kind* of causation — the kind present when we fail through laziness, but absent when we fail for stupidity, or when we steal from kleptomania. Actions can be praiseworthy (or blameworthy) only when they would have been different but for virtues (or defects) of character; we are responsible only for "free acts," viz., free such that they "could have been otherwise" *in the sense* that they would have been different if we had chosen differently, and that we would have chosen differently if we had had a different character. The Libertarian makes the mistake of thinking we are responsible only for an act free in the sense that it could have been different even if *everything* were exactly the same.

Nowell-Smith then tries (beginning with p. 677) to show *why* freedom in his sense, and only in his sense, is required for praiseworthiness or blameworthiness. The reason is manifest when we examine *what it is for an act to be blameworthy* (or "to be judged morally") — which, he says, is for it to be bad in view of its effects, and to be *fittingly blamed or punished*. For when is an act fittingly blamed or punished? Only, he suggests, when blaming or punishing can serve a good purpose. (Here is the utilitarian feature of his conception of responsibility.) And this will be the case when the blaming or punishing will *tend to prevent recurrence* of events like the one being blamed. Only "free" acts, in the above sense, are fittingly blamed or praised, because praise and blame will tend to affect the recurrence of acts of this kind, but not of "unfree" acts. Blame and punishment will tend to prevent the recurrence of poor work resulting from laziness, but not that resulting from stupidity. So it makes sense to distinguish the former kind of work by labeling it "free," the latter not. Blame or punishment will prevent the thief from stealing, but not the kleptomaniac, so deliberate theft is sensibly distinguished as "free," kleptomania not. The point behind our classifying acts as free or unfree is the fact that blame, praise, and punishment of an act will have good effects in some cases, not in others. When we see this, we shall be satisfied with continuing to use the criteria of utility of blaming or punishing as the criteria for whether an act is to be called free — criteria which we are already using, although not consciously and not always consistently.

From Patrick H. Nowell-Smith, "Free Will and Moral Responsibility," *Mind*, Vol. 57 (1948), pp. 45-61. Reprinted by permission of the author and of the editor of *Mind*.

Since the author no longer holds exactly the view expressed in this paper, there is added, in accordance with his wish, an appended commentary he prepared more recently, which appeared first in Sprague, Elmer, and Paul W. Taylor, eds., *Knowledge and Value, Introductory Readings in Philosophy*, published by Harcourt, Brace and Co., 1959, pp. 478-79, and reprinted with their permission.

FREE WILL AND MORAL RESPONSIBILITY

The traditional problem of free will has been so adequately covered in recent philosophical literature that some excuse must be offered for reopening it; and I do so because, although I believe that the traditional problem has been solved, I believe also that the solution leaves open certain further problems that are both interesting and important. It is to these problems that I propose to devote most of this paper; but, even at the risk of flogging dead horses, I feel bound to say something about the traditional problem itself.

I

The problem arises out of a *prima facie* incompatibility between the freedom of human action and the universality of causal law. It was raised in an acute form when universal determinism was believed to be a necessary presupposition of science; but it was not then new, because the incompatibility, if it exists at all, exists equally between human freedom and the foreknowledge of God. As it appears to the "plain man" the problem may be formulated as follows: "Very often I seem to myself to be acting freely, and this freedom, if it exists, implies that I could have acted otherwise than I did. If this freedom is illusory, I shall need a very convincing argument to prove that it is so, since it appears to be something of which I am immediately aware. Moreover, if there is no freedom, there is no moral responsibility; for it would not be right to praise or blame a man for something that he could not help doing. But, if a man could have acted otherwise than he did, his action must have been uncaused, and universal determinism is therefore untrue."

Broadly, there are two methods of resolving this, as any other, antinomy. We can either assume that the incompatibility is a genuine one at a certain level of thought and try to resolve it at a higher plane in which either or both the terms "freedom" and "necessity" lose their ordinary meaning or we can try to show by an analysis of these terms that no such incompatibility exists. If the latter method is successful, it will show that what is essential in our concept of freedom does not conflict with what is essential in our concept of causal necessity and that the incompatibility arises only because, at some stage in our development of one or both of these concepts, we have been tempted into making a false step. This method seems to me the better (provided always that it is successful), on the ground that it does not resort to any metaphysical conception imported *ad hoc* to solve this problem, which might be objectionable on other grounds. In the first two sections of this paper I shall give a brief outline of the analysis of the problem that I believe to be correct; and for this analysis I claim no originality. The method of presentation will, however, throw into relief the partial nature of the solution and help to indicate the further problems to be discussed in the last three sections. . . .

When I am conscious of being free, I am not directly conscious that my actions are uncaused, because absence of causation is not something of which one could be directly aware. That the plain man and the Libertarian philosopher are right in claiming to know directly the difference between voluntary and involuntary actions, at least in some cases, I have no doubt; but we can never have this direct knowledge that something is uncaused, since this is a general proposition and, like other general propositions, could only be established by reflection on empirical evidence. Fortunately it is not necessary here either to attempt an analysis of causality or to answer the question whether or not it is a necessary presupposition of science. It is now widely recognised that the considerations which lead scientists to suppose that strict determinism is not true are irrelevant to the problem of free will, since these considerations lend no support to the view that the phenomena with which we are concerned are not predictable; and it is to predictability, not to any special theory of the grounds of predictability, that the Libertarian objects. He claims that if our actions are predictable we are "pawns in the hands of fate" and cannot choose what we shall do. If, it is argued, someone can know what I shall do, then I have no choice but to do it.

The fallacy of this argument has often been exposed and the clearest proof that it is mistaken or at least muddled lies in showing that I could not be free to choose what I do *unless* determinism is correct. There are, indeed, grounds for supposing that strict determinism in psychology is not correct; but this, if true, constitutes not an increase but a limitation of our freedom of action. For the simplest actions could not be performed in an indeterministic universe. If I decide, say, to eat a piece of fish, I cannot do so if the fish is liable to turn into a stone or to disintegrate in mid-air or to behave in any other utterly unpredictable manner. It is precisely because physical objects have determinate causal characteristics that we are able to do what we decide to do. To this it is no answer to say that perhaps the behaviour of physical objects is determined while that of volitions is not. For we sometimes cause people to make decisions as well as to act on them. If someone shouts: "Look out! There is a bull," I shall probably run away. My action is caused by my decision to run; but my decision is itself caused by my fear, and that too is caused by what I have heard. Or, again, someone may try to influence my vote by offering me a bribe. If I accept the bribe and vote accordingly, the action is caused by the bribe, my avarice and my sense of obligation to the donor; yet this would certainly be held to be a blameworthy action, and therefore a voluntary one. A genuinely uncaused action could hardly be said to be an action *of* the agent at all; for in referring the action to an agent we are referring it to a cause.

In calling a man "honest" or "brave" we imply that he can be relied on to act honestly or bravely, and this means that we predict such actions from him. This does not mean that we can predict human actions with the same degree of assurance as that with which we predict eclipses. Psychology and the social sciences have not yet succeeded in establishing laws as reliable as those that we have established in some of the natural sciences, and maybe they never will. But any element of unreliability in our predictions of human actions decreases rather than increases the reliability of our moral judgements about them and of our consequent attributions of praise and blame. An expert chess-player has less difficulty in defeating a moderate player than in defeating a novice, because the moves of the moderate player are more predictable; but they could hardly be said to be less voluntary. In calling an action "voluntary" we do not, therefore, mean that it is unpredictable; we mean that no one compelled the agent to act as he did. To say that, on the determinist view, we are "mere pawns in the hands of fate" is to confuse causality with compulsion, to confuse natural laws (descriptions) with social laws (prescriptions) and to think of fate as a malignant deity that continually thwarts our aims. What the protagonist of freedom requires, in short, is not uncaused actions, but actions that are the effects of a peculiar kind of causes. I shall be as brief as possible in saying what these causes are, since this has often been said before. But it is one thing to state the criteria by which we decide whether or not an action is voluntary and another to say why this distinction is important for ethics. The problem which the analysts have not, in my view, sufficiently considered is that of analysing the peculiar relation of "merit" or "fitting-ness" that is held to exist between voluntary actions and moral responsibility.

II

If someone overpowers me and compels me to fire a gun which causes a death, I should not be held guilty of murder. It would be said that my action was not voluntary; for I could not, had I so wished, have acted otherwise. On the other hand, if I kill someone because I hope to benefit under his will, my action is still caused, namely by my greed; but my action would be held to be voluntary and I should be blamed for it. The criterion here is that, while in the first case the cause is external to me, in the second it is my decision. A similar criterion would be used to distinguish a kleptomaniac from a thief. A kleptomaniac is held to be one who steals without having decided to do so, perhaps even in spite of a decision not to do so. He is not held morally responsible for his action because his action is not held to be voluntary. But in this case it is not true, as it was in the last, that his action is called involuntary because it is caused by some outside force. The cause of kleptomania is obscure; but it is not external compulsion. And, if the cause is not external, how can we say that the kleptomaniac is "compelled"? As used by psychologists, the term "compulsion" is evidently a metaphor, similar to that by which we speak of a man's doing something when "he is not himself." Evidently our moral judgements imply not merely a distinction between voluntary and compelled actions, but a further distinction among actions that are not compelled.

A third example will make it clear that some such distinction must be made. Suppose that a schoolmaster has two pupils A and B, who fail to do a simple sum correctly. A has often done sums of similar difficulty before and done them correctly, while B has always failed. The schoolmaster will, perhaps, threaten A with punishment, but he will give B extra private tuition. On the traditional view his action might be explained as follows: "A has done these sums correctly before; therefore he could have done them correctly on this occasion. His failure is due to carelessness or laziness. On the other hand, B is stupid. He has never done these sums correctly; so I suppose that he *cannot* do them. A's failure is due to a moral delinquency, B's to an intellectual defect. A therefore deserves punishment, but B does not." This is, I think, a fair summary of what the "plain man" thinks about a typical case, and the points to which I wish to draw attention are these:

(*a*) Neither failure is said to be "uncaused."

(*b*) The causes assigned are divided into two classes, moral and intellectual. (Cases of physical deficiency, *e.g.* not being strong or tall enough would go along with the intellectual class, the point being that such deficiencies are nonmoral.)

(*c*) Praise and blame are thought appropriate to moral but not to nonmoral defects.

(*d*) The criterion for deciding whether a defect is moral is "Could the agent have acted otherwise?"

I do not wish to suggest that the reasoning attributed to the plain man in this case is in any way incorrect, only that, particularly in regard to point (*c*) and (*d*) it needs explaining.

It is evident that one of the necessary conditions of moral action is that the agent "could have acted otherwise" and it is to this fact that the Libertarian is drawing attention. His case may be stated as follows: "It is a well-known maxim that 'I ought' implies 'I can.' If I cannot do a certain action, then that action cannot be my duty. On the other hand, 'I ought' as clearly implies 'I need not'; for if I cannot possibly refrain from a certain action, there can be no merit or demerit in doing it. Therefore, in every case of moral choice it is possible for the agent to do the action and also possible for him not to do it; were it not so, there would be no *choice*; for choice is between possibilities. But this implies that the action is uncaused, because a caused action cannot but occur." The fallacy in this argument lies in supposing that, when we say "A could have acted otherwise," we mean that A, being what he was and being placed in the circumstances in which he was placed, could have done something other than what he did. But in fact we never do mean this; and if we believe that voluntary action is uncaused action, that is only because we believe erroneously that uncaused action is a necessary condition of moral responsibility. The Libertarian believes that an action cannot be a moral one if the agent could not have acted otherwise, and he takes no account of possible differences in the causes that might have prevented him from acting otherwise. The Determinist, on the other hand, holds that the objective possibility of alternative actions is an illusion and that, if A in fact did X, then he could not have done any action incompatible with X. But he holds also that differences in the various causes that might have led to X may be of great importance and that it is in fact from the consideration of such differences that we discover the criterion by which we judge an action to be voluntary, and so moral.

We all blame Nero for murdering Agrippina, and the Libertarian holds that this implies that Nero could have abstained from his action. But this last phrase is ambiguous. Even if we admit that it would have been impossible for anyone to predict Nero's action with the degree of assurance with which we predict eclipses, yet an acute observer at Nero's court might have laid longish odds that Nero, being what he was and being placed in the circumstances in which he was placed, would sooner or later murder his mother. To say that Nero might have acted otherwise is to say that he could have decided to act otherwise and that he would have so decided if he had been of a different character. If Nero had been Seneca, for example, he would have preferred suicide to matricide. But what could "If Nero had been Seneca . . ." possibly mean? Unfulfilled conditionals in which both terms are names of individuals constitute, admittedly, a thorny philosophical problem; but it is clear, I think, that if "If Nero had been Seneca . . ." means anything at all, it is a quasi-general proposition which can be analysed either as "If Nero had had the character of Seneca" or "If Seneca had been emperor" or in some similar fashion. None of these analyses are incompatible with the Determinist's contention that, as things stood, Nero could not have abstained. But, adds the Determinist, the cause of his inability to abstain was not external compulsion nor some inexplicable and uncharacteristic quirk. His action was predictable because it was characteristic, and it is for the same reason that he is held to blame.

But the Libertarian's case is not yet fully answered. He might reply: "But, on this analysis, I still cannot blame Nero which in fact I do, and feel that I do justly. If the murder was caused by his character, *he* may not have been to blame. For his character may have been caused by hereditary and environmental factors over which he had no control. Can we justly blame a man if his vicious actions are due to hereditary epilepsy or to the influence of a corrupt and vicious court?" To this the answer is that we can and do. So long as we persist in supposing that, to be moral, an action must be uncaused, we can only push the moral responsibility back in time; and this, so far from solving the problem, merely shows the impossibility of any solution on these lines. . . .

III

So far we have discovered nothing more startling than the fact that moral actions are the effects of a peculiar kind of causes, namely the voluntary actions of the agent. To sum up this part of the argument, I cannot do better than quote the words of Prof. Ayer: "To say that I could have acted otherwise is to say, first, that I should have acted otherwise, if I had so chosen; secondly, that my action was voluntary in the sense in which the actions say of the kleptomaniac are not; and, thirdly, that nobody compelled me to choose as I did: and these three conditions may very well be fulfilled. When they are fulfilled, I may be said to have acted freely. But this is not to say that it was a matter of chance that I acted as I did, or, in other words, that my action could not be explained. And that my actions should be capable of being explained is all that is required by the postulate of determinism." [1] With this I agree; but it leaves unsolved what is perhaps the most important part of the problem. Granted that we sometimes act "freely" in the sense defined by Ayer, in what sense is it rational or just or moral to praise or blame voluntary actions but not involuntary ones? It is surely not enough to say: "Actions of such-and-such a kind are given the name 'voluntary' and are praised and blamed; others are not." We need to explain the relation of "fittingness" that is held to obtain between voluntary actions and moral judgement. Suppose that A and B each kill some one. We apply Ayer's tests and decide that A's was a voluntary action and B's not. We hang A, and B is immured in an asylum or regains his liberty. What needs to be explained is (*a*) Why do we do this? and (*b*) Is it morally justifiable? . . .

IV

The theory that I wish to suggest is that in every so-called moral judgement there are two distinct elements, a value judgement and a moral judgement proper. About value judgements no special theory is implied. In particular, I do not intend to prejudice any of the following issues:

[1] "Freedom and Necessity," *Polemic* No. 5, p. 43.

(a) whether value judgements are or are not properly called "judgements" at all,

(b) whether there is or is not only one type of value (for instance, pleasure), and

(c) whether or not value judgements are subjective.

It will, however, follow that, whatever values there may be, there is no such thing as moral value, as such, but that when we attribute moral value to a thing we are saying in a misleading way that the thing has some value or other and is connected with a moral cause.

Whatever our reasons may be, we do in fact regard some states, objects and events as "good" or "valuable" and others as "bad" or "disvaluable"; the former we try to promote, the latter to prevent. Whatever may be the case with value judgements, the strictly moral element in a moral judgement is concerned with an empirical fact and is, therefore, objective. The difference between these two types of judgement can be made clear by an example. Suppose that, for whatever reason, I regard A's life as valuable. (I may hold that all human life is valuable as such, or that A is a good man and that the lives of good men are valuable, or merely that the existence of A is propitious to some scheme in which I am interested.) A may be murdered in cold blood by B or may be run over by C in circumstances over which the latter had no control. In each of these cases I should make the same value judgement, that A's death was "bad." But, while in the first case I should make the further moral judgement that B's action was criminal, in the second I should make no additional moral judgement at all.

The theory can be divided into four parts:

(a) Value judgements apply only to events (including their consequences), but not to their causes.

(b) Events that are "good" or "bad" constitute moral actions only when they are caused by someone's voluntary decision.

(c) "Good" and "bad" events that are also moral actions are fit subjects for praise and blame, while other good and bad events are not.

(d) This "fittingness" is a causal relation, discoverable neither by a special "moral sense" nor by intuition nor by a priori reasoning, but by reflection on experience.

Of these propositions (a) and (b) are recommendations to employ a certain terminology in ethical matters; (c) is a proposition which will, I think, be generally admitted, provided the suggested terminology is accepted. But it is (c) that requires explanation, and the explanation is contained in (d). If it is true that praise and blame are means employed to bring about good events and prevent bad ones, they are appropriate not to all good and bad events, but only to those that they can in fact bring about or prevent. Since a moral action is one that can be fittingly praised or blamed, it follows that a moral action is one that can be brought about or prevented by these means. Moral actions are a subclass of good and bad events, and the traditional criterion for deciding whether or not an event belongs to this subclass was, as we saw, "Was the action voluntary, *i.e.* caused by a decision of the agent?" But the application of this criterion involves two difficulties. It is sometimes difficult to decide to what cause an action was due. Is this a case of laziness or a case of stupidity? Was the prisoner in the dock mad or was he avaricious? This is an empirical difficulty and raises no question of principle. But the other difficulty that arises in applying the criterion of voluntariness is to find a rule for deciding what classes of actions are voluntary. If the criterion I have suggested is correct, then we should find that the class of actions generally agreed to be voluntary coincides roughly with the class of actions that are caused by characteristics that can be strengthened or inhibited by praise and blame. And this is what we do in fact find; moral characteristics, as opposed to intellectual and physical ones, are just those that we believe to be alterable in this way. Now the problem of deciding whether or not a characteristic is alterable may be difficult; but the difficulty is an empirical one only, and we know at least how to set about solving it.

This theory implies a utilitarian theory of punishment. Rewards and punishments (for the sake of brevity I shall in future refer only to punishment) are distributed not because certain actions directly "merit" them, but because some useful purpose is believed to be served by inflicting them. It should be noted that the theory that punishment is purposive does not imply that its purposes must always have been those that the Utilitarians had in mind. Furthermore, the fact that some systems of punishment do not in fact produce the intended results, an argument that is often urged against the utilitarian theory, does not tend to show that no result was intended. The performance of Sellenger's Round doubtless does nothing to keep the sun on its course; but that does not prove that it is not intended to do so by the performers. Failure to produce results argues not lack of purpose but lack of skill in the practitioner.

It may be objected that this theory fails to account for the retributive element in punishment and, before elaborating it on the positive side, I shall first suggest a possible explanation both of the fact that the retributive theory is believed and of the fact that its supporters claim to intuit its truth. To do this it is necessary to distinguish between the reasons for which the theory first came to be held and the reasons for which it is held now. An adequate account of the first point would require to be based on a wider knowledge of anthropology than I possess, and I do not claim that the account here suggested is true, even in its broad outlines. Nevertheless it is, I think, plausible to suppose that retributive punishment originally had *some* purpose, even if it was quite different from the one suggested here.

The primitive morality that demands an eye for an eye is by no means incompatible with the theory that punishment is not mere retribution, but is designed to bring about some end; and such practices as the punishment of idiots, animals and even inanimate objects do not prove that their practitioners were intuitionists who claimed to be directly aware that certain actions "ought to be punished," the morality of the punishment being in no way dependent on any supposed advantage to those who inflict it. Such practices are always found in conjunction with a special theological theory as to the nature of the universe. It is held that the Gods require certain sorts of conduct on the part of human beings and that they will visit breaches of the rules with their wrath in the form of plagues, famines and other undesirable events. It is to prevent these that punishment is inflicted; and this explains why it is that what *we* call the morality of the action, which includes the condition that it be voluntary, is not held to affect the morality of punishment, a point which orthodox retributionists have some difficulty in explaining. If the volition of the agent is held to be irrelevant to the operation of God's wrath, it will also be irrelevant to the morality of punishment, since the object of punishment is not to requite a voluntarily committed wrong but to ward off God's anger. Oedipus has committed parricide and incest. He must be punished, not because he did so, still less because he intended to do so, but because the tribe that harbours him will suffer if he is not. Punishment is expiation.

When a society holds theological beliefs other than our own we shall not be surprised to find that its moral ideas differ also. Retributive punishment does not have the object that punishment has with us, and it does not (we believe) achieve the results aimed at. But neither of these facts tends to show that it did not originally have some purpose, and it is a curious fact that the retributive practice tends to become mollified (in the form of purely ritual expiation) and finally abandoned, precisely when the crude theology on which it is based ceases to be believed. Now if retributive practices are due entirely to instinct or to an intuition of fittingness it is hard to see why this should be so. It is apparently a pure coincidence that the intuitive light grows dim precisely when a certain theological theory is abandoned. But if the purposive theory is true it is easy to see why the retributive element should tend to give way before the reformatory and deterrent elements when people abandon the belief that punishment will obviate the failure of crops but conceive (or retain) the belief that it will benefit society by inhibiting certain forms of action. When we abandon the belief that God will visit his wrath on a tribe that harbours an unwitting parricide, we no longer have any motive for punishing him. Consequently we call him innocent. A man is not punishable because he is guilty; he is guilty because he is punishable, that is to say, because some useful result is supposed to accrue from punishing him.

If this is true, we can also explain why it is that modern retributionists, who do not hold the crude theological beliefs with which I have suggested that the practice was originally linked, fall back on an intuition of fittingness. Here, as elsewhere, intuition is invoked to account for a belief that we are quite certain that we hold but for which we have forgotten the original grounds and cannot discover new ones. It often happens that a belief is retained after the theory on which it is based and which alone makes it plausible has been abandoned, and this is particularly liable to happen in ethics for the following reason. Metaphysical and scientific views are changed by the speculation of a few intellectuals, who are regarded by the many as harmless. But morals, as Hume said, excite our passions and produce and prevent action. The moral reformer, therefore, unlike the speculator, is treated as a danger to society; and for this reason morality tends to be more conservative than other branches of thought. Hence there sometimes arises a lack of logical relation between the metaphysical and scientific ideas of a society and its moral code; the latter being partly a survival from older modes of thought. When this process of survival occurs in a society not our own we call it a superstition or a taboo; when it occurs in our own we call it a Moral Law. Now the retributive theory has a logical justification if a certain theological view is accepted. That view having been abandoned, the justification no longer exists and we are forced to fall back on a direct intuition that punishment is fitting.

V

The analysis suggested at the beginning of the last section can now be applied to the examples used earlier in the paper. We saw that, apart from the empirical difficulty of deciding to what class an action belongs, there are two difficulties of principle. One is the problem of determining what classes of actions are voluntary; the other the problem of showing a connexion between being voluntary and being liable to praise or blame. It has, I think, usually been the practice to try to solve the first of these problems first; but this leaves us, as we saw, in the insuperable difficulty of libertarianism and also renders the second problem insoluble. If the theory I have suggested is correct, the second problem should come first and is simply the empirical problem of deciding what characteristics are alterable; and the solution to this problem then provides the criterion for deciding what actions are voluntary. The preliminary analysis of the case of the schoolmaster left unexplained the meaning of the vital sentence, "A could have acted otherwise, while B could not" and also the question "Why is laziness punishable and stupidity not?" It is not enough to say that A's failure was voluntary because he is known to have acted rightly before. Perhaps he was not lazy then but is now. And how do we know that his laziness now is not just as much beyond his control as was his industriousness then and as is B's stupidity now? . . . On the other hand, [however,] if, instead of assuming that A ought to be punished because he is morally guilty, we suppose that he ought to be punished for some other reason, the rationale of the schoolmaster's action becomes clear. He knows from experience that, if he adds the fear of punishment to the motives actuating A, then A will tend to get these sums right in future, which is, for him, the end to be achieved. On the other hand, if B is stupid, neither threats nor promises will cause him to do better. When we say that A could have done the sum correctly, had he so chosen, we do not imply that he could, on that occasion, have so chosen. But we do imply that A is such that, under certain circumstances, he will choose to act correctly; and those circumstances can be brought about. Rewards and punishments are means of varying the causal antecedents of actions so that those we desire will occur and those we wish to prevent will not occur. Cleverness and industriousness are both valuable characteristics; the latter is called a "moral" one and the former not, because we know from experience that the former cannot be induced by means of praise and blame, while the latter can. It is surely no accident that the characteristics that we believe to be alterable in this way are precisely those that we call moral; and this also explains why, to be moral, an act must be voluntary. To say that a man could have acted otherwise is to say that he might have been the sort of person who would have acted otherwise; and to attribute his acting as he did to his moral character, as opposed to some amoral defect, is to say that his action was due to one of the characteristics that can be altered by means of rewards and punishments.

It is not necessary to undertake an elaborate analysis of the other examples used. If a man kills someone because he is physically compelled to do so, he will not be prevented from doing so again in similar circumstances by the knowledge that the action will be severely punished. But if his action is due to his own decision, this knowledge may cause him to decide otherwise in future. In the same way the basis for the distinction between the kleptomaniac and the thief is that the latter is held to have decided to steal. Here the cause in both cases lies within the agent and the distinction of internal and external causation did not help us. The fact that one commits a voluntary action and the other does not is important, but by itself it does not account for the differential treatment of the two men. Why are men who steal as a result of a decision said to be worthy of punishment, while those who steal from some other cause are not? The reason is that we believe that the fear of punishment will affect the future behaviour of the thief but not that of the kleptomaniac. If a man steals because he has decided to do so, we can prevent his doing so again by causing him to decide otherwise. If he expects to be punished, then in addition to the motive that tends to make him steal there will be a powerful motive tending to make him refrain. Now the fear of punishment has no such influence on the kleptomaniac; on the other hand, psychoanalysis, by removing the subconscious cause of his tendency to steal, may achieve the desired result. Nor is this merely an interesting but unimportant distinction between kleptomaniacs and thieves; it is the very basis for the distinction. In each case we make the same value judgement, that the abstraction of one's neighbours' goods is undesirable. If we consider the actions of the thief and the kleptomaniac simply as events, without regard to their causes, they are identical and provide no possible basis for differential treatment. Therefore the different moral judgements that we in fact make and the different treatments that we accord cannot be based on the value judgement alone. The moral judgements are concerned with the causes of the actions. But to say that avarice is a reprehensible cause and kleptomania not explains nothing. For we cannot, without appeal to dubious intuitions, assert that of two similar undesirable events one is morally reprehensible and the other not. Nor is it enough to say with the positivists that the fact that we make these distinctions is simply a brute fact about our society and requires no explanation. Some basis must be found for the distinction, and I suggest that it is to be found in the fact that, while potential thieves will be deterred by the prospect of six months' hard labour, potential kleptomaniacs will not.

Generalizing from these instances, we can see that the relation that is held to exist between voluntary wrong-doing and punishability is neither an inexplicable sociological fact nor a mysterious relation of "merit" that some of us are able to intuit; it is a relation of cause and effect. If this is so, then, whatever views we may hold about the subjectivity of value judgements, moral judgements, being judgements of cause and effect, are all objective. Many moral philosophers have held subjectivist doctrines about other forms of value, such as pleasure or aesthetic taste, but have been unwilling to allow that moral judgements are subjective, and this in spite of the fact that the arguments leading to subjectivism in aesthetics appear to apply equally to morals. I think that their hesitation has been correct and has not always been due to the irrational considerations, such as the fear that subjectivity in ethics might undermine society, that have sometimes been attributed to them. If the proposed separation of the value element from the moral element in moral judgement be accepted, their unwillingness to accept a purely subjective theory of ethics will have been justified.

AUTHOR'S COMMENTARY

The main purpose of my article was to analyse the ideas of freedom and desert in terms of the empirical idea of "alterability by rewards and punishments" and thus reduce the number of intuitions required in this area. This attempt led me to conclude that "a man is not punishable because he is guilty; he is guilty because he is punishable, that is to say, because some useful purpose is supposed to accrue from punishing him." The question of freedom is too complicated for discussion in a postscript; something may be said about desert.

1. The idea that a punishment can and should "fit" a crime now seems to me to derive partly from a simple failure to distinguish punishment from damages, the purpose of civil law from the purpose of criminal law. It may be difficult to assess in monetary terms the amount of loss sustained by the plaintiff in a civil suit; but, once this is assessed, it is a simple matter to assess the damages which it is "fitting" for the court to award. For the purpose of the award is, as nearly as possible, to make good the loss. Since a *fine* of $100 awarded by a criminal court has the same effect on the pocket as an award of $100 *damages* in a civil court, we tend to confuse the two and

to suppose that the idea of "fittingness" between loss and reparation can be transferred to crime and punishment.

2. The major defect of the article lies in the failure to distinguish *cases* from *rules*, the judge's question, "Should this man in the dock, John Doe, be punished?" from the legislator's question, "Should acts of Type N be prohibited by law and, in consequence, people who do acts of Type N become liable to punishment?" When we say that John Doe deserves to be punished we certainly do not *mean* that it would be useful to punish him; nor would most of us subscribe to the *moral* view that it is just to punish him if and only if it is useful to do so. Desert is a matter of law. He deserves to be punished at all only if he has broken a law, and the severity of the punishment that he deserves is determined by what the law lays down. Considerations of utility can come in at this point only in so far as the law allows the judge a discretion to bring them in. But the legislator, I should now say, should be guided solely by considerations of utility. It is right to make a law forbidding acts of Type N only if (a) such acts are "bad" in the nonmoral sense referred to in the article and (b) the propensity to do them is one that can be weakened or eliminated by the threat of punishment.

3. In this modified theory the idea of a general fittingness between crime and punishment (as distinct from the fittingness of punishing this man in just this way) still has an important place. Deterring people from a particular type of act is never our sole aim; hence the deterrent effect of a penalty should not be the sole consideration of the legislator. While it still seems to me quite impossible to say that a certain type or degree of punishment is "fitting" to a certain type of crime, a more complex notion of fittingness is possible. Most people would agree that some types of crime are worse than others, whether or not they were prepared to analyse "worse" in terms of degree of disutility. If now we construct a scale of severity of punishment, it seems just that the punishment for a greater crime should be more severe than that for a lesser. This rule embodies a four-term relation of fittingness; it cuts across the principle of deterrence, since it may well occur that a milder penalty would deter people from the greater crime; and it can be accommodated within the framework of a utilitarian account. For a utilitarian will be more concerned to prevent greater crimes than lesser. If the penalty for a lesser crime were made equal to or greater than that for a greater crime — which it well might be if deterrence were our sole criterion — such a system, though tending to decrease the volume of the lesser crime, might increase the volume of the greater. For example, if the penalty for burglary is as great as that for murder, no doubt the number of burglaries will be reduced; but those burglars who are still not deterred will commit murder in order not to be caught. The purely deterrent rule would not then be the most "useful." As in all such matters our decision has to be made after considering the many different consequences of adopting one law rather than another. The admission of an idea of "fittingness" of this complex kind does

not seem to me to entail the falsity of my thesis that desert must, *in the end,* be explained in terms of alterability by punishment; but the explanation is a good deal more complicated than I used to think.

QUESTIONS

1. Does it seem to you that most people think that it would "not be right to praise or blame" a man if he could not have acted otherwise than he did? Is "being able to act otherwise" what is meant by "acting freely"?

2. Why does Nowell-Smith think that "the considerations which lead scientists to suppose that strict determinism is not true are irrelevant to the problem of free will"?

3. Does he offer sound reason for saying that "I could not be free to choose what I do *unless* determinism is correct"? What is his reason? Is he right that "in referring the action to an agent we are referring it to a cause"?

4. Cite some examples of actions we should ordinarily call "voluntary," and others of actions we usually classify as "involuntary." Do the two types differ in predictability? What do you think is our criterion for deciding to which class a given act belongs?

5. Do you agree that the "plain man" thinks an act is blameworthy only if it springs from a moral defect, not an intellectual one? Does he think the criterion for deciding whether a defect is moral is partly whether the agent "could have acted otherwise"?

6. Do you agree that the sense of "could have acted otherwise" which establishes a moral defect is "would have acted differently if he had chosen to, and would have chosen to act differently if he had had a different character"? What is the meaning of "character" which distinguishes it from any "non-character trait of personality" such as intellectual qualities?

7. Do you think people ought to be excused for their misdeeds if their deeds were caused by traits of character which were themselves caused by such influences as the heredity and childhood experiences of the agent? Would Nowell-Smith agree?

8. What is the essence of Nowell-Smith's proposal about *why* only those actions are praiseworthy or blameworthy which spring from a moral defect, which would have been otherwise if the agent's character had been different?

9. Do you agree that a defect is a defect of character if and only if it is a trait of mind which can be altered by punishment, praise, or blame?

10. Why, in his view, *is* blame suitable for a person whose action has sprung from a defect of character — and in that sense was "voluntary"? Why is it, in his view, that the thief is properly blamed, but not the kleptomaniac? the lazy student but not the dull one?

11. In view of Nowell-Smith's appendix, can we say that his theory makes room for the truth of the maxim, "The punishment should fit the crime"?

12. Can you think of any exceptions to his proposed rule that an action A is more reprehensible morally than an action B if and only if it is preferable, in view of the consequences, to punish offenses like A more severely than those like B?

Charles Arthur Campbell   (1897-   )

RESPONSIBILITY REQUIRES
CONTRA-CAUSAL FREEDOM

Some philosophers are convinced that the puzzle about freedom of choice, which has perplexed thinkers for many centuries, is by no means resolved as easily as writers like Nowell-Smith suggest. The best of the protests against the premature burial of the problem of freedom is the following paper by C. A. Campbell, who has been professor of logic and rhetoric at the University of Glasgow since 1938.

C. A. Campbell is a graduate of both Glasgow University and Oxford University, where he was a student at Balliol College. He has taught at the University of Glasgow since 1924, except for a period of five years at the University College of North Wales. Campbell has often criticized contemporary philosophical trends, on the ground that they have frequently overlooked important ideas and puzzles which lay behind traditional controversies. He is the author of *Scepticism and Construction* (1931) and *On Selfhood and Godhood* (1957).

The present article is an attack on the views about freedom of three philosophers — Moritz Schlick, P. H. Nowell-Smith, and C. L. Stevenson — whose resolutions of the "problem" of freedom have much in common. Campbell's article can be construed as a reply to our foregoing reading by Nowell-Smith. A major objection Campbell presents is that "moral responsibility" and "moral blameworthiness" are not the purely forward-looking concepts these authors make out they are; to say that a person is morally blameworthy, according to Campbell, is by no means to say that punishing or blaming him will have beneficial educative or deterrent effects. What thoughtful people believe about who is blameworthy — and to what extent they are to be blamed — is sharply at variance with what they would believe if what they meant by "blameworthy" were what these writers think is meant. Moreover, in order to be blameworthy in the sense this word really bears in ordinary thought, a person must have been *able to do what he ought to have done, even being exactly the kind of person he was*, and all the other conditions being exactly what they were. And for this to be true, there must be freedom of choice in a sense which is not compatible with the fact that human decisions are caused by prior states of affairs. Therefore, he concludes, the way of escape offered us by Nowell-Smith is really no way of escape at all. Campbell concludes his article by considering what strike him as the forceful reasons behind an opposite conclusion, and in particular a reason formulated in the article by Nowell-Smith, to the effect that the whole notion of contra-causally free action (action free in a sense incompatible with being wholly caused or wholly predictable) does not make sense because to be the agent of an action is the same thing as one's character being the cause of the action.

Campbell's positive view may be somewhat puzzling, but the reader will doubtless feel that there is much force in his critical arguments.

The "Verifiability Principle" to which he refers at the outset is the thesis that a statement about the world makes no sense if it cannot be supported by observations much as scientific statements can be. It also asserts that a question about the world makes no sense if in principle observation could not answer it.

C. A. Campbell, "Is 'Freewill' a Pseudo-problem?" *Mind*, Vol. 60 (1951), pp. 441-65. Reprinted by kind permission of the author and of the editor of *Mind*.

IS 'FREE WILL' A PSEUDO-PROBLEM?

I

In the days when the Verifiability Principle was accepted by its devotees as a secure philosophical truth, one could understand, though one might not agree with, the sweeping claim that many of the traditional problems of philosophy had been shown to be mere 'pseudo-problems.' It was easy to see how, given the Principle's validity, most of the leading questions which agitated our forefathers in metaphysics, in ethics, and in theology, automatically become nonsensical questions. What is perplexing, however, is that despite the pretty generally acknowledged deterioration in the Principle's status to that of a convenient methodological postulate, the attitude to these same questions seems to have changed but little. To admit that the Verifiability Principle is not an assured truth entails the admission that a problem can no longer be dismissed as meaningless simply on the ground that it cannot be stated in a way which satisfies the Principle. Whether or not a problem is meaningless is now something that can only be decided after critical examination of the particular case on its own individual merits. But the old antipathies seem in large measure to have survived the disappearance of their logical basis. One gets the impression that for at least many thinkers with Positivist sympathies the 'liquidation' of a large, if unspecified, group of traditional philosophic problems is still established fact. If that impression is mistaken, well and good. One may then hope for an early recrudescence of interest in certain problems that have too long suffered the consequences of an unhappy *tabu*. If the impression is correct, a real service would be done to philosophy if it were plainly stated which of the traditional problems are still regarded as pseudo-problems, and what are the reasons, old or new, for passing this sentence upon them. The smoke of old battles, perhaps understandably, darkens the philosophic air, to the considerable inconvenience of all concerned.

Fortunately, however, the obscurity complained of is not totally unrelieved. We do know of one traditional problem that is definitely on the black list of the *avant garde* — the problem of 'Free Will': and we do have pretty adequate information about the reasons which have led to its being placed thereon. This, so far as it goes, is satisfactory. A plain obligation now lies upon philosophers who still believe that 'Free Will' is a genuine problem to explain just where, in their opinion, the case for the prosecution breaks down. To discharge this obligation is the main purpose of the present paper.

There will be a clear advantage in making our start from the *locus classicus* of the 'pseudo-problem' theory, if *locus classicus* there be. And I think that there must be something of the sort. At any rate, the casual, and indeed slightly bored, tones in which so many contemporary philosophers allude to the traditional problem, and their contentment to indicate in only a sketchy manner the reasons why it no longer exists, strongly suggest that *somewhere* the matter has in their eyes been already effectively settled. At least one important 'document in the case' is, I suspect, Chapter VII of Moritz Schlick's *Problems of Ethics*, first published in 1931. This chapter, the title of which is 'When is a Man Responsible?' and the first section of which bears the heading 'The Pseudo-problem of Freedom of the Will,' presents in concentrated form, but with some show of systematic argument, most of the considerations upon which later writers appear to rely. It will be worth our while, therefore, to try to see just why Professor Schlick is so sure (and he is *very* sure indeed) that 'Free Will,' as traditionally formulated, is a pseudo-problem, begotten by mere confusion of mind.

II

I shall first summarise, as faithfully as I can, what I take to be the distinctive points in Schlick's argument.

The traditional formulation of the problem, Schlick points out, is based on the assumption that to have 'free will' entails having a will that is, at least sometimes, exempt from causal law. It is traditionally supposed, quite rightly, that moral responsibility implies freedom in *some* sense: and it is supposed, also quite rightly, that this sense is one which is incompatible with compulsion. But because it is further supposed, quite *wrongly*, that to be subject to causal or natural law is to be subject to compulsion, the inference is drawn that the free will implied in moral responsibility is incompatible with causal continuity. The ultimate root of the error, Schlick contends, lies in a failure to distinguish between two different kinds of Law, one of which does indeed 'compel,' but the other of which does *not*.[1] There are, first, *prescriptive* laws, such as the laws imposed by civil authority, which presume contrary desires on the part of those to whom they are applied; and these may fairly be said to exercise 'compulsion.' And there are, secondly, *descriptive* laws, such as the laws which the sciences seek to formulate; and these merely state what does as a matter of fact always happen. It is perfectly clear that the relation of the latter, the natural, causal laws, to human willing is radically different from the 'compulsive' relation of prescriptive laws to human willing, and that it is really an absurdity to talk of a species of natural law like, say, psychological laws, *compelling* us to act in this or that way. The term 'compulsion' is totally inept where, as in this case, there are no contrary desires. But the traditional discussions of Free Will, confusing descriptive with prescriptive laws, fallaciously assume 'compulsion' to be ingredient in Law as such, and it is contended accordingly that moral freedom, since it certainly implies absence of compulsion, implies also exemption from causal law.

It follows that the problem of Free Will, as traditionally stated, is a mere pseudo-problem. The statement of it in terms of exemption from causal law rests on the assumption that causal law involves 'compulsion.' And this assumption is demonstrably false. Expose the muddle from which it arises and the so-called 'problem' in its traditional form disappears.

But is it quite certain that the freedom which moral responsibility implies is no more than 'the absence of compulsion'? This is the premise upon which Schlick's argument proceeds, but Schlick is himself well aware that it stands in need of confirmation from an analysis of the notion of moral responsibility. Otherwise it might be maintained that although 'the absence of compulsion' has been shown not to entail a contra-causal type of freedom, there is nevertheless some *other* condition of moral responsibility that *does* entail it. Accordingly Schlick embarks now upon a formal analysis of the nature and conditions of moral responsibility designed to show that the *only* freedom implied by moral responsibility is freedom from compulsion. It was a trifle ambitious, however, even for a master of compression like Professor Schlick, to hope to deal satisfactorily in half-a-dozen very brief pages with a topic which has been so extensively debated in the literature of moral philosophy: and I cannot pretend that I find what he has to say free from obscurity. But to the best of my belief what follows does reproduce the gist of Schlick's analysis.

What precisely, Schlick asks, does the term 'moral responsibility' mean in our ordinary linguistic usage?[2] He begins his answer by insisting upon the close connexion for ordinary usage between 'moral responsibility' and

[1] *Problems of Ethics*, Ch. VIII. Section 2. (All references are to the English translation by David Rynin, published in New York in 1939.)

[2] *Loc. cit.*, Ch. VII, Section 5.

punishment (strictly speaking, punishment and *reward*: but for convenience Schlick virtually confines the discussion to punishment, and we shall do the same). The connexion, as Schlick sees it, is this. In ordinary practice our concern with the responsibility for an act (he tells us) is with a view to determining *who is to be punished for it*. Now punishment is (I quote) 'an educative measure.' It is 'a means to the formation of motives, which are in part to prevent the wrong-doer from repeating the act (reformation), and in part to prevent others from committing a similar act (intimidation).'[3] When we ask, then, 'Who in a given case is to be punished?'—which is the same as the question 'Who is responsible?'—what we are really wanting to discover is some agent in the situation upon whose motives we can bring to bear the appropriate educative influences, so that in similar situations in future his strongest motive will impel him to refrain from, rather than to repeat, the act. 'The question of who is responsible' Schlick sums up, 'is . . . a matter only of knowing who is to be punished or rewarded, in order that punishment and reward function as such — be able to achieve their goal.'[4] It is not a matter, he expressly declares, of trying to ascertain what may be called the 'original instigator' of the act. That might be a great-grand-parent, from the consequence of whose behaviour vicious tendencies have been inherited by a living person. Such 'remote causes' as this are irrelevant to questions of punishment (and so to questions of moral responsibility), 'for in the first place their actual contribution cannot be determined, and in the second place they are generally out of reach.'[5]

It is a matter for regret that Schlick has not rounded off his discussion, as one had hoped and expected he would, by formulating a precise definition of moral responsibility in terms of what he has been saying. I think, however, that the conclusion to which his argument leads could be not unfairly expressed in some such way as this: 'We say that a man is morally responsible for an act if his motives for bringing about the act are such as we can affect favourably in respect of his future behaviour by the educative influences of reward and punishment.'

Given the truth of this analysis of moral responsibility, Schlick's contention follows logically enough that the only freedom that is required for moral responsibility is freedom from compulsion. For what are the cases in which a man's motives are *not* capable of being favourably affected by reward and punishment? — the cases in which, that is, according to Schlick's analysis, we do *not* deem him morally responsible? The only such cases, it would seem, are those in which a man is subjected to some form of external constraint which prevents him from acting according to his 'natural desires.' For example, if a man is compelled by a pistol at his breast to do a certain act, or induced to do it by an externally administered narcotic, he is not 'morally responsible'; or not, at any rate, in so far as punishment would

3 *Ibid.*, p. 152.   5 *Ibid.*, p. 153.
4 *Ibid.*, p. 153.

be impotent to affect his motives in respect of his future behaviour. External constraint in one form or another seems to be the sole circumstance which absolves a man from moral responsibility. Hence we may say that freedom from external constraint is the only sort of freedom which an agent must possess in order to be morally responsible. The 'contra-causal' sort of freedom which so many philosophers and others have supposed to be required is shown by a true analysis of moral responsibility to be irrelevant.

This completes the argument that 'Free Will,' as traditionally formulated, is a pseudo-problem. The only freedom implied by moral responsibility is freedom from compulsion; and as we have rid ourselves of the myth that subjection to causal law is a form of compulsion, we can see that the only compulsion which absolves from moral responsibility is the external constraint which prevents us from translating our desires into action. The true meaning of the question 'Have we free will?' thus becomes simply 'Can we translate our desires into action?' And this question does not constitute a 'problem' at all, for the answer to it is not in doubt. The obvious answer is 'Sometimes we can, sometimes we can't, according to the specific circumstances of the case.'

III

Here, then, in substance is Schlick's theory. Let us now examine it.

In the first place, it is surely quite unplausible to suggest that the common assumption that moral freedom postulates some breach of causal continuity arises from a confusion of two different types of law. Schlick's distinction between descriptive and prescriptive law is, of course, sound. It was no doubt worth pointing out, too, that descriptive laws cannot be said to 'compel' human behaviour in the same way as prescriptive laws do. But it seems to me evident that the usual reason why it is held that moral freedom implies some breach of causal continuity, is not a belief that causal laws 'compel' as civil laws 'compel,' but simply the belief that the admission of unbroken causal continuity entails a *further* admission which is directly incompatible with moral responsibility; *viz.* the admission that no man could have acted otherwise than he in fact did. Now it may, of course, be an error thus to assume that a man is not morally responsible for an act, a fit subject for moral praise and blame in respect of it, unless he could have acted otherwise than he did. Or, if *this* is not an error, it may still be an error to assume that a man could not have acted otherwise than he did, in the sense of the phrase that is crucial for moral responsibility, without there occurring some breach of causal continuity. Into these matters we shall have to enter very fully at a later stage. But the relevant point at the moment is that these (not *prima facie* absurd) assumptions about the conditions of moral responsibility have very commonly, indeed normally, been made, and that they are entirely adequate to explain why the problem of Free Will finds its usual formulation in terms of partial exemption from causal law. Schlick's distinction between prescriptive and descriptive laws has no bearing at all upon the truth or falsity of these assumptions. Yet if these assumptions are accepted, it is (I suggest) really inevitable that the Free Will problem should be formulated in the way to which Schlick takes exception. Recognition of the distinction upon which Schlick and his followers lay so much stress can make not a jot of difference.

As we have seen, however, Schlick does later proceed to the much more important business of disputing these common assumptions about the conditions of moral responsibility. He offers us an analysis of moral responsibility which flatly contradicts these assumptions; an analysis according to which the only freedom demanded by morality is a freedom which is compatible with Determinism. If this analysis can be sustained, there is certainly no problem of 'Free Will' in the traditional sense.

But it seems a simple matter to show that Schlick's analysis is untenable. Let us test it by Schlick's own claim that it gives us what we mean by 'moral responsibility' in ordinary linguistic usage.

We do not ordinarily consider the lower animals to be morally responsible. But *ought* we not to do so if Schlick is right about what we mean by moral responsibility? It is quite possible, by punishing the dog who absconds with the succulent chops designed for its master's luncheon, favourably to influence its motives in respect of its future behaviour in like circumstances. If moral responsibility is to be linked with punishment as Schlick links it, and punishment conceived as a form of education, we should surely hold the dog morally responsible? The plain fact, of course, is that we don't. We don't, because we suppose that the dog 'couldn't help it': that its action (unlike what we usually believe to be true of human beings) was simply a link in a continuous chain of causes and effects. In other words, we do commonly demand the contra-causal sort of freedom as a condition of moral responsibility.

Again, we do ordinarily consider it proper, in certain circumstances, to speak of a person no longer living as morally responsible for some present situation. But *ought* we to do so if we accept Schlick's essentially 'forward-looking' interpretation of punishment and responsibility? Clearly we cannot now favourably affect the dead man's motives. No doubt they could *at one time* have been favourably affected. But that cannot be relevant to our judgment of responsibility if, as Schlick insists, the question of who is responsible 'is a matter only of knowing who is to be punished or rewarded.' Indeed he expressly tells us, as we saw earlier, that in asking this question we are not concerned with a 'great-grand-parent' who may have been the 'original instigator,' because, for one reason, this 'remote cause' is 'out of reach.' We cannot bring the appropriate educative influence to bear upon it. But the plain fact, of course, is that we do frequently assign moral responsibility for present situations to persons who have long been inaccessible to any punitive action on our part. And Schlick's position is still more paradoxical in respect of our apportionment of responsibility for occurrences in the distant past. Since in these cases there is no agent whatsoever whom we can favourably influence by punishment, the question of moral responsibility here should have no meaning for us. But of course it has. Historical writings are studded with examples.

Possibly the criticism just made may seem to some to result from taking Schlick's analysis too much *au pied de la lettre*. The absurd consequences deduced, it may be said, would not follow if we interpreted Schlick as meaning that a man is morally responsible where his motive is such as can *in principle* be favourably affected by reward or punishment — whether or not we who pass the judgment are in a position to take such action. But with every desire to be fair to Schlick, I cannot see how he could accept this modification and still retain the essence of his theory. For the essence of his theory seems to be that moral responsibility has its whole meaning and importance for us in relation to our potential control of future conduct in the interests of society. (I agree that it is hard to believe that anybody *really* thinks this. But it is perhaps less hard to believe to-day than it has ever been before in the history of modern ethics.)

Again, we ordinarily consider that, in certain circumstances, the *degree* of a man's moral responsibility for an act is affected by considerations of his inherited nature, or of his environment, or of both. It is our normal habit to 'make allowances' (as we say) when we have reason to believe that a malefactor had a vicious heredity, or was nurtured in his formative years in a harmful environment. We say in such cases 'Poor chap, he is more to be pitied than blamed. We could scarcely expect him to behave like a decent citizen with *his* parentage or upbringing.' But this extremely common sort of judgment has no point at all if we mean by moral responsibility what Schlick says that we mean. On *that* meaning the degree of a man's moral responsibility must presumably be dependent upon the degree to which we can favourably affect his future motives, which is quite another matter. Now there is no reason to believe that the motives of a man with a bad heredity or a bad upbringing are either less or more subject to educative influence than those of his more fortunate fellows. Yet it is plain matter of fact that we do commonly consider the degree of a man's moral responsibility to be affected by these two factors.

A final point. The extremity of paradox in Schlick's identification of the question 'Who is morally blameworthy?' with the question 'Who is to be punished?' is apt to be partially concealed from us just because it is our normal habit to include in the meaning of 'punishment' an element of 'requital for moral transgression' which Schlick expressly denies to it. On that account we commonly think of 'punishment,' in its strict sense, as implying moral blameworthiness in the person punished. But if we remember to mean by punishment what Schlick means by it, a purely 'educative measure,' with no retributive ingredients, his identification of the two questions loses such plausibility as it might otherwise have. For clearly we often think it proper to 'punish' a person, in *Schlick's* sense, where we are not at all prepared to say that the person is morally blameworthy. We may even think him morally commendable. A case in point would be the unmistakably sincere but muddleheaded person who at the cost of great suffering to himself steadfastly pursues as his 'duty' a course which, in our judgment, is fraught with danger to the common weal. We should most of us feel entitled, in the public interest, to bring such action to bear upon the man's motives as might induce him to refrain in future from his socially injurious behaviour: in other words, to inflict upon him what Schlick would call 'punishment.' But we should most of us feel perfectly clear that in so 'punishing' this misguided citizen we are not proclaiming his moral blameworthiness for moral wickedness.

Adopting Schlick's own criterion, then, looking simply 'to the manner in which the concept is used,' [6] we seem bound to admit that constantly people do assign moral responsibility where Schlick's theory says they shouldn't, don't assign moral responsibility where Schlick's theory says they should, and assign degrees of moral responsibility where on Schlick's theory there should be no difference in degree. I think we may reasonably conclude that Schlick's account of what we mean by moral responsibility breaks down.

The rebuttal of Schlick's arguments, however, will not suffice of itself to refute the pseudo-problem theory. The indebtedness to Schlick of most later advocates of the theory may be conceded; but certainly it does not comprehend all of significance that they have to say on the problem. There are recent analyses of the conditions of moral responsibility containing sufficient new matter, or sufficient old matter in a more precise and telling form, to require of us now something of a fresh start. In the section which follows I propose to consider some representative samples of these analyses — all of which, of course, are designed to show that the freedom which moral responsibility implies is not in fact a contra-causal type of freedom.

But before reopening the general question of the nature and conditions of moral responsibility there is a *caveat* which it seems to me worthwhile to enter. The difficulties in the way of a clear answer are not slight; but they are apt to seem a good deal more formidable than they really are because of a common tendency to consider in unduly close association two distinct questions: the question "Is a contra-causal type of freedom implied by moral responsibility?" and the question "Does a contra-causal type of freedom anywhere exist?" It seems to me that many philosophers (and I suspect that Moritz Schlick is among them) begin this inquiry with so firm a conviction that the contra-causal sort of freedom nowhere exists, that they find it hard to take very seriously the possibility that it is *this* sort of freedom that moral responsibility implies. For they are loath to abandon the common-sense belief that moral responsibility itself is something real. The implicit reasoning I take to be this. Moral responsibility is real. If moral responsibility is real, the freedom implied in it must be a fact. But contra-

[6] *Loc. cit.*, Ch. VII, Section 5, p. 151.

causal freedom is not a fact. Therefore contra-causal freedom is not the freedom implied in moral responsibility. I think we should be on our guard against allowing this or some similar train of reasoning (whose premises, after all, are far from indubitable) to seduce us into distorting what we actually find when we set about a direct analysis of moral responsibility and its conditions.

I V

The pseudo-problem theorists usually, and naturally, develop their analysis of moral responsibility by way of contrast with a view which, while it has enjoyed a good deal of philosophic support, I can best describe as the common view. It will be well to remind ourselves, therefore, of the main features of this view.

So far as the *meaning*, as distinct from the *conditions*, of moral responsibility is concerned, the common view is very simple. If we ask ourselves whether a certain person is morally responsible for a given act (or it may be just "in general"), what we are considering, it would be said, is whether or not that person is a fit subject upon whom to pass moral judgment; whether he can fittingly be deemed morally good or bad, morally praiseworthy or blameworthy. This does not take us any great way; but (*pace* Schlick) so far as it goes it does not seem to me seriously disputable. The really interesting and controversial question is about the *conditions* of moral responsibility, and in particular the question whether freedom of a contra-causal kind is among these conditions.

The answer of the common man to the latter question is that it most certainly *is* among the conditions. Why does he feel so sure about this? Not, I argued earlier, because the common man supposes that causal law exercises 'compulsion' in the sense that prescriptive laws do, but simply because he does not see how a person can be deemed morally praiseworthy or blameworthy in respect of an act which he could not help performing. From the stand-point of moral praise and blame, he would say — though not necessarily from other stand-points — it is a matter of indifference whether it is by reason of some external constraint or by reason of his own given nature that the man could not help doing what he did. It is quite enough to make moral praise and blame futile that in either case there were no genuine alternatives, no open possibilities, before the man when he acted. He could not have acted otherwise than he did. And the common man might not unreasonably go on to stress the fact that we all, even if we are linguistic philosophers, do in our actual practice of moral judgment appear to accept the common view. He might insist upon the point alluded to earlier in this paper, that we do all, in passing moral censure, 'make allowances' for influences in a man's hereditary nature or environmental circumstances which we regard as having made it more than ordinarily difficult for him to act otherwise than he did: the implication being that if we supposed that the man's heredity and environment made it not merely very *difficult* but actually *impossible* for him to act otherwise than he did, we could not properly assign moral blame to him at all.

Let us put the argument implicit in the common view a little more sharply. The moral 'ought' implies 'can.' If we say that A morally ought to have done X, we imply that in our opinion, he could have done X. But we assign moral blame to a man only for failing to do what we think he morally ought to have done. Hence if we morally blame A for not having done X, we imply that he could have done X even though in fact he did not. In other words, we imply that A could have acted otherwise than he did. And that means that we imply, as a necessary condition of a man's being morally blameworthy, that he enjoyed a freedom of a kind not compatible with unbroken causal continuity.

V

Now what is it that is supposed to be wrong with this simple piece of argument? — For, of course, it must be rejected by all these philosophers who tell us that the traditional problem of Free Will is a mere pseudo-problem. The argument looks as though it were doing little more than reading off necessary implications of the fundamental categories of our moral thinking. One's inclination is to ask 'If one is to think morally at all, how else than this *can* we think?'

In point of fact, there is pretty general agreement among the contemporary critics as to what is wrong with the argument. Their answer in general terms is as follows. No doubt A's moral responsibility does imply that he could have acted otherwise. But this expression 'could have acted otherwise' stands in dire need of analysis. When we analyse it, we find that it is not, as is so often supposed, simple and unambiguous, and we find that in *some* at least of its possible meanings it implies *no* breach of causal continuity between character and conduct. Having got this clear, we can further discern that only in one of these *latter* meanings is there any compulsion upon our moral thinking to assert that if A is morally blameworthy for an act, A 'could have acted otherwise than he did.' It follows that, contrary to common belief, our moral thinking does *not* require us to posit a contra-causal freedom as a condition of moral responsibility.

So much of importance obviously turns upon the validity or otherwise of this line of criticism that we must examine it in some detail and with express regard to the *ipsissima verba* of the critics.

In the course of a recent article in MIND,[7] entitled 'Free Will and Moral Responsibility,' Mr. Nowell Smith (having earlier affirmed his belief that 'the traditional problem has been solved') explains very concisely the nature of the confusion which, as he thinks, has led to the demand for a contra-causal freedom. He begins by frankly recognising that 'It is evident that one of the necessary conditions of moral action is that the agent

[7] January, 1948.

"could have acted otherwise" ' and he adds 'it is to this fact that the Libertarian is drawing attention.' [8] Then, after showing (unexceptionably, I think) how the relationship of 'ought' to 'can' warrants the proposition which he has accepted as evident, and how it induces the Libertarian to assert the existence of action that is 'uncaused,' he proceeds to point out, in a crucial passage, the nature of the Libertarian's error:

The fallacy in the argument (he contends) lies in supposing that when we say 'A could have acted otherwise' we mean that A, *being what he was and being placed in the circumstances in which he was placed*, could have done something other than what he did. But in fact we never do mean this.[9]

What then *do* we mean here by 'A could have acted otherwise'? Mr. Nowell Smith does not tell us in so many words, but the passage I have quoted leaves little doubt how he would answer. What we really mean by the expression, he implies, is not a *categorical* but a *hypothetical* proposition. We mean 'A could have acted otherwise, *if he did not happen to be what he in fact was*, or *if he were placed in circumstances other than those in which he was in fact placed.*' Now, *these* propositions, it is easy to see, are in no way incompatible with acceptance of the causal principle in its full rigour. Accordingly the claim that our fundamental moral thinking obliges us to assert a contra-causal freedom as a condition of moral responsibility is disproved.

Such is the 'analytical solution' of our problem offered (with obvious confidence) by one able philosopher of to-day, and entirely representative of the views of many other able philosophers. Yet I make bold to say that its falsity stares one in the face. It seems perfectly plain that the hypothetical propositions which Mr. Nowell Smith proposes to substitute for the categorical proposition cannot express 'what we really mean' in this context by 'A could have acted otherwise,' for the simple reason that these hypothetical propositions have no bearing whatsoever upon the question of the moral responsibility of A. And it is A whose moral responsibility we are talking about — a definite person A with a definitive character and in a definitive set of circumstances. What conceivable significance could it have for our attitude to A's responsibility to know that someone with a *different* character (or A with a different character, if that collocation of words has any meaning), or A in a different set of circumstances from those in which A as we are concerned with him was in fact placed, 'could have acted otherwise'? No doubt this supposititious being *could* have acted otherwise than the definitive person A acted. But the point is that where we are reflecting, as we are supposed in this context to be reflecting, upon the question of A's moral responsibility, our interest in this supposititious being is precisely *nil*.

The two hypothetical propositions suggested in Mr. Nowell Smith's ac-

[8] *Loc. cit.,* p. 49.
[9] *Loc. cit.,* p. 49.

count of the matter do not, however, exhaust the speculations that have been made along these lines. Another very common suggestion by the analysts is that what we really mean by 'A could have acted otherwise' is 'A could have acted otherwise *if he had willed, or chosen, otherwise.*' This was among the suggestions offered by G. E. Moore in the well-known chapter on Free Will in his *Ethics*. It is, I think, the suggestion he most strongly favoured: though it is fair to add that neither about this nor about any other of his suggestions is Moore in the least dogmatic. He does claim, for, I think, convincing reasons, that "we *very often* mean by 'could' merely 'would, *if* so-and-so had chosen.' " [10] And he concludes "I must confess that I cannot feel certain that this may not be all that we usually mean and understand by the assertion that we have Free Will." [11]

This third hypothetical proposition appears to enjoy also the support of Mr. C. L. Stevenson. Mr. Stevenson begins the chapter of *Ethics and Language* entitled 'Avoidability-Indeterminism' with the now familiar pronouncement of his School that 'controversy about freedom and determinism of the will . . . presents no permanent difficulty to ethics, being largely a product of confusions.' A major confusion (if I understand him rightly) he takes to lie in the meaning of the term 'avoidable,' when we say 'A's action was avoidable' — or, I presume, 'A could have acted otherwise.' He himself offers the following definition of 'avoidable' — ' "A's action was avoidable" has the meaning of "If A had made a certain choice, which in fact he did not make, his action would not have occurred." ' [12] This I think we may regard as in substance identical with the suggestion that what we really mean by 'A could have acted otherwise' is 'A could have acted otherwise *if* he had chosen (or willed) otherwise.' For clarity's sake we shall here keep to this earlier formulation. In either formulation the special significance of the third hypothetical proposition, as of the two hypothetical propositions already considered, is that it is compatible with strict determinism. If this be indeed all that we mean by the 'freedom' that conditions moral responsibility, then those philosophers are certainly wrong who hold that moral freedom is of the contra-causal type.

Now this third hypothetical proposition does at least possess the merit, not shared by its predecessors, of having a real relevance to the question of moral responsibility. If, *e.g.* A had promised to meet us at 2 p.m., and he chanced to break his leg at 1 p.m., we should not blame him for his failure to discharge his promise. For we should be satisfied that he *could not* have acted otherwise, even if he had so chosen; or *could not*, at any rate, in a way which would have enabled him to meet us at 2 p.m. The freedom to translate one's choice into action, which we saw earlier is for Schlick the *only* freedom required for moral responsibility, is without doubt *one* of the conditions of moral responsibility.

10 *Ethics*, p. 212.
11 *Loc. cit.*, p. 217.
12 *Ethics and Language*, p. 298.

But it seems easy to show that this third hypothetical proposition does not exhaust what we mean, and *some*times is not even *part* of what we mean, by the expression 'could have acted otherwise' in its moral context. Thus it can hardly be even part of what we mean in the case of that class of wrong actions (and it is a large class) concerning which there is really no question whether the agent could have acted otherwise, *if* he had chosen otherwise. Take lying, for example. Only in some very abnormal situation could it occur to one to doubt whether A, whose power of speech was evinced by his telling a lie, was in a position to tell what he took to be the truth *if* he had so chosen. Of *course* he was. Yet it still makes good sense for one's moral thinking to ask whether A, when lying, 'could have acted otherwise': and we still require an affirmative answer to this question if A's moral blameworthiness is to be established. It seems apparent, therefore, that in this class of cases at any rate one does *not* mean by 'A could have acted otherwise,' 'A could have acted otherwise *if* he had so chosen.'

What then *does* one mean in this class of cases by 'A could have acted otherwise'? I submit that the expression is taken in its simple, categorical meaning, without any suppressed 'if' clause to qualify it. Or perhaps, in order to keep before us the important truth that it is only as expressions of *will* or *choice* that acts are of moral import, it might be better to say that a condition of A's moral responsibility is that he could have *chosen* otherwise. We saw that there is no real question whether A who told a lie could have acted otherwise *if* he had chosen otherwise. But there is a very real question, at least for any person who approaches the question of moral responsibility at a tolerably advanced level of reflexion, about whether A could have *chosen* otherwise. Such a person will doubtless be acquainted with the claims advanced in some quarters that causal law operates universally: or/and with the theories of some philosophies that the universe is throughout the expression of a single supreme principle; or/and with the doctrines of some theologians that the world is created, sustained and governed by an Omniscient and Omnipotent Being. Very understandably such world-views awaken in him doubts about the validity of his first, easy, instinctive assumption that there are genuinely open possibilities before a man at the moment of moral choice. It thus becomes for him a real question whether a man could have chosen otherwise than he actually did, and in consequence, whether man's moral responsibility is really defensible. For how can a man be morally responsible, he asks himself, if his choices, like all other events in the universe, could not have been otherwise than they in fact were? It is precisely against the background of world-views such as these that for reflective people the problem of moral responsibility normally arises.

Furthermore, to the man who has attained this level of reflexion, it will in *no* class of cases be a sufficient condition of moral responsibility for an act that one could have acted otherwise *if* one had chosen otherwise —

not even in these cases where there *was* some possibility of the operation of 'external constraint.' In these cases he will, indeed, expressly recognise freedom from external constraint as a *necessary condition,* but not as a *sufficient* condition. For he will be aware that, even granted *this* freedom, it is still conceivable that the agent had no freedom to choose otherwise than he did, and he will therefore require that the latter sort of freedom be added if moral responsibility for the act is to be established.

I have been contending that, for persons at a *tolerably advanced level of reflexion,* 'A could have acted otherwise,' as a condition of A's moral responsibility, means 'A could have chosen otherwise.' The qualification italicised is of some importance. The unreflective or unsophisticated person, the ordinary 'man in the street,' who does not know or much care what scientists and theologians and philosophers have said about the world, sees well enough that A is morally responsible only if he could have acted otherwise, but in his intellectual innocence he will, very probably, envisage nothing capable of preventing A from having acted otherwise except some material impediment — like the broken leg in the example above. Accordingly, for the unreflective person, 'A could have acted otherwise,' as a condition of moral responsibility, *is* apt to mean no more than 'A could have acted otherwise *if* he had so chosen.'

It would appear, then, that the view now favoured by many philosophers, that the freedom required for moral responsibility is merely freedom from external constraint, is a view which they share only with the less reflective type of layman. Yet it should be plain that on a matter of this sort the view of the unreflective person is of little value by comparison with the view of the reflective person. There are some contexts, no doubt, in which lack of sophistication is an asset. But this is not one of them. The question at issue here is as to the kind of impediments which might have prevented a man from acting otherwise than he in fact did; and on this question knowledge and reflexion are surely prerequisites of any answer that is worth listening to. It is simply on account of the limitations of his mental vision that the unreflective man interprets the expression 'could have acted otherwise,' in its context as a condition of moral responsibility, solely in terms of external constraint. He has failed (as yet) to reach the intellectual level at which one takes into account the implications for moral choices of the world-views of science, religion, and philosophy. If on a matter of this complexity the philosopher finds that his analysis accords with the utterances of the uneducated he has, I suggest, better cause for uneasiness than for self-congratulation.

This concludes the main part of what it seems to me necessary to say in answer to the pseudo-problem theorists. My object so far has been to expose the falsity of those innovations (chiefly Positivist) in the way of argument and analysis which are supposed by many to have made it impossible any longer to formulate the problem of Free Will in the traditional manner. My contention is that, at least so far as these innovations are concerned, the simple time-honoured argument still holds from the nature of the moral ought to the conclusion that moral responsibility implies a contra-causal type of freedom. The attempts to avoid that conclusion by analysing the proposition 'A could have acted otherwise' (acknowledged to be implied in *some* sense in A's moral responsibility) into one or other of certain hypothetical propositions which are compatible with unbroken causal continuity, break down hopelessly when tested against the touchstone of actual moral thinking. It is, I think, not necessary to defend the procedure of testing hypotheses in the ethical field by bringing to bear upon them our actual moral thinking. If there is any other form of test applicable, I should be much interested to learn what it is supposed to be. Certainly 'logical analysis' *per se* will not do. That has a function, but a function that can only be ancillary. For what we are seeking to know is the meaning of the expression 'could have acted otherwise' not *in the abstract*, but in the context of the question of man's *moral responsibility*. Logical analysis *per se* is impotent to give us this information. It can be of value only in so far as it operates within the orbit of 'the moral consciousness.' One may admit, with some qualifications, that on a matter of this sort the moral consciousness without logical analysis is blind: but it seems to me to be true without any qualification whatsoever that, on the same problem, logical analysis without the moral consciousness is empty.

V I

There are times when what seems to a critic the very strength of his case breeds mistrust in the critic's own mind. I confess that in making the criticisms that have preceded I have not been altogether free from uncomfortable feelings of this kind. For the arguments I have criticised, and more particularly the analyses of the conditions of moral responsibility, seem to me to be in many cases quite desperately unplausible. Such a state of affairs ought, I think, to give the critic pause. The thought must at least enter his mind (unless he be a total stranger to modesty) that perhaps, despite his best efforts to be fair, he has after all misrepresented what his opponents are saying. No doubt a similar thought will enter, and perhaps find lodgment in, the minds of many readers.

In this situation there is, however, one course by which the critic may reasonably hope to allay these natural suspicions. He should consider whether there may not be certain predisposing influences at work, extrinsic to the specific arguments, which could have the effect of blinding the proponents of these arguments to their intrinsic demerits. If so, he need not be too much disquieted by the seeming weakness of the case against him. For it is a commonplace that, once in the grip of general prepossessions, even very good philosophers sometimes avail themselves of very bad arguments.

Actually, we can, I think, discern at least two such influences operating powerfully in the case before us. One is sympathy with the general tenets of Positivism. The other is the conviction already alluded to, that man does not in fact possess a contra-causal type of freedom; whence follows a strong presumption that no such freedom is necessary to moral responsibility.

About the first of these influences I propose to say very little. I wish merely to indicate how strict adherence to Positivist tenets precludes one in principle from understanding moral responsibility as the ordinary man understands it, and how Positivists are therefore bound, when they attempt to define the conditions of moral responsibility, to say things that seem monstrously unplausible.

That the Positivist — who has certainly not been drawn initially to this way of philosophising by reflexion upon the phenomena of the moral life — should approach the problems of ethical analysis with certain strong prepossessions, is only to be expected. The most crucial of these is that (non-tautologous) statements in this field, as in every other field, can have no meaning — or at any rate no cognitive meaning — unless they are, at least in principle, sensibly verifiable. The consequence of that prepossession must be to close the mind in advance, more or less absolutely according to the extent to which the Verifiability Principle is maintained as unshakeable dogma, against the common view of the moral ought — which happens also to be the view in terms of which the problem of moral responsibility historically and habitually arises. For on this view the moral ought as apprehended by the moral consciousness is most certainly an object neither of 'outer' nor of 'inner' sense. One need not wonder, therefore, that the Positivist should recommend analyses of the conditions of moral responsibility, such as the hypothetical propositions offered as the meaning of the expression 'could have acted otherwise,' which to anyone who understands the moral ought in the ordinary way seem little short of fantastic. By an *a priori* prejudice he has effectively debarred himself from appreciating what ordinary men mean by moral obligation and moral responsibility. I cannot forbear adding that in view of the doom which has so swiftly attended the very various attempts so far made to define moral obligation in Positivist terms, the case for at least a temporary suspension of belief in Positivist presuppositions in the ethical field would appear to be a strong one.

Of far wider and more permanent interest, in my judgment, is the second of the 'predisposing influences' — the conviction that there just *is* no contra-causal freedom such as is commonly alleged to be a condition of moral responsibility. A natural desire to 'save' moral responsibility issues, logically enough, in attempts to formulate its conditions in a manner compatible with unbroken causal continuity. The consequent analyses may be, as I have urged, very unsatisfactory. But there is no doubt that the conviction that motivates the analysis is supported by reasons of great weight: well-known arguments that are the property of no particular school and which most of us learned in our philosophical cradles. A very brief summary of what I take to be the most influential of these arguments will suffice for the comments I wish to make upon them.

A contra-causal freedom, it is argued, such as is implied in the 'categorical' interpretation of the proposition 'A could have chosen otherwise than he did,' posits a breach of causal continuity between a man's character and his conduct. Now apart from the general presumption in favour of the universality of causal law, there are special reasons for disallowing the breach that is here alleged. It is the common assumption of social intercourse that our acquaintances will act 'in character'; that their choices will exhibit the 'natural' response of their characters to the given situation. And this assumption seems to be amply substantiated, over a wide range of conduct, by the actual success which attends predictions made on this basis. Where there should be, on the contra-causal hypothesis, chaotic variability, there is found in fact a large measure of intelligible continuity. Moreover, what is the alternative to admitting that a person's choices flow from his character? Surely just that the so-called 'choice' is not *that person's* choice at all: that, relatively to the person concerned, it is a mere 'accident.' Now we cannot really believe this. But if it *were* the case, it would certainly not help to establish *moral* freedom, the freedom required for *moral* responsibility. For clearly a man cannot be morally responsible for an act which does not express his own choice but is, on the contrary, attributable simply to chance.

These are clearly considerations worthy of all respect. It is not surprising if they have played a big part in persuading people to respond sympathetically to the view that 'Free Will,' in its usual contra-causal formulation, is a pseudo-problem. A full answer to them is obviously not practicable in what is little more than an appendix to the body of this paper; but I am hopeful that something can be said, even in a little space, to show that they are very far from being as conclusive against a contra-causal freedom as they are often supposed to be.

To begin with the less troublesome of the two main objections indicated — the objection that the break in causal continuity which free will involves is inconsistent with the predictability of conduct on the basis of the agent's known character. All that is necessary to meet this objection, I suggest, is the frank recognition, which is perfectly open to the Libertarian, that there is a wide area of human conduct, determinable on clear general principles, within which free will does not effectively operate. The most important of these general principles (I have no space to deal here with the others) has often enough been stated by Libertarians. Free will does not operate in these practical situations in which no conflict arises in the agent's mind between what he conceives to be his 'duty' and what he feels to be his 'strongest desire.' It does not operate here because there just is no occasion for it to operate. There is no reason whatever why the agent should here even contemplate choosing any course other than that prescribed by his strongest desire. In all such situations, therefore, he naturally wills in accordance with strongest desire. But his 'strongest desire' is simply the specific *ad hoc* expression of that system of conative and emotive dispositions which we call his 'character.' In all such situations, therefore, whatever may be the case elsewhere, his will is in effect determined by his character as so far formed. Now when we bear in mind that there are an almost immeasurably greater number of situations in a man's life that conform to *this* pattern than there are situations in which an agent is aware of a conflict between strongest desire and duty, it is apparent that a Libertarianism which accepts the limitation of free will to the *latter* type of situation is not open to the stock objection on the score of 'predictability.' For there still remains a vast area of human behaviour in which prediction on the basis of known character may be expected to succeed: an area which will accommodate without difficulty, I think, all these empirical facts about successful prediction which the critic is apt to suppose fatal to Free Will.

So far as I can see, such a delimitation of the field of effective free will denies to the Libertarian absolutely nothing which matters to him. For it is precisely that small sector of the field of choices which our principle of delimitation still leaves open to free will — the sector in which strongest desire clashes with duty — that is crucial for moral responsibility. It is, I believe, with respect to such situations, and in the last resort to such situations alone, that the agent himself recognises that moral praise and blame are appropriate. They are appropriate, according as he does or does not 'rise to duty' in the face of opposing desires; always granted, that is, that he is free to choose between these courses as genuinely open possibilities. If the reality of freedom be conceded *here*, everything is conceded that the Libertarian has any real interest in securing.

But, of course, the most vital question is, can the reality of freedom be conceded even here? In particular, can the standard objection be met which we stated, that if the person's choice does not, in these situations as elsewhere, flow from his *character*, then it is not *that person's* choice at all.

This is, perhaps, of all the objections to a contra-causal freedom, the one which is generally felt to be the most conclusive. For the assumption upon which it is based, *viz.* that no intelligible meaning can attach to the claim that an act which is not an expression of the self's *character* may nevertheless be the *self's* act, is apt to be regarded as self-evident. The Libertarian is accordingly charged with being in effect an *In*determinist, whose 'free will,' in so far as it does not flow from the agent's character, can only be a matter of 'chance.' Has the Libertarian — who invariably repudiates this charge and claims to be a *Self*-determinist — any way of showing that, contrary to the assumption of his critics, we *can* meaningfully talk of an act as the self's act even though, in an important sense, it is not an expression of the self's 'character'?

I think that he has. I want to suggest that what prevents the critics from finding a meaning in this way of talking is that they are looking for it in the wrong way; or better, perhaps, with the wrong orientation. They are looking for it from the stand-point of the *external observer*; the stand-point proper to, because alone possible for, apprehension of the physical world. Now from the external stand-point we may observe processes of change. But one thing which, by common consent, *cannot* be observed from without is *creative activity*. Yet — and here lies the crux of the whole matter — it is precisely creative activity which we are trying to understand when we are trying to understand what is traditionally designated by 'free will.' For if there should be an act which is genuinely the self's act and is nevertheless not an expression of its character, such an act, in which the self 'transcends' its character as so far formed, would seem to be essentially of the nature of creative activity. It follows that to look for a meaning in 'free will' from the external stand-point is absurd. It is to look for it in a way that ensures that it will not be found. Granted that a creative activity of any kind is at least *possible* (and I know of no ground for its *a priori* rejection), there is one way, and one way only, in which we can hope to apprehend it, and that is from the *inner* stand-point of direct participation.

It seems to me therefore, that if the Libertarian's claim to find a meaning in a 'free' will which is genuinely the self's will, though not an expression of the self's character, is to be subjected to any test that is worth applying, that test must be undertaken from the inner stand-point. We ought to place ourselves imaginatively at the stand-point of the agent engaged in the typical moral situation in which free will is claimed, and ask ourselves whether from *this* stand-point the claim in question does or does not have meaning for us. That the appeal must be to introspection is no doubt unfortunate. But he would be a very doctrinaire critic of introspection who declined to make use of it when in the nature of the case no other means of apprehension is available. Everyone must make the introspective experiment for himself: but I may perhaps venture to report, though at this late stage with extreme brevity, what I at least seem to find when I make the experiment myself.

In the situation of moral conflict, then, I (as agent) have before my mind a course of action X, which I believe to be my duty; and also a course of action Y, incompatible with X, which I feel to be that which I most strongly desire. Y is, as it is sometimes expressed, 'in the line of least resistance' for me — the course which I am aware I should take if I let my purely desiring nature operate without hindrance. It is the course towards which I am aware that my *character*, as so far formed, naturally inclines me. Now, as actually engaged in this situation, I find that I cannot help believing that I *can* rise to duty and choose X; the 'rising to duty' being effected by what is commonly called 'effort of will.' And I further find, if I ask myself just what it is I am believing when I believe that I 'can' rise to duty, that I cannot help believing that it lies with me here and now, quite absolutely, which of two genuinely open possibilities I adopt; whether, that is, I make the effort of will and choose X, or, on the other hand, let my desiring nature, my character as so far formed, 'have its way,' and choose Y, the course 'in the line of least resistance.' These beliefs may, of course, be illusory, but that is not at present in point. For the present argument all that matters is whether beliefs of this sort are in fact discoverable in the moral agent in the situation of 'moral temptation.' For my own part, I cannot doubt the introspective evidence that they are.

Now here is the vital point. No matter which course, X or Y, I choose in this situation, I cannot doubt, *qua* practical being engaged in it, that my choice is *not* just the expression of my formed character, and yet *is* a choice made by my *self*. For suppose I make the effort and choose X (my 'duty'). Since my very purpose in making the 'effort' is to enable me to act against the existing 'set' of desire, which is the expression of my character as so far formed, I cannot possibly regard the act itself as the expression of my *character*. On the other hand, introspection makes it equally clear that I am certain that it is *I* who choose; that the act is not an 'accident,' but is genuinely *my* act. Or suppose that I choose Y (the end of 'strongest desire'). The course chosen here is, it is true, in conformity with my 'character.' But since I find myself unable to doubt that I *could* have made the effort and chosen X, I cannot possibly regard the choice of Y as *just* the expression of my character. Yet here again I find that I cannot doubt that the choice is *my* choice, a choice for which *I* am justly to be blamed.

What this amounts to is that I *can* and *do* attach meaning, *qua* moral agent, to an act which is not the self's character and yet is genuinely the self's act. And having no good reason to suppose that other persons have a fundamentally different mental constitution, it seems to me probable that anyone else who undertakes a similar experiment will be obliged to submit a similar report. I conclude, therefore, that the argument against 'free will' on the score of its 'meaninglessness' must be held to fail. 'Free Will' does have meaning; though, because it is of the nature of a creative activity, its meaning is discoverable only in an intuition of the practical consciousness of the participating agent. To the agent making a moral choice in the situation where duty clashes with desire, his 'self' is known to him as a creatively active self, a self which declines to be identified with his 'character' as so formed. Not, of course, that the self's character — let it be added to obviate misunderstanding — either is, or is supposed by the agent to be, devoid of bearing upon his choices, even in the 'sector' in which free will is held to operate. On the contrary, such a bearing is manifest in the empirically verifiable fact that we find it 'harder' (as we say) to make the effort of will required to 'rise to duty' in proportion to the extent that the 'dutiful' course conflicts with the course to which our character as so far formed inclines us. It is only in the polemics of the critics that a 'free' will is supposed to be incompatible with recognising the bearing of 'character' upon choice.

"But what" (it may be asked) "of the all-important question of the *value* of this 'subjective certainty'? Even if what you say is sound as 'phenomenology,' is there any reason to suppose that the conviction on which you lay so much stress is in fact *true?*" I agree that the question is important; far more important, indeed, than is always realised, for it is not always realised that the only direct evidence there *could* be for a creative activity like 'free will' is an intuition of the practical consciousness. But this question falls outside the purview of the present paper. The aim of the paper has not been to offer a constructive defence of free will. It has been to show that the problem as traditionally posed is a real, and not a pseudo, problem. A serious threat to that thesis, it was acknowledged, arises from the apparent difficulty of attaching meaning to an act which is not the expression of the self's character and yet *is* the self's own act. The object of my brief phenomenological analysis was to provide evidence that such an act *does* have meaning for us in the one context in which there is any sense in *expecting* it to have meaning.

VII

My general conclusion is, I fear, very unexciting. It is merely that it is an error to suppose that the 'Free Will' problem, when correctly formulated, turns out not to be a 'problem' at all. Labouring to reinstate an old problem is dull work enough. But I am disposed to think that the philosophic situation to-day calls for a good deal more dull work of a similar sort.

QUESTIONS

1. Why does Campbell think acceptance of the Verifiability Principle disposes philosophers to conclude there is no "problem of free will"?
2. Campbell and Schlick agree that moral responsibility is not present (*i.e.*, an agent's acts are not properly held blameworthy or praiseworthy) unless an action is free at least in the sense of not being compelled. What confusion did Schlick think led to the supposition that moral responsibility requires that an act not be completely *caused?*
3. If Schlick is right that a man is morally responsible for an act if punishing him would tend to produce motives, in him or others or both, that will help to prevent recurrence of this kind of act, then does it follow that lack of compulsion is sufficient for being morally responsible, as Schlick says?
4. What two assumptions does Campbell think are behind the traditional claims that moral responsibility requires exemption from causal law?
5. Does Campbell successfully refute Schlick's view of moral responsibility by showing that we (a) think animals' acts are not morally blameworthy, (b)

think that the past acts of long-dead persons were blameworthy, and (c) think that a bad heredity or upbringing reduces culpability?

6. Do you agree with Campbell that a deed is not blameworthy if the agent's own bad character is the only thing that prevents his acting rightly? Must it have been possible for an agent to have acted otherwise, despite his bad character?

7. What argument does Campbell offer to show that it is not enough, for moral responsibility for an act, that the agent would have done otherwise *if* he had chosen or tried to, but that what is required is that he also could have *chosen* otherwise?

8. Which two arguments against "contra-causal freedom" does Campbell think "worthy of respect"? In what circumstances does Campbell think "free choice" operates?

9. In the course of attacking the objection that it is meaningless to say that an act is one's own act but not an expression of one's character, Campbell is led to draw a line between the "line of least resistance" to which character inclines one, and rising to duty by an "effort of will." Do you see any reason why the fact that one rises to do one's duty is *not* indicative of, or an expression of, one's character, or why one's character is supposed to be expressed only in what one finds most enticing, or the line of least resistance? What do you think is sufficient reason for saying of any occurrence or result, "I did it"?

CHAPTER 7 SUGGESTIONS FOR FURTHER READING

Benn, S. I., and R. S. Peters. *Social Principles and the Democratic State.* London: Allen & Unwin, 1959, Ch. 9.

Bourke, V. J. *Ethics.* New York: Macmillan, 1955, Chs. 3, 6, 8. A Thomistic analysis.

Brandt, Richard B. *Ethical Theory.* Englewood Cliffs, N. J.: Prentice-Hall, 1959, Chs. 18 and 20.

Carritt, E. F. *Ethical and Political Thinking.* Oxford: Clarendon Press, 1947, Ch. 12.

Ewing, A. C. *Second Thoughts in Moral Philosophy.* New York: Macmillan, 1959, Ch. 5.

Hobart, R. E. "Free Will as Involving Determinism," *Mind,* Vol. 48 (1934), pp. 1-27.

Hook, Sidney, ed. *Determinism and Freedom.* New York: New York Univ. Press, 1958. Essays representing different positions.

Hume, David. *An Enquiry Concerning the Human Understanding.* Many editions, Ch. 7.

Mabbott, J. D. "Freewill and Punishment" in Lewis, H. D., ed. *Contemporary British Philosophy.* London: Allen & Unwin, 1956.

Moser, S. "Utilitarian Theories of Punishment and Moral Judgments," *Philosophical Studies,* Vol. 8 (1957), pp. 15-19. Critique of utilitarian views.

Nowell-Smith, Patrick. *Ethics.* Baltimore: Penguin Books, 1954, Chs. 17-20.

Ross, Sir William David. *Foundations of Ethics.* (Gifford lectures) New York: Oxford Univ. Press, 1939, Ch. 10.

Sidgwick, Henry. *The Methods of Ethics.* 7th ed. New York: Macmillan, 1874, pp. 56-66.